PERU 1890–1977: GROWTH AND POLICY IN AN OPEN ECONOMY

The Columbia Economic History of the Modern World

GENERAL EDITOR: STUART W. BRUCHEY

PERU 1890–1977

GROWTH AND POLICY
IN AN OPEN ECONOMY

Rosemary Thorp
and
Geoffrey Bertram

New York   Columbia University Press   1978

Published in 1978 in Great Britain by The Macmillan Press Ltd and
in the United States of America by Columbia University Press

Printed in Great Britain

Library of Congress Cataloging in Publication Data

Thorp, Rosemary.
  Peru, 1890–1977.
  (Columbia economic history of the modern world
  series)
  Bibliography: p.
  Includes index.
  1. Peru – Economic conditions. 2. Peru –
Economic policy. I. Bertram, Geoffrey, joint
author. II. Title. III. Series.
HC227.T485 1978   330.9′85′063   77–27925
ISBN 0–231–03433–4

For
BRIDGET
and
TIM

Contents

List of Tables

List of Figures

List of Symbols

£   British pound sterling.
$ United States dollar.
Lp   Peruvian Libra of ten soles, in use from 1898 to 1930, and originally at par with the £.
S/   Peruvian sol.

Preface

Once a book is completed, the author or authors become painfully aware of what it is not. We claim to have written a book about 'Peru'— but we are well aware that it is a book which principally concerns only one 'Peru': that accessible through published data and the limited amount of archive material we were able to tap in the time available. Further, for all our proclaimed sensitivity to the importance of social and political structures, it remains essentially the viewpoint of economists. Our hope is that we have provided documentation on which others may build at least a few of those other books the need for which has been vividly brought home to us in the course of our own work.

Even with its limitations, however, this book would have been impossible without the cooperation of many people. We owe particular thanks to all our Peruvian friends who facilitated our access to materials in many different ways. Ricardo Cubas and Drago Kisic worked especially hard for us. Graciela Sanchez Cerro and her staff in the Sala de Investigaciones of the Biblioteca Nacional, and Rosa Chavez in the library of the Banco Central, all went out of their way to be helpful, as did the staff of the *Peruvian Times*, who allowed us to use their archive. Raul Arrieta, Gabriel Palma, Donald Tarnawiecki and Susan Watt all provided research assistance at various times. We also owe our thanks to the numerous researchers who answered our queries and gave us access to their preliminary work, especially Bill Albert, Bill Bell, Peter Blanchard, José Maria Caballero, Valpy Fitzgerald, Denis Gilbert, Shane Hunt, Alaine Low, Alison McEwan, Rory Miller, Bryan Roberts, Christopher Scott, Bill Warren and Richard Webb. Valpy Fitzgerald, Christopher Platt and Stuart Bruchey commented extensively on an earlier version of the book.

Finally, we owe our thanks to the Social Science Research Council of the United Kingdom for financial assistance over three years, and to the Director, Teddy Jackson, and the Staff of the Institute of Economics and Statistics, Oxford, for the innumerable forms of moral and practical support required to complete our task.

Oxford, 1977   *R.T.*
                                                             G.B.

Part I

Background

1 The Setting: an Introduction

Peru is today a country containing some of the most acute poverty in Latin America, with a *per capita* national income below the continental average and ranking among the most unequal in terms of income distribution. To understand how a country famous for the richness of its natural resource base can yet have apparently achieved so little, we must turn to Peru's history as a trading nation in the world economy. In the sixteenth century, Peru's original integration into world trade occurred during the 'plunder' phase of European overseas expansion and, notwithstanding Peru's immense natural wealth, the greater part of the 'gains from trade' went to Spain, not to Peru. Independence from Spain in 1824 brought little improvement; the early decades of republican government were corrupt, racked by civil war, and characterised by general economic decline. The celebrated 'Guano Age' which followed in the mid-nineteenth century made Peru one of the classic examples of a monoproduct export economy, but failed to result in a process of self-sustaining growth. Exhaustion of the best guano deposits and war with Chile at the end of the 1870s virtually wiped out even the meagre economic achievements of the guano period. Not surprisingly, many writers have pointed to Peru as a prototype of the evil effects of exploitation, a country which has been 'underdeveloping' rather than 'developing' over the long run.[1]

This book concerns the period of nearly a hundred years which has elapsed since the ending of the guano age, a period about which very little has yet been published in the way of quantitative analysis. Our first task therefore is documentation:[2] what growth was there, in which sectors, and to whose benefit? Our second task is to interpret and explain the most important trends, drawing in particular upon the theoretical perspectives which are outlined in Chapter 2. Our third task is to evaluate the present stage of Peru's economic evolution and the problems which the country faces, in the light of historical experience.

We begin, in this chapter, with brief summaries of the main long-run trends of the economy since the War of the Pacific (1879–82) and of the geographical setting within which the events described in this book took place.

1.1 SOME LONG-RUN TRENDS

Peru's post-colonial economic history can be visualised as a series of major export cycles, and it will become apparent as we proceed that the export sectors have been central to the process of economic change in Peru even in the 1970s. Figure 1.1 shows that the history of export performance divides into three distinct phases of about fifty years each. The first period, the Guano Age, ran from the 1830s through to the War of the Pacific (1879–81) in which Peru was defeated by Chile, the country occupied, and the export economy virtually destroyed. The second period began with post-war reconstruction in the 1880s and continued along a path of sustained export growth (with a boom during the First World War) until the 1920s, ending in 1930 with the onset of the Great Depression. The third period runs from the post-Depression recovery of the 1930s (with a dip corresponding to the Second World War) through the rapid export-led growth of the 1950s and early 1960s and into the incipient export crisis of the late 1960s and early 1970s, coming to an end with the collapse of the world commodity price boom in 1974–5.

Over the long run, the growth of the export sectors has been relatively modest. From 1900 to 1959 (years which appear to be on the long-run overall trend in Figure 1.1) the average growth rate of export earnings, in undeflated dollars, was 4.5 per cent per annum. In *per capita* terms, this gives an annual growth rate somewhat over 3 per cent, which allowing for price rises represents a 'real' rate of growth of the order of one per cent[3]. However, the years within each of the growth phases have been remarkable for a high rate of export expansion sustained over a period of decades, and for the stability of this rate. From 1830 to 1870 the export quantum grew at an average annual rate of nearly seven per cent, and from 1890 to 1929 a similar rate of growth was achieved by both quantum and value indices. From 1942 to 1970, in the most recent growth phase, the rate of growth of export earnings was nearer to 10 per cent. These rates of growth indicate that, in each of the upswings, external market opportunities produced a strong supply response from Peru over periods of thirty years or so; whilst the stability of the growth path (once established) reflects the diversified character of Peru's exports, which makes the country less vulnerable than many of its Latin American neighbours to market fluctuations in one or two products.

It is no surprise to find that the periods of greatest political stability and conservatism in Peru's history—the 'aristocratic republic' and '*oncenio*' from 1895 to 1930, and the Odría and Prado regimes of 1948–62—corresponded to the long upswings of the export economy, whilst the years of political flux—1882 to 1895, 1930 to 1948, and the late 1960s—corresponded to periods in which the export economy had

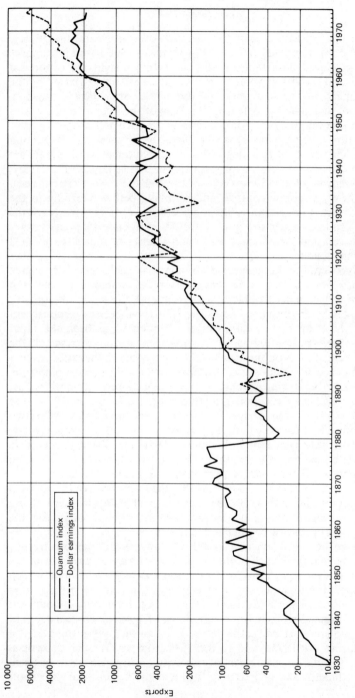

FIGURE 1.1 Exports 1830 to 1975: Indices of volume and dollar value (1900 = 100)

Sources: Quantum index from Hunt (1973), pp. 28—9, 64—5. Dollar earnings derived from *Extracto Estadístico* and Banco Central, *Cuentas Nacionales*. For Quantum index 1963—74, see Table 12.9. For 1830—90 we give only the quantum index since reliable figures on the total value of exports are not available for most of the nineteenth century.

entered into crisis and ceased to generate clear guidelines for policy. Each of the three phases outlined above came to an end in circumstances which produced uncertainty about the future viability of export-led growth, and reconsideration of the role which should be played by the government in the economy. In the 1890s, after Peru's crushing economic and political defeat in the War of the Pacific, new lines of economic development were explored and the issue of 'free trade' versus 'protection' was hotly debated. The Great Depression and the Second World War prompted a degree of disenchantment with export-led growth and renewed interest in industrialisation as a possible strategy; as renewed export growth was delayed through the 1940s, Peru entered a brief era of economic controls and rationing before returning to the time-honoured policies of economic liberalism in 1948. Finally, as the export economy again ran into difficulties in the late 1960s, a military junta seized power and embarked upon a series of radical-nationalist economic policies.

Reconsideration of economic strategy has each time been made imperative by the recurring tendency of the economy to run into balance-of-payments trouble towards the end of each of the growth phases, but before the upward trend of exports has been exogenously cut short. The main manifestation of this tendency has been the rapid increase of the public foreign debt, as governments sought to sustain the growth rate of the economy at a level above that which the export sectors could by themselves support. There has been a clear cyclical pattern in government borrowing abroad, with a heavy concentration in the last decade of each of the export-growth phases: the 1870s, the 1920s, and the period from the early-mid 1960s to the mid-1970s.[4] On two occasions the collapse of the export economy was accompanied by default on the foreign debt. Following the War of the Pacific, the holders of the defaulted bonds were eventually compensated, in 1890, by being given control of the country's railways and guano exports in the so-called 'Grace Contract'; while, following the Depression of the 1930s, it was not until the early 1950s that Peru re-established its international credit by negotiating a settlement with the bondholders for the resumption of service payments in 1953.

Foreign direct investment has tended to move into Peru most strongly during the middle of each of the export growth phases, when the initial problems of recovery from earlier economic collapse had already been overcome. The high periods of foreign direct investment in Peru were 1901–29 and 1950–68 (during the Guano Age foreign investment was largely confined to mercantile activities and government bonds). The implication, confirmed by the detailed discussion later in this study, is that during the 1890s, and in the 1930s and 1940s, such growth as occurred in the economy was of necessity locally-generated, in terms both of finance and of initiative. In the course of each of the export growth phases the degree of foreign domination of the economy increased dramatically, but over the longer run the trend was less pronounced.[5]

Our study takes up the detailed story as the new directions of the first period of transition began to be explored in the 1890s. It concludes as the most recent period of transition runs into the economic crisis of mid-late 1975.

1.2 THE PHYSICAL SETTING AND NATURAL RESOURCES[6]

Peru is divided geographically into three major regions—Coast, Sierra and Selva. The narrow coastal strip, 12 per cent of the national territory, contains today around 45 per cent of the population.[7] The soil is highly fertile but requires irrigation, when it produces cotton, rice, or sugar, according to the region, and can produce a wide range of other crops (though historically these have been less productive than the three already mentioned). The North contains important oil deposits (now largely exhausted); and some minerals (particularly iron, phosphates, and some copper and gold) are encountered elsewhere along the Coast. The land tenure system that prevailed throughout most of our period[8] was unequal, but varied with the crop: sugar was grown in large plantations, becoming increasingly mechanised over time, while cotton and rice were mostly grown under a system of *yanaconaje* (sharecropping) or by small-holders. The main centres of population and industry are on the Coast, while within the coastal area the concentration of both population and industry in Lima has increased steadily throughout the century.[9]

The Sierra comprises three Andean ranges running north to south down the country, presenting severe problems of transport and of poorly-yielding land. About half of the population live in the Sierra, many in a subsistence economy. The major centres of population and of integration into the market economy are the mining towns, since it is in the Sierra that the bulk of Peru's rich mineral deposits have been found. Gold, silver, copper, lead, and zinc have all in their turn been taken out in massive quantities. The landholding structure before agrarian reform was more unequal than on the Coast, though the vast areas of poor grazing land somewhat distort the picture. The main agricultural activities are livestock raising and the production of such crops as wheat, maize, and potatoes on a basis of very low yields, little or no technical progress and small marketed surpluses. The building of the Central Highway in the 1920s opened a limited area of the Sierra to the Lima market, and Lima now gets nearly half its food supplies from the Sierra,[10] but this has affected a relatively small proportion of the total area.

The Selva, or jungle – the unknown quantity in Peru – has been the constant hope of policy-makers. Covering 60 per cent of the area of the country, it has a population estimated at six per cent of the national total and its terrain is still only partly explored. Systematic colonisation schemes began late in the nineteenth century but have generally been unsuccessful owing to the lack of the enormous infrastructural support required to overcome the difficulties of terrain and climate. The one major population centre, Iquitos, became important during the rubber boom at the turn of the century, a boom which by virtue of the area's isolation came and went with remarkably little impact on the rest of the country.

1.3 A POSTSCRIPT ON SOURCES

Our principal reliance has been on primary data, basically the abundant material produced by the numerous Peruvian statistical agencies throughout this century. The quantity and quality of this material proved very impressive, though inevitably it is limited almost entirely to the modern economy. We are convinced that more can be done to explore the evolution of the traditional sectors, using monograph literature and local archives, but as the preface explains, this was not our objective here.

Other important sources were contemporary Peruvian analyses—particularly for the first years of our period—and business periodicals such as *El Economista* and the *West Coast Leader* (later the *Peruvian Times*), a journal aimed essentially at the Anglo-Saxon business community. It is an unfortunate corollary of the pattern of development which comprises our main theme that long periods of rising foreign influence leave their mark firmly on the business press, with the result that we find the Peruvian weeklies flourishing only in the brief interludes of relative autonomy.[11] We mention this only to make the point that we are well aware of the bias in the foreign business press and have taken care to rely on such periodicals for factual material rather than for policy analysis.

Finally, in the last five years there has been a dramatic increase in the amount of research on Peruvian problems both within and without the country. This has proved invaluable to us, and we stress again our appreciation to those researchers who have freely allowed us to use their preliminary work.

2 The Framework of the Study

It will be evident already from the brief description in Chapter 1 that Peru ranks as an acutely underdeveloped component of the world capitalist economy. By this we imply a country not only poor but also characterised by serious rigidities which inhibit a process of structural change. Such rigidities comprise imperfections in product and factor markets; and their result is the dualistic structure which we find acutely manifest in Peru, as shown in Table 2.1. In Peru the 'modern' sector generates 67 per cent of gross domestic product but employs only 35 per cent of the population. Large modern capital-intensive enterprises coexist with 'traditional' small-scale non-corporate units of low productivity, *within* the same economic sector. The structural rigidities behind this dualistic structure result in a highly unequal income distribution (portrayed in Table 2.2), and a widespread under-utilisation of resources, both capital and labour.

Our first preoccupation in an effort to understand the emergence and

TABLE 2.1 The dual structure of the economy, 1968

	Output (per cent of GDP)			Employment (per cent of economically active population)		
	Corp-orate	Non-corporate	Total	Corp-orate	Non-corporate	Total
Primary sector	18	8	26	14	37	51
Secondary sector	23	6	29	7	11	18
Tertiary sector	26	19	45	14	17	31
TOTAL	67	33	100	35	65	100
Lima-Callao	38	19	57	14	10	24
Rest of Peru	29	14	43	21	55	76

Source: Fitzgerald (1976c).

Peru 1890–1977

TABLE 2.2 Personal income distribution, 1961

Proportion of labour force	Share of personal income
Top 1 per cent	25
Top 5 per cent	39
Top 20 per cent	64
Middle 40 per cent	28
Lowest 40 per cent	8

Source: Webb (1972a).

survival of such characteristics, must be with the non-emergence of forces that could remove the structural obstacles to growth. In other countries, at other times, this role was played by agents such as the State, by the banking sector, by particular entrepreneurial groups, or by ideology.[1] In Peru, the performance of both public and private sectors within the society was inadequate to effect the necessary structural transformation. Secondly, we need to understand the evolution through time of the structural obstacles themselves, and to ask whether there have been forces at work which increase structural problems over time, even in the context of economic growth.

It has almost become part of the new orthodoxy that the framework for such an analysis is to be found by studying the historical significance of Peru's place in the world economy. The pure Rostovian view — that underdeveloped countries were repeating now the experience of European economies two centuries previously — has been replaced by a widespread acceptance of the fact that being a late-comer profoundly affects one's options. The earliest analyses along these lines, however, offered only partial insights. Prebisch, for example, saw the problem in terms of the inability of an underdeveloped economy to adjust to unfavourable trends in the terms of trade, as a result of structural rigidities such as the land tenure system and weak tax structures; rigidities, in other words, which were themselves independent of the external system.[2] Kuznets commented on the negative aspects of the international availability of technology, and the unsuitability for development of the value systems and social structures resulting from colonialism, formal or informal.[3] Myrdal developed the notion that the international system embodied cumulative tendencies working to the advantage of the dominant economies of the 'centre' and to the disadvantage of the others.[4]

Recently, however, a number of attempts have been made to broaden the scope of this analysis, and in particular to attempt to contribute more to the first issue mentioned above: why agents of change fail to emerge from within the system. This line of thought, known as the 'dependency school',[5] is of particular importance for our study, for two reasons. The first is its influence in Peru in recent years: as we shall argue, the nationalist military regime which took power in 1968 represented one of the most explicit attempts yet seen in Latin America to implement the policy prescriptions of the school, albeit in a damagingly over-simplified form. The second is that, despite a number of problems which we outline below, the dependency model offers insights which are of considerable help in understanding the economic history of the country. We therefore turn to a brief description of its evolution and main hypotheses.

The school in Latin America evolved out of a combination of empirical and theoretical developments. First, the 'structuralist' framework of analysis of the fifties and sixties, stemming from the work of Prebisch, had reached a point of bankruptcy. Its policy prescriptions — industrialisation, tax and land reforms, public foreign aid to facilitate structural transformation — had proved inadequate to resolve the problem of development. Industrialisation had brought far more limited gains than had been anticipated, while meaningful reforms proved impossible in the face of the existing political structure — a factor which was exogenous to the structuralist model. By the end of the sixties, this was provoking a desire to deepen the analysis[6] and above all to integrate policy-making and political structures into the model.

Secondly, it was becoming clear that the character of the international capitalist system was altering.[7] In particular, multi-national corporations were now characteristically moving into manufacturing sectors, as opposed to their earlier concentration on primary products. This was seen as connected with the poor results of industrialisation, but it was obvious that the connection had to be carefully explored.

Thirdly, and at the same time, new insights were being offered by Marxian analysis. Classical Marxist theory had seen the expansion of capitalism into underdeveloped countries as simply a process of destruction and replacement of pre-capitalist structures, with little attention to the details of the model. However Baran in the 1950s, and Frank in the early 1960s, turned their attention to a more detailed analysis of the repercussions of imperialism in the periphery. Their analysis was a direct challenge to the analysis of Prebisch and the structuralists: structural rigidities were not independent of the international system but were actually created by it, in a twin process of exploitation and distortion. This idea, although developed rather crudely by Frank, directly stimulated both Marxist and non-Marxist writers. The result was the introduction of a new term, 'dependence'.

'Dependence' is a situation which may be located at one end of a continuum, the opposite pole of which may conveniently be labelled 'autonomy'. Autonomy is not the same as total isolation, but involves rather the ability of a national economy to achieve self-sustaining growth within a capitalist framework. (Socialist alternatives, whatever their appeal for the future, are not relevant to explaining the historical problems of capitalism in Peru.) Among the main requirements for the achievement of autonomy are local control of the economic surplus,[8] local ability to innovate and to adapt technology, local ability to produce capital goods of a type appropriate to the country's resource endowment, and endogenous sources of economic dynamism (as distinct from dependence upon the growth of world markets). Dependence is not to be equated with underdevelopment;[9] the key empirical hypothesis of the dependency writers is rather that dependent economies are particularly prone to suffer from continuing under-development, or (what often amounts to almost the same thing) to undergo a distorted process of growth, the end product of which differs very greatly from the usual image of a 'developed' economy and society. Where dependence and underdevelopment coincide, mutually-reinforcing elements come into play; an underdeveloped country in the modern capitalist system tends to become dependent, while a dependent economy tends to remain underdeveloped.

The detailed mechanisms suggested by various writers differ widely, as do the specific circumstances of different countries within the international system. A number of empirical hypotheses can, however, be said to command wide support in the literature. For example:

(i) Foreign ownership of the sources of economic surplus leads to resource-allocation decisions which reduce, on balance, the economy's long-run growth potential—principally by remitting surplus abroad. (In the more rigorous versions of the theory, full account is taken of the initial contribution of foreign ownership to the growth of the surplus. For a full discussion of the methodological complexities involved see Chapter 5 below, where we explore the hypothesis for the case of Peru.)

(ii) Foreign monopolisation of opportunities may in addition have stultifying effects upon the development of local capabilities, and may lead to the export or consumption of locally-controlled investible funds.

(iii) The lack of domestic technological capacity exposes an economy to losses, as a result of the monopolisation of the sources of technology by international corporations. The losses take the form partly of the royalty payments which the multinationals are in a position to demand and partly of the costs implied by the inability to modify otherwise inappropriate technology. (These costs are of course accompanied by gains. The argument is not (usually) for zero borrowing, but for more selective borrowing and for policies to counteract any undesirable effects of the easy availability of foreign technology.)

(iv) While the source of dynamism of an economy remains external, and especially when it depends upon world demand for some primary commodity, that economy is always vulnerable to fluctuations in demand, and to the danger of substitution of other commodities in world consumption.

(v) The form of the external relationship may generate internal dualism. For example, the importation of demand patterns and technology may result in a productive structure that accentuates inequality.

(vi) The emergence of agents of change, who might for example bargain or compete more effectively with foreign capital, or achieve greater diversification of the economy by modification of the international relative price structure, is profoundly conditioned by the international system, which in different ways at different times provides for a harmonisation of interest between local ruling classes and international capital.

In recent years, it is argued, the changing *modus operandi* and focus of interest of the multinationals has implied a shift in the characteristics of dependent underdevelopment. Since investment in manufacturing for local markets implies an interest in the growth of those markets, more growth is to be expected, especially industrial growth. But this will be combined with continuation of dualism, unemployment, disarticulation and external control of resource allocation decisions.[10]

A simultaneous stress on both economic growth and increased equality, as vital components of a successful development process, is one of the hallmarks of the dependency writers. This springs partly from their definition of 'development': growth in their view counts as development only if it incorporates a measure of structural change such that access to income opportunities is significantly broadened, making greater income equality at least possible. In addition to this value judgement, however, these writers propose or imply two empirical hypotheses which treat growth and equality as mutually reinforcing in practice: first, that greater equality of opportunity is the necessary route to the release of a society's potential entrepreneurial, administrative and technical abilities, on which increased autonomy must be based; and second, that more equal income distribution contributes to the interdependence of local demand and supply which is necessary if the dynamism of the economy is to be successfully internalised. This is one aspect of the way in which more development and more autonomy can each sustain the other, while dependence and underdevelopment can be similarly mutually-reinforcing.

For all the intuitive appeal of the dependency analysis, it embodies several areas of difficulty and imprecision, which need to be spelt out. First is the problem of defining and making operational the notion of 'dependence' itself. The version we have given above is that which appears to us the most precise and useful definition, but the literature contains many variations and ambiguities.

A second problem is the relative weight to be assigned to international inequality on the one hand, and internal features of the dependent countries on the other. At one extreme Frank[11] appears to regard the conditioning process as absolute, so that the dependent economy's evolution is entirely determined by its 'satellite' status in the international system. At the other extreme are writers who treat the international system as irrelevant and concentrate on internal social and economic processes, implying that 'dependence' in the international sense is at most a secondary issue. (It is, for example, quite possible to argue that increasing inequality of income distribution is the inevitable concomitant of a particular stage of capitalist development, and has nothing to do with a country's international position.[12])

A third problem is to determine whether, and to what extent, there exist real possibilities for more rapid and autonomous development within the system. The most pessimistic writers appear to consider that no escape or modification is possible — a purely deterministic stance which makes the question of alternatives irrelevant. Other writers evidently believe that there is scope for change (whether by a revolutionary break with the system, or manipulation of policy within it), but are generally very imprecise in their description of the conditions which may lead to more or less autonomy.

This imprecision stems from a further and fundamental weakness: the lack of a developed economic model underlying the notion of 'relatively greater autonomy'. It is the vagueness of the model which has permitted the coexistence under one umbrella of such diverse views of the alternative. It is this vagueness also which has tended to lead to a dangerous simplification of its policy prescriptions in its 'popular' version. As we have mentioned, in Peru in the late 1960s a radical nationalist government engaged itself in a serious attempt at implementing the prescriptions of the school. But while the need to break the power of certain groups, both internal and external, was clear, what should follow was not.

Such problems notwithstanding, it remains important to make use of the insights which the dependency writers provide.

First, the relationship between developed and underdeveloped economies is viewed from a very broad perspective. Rather than focusing, as many radical development economists have done, upon some specific problem such as factor movements or the terms of trade, the new approach probes all facets of the international system and its ramifications within the dependent economy, considering, for example, market relations, corporate organisation, options for borrowing or bargaining, the impact of imported technology, the determinants of consumption patterns, and the direction of sectional biases in policymaking, to mention only the most important issues of relevance to a full understanding of the impact of the total system upon a particular country.

The second feature, closely related to the first, is the emphasis placed upon the impossibility of understanding the whole by focusing upon a division into neat analytical compartments, and hence upon the need for research to bridge various disciplines of the social sciences. Although most authors tend to develop either the political or the economic aspects of the analysis, at least the need for integrated research is acknowledged and a number of points of contact made.

The third important contribution of the dependency approach is that it makes intelligible the apparent paradox of countries which enjoy full political independence, yet fail to remedy the distortions induced by the international system. Often, indeed, policies are followed which accentuate rather than reduce these distortions. The explanation proposed is twofold: first, that in some matters the range of options open to dependent countries is artificially restricted, to the advantage of the dominant participants in the international system; while second (and equally important), a process of 'conditioning' takes place which leads policymakers in the dependent country to make choices which are obviously inappropriate to the 'local interest'.[13] The key to understanding such policy choices lies in the effects of the international system on class formation and class interests within the dependent country, and especially in the process whereby the ruling classes in a peripheral country are drawn by self-interest into alliance with the dominant elements in the international system. This alliance is then reinforced by the provision of outside support for that ruling class, against local challenges to its power from other groups which oppose the alliance. On this argument, the ill-effects of 'dependence' flow as much from local failure to solve the problem of state power in a direction favourable to the pursuit of independence, as they do from the direct impact of unequal market relations among countries in the international sphere.

In the study that follows we cannot attempt to tackle the theoretical and empirical clarification needed to resolve the problems we have outlined. Our design is much more limited. In the course of our research, we have found that the perspective described above has provided certain insights of particular relevance to understanding the economic history of Peru. At the same time, we see Peru as an example of peculiar interest for exploring the value of this perspective, since, as we have indicated, from 1968 to the mid-1970s the Peruvian Government was engaged upon one of the most interesting and serious of recent attempts in Latin America[14] to break with certain aspects of the international system, and find a more independent route to development, *without* a clearcut break with the capitalist system. In the longer run (our primary focus), Peru is an excellent case study of an economy which has passed through alternating periods of relative autonomy and renewed dependence. Both the emergence of the present Military Government, and the problems it has encountered, can best be understood as part of this historical process.

Several themes are suggested by the dependency perspective as the framework for this analysis.

First, we must seek to evaluate the significance which more or less 'autonomy' might have had for Peru's long-run development. It is in this context that we tackle the difficult question of the role of foreign investment, as a core element in the relations of Peru with the outside world.

Second, granted the significance of a greater degree of autonomy as we have defined it, the points in Peru's history when the economy seemed to be turning towards greater autonomy and a more complex and diversified structure require close investigation, to identify the forces which either encouraged or obstructed such movements towards autonomy, and to consider the extent to which these forces were open to manipulation by government policy.

This leads us to a third theme: the relationship between economic events and policy-making. What, or who, were the potential agents of change, who might have generated or consolidated such movements, and why did their interests apparently lie elsewhere? In particular we seek to trace the impact of export booms and slumps on the interests and strategies of the main protagonists in the economic arena – the government, local and foreign entrepreneurial groups, the emerging working class and the middle sectors.

Lastly, we give special attention to forces helping or hindering industrialisation *per se*. This focus is justified in so far as greater autonomy is accepted as desirable, since industry clearly plays an important role in an autonomous economy, both because of its central role in creating the intersectoral linkages which could lead to a greater endogenous stimulus to growth, and because of its potential role as a source of locally-produced capital goods and of technology.

The study that follows is first and foremost an essay in economic history. We have tried to show here how the questions we asked in attempting to explain that economic history were influenced by a particular perspective. Although at different points in the study we can provide evidence on specific hypotheses implied by that perspective, we cannot claim to have tested it *per se*: it is indeed too diffuse to be tested in a single study.[15] Nevertheless the coherence or otherwise of our analysis will reflect on the value of our initial viewpoint.

2.1 SOME TOOLS OF ANALYSIS

Before proceeding with the study, it may be helpful to elaborate on certain of the concepts used. First, two terms in particular have been the subject of confusion – 'duality' and 'foreign' ownership. Secondly, the relationship between exports and the rest of the economy features so prominently in the analysis that for the non-specialist it seems worth clarifying its major features.

Duality
Duality, or dualism, in its strict sense refers to the coexistence within a single economy of units with widely differing factor endowments and productivity. The use of the concept is occasionally taken to imply an approach which conflicts directly with that of dependency writing. However, this is to confuse the concept with the use made of it by a particular school: the so-called 'agricultural surplus' writers,[16] who use the notion of a dual structure to build a model wherein the availability of surplus from one sector facilitates the dynamic growth of the other, via the operation of the market, such a process being labelled 'development'. Such an approach to development is diametrically opposed to that of dependency writing, as will be evident from our earlier discussion. We use the term 'dualism' here in a purely descriptive sense, to identify one of the most fundamental attributes of present-day Peru: the coexistence both within and between sectors of units with vastly different resource endowments. The way is thus left open for a discussion of the form of the relationship between the units and the part played by such interaction in the development process.

The issue of nationality
For the purposes of the present study we shall treat as 'foreign' any firm which is organised on an international basis and whose centre of decision-making and capital-accumulation is external to Peru. We shall not treat as 'foreign' the operations of resident immigrants (and any capital brought in with them), nor internationally-organised firms whose centre of decision and accumulation is in Peru. To some extent, obviously, this distinction is an arbitrary one, to be justified in the light of the use to which we put it. Our distinction is designed to provide a convenient dividing-line between those enterprises which are more likely and those which are less likely to return to the local economy the surplus generated in production. The distinction may be clarified by defining a local firm as one which can be expected to accumulate locally unless there are special reasons to accumulate abroad; whereas a foreign firm is one which will normally accumulate abroad unless there are special reasons to accumulate locally.

As the above discussion indicates, we believe the most important effects of foreign ownership to be upon the allocation of net profits, which in turn generates a number of external effects upon local 'capabilities'. Further significant effects, especially today, derive from differential access to technology and to markets. We would suggest, however, that it is easy to exaggerate the differences in ability and in behaviour between local and foreign firms. In the course of this study, we shall encounter situations in which local firms behave in the manner commonly attributed to 'foreign capital', as well as numerous cases where the widely-touted 'superiority' of international firms proves to rest simply upon their success in consolidating monopoly positions or securing privileged access to funds for investment (rather than upon any inability of 'local' firms to undertake the activity).

The operation of an export economy[17]
Despite the frequent references in the literature to exports as an 'engine of growth', an engine is only useful once its power is harnessed. In the case of exports this means that the benefits an economy actually receives depend upon the effectiveness with which export earnings are transmitted to other sectors of the economy, and the efficiency with which those other sectors make use of the resulting stimulus. These links between export sectors and the rest of the economy are susceptible to measurement, or at least to estimation, and we have endeavoured to identify and trace them in some detail. The framework for such an analysis rests upon an understanding of the twofold role played by export sectors in an underdeveloped economy.

In the first place, they are the only productive sectors responding to external demand and therefore not constrained by the size of the internal market. Hence, given an external market, they are able to grow as rapidly as the necessary factors of production can be mobilised, and in hiring those factors of production they inject effective demand into the local economy. This injection of demand is automatically accompanied by increased availability of foreign exchange, and multiplier effects are therefore likely to be able to work their way through the system without encountering a foreign-exchange bottleneck (such as may arise in the case of endogenously-created demand in an open dependent economy). In addition to factor payments, export sectors also boost local demand by such purchases of material and equipment as they make locally (the so-called 'backward linkage' effect).

In the second place, export sectors taken together have historically been the most important source of investment funds in Latin American countries. The combination of externally-determined world prices and local comparative-advantage in production usually leads to the generation of large rents, which constitute the main potential source of local savings and investment, not only for the export sectors themselves, but for other sectors. Consequently, ownership of and thereby access to the surplus generated in export sectors implies also command over a vital part of the domestic economic surplus.[18]

When we come to measure the contribution of export sectors to economic growth, therefore, two questions have to be answered: first, what proportion of the total value of exports is 'returned' locally – hence the phrase 'returned value'[19]—and second, what proportion of the surplus returned from export production is invested locally? There are three main determinants of returned value. The first is the production function for the sector, which determines the amounts which must be spent on inputs, and the distribution of those payments among various factors of production and suppliers. The second is the willingness of the local government to tax the surplus which remains after meeting costs of production. The third is the savings, investment, and consumption behaviour of the capitalists who control the sector, and who receive that part of the surplus which is not appropriated by the government. These aspects provide the framework for the chapters of this book which are devoted to detailed analysis of the leading export sectors in Peru.

All of these issues will be developed further as we proceed. It is time now to turn to our main subject: the Peruvian economy since 1890.

Part II

The Rise and Fall of a Local Development Effort: 1890–1930

Introduction

During the mid-nineteenth century the Peruvian export economy had ridden high on a wave of prosperity generated by one of the most remarkable export commodities of the century, guano. The failure to convert the finite guano boom into a more lasting and self-sustaining growth process is well-known, although the reasons for the failure remain in dispute.[1] During the 1870s the Peruvian economy suffered a process of gradual disintegration, as revenues from guano fell behind the spending commitments of the government, and the development of southern nitrates to replace the declining guano reserves was delayed by short-sighted official policies.[2] The second half of the decade witnessed the collapse of the financial structure, the failure of most of the country's banks, the resort to paper money and inflationary finance for the government sector, and finally Peru's crushing defeat by Chile in the War of the Pacific (1879–81).

As post-war reconstruction began, there was little indication that the route would be one of increased autonomy. Most of the Peruvian élite (or what was left of it after the disasters of the 1870s) were of the opinion that the economy's future depended upon development of Peru's natural resources for export purposes, and that a necessary condition for such development was large-scale foreign investment. During the decade after 1884, when Peru was governed by General Caceres or his nominees, all policies were directed to this end. The primary task of the Government was felt to be the re-establishment of Peru's international credit-worthiness, the attraction of foreign investment, and (if possible) further government borrowing abroad, on the pattern of the guano era. Of various measures taken to this end, the two most important were the removal from circulation of the devalued paper currency (1887–8), and the negotiations with the foreign holders of the Peruvian Government bonds defaulted in the 1870s.[3] These negotiations began in 1886, and in 1890 resulted in the signing of the Grace Contract, one of the milestones of Peruvian economic history.[4] The Grace Contract cancelled the claims of the bondholders against the Government; in exchange they obtained control of the railway system, what was left of the guano export business, and various other lesser concessions. Michael P. Grace, the merchant who played a central role in the negotiations, subsequently promoted a series of large investment projects, as a result of which British capital between 1890 and 1892 showed a real interest in the expansion of the railways, the oil industry, mining, cotton textile manufacture, and in some areas, the sugar industry.[5] The Peruvian economy seemed set on the road to foreign control.

This trend, however, was shortlived. British confidence in Peru's credit-worthiness had hardly been re-established when the Baring Crisis gave all South American ventures a bad name in London. At the same time, the world silver price was falling, with the result that countries whose currencies were on the silver standard (Peru among them) were unable to maintain monetary stability, as the previous gradual depreciation of their currencies became headlong collapse in 1892. Besides causing a severe commercial recession in Peru, the falling silver price abruptly reduced the interest of British capitalists in the silver mines of Peru (the attraction of which had been the main motive behind the extension of the Central Railway to Oroya in 1890–3). Added to these economic troubles, the governing coalition in Peruvian politics weakened steadily after Caceres' departure from the Presidency in 1890, and Congressional criticism of Government policy sharpened, focusing particularly upon the terms of the Grace Contract. Relations between the Government and the Peruvian Corporation (the company set up by the former bondholders) deteriorated rapidly after Congress in 1892 revoked the Corporation's disputed rights to the drainage concession for the mines at Cerro de Pasco.[6] Against this background of economic disintegration and political instability, the accusations exchanged between the Government and the Peruvian Corporation put an end to the brief honeymoon with British capital. A new excursion into foreign-financed growth had to await the awakening of U.S. interest in Peru; meanwhile, from 1892 until the early twentieth century, economic expansion had to be organised, financed and controlled locally.

The challenge evoked its response. In a few years during the second half of the 1890s, Peruvian and immigrant capitalists constructed a remarkably successful framework for autonomous local development. As we shall see, an intensive mobilisation of local resources permitted the simultaneous development of new export sectors and of a rapidly-expanding urban manufacturing and utilities sector. A thriving financial system – banks, insurance companies, and a Stock Exchange – was created almost from scratch, to capture and allocate the economic surplus generated in the export industries. Moreover, the regional effects of growth at this time were remarkably widespread. Export growth was not limited to the Coast, but included also silver, gold and copper mines dispersed throughout the Sierra, production of coffee and cocaine in the central and northern 'montana', and the rubber boom in the Amazon Basin. Most regions of the country had their own growth poles, and integration among them was increasing—a trend most noticeable in the labour market, as inter-regional migration revived and a new working class began to form in mines, plantations, and factories.

Not only could contemporary observers point to Peru as one of the fastest-growing Latin American economies,[7] but they were also aware of the unusually 'national' character of that expansion.[8] The events of the 1890s demonstrated that, given a suitable conjuncture of circumstances, Peru could produce a capable class of entrepreneurs, mobilise substantial resources for investment, and sustain a process of growth in which the profits of export sectors were channelled into the expansion of other areas of the economy.

The period beginning in the 1890s is therefore one of exceptional significance in terms of our general framework. The unusual circumstances which generated relative isolation from international factor movements without implying a disruption of international commodity markets permitted a strong expansion, while yet more unusual circumstances directed that expansion into new channels of potential long-run significance. The period therefore provides an unusually solid base on which to evaluate certain types of argument accounting for underdevelopment, namely those based on lack of local capacity to undertake the task of development. It also provides a clear-cut opportunity to study the forces operating for and against the continuation of the process in the years which followed.

Chapter 3 documents the process of growth and diversification, analysing what made it possible, and concluding by examining the conditions that would have been required for its continuation. The chapters which follow indicate the degree to which these conditions were present in the following thirty years, and in this light examine what became of the early effort.

3 The 1890s: Growth and Diversification

The driving force for rapid economic growth during the 1890s was the expansion of exports during the second half of the decade. Referring back to Figure 1.1, we see that the gradual recovery of export volume after the War of the Pacific was cut short in 1893–4 with a fall in both volume and value. This fall was attributable both to the local recession caused by the collapse of silver prices in 1892,[1] and more particularly to the civil war which swept through Peru in those years, culminating in the victory of Pierola in March 1895. With the re-establishment of civil peace and political stability came a revival of business confidence and activity, and export production embarked on a rapid long-run expansion which was to continue until the 1920s. Data problems make export earnings difficult to trace, but we have assembled estimates of the CIF value of the eight main export products other than guano, with results which are summarised in Table 3.1.[2] Our series shows a slight upward trend in export earnings during the years 1887–92, a fall in 1893–4, and then a dramatic expansion of 19 per cent a year from 1895 to 1900, led by sugar, metals and rubber. From 1900 to 1903 there was a pause in export expansion due mainly to a sharp fall in international commodity prices and a reduction in the volume of metals exports (for reasons discussed in Chapter 5 below). Rapid growth then resumed until 1907 when another recession began.

The very rapid export expansion from 1895 to 1900 is attributable mainly to exchange depreciation and accumulated investment. Price data for Peru's main export products[3] indicate that in the mid-1890s world prices were generally lower than in the 1880s; but this downward trend in world markets was more than offset by the rapid depreciation of Peru's silver-based currency in the years 1892–4 as world silver prices fell sharply. The Peruvian sol, which in 1890 had been worth 37 pence, had fallen to 24 pence by 1894,[4] a devaluation of 35 per cent. This produced an initial recession (due to the impact of falling prices on the silver-mining industry and the economy's import capacity),[5] but in the longer run boosted the profits of most export producers and also of local import-competing industry. Meantime, so far as investment was concerned, the 15 years after the War of the Pacific had been a period of reconstruction from which several export sectors emerged reorganised

TABLE 3.1 CIF value of eight main export products (Sugar, cotton, wool, alpaca, coffee, silver, copper and rubber), 1880–1910
(thousands of pounds sterling)

	CIF Value		CIF Value
1880	1,943	1896	2,091
1881	1,652	1897	2,477
1882	1,697	1898	2,812
1883	1,421	1899	3,302
1884	1,808	1900	3,892
1885	1,672	1901	3,571
1886	1,641	1902	2,883
1887	1,551	1903	3,527
1888	1,849	1904	3,996
1889	2,046	1905	4,175
1890	1,781	1906	4,659
1891	1,909	1907	5,278
1892	2,120	1908	4,462
1893	1,968	1909	5,023
1894	1,532	1910	6,231
1895	1,663		

Source: Appendix 1.

and re-equipped. The increased profitability consequent upon exchange-rate depreciation quickly called forth further heavy investment in these sectors.

The detailed histories of the various export sectors are discussed in later chapters. In this chapter we look first at the interaction of the export sectors with the rest of the economy, then examine in detail the evidence for the remarkable diversification which we shall show occurred.

It is often argued that rapid export growth discourages, rather than promotes, economic diversification, for three main reasons: first, because rising profitability and expectations of producers tend to encourage reinvestment of profits in the export sectors themselves (with diversification more likely to occur during periods when expectation of profits in export production are lower); second, because abundant foreign exchange earnings lead to an exchange rate which favours imports against local production; and third, because buoyant exports lead to increased tax revenue and foreign-borrowing options for government, thus reducing the revenue motive for raising tariffs on imports. Where such conditions hold, the expected pattern of economic growth may be summarised as a concentration of investment in export sectors, a strong exchange rate supported both by export earnings and by the capital inflow which they encourage, and relatively low tariffs which fail to compensate local import-competing industry for the economy's high import capacity. In so far as surplus is generated in excess of the investment needs of export sectors, it tends to be invested abroad (especially when foreign firms are significant among export producers) or spent on capitalists' consumption.

Peru in the 1890s diverged from this pattern. Export growth went hand in hand with economic diversification and industrialisation. An examination of the circumstances in which this occurred reveals an unusual conjuncture: successful export sectors with high returned value, generating large demand effects in the local economy and leaving surplus in the hands of local capitalists over and above that required for re-investment in further export expansion; yet, at the same time, a relative-price situation which made urban manufacturing sufficiently profitable to attract investment capital. The discussion which follows considers each of these elements in turn.

3.1 RETURNED VALUE

Around the turn of the century, most of the major Peruvian export sectors were returning a high proportion of their foreign-exchange earnings to Peru.[6] Despite tendencies towards increasing concentration and capital-intensity (especially in the sugar industry), techniques of production were still relatively labour-intensive; in the mid-1890s, 24,000 workers were employed in sugar production,[7] and 66,600 in mining.[8] In addition to the stimulus to local demand from the wage bill of the export sectors, both sugar production and mining generated linkage effects of some importance, especially by their purchases of capital goods from local foundries. These foundries had long been supplying equipment for sugar mills (even in some cases complete mills), while in the 1890s the building of smelters to process silver and copper ores created a new demand for equipment since many of the smelters erected during the 1890s and early 1900s were of local manufacture.[9] The engineering workshops attached to the railways also constituted important centres of capital goods production.

Local ownership was the rule in the leading export sectors, and the profitability of those sectors provided local capitalists with surplus funds over and above their re-investment needs.[10] Once confidence was re-established after the civil war, large sums were available for investment in any activity which promised to return a good profit; by 1899 President Pierola was remarking on the mobilisation and investment of 'capital previously concealed, unproductive, or diverted to foreign countries.'[11]

3.2 RELATIVE PRICES

Strong local demand and large supplies of funds for investment, however, do not suffice to generate a diversification process in an open economy. Demand can be met by imports as well as by local production; funds can be invested in export sectors or abroad, or used for luxury consumption, rather than invested in non-export activities. Only sectors which are protected from import competition by their very nature (utilities, for example, and products with very high weight-to-value ratios) can expect to benefit automatically from such a situation. In Peru during the 1890s, however, relative prices shifted sharply in favour of import-substituting industry, which as a result became profitable enough to attract investment capital. Both a depreciating exchange rate and large increases in tariffs accompanied the expansion of demand fuelled by the export sectors. The falling exchange rate (a result of world developments rather than domestic price movements) created a price advantage for local industry which was amplified by an increase in effective tariff protection.

The depreciation of the exchange rate is shown in Table 3.2. Between 1890 and 1897 the fall was nearly 40 per cent, a result simply of the effect

TABLE 3.2 Value of the sol in
British pennies, 1883–1900

	Exchange rate
1883	39.67
1887	35.28
1890	36.92
1891	35.80
1892	31.14
1893	26.71
1894	24.18
1895	24.22
1896	23.53
1897	23.19
1898	24.01
1899	24.00[a]
1900	24.00[a]

Source: Calculated from *Extracto Estadístico*, 1934–5, pp. 34–7. Rates are averages of high and low rates for all months.
[a] Gold Standard par.

on a silver-based currency of the fall in world silver prices which occurred once the U.S. ceased to support the price in 1892. Domestic price data for this period are non-existent, but the qualitative evidence indicates that it was only by 1898 that the problem of inflation had become serious.[12] Wages in the meantime rose more slowly,[13] widening the margin of profitability for local industry.

The increase in tariff rates was a result of the Government's need for revenues. An export boom might have been expected to relieve any revenue constraint, by increasing the yield from export taxes and the Government's ability to borrow abroad. In Peru, however, export taxes did not exist in the 1890s, as during the high prosperity of the guano era these and various other taxes (notably the poll tax on the Indian population) had been allowed to lapse. After 1880 the political strength of the export producers enabled them to resist the imposition of export taxes: mining was granted a fifteen-year exemption in 1890,[14] and the sugar producers were able to prevent any taxation of agricultural exports.[15] Foreign borrowing was impossible, given Peru's reputation as a recent defaulter, combined with the effects of the Baring Crisis on the London financial market. Inflationary financing of the government sector had been ruled out by the monetary reform of 1887. To cap all this, the transfer of guano export earnings from the Government to the Peruvian Corporation as part of the 1890 Grace Contract abruptly cut fiscal income by about half. Of the few tax options which remained open to maintain solvency, tariffs on imports were the easiest to apply, and encountered the least resistance.

In the 1860s, the highest rate of import duty had been 30 per cent *ad valorem*, and the average was about 20 per cent. The first increases were introduced in 1874–5:[16] by 1891 the average incidence of duties on the 80 per cent of import items subject to duty was 39 per cent, giving an overall incidence of 31 per cent.[17] After long debate a new customs schedule was introduced in 1889–90, and an 8 per cent surcharge on all import duties was added in January 1893.[18] In 1894 an attempt by the Government to impose sweeping increases to finance the suppression of the Pierolista revolt was blocked by Congress,[19] but the following year the new Pierola regime, still in search of additional revenues, pushed through a doubling of the rates on a number of consumer goods[20] and even greater increases in certain cases—for example, matches, the duty on which was raised from 40 per cent to 250 per cent.[21] In the key area of cheap cotton textiles, the duty per yard more than doubled between the 1870s and the 1890s.[22] In addition, the effectiveness of the decreed rates of duty was increased in the 1890s by reform of the Customs administration (reducing corruption and misreporting)[23] and by the more stable conditions which followed the ending of the civil war in 1895. Contemporary comment reflects the effectiveness of all these measures in providing protection for local industry; the head of the

Customs, for example, complained in 1894 that 'the Customs are expected to produce revenues, yet these are only reduced by protectionist tariffs.'[24]

Until the mid-1890s, tariff increases had been designed without much thought for protectionist aims (many of the high-duty luxury import categories, for example, were goods unlikely to be produced in Peru, as critics noted,[25] the result being an increase in smuggling of these lines rather than more local production).[26] The political strength of export interests, however, had ensured that high duties were imposed on consumer goods rather than on such items as machinery and equipment or many intermediate goods, and the Pierola regime in 1895 removed several of the duties which did apply on these classes of goods.[27] Effective protection (as distinct from nominal tariffs) was thus sharply increased.

For those consumer-goods industries which could be quickly established or expanded, the combined effects of high effective protection and exchange depreciation made local production profitable in competition with imports, at a time when the expansion of export earnings was providing a strong and sustained boost to local demand. Capital poured into industry,[28] to the alarm of local defenders of the theory of free trade and comparative advantage, and in the closing years of the century debate over the merits or otherwise of protectionism raged in the press and in Congress.[29]

The heat of the debate owed much to the fact that among the promoters of non-export ventures were many of the country's leading export producers and merchants. Sugar planters were particularly prominent; Jose Pardo, for example, established the Fabrica de Tejidos La Victoria in 1897, and was manager of the factory until he became President of Peru in 1903.[30] The Pardo family were also involved in a series of banks and insurance companies in Lima, as were the Aspillaga family (like the Pardos, planters from Lambayeque). Investments by the Aspillagas reported in the contemporary business press[31] included two insurance companies, two banks, a tax-collecting company, an electricity-generating plant, a tramways company in Lima, the Salaverry wharf company, a mining company, and an unsuccessful venture into jute sack manufacturing. Various other leading planters and mine-owners appear on the directorates of companies listed by Yepes.[32] Export capitalists who were not themselves directly involved in the promotion of new projects could contribute funds to the process through the rapidly-expanding system of financial intermediaries which emerged at this time, particularly the new banks. The principal organising genius of this financial network was the banker and businessman Jose Payan.[33]

We have seen, therefore, how the favourable situation for industry had arisen not out of deliberate government strategy, nor from determined pressure applied by any politically-powerful group, but out of a chance combination of circumstances. By the end of the 1890s circumstances were changing. Peru went on to the gold standard in 1897, thus halting exchange depreciation,[34] and the establishment of efficient tax-collecting companies made possible a switch to excise taxes on sugar, alcohol and tobacco as a major new source of government revenues after 1900, thus reducing the role of import tariffs. The preservation of protection for local industry would have required, at the very least, the existence of a large and politically-powerful industrialist class. Instead, the new industrial sector was controlled by exporters, merchants, financiers, and relatively recent immigrants.

3.3 THE EVIDENCE

Before we turn, in the conclusion to this chapter, to spell out more fully the conditions which would have been required for the further development of these promising beginnings, we must first present the evidence for our claim that diversification made significant progress at this time. As we have indicated, the three non-export sectors which led the process were import-substituting industry, public utilities and financial institutions. In the remainder of this section we survey the evidence for the growth of these three sectors, and particularly manufacturing.[35]

In no case, of course, did the growth appear out of nowhere. Particularly in manufacturing, the years following the War of the Pacific had witnessed the establishment of a number of enterprises which were forerunners of the industrial boom of the late 1890s. Responsibility for most of these ventures rested with either foreign (mainly British) capital, or immigrant entrepreneurs seeking to establish themselves in Peru and finding the urban economy the easiest point of entry. Several immigrant groups had already begun to move into particular lines of industrial production before the War—Germans in brewing, Italians in macaroni, British in flour milling and small engineering works.[36] The years following the war saw many of these enterprises built up to larger-scale operations, while their ranks were swelled by new entrants.[37] The establishment by the Italian colony of the Banco Italiano in 1889 was a milestone for industrial development, as this bank provided the financial basis for a growing number of small Italian-owned ventures, especially in foodstuffs.[38] Further, while immigrant and foreign capital made their appearance at the top of the industrial structure, the 1880s and early 1890s also witnessed a revival of artisan manufacturing,[39] with the emergence of a local petty-bourgeoisie in sectors such as leather tanning, cigarettes, furniture, shirt manufacture, and various food products.[40]

TABLE 3.3 Share of manufactured consumer goods (excluding foodstuffs) in total imports, 1891–1907

| | Percentages of total imports by value | | | | |
	Textiles	Clothing	Other non-durables[a]	Durables	Total
1891–2 (av.)	29.2	7.0	15.2	6.2	57.6
1897	29.5	6.0	11.7	7.1	54.3
1900	25.2	6.3	11.0	6.9	49.4
1902	22.0	6.0	9.3	6.4	43.7
1907	14.7	6.7	10.4	7.2	39.0

Source: Bertram (1976).
[a] The exclusion of foodstuffs accounts for the difference between our totals and those in Bertram (1976) Table 10.

With the 1890s, however, came a swift acceleration. Industrial production data are very scarce for this decade, but other indicators are available. Most significant is the falling share of consumer goods (including textiles) in the total import bill between 1891 and 1907, traced in Table 3.3. From 58 per cent of total imports in 1891–2, these categories of goods had fallen to 49 per cent by 1900 and to 39 per cent by 1907. The most dramatic fall was registered in textiles, the share of which in total imports fell by half between 1897 and 1907. This change in the composition of Peruvian imports was due mostly to import-substituting industrialisation. (The other possible explanation for the altered import composition, namely a change in the structure of local demand, is unlikely to have had more than a slight effect over such a short period, and is not indicated by any of the contemporary literature.) Several observers during the 1890s and early 1900s commented on the inroads which native manufactured goods were making into markets traditionally dominated by imports. Comparing the import statistics for 1891 and 1897–8, Gubbins demonstrated steep declines in both the quantity and the value of imports of beer, candles, soap, cigarettes, shoes, shirts, furniture, wines, and textiles, all of which had been subject to substitution.[41] A heated debate in the Lima press in 1901 focused upon the revenues lost to the Government as a result of the success of the two recently-established local match factories in displacing imported matches from the market of Central Peru.[42] The expansion of these new industrial sectors is most strikingly illustrated by the case of cotton textiles.

Until the 1890s there had been only one cotton-textile mill in Peru (the Vitarte plant which was taken over in 1890 by British capital). New mills were established in 1892, 1897 (two), 1898, 1901 and 1902, all except one financed and controlled by local capitalists (the U.S. merchant firm

W. R. Grace and Company took a one-third share in the 1902 venture).[43] As the new mills came into production, local output of cotton textiles rose to eight million yards per year by 1899 and to 20 million yards by 1904 (see Table 3.4). Substitution was initially in the cheap grades, particularly *tocuyo*[44] (while growing demand for more expensive fabrics continued to be met by imports). As a percentage of total supply of cotton textiles, local production rose from less than 5 per cent in 1890 to 42 per cent by 1906.

TABLE 3.4 Local production of cotton textiles, 1891–1908
(in million yards)

	(1)	(2)	(3)	(4)	(5)
	Local production	Imports	Total supply	Exports	Local production as a percentage of total supply
1891	1.5	28.5	30.0	–	5
1898	8.0	31.2	39.2	–	20
1901	15.0	29.3	44.3	1.2	34
1902	18.0	27.4	45.4	1.2	40
1903	20.0	n.a.	n.a.	n.a.	n.a.
1904	23.5	30.9	54.4	2.4	43
1905	25.0	31.9	56.9	1.9	44
1906	22.0	30.4	52.4	1.8	42
1907	21.5	31.6	53.1	1.1	40
1908	25.0	27.8	52.8	1.1	47

Sources: Column 1 was assembled from various sources—
1891 based upon a statement in *Financial News* (London) March 21, 1891 (Council of Foreign Bondholders, Press clippings file, Guildhall Library, London) that the capacity of the sole existing textile mill at Vitarte would be raised to 2.5 million yards by a large investment programme.
1898 from Gubbins (1899) p. 5.
1901 from Garland (1902a).
1902–7 estimated from the trend of mill consumption of locally-ginned cotton (Appendix II). These data indicate that the output estimate of 20 million yards given by Garland (1905) is almost certainly for 1903, while the 25 million yards output given in Cisneros (1906), p. 157, is clearly for 1905. 1908 is from U.K. Parliamentary Papers, Vol. CXV, 1908, p. 33.
Columns 2 and 4 are from *Estadística del Comercio Especial*, various years; imports converted to yards at 1 kilo = 8 yards; exports converted at 1 kilo = 6 yards.

Evidence on the general expansion of manufacturing is also provided by the number of new firms established in the sector during the 1890s and early 1900s. The first industrial census, conducted in 1902 by Alejandro Garland, found 256 firms of factory size (the precise criterion was not specified) of which 83 were export processing enterprises (sugar, cocaine, oil) and 32 were rural processing (cottonseed mills and rice mills). Adding eight foundries which Garland omitted, we have 264 firms, of which 149 are clearly identifiable as urban manufacturing.[45] We have been able to identify 120 of these 149 firms and to determine the date of establishment of 87. Forty-two had begun during the 1890s, and over half of these were from the years 1896–9. Twelve firms dated from the 1880s, and 22 were survivors from the years before the War of the Pacific. The remaining 11 had been established during the years 1900–2. Thus of our sample of 87 firms operating in 1902, roughly 60 per cent had been established since 1890.

In 1905 Garland conducted a second census, which showed a total of 173 urban manufacturing firms (again excluding export processing and rural processing); net additions to the sector in 1902–5 thus totalled 24. Combining this with our data on the 87 firms analysed above, we can say that of a sample comprising 111 (64 per cent) of the urban manufacturing firms operating in 1905, 77 firms (69 per cent) had been established since 1890. This is not, of course, a representative sample; the 87 firms from the 1902 census constituted the top half of the industrial sector— firms large enough to have merited individual mention by contemporary observers. We would suggest that for the remainder of the population of industrial firms, the proportion originating since 1890 would have been still higher.[46]

Alongside the growth of urban manufacturing went the expansion of privately-owned utilities companies. The first electrical generating plant was established in Lima in 1895 to supply power for industrial use,[47] and in the following six years two other large electricity companies were formed,[48] as well as four new electric-tramways companies to serve the outlying suburbs.[49] The 1890s saw water-supply and wharf-operating companies established throught the country, all under local control. In 1906 the Lima electricity, gas, and tramways companies were merged into a single giant firm, Empresas Electricas Asociadas, headed by the two leading promoters of utilities development, Mariano Ignacio Prado and Jose Payan.[50] In the first decade of the twentieth century Lima was unique among Latin American capitals in having its utilities locally owned and operated, with hardly any British investment.[51]

Turning to developments in the capital market and financial system, we immediately encounter the towering figure of Jose Payan, a Cuban-born immigrant who had become manager of a local bank in 1879.[52] This, the Banco de Callao, was the sole survivor of the banks set up before the War of the Pacific. Although the late 1880s produced a second bank[53] and an important new piece of financial legislation (the 1889 Mortgage Law, designed by Payan)[54] it was not until peace returned with the establishment of the Pierola regime in 1895 that the main period of expansion began. Thereafter new developments followed one another in rapid succession, with Payan and his associates at the centre of a spreading web of financial institutions. In 1897 the Banco de Callao became the Banco del Peru y Londres, with direct links to the London financial market,[55] while between 1895 and 1904 local interests established two new banks,[56] seven insurance companies,[57] and a Stock Exchange.[58] Parallel with the growth of the financial firms, and linked to them, went the establishment of new enterprises engaged in tax-collecting.[59]

The expansion of the financial system in its early years was very rapid. Total paid-up capital of the banks increased from Lp 375,000 in 1897 to Lp 1 million by 1906, while in the same nine-year period deposits rose from Lp 1.4 million to Lp 3.8 million.[60] In the first three years after the establishment of the Stock Exchange successful company flotations totalled over Lp 1.3 million,[61] and by 1900 there were 55 enterprises listed on the Exchange.[62] Perhaps the most interesting and symptomatic event of the period, however, was the use of legislation to encourage the development of locally-owned insurance companies between 1895 and 1901.[63] In 1895 the Government, alarmed at the large outflow of funds resulting from the operations of the fifteen offices of foreign insurance companies then active in the country, decreed that each company had to maintain in Peru a minimum effective capital of S/100,000, of which 30 per cent had to be invested in Peruvian securities. Foreign companies began to withdraw from Peru in protest, and their place was quickly taken by new local companies, which captured a rapidly-growing share of the market. By 1901 the local companies had become powerful enough to push through further legislation raising the minimum local capital to S/200,000, 50 per cent to be invested in local securities. All but one of the foreign companies withdrew at this stage, leaving the field clear for another wave of new Peruvian entrants.

Thus within a very few years, an effective and very profitable[64] network of financial intermediaries was established and the ability of the local economy to mobilise capital was greatly increased—a fact manifested by the ability of the Government in 1898 to finance its budget deficit by floating an internal loan.[65]

3.4 CONCLUSION: THE PRECONDITIONS FOR AUTONOMOUS DEVELOPMENT

This chapter has shown that Peru in the 1890s achieved at least some degree of 'autonomous development': a dynamic, locally-controlled, and broadly-based expansion, laying the groundwork for a more diversified economy, with increasing technological capacity and a local capital-goods sector. During the first thirty years of the twentieth century, however, the economy changed direction, returning to the more familiar patterns of a dependent export-led system. This process provides the subject of the next three chapters. To conclude our discussion here of the brief experiment with autonomous growth, we shall attempt to spell out the conditions which might have led to further growth along the lines of the years from 1895 to about 1907.

The first obvious requirement would have been a continuing stimulus to economic activity, whether derived from exports, investment or government spending. In the case of Peru such stimulus would have had to depend primarily upon growing exports; in order to generate a rapid growth both of internal demand and of investible surplus, export growth would have had to be characterised by

(i) High returned value, so that rising export earnings fed through to the local economy,

(ii) Strong linkage effects, particularly as regards capital goods (otherwise local technological capability would tend to decay), and

(iii) Substantial profits retained locally and exceeding the reinvestment needs of the export sectors themselves.

One obvious implication of the above list is that increased foreign ownership of export sectors, in so far as it led to a fall in returned value and/or an increase in the leakage of surplus out of the country, could threaten the prospects for autonomy.

A second requirement would have been relative prices which sustained the economic viability of non-export sectors, and thereby prevented an undue draining-off of resources from those sectors to export production or unproductive use. If such incentives to local manufacturing and non-export agriculture were not forthcoming in a *laissez-faire* environment, some form of policy intervention would have been required.

Obviously, this leads on to a third requirement, which is the existence of some politically-powerful interest group committed to obtaining appropriate policy measures from the government (and capable of resisting pressures from other groups for inappropriate policies). Examples of such groups would be a well-connected industrialist class determined to sustain the viability of local industry; or a strong organised working-class committed to goals such as industrial employment; or a powerful farming interest excluded from export production and hence eager to obtain more incentives for non-export agriculture.

Finally, and again following from the above, policy intervention on strategic economic issues could have come about only if the government itself had been willing to accommodate the demands of the relevant interest groups. This could have occurred either as a result of control by such groups over the political process; or for entirely separate reasons, such as the strong desire of government in the 1890s to increase its revenues at a time when import tariffs offered the easiest option.

The chapters which follow will indicate the degree to which these various elements were present in Peruvian development from 1900 to 1930. Chapters 4 and 5 analyse the main export sectors and their contribution to economic growth. Chapter 6 considers the repercussions of export growth on the rest of the economy, and the importance of other local developments, with particular reference to two leading non-export sectors, manufacturing and domestic agriculture. Chapter 7, which concludes this section of the book, reviews Peru's experience in the period between 1890 and 1930, and considers the stage the economy had reached by the time Peru was struck by the major external disaster of the World Depression of 1930.

4 Export Crops, 1890-1930

4.1 INTRODUCTION

In this chapter and the next we examine the mainspring of the economy: the export sectors. In each case-study we begin by analysing the rate of growth in different periods, and the extent to which this was determined by the changing opportunities presented by world markets. We then go on to consider the relationship of developments in each export sector with trends in the rest of the economy; this entails in particular a study of the mode of production and nature of ownership within each sector, and the consequent linkages (or lack of them) with other sectors. The underlying hypothesis of these two chapters is that the failure to sustain the process of relatively-autonomous growth is to be explained in large part by developments within the export sectors.

Peru's exports were unusually diversified by Latin American standards, as shown in Table 4.1, no single product accounting for more than one-third of total earnings. The balance among the seven products shown, however, shifted over time as first one sector, then another, took the lead in export growth. Sugar, followed by copper, led the export growth of the 1890s, while in the first decade of the twentieth century cotton and rubber were the products whose share increased. In the 1910s the decline of rubber was partly offset by the appearance of petroleum as a major export. The main beneficiaries of the booming commodities markets during the First World War and the immediate post-war years, were the agricultural products sugar and cotton, but in the 1920s these two sectors suffered an eclipse as mineral exports moved into an unchallenged lead.

Corresponding to these shifts in the composition of exports came changes in the structure of the export economy itself. The leading export sectors of the 1890s and early 1900s (including silver and copper at that time) were geographically dispersed, locally controlled, and had relatively close links with the rest of the economy. (The only exception was the rubber industry on account of its geographical location.) By the First World War, when export earnings soared to an unprecedented peak, the export economy was becoming increasingly concentrated on the Coast (where sugar, cotton and petroleum production were expanding), while the established export industries of the Sierra and Selva (rubber, silver, wool, coffee and cocaine) were heading into a relative decline. Of the

TABLE 4.1 Composition of exports by value,[a] 1890–1930 (percentage shares)

	Sugar	Cotton	Wool[b]	Silver	Copper	Rubber	Petroleum
1890	28	9	15	33	1	13	–
1895	35	7	15	26	1	14	–
1900	32	7	7	22	18	13	–
1905	32	7	8	6	10	16	–
1910	20	14	7	10	18	18	2
1915	26	11	5	5	17	5	10
1920	42	30	2	5	7	1	5
1925	11	32	4	10	8	1	24
1930	11	18	3	4	10	–	30

Sources: 1890–1900 calculated from the eight-product data in Appendix I, Table 3; 1905–1930 from *Extracto Estadistico* 1939, pp. 247 and 238–9, with the exception of silver and copper, which were calculated by the method used in Appendix I for the whole period, since in the data in *Extracto Estadistico* the silver content of copper ore is not shown.

[a] The percentage shares are only very approximate, since some exports were valued fob, some cif—it often being unclear what the practice was. (On problems of valuation, see Thorp, 1975). The rows sum to less than 100 % owing to the exclusion of minor export items.
[b] Including alpaca.

Sierra's export products only copper retained its dynamism; and, in contrast to the declining sectors, copper production was regionally highly-concentrated, the great bulk of production occurring at Cerro de Pasco and Morococha in the central Sierra.

The balance between local and foreign capital also shifted in the latter's favour. Copper, silver and oil had all, by 1910, become dominated by large foreign firms, although sugar, cotton and wool remained in local hands. The rise of mineral exports, which became especially pronounced in the 1920s, therefore implied the rise of foreign capital, while export sectors owned by local firms went into first a relative and then an absolute decline during the 1920s. The surplus generated in export production became increasingly concentrated in foreign rather than local hands, at the same time as the regional focus of the economy became narrower.

The sugar, cotton, wool and rubber sectors, which played leading roles in export growth up to the late 1910s but then dropped behind, form the subjects of the present chapter. The mineral products copper and oil, which had risen to dominate the export economy by the 1920s, are considered in the next.

4.2 THE SUGAR SECTOR

Like cotton, sugar was a coastal crop, and in the 1890s was grown in irrigated valleys scattered throughout the length of the country. In contrast to cotton, sugar was a sector in which economies of scale and the greater efficiency of mechanised processes dictated a trend towards large-scale enterprises organised on entirely capitalist lines and employing wage labour on a regular basis. The chief characteristic which distinguished the Peruvian sugar industry from its counterparts elsewhere in the world, and which strongly reinforced the trend towards large-scale units, was the absence of seasonality in production: sugar in Peru can be harvested all the year round, and favourable ecological conditions result in exceptionally high yields.[1] The labour force is therefore relatively constant throughout the year, with little need for seasonal hiring of temporary workers, and the most efficient production system is that of the large wage-labour plantation.[2]

Consequently, one of the main features of the period was a steady increase in the concentration of ownership of sugar land. This had begun in the 1860s, and in the period following the War of the Pacific most areas experienced further concentration.[3] The best-known case is that of the Chicama Valley in La Libertad, where the dominant families of the pre-war era were bought out by three expanding enterprises.[4] These were the Larco family (Italian immigrants of the 1850s, who had bought their first sugar plantation in the area in 1872); the Gildemeister family (immigrant German merchants, who bought the *hacienda* Casagrande from another German, Luis Albrecht, in 1889); and the merchant house W.R. Grace and Co., which acquired the *hacienda* Cartavio from the Alzamora family in 1882 by foreclosure on a loan. All three enterprises enjoyed an advantage over the other landowners of the valley in their access to adequate capital or credit facilities, which enabled them to survive the difficult times up to 1894 and after 1900, and to finance the purchase of the estates of others less well-placed.[5] The Gildemeister and Larco families had between them bought up at least sixteen properties by the mid-1890s, and during the depressed years of the early twentieth century they added another fourteen.

In the neighbouring Santa Catalina Valley a similar steady concentration of properties in the hands of the Chopitea family resulted in the expansion of the Laredo plantation,[6] while in the Cañete valley south of Lima the Scottish immigrant planter Henry Swayne had built up the Santa Barbara plantation from a number of smaller properties.[7] In several other areas, although concentration was less marked, properties passed into the hands of creditors in the 1880s.[8]

The most stable area so far as the post-war pattern of ownership went was Lambayeque, where the impact of the War of the Pacific was evidently less drastic than farther south. The two leading sugar-planting families of this area, the Pardos and Aspillagas, had both established themselves on a fairly large scale before the war, and were able to survive and expand with the help of credit from merchant houses. Ownership transfers in the other estates of the valley, in so far as they occurred, did not imply changes of the sort experienced farther south.[9]

The boom of the late 1890s brought a new set of changes in ownership as capital for investment was mobilised. The usual pattern in coastal areas close to Lima was the formation of partnerships or incorporated joint-stock companies bringing together landowners and financiers for the construction of large new mills, some of them designed to operate as *centrales* (milling cane from a number of properties).[10] In the far north and south of the Coast, farther from the stock market and banks of Lima, family enterprises of the old variety remained the rule, and capital from outside, when needed, was obtained through informal credit links with merchant houses rather than by floating new companies.

By the first decade of the twentieth century the process had slowed down, apart from the continuing expansion of the two main Chicama Valley estates, and a probable increase in the amount of sugar land around Lima controlled by members of the country's financial, industrial, and mining élite.[11] The 1910s brought few major ownership changes; three plantations were bought by foreign merchant houses during the decade, but all three were resold to Peruvians in the 1920s.[12] The main events of the 1920s were the consolidation of the Gildemeister holdings in the Chicama Valley through the acquisition of Roma, the bankrupt Larco estate; and the sale of the Paramonga plantation by its local owners to W.R. Grace and Co. in 1926.[13]

In summary, the 1880s and 1890s witnessed widespread changes and reorganisation in the ownership structure of the industry, while by the early twentieth century the new order had become established. Over the succeeding thirty years there was a steady but gradual trend towards concentration of sugar production in the hands of about a dozen leading enterprises, due partly to further takeovers of smaller enterprises by the leaders (mainly in Chicama), but more importantly to the regional concentration of production discussed below, as many planters in the Centre and South withdrew from sugar growing during the 1910s and 1920s. By the end of the 1920s the industry was dominated by a few large enterprises located mostly on the north Coast, and the list of 'sugar barons' had shrunk dramatically from the great days of the 1890s.

As the above discussion has indicated, foreign capital played only a subsidiary role in the development of the sugar industry, despite the widely-accepted stereotype of sugar as a 'foreign-controlled' sector.[14] While many of the sugar growers relied on foreign merchant houses for short-term financial assistance as well as marketing services, actual control of the industry and the bulk of its profits remained in local hands. Hostile comments on the 'foreign-ness' of the sugar growers[15] generally referred to the immigrant origin of many of the leading families, examples being the Gildemeister, Larco, Aspillaga, Swayne, and De la Piedra families. In only a few plantations did foreign firms actually take control, and in most cases this was due not to any deliberate strategy of penetration, but to the attempt to recover debts; both Grace and Locketts entered the industry by this means. In the case of Grace, the firm seems to have been slow to press on with development at Cartavio, and it was Peruvian, not foreign, capital which installed and operated the new mill of the late 1890s. By the 1920s, when Grace purchased Paramonga, the company had obviously become committed to sugar production; but other foreign merchant firms which at various times acquired plantations generally sold out when a good opportunity offered (Milne, Barber Vargas, Locketts), or were content to remain minor operators on the fringes of the industry (Fraser Luckie and Co. at Andahuasi). Sugar, in summary, was a 'Peruvian' sector, and its periods of rise and decline were consequently periods of rise and decline also for an important fraction of Peruvian capital.

Sources and patterns of growth

Figures on the expansion of sugar production will be found in Appendix 2. By decade, the percentage increase in production was as follows:

1889–1900	83
1900–1910	38
1910–1920	77
1920–1930	28
1930–1940	18

Production and exports grew very rapidly during the period 1894–7, and again from 1914 to 1916. In both of these periods the sudden surge of growth carried sugar into the lead among Peru's exports; in the 1900s and 1920s other products took the lead and the share of sugar fell. The 1920s brought a particularly steep decline in the sugar industry's share of export earnings as falling prices more than offset the continuing growth of production; and by the 1930s the sector had sunk into virtual stagnation.

The aggregate figures conceal the fact that during the first thirty years of the century the production of sugar became regionally very concentrated, a process which is traced by Table 4.2. The north Coast, which in the 1890s had accounted for less than half of the total production, was the scene of almost all the twentieth-century expansion of the industry, while other sugar growing areas turned to other crops. By the early 1920s the north's share of output had reached 75 per cent, and by the 1930s it was over 80 per cent.

The expansion of exports after the War of the Pacific appears to have corresponded closely to the 'vent for surplus' model of export growth. At the turn of the century, local consumption of sugar absorbed only

TABLE 4.2 Regional distribution of sugar production, selected years (percentages)

	North Coast	Central Coast	South Coast	Sierra
1894	49.9	41.5	5.9	2.8
1912	66.8	29.4	1.1	2.7
1916	70.0	27.2	1.2	1.6[a]
1922	73.4	23.7	1.6	1.3
1927	76.8[b]	20.3	1.8	1.2
1932	83.0[b]	16.6	2.3	2.0
1937	88.4	6.9	2.1	2.6[c]
1941	90.0	5.6	1.7	2.6[c]

Notes 'North Coast' comprises Piura, Lambayeque, La Libertad and Ancash. 'Central Coast' comprises the Department of Lima (including the valleys of Pativilca and Canete). 'South Coast' comprises Ica, Arequipa, Moquegua and Tacna. 'Sierra' includes production of the montana.
[a] In this year the statistics gave no production figure for the Sierra; an estimate of 4,500 tons has therefore been interpolated on the basis of 1912 and 1922 data, and the total production adjusted accordingly.
[b] Including the category 'other Coast', comprising Piura, one Lambayeque property, and Camana (this last is in the South, but of very small weight).
[c] Including some small coastal properties not providing detailed information.

Sources: 1894 is from Garland (1895). 1912 onwards is from the annual official statistics published in *Estadística de Producción de Azúcar*, and reproduced in the following sources from which the figures were taken:
1912 from Scott (1972) p. 10.
1916 from *Extracto Estadístico del Perú*, 1918, p. 97.
1922 from *Extracto Estadístico del Perú*, 1922, p. 88.
1927 to 1941 from the annual *Memoria de la Sociedad Nacional Agraria*.

about 15 per cent of output, and this proportion remained virtually unchanged until the mid-1930s. The rapid expansion of production thus was not a response to local needs; nor, as the price data for the 1890s indicate,[16] was world demand creating an especially strong pull. The key to rapid growth of the industry in the 1890s was the success of Peruvian planters in increasing their yields and cutting costs by means of technical innovation and reorganisation of the relations of production.[17]

These developments were induced by the problems faced by sugar planters after the War of the Pacific: especially the shortage of labour. The trade in indentured Chinese labour had been ended in the 1870s by diplomatic pressure from Britain and China,[18] and as the contracts of the existing Chinese labour force on the plantations expired, a growing labour shortage became apparent. Although increased use of temporary migrants from the Sierra made up some of the industry's requirements,[19] there was a strong incentive for planters to invest in labour-saving innovations despite low world sugar prices (which had failed to recover from the collapse of 1878) and the acute shortage of bank credit.[20]

The ensuing wave of mechanisation affected mostly the cultivation of cane; the outstanding innovations were the introduction of steam ploughs, and light railways to carry cane to the mill.[21] From there it was a short step to the introduction of improved milling machinery to raise the efficiency of extraction of sucrose from the cane, and by the early 1890s a number of plantations were laying plans for a new generation of large mills, although finance remained a problem. The pessimism of some contemporary observers concerning the alleged 'apathy and inertia' of sugar planters, and unsuitability to modernisation of the 'feudal latifundio',[22] was thus misplaced.

By the mid-1890s, the foundations had been laid. The ending of the civil war in 1895, the ensuing greater political standing of the planters, and the competitive edge in world markets which the sector derived from depreciation of the silver currency, provided favourable conditions for a take-off of production. At the same time, access to the neighbouring Chilean market was improved and safeguarded when, in 1893, Chile imposed a special tariff on imports of refined sugar, to protect Chilean refiners of Peruvian raw sugar from the competition of subsidised German beet sugar.[23] Shortly afterwards, Peruvian access to the U.S. market improved as a result of the Cuban revolution of 1895 and the subsequent Spanish-American War. The U.S.A. which had taken only one per cent of Peruvian sugar exports in 1897, was taking over half by 1901.

In response to these conditions, investment in the industry boomed. Railways and steam ploughs were introduced at an accelerated rate, while in several plantations the first of a new generation of modern mills were installed.[24] Milling capacity in 1894 had been estimated as 85,000 tons per year,[25] yet by 1897 production had risen above 100,000 tons. Suggestive figures on the scope of the investment are provided by the occasional estimates of the sugar sector's total capital stock. In 1894 Garland calculated fixed capital in the coastal plantations as S/31.9 million, with working capital a further S/2.5 million.[26] By late 1896 the Lima journal *El Economista* estimated that investment in sugar had reached S/40 million,[27] and in 1901 Garland gave total capital as S/50 million or more.[28] Since investment in improved mills often involved the replacement of existing equipment, the actual funds committed to the industry during the six years after 1894 would have been above the S/20 million implied by the above figures. The investment effort received support at governmental level, with the foundation of an Agricultural College in 1901[29] and an Experimental Station in 1906.[30]

Increased production came in part from an increase in the area under sugar, from 36,000 hectares in 1894[31] to 50,000 hectares by 1901.[32] But this accounted for less than half the increase in output; more important was an increase in productivity as the investments of the 1890s bore fruit. Average production in 1894 had been around 5,000 kilos of sugar per hectare of cane cut, or roughly 2,000 kilos of sugar per hectare of total area under cane.[33] By 1901 production was 2,700 kilos per hectare under cane,[34] suggesting that yields of sugar per hectare harvested were up to around 6,750 kilos per hectare. By 1910 the figure was 7,500 kilos.[35] On the plantation Cartavio, 2.4 tons of sugar were produced per hectare under cane in 1896; by 1900 the figure was 3.43 tons, and by 1905, 4.35 tons.[36] Much of this gain was undoubtedly attributable to improved milling techniques.

The worldwide increase in sugar production at this time, in both cane- and beet-growing areas, led to depressed world markets, and in 1902 there was a sharp fall in world prices.[37] For Peruvian planters, conditions were becoming increasingly difficult in the early years of the century,[38] and the pace of new investment slowed. Cotton prices improved greatly relative to those for sugar, and the 1903 imposition of excise taxes on cane alcohol and sugar sold on the local market provided an additional incentive for marginal planters to switch their land out of sugar. In 1904 the total area under cane was still roughly 50,000 hectares,[39] equal to 1901, but by 1912 this had fallen back to 37,000 hectares (the 1894 level) as planters in areas such as Ica, Camana, Tacna, and Piura shifted out of sugar; while the plantations of Lambayeque, La Libertad, and Lima accounted for most of the increase in production. By 1912 the first two of these departments had raised their share of output to over 60 per cent (Table 4.2, above).

In general, the decade after 1900 was characterised by uncertain world markets and unstable prices which deterred further heavy investment, although once the worst of the 1902 crisis was over the installation of mill machinery in some plantations was resumed.[40] An exceptionally good year for the industry in 1905[41] was followed by severe drought and economic recession in 1907,[42] and it was not until the end of the decade that serious interest in further expansion revived. Many large plantations then began laying plans for the installation of new machinery, one of the leaders being the Gildemeisters' estate, Casagrande, which in 1910 raised from German partners the finance to purchase a giant new mill which gave this plantation undisputed leadership in the sector.[43] Other large plantations which installed new mills in the following few years included Santa Barbara in Cañete, Laredo in La Libertad, and Tuman, Patapo, Pucala, and Cayalti in Lambayeque.[44] The Peruvian industry was thus in good shape to respond to the unprecedented rise in world prices which occurred during the First World War, and sugar once again set the pace in export growth, with enormous profits being reaped by those planters whose additional milling capacity and cane plantings came into production at precisely the right time, 1914–15.

With the spur of improving prices, the total area under cane began to rise about 1912, reaching 50,000 hectares by 1921, most of this increase taking place in the north (see Table 4.2, above).[45]

Production, having remained virtually stationary at around 170,000 tons from 1906 to 1912, had soared to 270,000 tons by 1916, evidently close to full capacity, as no further large-scale production increases were recorded until after the war. Wartime shortages of capital goods held back further heavy investment in sugar production until 1919–20. In those two years, however, with world prices still rising and the European beet industry prostrate, capitalists in Peru (as in other cane-sugar producing countries) scrambled to invest in the sugar industry. Wartime savings totalling at least $10 million were poured into the purchase of sugar land and the installation of new mills.[46] Over half of this sum was spent by groups of Peruvians in the purchase of four large plantations from foreign firms; the latter, all merchant houses and no doubt well aware of the fragility of the boom, were happy to sell out at the peak of the market.[47] The remainder of the new capital went into the purchase of machinery and the carrying-out of improvements. By the early 1920s productive capacity had been raised to around 320,000 tons, nearly double the pre-war level.

This commitment to the sugar industry of a large part of the local capital accumulated during the war proved a disastrous mistake. High world prices were stimulating a similar productive effort not only among other cane producers, but also in the reviving sugar-beet industry. The market broke in late 1920, just as enormous investments in the world sugar industry were coming to fruition, and the following decade was characterised by a steadily-worsening crisis of oversupply which kept prices low. By 1930 accumulated world sugar stocks had reached a third of annual production and, with brief exceptions in 1923 and 1927, world prices had maintained a steady downward trend for ten years.[48] In Peru planters who could move out of sugar into other more profitable crops did so (mainly in the Centre and South).

Planters in the North, unable to switch, cut back their investment programmes and held production up at full capacity in the attempt to offset low prices. One large estate (Roma) went bankrupt and one other (Paramonga) was sold off to a foreign firm,[49] but on the whole the remaining planters were able to weather the crisis. Profits, however, were low (though positive)[50] and both economically and politically (see below) the sugar industry went into eclipse, while the local economies of the sugar-growing areas (particularly La Libertad) went into decline.

Sugar and the economy

Of the contributions made by the sugar industry to Peru's economic growth the most important was its role in technological advance and capital formation during the crucial years of the 1890s. The close ties between the sugar planters and the urban financiers from 1895 on made possible not only the financing, through the Lima capital market, of major investment programmes in the sugar sector itself, but also the rapid diversification of their investments by the more successful sugar planters, a process described in Chapter 3. Planters became directors and shareholders in a wide variety of new urban enterprises, and supplied a large part of the deposits in the new banks which they helped to establish.

The existence of a modern sugar industry also generated important external effects. The sugar workers constituted an important section of the nascent industrial labour force, while the training in modern industrial techniques afforded by the plantations and mills contributed substantially to the raising of skills and the emergence of a new class of native engineers. In the early years, also, the sector made important purchases of capital equipment from the Lima foundries, assisting the growth of the local capital-goods industry, although from the turn of the century this linkage effect was rapidly eroded by competition from imported machinery.[51]

In considering the effect of increased demand in the local economy, it is necessary to be more cautious. By 1895 the industry employed some 24,000 workers, but during the following thirty years, while output more than quadrupled, employment hardly changed, and real wages showed a downward trend (Table 4.3).[52] Thus, although it is probable that the change from Chinese coolie labour to local wage-labour during the

TABLE 4.3 Real wages and employment in sugar production

	Indices of real wage bill		Number employed, field and mill workers
	Sugar field workers	Sugar mill workers	
1895	111	n.a.	(24,000)
1912	139	n.a.	23,745
1914	127	n.a.	25,681
1916	105	92	23,456
1918	101	94	25,081
1920	93	87	28,860
1922	96	95	28,938
1924	100	100	30,051
1926	85	95	28,207
1928	98	105	30,151

Source: Hunt (1974c), Tables 4–8 and 4–17. The 1895 employment estimate is based on Garland (1895), pp. 23–4.

1880s and early 1890s resulted in a once for all increase in the contribution of sugar workers' wages to total demand,[53] in the long run the growth of the sector did not translate readily into increased local demand. In addition, the tax burden on the industry was negligible in the 1890s, and was only slightly increased by the establishment of excise taxes in the early 1900s. Not until 1916 were export taxes imposed on all commodities, including sugar, and since these taxes were linked to prices, the long depression of sugar markets which began in 1920 meant that the Government's share in sugar earnings was not very high: by 1928 prices had fallen below the cut-off level for export tax.[54]

In addition to this rather small contribution to the local economy via wage and tax payments, the sugar industry played a less and less positive role from the point of view of capital formation as time went by. During the first decade of the twentieth century, incentives to invest in other sectors were decreasing (for reasons analysed in later chapters), and although investment activity by the planters revived from 1910 onwards, it was concentrated in the further expansion of sugar production itself, rather than in a diversification of investments into other sectors. The First World War market boom for export commodities yielded extremely high profits, but simultaneously made non-export sectors relatively less attractive as possible investment outlets. During the War sugar planters and other exporting groups held large sums of cash abroad, in expectation of an easing of wartime restrictions on the supply of capital goods for further development of export production;[55] and, as we have already seen, following the end of the war the sugar sector absorbed and subsequently immobilised large amounts of local capital. As the industry moved into the long recession of the 1920s there was no sign that the surviving planters were transferring their capital out to other, more lucrative sectors of the local economy. While most of them maintained an opulent lifestyle (which absorbed a good part of the sector's reduced surplus), their capital accumulation, such as it was, seems to have occurred outside Peru, continuing the wartime tendency to hold savings in foreign banks. This tendency was presumably accentuated by the reduced weight of the sector in national politics, which was one of the most important consequences of the regional concentration we described above. This political decline occurred particularly with the decline of cane-growing in the valleys around Lima, where many members of the business élite of the capital had been active in sugar up to the First World War. With the decrease of a major asset—local political access—which had distinguished local from foreign capital, the former now lost its chief behavioural characteristic: local reinvestment. The two largest financial windfalls for sugar planters during the 1920s—Victor Larco's receipt of £500,000 net from the sale of Roma to the Gildemeisters, and the £600,000 received by the sellers of Paramonga in 1926[56]—did not result in any identifiable gains for the local economy in terms of capital formation, and it seems probable that this capital went abroad.

Two basic conclusions follow from the above discussion. The first is that the fact of local, as distinct from foreign, ownership did not prevent the sugar industry growing by the use of capital-intensive techniques. The result was that employment hardly expanded at all while virtually all the gains from growth were captured by the sector's capitalists, since the real wage bill remained stationary and government participation via taxation remained low. This meant that the sector was a relatively inefficient generator of positive demand stimuli for the local economy (although the depression of sugar markets in the 1920s had a clear connection with the problems of the regional economy of La Libertad, contributing to the growth of the radical APRA party in that area[57]). The high and increasing profit share, however, meant that the sugar industry was a leading sector in the process of capital accumulation.

The second important conclusion is that the fact of local ownership of the sector, and hence local control of the surplus generated, was not a sufficient condition for sustaining the process of diversified investment of that surplus. In the 1890s the sugar planters were leaders in the diversification of the economy, as we have seen, but while they were happy thus to take advantage of profit opportunities created by largely exogenous circumstances, they did not use their considerable political power to press for *policies* designed to perpetuate that process of diversification. On the contrary, three Presidents who were actual or former sugar planters[58] governed Peru for most of the period 1900–30 without taking any serious steps to sustain the growth model of the 1890s, or to check the decay of non-export sectors (and several export sectors) after 1900. When local opportunities ceased to provide attractive investment options, and when their political influence waned, sugar planters were well enough integrated into the international economy to think in terms of holding their funds abroad to be spent on the education of children, on frequent overseas trips, and no doubt in investments in the industrialised countries.

In summary, the returned value to the local economy from sugar exports was very high in the 1890s and early 1900s, with a large element of economic surplus which was deployed to fuel the local development effort of those years. During the First World War the proportion of actual returned value fell as prices rose, with windfall profits held abroad, and later spent in part upon imports of equipment whose economic return proved rather low. In the 1920s, low world prices virtually eliminated sugar as a major earner of surplus, and such disposable funds as were generated tended to leak abroad, so that, although the sector remained largely free of foreign control, its economic performance became increasingly similar to that expected of a foreign-owned export industry. Similarly, the choice of technique in sugar production during the first thirty years of the century was independent of nationality, since both foreign and local firms faced the same sets of relative factor prices. Acting as rational capitalists within an exogenously-given international system, the local planters were drawn steadily into the patterns of operation characteristic of a dependent economy.[59]

4.3 THE COTTON SECTOR

Of all the products considered in this chapter and the next one, cotton had by far the greatest long-run impact on the level of internal demand. Conditions suitable for cotton-growing occur the whole length of the Coast,[60] and once early difficulties with pests and disease had been overcome, cotton steadily displaced sugar from large areas of coastal land. This switch involved the replacement of an industry with relatively low demand linkages by one with exceptionally high demand effects—a function of the relations of production in cotton-growing.

Production relations and nationality of control
The commercial cultivation of cotton in Peru began as a plantation activity, using slave labour on the same basis as the cotton sector in the south of the U.S.A.[61] Production was directly organised by the large landowners, and the processing of cotton was conducted in gins owned by the landowners and located on the estates. The abolition of slavery in the 1850s led in cotton growing, as in the sugar industry, to the use of Chinese coolie labour on many estates, until the ending of this source of labour in the 1870s. In the years following the War of the Pacific, confronted with a general shortage of agricultural labour on the Coast, landowners resorted to new types of production systems. Sugar, which had a year-round need for large masses of labour, moved as we have seen towards a wage-labour plantation regime. Cotton-growing, on the contrary, had somewhat different labour requirements, and this sector of commercial agriculture moved in a different direction, towards sharecropping, variously described as *yanaconaje* or the *partidario* system.[62]

The key point here was that cotton production was a seasonal activity, with heavy labour requirements during harvesting and planting, but relatively low labour needs during the remainder of the year. In order to maintain a permanent agricultural labour force on the *hacienda*, landowners found it convenient to divide up a large part of their land among small tenant cultivators on a 50–50 crop-sharing basis, and rely upon seasonal migration from the Sierra for only their temporary excess labour requirements. Along much of the Coast, therefore, cotton-growing became the work of a new class of tenant peasantry, with landowners living on their share rentals and on their profits from the compulsory handling of cash crops produced by their tenants.[63] There were also large numbers of small peasants working land of their own.

It remained true, nevertheless, that the sector was dominated by the large landowners.[64] The best cotton land was firmly under *hacendado* control, as was preferential access to irrigation water in many areas.[65] Furthermore, the balance of ownership of cotton land between large and small proprietors swung considerably in the formers' favour during the first two decades of the twentieth century, since much of the additional land sown to cotton was reclaimed from desert, swamp, or scrub areas controlled or bought up by large landowners.[66]

It was the rationality of the small-scale sharecropping mode of production which preserved the sector from the invasion of foreign firms. On the one hand, there were few if any gains from larger-scale production; on the other, foreigners were not anxious to become involved in small-scale semi-feudal relations of production.[67]

Matters were quite otherwise, however, in the related activities of cotton ginning, finance, and marketing. Working capital for cotton growers came largely in the form of short-term loans from merchants, secured on the forthcoming crop; and from the beginning of the twentieth century, when commercial cotton-growing began to expand, the role of the foreign merchant houses became steadily more important. The leading cotton dealers of the period were British houses such as Duncan Fox, Graham Rowe, and Locketts, and for many years these firms had a virtual monopoly of lending to growers. The Lima commercial banks were wary of supporting cotton-growing (in part because this sector lacked the large, capitalist-style enterprises characteristic of sugar) and it was not until 1918 that one of them, the Banco Italiano, entered the 'habilitation' business (the provision of short-term loans against the year's crop).[68] Beginning in the 1890s, cotton growers had been involved in the campaign to establish an Agricultural Bank to provide working capital,[69] but no concrete progress in that direction was made until 1927, when the Leguía Government established (reluctantly and on a rather uncertain basis) the Credito Agricola, forerunner of the present Banco de Fomento Agropecuario.[70] In the intervening period, cotton financing was mostly in the hands of the merchants.

Control of cotton ginning also began to pass out of the hands of the large landowners and into the control of the merchant firms. The various gins installed before 1900 were almost all located on and owned by large estates.[71] During the first decade of the twentieth century, however, several of the merchant houses began installing 'central' gins in the towns of the cotton areas, integrating this processing of the crop with their financing and marketing activities.[72] By the 1920s the leading cotton merchants, Duncan Fox, were operating large cotton processing plants (ginning and cottonseed oil extraction) in Pisco, Huacho, Tambo and Lima,[73] integrated with their expanding interests in cotton textile manufacture.[74] Not all of the new generation of 'central' gins were foreign-owned: a number of local firms such as Coloma, Rehder & Co. (Tambo de Mora),[75] Luis Albizuri (Pisco),[76] and M. B. Sayan Palacios (Huacho)[77] also established central gins during the first twenty years of the century. In addition, the merchant-controlled gins did not reach the stage of complete domination of the processing stage of cotton until after the Depression of the 1930s; most large *haciendas* continued to gin their own cotton at least until the end of the 1920s.[78]

Increasing foreign control of marketing, finance, and eventually ginning did not, however, have major repercussions for the sector. The large and increasing number of merchant houses[79] meant a competitive situation which kept margins down, while, as we have shown, many *haciendas* continued to gin their own cotton. In both cotton and sugar exporting, it appears that the bulk of the profits accrued to the local producers, with a relatively small margin taken by the merchants in commissions and interest on loans. In 1922 a careful estimate of the balance of payments indicated that 'profits of foreign-owned sugar and cotton estates, including profits on sugar and cotton handled by foreign merchant firms' came to no more than seven per cent of the gross earnings of those two export sectors.[80] Admittedly the period covered by this estimate came immediately after a year of economic crisis; nevertheless this seven per cent figure is consistent with other evidence that most of the earnings of the sectors remained in local hands. In 1923, with production costs totalling roughly S/30 per bale of Tanguis cotton, growers were receiving S/80 per bale from Lima buyers at the end of the season, a clear profit of well over half the gross export value.[81] While 1923 was an exceptionally good year, it seems reasonable to state that the lion's share of the benefits from cotton exports went to the producers.

Cotton, in summary, was a locally-controlled sector using merchant firms (several of them foreign) for credit and marketing services, and also to an increasing extent for the processing of cotton for export. In the early twentieth century cotton was grown largely by tenants and small holders, with few production units organised on a large scale; and consequently the owners of large areas of cotton land were often as much rentiers as capitalists. From the First World War, this situation gradually began to change, as larger and more capitalistic production units became more common,[82] particularly as sugar land was switched to cotton. By the end of the twenties, however, this trend had not reached the point where it seriously modified the structure of the sector.

The sources of growth in the cotton sector
The overall performance of cotton exports and production is shown in

Fig. 4.1. It will be seen that growth was consistent and rapid in all but a few years of the period. In the years of most rapid expansion, 1905 to 1920, the rate of growth of the volume of exports averaged over 10 per cent a year.

The dominant factor in generating such a rate of growth was the world market. In the nineteenth century Peruvian long-staple cotton had been unable to compete with the short-staple cotton produced by the Southern States of the U.S.A. The sector had experienced a brief growth phase in the 1860s during the U.S. Civil War, when production and exports of the Southern States were curtailed,[83] but following the re-entry of the U.S. into full production, cotton-growing in Peru stagnated again during the succeeding three decades. It was only with technical innovations in the British textile industry which made possible the blending of the native long-staple 'Peruvian rough' ('*Aspero*') cotton with wool, that exports began to expand in the late 1880s.[84] The 1890s brought rather depressed cotton prices,[85] but in 1900 markets improved dramatically, and growing British demand for cottonseed cake (the residue left after extraction of cotton fibre and oil) provided a profitable outlet for an otherwise useless by-product.[86] The First World War brought an initial fall in prices in 1914–15 which, combined with shipping difficulties, contributed to a pause in growth of output; but thereafter prices were exceptionally high, and the wartime interruption of Egyptian cotton exports provided Peruvian growers with the opportunity to penetrate U.S. markets for long-staple cotton.[87] In 1921, the U.S. cotton crop was struck by a plague of boll weevil, and it was not until the recovery of U.S. production in 1925 that cotton markets followed those for sugar and other agricultural staples into recession.[88] Meantime non-U.S. producers such as Peru enjoyed a market bonanza in 1922–4.

While this sustained rise in the world market provided the main incentive for the expansion of cotton cultivation in Peru, the importance of the local market should not be overlooked. As was shown in Chapter 3, the late 1890s and early 1900s were a period of rapid expansion for the local cotton textile industry, and this caused a rapid increase in local demand for raw cotton. In 1901, 17 per cent of total cotton production was destined for local mills; by 1904 the figure had risen to 24 per cent. The regional impact was concentrated particularly in the valleys of the Centre such as Cañete (Table 4.4), where sales of cotton to the local market increased eight and a half times between 1900 and 1909, although total production increased only three times. From less than 20 per cent of Cañete cotton production in 1900, the local market was by 1909 absorbing over 40 per cent. The expansion of the local textile industry, however, slowed at the end of the 1900s,[89] and, as cotton exports continued to grow, the proportion of Peruvian production absorbed locally fell to only eight per cent by the 1920s.

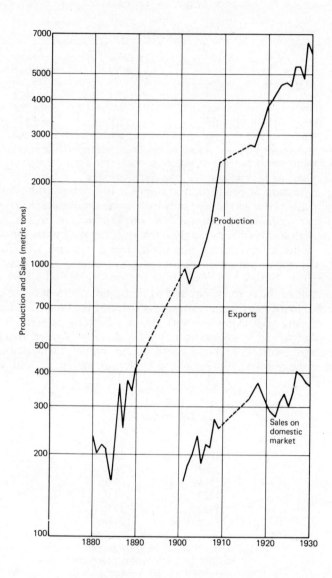

FIGURE 4.1 Cotton production: total[a] and for the internal market

Sources: Table A.2.3, Appendix 2; Table A.1.1, Appendix 1.
[a] Production: 1880–91, exports as proxy; 1916–30, official production figures; 1901–9, sum of exports and local consumption.

TABLE 4.4 Production and exports of cotton in the Cañete Valley, Peru, 1900– 9[a]

(metric tons)

	Exports	*Local sales*	*Total production*
1900	510	111	621
1903	805	403	1,208
1906	1,109	469	1,577
1909	1,499	1,046	2,544

Source: Martin (1911). p. 174.

[a] Components may not exactly add to total, due to rounding.

The expansion of production in response to the favourable market situation after 1900 was limited only by the amount of suitable irrigated land made available for cotton cultivation. The average yield of cotton land in Peru has been remarkably stable over the sixty years for which regular statistics have been published,[90] and it seems that for all practical purposes output can be treated as a function simply of the area under cotton. Table 4.5 shows that the area under cotton doubled in the first decade of the century, doubled again between 1916 and 1920, and continued to increase, but at a slower pace, during the 1920s. The land to accommodate such expansion was obtained both by extension of the irrigated area, and by switching part of the existing irrigated area from other crops to cotton. In the far north, cotton competed with rice; in the centre of the country, with sugar and foodcrops; and in Ica, with vines.

TABLE 4.5 Area sown to cotton, 1901–29

(000 hectares)

1901	22.9
1905	28.7
1909	56.7
1916	55.6
1920	104.0
1925	119.0
1929	127.0

Source: for 1916–29, *Extracto Estadístico del Perú*; for 1901 to 1909 the figures are estimates based on the yield of ginned cotton per hectare in the 1910s. Yields being ecologically given, this assumption is reasonable; if anything, these figures understate the rise in area since, as more marginal land was drained and utilised, yields might well have fallen.

Any re-allocation of land of course depended upon the relative prices of different crops; high cotton prices led to re-allocation of land only when markets for other crops were less strong.

The increase in cotton area in the early twentieth century was due both to new irrigation projects and to such a re-allocation of cultivated land. Irrigation projects had on various occasions before 1900 been carried out by private initiative, especially in Piura. In the brief cotton boom of the 1860s several landowners had embarked on irrigation schemes, several of which used steam-powered pumps.[91] In 1891–2 heavy rains in Piura[92] resulted in a dramatic extension of the area which could be planted to cotton in those years, to the benefit of both *hacendados* and local peasant communities, and plans for permanent irrigation works in the area were made in the following years.[93] In 1902 one of the Piura landowners, Miguel Checa, formed the Empresa de Irrigacion de Chira to complete the construction of a canal to irrigate part of the right bank of the Chira River; this project appears to have reclaimed between 4,000 and 7,000 hectares of land suited to the growing of Aspero cotton.[94] Elsewhere along the coast landowners were similarly reclaiming land for cotton cultivation. The scope of feasible privately-organised irrigation projects, however, was inevitably limited, and large-scale schemes could be carried out only by government action.[95] In response to pressure from agricultural and mining interests, the 'Cuerpo de Ingenieros de Minas y Aguas' was established in 1901 in the Ministerio de Fomento to carry out technical studies of the development possibilities in both mining and irrigation work. During the first decade of the century this institution produced a mass of reports,[96] and the Leguía regime of 1908–12 brought in a U.S. engineer, Charles Sutton, to advise on possible public-works irrigation schemes. In the event, however, it was not until Leguía's second presidency in the 1920s that the first large State projects were launched.

Meantime, private reclamation of land was supplemented by the re-allocation of large areas of already-cultivated land into cotton-growing. In the years after 1900 sugar prices were depressed and uncertain, and the introduction in 1903 of a tax on alcohol provided an incentive for both sugar planters and vine-growers to change to cotton. In areas such as Cañete and Ica (sugar- and vine-producing valleys respectively) considerable areas were planted to cotton.[97] By 1910 however this process was encountering increasing constraints, and from 1910 until 1916 there was no further expansion of cotton-growing. The constraints were basically two: first, the improvement of sugar prices after 1910, which halted the contraction of the area planted to cane; and second, the difficulties of establishing long-staple varieties of cotton in the central Coast in the face of severe losses caused by wilt disease.[98]

The response to the latter constraint provides a remarkable study in successful agricultural innovation. A Pisco cotton-grower, Fermin

Tanguis, began selective breeding of cotton varieties in 1908, and in 1912 succeeded in producing a new long-staple variety which was resistant to wilt and suited to the ecological conditions of the central and southern Coast.[99] In 1915 Tanguis made his new variety available to other cotton growers, and in 1919, at the height of the post-war market, Tanguis cotton made its appearance as an export crop. In that year, the new variety accounted for 12 per cent of cotton exports by weight. By 1924 this had risen to 67 per cent and by 1926 to 80 per cent (see Table 4.6). The advantages of the new cotton were its high quality, long staple, and high yield, as well as resistance to disease; its introduction revolutionised the economics of cotton-growing in Peru. As Table 4.5 indicates, in the years following the appearance of the new variety the area under cotton resumed its rapid expansion, continuing into the 1920s as the decline of sugar prices induced most plantations around Lima to change over to cotton. A 1924 observer reported from Pisco:[100]

> The price and profitability of the cotton crop has in recent years relegated Pisco, the drink, into a place of very minor importance in Pisco, the port . . . . Old vineyards have been planted to cotton, stills have been replaced by the oil mills and the wine press has been succeeded by the cotton press . . . . This year of record profits is likely to see the last of the big vineyards in Ica and the other valleys contributory to Pisco, uprooted.

In Cañete, formerly a major sugar-producing area, a 1926 study reported that cotton accounted for 90 per cent of all irrigated land in the province.[101]

The adoption of Tanguis and subsequent expansion of cotton-growing indicate a lively awareness of commercial advantage among producers, particularly significant when it is remembered that a large part of the crop came from small peasant or sharecropper planters.[102] Furthermore, as Table 4.6 indicates, the experience with Tanguis in the Centre was not an isolated case. In the northern region of Piura an extra-long-staple variety, Pima, brought from the U.S.A. in 1918 by a local merchant, Emilio Hilbck, rapidly displaced the native Aspero cotton from land in the department. By 1930, Pima accounted for the bulk of exports of non-Tanguis cotton.[103]

By the mid-1920s, cotton was the only export crop (and the only locally-controlled export sector) with a recent record of success (high prices and rapid expansion). The trouble which had already overtaken other agricultural staples at the beginning of the decade—chronic oversupply and falling world prices—had been avoided in the case of cotton by the historical accident of the U.S. boll-weevil plague of 1921. By 1925, however, the U.S. crop had recovered, cotton markets fell steeply, and the good days were over. Along the Peruvian coast 1925 was also a year of disastrous floods which wiped out much of the crop. Just

TABLE 4.6 The rise of Tanguis and Pima cotton

	Tanguis as per cent of all types of cotton ginned	*Pima as per cent of all types of cotton ginned*	*Tanguis as per cent of ginned-cotton exports, by volume*	*Pima as per cent of ginned-cotton exports, by volume*
1917	–	–		
1918	8	–		
1919	20	–		
1920	31	–	27	
1921	31	–		
1922	34	–	37	
1923	47	–		
1924	61	–	67	
1925	67	–		
1926	69	3	79	3
1927	71	3		
1928	83	5	82	8
1929	n.a.	n.a.		
1930	n.a.	n.a.	83	11
1931	89	7		

Sources: Columns 1 and 2 calculated from *Extracto Estadístico* 1934–5, p. 168. Columns 3 and 4 calculated from *Estadística del Comercio Especial*, various issues.

as the local capital invested in the sugar industry in 1919–20 had become trapped in a declining sector, so the planters who committed their resources to cotton in the early 1920s soon found themselves similarly trapped.[104]

Cotton in the economy
The outstanding characteristic of the cotton sector was the high returned value from its export earnings, due both to local ownership of cotton land and to the relatively low import requirements of production. The character of the production system, described above, meant that much of the income derived from exports was distributed among a large number of peasant or tenant cultivators permanently resident in the growing areas, as well as providing the most important source of cash income for migrants from the Sierra during the slow season in highland agriculture (which roughly coincides with the cotton harvest).[105] The booms and slumps of the cotton market translated directly into gains or losses for a large part of the rural population. Hence, any inclination among large landowners towards import-intensive consumption or capital flight would have had only a relatively slight dampening effect on the stimulus to the local economy. As the sugar industry went into

decline, the importance of cotton to the local economy became strikingly evident during the 1920s, when numerous observers agreed that the state of the cotton harvest and level of cotton prices were the main determinants of exchange-rate fluctuations.[106]

There exist no reliable figures on the distribution of the earnings of cotton up to 1930, but some general points can be made. In the first place, the import requirements of the sector were low in relation to its export earnings; the most important single purchased input in cotton production was guano fertiliser, produced within Peru, and imports consisted mainly of simple cultivation tools and the relatively small-scale equipment for the processing plants. Unfortunately, the detailed import statistics did not distinguish cotton-processing machinery from machinery destined for the sugar, oil, and mining sectors, with the result that no direct estimate can be made of the level of capital-goods imports. The commissions earned by foreign merchant houses on the exporting of cotton constituted a further leakage; here again no detailed data are available, but we do have the balance-of-payments estimate for 1922 mentioned above, which gave a figure of around seven per cent of gross export earnings of the sector, in a moderately good year—an estimate which is consistent with the degree of competition among merchant firms. A reasonable assumption would be that not less than 85 per cent of gross foreign-exchange earnings of the cotton sector, and very likely more than this, returned to Peru in the first round, and even allowing for a possible high import-propensity of some of the larger landowners in the second round, the generalised income effects of the sector were high relative to export earnings.

The share of the labour force, and hence the magnitude of general demand effects, presents a problem. We know that the expansion of production was accompanied by a significant increase in employment, from 21,000 in 1916 to 41,000[107] in 1923, with possibly some rise in wages.[108] But this refers only to the seasonal labour force, and nothing is known as to how sharecropping arrangements might have altered over time. What is clear is that the depressive effect of a decline in prices was swiftly passed on to the labour share. Employment held constant between 1923 and 1930, while real wages dropped abruptly, by over 30 per cent in the same period, to below their level at the start of the series in 1916.

In addition to the income effects, it is important to recognise that cotton production in Peru was an activity with significant 'forward linkages' into industrial development. In the 1890s the existence of a local source of raw material encouraged the development of the local cotton textile industry, while in the first decade of the twentieth century the processing of cotton by-products, into cottonseed oil, soap, and candles, was one of the leading areas of industrial growth. In the 1910s the development of the necessary technology for production of edible lard from cottonseed oil was the basis of the successful Compania Industrial de Huacho, which by the late 1920s was exporting its product to neighbouring countries as well as supplying the local market.[109] The switch to production of Tanguis cotton in the central Coast during the 1920s meant that local textile mills were working with a higher-quality raw material, and may thereby have gained some advantage in competing with imports.[110]

The strong demand and linkage effects of the sector were not matched in the areas of mobilisation of surplus and incentives to diversification. The leading capitalists in the development of cotton in Peru were not, on the whole, prominent in the promotion of large ventures in other sectors of the economy before 1930 (this distinguishes them sharply from the sugar planters). In part this may have been because profits in cotton, while satisfactory before the First World War, were not at the levels achieved by the larger enterprises in sugar production during the boom periods. In part, it appears that cotton planters were more likely to concentrate their investment activity in their local areas—the installation of cottonseed oil mills, soap and candle factories, local utilities (railways and wharves), shipping and general merchandising business in regional towns, and so on—whereas sugar planters operated on a grander scale and consequently made more impact on the contemporary literature. Possibly also cotton planters were slow to develop the entrepreneurial and administrative skills required for successful urban entrepreneurship, since few cotton *haciendas* (in contrast to sugar) were organised along the lines of large-scale capitalist enterprises before the First World War. It is of interest to note that in the 1920s, as large-scale commercial operations in cotton became more common, especially in ginning, several of the leading entrepreneurial figures in the construction boom in Lima and in the few large manufacturing ventures of the decade were drawn from the ranks of the successful cotton capitalists—particularly the owners of ginning and oil-extracting factories.[111]

Finally, the lesser political importance of cotton growers might have allowed for the mobilisation of surplus from the sector via taxation. In fact, however, for over half our period export taxes were non-existent. In 1916, as noted above, export taxes were introduced on all sectors; on average over the years 1916 to 1925 the revenue yield from cotton was only two per cent of the total value of cotton exports,[112] and thereafter fell almost to zero as cotton prices fell.

To sum up: in the period 1890–1930, efficient production in the cotton sector dictated a small-scale production structure with widespread demand effects. This situation was responsible for the maintenance of local control, rather than vice versa. We have found that, despite the 'pre-capitalist' and peasant character of the sector, there was a strong supply response to market opportunities, including the adoption of new varieties. But these conditions, which appear to have favoured the sector's growth and maximised its spread effects, were not so favourable for the mobilisation of surplus for investment outside the sector. Cotton, in short, was an efficient 'engine' for keeping local demand buoyant, but rising cotton exports could not by themselves lead to a process of economic diversification. For that, the participation of large surplus-generating sectors was required, together with conjunctural conditions of the sort already described for the 1890s. At the time when cotton played a leading role in export growth, from 1916 to 1925, the economy's surplus was becoming increasingly concentrated in the hands of petroleum and mining companies which played no role in domestic capital formation (see Chapter 5 below), while sugar, the traditional source of capital for non-export sectors, had ceased to fulfil this function. The stimulus from successful cotton exports, consequently, was largely dispersed or directed towards import demand, a process which is analysed in more detail in Chapter 6.

4.4 THE WOOL SECTOR

Of the six export sectors singled out for individual discussion in these chapters, wool was quantitatively the least important, having made up more than 10 per cent of export earnings only in a few scattered years in the 1890s, in 1903, and in 1918–20. Nevertheless, wool is significant for our study, partly because of its role in the rise and fall of Peruvian-controlled export sectors, and partly because of its role in the growth of regional inequality.[113] Peruvian wool is produced from the high grazing lands of the Sierra, mainly in the south of the country. Although the Central Sierra is also a wool-producing region, its pastoral economy is split between wool and cattle-raising, while in the north, cattle predominate in commercial livestock production. In the regional economy of the south, wool remained by far the most important market-oriented productive sector until the opening of the Toquepala copper mine in 1960. From 1916 to 1930, of total exports through the port of Mollendo worth $80 million, wool of various kinds accounted for no less than 73 per cent.[114] The wool trade formed the basis of the economy of the commercial city of Arequipa, located on the Southern Railway between the Sierra and the Coast, and the cyclical fluctuations of the wool market had a profound influence on the entire region.

The mode of production contrasts sharply with the sectors discussed above, since it straddled the structural divide between the 'modern' and the 'traditional' sectors of the economy. Whereas other export sectors in Peru grew by drawing labour out of traditional agriculture into modern-sector enterprises, organised with capitalist relations of production (mining, sugar) or with special forms of non-capitalist relations (the *yanacona* system in cotton), wool was already produced and traded within the 'traditional' economy, and the export trade in wool was established by bringing small peasant producers into the market through exchange mechanisms, as much as by expansion of the production of wool in the large-scale sector (the *haciendas*). As a result, there developed a triangular structure of great importance for understanding the evolution of the sector, the three poles being the small-scale producers, the large-scale producers (*haciendas*), and the merchants who handled the exporting of wool. It is the first group, the Indian herdsmen of the Sierra, who have always produced the high-grade wools coming from the native cameloids, especially alpaca,[115] whereas the lower-quality sheep wool (although also produced to some extent by the small-scale sector) has been the main product of the large livestock *haciendas* of the south. The large landowners and merchants, comprising between them the core of the economic élite of the South, were always relatively independent of the rest of Peru, and links between that élite and firms operating in the Centre and North were little developed. The scope which this left for transfer of interests within the southern economy, however, was considerable, especially for the landowners of the Sierra, most of whom possessed professional occupations in addition to their landed interests, and could survive comfortably as absentee *rentiers*, a characteristic which obviously reduced their commitment to the progress of the sector once obstacles arose. Nor was the structure of the merchant sector such as to encourage progress: the central preoccupation of the merchant families of Arequipa seems to have been with maintaining and extending their shares of the wool trade, rather than in financing any expansion of global output. Despite the ties of marriage and mutual interest which might have been expected to produce a common front among Arequipa interests, competition in fact was fierce, and many of the leading houses were driven to the wall during the first half of the twentieth century.

From relatively early in the history of the sector, all available land had been absorbed by one or other of the two producer groups. Production was divided between the internal and the external market, although the exact division is impossible to estimate.[116] Response to improved international prices could take the form of diversion of supplies, or of more frequent shearing (the latter at the expense of quality).[117] However, only a limited increase in export supply could come from these sources. In the absence of productivity-raising technical change the response to improved prices consisted mainly of increased conflict between *haciendas* and peasantry over access to grazing land. Attempts by the large landowners to introduce technical changes aimed at raising productivity were generally blocked by the Indians, since these changes implied enclosures, which in turn implied the exclusion of small-scale producers from the grazing rights within the *haciendas* to which they were entitled under the traditional labour-service system.[118] Not

surprisingly, relations between large landowners and independent
peasantry in the Peruvian Sierra were characterised by a high level of
conflict and violence, much of which resulted from attempts to reap
commercial advantage by shifting the balance of class forces in the
region.[119]

These factors dominate the story of the rise and fall of wool. Its
commercial export began with the development of a market for alpaca
wool in Britain in the 1830s (as Table 4.7 indicates, it was not until the
1850s that exports of sheepwool became significant). Exports expanded
rapidly in the mid-nineteenth century as the producers were integrated
into the international market, with the establishment of annual fairs
throughout the southern Sierra at which travelling buyers purchased
local production. In the Sierra, as elsewhere in Peru, the War of the
Pacific, Chilean occupation, and subsequent political troubles were a
setback to the regional economy, and only in the 1890s did exports
recover to the level of the 1870s. In the mid-1890s, however, depreciation
of the silver sol and the return of political peace coincided with the
completion of the Southern Railway extension to Sicuani in 1894.[120]
Wool production became more profitable, encouraging the large-scale
producers to seek to expand their enterprises at the expense of the small-

TABLE 4.7 Exports of wool from Peru, 1830–1929
(metric tons, annual averages)

	Alpaca	Sheepwool	Total
1830–9	342	8	350
1840–9	1,162	64	1,226
1850–9	924	1,006	1,930
1860–9	1,167	1,671	2,838
1870–9	1,582	1,589	3,171
1880–9	1,584	1,040	2,624
1890–9	1,821	1,288	3,109
1900–9	2,492[a]	1,336[a]	3,867
1910–9	3,097[b]	2,700[b]	5,286
1920–9	2,730	1,840	4,570

Sources: 1830–99 from Hunt (1973a) Table 14; 1913–29 from *Estadística del Comercio
Especial*, annual volumes; 1900–13 totals from *Anuario Estadístico del Perú*, 1944–5, p.
360; breakdown into alpaca and sheepwool from *Estadística del Comercio Especial* for
1904, 1905 and 1908; other years 1900–09 estimated using Hazen (1974), Table 1, p. 19.
(Official trade statistics were not available to us for the other years.)

[a] Excluding 1901, 1903 and 1907. Of the other years of the decade, the breakdown for
alpaca versus sheepwool was estimated for 1902, 1906 and 1909 on the basis of a series for
Mollendo exports, assuming Mollendo accounted for 95 per cent of total alpaca exports.
[b] 1913 to 1919. Note that the variation in the period covered by the data explains why for
certain years the components do not sum to the total.

scale sector, by displacing the small herdsmen from grazing land.[121] The expansion of *haciendas* at the expense of the independent peasant communities of the region became a political issue in the first decade of the twentieth century, and by the 1910s this process, combined with attempts by the *hacendados* to stamp out the capacity of the Indians to resist, was producing a growing wave of peasant revolts in the area.[122]

As physical expansion of the area of land controlled by the large-scale sector became more difficult, and wool prices soared to unprecedented heights during the First World War, several of the large-scale operators began to think in terms of modernisation to raise productivity. In the Central Sierra the British merchant firm of Duncan Fox had introduced modern techniques of fencing, selective breeding, and disease eradication on their Atocsayo property, bought for the purpose in 1905.[123] In the 1910s widespread interest in these innovations was evident among the large landowners of the south,[124] and under pressure from them and from the Peruvian Corporation (owners of the Southern Railway, which stood to gain from any expansion of wool output) the Government in 1919 established a model experimental livestock ranch at Chuquibambilla.[125] Before most of the proposed projects could bear fruit, however, the wool market collapsed in 1920; and since the Arequipa merchant houses had been carrying large speculative stocks of wool at the time, their buying activities in the Sierra were sharply curtailed in subsequent years. At the same time the modernisers among the large landowners were encountering strong peasant resistance to enclosures and other measures.[126] This opposition, combined with the depressed world market, doomed to failure a series of schemes promoted by the Peruvian Corporation in an attempt to develop a gigantic wool syndicate in Puno, between 1921 and 1924.[127] Most of the leading landowners departed to their town residences in Arequipa and their alternative careers as merchants, lawyers or administrators.

Capitalist relations of production thus failed to make headway in the southern Sierra, and the region's agrarian system remained as before, with a large independent peasantry co-existing with large properties worked on a labour-service basis. As Table 4.7 shows, the supply of wool for export reached its peak during the period of the First World War boom, falling back again in the 1920s. (The actual extent of the fall is understated in the table because substantial stocks built up by the Arequipa houses in 1918–20 were exported after 1920, boosting the export figures.)[128] It is interesting to note that from the 1890s to the 1910s the most rapid expansion was recorded by sheepwool (the *hacienda* product), while in the 1920s and 1930s it was this product which displayed the greater recession of export supply. Alpaca exports held up better in the 1920s, and recovered to almost the First World War level in the 1930s. In an indirect fashion, this provides some confirmation of an expansion of large-scale production at the expense of small-scale in the early twentieth century, although the switch appears far less dramatic than some of the qualitative literature on *hacienda* expansion would suggest. It also seems possible that the figures reflect a tendency after 1920 for the small Indian herdsmen to gain increased access to *hacienda* grazing lands, as the market incentive for large landowners to exclude tenants' flocks diminished. However, the acceleration of population growth would have meant that this was hardly reflected in any *per capita* improvement.

TABLE 4.8 *Per capita* export earnings: Peru and the South, 1910–35
(indices 1910 = 100)

	Peru	*Southern Peru*[a]
1915	151	91
1920	362	139
1925	215	85
1930	176	59
1935	142	39

Source: Bertram (1976a), Table 2.
[a] Figures for exports through the ports of Mollendo and Puno. Population was estimated by interpolation between the census totals for the South in 1876 and 1940.

The consequences of the relative decline in wool for the regional economy of the South are indicated in Table 4.8, which shows that, compared with the national average in *per capita* terms, southern exports rose less up to 1920 and fell more sharply thereafter. The result was a recession of the regional economy during the 1920s—a recession which received little or no relief from Central Government, since (as Chapter 6 describes in more detail) the determinants of economic policymaking in those years did not include any desire to alleviate regional inequalities, nor any interest in fostering the sort of diversified, inward-directed economic growth which might have benefited at least some of the declining regions. The professional and commercial activities to which the landowners of the South retired in times of trouble for the wool industry were essentially parasitic; but, given the circumstances of the period, the choice for such men was between operation as local parasites, or migration to the still-active economy of Lima (where parasites also proliferated in the 1920s).

4.5 THE RUBBER SECTOR

Rubber, like wool, was an export product the fortunes of which were closely linked to those of a particular regional economy—in this case, the jungle region east of the Andes. Of the various export products of the late nineteenth and early twentieth centuries, rubber is the most obscure, and in a sense the least important, despite its considerable weight in the total value of exports, because of the almost-total isolation of the jungle region (communication with Lima was quicker by the sea route around Cape Horn than overland by the Pichis Trail). The industry was operated on an extremely primitive basis, the workers simply collecting rubber from scattered stands of wild rubber trees, with no attempt to establish concentrated plantations such as were being started in the Far East by the turn of the century. The labour force was a mixture of opportunistic adventurers and exploited local Indians; in one region, along the Putumayo River, the treatment of local Indians by the Peruvian Amazon Company became an international scandal in 1908– 1912.[129] The economy of the region was oriented toward Iquitos, not Lima; all consumption goods not locally produced were imported from abroad (the industry generated virtually no internal trade in Peru); the national Government's control over the region was at best tenuous; the leading firms of Iquitos were locally-based merchants, entirely independent of and unconnected with any companies west of the Andes; and the same was true of the banking system, such as it was. Central government authority was wielded by officials who regarded their first duty as self-enrichment, and the collection of statistics and enforcement of taxes was haphazard, to say the least.

Rubber was produced in two forms: *caucho*, obtained by felling trees of the *castilloa* species, and *jebe*, a more valuable product obtained by tapping *hevea* trees.[130] Rubber was one of the very few products subject to export taxes after the Pierola reforms of 1896, and although the tax was lower than those charged by Bolivia and Brazil,[131] the incentive to export rubber through contraband rather than official channels was strong enough to render official statistics of the industry before 1900 completely worthless (see Appendix 1). Brazilian statistics and qualitative information, however, make it possible to sketch in outline the rise and decline of the rubber industry.

The history of the world wild-rubber industry is simply told.[132] During the second half of the nineteenth century the consumption of rubber by the industries of Europe and the U.S.A. increased steadily from around 400 tons in 1850 to between 50,000 and 60,000 tons in 1900. All of this increase in demand was supplied from the wild-rubber producing areas of Africa and the Amazon Basin, with Brazil the leading producer; and as the accelerating growth of world consumption began to run ahead of wild rubber production in the 1890s, rising prices[133] provided windfall profits for producers. Production from the world's wild-rubber areas continued to expand until 1912, when an all-time peak of 70,000 tons was reached. Thereafter, however, wild-rubber producers were quickly eclipsed by the new plantation-rubber producers of the Far East. Plantations had first been established in the late 1880s, and from 1900 on the very high prices prevailing for rubber (due to inelastic supply) resulted in very rapid expansion of these plantations, which by 1910 were exporting over 8,000 tons annually. During the following decade, plantation rubber became the dominant source of world supply, and as production caught up with demand, prices fell to the point where wild-rubber production became uneconomic. Attempts to start plantations in Brazil in the early twentieth century failed, while Peru and Bolivia made no attempt at all to move on from wild-rubber collection to more organised production. Consequently, by 1920 the South American countries had practically disappeared from the world rubber scene.

In 1851 the Peruvian town of Iquitos was a fishing village with fewer than 200 inhabitants. By the early 1900s the population was 20,000[134] and the town possessed a wealthy merchant élite, fine public buildings, and a thriving trading economy. To judge from the available statistics, the boom dated from the mid-1880s, and by the early 1890s exports had reached a level not to be surpassed until 1904.[135] During the following twenty years prices continued to rise and immense fortunes were made, most of which seem to have been squandered on imported luxuries (prices of which in Iquitos were often absurdly high) or sent abroad. The banking business of the region was handled by the Commercial Bank of Spanish America, a London-based firm with no other interests in Peru.[136]

By 1912 the Peruvian Amazon had reached peak production of around 3,200 tons annually, and although this level of output was sustained (with fluctuations) until 1919, falling prices reduced actual receipts from the sale of rubber to one-third of their 1912 level by 1919. The years 1920–1 brought the complete collapse of the rubber economy as prices fell still further, and although some rubber continued to be produced throughout the 1920s, it did not suffice to keep the regional economy afloat. Hopes that cotton-growing could replace rubber as a source of income proved unfounded, and the entire regional economy sank into a state of decadence. The post-war collapse of the industry prompted demands for government aid, and, when none was forthcoming, Iquitos mounted an unsuccessful armed revolt against the Leguía government.[137] Political discontent at the failure of the Government to rescue the region's economy evidently continued to simmer and in 1932 Loreto was one of the Departments won by the APRA party in the national elections.[138]

Ownership, control and production

The population of the Peruvian jungle when the rubber boom began was very small, and, since the region was cut off from the main centres of population, it is not surprising to find that several of the pioneers of rubber were immigrant foreigners such as the merchants Kahn and Israel. Peruvians, however, were also prominent. Carlos F. Fitzcarrald, the 'rubber king' of the 1890s, was from Ancash,[139] while Julio C. Arana, the founder of the Peruvian Amazon Company and leading figure of the 1900s, appears to have been also of Peruvian origin.[140] These had all been active in the region since the 1880s.

Serious interest in the rubber industry on the part of the Government began in the late 1890s, when Peru and Brazil made a joint attempt to put an end to contraband rubber exports.[141] In 1898 a law was passed to control the development of the industry: the Government would grant concessions to developers, on condition that they paid both a small lease and a royalty on rubber produced. The practice of cutting down trees in order to obtain rubber was prohibited.[142] Under the new law a number of large new enterprises entered the industry during the 1900s,[143] probably the two most important being the Inca Rubber Company (set up as an offshoot of the gold-mining activities of the U.S.-owned Inca Mining Company in the Madre de Dios[144]) and the Peruvian Amazon Company started by Arana in 1904 in alliance with British interests. These and other enterprises of the 1900s vanished during the following decade. Of the individual leaders of the rubber boom, several of the merchants remained in business in Iquitos after 1920, although on a more modest scale than hitherto—notably Kahn and Co., Israel and Co., Arana y Hermanos, and Luis F. Morey.[145] Julio Arana, despite his involvement in the Putumayo scandal, cultivated his relationship with President Leguía (in office from 1908 to 1912 while the diplomatic pressure over the Peruvian Amazon Company was on) and in 1919 moved to Lima as Senator for Loreto under the second Leguía administration.[146] There he appears to have spent much of his remaining money on living well, and certainly did not figure as an entrepreneur.

Rubber and the economy

The central fact about the rubber boom of the 1890s and 1900s is that it had very little effect indeed on the remainder of the Peruvian economy, except in so far as high profits in rubber influenced the expectations of politicians and businessmen concerning the future development of the jungle region. In the jungle region itself, prosperity was entirely dependent upon monoproduct rubber exports; there was no drive to diversify or develop the local economy, and once deprived of its import capacity the region sank immediately into stagnation. The population of Iquitos had dropped to 15,000 by the 1930s.[147] Looking back in 1924, a

Peruvian observer wrote the following epitaph for the sector:[148]

> The crash came, and contrary to all morals and maxims, the lucky ones were the spendthrift, for they at least had had a good time. [T]hose who reinvested their profits in the industry lost everything. There was nothing left. No other industry had been developed or even thought of. Practically all food had been imported. Labour was too valuable for rubber gathering to waste it on the development of farms and the production of foodstuffs. . . . Rubber, at first promising so much, became a dead issue, and instead of developing the country, retarded real progress that would have been of permanent value. After years of hectic exploitation, Eastern Peru was not benefited one iota, but sank back to the economic stagnation of fifty years ago.

4.6 CONCLUSION

The unifying characteristic of the four export sectors discussed in this chapter was the predominance of local as distinct from foreign control. In all cases, we have encountered evidence of the capacity of such locally-owned sectors to respond to market opportunities. Even in the case of wool, where modernisation ran into resistance which defeated it, the evidence refuted the common stereotype of the Peruvian élite as backward and uninterested in entrepreneurial experiment. In all cases, also, we found that the fact of local ownership did not, by itself, provide any guarantee that the expansion of export production would stimulate a sustained drive towards relatively autonomous, diversified growth. On the contrary, our discussion indicated that the sugar industry gradually ceased to operate as a net supplier of capital to other sectors, and by the end of the First World War had become a net absorber of funds, before sinking into prolonged and severe recession. Cotton stimulated demand from 1916 on, but in the absence of other conditions favouring autonomous growth this stimulus was dissipated. Wool and rubber failed to provide much impetus to other sectors, and both in turn dragged their regional monoproduct economies into severe recession by the 1920s (while the crisis of sugar had a similar effect on the economy of La Libertad). These various problems were unrelated to the issue of local versus foreign control *per se*; rather, the emergence of the patterns of a dependent economy was determined by rational response to the signals of the international market and its effects upon the local economy.

Faced with this situation, government policy was not powerless, in principle at least. But government in Peru existed, and designed its policies, primarily to serve the interests of the classes who owned the export sectors discussed here, or who otherwise benefited (for example, as merchants or bankers) from the operation of those sectors. It was the exporting interests themselves who determined (via their influence on economic policy) that the autonomous growth process of the 1890s should be allowed to die out; that taxation of export sectors should be avoided altogether until 1916 and then applied only lightly; and that the central government's taxing and spending powers should not be used to alleviate the decline of regions whose export industries were failing.[149] While in principle it is thus possible to specify alternative policies which might have retained the dynamic of the 1890s, it would be unrealistic to claim that a Peruvian government of the period could have been readily persuaded to adopt such policies—although strong advocacy of a revised economic strategy is to be found in the early publications of the APRA party.[150]

We have not, however, completed our survey of leading export sectors, nor tackled directly the issue of whether foreign direct investment helped or hindered economic growth in Peru. Such is the task of the next chapter.

5 The Extractive Export Sectors, 1890–1930

This chapter explores the role played by metals mining and petroleum in the Peruvian economy up to 1930. Since increasing penetration by foreign capital features prominently in the histories of both sectors, an attempt is made to evaluate the effects of foreign control, both upon the performance of the sectors themselves, and upon their contribution to the growth of the local economy as a whole.

5.1 METAL MINING: EXPANSION AND DENATIONALISATION

The history of metal mining in Peru is complicated by the variety of products: at different times since 1890 the list has been headed by gold, silver, copper, lead, zinc and iron, with many other secondary metals bringing up the rear. Peruvian ores tend to be complex and it is common for a number of metals to be found in the same mine. In the period covered by this chapter, the sector was undergoing radical changes which profoundly affected its impact upon the economy.

Up to 1900, mining comprised a large number of small-scale operations, spread throughout the Sierra and concentrating on the production of precious metals. At the turn of the century, however, these metals were displaced by copper (hitherto a little-valued by-product) and it was copper which dominated the history of the thirty years up to 1930. With the expansion of copper production came also U.S. capital, which in a short period totally dominated mining in Peru. Incidental to these trends in product markets and in ownership was also a pronounced regional concentration of mining activity.[1]

To evaluate the later developments, and in particular the rise of foreign capital after 1901, we must first consider the history of precious-metals mining at the end of the nineteenth century. For it was the local mine-owners, previously involved in the expansion of silver and gold mining, who initiated the development of copper in the 1890s and then sold out to foreign mining companies early in the twentieth century. The history of the 1890s provides evidence of the constraints faced by the sector, and of the degree of competence displayed by Peruvian miners—

both important issues for any assessment of the role of foreign capital.

The sector under local control

Peru has a mining tradition stretching back before the Conquest, and the precious metals, silver and gold, had been the mainstay of Peru's exports during most of the Colonial period.[2] The basic technology of mining was well known, and on occasion Peruvians had been notable for their willingness to adopt innovations.[3] The nineteenth century, however, brought a prolonged stagnation of mining (although the boom product of the century, guano, was in a sense a branch of mining/quarrying). Mercury for use in amalgamation plants had become scarce and expensive after the collapse of the Santa Barbara mine at Huancavelica in the 1780s; the Wars of Independence caused widespread destruction of mining installations; drainage problems hindered exploitation of lower-level ores at the richest mining centre, Cerro de Pasco; and throughout Peru the best oxide ores (susceptible to treatment by mercury amalgamation) were being exhausted, while the technology for treatment of sulphide ores was little developed. Mining, in short, was a relatively difficult and risky area for investment, and in the Guano Age the sector attracted little interest from large-scale capital.

From 1870 on, however, and particularly following the War of the Pacific, there was a revival of silver mining. Rapid depreciation of the paper peso had raised the profitability of silver,[4] while the growing number of Peruvian-trained mining engineers from the School of Mines (established in 1876)[5] improved the quality of exploration and survey work. Major advances now followed on two fronts: discovery and technology. Discoveries of new deposits led in the 1880s to rapid expansion of silver mining at Casapalca, where Ricardo Bentín's 'Aguas Calientes' mine served as the basis for one of the largest family fortunes in Peru.[6] In the mid-1890s major discoveries at Morococha (also in the Central Sierra, and close to the Central Railway extension completed in 1893) brought fortunes to a new group of enterprising operators.[7] In technology, the two main developments were the rapid extension of smelting to treat lead-silver ores[8] and the arrival in 1890 of the Patera leaching process (lixiviation) which, following its introduction in the silver-mining centre of Hualgayoc, rapidly spread to other parts of the country.[9] By 1898 Hualgayoc had four smelters and nine leaching plants operating.[10] Near Cerro de Pasco the Huamanrauca smelter was expanded and re-equipped during the 1880s and 1890s.[11] In 1889, also, the immigrant U.S. engineers Jacob Backus and J. Howard Johnston established a custom smelter at Casapalca.[12] By 1897, according to a list published in *El Economista*, there were thirteen lixiviation plants, thirteen smelters, seventeen large amalgamation mills (including two gold companies) and six diversified installations (including at least two smelters and two lixiviation plants) in Peru.[13] Most of this investment had been the work of Peruvian and immigrant entrepreneurs; the *Economista* list included only two clearly-identifiable foreign firms (John T. North's Maravillas British Silver Mining Company and the U.S.-owned Inca Gold Mining Company), though it missed one major foreign venture, the London-based Caylloma Silver Mining Company.[14]

TABLE 5.1 Peruvian silver production, 1860 to 1920
(metric tons, annual averages)

| | Silver-mine output[a] | Copper-mine by-product[b] | Total | Production of silver from | |
				Cerro de Pasco	Other mining areas
1860–1869	70	–	70	48	22
1870–1879	82	–	82	44	38
1880–1889	68	–	68	30	38
1890–1894	89	–	89	37	52
1895–1899	136	c	136	36	100
1900–1904	193[d]	c	193[d]	n.a.	n.a.
1905	151	40	191	n.a.	n.a.
1910	84	169	253	n.a.	n.a.
1915	64	230	294	172[e]	164[e]
1920	54	223	277	140	137

Source: 1860–1904 from Hunt (1973a), Tables 3 and 21. Pre-1900 production converted from marks (1 mark = 8 oz). 1905–1920 from annual official mining statistics.

[a] Comprises the silver content in silver bars, silver-lead bars, lixiviation precipitates, and export-grade ores.
[b] Comprises the silver content of copper bars and copper matte.
[c] Included in silver-mine output.
[d] Exports.
[e] 1916.

As a result of this new surge of activity, production began to expand rapidly. Table 5.1 shows that, although Peruvian silver production did not rise above the level of the mid-nineteenth century until the 1890s, the total concealed a steady shift after 1870, away from the declining mines of Cerro de Pasco towards the expanding silver-mining centres, both in the central Sierra (Casapalca, Morococha, Yauli) and elsewhere (Quiruvilca, Hualgayoc, Ancash, Castrovirreyna, Cailloma). By the mid-1890s production was booming, with most of the expansion coming from this latter group of mining centres, where the new processing technology (smelting and leaching) had its main impact. At Cerro de Pasco, where the problem was drainage rather than ore treatment,[15] production remained stationary and profitability fell as the grade of accessible ores dropped.

The 1890s, however, also brought a dramatic shift in metals prices on world markets. Silver prices collapsed in 1892[16] and, despite the efforts of the U.S. Government, continued downward for the rest of the decade. For a time the position of some Peruvian silver mines was alleviated by their assured local market for coinage purposes; but in 1897 the Pierola Government, alarmed at the instability of the silver currency, suspended the coinage of silver and closed the Cerro de Pasco mint.[17] Although silver exports increased 150 per cent in volume between 1890 and 1900 (due to the heavy investments in new technology in the early 1890s and the opening of new mines), the value of those exports rose no more than 47 per cent.[18] Silver had ceased to be a high-profit sector.

The result was that production of silver began to decline again. From 151 tons in 1905, the volume of silver produced outside the copper-mining sector had dropped to 84 tons by 1910 and to only 64 tons by 1915.[19] Production of silver as a by-product of copper smelting rose rapidly, however, from 46 tons in 1903 to 169 tons in 1910 and 230 tons in 1915; but this is to anticipate our story.

The rise and subsequent decline of silver production was echoed after 1890 in the history of the other precious metal, gold. As Table 5.2 shows, exports of gold increased eight-fold during the 1890s, reflecting the exploitation of new deposits and introduction of technological innovations, as had been occurring in silver mining. On the other hand, the sale of the country's leading gold mine to U.S. capitalists in 1895 was the first step in the general denationalisation of mining which was to follow from 1900 on, and links the history of gold to that of copper—both of them, in the 1890s, products which attracted a wave of new investment and exploration by Peruvians, and important in the general mobilisation of local capital during the decade, yet which subsequently passed under foreign control.

The history of gold mining in Peru over the last century has been intimately linked to developments in the monetary field. The price of gold has been institutionally fixed for long periods, separated by sharp upward revaluations corresponding to periods of monetary crisis: the 1890s, the 1930s, and the 1970s. During the 1890s, as the value of silver fell relative to gold, the price of gold in local currency naturally rose, leading to a series of attempts to revive the gold-mining industry. Gold in Peru occurs in both quartz and placer deposits, and had been extensively mined during the Colony. Thereafter, activity had virtually ceased; the easily-processed oxide ores had been mostly exhausted, and the nineteenth-century emphasis was on silver. The revival of interest in gold mining in the 1890s, in response to improving prices, was made

TABLE 5.2 Production and exports of gold and copper, 1890–1905

	Gold (kilos)		Copper (tons)	
	Exports	Production	UK imports from Peru	Estimated production
1890	208		150	180
1892	231		290	348
1894	224		440	528
1896	350		740	888
1898	945		3,040	3,649
1899	1,294		5,165	6,195
1900	1,633		8,220	9,865
1901				11,414
1902				9,096
1903		1,078		9,497
1904		601		9,504
1905		777		12,213

Sources: Column 1 from Hunt (1973a), Table 21. Column 2 from 'Estadística Minera en 1914' (*BCIM* No. 82, 1916) p. 46. Column 3 from 'Estadística Minera del Perú en 1903' (*BCIM* No. 14, 1904) p. 36. Column 4, 1897–1903 from 'Estadística Minera del Perú en 1903' p. 36; years 1897 to 1902 were there obtained by marking up U.K. imports by roughly 20 per cent (the ratio applicable for 1903, when the first Peruvian direct estimates of production became available). 1890–6 have here been interpolated on the same, admittedly shaky, basis. 1904–5 from 'Estadística Minera en 1914', p. 74.

possible, as in silver mining, by two new developments, in technology and discovery. The most important technological advance was the invention of the cyanide process for the treatment of sulphide ores, which made feasible the reopening of mines whose oxides had been worked out; this process was first introduced to Peru by the Compania Minera El Gigante, which in 1894 embarked on an attempt to revive mining in the Pataz district of La Libertad.[20] This and other projects based upon cyaniding, however, failed to achieve much, because of the extreme difficulty of transport and the fact that the new technology took several years to adapt to Peruvian ores.[21]

More important was a series of new discoveries and rediscoveries of gold deposits rich enough to be worked on a large scale using either amalgamation or sluicing. The two principal examples were the Santo Domingo mine in Puno, discovered in 1890, which for the following forty years was Peru's leading gold mine;[22] and the Ccochasayhuas mine in Apurimac, which had been abandoned in 1639 during an Inquisition witchhunt and was rediscovered only in 1893.[23] Of the placer deposits in Puno which had once been worked by the Spaniards, Aporoma and San Antonio de Poto attracted renewed interest.[24]

It was the Santo Domingo mine which set the pace. Shown by the

Indian discoverer to two Macusani citizens, it was 'denounced' by them (the process of 'denouncement' in Peruvian mining law is equivalent to claim-staking) and within four years had reached an output of nearly a ton of fine gold per year. In 1894 this extremely successful enterprise was sold for $210,000 to a syndicate of U.S. capitalists, who formed the Inca Mining Company, the first of the series of large foreign firms which were to dominate Peruvian mining by the 1920s.

The success of Santo Domingo and the high gold price, combined with the new business climate of 1896–7 in Lima, produced a gold-rush atmosphere in those two years. Syndicates were formed of Lima capitalists and local miners and prospectors to stake out gold claims. Among the promoters and investors in new gold-mining ventures were the leaders of the business élite of the country: Payan, Pardo, Aspillaga, Leguía, Candamo, Barreda and many others.[25] The gold boom was shortlived, however. Stabilisation of the silver price and the Peruvian monetary reform of 1897 were followed by a narrowing price premium on gold as domestic inflation caught up with the previous exchange-rate depreciation; in addition the difficulties of transport and technology encountered by the new enterprises were severe. Of all the Peruvian companies launched, only two survived until 1914.[26]

As the considerable risks and great difficulties of gold mining became evident, the interest of local capitalists swung towards other sectors where profit opportunities were greater. Outstanding among these was copper mining. Copper had been a product of little interest in Peru until the 1890s. High prices in the 1860s had prompted the exploitation of small but rich veins around Nazca and Ica on the coast, where from 1875 to 1884 the Canza mine had exported some 23,000 tons of ore,[27] but with the closure of this mine the industry became insignificant until the mid-1890s. In the Sierra, although a number of large copper deposits were known, technical problems and the absence of rail transport had made them uneconomic to work.[28] In 1893, however, the Central Railway was pushed through to Oroya, putting the rich mineral district of Morococha within reach of cheap transport, and in the following year the Backus and Johnston custom smelter at Casapalca began for the first time to pay for the copper content of ores purchased from local miners (previously only lead and silver had been paid for), as the smelter moved into production of copper matte. There was an immediate rush to locate and stake claims to the rich copper deposits which were known to exist at Morococha, and production of copper ore expanded rapidly both to supply the Casapalca smelter and for direct export over the railway.[29]

At Cerro de Pasco, where there were large deposits of high-grade copper ore in the drained levels of the existing silver mines, the rising prices of the mid-1890s[30] and the possibility of sending ores by llama and mule down to Oroya for rail shipment to Casapalca led to a general swing into copper mining during 1897.[31] In the first two years of intensive copper mining at Cerro de Pasco the copper content of ore averaged betweed 30 per cent and 60 per cent,[32] rich enough to justify sending it out without further treatment. But it was 100 miles to the railhead at Oroya, and pressure on the supply of llamas and mules quickly pushed up transport costs, with the result that ores of 25 per cent or less copper content could be profitably worked only if they could be smelted locally into high-value matte.[33] In mid-1897 the English immigrant mine-owner George Steel was organising the first syndicate to build a smelter at Cerro de Pasco,[34] and his example was followed by other entrepreneurs. By 1898 two copper smelters were operating successfully and several others were coping with teething troubles.[35] A year later five plants were operating and two others were under construction.[36] By 1900 there were eleven smelters in Cerro de Pasco itself and four in the surrounding area.[37] The logical next step, from small-scale smelting of copper matte to the large-scale production of blister copper,[38] was simply a matter of time; in the early 1900s plans began to circulate among the Lima business community for the establishment of a large central smelter for the Cerro de Pasco region,[39] and had the mines remained in local hands the project would no doubt have come to fruition.

By 1900, however, copper mining at Cerro de Pasco was running into constraints similar to those which had earlier afflicted silver mining in the area. Drainage of the mines below the level of the Quiulacocha tunnel (dug in the 1820s) awaited the construction of the lower-level Rumihallana tunnel, planned since the 1870s (when the tunnel had been begun by Henry Meiggs shortly before his bankruptcy and death).[40] Flooding prevented access to the large volume of high-grade ores lying below the water table, and for reasons which are not altogether clear (probably the shortage of fuel) there had been no attempt to repeat the Trevithick pumping experiment of the early nineteenth century.[41] Above the water table there remained large tonnages of the lower-grade ores which could be reduced by smelting, but the shortage and high cost of fuel forced the existing smelters to work far below capacity (the coal mines were 35–50 km distant, and the only means of transport was by llama).[42] These two problems—drainage and fuel—imposed the critical constraints on copper production. Other problems, such as a railway from Oroya to Cerro de Pasco to carry out the copper, and the achievement of a more efficient scale of operation in mining and smelting, were soluble if the first two could be dealt with, as the Sociedad Nacional de Mineria pointed out in 1899.[43]

As in the case of the central smelter, these constraints would have been overcome, given time. Proposed government concessions for. construction of a drainage tunnel, a railway to the coalfields, and a rail or road connection to the Central Railway at Oroya, were the subject of manoeuvre and debate during the 1890s as various interests (both local and foreign) sought to obtain rights over the mines in exchange for constructing one or more of these infrastructure works.[44] In 1900 matters finally began to move, with the formation of a syndicate of Lima capitalists headed by Isaac Alzamora, Jose Payan and Ramon Aspillaga, to construct the drainage tunnel. Having obtained a concession from the Government and reached agreement with the Cerro de Pasco miners' guild, the Empresa Socavonera del Cerro de Pasco proceeded with construction of the tunnel, which was eventually completed early in 1908.[45] The concession for a railway to the Champa Cruz coal deposits was granted in late 1899 to Isaac Alzamora and Pedro Davalos y Lisson, but the project had still not been financed when in 1901 the Cerro de Pasco copper-mining industry ran into a short-run economic crisis and was bought up by U.S. capital.

To sum up, the last decades of the nineteenth century were a period in which Peruvian and immigrant capitalists demonstrated their capacity to mobilise funds and introduce new technology, the result being a rapid increase in the production, first of silver, and later of gold and copper, as market opportunities changed. There seems no reason to suppose that the process could not have continued into the twentieth century and, despite the constraints which were limiting expansion at one of the new copper-mining centres,[46] we would argue that, regardless of who controlled the sector, copper was clearly marked out as a major growth area of the next couple of decades. As matters turned out, the process of development under local control did not have the opportunity to run its course. U.S. mining capital was expanding its interests abroad, and Peru was one of the countries which attracted attention for its rich mineral resources. In the twenty years after 1900, local capital was largely displaced from the development of Peruvian mining.

The denationalisation of mining, 1901–30
In the first decade of the twentieth century, the growth areas in mining were copper and a new metal, vanadium. The remarkable feature of the period after 1900 was that, instead of continuing to move into these new and promising lines of production, Peruvian capital was being displaced from them as foreign capital moved in. The event which was to dominate not only the development of mining, but the evolution of the entire economy of central Peru, was the formation in New York in 1901 of the Cerro de Pasco Mining Company, to buy up the locally-owned mines of Cerro de Pasco. This U.S. company subsequently moved into Morococha as well, and at the end of the First World War consolidated its position by taking over the Backus and Johnston interests at Casapalca. Other U.S. companies also moved in on Peruvian mining during the first twenty years of the century. The world's largest known vanadium deposit was sold to a U.S. company in 1905; the Anaconda company took control of the Cerro Verde copper deposit in the south in 1916–20;

and between 1919 and 1924 the American Smelting and Refining Company (through its subsidiary Northern Peru Mining and Smelting Company) built up what amounted to a monopoly position in copper, silver and gold mining in the Department of La Libertad in the north.[47] This foreign penetration involved not merely the transfer of control of natural resources; the giant smelters installed by the foreign firms pushed out the locally-owned smelters, virtually none of which remained in operation by 1930.[48]

TABLE 5.3 The volume and composition of metals production

	Quantum index of output (1915 = 100)	Percentage of total value of metal production						
		Copper	Silver	Gold	Lead	Zinc	Vanadium	Other
1903	36.9	39.5	48.1	12.0	0.4	–	–	–
1905	42.8	46.2	46.4	6.7	0.4	–	–	0.3
1910	78.7	55.3	31.1	3.8	0.1	–	9.3	0.4
1915	100.0	61.0	23.2	5.7	0.7	–	7.4	2.0
1920	96.1	44.3	33.4	5.0	0.2	–	16.9	0.2
1925	139.3	37.1	46.6	7.1	2.3	1.0	5.9	–
1930	150.3	47.7	20.3	7.6	8.3	3.9	12.1	0.1

Source: Calculated from current-price valuations in annual mining statistics, 1903 to 1932. The quantum index is calculated from *Extracto Estadístico* 1934–5, using 1915 prices from the *Boletín del Cuerpo de Ingenieros de Minas*.

Table 5.3 traces the expansion of metals mining from 1903 to 1930. The extent to which copper dominated the sector is understated by these figures because of the considerable weight of metals such as silver and gold produced as by-products of copper smelting. By the 1920s Cerro de Pasco Copper Corporation and Northern Peru Mining accounted for virtually all copper production, and the great bulk of gold and silver. Cerro opened a huge new central smelter at Oroya in 1922, causing the closure not only of the two existing smelters of this company (at Tinyahuarco and Casapalca) but also of the last two surviving independent smelters in the central Sierra.[49] In La Libertad, Northern Peru Mining opened its copper smelter at Shorey (near Quiruvilca) in 1927,[50] and between 1920 and 1930 these two companies between them accounted for 22 per cent of total Peruvian export earnings. A third large foreign firm, Vanadium Corporation, monopolised vanadium production.

Peruvian owners of promising mineral deposits offered them as a matter of course for sale or lease to the foreign giants. The capable and effective local mining capitalists of the 1880s and 1890s, with very few exceptions, welcomed and cooperated with foreign penetration, while they themselves mostly retired to a comfortable life in Lima or on *haciendas* bought with their new wealth. The very few local mine-owners who continued to work mines of their own on a significant scale (Fernandini, Proaño, Arias, Mujica, Marcionelli) were no more than satellite suppliers of the Oroya smelter—a role, however, which suited them well and yielded them large profits.[51]

The reasons for which local entrepreneurs relinquished control to foreigners are crucial to an evaluation of the role of foreign capital. Did the sellout indicate some insuperable constraint of technology, finance, or market access? How and where did the sellers of mines redeploy their resources? To answer these questions we first describe the process of denationalisation in more detail, then examine its repercussions.

At Cerro de Pasco, as we have already indicated, the expansion of copper mining was by 1900 encountering drainage and transport constraints, the removal of which required several years of infrastructure investment before the area's full productive potential could be realised. On the evidence of the subsequent performance of the Empresa Socavonera and the Cerro de Pasco Mining Company in undertaking these investments, it seems reasonable to suppose that, in the absence of foreign investment, the installation of the drainage tunnel, the railway, and a large central smelter would have taken between five and ten years.[52] In 1901, however, world copper prices slumped sharply, and operation of many of the smelters became uneconomic at prevailing costs of fuel and transport.[53] With short-term profits low, and with long-term profits dependent upon a number of uncertain factors (the movement of world prices, and the date of completion of the drainage and transport facilities), the atmosphere in Cerro de Pasco in 1901 was one of pessimism. On top of the economic problems of the miners there was a genuine fear that, should the copper industry return to prosperity, the Peruvian Corporation (which was still pressuring the Government to recognise its supposed rights at Cerro de Pasco) might at some stage win over a future President and obtain a new concession. As one observer remarked, given all the above factors,[54]

> if tomorrow a person were to arrive in Cerro with one million soles in cash, it is absolutely certain that in eight days he could buy up half of all the mines.

At the end of 1900 the promoter Juan Garland had secured options of purchase on 260 mines (about one-third of Cerro de Pasco) for a total of £200,000,[55] but the necessary (foreign) finance was not forthcoming (the copper market was collapsing) and the deal fell through. Later in 1901, however, Alfred W. MacCune, an associate of the U.S. mining millionaire James B. Haggin,[56] arrived in Peru to look at the Cerro de Pasco mines, and in September he began buying. By late October purchase contracts totalling £500,000 had been concluded,[57] and by late November the Haggin-MacCune interests had control of 80 per cent of

TABLE 5.4 Sellers of mines at Cerro de Pasco to U.S. syndicate, 1901–10

Name of Seller	Amount paid for properties in £ Sterling
Miguel Gallo Diez	100,000
Elias Malpartida	50,000
Jorge Eduardo Steel	48,500
Felipe Salomon Tello	45,000
Languasco family	36,000
Ignacio Alania	32,000
Matilde Puch de Villaran	32,000
Herminio Perez	28,000 +
Gallo Hermanos	20,800
Romualdo Palomino	20,000
Ortiz family	20,000
Lagravere/Scheuermann family	16,000
Francisco Martinench & Jesus Chavez de Martinench	15,000
TOTAL, thirteen sales	463,300
Other recorded sales	220,000
TOTAL recorded sales	683,300

Source: Title documents of the Cerro Corporation held in the Corporation archives at Cerro de Pasco.

the total mineralised zone.[58] As further properties were added to the list over the following few years, the outlays by the U.S. group on purchases of mines at Cerro de Pasco reached a total of over £700,000.[59] Table 5.4 lists the thirteen biggest individual deals, and indicates that, of the total, nearly 70 per cent was concentrated in the hands of twelve sellers, and over half in the hands of only seven. The sums involved were considerable fortunes by the standards of the day, and the new U.S. group, soon constituted as the Cerro de Pasco Mining Company, paid prices well above those which Garland had been offering earlier in the year.

The new owners closed down many of the mines at Cerro de Pasco for five years while the infrastructure for large-scale exploitation was laid. A railway to Oroya was constructed in 1904, and a large smelter at Tinyahuarco near Cerro began production in 1906. In early 1908 the Peruvian-owned Empresa Socavonera completed its drainage tunnel, which (despite the fact that the U.S. company was using pumps successfully to drain the mines) entitled the tunnel builders to claim a 20 per cent royalty on production. Having fought unsuccessfully to block the tunnel company's concession, and subsequently used physical sabotage in an attempt to stop the construction of the tunnel, Cerro came to terms and bought out the Empresa Socavonera for $3 million worth of Cerro shares.

As Table 5.2 above indicates, the copper boom did not come to an end with this closure of the mines bought by the U.S. group. The total output of copper in Peru, after falling from over 11,000 tons to around 9,000 tons with the closure of the U.S.-purchased mines, grew steadily through the period of suspension of operations by Cerro, reaching 12,213 tons in 1905 (the year before the new Cerro smelter opened). Most of this increase was attributable to the rapid expansion of output at Morococha.[60]

The surge of production at Morococha in 1905 coincided with a sharp recovery of world copper prices. The Morococha mines faced drainage problems far less severe than those at Cerro de Pasco, while the district had been directly on the Central Railway since 1902, when the Government constructed a spur line over the pass at Ticlio. In sharp contrast to Cerro de Pasco in 1901, the outlook in Morococha in 1905 was one of rapid expansion. Nevertheless, it was in 1905–7, at the peak of the copper market, that the Cerro de Pasco Mining Company interests secured control of most of Morococha for an outlay of some £360,000 (U.S. $1.7 million). Further purchases in later years raised this to over £400,000 by 1917. In 1919, by taking over Backus and Johnston's interests, Cerro finally consolidated its position.

Table 5.5 lists the main purchases at Morococha between 1905 and 1912. Of the sellers listed, most were happy with the price received, and at least one family (the Pfluckers) subsequently squandered the money on luxury consumption. It should be noted, however, that of the various owners of mines at Morococha the Pfluckers, besides being the longest-established, were among the least dynamic by 1900, and the head of the family is reputed to have visited the mines only once in his life.[61] More interesting were the sales of mines by the entrepreneurs who had built up copper mining in the district since the mid-1890s: the Valentine family, David Stuart, the Pehoaz family, and Lizandro Proaño. With the exception of the last, all of these willingly sold. Proaño, who had been building up an integrated operation of his own, with a new smelter at Tamboraque due to open in 1906, was the only mine-owner actively to oppose the spread of foreign control. Forced by lawsuits and pressure to sell part of his mining interests to the Cerro group in 1907,[62] he lost control of the remainder to Backus and Johnston in 1911 when the latter company illegally (but effectively) manipulated a board meeting in their favour.[63] (Backus and Johnston, it may be noted, had by the 1910s become a U.S. rather than a local firm; in 1919 it was merged with Cerro).

The number of local mine-owners who did not sell to the Haggin

TABLE 5.5 Sellers of mines at Morococha to Haggin interests, 1905–12

Name of Seller	Amount paid in £ Sterling
Pflucker family	120,000
Lizandro A. Proaño	95,000
Octavio Valentine	39,500
David A. Stuart	28,000
Montero family	27,000
Pehoaz family and associates	20,480
N. B. Tealdo Peri y Cia	20,000
Sociedad Minera Puquiococha interests	20,000
TOTAL, eight sales	369,980
Other recorded sales	29,000
TOTAL recorded sales	398,980

Source: Titles documents of Cerro Corporation in the Corporation archives at La Oroya.

group at Cerro de Pasco and Morococha was remarkably small, and in most cases the reason was that their mines had relatively low grades of copper which did not attract foreign interest.[64] At Cerro de Pasco only one of the existing mine-owners, Eulogio Fernandini, continued to expand as an independent,[65] while at Morococha Proaño's resistance to denationalisation was an isolated case. Can one explain the willingness, or even eagerness, of Peruvians to sell their mines by reference to economic crisis or justifiable pessimism about the future? At first the case of Cerro de Pasco in 1901 might be taken as evidence for such a view, but examination of the history of other purchases of mines by foreign capital marks out Cerro de Pasco as the exception which proves an entirely different rule.[66]

The Santo Domingo gold mine, it will be recalled, was sold to U.S. capitalists in 1894 at a time when its production was expanding rapidly and the gold price was rising. The Morococha copper mines were sold to Haggin under similar circumstances in 1905. Next to go was the Mina Ragra vanadium mine, discovered and claimed by Eulogio Fernandini in 1905. Fernandini, notwithstanding his position as the leading independent operator in the Cerro de Pasco area, sold Mina Ragra immediately to the newly-formed American Vanadium Company of Pittsburgh for $10,000 cash and a 10 per cent shareholding. Without being called upon to perform any entrepreneurial function in the development of the property, Fernandini shared in the enormous profits made by the firm during the First World War vanadium boom, when this mine was the chief world source of the metal, and remained as a director on the board of the successor company, Vanadium Corporation, which bought up the mine in 1919.

The next important development came during the First World War, when the Anaconda company in 1916 secured an option on the Cerro Verde copper deposit near Arequipa, then being worked on a small scale by Carlos Lohmann, and in 1920 the mine was purchased for $200,000. Shortly afterwards, in 1921, the American Smelting and Refining Company obtained an option on the Gildemeister family's copper mines at Quiruvilca in La Libertad, which had been doing well during the First World War and where a smelter and cart-road were under construction; the mines were bought for $850,000 in 1923, while $225,000 more was paid for neighbouring copper claims of other Peruvians. Meanwhile ASARCO had also leased most of the silver mines at nearby Mill-huachaqui, and there in 1924 obtained an option on 'La Guardia', owned by the Boza family, the most successful silver mine in Peru and the pioneer in introduction of the flotation concentrator to Peru. Control of various other promising deposits in the north passed during the 1920s into the hands of the new ASARCO subsidiary, Northern Peru Mining and Smelting Company.

Back in the Central Sierra the leading Peruvian operator remaining in Casapalca, Ricardo Bentin, sold his Aguas Calientes property to Cerro in 1919 for £400,000,[67] while the rich but isolated copper deposit of Yauricocha, after several years in the hands of a group of local immigrant promoters, was sold to Cerro in 1927.

Such, in summary, was the course of events in the main mining centres.[68] The lessons to be drawn are of great importance. The key factor in denationalisation, without any doubt, was the ability of foreign firms to outbid Peruvians for control of mineral resources. During the whole period from 1894 to 1930, foreign firms operating in Peru did not discover a single new mine, and in only one case (vanadium) did a foreign firm undertake the development of a mine from scratch. Most foreign penetration consisted of the takeover of locally-owned mines which were already operating, usually with records of success, at the time of sale. In addition, with the partial exception of Cerro de Pasco (where the mine-owners confronted serious constraints on expansion, discussed above), the mines sold to foreigners were virtually all in the midst of development programmes, or in the hands of local owners fully capable of undertaking such development.[69] In no sense is it accurate to think of the majority of local mine-owners as having been forced to sell by economic crisis or by their own inability to develop. The decision to sell was purely and simply a matter of price: the foreign firms, for some reason, valued Peruvian mineral deposits more highly than did the Peruvians; and no capitalist, offered more than his own estimate of the capital value of his property, could be expected to refuse such a bonanza.

The nature of the imperfections in international capital markets which may lead to such a situation have been much-discussed in the literature on international firms,[70] but any attempt to determine the precise mechanisms which operated in the case of Peruvian mining cannot be more than speculative. It may be noted that in 1901, interest rates in Peru were much higher than those in the U.S.A., where James Haggin found himself in 1901 with over $7 million of ready cash in search of a high-yielding investment opportunity.[71] Probably Haggin's inside knowledge of cartel manipulation of the international copper market[72] enabled him to forecast the future of that market more accurately than could the distant Peruvians. It may well be that Peruvian capitalists, limited to a single underdeveloped economy, applied higher risk and uncertainty discounts in their decision-making than was appropriate for the international operators Haggin and ASARCO. These international companies, by integrating Peruvian mines into their worldwide operations, could probably anticipate greater profits than could the Peruvian capitalists, who had to market their exports through merchant houses which naturally charged commissions. Whatever the reason, the foreigners' valuation of Peruvian mines exceeded the Peruvians' valuation. In deal after deal, foreign firms were left in control of the country's best mineral deposits, and local capitalists were left with enormous sums of cash in their hands. By the conscious decision of the former owners, the local mining sector, local mining and smelting technology, and the local institutions which had serviced the early growth, faded away.

The repercussions for Peru of this denationalisation of mining are difficult to evaluate. On the one hand, the expansion of copper mining probably took place more rapidly under foreign control than would have been possible under local control, especially in the case of Cerro de Pasco. On the other hand, foreign control implied the leakage abroad of the sector's profits (with consequent lower returned value) as well as the stunting of local enterprise in this sector, so that the local economy might have been better-off with less rapid expansion under local control. In order to clarify these issues we shall examine in more detail the gains and losses associated with the operations in Peru of the Cerro de Pasco Copper Corporation.

For the years from 1916, enough information is available to permit a reconstruction of the division of Cerro's earnings between local expenditures (returned value) and expenditure abroad (imported requirements, and profits). These figures appear in Table 5.6, for the period 1916 to 1937. With the exception of the worst years of the Depression (when profits were low), returned value averaged slightly over half of the value of the company's earnings from Peruvian operations. The division of the remaining 40–50 per cent or so between imported requirements and profits is somewhat speculative, but a comparison of the results obtained from Peruvian data in Table 5.6, with

TABLE 5.6 Direct balance-of-payments effect of Cerro, 1916–1937
(U.S. $million)

	(1)	(2)	(3)	(4)	(5)	(6)
	Payments within Peru to			Total returned value	Cerro gross earnings in Peru	Per cent returned value
	Labour	Suppliers	Government			
1916				12.0	20.8	58
1917				11.5	22.6	51
1918				10.6	22.2	48
1919				10.3	18.5	56
1920				9.6	18.8	51
1921				13.5	18.6	73
1922	3.7	3.9	0.5	8.1	18.1	45
1923	4.7	4.1	0.9	9.7	22.0	44
1924	4.1	4.2	0.9	9.1	15.9	57
1925	3.9	4.8	1.0	9.7	18.4	53
1926	4.5	6.7	0.9	12.1	17.7	68
1927	5.4	5.9	1.0	12.3	19.9	62
1928	5.9	6.6	1.2	13.7	25.4	54
1929	6.9	6.2	1.7	14.7	31.3	47
1930	6.6	3.7	1.2	11.4	19.6	58
1931	4.5	1.9	0.6	7.0	9.8	71
1932	2.1	0.6	0.2	3.0	3.3	91
1933	1.6	0.9	0.2	2.7	5.2	52
1934	2.2	1.2	0.3	3.8	7.4	51
1935	3.1	1.5	0.7	5.3	11.8	45
1936	3.8	2.6	1.0	7.4	12.5	59
1937	4.2	3.4	1.4	9.0	15.3	59
TOTAL						
1916–37	n.a.	n.a.	n.a.	206.5	375.1	55

Sources: Bertram (1974), pp. 169 and 381, on the basis of information drawn from the following sources: returned value 1916–21 estimated very roughly from Cerro de Pasco Corporation *Annual Report and Balance Sheet*; returned value 1922 from Fernández (1923), p. 9; returned value 1923–31 from Alvarez Calderón (1934), p. 92; returned value 1932–7 from *BCIM*, No. 122, 1938, p. 262A; gross earnings are estimated Cerro exports from annual issues of *Estadística del Comercio Especial del Perú*, plus estimated income from the railway and *haciendas* owned by the company, based upon data in Cerro *Annual Report and Balance Sheet*.

information drawn from the consolidated accounts of Cerro in New York (Table 5.7) provides helpful guidelines (as well as confirming the accuracy of the orders-of-magnitude in the Peruvian data).

To sum up very crudely the results: of some $375 million gross earnings of Cerro in Peru 1916–37 (the great bulk of which was from exports of metals), $207 million (55 per cent) were returned to the local

TABLE 5.7   Comparative data on the operations of Cerro, 1916–1937
(millions of U.S. dollars)

	(1)	(2)	(3)	(4)	(5)
	Gross earnings		*Imports plus repatriated funds*	*Gross profits of Cerro New York*	*Distributed profits of Cerro New York*
	Cerro Peru	*Cerro New York*			
1916	20.8		8.8		2.7
1917	22.6	26.3	11.1	12.7	4.0
1918	22.2	23.6	11.6	8.7	4.4
1919	18.5	16.2	8.2	5.7	3.6
1920	18.8	13.8	9.1	4.3	3.6
1921	18.6	18.9	5.5	1.0	0.4
1922	18.1	19.4	10.0	5.2	–
1923	22.0	22.8	12.3	9.3	3.0
1924	15.9	22.8	6.8	8.1	4.4
1925	18.4	22.0	8.7	10.3	5.6
1926	17.7	28.6	5.5	9.4	5.6
1927	19.9	22.5	7.6	7.8	4.5
1928	25.4	26.6	11.7	10.2	4.1
1929	31.3	30.3	16.5	10.3	3.8
1930	19.6	21.0	8.2	3.2	6.2
1931	9.8	8.2	2.9	− 0.2	1.5
1932	3.3	4.3	0.3	− 0.6	0.3
1933	5.2	7.6	2.6	3.4	–
1934	7.4	9.1	3.6	4.0	–
1935	11.8	17.7	6.5	7.0	3.4
1936	12.5	17.9	5.1	6.7	4.5
1937	15.3	22.8	6.4	11.0	6.5
TOTAL 1916–37	354.3[a]	402.4[a]	168.6	137.5[a]	72.1

Sources: Columns 1 and 3 from Table 5.6; column 3 is the residual from columns 4 and 5 of Table 5.6; columns 2, 4 and 5 from Cerro de Pasco Copper Corporation *Annual Report and Balance Sheet.* Gross profits here are defined as income minus costs and taxes plus changes in stocks. (The Corporation's report provides no distinction between U.S. and foreign taxes). 'Gross earning' is income from metal sales and other sources, but excluding changes in stocks.
[a] Excluding 1916.

economy and $169 million (45 per cent) went abroad to pay for imports and profits. During the 22 years, the distributed profits of Cerro totalled $72 million. Taxes paid to the U.S. Government probably accounted for a further $15–20 million, and Cerro's investments of its undistributed profits in the U.S.A. in stocks and bonds, cash, and the subsidiary American Metals Company (acquired about 1921) had a book value of $18 million by 1937, bringing total repatriated funds to a minimum of $110 million. The scope for error in the above figures is not unduly great. The most important error is likely to be in the gross earnings figure, based as it is on Peruvian official valuations of minerals exports, which may have been done cif in the early years. If we make the correction most favourable to the company, assuming that imports for Peruvian operations totalled $35 million[73] and taking the remaining $24 million unaccounted for to have represented overvaluation of Cerro exports, then gross earnings in Peru would be reduced to $351 million, returned value would rise to 59 per cent, foreign charges would fall to 41 per cent, and distributed profits of Cerro (assuming, not too unreasonably, that all of these should be attributed to Peruvian operations) would rise from 19 per cent of gross earnings to 21 per cent.

In evaluating these results, it should first be pointed out that the level of returned value was surprisingly high for the time and place. During the 1920s, when our data indicated Cerro to have been returning between 50 per cent and 60 per cent of its gross earnings to Peru, the equivalent figure for three large foreign copper companies in neighbouring Chile was only 30–40 per cent,[74] while in Peru itself the foreign oil companies (discussed below) were yielding results lower still. Compared with other foreign-owned companies in Latin American extractive industries, Cerro thus performed rather well. (The key to this situation was the corporation's large purchases of custom ores from a number of locally-owned mines, notably those of Fernandini and Proaño).

It is more important, however, to compare Cerro's actual contribution to the Peruvian economy with the contribution which would have been made, in the absence of foreign capital, by a locally-owned mining sector, built upon the foundations laid during the 1890s. The entry of foreign capital, obviously, excluded Peruvian capital from access to the main mineral deposits—and one of the first principles of cost-benefit analysis is that if two projects are mutually-exclusive, the net benefits of the excluded project should be treated as part of the costs of the project actually undertaken. Cerro's net contribution to the Peruvian balance of payments over the 22 years from 1916 to 1937 was therefore not equal to the returned-value shown in Table 5.6. To take, for a moment, the most extreme case: if a local company or companies had existed instead of Cerro, with *identical* output and costs (but receiving profits and paying taxes locally rather than abroad), returned value would have been, not $207 million, but $317 million[75]—that is, more than 50 per cent greater. Furthermore, this 50 per cent addition to returned value would have represented not wages and other costs, but potential economic surplus—resources potentially available for further local investment.

Of course, the defender of the foreign firm would be quick to point out that it is quite unrealistic to assume that a locally-controlled mining sector would have been identical to Cerro. He would probably also claim that local mining companies would have been far less efficient and productive than Cerro in the 1910s and 1920s. We would accept the first of these points, but our discussion earlier of the development capacity of local mining capitalists makes us dubious about the second. Can anyone convincingly argue that Peruvian mining output would have been lower in the long run without foreign investment? No doubt development would have been rather slower under local control, if only because of the much greater liquidity of the foreign firms at the time of their entry; but we suspect that by the time of the First World War, a locally-owned mining sector would have raised copper production to very nearly the levels actually achieved by Cerro. The impressive contemporary performance of the locally-owned tin-mining industry in neighbouring Bolivia seems to give support to this hypothesis.[76]

For the sake of argument, however, let us suppose that a locally-controlled mining industry would have produced less than did Cerro in fact. Let us assume that the ratio of imported materials to total exports of metals was fixed, so that the proportion of export earnings returned to Peru by a locally-owned sector would have been 85 per cent[77] compared to the 55 per cent of Cerro. Peru would have been better-off, so far as the balance of payments went, with any firm or firms which returned more than the $207 million which was actually returned by Cerro; that is, with any locally-owned alternative which produced more than $244 million worth of exports (only 65 per cent the level of output achieved by Cerro).[78] That a locally-controlled mining sector would by the 1920s have reached a level of output at least 65 per cent as large as that of Cerro is in our view beyond any doubt. On the assumption that local firms would have brought their profits back into Peru, the effect of foreign investment on the balance of payments over the long run was negative, in the sense that the balance of payments would have been stronger without the foreign firm and its capital.

The above discussion, of course, would still not satisfy the defender of the foreign firm. We have assumed, he would point out, that local capital diverted from investment in mining was not used to expand other productive sectors, and thereby contribute to foreign-exchange earnings (any such extra foreign-exchange earnings could in a sense be attributed to the foreign investment in mining which freed those local resources for reinvestment elsewhere). And we have assumed that local firms would have retained and spent their profits in Peru rather than abroad, when the evidence not only of the Bolivian tin-miners, cited above in support of our case, but also of Peruvian sugar planters in the 1920s, suggests precisely the contrary—that locally-owned firms could be just as willing to send their profits abroad as any foreigner.

Let us consider these two points further. The first is of particular importance, for if an underdeveloped economy is considered to have a scarcity of capital and an abundance of natural resources, surely an inflow of foreign capital must supplement its total supply of capital, raising total investment and speeding-up the whole growth process? Various sources suggest that roughly $16 million was invested in Peru by Cerro between 1901 and 1907: $6 million on the purchase of mines and other property, $3.5 million on local development and installation costs, and $6.5 million on imports of machinery and equipment. The straight-forward cash injection into the economy thus amounted to $9.5 million, of which $6 million went as cash payments to local capitalists, and could be considered to have been made available for reinvestment in other sectors of the economy. A further $3 million worth of Cerro shares was handed over to shareholders in the Empresa Socavonera in 1908, bringing total payments to local capitalists to $9 million[79] (although these shares were converted into cash only gradually over a period of years). Against this should be set the loss of the capital invested in the independent smelters forced to close down after 1901 by the Cerro monopoly—say, $0.5 million. After 1907, with the mines and smelter in operation and earning large profits, Cerro became self-financing, and further new injections of outside capital were not required.

What, then, happened to the $8.5 million[80] which were added to the liquid resources of local capitalists by Cerro's entry during the first decade of the century? In the first place, this inflow undoubtedly helped to tide the economy over the export recession of 1901–4 (see Table 3.1) without putting pressure on the new gold-standard exchange rate; whether this is regarded as a blessing or a curse is open to debate.[81] It can be argued, however, that the inflow of these enormous amounts of sterling (Cerro made all its payments locally in sterling) did not translate readily into an increased rate of capital formation in the economy. One of the leading capital-absorbing sectors had been closed to local capital, while simultaneously very large sums of liquid funds had been released into the system. In a closed economy this might have driven down the interest rate and thus encouraged the financing of new marginal investment projects promising returns below the previous cut-off level;[82] but in an open economy the possibility clearly existed that (provided local capitalists' profit expectations remained unchanged, or at least were not reduced) the injection of new funds might result in increased consumption, inflation and capital flight as well as in additional savings and investment.[83]

The point is perhaps made clearer by reference to Baran's distinction between the economic surplus actually mobilised and invested by an economy, and the 'potential surplus' which could be obtained by restricting consumption to the subsistence level, and capturing the remainder of national income for investment.[84] In an economy where potential surplus already exceeds realised surplus by a large amount (and we suspect, with Baran, that this was the case with countries such as Peru), additional injections of outside funds will certainly increase the potential surplus, but may have little effect on realised surplus.

In the absence of quantitative evidence, we have resorted to a qualitative approach to this problem. The number of individuals who received large sums of money from the sale of mines to Cerro was fairly small, and their entrepreneurial performance after the sales can be traced by biographical research. Such an exercise has been conducted by Low,[85] with the following results.

Low has carried out detailed studies of 16 families, of whom 13 figure among the main sellers of mines listed in Tables 5.4 and 5.5, and received £642,800 out of the £1.1 million total. Of the thirteen families, seven[86] can be definitely said to have spent their money on luxury consumption and trips abroad (four families), or capital export (emigration of the former mine-owner with his money) (three families). These seven received £332,000 of the £642,800 paid to the sample group. The remaining six families remained active as entrepreneurs in various sectors of the Peruvian economy after the sale of all or part of their mining interests to Cerro, and it may be presumed that a good deal of the money received by them, £310,800, was used to finance investment in these subsequent ventures. Miguel Gallo was active in two Lima banks and three insurance companies and, more significantly, helped to launch his son-in-law Manuel Mujica y Carassa as a successful mine-owner and landowner in the Central Sierra. The Malpartida family purchased coastal land and participated in the expansion of sugar and cotton-growing. The Tello family established the electricity supply company for Cerro de Pasco, and bought up land in what is now the centre of Miraflores, thereby guaranteeing themselves an important place in the real-estate boom of the 1920s. Gallo Hermanos continued to operate their merchant house in Cerro de Pasco, and retained control of mines at Vinchos; in the 1930s they launched the Atacocha mining company, one of the great post-1930 success stories (see Chapter 8), although the finance for this venture would have been only peripherally derived from their pre-1910 sales of mines. Proaño retained important mines at Morococha and his smelter at Tamboraque, in which much of the £95,000 he received from Cerro was probably reinvested. Last in this group, the Alania family retained some small mines at Cerro de Pasco, and purchased a small *hacienda* in the Sierra, although the bulk of their money was apparently used to buy and maintain several large family houses in Lima.

Although not included in Low's sample, the eight other families appearing in Tables 5.4 and 5.5 can be roughly classified, on the basis of the available evidence, into one group of three families[87] with ongoing entrepreneurial records, who probably used the £60,480 from their sales to help finance other activities; and a second group of five families[88] who appear to have used their £98,000 for generally non-productive purposes.

In summary, of the £833,280 paid to mine-sellers identified in Tables 5.4 and 5.5, a total of £403,280 (48 per cent) went to families who had at least some identifiable propensity to reinvest, while 430,000 (52 per cent) went to unproductive spenders. If we assume similar proportions to have applied to the remaining £249,000 worth of sales not shown in detail in our tables, then £519,500 out of £1,082,280 can be estimated to have been received by potential investors.[89] Precisely what the propensity of this group to save and invest would have been we cannot say; certainly, in common with all upper-class Peruvians of the period, they would have expected to maintain a comfortable lifestyle, and part of their income from mine sales would have been spent on Lima houses and high society. If we assume that about three-quarters of their receipts from sales of mines was saved, then the total addition to the local economy's investment funds would have been £400,000 (slightly less than $2 million) spread over a period of nearly ten years. This, however, overstates the gains to actual investment, because, as the summaries above indicated, a considerable amount of the 'investment' by the sellers of mines took the form of purchases of land in various parts of the country, presumably from other Peruvians who may well have utilised the proceeds for consumption rather than investment. In addition, as already noted, it is unrealistic to expect that the injection of an extra £400,000 into the local capital market would have translated into extra saving and investment equal to this sum, since the effect could well be to deter other potential investors from supplying funds to the market (leading them instead towards consumption and/or capital flight).

In brief, Cerro's entry added perhaps $2 million directly to the economy's supply of savings, in addition to financing $10 million of capital formation, all spread over the years 1900–1916 when Peru's exports were worth $15–20 million *annually*. We doubt that this compensated for the $100 million-odd lost to the local economy from 1916 to 1937 as the result of Cerro's presence (again assuming that local companies would have rivalled Cerro in scale).[90]

Low's findings are consistent with more general evidence from the record of the 1900s. The impression which one obtains from a reading of the qualitative literature on the decade is of a period in which developmental entrepreneurship and investment were slowing down rather than speeding up, and it is noteworthy that although attractive corporate ventures floated in the early 1900s tended to be quite heavily over-subscribed,[91] the rate of new company flotations on the Lima stock exchange was declining fast.[92] In summary, it seems probable that only a rather small part of the liquid funds generated by Cerro's entry

found profitable investment opportunities, while those which did find
such opportunities may well, in doing so, have excluded other potential
investors.

The second of our earlier assumptions that might be queried was that
local firms, operating the mines in the absence of Cerro, would have
returned all their profits to the economy. The difficulty here is that the
decision of local firms to invest or consume locally or abroad is
dependent upon the circumstances in which the local economy finds
itself. In the 1890s, we have already seen, local firms returned the great
bulk of their profits; in the 1920s, as we shall see, the record was less
encouraging. We must, therefore, introduce a qualification to our earlier
argument that Cerro's contribution to the balance of payments was
negative in the years 1916–37. A locally-controlled mining sector would
have performed better than Cerro only in so far as it was operating in an
economic setting which encouraged the local accumulation and spending of profits—that is, in a local economy which was continuing to grow
and to offer attractive investment opportunities in a number of sectors.
Peru without foreign capital after 1900 would still have been an
economy enmeshed in the international system; and just as Bolivian
mining capitalists, in such a situation, sent their profits abroad, so might
Peruvian capitalists have done in a local economy which failed to modify
the terms of its integration into the international system. As Chapter 2
noted, the most difficult problem with dependency theory is that the
parts cannot be properly considered in isolation from the whole. Peru
without Cerro would have been *potentially* much better-off; but the
benefits of local control would have been enjoyed only in so far as other
elements of the economy's increasing dependence could have been
mitigated. (Looking on the brighter side, even capital flight can be
viewed as investment in assets abroad, which brings some return to local
capitalists whether or not they actually repatriate the earnings from their
overseas funds. To bring matters such as this into our calculations,
however, merely complicates matters greatly without clarifying the
outcome.)

The problems of putting a discussion such as the above into a formal
cost-benefit framework are, obviously, enormous, and the effort does
not contribute much more to our evaluation of Cerro. We have
undertaken the exercise elsewhere,[93] and will simply note here that the
results of our formal quantitative model were rather inconclusive,[94]
although tending to show that Cerro's presence reduced national
income below the level it would otherwise have reached, even on *ceteris
paribus* assumptions. Relaxation of *ceteris paribus* conditions (to take
into account the dynamic gains from 'learning by doing', increased
capital-absorptive capacity, stimulus to local technology, mobilisation
of entrepreneurial capacities, and so on) strengthened the case against
foreign investment in mining.

We conclude, thus, that the entry of Cerro to Peru (i) made only a small difference to the total amount of investment actually realised in the economy during the 1900s; (ii) caused foreign-exchange receipts from the First World War onwards to fall below the level which they would otherwise have attained; (iii) excluded local entrepreneurship and management from the development of the mining sector, contributing thereby to the erosion of local technological competence and the under-mobilisation of the society's creative potential; (iv) strongly reinforced the general trend towards increased dependence, including the tendency for government to allow foreign capital to operate without effective regulation; and (v) was welcomed and applauded by almost all influential Peruvians. The 'invisible hand' was not much help to local economic growth, at least so far as mining was concerned.[95] What then of Peru's experience as an oil producer?

5.2 THE PETROLEUM SECTOR

The denationalisation of one of the main extractive export sectors has now been described, and the costs and benefits of foreign control assessed. This section will consider another extractive sector which became increasingly the preserve of foreign firms during the period from 1890 to 1930—oil. We begin with a survey of the main developments in the sector, and the nature of ownership and control. We then review the record of oil exports from the point of view of local development, reaching conclusions so pessimistic (and so unfavourable to the foreign firms involved) as to invite incredulity that any supposedly independent country could tolerate, let alone welcome, foreign investment on such terms. We therefore conclude with a closer look at the interaction between oil company pressures and Peruvian policymaking.

General trends, 1890–1930
The development of the oil industry in Peru began in the 1860s, but for the first forty years growth was slow.[96] During the late 1890s and early 1900s the pace began to pick up, with a sharp increase in the amount of exploration and with the formation of new companies; but oil still lagged behind the leading export sectors of the period. The oilfields which became actual producers at that time were (with the sole exception of the small Pirin field in Puno) clustered in the coastal desert of the far northwest. Most important was the Negritos oilfield beneath the Hacienda La Brea y Parinas; this area had been known since the Colony as a tar producer, was drilled for oil by Meiggs and others in the 1870s, and in 1889 became the property of a British company, London and Pacific Petroleum. Second in importance was the Lobitos field north of Negritos, discovered by wildcat drilling in 1901, and developed by

another British firm, Lobitos Oilfields. Third was Zorritos, further north again, a small and geologically-complex field first developed in the 1860s, and controlled from 1883 on by the immigrant Callao merchant Faustino G. Piaggio.

After the 1901 discovery of Lobitos, only two other significant producing areas remained to be located in the north (at least until the present day): the small Los Organos field discovered in the 1940s and the offshore oil developed in the 1950s and 1960s. The presence of oil in the jungle east of the Andes was suspected, but no actual strikes were made until the 1930s; while on the altiplano of Puno the Pirin field, discovered and worked in the first decade of the twentieth century, was quickly exhausted.

Figure 5.1 shows the crude oil production of the various oilfields between 1890 and 1930. Until 1900 the Piaggio company and the London and Pacific Company at Negritos were operating on a similar scale, but the much greater size and productivity of the Negritos field became increasingly evident thereafter. From 59 per cent in the 1890s, the share of Negritos in total output rose to 63 per cent in the 1900s, 80 per cent in the 1920s and 83 per cent in the 1930s. The locally-controlled field at Zorritos had reached full-capacity production by the early years of the twentieth century, and by the 1930s was nearing exhaustion; from 41 per cent of output in the 1890s this field had dropped to one per cent by the 1920s, although its share of the local market for oil products (the Piaggio firm exported little after 1910) remained close to 10 per cent. The third company. Lobitos, never made any significant attempt to penetrate the local market before 1930, concentrating on the export of crude oil, although some sales were made to the IPC refinery at Talara.

Looking at the overall rate of growth in Fig. 5.1, we see that output expanded very rapidly from the mid-1880s until 1892, due at first to the growth of the Piaggio company at Zorritos, and then (1890–2) to the establishment of the London and Pacific Petroleum Company at Negritos. In 1893, however, the London and Pacific company (in common with other British enterprises established during Michael P. Grace's period of promotional activity) cut back its investment in Peru and by 1897 this company's output had fallen below one-quarter of the 1892 peak. Steady expansion by Piaggio offset much of the drop, but by 1898 total Peruvian production was still below the 1892 level. In that year reorganisation of the London and Pacific board and settlement of the company's dispute with Michael Grace[97] resulted in rehabilitation of the Negritos field, and from then until 1900 both the leading companies were expanding rapidly, in line with developments in other sectors of the economy.

In the first years of the twentieth century, oil prices in Peru fell heavily, and expansion came to a halt again until 1905, when the Lobitos field began commercial production. This coincided with an improvement in

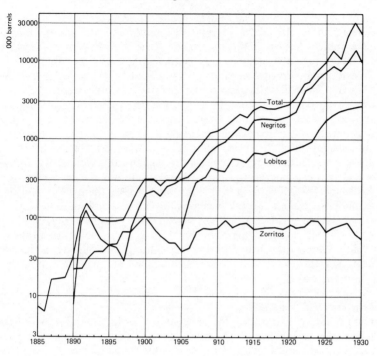

FIGURE 5.1 Crude oil output, 1885–1930 (North Coast)

Source: Estadística Petrolera del Perú 1948–9, pp. 43–4.

the sector's prospects. Up to that point, oil's role in the Peruvian economy had been very limited, in contrast to that of sugar, cotton or silver. Its only use was as domestic kerosene, and exports were very small. The take-off of the industry after 1904 was encouraged by the emergence of a large Peruvian market for fuel oil, as the Central Railway and the Peruvian Steamship Company switched from coal to oil; at the same time international demand was rising fast, and exports from Peru on a large scale began about 1908. Prices rose until 1920, and from 1908 to 1915 Peruvian production expanded steadily. The First World War years, however, were a period of stagnation. The shortage of shipping during the war was responsible to some extent; but more important was the tense political situation which developed around the oil industry in the years following the 1913 takeover of the Negritos oilfield by Standard Oil of New Jersey (see below). As is described below, confrontation between the Government and Standard Oil over the terms

of the latter's title to the oilfield produced fears of possible expropriation, and both of the foreign oil companies cut back on further
development until a definite settlement of the issue was in view in 1921–
2. Uncertainty was ended in 1922, with a compromise agreement on La
Brea-Parinas (Negritos) and the promulgation of a new Petroleum Law
to govern future development of the industry; the 1920s were a decade of
rapid expansion, oil becoming the leading Peruvian export in 1924, and
accounting for 30 per cent of total export earnings by 1929.

From the outset the development of oil in Peru was accompanied by
the installation of refineries, initially to produce kerosene (the basis of
the industry's early success) and later, gasoline and fuel oil. Two small
refineries were operating before the War of the Pacific (both were
destroyed in the war), and by the later 1890s there were working
refineries at Talara (on the Negritos field) and Zorritos, as well as an
expensive but unsuccessful plant installed by a French company. The
Zorritos and Talara refineries both grew and diversified during the first
twenty years of the century, the latter becoming dominant as production
from Negritos expanded. In the 1920s a small natural-gasoline extraction plant was also started by the Lobitos company.[98]

Reasons for foreign control
The primary constraint on the development of the oil industry in Peru
was access to commercially-exploitable oil reserves. Under the 1877
Peruvian Mining Law, control over any mineral deposit could be
secured by simply staking a claim to it, and the claim could be held for an
indefinite period on the sole condition that the annual surface tax (S/30
per block or *pertenencia*) was paid.[99] Once the three main oilfields had
been staked, the pace of their development was determined entirely by
the companies in control, who could not be legally displaced regardless
of how many other enterprises wished to enter. The fact that the two
biggest oilfields came into foreign hands (Negritos by purchase, Lobitos
by discovery) meant that the timing and pace of development was
determined by the strategies and resources of the parent companies.
Peruvian crude oil was of high grade (particularly suitable for fuel, less
suitable for the production of lubricants, in which Peru never became
self-sufficient); and the fields were located on the Coast, so that export
production could be piped directly on to tankers without heavy
investment in infrastructure. The industry was thus not subject to any
transport bottleneck, and output grew as fast as new wells were drilled.

Under these circumstances, the early entry and consequent predominance of foreign firms is particularly important. Peru's oil resources were limited, and foreigners got to them first, up to forty years
before Peru became a significant oil exporter. The first well was sunk on
the Zorritos field in 1863 by a local syndicate, which brought in U.S.
drilling crews in 1865. Despite four successful wells, the enterprise failed

financially, and it was a Pennsylvania oilman, Prentice, who established the first successful refinery at Zorritos in 1876, after nine years of prospecting and drilling on the field. Another U.S. operator, Henry Smith, had begun drilling at Zorritos in 1870, and in 1875 or 1876 (sources differ) he entered partnership with the immigrant merchant Faustino Piaggio. Meanwhile, on the Negritos oilfield further south, Henry Meiggs had been prospecting and drilling; in 1873 he established a refinery at Callao.[100] By the time the Chilean navy destroyed all the oil installations in 1879, the industry was thus already dominated by U.S. capitalists.

The initial phase of post-war reconstruction brought the first, and only, successful large-scale local venture. By 1883 Piaggio, taking over as Smith's creditor, had begun the rehabilitation of the Zorritos field, and in 1884 his Establecimiento Industrial de Petroleo de Zorritos began work on port facilities and a new refinery, and brought in modern drilling equipment. In the conditions of the 1880s the local kerosene market (in which by 1886 Piaggio was supplying an estimated 30 per cent of annual consumption of a million gallons)[101] was becoming increasingly profitable, but most Peruvian capital was being absorbed by the post-war economic recovery of Lima and the sugar and mining sectors: interest in the oil industry remained confined to a very limited group of local capitalists. Apart from Piaggio, indeed, the only Peruvian with a major interest in oil was Genaro Helguero, owner of the Hacienda La Brea-Parinas beneath which lay the Negritos oilfield, but his main concern was to capitalise his asset through sale. Having obtained (by manoeuvres of dubious legality) a virtual tax exemption for the property, coupled with a consolidation of surface and subsoil rights, Helguero sold it in 1888 to an international oil speculator, Herbert Tweddle,[102] for £18,000. Tweddle formed a company in Britain, the 'London and Pacific Petroleum Company,' in which he sold his interest in 1890, at a large profit. For the following fifteen years Piaggio and the London and Pacific Company were the only firms controlling proven and producing oilfields.

In the 1890s a number of attempts to find a third commercial field met with failure. Most of the enterprises were by then either Peruvian or Peruvian-foreign joint ventures.[103] In 1900, however, it was the British merchant Alexander Milne who struck oil at Lobitos and in 1901 formed a company in London to finance development. Production began in 1904–5, and in 1908 the firm was reorganised, becoming the Lobitos Oilfield Co. Ltd. The only other successful entrant into the industry was the small Lagunitas Oil Co., with four square miles of claims near Talara.[104]

After 1900, the rapidly increasing prosperity of the industry aroused increasing interest among Peruvian entrepreneurs. Peruvians tried, and failed, to find new oilfields in 1904 (J. Taiman, at Quebrada Siches);

1905–7 (Taiman again, at La Breita);[105] 1910 (Elias Montefiore at Cabo Blanco); 1912 (at La Garita); 1913 (a 'Peruvian syndicate', at Lechusal); and 1913–14 (Bocapan Oilfields Ltd, a Lima syndicate, at Boca Pan)—all in the northwest. Various parallel new foreign attempts met an equal lack of success.[106]

After 1910 further development efforts were delayed by the problem of establishing legitimate title to oil claims. Adequate cadastral surveys of the northern Coast had never been undertaken, and as renewed growth of production after 1905 brought a wave of claim-staking in the region by hopeful new entrants, the problem of overlapping and conflicting claims became serious. In September 1910 the Government suspended all further registration of new claims in the area until a cadastral survey had been conducted.[107] As the years passed without any survey, and enterprises formed to explore pre-1910 concessions met with no success, interest in the oil industry among Peruvian capitalists virtually ceased. The moratorium on new claims lasted until 1922, during which period the three established companies were assured of freedom from new competition.

In the meantime, foreign control was being consolidated by the arrival of a giant. Shortly before the First World War, Standard Oil of New Jersey[108] arrived in Peru to buy up oilfields. The obvious candidates were the British firms. In 1913 Standard bought control of London and Pacific, and Lagunitas followed in 1914. The two enterprises were consolidated under the control of the International Petroleum Company (IPC), a Canadian subsidiary of Jersey Standard: and the West Coast Fuel Company (the sole oil-distributing network on the Pacific coast, and the key to the Chilean market) was taken over at the same time.[109] Negritos became an integral part of the worldwide activities and strategy of Standard Oil; and since world oil markets were subject to growing oligopolistic control and the IPC offered an easy means of access to those markets, the other major exporting firm in Peru (Lobitos Oilfields) entered a working alliance with the Standard interests, selling all Lobitos oil through the IPC. Piaggio, the Peruvian firm, had by this time almost ceased to operate as an exporter, since domestic demand was sufficient to absorb all the output from Zorritos and local prices were good.

The year 1922 was a turning point for the industry. The new Petroleum Law, promulgated in January 1922, imposed a 10 per cent royalty limit on crude oil output, provided for a new structure of surface taxes with high rates for unworked claims and low rates for productive claims, and ended the moratorium on registration of new claims in the north. (The 1922 agreement with IPC, discussed below, was designed specifically to exempt the company from this new law.)

The most important effect of the new law was a rush to stake oil claims. The industry was by this time rapidly growing and highly profitable,[110] while other sectors of the economy were suffering unfavourable conditions. Although IPC and Lobitos, the two large foreign firms, moved quickly to extend their control over the most promising areas (both companies had been exploring the region during the moratorium on claims), the wave of new activity included others as well. The number of oil claims registered in the north rose from 43,051 in 1922 to 206,824 by 1924. Of this increase of over 160,000 claims, the IPC accounted for some 50,000 and Lobitos Oilfields for part of the rest. Large numbers of Peruvian capitalists from other sectors of the economy, however, also took the opportunity to gain a foothold in the north. Of these the most active was Carlos Cilloniz, a Cañete cotton planter, who drilled three unsuccessful wells on his concession before abandoning the search.[111] Many of the other Peruvian holders of claims granted options to a Shell subsidiary which entered the area and began prospecting in 1924, but the venture ended when Shell withdrew, evidently under a secret agreement with Standard Oil.[112] Much of the north reverted to the State, which brought in Phillips Petroleum to explore for oil in 1927–8, without result.[113] Another Peruvian group headed by Carlos Ortiz de Zevallos contracted with the German Company, Stinnes, for exploration work, but equally without success.

These explorations of the 1920s all focused on the huge empty desert area known as the Sechura, which, it was generally believed, must contain further oilfields in addition to those discovered prior to 1910. This belief was not confined to the uninitiated; IPC drilled 22 unsuccessful exploration wells in the Sechura during the mid-1920s, and Lobitos Oilfield also carried out exploratory drilling.[114] Neither then nor since, however, has any significant oilfield been found in the Sechura.

Among the claim-stakers and explorers of the 1920s the conspicuous absentee was the only successful Peruvian oil company, the Piaggio enterprise. This lack of initiative is explained by the advancing age of Faustino Piaggio, who had migrated to Peru in 1861 and was in poor health in the early 1920s. He died in 1924[115] and the firm suffered for some time thereafter from management difficulties.

The story of foreign control is thus relatively straightforward. The Peruvian oil industry was dominated by foreign firms principally because foreign oil speculators developed an interest in Peru twenty years before the country became a significant exporter, and bought control of the largest oilfield very cheaply at that time. The sole remaining large field in the north, at Lobitos, was staked out by British interest—whether by superior energies, or by pure chance, remains unclear. Thereafter, the fact that no large new fields remained to be found constituted an effective barrier to entry, and assured the oligopolistic position of the three main successful firms. The key to this situation was the London and Pacific Company's control over the entire

640 square miles of the Negritos oilfield—a large (by Peruvian standards) resource base which could equally well have supplied a number of smaller firms.

What then would have happened to the oil industry in Peru in the absence of foreign capital? In the case of metal mining, our answer to this question had to rest on hypothetical arguments about whether local firms would have possessed the necessary competence to develop the sector on their own. In the case of oil, one of the three successful firms was locally-controlled throughout the period considered here, and its performance enables us to state without hesitation that local development of the industry would have been perfectly feasible. Apart from a price-fixing deal with IPC, Piaggio operated in complete independence from the foreign firms. Up to 1920 his company was as efficient as the IPC,[116] and contemporary opinion was that its products were of higher quality than those of the IPC, and fetched a corresponding premium in price.[117] After 1920, the comparison between Piaggio and IPC loses meaning, because of the senility of Piaggio himself, and the pending exhaustion of the Zorritos field, which discouraged further investment at a time when IPC was still bringing Negritos up to peak production. There was, however, no mystery to oil production and refining; Piaggio or anyone like him could have undertaken the development of the Negritos and/or the Lobitos oilfields with every expectation of success. The foreign companies controlled the oilfields with the full acquiescence of the local élite and government, but if they contributed any unique ability to the development of the sector, it could only have been in respect of their privileged access to international markets, where cartel arrangements were increasingly tight.[118] The section which follows, however, indicates that any benefits derived from such access were benefits for the companies—not for the local economy.

Oil and the economy

Of the major export products of the 1890–1930 period, oil was the one which conformed most closely to the popular stereotype of the foreign-owned enclave. The producing oilfields were located in the far northwest, 600 miles from Lima, in the middle of a desert region and lacking effective communication with the rest of the country except by sea. Most equipment and materials were imported directly through the company ports, and export production left directly from the fields by tankers. The industry generated virtually no backward linkages in Peru, so that the stimulus to the local economy from oil exports was confined to payments by the two large foreign firms to their labour force and to the government.[119]

In one important way, however, oil diverged from the enclave stereotype. Peru was itself a rapidly-growing market for oil products, and in the absence of good domestically-produced coal, oil was the main fuel for industry and transport, while kerosene was the main cooking fuel. Somewhat over 10 per cent of the oil industry's total sales were to the Peruvian market. It would however be wrong to suggest that local sales of oil products generated 'forward linkages,' since IPC and Piaggio maintained a price-fixing agreement which held local prices equal to the cif value of imports; for Peruvian consumers, therefore, domestically-produced oil was not significantly cheaper than imports would have been. Although costs of production in Peru were very low, the Government did not pursue policies designed to force down local prices; rather, the threat of such policies was used by the Leguía regime in the 1920s to blackmail the IPC into providing financial aid for the Government.[120]

The result of the very wide margin between cost and price was that oil production in Peru was an exceptionally profitable activity; one critical observer indicated in 1930 that at least 50 per cent of the wholesale price of oil products sold in Lima was clear profit for the companies.[121] More significant, the same observer pointed out, was the fact that for the IPC the profits on its sales of products *within* Peru were sufficient to meet the entire local-currency cost of producing for export, with the result that the IPC, despite its role as the leading single export enterprise of the 1920s, played virtually no part in the actual supply of foreign exchange to the market.

A summary of the IPC's local outlays (returned value) compared with income is given in Table 5.8, and estimates for imported materials and equipment and repatriated profit are shown in Table 5.9. (Note that repatriated profit is net of reinvestment in Peru, which is included in the figures on operating outlays.) Table 5.10 presents consolidated results for IPC and Lobitos Oilfields. While these figures cannot claim to be absolutely precise,[122] they are accurate enough to support certain clearcut conclusions. In only six of the twenty years did income from sales to the local market fail to cover the company's total local-currency expenditures, and total returned value for the twenty years was only $1.4 million above total local income. Since the fictitious contingencies item in our returned-value estimates came to $5.6 million over the same period, we are able to state with certainty that over those twenty years the net amount of foreign exchange contributed to the local economy by IPC was insignificantly different from zero.[123] This rather startling result is *not* due to the character of IPC as an enclave, but to the fact that the company, as the main supplier of the local market, was able to extract enough revenue from local consumers to cover its entire local operating costs. Oil export receipts ($346 million over the period) were divided between payment for imported equipment and materials (17 per cent) and clear profit for the company (83 per cent). In terms of the global totals, shown in Table 5.9, no less than 70 per cent of the company's total earnings were clear profit. Payments to the labour

TABLE 5.8   Returned value from operations of the International
Petroleum Co., 1916 to 1934
(thousands of U.S. dollars)

	(1)	(2)	(3)	(4)	(5)	(6)	(7)
	Local-economy payments to			*Total local-currency expendi-tures*	*Local sales income*	*Total sales[d] income*	*Returned value as per cent of total sales*
	Labour[a]	*Govern-ment[b]*	*Other[c]*				
1916	875	250	111	1,236	702	7,018	18
1917	803	364	115	1,282	1,118	5,993	21
1918	739	444	116	1,299	2,059	7,756	17
1919	1,230	590	182	2,002	2,007	11,631	17
1920	1,538	574	211	2,323	2,744	8,827	26
1921	1,393	484	188	2,065	2,191	15,353	13
1922	1,455	1,875	231	3,561	1,956	21,837	16
1923	1,648	937	255	2,840	2,885	18,618	15
1924	1,669	1,385	304	3,358	3,495	24,814	14
1925	2,240	988	324	3,552	4,948	23,132	15
1926	2,448	1,704	417	4,569	3,984	27,082	17
1927	2,678	1,690	436	4,804	4,916	37,352	13
1928	2,755	2,152	492	5,399	5,923	45,675	12
1929	2,452	2,676	452	5,580	5,884	50,520	11
1930	1,878	1,878	374	4,130	5,080	24,968	17
1931	1,057	1,589	265	2,911	3,867	15,760	18
1932	1,581	1,193	277	3,051	2,500	15,643	20
1933	1,327	2,122	345	3,794	2,312	17,926	21
1934	1,796	3,349	514	5,659	3,486	28,194	20
TOTALS	31,562	26,244	5,609	63,415	62,057	408,093	16

Source: Bertram (1974), Appendix B.

[a] Including expenditures on company schools, hospitals, etc.
[b] Including special payments made in 1922 and 1929 in connection with special agreements with the Government (the 1922 Laudo and the 1929 petroleum monopoly case).
[c] This column is an entirely fictitious contingencies item, since no payments to local suppliers could be traced. We have simply taken 10 per cent of the wage bill and normal tax costs.
[d] Local sales plus exports through Talara.

force, including social benefits, took eight per cent, payment to government six per cent, and our contingencies allowance for possible unrecorded local expenditures one per cent. The remaining 15 per cent went to pay for imports. Of these figures, the one most likely to be an underestimate is that for profits.

Furthermore, it is evident from Table 5.9, column 6, that the long-run tendency of the profit share was, if anything, upward, a result

TABLE 5.9   International Petroleum Co.: operating costs and estimated profits (thousands of U.S. dollars)

	(1)	(2)	(3)	(4)	(5)	(6)
	Returned value	Imported materials and equipment	Total operating costs (1) + (2)	Total sales	Estimated profit (4) − (3)	Profits as per cent of sales
1916	1,236	1,539	2,775	7,018	4,243	60
1917	1,282	1,697	2,979	5,993	3,014	50
1918	1,299	1,531	2,830	7,756	4,926	64
1919	2,002	1,919	3,921	11,631	7,710	66
1920	2,323	2,479	4,802	8,827	4,025	46
1921[a]	2,065	7,328	9,393	15,353	5,960	39
1922	3,561	1,964	5,525	21,837	16,312	75
1923	2,840	3,370	6,210	18,618	12,408	67
1924	3,358	3,807	7,165	24,814	17,649	71
1925	3,552	4,480	8,032	23,132	15,100	65
1926	4,569	6,547	11,116	27,082	15,966	59
1927	4,804	6,416	11,220	37,352	26,132	70
1928	5,399	4,049	9,448	45,675	36,227	79
1929	5,580	3,800	9,380	50,520	41,140	81
1930	4,130	2,330	6,460	24,968	18,508	74
1931	2,911	1,589	4,500	15,760	11,260	71
1932	3,051	789	3,840	15,643	11,803	75
1933	3,794	941	4,755	17,926	13,171	73
1934	5,659	1,981	7,640	28,194	20,554	73
TOTALS	63,415	58,576	121,991	408,093	286,102	70

Source: Columns 1 and 4 from Table 5.8.
Column 2 from Bertram (1974), p. 349. These import estimates were obtained by assigning to IPC slightly over 70 per cent of total imports through the port of Talara, the remainder being destined for Lobitos Oilfields (20 per cent) and consumption of the local population (including expenditure of the company wage bill in the second-round). The result is an upper-bound estimate, since second-round import expenditures were certainly higher than assumed.
[a] It may be noted that 1921 was a year of exceptionally heavy imports of investment goods for development of the oilfield.

attributable directly to the complete absence of governmental regulation and the astonishingly low taxation imposed on the company. IPC's success in maintaining its profitability through the Depression is especially striking, and it is easy enough to see that for a firm earning clear profits of $11 million annually at the lowest point of the Depression, it was easy to spare some cash for the purpose of retaining the friendship of the Government. Various recent studies of the IPC's history have emphasized the use made by the company up to the 1940s of a combination of diplomatic pressure, 'soft' loans to the Government,

TABLE 5.10 Returned value from Lobitos Oilfields operations, and consolidated results for foreign firms (thousands of U.S. dollars)

| | Lobitos local-economy payments to | | | | Lobitos total sales[c] | Returned value as per cent of income | Consolidated figures, Lobitos + IPC | | |
	Labour[a]	Government	Other[b]	Total			Returned value	Total sales	Percent returned value
1916	245	58	29	332	495	67	1,568	7,513	21
1917	230	115	34	379	898	42	1,661	6,891	24
1918	206	153	37	396	1,214	33	1,695	8,970	19
1919	349	202	54	605	1,712	35	2,607	13,343	20
1920	450	161	60	671	909	74	2,994	9,736	31
1921	458	94	54	606	1,097	55	2,671	16,450	16
1922	481	212	69	762	2,067	37	4,323	23,904	18
1923	736	436	119	1,291	2,478	52	4,131	21,096	20
1924	1,041	587	162	1,790	3,009	59	5,148	27,823	19
1925	1,324	720	204	2,248	4,292	52	5,800	27,424	21
1926	1,432	826	227	2,485	4,479	55	7,054	31,561	22
1927	873	1,015	190	2,078	5,450	38	6,882	42,802	16
1928	699	985	167	1,851	5,264	35	7,250	50,939	14
1929	856	1,032	188	2,076	6,980	30	7,656	57,500	13
1930	646	858	152	1,656	4,900	34	5,786	29,868	19
1931	371	792	117	1,280	2,913	44	4,191	18,673	22
1932	606	580	119	1,305	3,322	39	4,356	18,965	23
1933	558	522	107	1,187	2,252	53	4,981	20,178	25
1934	792	765	156	1,713	3,229	53	7,372	31,423	23
TOTALS	12,353	10,113	2,245	24,711	56,960	43	88,126	465,053	19

Source: Bertram (1974), Appendix B.
[a] Including social-security and fringe benefits
[b] As with IPC, a 10 per cent contingencies addition
[c] Exports through the port of Lobitos

and direct bribery to protect its interests in Peru.[124] (Lobitos Oilfields, while less prominent in its resort to such tactics, was to be found backing-up IPC pressure at crucial moments.)[125] The oil industry's performance in Peru fully justified the charges of its most hostile nationalist critics.

To bring out the implications of the above figures more clearly, let us ask what gains Peru would have obtained from retaining (or restoring) local control over the Negritos oilfield. The total costs incurred by the IPC in producing $408 million of oil products between 1916 and 1934 came to $122 million (Table 5.9, column (3)). If we assume that, for any level of output of a local firm replacing the IPC, the ratio of costs to earnings would have been the same (i.e. 30 per cent), then rough estimates are possible of the benefits which the local economy would have derived from such replacement. A counterfactual firm identical to IPC would have yielded returned value of $350 million[126] compared to IPC's actual $63 million; or, if we subtract the income from local-market sales, $285 million compared to IPC's zero. In either case, the net gain would have been $285 million approximately. Conceivably, cartel control of the international oil market might have made it difficult for a local firm to export at the levels achieved by IPC, since markets might have been restricted to the neighbouring Latin American countries (particularly Chile). The local economy would still have remained better-off with the replacement firm so long as exports sufficed to cover the foreign-exchange cost of imported inputs (which we assume, on the basis of the IPC's production function, to have averaged 14 per cent of total sales). Simple calculation shows that the break-even point (where import costs equal export earnings) would have been that at which exports were $10 million[127]—roughly three per cent of the IPC's actual exports over the period 1916–34. In effect, Peru would have been better-off with a locally owned oil industry restricted virtually to import-substitution, than with the IPC as its leading export enterprise. Considering the possibility that local firms might have incurred lower proportional import costs than did IPC, this conclusion is strengthened.

On any reasonable assumptions, Peru would have been better-off without the IPC. We have discussed these issues elsewhere in a detailed cost-benefit framework,[128] with results which unequivocally favour replacement of the IPC by local firms—in other words, exclusion or expropriation of the company, with or without modest compensation. An alternative means of increasing the local economy's gains from the company's presence might have been to raise taxation very steeply, capturing more of the surplus generated by the sector. Either course would have involved a major change in government policy, but perhaps the most important lessons of the IPC story is that not only did successive Peruvian governments explicitly turn down clear opportunities to expropriate the company, but they also consistently allowed the company to operate under a privileged low-taxation arrangement. (As Table 5.10 indicates, the neighbouring Lobitos company paid 18 per cent of its income in taxes compared with IPC's 6 per cent). Part of the trouble was that foreign capital in countries such as Peru tended (and tends) to operate as an indivisible whole; governmental action against one foreign company, however absurdly exploitative that company's record might be, would be greeted by solid opposition from all other foreign firms operating locally, backed by diplomatic and financial pressure from the British and U.S. Governments.[129] Given the importance of this issue, the record of government negotiations with the IPC deserves closer scrutiny.

Government policy and the IPC

In 1824 Simon Bolivar broke with Latin American legal precedent by granting outright ownership of the subsoil on part of the *hacienda* La Brea-Pariñas to one of his followers. Subsequent Peruvian legislation reaffirmed the traditional claim of the State to be the sole owner of subsoil resources, with private firms granted rights of exploitation only under governmental concessions. When the 1877 Mining Law made the payment of 'surface taxes' a necessary condition for the continued holding of concessions to mineral deposits, however, the owners of Negritos at first claimed to be exempt, on the grounds that they held the oil deposits not in concession but in fee simple. The dispute was resolved, but the issues merely confused, by an 1887 compromise under which the oilfield was registered as comprising 10 claims with annual tax of S/300 per year, although the Helguera family continued to regard themselves as outright owners of the subsoil (and claimed furthermore that this ownership extended beyond the very limited area indicated in the 1824 title, to cover the entire Negritos oil field.)[130] This position was inherited by the London and Pacific Petroleum Company, and subsequently by the IPC. These foreign companies considered themselves legally exempt from any additional taxes on their property beyond the S/300. Consequently, until the imposition of export taxes in 1916, the tax burden on Negritos was negligible.

This was of little concern to the central Government at first, since oil production was conducted in an isolated area and with a very low profile. However, the mounting concern in 1910 over the need for clearer measurement of oil concessions (see above) brought as a by-product the revelation in 1911 that the largest oil company, while paying tax for only 10 claims, was in fact occupying an area equivalent to more than 41,600.[131] Taxing the property at the rate applying to all other mineral deposits in the country would have netted the Government S/1,250,000 annually; but the company flatly refused to accept any remeasurement, and President Leguía hesitated to press the issue.

In 1914–5 the military regime of Benavides, seeking new revenue sources (and perhaps less subject to company pressure) had the Negritos property remeasured despite determined opposition from the IPC, and the field was officially registered as comprising 41,614 claims. Two decrees were then issued ordering payment of the appropriate tax, but to no effect. IPC, a Canadian-registered company with a U.S. parent, called for diplomatic intervention from both the U.S. State Department and the British Foreign Office, alleging that it was being subjected to unfair and confiscatory taxation. The State Department was unwilling to help[132] but the British were enthusiastic and treated the case as a direct affront to a British enterprise.[133] The British Minister in Lima presented the Government with a Note which, as one recent student of the affair comments, 'distorted the situation in nearly every substantive reference',[134] and peremptorally demanded withdrawal of the tax decrees. Again the Government (now in the hands of Pardo) did not press the issue, preferring to arrange a negotiated transaction whereby IPC's parent Esso would help Peru to raise a $15 million loan in the U.S.A., in exchange for the imposition of only modest taxation on the oilfield and a concessionary rate of export tax.[135] The loan, however, was blocked,[136] and the tax issue became the centre of bitter political debate until 1918, during which time the British Minister continued to act as an agent for the company while the congressional opposition sought to block any further attempt to grant tax exemptions. By 1918 it was clear that the IPC would not accept full taxation, while neither Congress nor Pardo could afford politically the responsibility for granting concessions to the company. In an attempt to break the deadlock the IPC resorted to use of the 'oil weapon.' One of the two tankers supplying the Peruvian market disappeared in January, allegedly requisitioned for war duties,[137] and in July the company slowed down work and laid off part of the work force. In September a total stoppage of work was announced, and the sole remaining tanker was withdrawn from service, leaving Lima without supplies of fuel in October. The Government's response to this rather crude blackmail (which could well have been used as justification for expropriating the company) was weak and slow; only in early November did a decree appear prohibiting any of the oil companies from exporting oil until the domestic market was supplied,[138] and by then a secret agreement had been reached to send the tax issue to arbitration. Congress, having been a party to this deal in mid-October, staged a final one-month showpiece debate before passing the arbitration bill.[139]

IPC's title to the oilfield was still unconfirmed when in 1920 the recently-installed President Leguía, having been financed in his bid for power by various foreign interests including Royal Dutch Shell,[140] began to consider granting Shell a large concession on the north coast. Alarmed, IPC obtained more diplomatic support (this time from the U.S. State Department) and was informed by Leguía that, as in 1916, the price of security would be a large sum in cash, and assistance in placing Peruvian loans in the U.S.A. After two further years of negotiation a final agreement was reached in March 1922 which in its essentials was identical to that previously reached with Pardo in 1916. IPC was assured of security in its control of the whole oilfield, and was obliged to pay normal surface tax only on those claims in active production, idle claims being subject to a virtually negligible special tax. The company was exempted from payment of royalties on its production, and its export tax liability was frozen for fifty years. In exchange for this extraordinary charter, IPC paid $1 million in cash and assisted in the placing of $2.5 million of Petroleum Bonds in the U.S.A. in July 1922.[141] The agreement was enshrined in international law by convening, under the 1918 law, an 'international arbitration tribunal' to rubber-stamp the document and declare it the final settlement of a dispute between the British and Peruvian Governments. The issue originally at stake, namely whether or not the Negritos oilfield was State property, granted by concession to the private company, and hence subject to the normal law of the land, was simply ignored in the 1922 document.

Three Peruvian presidents in turn, thus, were content to use the promise of future security for IPC merely as a lever to pressure the company into providing short-term financial support for the government. Studying the record, it is impossible to avoid the conclusion that these governments were not taking the long-run costs and benefits for the local economy into account. Their overriding interest was to survive their relatively brief terms of office (five years or less) without undue fiscal crises, and negotiations with the IPC were pursued seriously only at times when the fiscal deficit reached alarming proportions, which it did in 1915–16 and in 1921–22. For a President who looked no more than four or five years ahead, the benefits of expropriating the company or enforcing increased taxation would no doubt have appeared rather distant by comparison with the short-run political and diplomatic unpleasantness which would have resulted, and the hard work of actually administering a radical policy. One therefore cannot say that Peruvian governments were acting 'irrationally' in allowing the IPC to strip the country's richest oilfield virtually tax-free, since 'rationality' itself is determined by such matters as the time-horizon chosen by decision-makers, and their evaluation of the relative weight to be assigned to fiscal short-run benefits as against long-run costs to the local economy.

In the literature on foreign direct investment it is often assumed that such investment will be permitted only where there are benefits for the host economy as well as for the foreign firm, and furthermore that a process of bargaining takes place in which a responsible nationalist government maximises the benefits for the host economy.[142] This assumption bears no resemblance to the situation outlined in this chapter: there were no benefits for the host economy (more specifically, there were substantial losses), and government at no stage pushed its bargaining position anywhere near the limit. This was not so much because Peru's rulers were ineffective bargainers (quite the contrary), as because their selection of bargaining objectives and strategy was based on narrow sectoral interests, excessively short-time horizons, and the justified expectation that the bargainers on the Peruvian side could expect to profit personally from an outcome favourable to the foreign firm. With such governments, a country such as Peru stood little chance of achieving an economic breakthrough.

5.3 CONCLUDING REMARKS

Our findings in this chapter have not been kind to the foreign investor, and on that account may be controversial. We feel therefore bound to remind the reader at this point of the conclusion reached in Chapter 4, that local control of sectors such as sugar and cotton proved far from sufficient, in the absence of other necessary pre-conditions, to ensure development or diversification of the local economy. Consequently, it does not follow from our conclusions in this chapter that the mere ab<ence of foreign investment would *by itself* have been sufficient to guarantee autonomous development. As Chapter 3 indicated, a wider focus is needed to understand the failure of Peru to build on the foundations of the 1890s. We rest our case here on the claim that a dramatically different attitude towards foreign capital on the part of Peruvian investors and government would have been a necessary (though insufficient) condition for autonomous growth.

6 The Non-export Economy, 1900–30: Industrial Relapse and Lagging Agriculture

As we have indicated in the discussion of export sectors, the increasingly autonomous growth trend of the 1890s was not sustained long beyond the turn of the century. We have also indicated that the change to a more dependent model is to be understood as the result of the economy's response to market signals (both internally- and externally-generated) in a *laissez-faire* environment. Chapter 3 suggested a number of prerequisites for autonomous growth. It is clear from our study of the export sectors that two such prerequisites continued for a substantial part of the following thirty years: buoyant aggregate demand, providing an expanding local market, and a surplus available for investment. But these two elements by themselves were not sufficient to induce rapid development of, for example, import-substituting manufacturing or non-export agriculture. The investment of the economy's surplus in such sectors depended upon a third pre-requisite: favourable relative prices, and hence relative profitability, sufficient to attract investment funds away from alternative uses. Our central argument in this chapter will be that, in the absence of effective intervention by government, price trends in the growing export economy worked against the development of non-export sectors.[1] We begin by analysing trends in aggregate demand and income distribution, then go on to look in some detail at the forces which helped or hindered the development of industry and agriculture after 1900.

6.1 TRENDS IN DEMAND, 1890–1930

The three main sources of demand stimulus in the Peruvian economy were: first, returned value from export earnings; second, net inflows of foreign capital; and third, government expenditure.[2] Figure 6.1 sums up the available data on trends in aggregate returned value and government

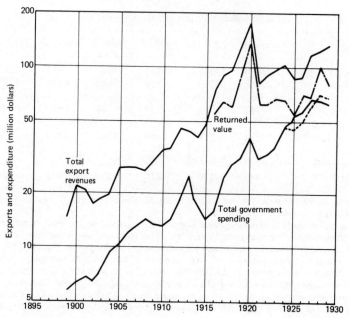

FIGURE 6.1 Exports and government expenditure, 1899–1929
(millions of U.S. dollars)

Sources: Extracto Estadístico, various years. For returned value: estimates taken from
Bertram (1974), p. 339.
Note that the increase in government spending 1916–19 is exaggerated by the exchange
rate.

spending, while Table 6.1 assembles estimates of the deficit in the
commercial balance (adjusted for gold movements), which we shall take
as an approximation for the net effect of foreign investment on the
balance of payments.

It is obvious that the first twenty years of the century were a period of
exceptional buoyancy in demand. Both export earnings and returned
value displayed sustained long-run growth; and the years of relatively
slow export growth (1901–4, 1906–8, and 1913–14) were coinciden-
tally years which witnessed a considerable inflow of foreign investment,[3]
at least part of which was spent in the local economy on factor
payments, materials, and purchases of property.[4] The leading role in
export growth for most of the period 1900 to 1920[5] was taken by
agricultural export sectors which were closely linked to the coastal

TABLE 6.1 Estimated balance of payments, two-yearly averages (000Lp.)

	1898–9	1900–1	1902–3	1904–5	1906–7	1908–9
Exports[a]	2440	3526	3403	4421	5148	5387
Imports[a]	2662	3524	4356	5665	6845	6222
BALANCE	−222	2	−753	−1244	−1697	−835
Net capital movements [b]	338	178	969	1542	2109	871
Net gold movements (inflow −)	−116	−180	−216	−298	−412	−36

Source: Extracto Estadistico, but see note below; *Foreign Commerce and Navigation of the USA; Statistical Abstract for the UK.*

[a] The visible trade figures have been substantially corrected on the basis of a detailed comparison of trade data as given by Peru and by her main trading partners, the U.K. and the U.S. The details of the comparison are available in a working paper (Thorp, (1975b)). The analysis is unfortunately not very conclusive, but suggests substantial undervaluation of imports in the early 1900s, of the order of 30 per cent, and a somewhat greater degree prior to 1901, when revised 'official' import prices were introduced. Exports appear to have been overvalued by the use of cif rather than fob values, especially for mineral products. The order of magnitude here is some 10 per cent, but perhaps as high as 20 per cent prior to 1902.

[b] Derived as a residual and representing only the crudest order of magnitude. Included here also are debt service payments and profits, both very low at this period.

economy—cotton, sugar, and wool. (Rubber, which went into sharp decline after 1910, was an industry confined to the isolated Amazon Basin, and the demand impact of its collapse was confined to the regional economy.) These export sectors were locally-owned, with quite high returned value; and the rising share of cotton in total export earnings must have accentuated the dynamic impetus to demand, since (as we have already seen) cotton was the export product with strongest demand effects.

Turning to government spending, we see that up to 1920 this tended to grow at roughly the same rate as exports, and to fluctuate in parallel with export earnings rather than counter-cyclically. Further, even the sharp increase which occurred under Pardo in the years 1903–8, with Leguía as Minister of Finance, was largely counterbalanced by increases in taxation.

In the years up to 1920, then, there was strong demand expansion propelled by exports and private capital inflow, with the government sector playing a minor role in terms of aggregate demand. By contrast, the years from 1920 to 1930 present a completely different picture. Export growth slowed down somewhat after the wartime boom, and the lead was taken by foreign-owned mineral export sectors whose returned value was far below that of the agricultural sectors. The gap between total export earnings and aggregate returned value thus widened rapidly and, during the decade, total returned value was static or declining, with all of the increase in export earnings absorbed by the costs of servicing the foreign-owned sectors. The net inflow of funds attributable to private capital had become a net outflow, as foreign-owned sectors became self-financing and repatriated profits increased. Demand expansion now became entirely dependent upon the government sector.

As Fig. 6.1 indicates, one of the chief characteristics of the second administration (1919–30) of Augusto Leguía was his determination to continue to expand the government sector at the rate which sustained export expansion had previously permitted. Despite the post-1920 stagnation of export-derived demand, the achievement of Leguía's goal was made possible by the fact that (in sharp contrast to the 1890s) the climate in international financial markets had changed in favour of loans to Latin American countries. Leguía could now borrow abroad, mainly by issuing government bonds to the New York market, and the net increase in the funded foreign debt was $105 million between 1920 and 1928.[6]

The resulting expansion of demand was somewhat less than the simple totals for government spending indicates, since large sums were spent on external debt repayment. The dotted line in Fig. 6.1 for 1921–9 shows the trend of expenditure net of external repayments. Even with this adjustment made, it will be seen that there was still a significant expansion. The extra funds were spent on public works: irrigation, roads, railways, and the modernisation and expansion of Lima.[7] The period was one of exceptional corruption, many of the most expensive projects were failures or never completed,[8] and the spending of the fortunes made by friends of the Government tended to be oriented towards luxury consumption and capital flight. The rapid expansion of the government sector under Leguía thus generated relatively meagre gains in terms of capital formation in the economy, but did nevertheless help to hold up the level of internal demand, particularly in the bad years 1925 and 1926.[9] When U.S. investors ceased providing new finance for the Government, however, the consequent rapid contraction of local spending in the years 1929 and 1930 served to intensify the impact of world depression in the latter year.

Turning to the income distribution associated with these developments in aggregate returned value and government spending, we encounter our most severe data limitations. It is only possible to examine modern sector wages and employment, and even here the data are patchy.

The scattered data available on wage incomes have been assembled in a study by Hunt, the main results of which are summarised in Table 6.2.

TABLE 6.2 Real wages and salaries in selected modern sectors, 1896–1930 (indices, 1924 = 100)

	Petroleum (peones)	Metal mining (obreros)	Sugar field workers	Rice	Cotton[a]	Government	
						Clerks	Administrative employees
1896	...	...	111	...	...	196	132
1900	112[b]	...	...	...	...	171	128
1912	...	105	139	...	...	161	125
1915	...	...	124	108	75[c]	126	93
1920	101	...	93	105	96	73	62
1925	94	91	93	94	...	122	96
1930	130[d]	133	...	...	...	143	117

Source: Data selected from Tables 4–17, 4–18 and 4–19 in Hunt (1974c).
[a] 1923 = 100, [b] 1901 figure, [c] 1916 figure, [d] The index stops in 1925. The 1930 figure was estimated from an overlapping series for *obreros* in the petroleum sector.

It will be seen that, despite the incomplete data, a rather consistent picture emerges of a stagnation of average wage incomes in the modern sector throughout the first twenty years of the century; in the case of the government and sugar sectors there is clear evidence of decline. However, total employment increased considerably (see Table 6.3) so that, despite the increasing capital intensity and declining wages of the sugar sector, the overall feed-through effect of export expansion was considerable. The increasing labour supply from the 1910s onwards[10] meant that growth in numbers rather than average earnings was the logical outcome.

TABLE 6.3 Employment in agriculture and mining, 1908–29

(i) Indices 1920 = 100

	Agriculture	Mining
1908	56	75
1920	100	100
1929	129	126

(ii) Annual growth rate of employment in modern[a] primary sectors

1908–20	4.2
1920–9	2.9

Source: Hunt (1974c), Tables 4.10 and 4.11 (industry deducted).
[a] Includes sugar, cotton, rice, extractive sectors.

In the 1920s the level of real wages increased in the mineral extractive sectors, but total employment in agriculture and mining grew only 70 per cent as rapidly as in the preceding decade (Table 6.3) and much[11] of that expansion was due to increased employment in rice growing, where wages were low compared with sugar or cotton. In keeping with the new role of the State under Leguía, public sector salaries regained ground, and the wage bill of the government sector compensated at least partially for the depression of several primary sectors—but with strong regional bias, since the rise was concentrated in the urban sector whilst rural areas either stagnated or were actually depressed.[12]

More striking than the effect of the 'official' rise in salaries during the 1920s was the impact of government finance on income distribution via more unofficial means. Leakages into bribery and pay-offs of various forms became an open scandal, the most notorious fortune being made by the son of the President himself.[13] In contrast to the rather broadly-based effects of a rise in, say, cotton sector incomes, a few became very rich, and typically these few were characterised by a preference for high living and expenditure abroad.[14]

In summary, then, while income distribution probably worsened steadily between 1900 and 1930 (bearing in mind that those who gained in the 1920s were certain of the élite groups and the already better-off members of the labour force), expansion of employment was sufficient in the first two decades after 1900 to ensure only a slight check to the strong demand expansion already identified for that period. In the 1920s, the very limited growth of real wages and salaries was accompanied by a slowdown in the growth of employment in mining and agriculture, and a strong tendency towards regional concentration of income opportunities. Expansion of the government sector's wage and salary payments only partially compensated for the stagnation of returned value from exports.[15]

We can therefore distinguish two separate periods so far as demand trends are concerned: one of strong expansion up to 1920 (continuing the upswing begun in the 1890s); and a second period, with relative stagnation of demand, and sharply-increased income inequalities, beginning in 1920. Other things being equal, this might suggest that the development of non-export sectors of the economy should have continued at a rapid pace up to 1920, particularly since our previous discussion of the various export sectors indicated that until the end of the wartime commodities boom in 1920, large profits continued to accumulate in the hands of local export capitalists (it was only in the 1920s that foreign control over the bulk of the surplus was consolidated). Funds for investment in non-export sectors were therefore available. The third of our prerequisites for economic diversification—a favourable relative-price situation—therefore emerges as the key to an understanding of the poor performance of non-export sectors described in the remainder of this chapter.

6.2 THE DECLINE OF INDUSTRIALISATION

Despite the continuing stimulus to demand from export growth, and the availability of resources for investment, the rapid pace of industrialisation was not sustained. Table 6.4 shows that the decline of the share in total imports of textiles and consumer goods, which had been dramatic over the period 1891 to 1908, eased off thereafter. Having fallen from nearly 60 per cent of total imports in the early 1890s to 38 per cent fifteen years later, these categories then fluctuated between 30 per cent and 40 per cent of the total until the mid-1920s, when the share fell to 26 per cent. Table 6.5 presents output data for the leading industrial sector, cotton textiles, revealing a similar trend. Having trebled in the decade 1898–1908, textile production increased only about 50 per cent in the following decade, after which growth ceased altogether. The proportion of the total supply of cotton textiles contributed by local mills had reached 56 per cent by 1916; thereafter no further gains were recorded until the 1930s.

TABLE 6.4 The share of textiles and consumer goods[a] in total imports
1891–1930
(percentage of total imports)

	Textiles	Clothing	Other non-durables[a]	Durables	Total consumer goods and textiles
1891–2	29	7	15	6	58
1907–8	15	7	10	7	38
1911–12	14	8	10	9	41
1913–14	11	7	9	8	35
1915–16	11	6	9	6	32
1917–18	16	5	8	9	38
1919–20	8	6	11	9	33
1921–2	11	5	7	7	31
1923–4	14	4	5	8	32
1925–6	10	3	5	8	26
1927–8	10	3	7	8	26
1929–30	10	3	8	8	29

Source Bertram (1976). Totals may not add exactly due to rounding.
[a] Excluding foodstuffs.

Data problems make it difficult to date exactly the ending of the industrialisation boom, but Tables 6.4 and 6.5 indicate that momentum was sustained until the economy was overtaken by recession in 1907.[16] Thereafter, stagnation became increasingly apparent.[17] In contrast to the 42 enterprises which we have been able to date definitely as having been started in the 1890s (see Chapter 3), only 25 significant new industrial ventures could be traced to the 1900s and, of these, 18 dated from the years 1900–5.[18] On these somewhat impressionistic grounds it seems probable that much of the industrial growth of the years after 1900 consisted of the expansion of factories established earlier, at the height of the boom. In one industrial sector, foundries and machine

TABLE 6.5 Local production of cotton textiles, 1890–1930
(million yards)

	(1)	(2)	(3)
	Local output	Domestic consumption plus exports	Local output as per cent of domestic consumption plus exports
1908	25.0	52.8	47
1916	32.0	57.0	56
1917	34.0	n.a.	n.a.
1918	37.0	n.a.	n.a.
1919	33.5	n.a.	n.a.
1920	30.7	n.a.	n.a.
1921	28.8	n.a.	n.a.
1922	28.2	55.6	51
1923	31.9	67.3	47
1924	34.2	73.9	46
1925	30.9	59.1	52
1926	35.2	62.9	56
1927	41.4	69.3	60
1928	39.5	68.8	57
1929	37.6	71.5	53
1930	36.6	66.8	55

Sources: For output 1898–1908 see Table 3.4 above. 1916 to 1930 was calculated from data on raw materials inputs: locally-produced cotton purchased by the mills, plus imports of yarn for textile production. For methodological details see Appendix 4.

Column 2, showing total available supply of textiles (including textiles exported from Peru) is obtained by adding to Column 1 the imports of cotton textiles for the relevant years, as shown in *Estadística del Comercio Especial*. After 1908 exports were negligible.

shops, actual decline had set in by 1905 as falling international freight costs and determined penetration of the local market by US firms combined to squeeze out the promising capital-goods sector of the 1890s.[19]

As the economy began to lift out of recession from 1910 onwards with rapidly-expanding exports of sugar, cotton and copper, there was undoubtedly some response from the manufacturing sector. Demand pressures strengthened further as the wartime commodities boom took hold and, in several branches of manufacturing, production moved up to full capacity again. The decade after 1910 saw the establishment of three new cotton textile mills and one new woollen textile mill.[20] A survey of nearly 50 new manufacturing firms which we have been able to identify as having been established during the 1910s (mostly in the years 1911–13 and 1916–19) indicates that the main areas of expansion, apart from textiles, were leather tanning, shoes, and beverages; the industrial sector, in other words, was broadening but not deepening.[21] After 1918 even in these lines there was a renewed decline in the rate of establishment of new ventures.

Analysing the ownership of the 50 new ventures identified, we find that these projects were promoted not by the élite who had led the process in the 1890s, but by immigrant and local small-scale entrepreneurs, or in the case of certain larger projects, foreign firms—particularly in textiles. Foreign firms had controlled 29 per cent of capacity in cotton textiles in 1902; by 1910 the figure was 45 per cent, by 1918 55 per cent, and by 1935, over 80 per cent (see Table 6.8 below).

Further evidence can be drawn from information on numbers of industrial establishments. Table 6.6 summarises the results of various semi-official industrial censuses.[22] Unfortunately, it is beyond doubt that the survey of 1918 was more thorough than that of 1905: the increase in number of plants therefore reflects to an unknown degree the greater coverage of the later source. An extreme example is the beverage sector, which apparently rises between 1905 and 1918 from eight to 104 plants, mostly comprising bottling plants. Of the 1918 figure of 104, only half a dozen plants were enterprises of significant size, and most (possibly all) of these dated from before 1906. The remainder were backyard operations of negligible quantitative importance. Removing the beverages sector entirely, we can however conclude that, even without allowing for other non-detectable increases in coverage, the increase between 1905 and 1918 was not rapid—only some three per cent a year. Comparing the number of firms known to originate in 1895–1905 with that from the period 1905–15 we find a fall of more than half.

Turning to the 1920s, the evidence of stagnation is unequivocal. The census results in Table 6.6 show that between 1918 and 1933 the net increase in the number of firms was not more than 42 in total, i.e. 13 per cent in fifteen years. Data on employment from the same censuses, shown in Table 6.7, indicate that employment in the key cotton textiles industry fell during the period, while increases were recorded in only a few cases—tanning, macaroni, soap, and woollen textiles—and in other industries there was very little change over the sixteen years. The few gains in output which can be identified from census sources are likewise unimpressive (and in several cases probably derive from the response to import shortages in the early 1930s, i.e. after the end of the period considered in this chapter).

Also significant is the nature of the few successful new ventures launched in manufacturing during the 1920s. The postwar boom in urban construction in Lima, which lasted from about 1918 to 1926, generated a rapidly-expanding market for construction materials, which in turn led to the establishment of related industrial enterprises. The most important of these, a cement factory, was developed and

TABLE 6.6 Number of factories, 1902–33[a]

Activities aimed at local market	1902	1905	1918	1933
Textiles and clothing	25	24	30	39
Tanneries	16	17	35	40
Shoe factories	2	1	7	11
Candles and wax	5[b]	10	19	10
Furniture	2	3	11[b]	19
Construction materials	6	8	12[b]	13[b]
Soft drinks	3	5	71 ⎫	90
Wines and liquors	5	4	33 ⎭	
Breweries	6	5	10	4
Food and food processing	70[b]	85[b]	128	144
Other	34[b]	42	79	93
A TOTAL	174	204	435	463
A′ TOTAL EXCLUDING SOFT DRINKS, WINE and LIQUORS	166	195	331	373
Export processing				
Cottonseed oil	7	8	25	24
Sugar mills	60	55[b]	33	25
Oil refineries	2	2	2	2
Cocaine	21	22	10	0
B TOTAL	90	87	70	51
A′ + B SUM	256	282	401	424

Sources: Garland (1902a) and (1905); Jimenez (1922); Hohagen (1936).
[a] See the text and Appendix 4 for comments on the varying coverage of the different years. In the Appendix we give details of the revisions and interpolations we have carried out.
[b] Some component has been interpolated.

controlled by a U.S. construction firm, the Foundation Company. This company, heavily involved in the public-works construction programmes of the Leguía era, was also the moving force in the two other most important new ventures: the 1926 reorganisation of a glass-bottle factory begun by Peruvian-U.S. interests in 1922, and a large freezing works and slaughterhouse in Callao. Such enterprises represented either vertical or horizontal integration of the Foundation Company's interests,[23] and therefore reflect special considerations rather than a general climate favouring manufacturing expansion. Similar comments

TABLE 6.7 Employment in various manufacturing industries

Industry	Number of workers reported in			
	1902	1905	1918	1933
Cotton textiles	850	1,000	3,100	3,050
Woollen textiles	600	600	791	1,838
Hat manufacture	n.a.	80	200	255
Cottonseed oil mills	n.a.	n.a.	536	600
Soap and candles	150	150	600	708
Cigarettes	2,000	500	320	n.a.
Matches	210	120	180	0
Shoes	110	n.a.	300	381
Tanning	n.a.	n.a.	460	690
Wine, liquors and soft drinks	n.a.	n.a.	375	420
Sawmills	210	210	n.a.	266
Brewing	n.a.	n.a.	600	517
Spaghetti	200	200	250	426
Flourmilling	n.a.	130[a]	430	456
Biscuits and chocolate	n.a.	100[a]	550	588
Shirt manufacture	n.a.	250	n.a.	402

Sources: Garland (1902a) and (1905); Jimenez (1922); Hohagen (1936), passim.
[a] One factory only (i.e. incomplete coverage).

TABLE 6.8 Installed capacity and employment in cotton textiles, 1902–33

	Employment			Looms operating		
	Local firms	Foreign firms	Total	Local firms	Foreign[a] firms	Total
1902	n.a.	n.a.	850	725	290	1,015
1905	n.a.	n.a.	1,000	705	600	1,305
1910	n.a.	n.a.	n.a.	980	809	1,789
1918	1,587	1,513	3,100	1,365	1,684	3,049
1920	n.a.	n.a.	n.a.	n.a.	n.a.	3,400
1931	n.a.	n.a.	n.a.	925	2,882	3,807
1933	n.a.	n.a.	3,050	n.a.	n.a.	n.a.
1936	n.a.	n.a.	n.a.	841	3,661	4,502

Sources: Garland (1902a), pp. 22–4; Garland (1905), pp. 115–17; Martin (1911), p. 317; Jimenez (1922), pp. 3–19; Gurney (1931), p. 36; Hohagen (1936), p. xix; West Coast Leader, Industrial Number 1936, p. xci.
[a] Part of the increase in the foreign sector shown above reflects takeovers of Peruvian-owned mills rather than actual expansion by the foreign mills.

apply to the expansion of capacity in cotton textiles which, as Table 6.8 shows, was quite considerable: the output series indicates that much of this new capacity must have been under-utilised in the 1920s; and reference to the detailed history of the industry confirms that the capacity increases of the 1910s and 1920s were the result primarily of the business strategies of two foreign firms which were undertaking at that time a drive for control of the textile industry, and for whom their involvement in the marketing of imported textiles and the exporting of cotton created a unique opportunity for spreading risk and maximising profits as market conditions changed.[24]

The poor performance of manufacturing in the 1920s is understandable enough in view of our earlier discussion of the stagnation of demand during the decade. However, the evidence that decline set in at an earlier stage remains to be explained, as does the rather obvious lack (until the late 1920s) of any attempt to prevent the stagnation of local industry by policy intervention. We now turn, therefore, to the determinants of profitability in the manufacturing sector, our main theme being that, however favourable the conditions of effective demand and capital supply, industrial expansion would occur only if the effect of export expansion on relative profitability was compensated in some way. Otherwise, demand could be satisfied by imports, and capital could be invested or consumed elsewhere.

Determinants of industrial profits

As the discussion of the 1890s in Chapter 3 made clear, the key variables determining the competitiveness and profitability of local manufacturing were the exchange rate and the level of tariff protection. Both of these were to some extent policy variables, and hence the objects of strong political pressures from various interest groups. It is possible to conceive of a situation in which devaluation and/or tariff protection might have been espoused by powerful groups—for example, by exporters anxious to create profitable local opportunities for diversifying their investments; or by established industrial capitalists who identified their future with the future of manufacturing and were deprived of attractive alternative options; or by an organised working class committed to the expansion of employment in manufacturing; or even by the Government itself, looking to tariffs to meet revenue needs. The Peruvian experience from 1900 to 1930, however, displayed no such patterns; the period was characterised by a stable exchange rate and by declining tariff protection. Meantime, domestic inflation and falling international freight rates eroded the competitiveness of local industry.

We begin with the period of strong demand stimulus up to 1920. The trends which brought industrialisation to a halt during that period are summarised in Table 6.9. Between 1902 and 1911 the domestic price level rose 82 per cent while import prices rose only 16 per cent; and from

1911 until 1918 local prices rose 126 per cent while import prices rose 102 per cent. Only at the end of the decade was there a slight reversal of this long-run shift of relative prices. The tendency for internal price inflation to run ahead of import prices meant, naturally enough, that increases in aggregate local demand were increasingly channelled towards the purchase of imports rather than the products of local industry; while at the same time, the increasing cost of local inputs put pressure on manufacturing profits. The result was an extremely rapid rise in imports, shown in Table 6.1 above, amounting to some 20 per cent per year between 1900 and 1907.

TABLE 6.9 Import and domestic prices and tariff levels, 1902–20

	Indices		Duties as per cent of value of imports
	Import price in domestic currency	Domestic wholesale prices	
1902	79	(55)ᵃ	27
1908	91	(94)ᵃ	22
1911	92	(94)ᵃ	22
1913	100	100	22
1916	130	146	12
1918	186	212	10
1920	267	238	10

Sources: Import price index: a rough approximation calculated from U.S. and U.K. export prices. The weights used were shares of the two countries in Peruvian import trade. For 1902 to 1911, the average share for 1901–3 was used. For subsequent years, the 1921 share was used. The data were obtained from U.S. Department of Commerce, *Statistical Abstract of the United States*; Schlote (1952); *Extracto Estadístico*. Wholesale prices: *Extracto Estadístico*. Import values and duties: *Estadística del Comercio Exterior*, annual numbers.
ᵃ Estimates based on partial information. See Table 6.16 below for 1902–8. Martin (1911) provides the basis for assuming that the rise slowed down 1908–11.

The movement of relative prices against local manufacturing was due to several factors, including growing competition in world markets for manufactures, falling shipping costs, and the wave of foreign investment in Peru in the early 1900s which, as we suggested in Chapter 5, contributed to the process of local inflation by rapid expansion of the money supply. Most important, however, was the fixed exchange rate which prevailed after Peru went on to the gold standard in 1897. With the Peruvian Libra (S/10) at par with the pound sterling, and the exchange rate well protected by rising exports and capital inflow, domestic inflation could proceed for a time without pushing down the exchange rate, and a growing gap was thus opened up between local prices and import prices.

The First World War brought steep increases in international prices, evident in Table 6.9, but this did not result in an increase in the competitiveness of import-substituting industry. On the contrary, good prices for Peruvian exports resulted in upward pressure on the exchange rate, and when the U.S. Government prohibited gold exports in 1917 (thereby cutting off the equilibrating mechanism in the gold standard system) the Peruvian exchange rate appreciated to nine per cent above par in 1918, contributing to a relative reduction in import prices. Meantime, internal inflation continued at a rapid pace.

Turning to the second major variable, the level of protection afforded by tariffs, Table 6.9 shows that the increase in protection which had occurred by the late 1890s ceased after 1900,[25] and between 1911 and 1918 the tariff level suffered an unprecedented decline. Peru at this time was using a system of tariffs common to a number of Latin American countries, whereby so-called 'specific' duties were imposed, that is, a fixed figure per unit of volume, rather than *ad valorem* percentages.[26] As import prices rose, the rate of duty therefore fell, unless frequent upward adjustments were made. Although the customs administrators were aware of this problem,[27] successive Governments were slow to realise that the decline in the revenue from tariffs was due in part to changing import prices.[28] By 1916 the growing fiscal crisis had impressed upon the Government the inadequacy of the customs statistics, and a new schedule of import valuations was introduced to improve the realism of the statistics. No attempt was made, however, to return the rates of duty to their pre-war levels, from which they had fallen by roughly half. More damaging still to manufacturing profits was the fact that the few duty increases which were legislated in 1915 were on capital goods and intermediate goods, so narrowing the margin of effective protection.[29]

Why was it that such an erosion of tariff protection could be allowed to pass almost without protest from any of the groups affected? In large part, the answer lies in the extremely successful performance of export sectors during the 1910s; these sectors attracted capital and entrepreneurs away from manufacturing, and displayed such high capital-absorptive capacity during the wartime period that surplus funds were held for reinvestment, and not used to finance diversification.[30] The well-developed banking system provided a channel through which resources from one sector could be readily transferred to others when opportunity arose. By the 1910s, therefore, there were no longer many manufacturing ventures in which the ruling class had a direct interest; élite figures had withdrawn from manufacturing, or relegated their industrial interests to secondary importance. Entrepreneurs who remained in manufacturing did not constitute a social group either powerful or cohesive enough to influence policy.

A further relevant point in explaining the absence of protectionist policies in Peru concerns sources of fiscal revenue. In Latin America, tariff increases often resulted principally from a need for revenue rather than a conscious protectionist urge. But Peruvian governments in the early twentieth century could increase their income in other ways. The guano era of the nineteenth century had been notable for an almost total dependence upon guano as the source of revenue. In the 1880s and 1890s, when the financing of government spending had again become dependent upon other sources of income, the immediate reaction was, as we have seen, to raise tariffs[31] rather than domestic taxes. By the first years of the twentieth century, therefore, Peru was still exceptionally 'under-taxed,' and it was possible for Leguía as Minister of Finance in 1903–5 to institute or raise numerous taxes and produce a rapid rise in revenue.[32] Further, in 1915 taxes on exports became an option. The twenty-five year exemption of mining and petroleum from any form of export tax, legislated in 1890, ended in October of that year; in November a tax was introduced on those two sectors and subsequently extended to others.[33] The Government, thus, had other revenue options besides tariff increases—which in any case were politically unpopular in the 1910s because of the rising cost of living. This was the more relevant, given that the craft unions (which in the nineteenth century had pressed for increased protection) had by this time shifted somewhat in their composition. As the views of urban wage workers emerged more strongly relative to those of artisans, so the mood of the working-class movement, such as it was, had swung against tariffs and in favour of reductions in the cost of living.[34] No Government in the 1910s could afford to ignore this current of opinion.

Even granted that government policy acquiesced in a steady erosion of the competitive position of local industry, and that entrepreneurship for the industrialisation that did occur came from middle-class rather than élite sources, it must be recognised that, from 1914 on, the special conditions of wartime went some way to counteract these factors. Worldwide, supplies of many categories of manufactured goods became scarcer as the industries of belligerent countries went over to war production; whilst shortages of shipping pushed up freight rates and delayed deliveries. In several Latin American countries this resulted in a strong impetus for native industries—especially in Chile and Brazil.[35] Other countries showed less response, however. Argentina, with exceptionally high stocks of goods in 1914 and a long recession of internal demand during the war[36] was one case; Peru was another. As Table 6.10 suggests, Peru and Colombia had already switched from European to U.S. suppliers for a large part of their manufactured imports, so that the cutting-off of European exports to Latin America hit least hard at these countries. In addition, Japan took the opportunity to establish a beachhead for her industrial goods in the markets of the Pacific Coast,

TABLE 6.10 Latin American imports from the U.K. and the U.S., 1912–20
(at 1913 prices)

	Peru	Argentina	Brazil	Chile	Colombia
Share of imports from U.K. in U.K. + U.S. imports, 1912	54	66	60	66	51
Indices (1912 = 100):					
1913	115	108	97	100	115
1914	85	64	52	69	83
1915	78	63	52	54	94
1916	112	68	57	32	119
1917	123	59	52	95	76
1918	109	57	45	101	55
1919	121	72	70	73	105
1920	192	90	90	74	229

Sources: U.S. Department of Commerce, *Statistical Abstract of the United States*, U.K.
Board of Trade, *Statistical Abstract* for the United Kingdom. Deflated by export or
wholesale price indices for the U.S. and U.K., the U.S. from the same source, the U.K.
series from Schlote (1952).

again alleviating the supply constraint.[37]

In short, the war did not cut the supply of imported consumption
goods sufficiently to induce more than a relatively slight impetus to
Peruvian manufacturing; and wartime shortage of capital goods,
although genuine enough, could not provide the basis for a new wave of
local production of machinery and equipment.[38]

To summarise, the boom in Peru's export earnings up to 1920 did feed
through to domestic demand (the first requirement for a process of
diversified export-led growth), but this surge in demand was not a
sufficient condition for the expansion of non-export industries. In fact,
export expansion was itself an important reason why the depreciating
exchange and rising tariffs of the 1890s gave way after 1900 to a stable
and even appreciating exchange rate, falling protection from tariffs, and
rapid domestic inflation. Local manufacturing became less competitive
with imported goods, and demand was increasingly channelled towards
the latter.

Demand stagnation in an open economy: the 1920s
If the period before 1920 demonstrates that export growth may hinder
rather than help industrialisation, the decade of the 1920s provides a
case study of what may happen when export stagnation occurs in a

country which remains closely integrated into a prosperous international economy. After 1920 the export boom did at last level off, as we have seen, but the circumstances were far from conducive to a transfer of resources to other productive activities.

The ending of rapid growth in those export sectors still controlled by local capital might have been expected to induce such a transfer, both by causing downward pressure on the exchange rate (raising the relative profitability of investment in non-export sectors) and by increasing the political and economic pressures for increased import tariffs, as former export-sector capitalists sought to create new fields of activity. Even in the context of stagnant aggregate demand, such measures could result in a dynamic stimulus for manufacturing growth, by causing a diversion of existing demand away from imports towards local production.

As it turned out, events in Peru after 1920 took a different course. The stagnation of demand was accompanied by a sharp decline in the amount of surplus available for local investment, because of the decline of the sugar industry and the rise of foreign-controlled export sectors. Secondly, those local groups which did possess surplus funds (including several of the sugar planters even during the 1920s) were able to export those funds for investment or expenditure abroad—local capitalists, in other words, were not obliged to think in terms of the creation of profit opportunities locally. Thirdly, in so far as funds were employed for investment in local non-export sectors, the rapid growth of government spending during the 1920s created a series of profitable investment opportunities, most notably in private and public construction work, and real-estate speculation;[39] funds were thereby diverted from possible investment in industry or agriculture.

We can thus understand why exporters thinking in terms of the possible export of capital sided with bankers, merchants and the Government itself[40] in deploring depreciation of the exchange rate, with the result that the slide of the Peruvian Libra following the end of the export boom in 1920 was reversed as soon as possible by government intervention in the exchange market. During 1922 the Central Bank sold off a large part of its reserves of gold and foreign exchange in an attempt to bring the exchange rate back up to par, and in the mid-1920s the Government raised a series of huge foreign loans, one of the explicit goals of which was exchange stabilisation.[41]

In Table 6.11 it will be seen that, partly as a result of such action, import prices after 1920 continued their pattern of relative decline. The Table does reveal some increase in levels of protection, mostly resulting from the imposition of revenue surcharges on the existing rates of duty. Since these surcharges applied on *all* duties, the increase in effective protection which they produced was modest at best. Some significant increases in duty were embodied in the tariff reforms of 1923 and 1928,[42] but these produced only relatively slight jumps in the overall level of

TABLE 6.11 Import prices, wholesale prices and tariff incidence, 1919–29

	Indices, 1919 = 100		Import tariff incidence (percentage of total imports)	
	Import prices in domestic currency	Wholesale prices	Duties only	All customs charges
1921	93	93	9	11
1923	79	86	13	17
1925	82	92	12	18
1927	78	92	11	18
1929	70	85	15	21

Source: as Table 6.9, except for duties including all customs charges, which come from *Extracto Estadístico*, 1934–5, p. 280.

tariffs—regaining the pre-war levels but not taking the form of a determined policy of industrial promotion.

The lack of successful pressure for a significant increase in effective protection is understandable in terms of the factors outlined above. But there was an additional reason: the growing participation of foreign merchant firms in the manufacturing sector, particularly in textiles. The latter sector had become increasingly the preserve of two foreign merchant houses, Grace and Co. and Duncan Fox and Co.,[43] for whom the control of textile mills was not simply a profit-making exercise in itself but also an invaluable addition to their sources of supply. After 1920, when it became more profitable for these firms to handle imported textiles rather than produce locally, and when the boom in export prices for cotton made it more profitable to export the raw fibre than to convert it into cloth, these firms had no reason to press for immediate protection, and were content simply to cut back their production. Imports of cotton textiles soared, while as the figures of Table 6.12 on consumption of cotton by the textile mills indicate, the foreign firms were responsible for most of the depression of output in the early 1920s.

The significance of this attitude of the dominant firms in the cotton textile industry was considerable, since this was the only industrial sector with sufficient political influence to have much impact on overall policy. It was only in 1925, when cotton export markets again became depressed and the Peruvian balance of payments became critical (with renewed depreciation of the sol) that the textile industry began to provide leadership for a campaign for more protection, the immediate result of which was the 'emergency tariff' approved in November 1926

TABLE 6.12 Consumption of raw cotton by mills (1918 = 100)

	Foreign-owned mills	Local-owned mills	Total
1920	85	78	83
1922	67	92	75
1924	78	115	91
1926	84	112	94

Source: Based on Tizon y Bueno (1930).

and applied in 1927.[44] The effects of the new tariff rates, however, were over-shadowed by the deepening recession of the entire economy, which offered little in the way of a dynamic impulse to new industrial growth.

The urban economy
We have centred this account around the industrial sector, for practical reasons of data availability and the necessity to limit an already wide study, as well as because industry is of central importance as the chief potential agent of greater independence. But before turning to agriculture we wish briefly to make the point that the experience of industry was shared by the other sectors of the urban economy which showed so much vitality in the 1890s: the financial system and public utilities. Both had been unusual for their degree of local control and dynamism at that time. But with the general rise of foreign investment and influence the pattern changed, here as elsewhere.

Branches of foreign banks reappeared in Peru in 1904–5,[45] and in the 1910s and 1920s the relative importance of foreign banks in the financial system increased rapidly. Foreign insurance companies re-entered Peru from about 1910 on,[46] while the utilities sector turned increasingly to foreign sources of finance from 1906 on; the dominant Empresas Electricas Asociadas became registered in London as Lima Light and Power Company in 1910, and later in 1923 became an affiliate of Latina Lux of Milan. The number of firms quoted on the Lima Stock Exchange reached a peak of 57 in 1905, falling thereafter to only 42 by 1915. Thus, although the expansion of most of the financial system continued in line with that of the broader economy, the distinctively local character of that system became increasingly diluted. The channels for intersectoral resource transfer through the banks and Stock Exchange, which in the 1890s had served the purposes of economic diversification, served equally well for the purpose of draining resources from non-export activities when they ceased to prove sufficiently profitable; and as the proportion of the economy's surplus which was controlled by local firms fell, the climate in the capital market became ever more unfavourable to ventures of the kind which had flourished in the 1890s.

6.3 NON-EXPORT AGRICULTURE

The second major sector of the non-export economy which we here single out for separate discussion, is food production for the internal market. Apart from the obvious and enormous importance of the sector in determining the welfare of vast numbers of the rural population, the sector is of special importance in relation to export expansion. A continual accusation levelled at the impact of international market forces on Peru has been that the resulting focus on export crops has been directly at the expense of production for the local market, resulting in both inflation and an 'unhealthy' dependence on imported food.

A coherent discussion of the sector for the years here in question, 1890–1930, is almost impossible given the lack of data. The indications are, however, that despite the widespread indictment of export crops on this count among contemporary commentators, the charge is at the least exaggerated.

Let us first examine the geography of the food supply situation and the role of imports. Food production for local consumption was (and still quite largely is) concentrated close to the market. Lima in the 1920s was still fed extensively from truck gardens and small plots around the city—with the exceptions of wheat, rice and meat. This can be seen from the data on area cultivated in the provinces of Lima and Callao in 1920–1, shown in Table 6.13. If we take the estimate made by Twomey,[47] that in 1918 the city of Lima needed 7,000 hectares to feed it, excluding livestock and rice, we see that the province itself provided almost enough

TABLE 6.13 Crop area cultivated in the Provinces of Lima and Callao, 1920–21 and 1929
(hectares)

	1920–21	1929	Percentage change
Non-export food crops	6332	6910	+9
of which			
Maize	2605	2642	+1
Potatoes and			
sweet potatoes	1997	2335	+17
Sugar	5528	4217	−24
Cotton	10234	17723	+73
TOTAL[a]	22094	28850	+31

Source: Ministerio de Fomento (1921) and (1932).
[a] Excluding pastures, both cultivated and natural.

land on its own. Meat came largely from the Sierra,[48] while rice came from other Coastal provinces more suited to it, and from imports. Wheat was imported.

TABLE 6.14 Food imports as percentage of total imports, 1925

Wheat and flour	9
Rice	4
Lard	3
Dairy products	2
TOTAL	18
TOTAL FOOD IMPORTS	24

Source: *Estadística del Comercio Especial del Perú* (1925).

The composition of the food import bill in the 1920s is shown in Table 6.14. It will be seen that wheat, flour, rice and pork lard alone accounted for two-thirds of food imports. Rice and lard are products which compete directly for cotton land; in the late nineteenth century maize was grown on the Coast for fattening pigs, but with disease problems among pigs in the early twentieth century local production ceased to supply the market and tariff protection was reduced.[49] Wheat was eliminated from the Coast some centuries ago by rust disease and no success had been achieved by the 1920s in finding a rust-resistant variety;[50] in any case wheat could not compete in yield with sugar or cotton.[51] The climate in the Sierra does not suit wheat either (since the temperature is too low for successful ripening), and it was grown only on slopes too steep for potatoes. Further, consumers preferred the quality of imported flour, which made a finer grade of bread.[52] Dairy products, the next largest category, reflected the deficiencies of local livestock rearing. This was principally, as we have said, a Sierra activity, in which small units predominated,[53] and where the extremely low productivity was a result principally of climate and poor soil, but also of the difficulties of improving breeds, given the lack of fencing and the predominance of small units.

Thus about half the food import bill consisted of products whose production was barely if at all affected by the expansion of export crops. The other half, consisting of products such as rice, vegetables, and lard, requires further analysis.

The overall allocation of cultivated land on the Coast is shown in

Table 6.15. The 47 per cent increase in area cultivated in 24 years indicates the possibilities which were still open at that time for incorporating marginal land as the profitability of cotton and sugar rose, by improving drainage and irrigation schemes and the management of water rights, and putting pasture land under crops as tractors replaced oxen.[54] Little was actually added by official irrigation schemes until the 'Pampas Imperial' project in Cañete was completed in 1923,[55] adding 5,000 hectares to the area under cotton. Nevertheless Table 6.15 indicates that the steady expansion of the total cultivated area by private initiative sufficed to accommodate all the expansion of export crops between 1905 and 1930, with the result that the total area under non-export crops remained virtually constant. In the aggregate, thus, export crops did not force an absolute contraction of the area under foodcrops, although export crops obviously had preferential claim on increments in cultivated area.

TABLE 6.15 Area cultivated on the Coast, 1901–29
(000 hectares)

	a	b	c	d	$e = d - c$	f
	Cotton	Sugar	Cotton plus sugar	Total area cultivated, Coast	Non-export food crops as residual	Of which rice
1901	23	50	73	n.a.		
1905	29	50	79	262	183	n.a.
1909	57	38	95	n.a.		
1916	56	41	97	n.a.		
1918	78	50	128	(320)	(192)	31
1920	104	49	153	n.a.		
1929	127	78	205	384	179	47

Sources: Total area cultivated: for 1905, Twomey (1972), p. 8, based on *BCIM*; for 1918, Twomey (1972), p. 60, apparently based on interpolation; for 1929, Ministerio de Fomento (1932). Cotton, sugar and rice: for 1901–9, based on production and yield estimates (see above pp. 46, 56); for 1916–29, *Anuario Estadístico*.

The same picture emerges in the case of the only province and period for which we have more detailed data: that of Lima, where as shown in Table 6.13 both food crops and cotton were able to expand as a result of a 31 per cent increase in area cultivated during the 1920s.

This would still be compatible with accusations of export expansion at the expense of the local market if, in the face of rising demand, the absorption of all new land by export crops left local supplies deficient and the economy subject to inflation on the one hand and a rising import bill on the other. The role of food shortages and rising food prices was the dominant theme of commentaries on the cost of living in the early 1900s and during the First World War. The evidence, however, suggests that the political sensitivity of food prices caused undue attention to be focused on them.

TABLE 6.16 Retail price movements, 1902–8
(percentage change between the two years)

Food items		Non-food items	
Beef	61	Coal	67
Pork	78	Water	27
Poultry	24	Rents	78
Eggs	50	Matches	100
Milk	44	Boots	75
Potatoes	100		
Rice	100		

Source: U.K. *Parliamentary Papers*, Vol. CXV, 1908, p. 33.

Table 6.16 presents the available figures on price increases during the first decade of the century—a period in which, as already noted, domestic inflation became rapid. There is no sign in the Table of any tendency for food prices to increase more rapidly than the general price level, and hence no reason to single out food shortages as the prime cause of the inflation. It is true, however, that food imports rose extremely rapidly during the first decade of the century, a trend illustrated by Figure 6.2. The share of food in total imports rose from 11–12 per cent at the turn of the century to 16–17 per cent by 1907–8, and it might be suggested that this was attributable to falling local food supplies as a result of the expansion of export crops—particularly since the rise in food imports pre-dated the bad harvests of 1905 and 1907.[56] Referring back to Table 6.15, however, it will be seen that the sharp rise of food imports also pre-dated the big expansion of cotton cultivation and occurred during a period when the area under sugar was showing signs of decline. It seems, therefore, that the rapid rise in food imports during the 1900s is to be attributed to the strong pressure of demand expansion during those years, which generated also the general rise of internal prices.

Relative price movements for the years after 1910 are shown by Table 6.17, where we encounter dramatic evidence of the effects of the wartime commodity prices boom upon the relative profitability of production for

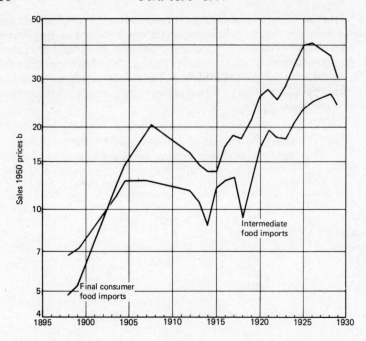

FIGURE 6.2 Imports of food *per capita*, constant prices; 3 year moving average[a]

Sources: Imports: Bertram (1976). Prices: see Table 6.9. Population: Direccion General de Estadística (1944), Vol. I.
[a] 1904–5 and 1907–8 are two-year averages only.
[b] The data have been deflated by an import price index. For the sources used see Table 6.9 above. The figures are in 1950 prices only in the sense that 1950 = 100 in the final series; different weights were used for different periods.

export compared with production for the local market. Between 1913 and 1919 the price index for export crops increased 237 per cent while that for locally-marketed food rose only 104 per cent. Despite this, the price series reveal no tendency for food prices to rise more rapidly than the average price level during the 1910s, which in turn suggests that supply shortages were no worse for food than for other goods. The strong bias of price movements in favour of export production undoubtedly was responsible for the 58 per cent increase in the area planted to export crops between 1916 and 1920 (Table 6.15); but this expansion was evidently achieved without causing any severe contraction in the area planted to foodcrops, which was greater in 1918 than in either 1905 or 1929 (the area under rice, for example, expanded steadily through the decade). Figure 6.2 indicates, furthermore, that the 1910s were by no means a period of steeply-rising food imports; on the

TABLE 6.17 Relative price movements, 1911–29
(indices, 1913 = 100)

	Export crop price index	Wholesale food price index	$\dfrac{Export\ prices}{food\ prices} \times 100$	Cost of living Ratio of food prices to total × 100
1911	65	94[a]	69	n.a.
1913	100	100	100	100
1914	146	102	143	103
1915	228	115	198	103
1916	232	128	181	100
1917	261	143	183	102
1918	285	171	167	99
1919	337	204	165	100
1920	335	226	148	99
1921	292	204	143	92
1922	248	187	133	92
1923	325	193	168	92
1924	294	192	153	90
1925	234	207	113	90
1926	234	219	107	91
1927	270	218	124	91
1928	244	194	126	89
1929	205	189	108	90

Source: Calculated from *Anuario Estadístico*, various years.
[a] Assumed equal to retail food price index from Hunt (1974c), Table 4.16.

contrary, the 1907 level of *per capita* food imports was not exceeded until 1920.

In summary, the expansion of export crops from 1900 to 1919 was not accompanied by any significant decline in the area devoted to foodcrops along the Coast; the data on prices and food imports *per capita* appear to refute the claim that the 1910s were characterised by severe shortages. It is probable that any tendency of food production to fall behind population growth during the 1910s was compensated for by the reduced *per capita* demand for wage goods as income distribution became more unequal. As we showed earlier in this chapter, there was a tendency for real wages in some sectors to decline during the First World War.

In so far, then, as there did occur food shortages, these must have been regionally-concentrated, and matched by surpluses elsewhere. It is only when we turn to the 1920s that we encounter evidence that export expansion was achieved at the expense of non-export agricultural production. After 1919 the rise in *per capita* food imports became very marked (Fig. 6.2) and the share of food imports in total imports jumped from around 15 per cent to around 23 per cent (Table 6.18). Table 6.19 shows that most of this increase was caused by higher imports of rice, lard and dairy products, and it appears that the first two of these were commodities the local production of which was reduced by the expansion of cotton during the first half of the 1920s. As Table 6.14 showed, the area under cotton increased very rapidly during those years, while the area under rice fell from 36,000 hectares in 1922 to 26,000 hectares by 1926—a trend directly attributable to cotton expansion. In 1925, however, cotton prices fell sharply (the effect can be seen in Column 3 of Table 6.17), and shortly afterwards increased tariffs were imposed on imports of rice and lard as part of a policy of promoting

TABLE 6.18 Food imports as percentage of total imports

	Total	Final food imports	Intermediate food imports[a]
1891–2 av.	14	8	5
1897–8 av.	12	5	7
1900	13	6	7
1902	11	5	6
1904	13	7	6
1908	12	7	5
1912	16	8	8
1913	13	8	5
1914	13	8	5
1915	21	12	8
1916	19	9	10
1917	14	10	4
1918	15	9	5
1919	15	10	5
1920	23	15	9
1921	21	12	9
1922	22	12	10
1923	18	11	7
1924	22	14	8
1925	24	15	9
1926	23	15	8
1927	22	14	9
1928	21	13	8
1929	19	10	9

Source: Bertram (1976).
[a] Virtually entirely wheat and flour.

production of these two foodstuffs.[57] The relative importance of rice
and lard imports fell again (Table 6.19) and by the end of the 1920s the
share of food in total imports had begun a downward trend which was to
continue into the 1930s.

TABLE 6.19 Composition of change in the share of final food imports
in total imports, 1916–29
(percentage share of total imports)

Total increase in final food imports			
1916 to 1925		+ 6	percentage points
of which	Rice	+ 2.6	
	Lard	+ 1.9	
	Dairy products	+ 1.4	
	TOTAL	+ 5.9	
Total fall in final food imports			
1925 to 1929		− 4.7	percentage points
of which	Rice	− 2.7	
	Lard	− 1.6	
	TOTAL	− 4.3	

Source: Calculated from *Estadística del Comercio Especial*, 1916, 1925, 1929.

In the meantime, there had certainly been no pressure on food prices
during the 1920s. As Table 6.17 shows, food prices led the deflation of
the early 1920s, and the general stagnation of demand in the economy
combined with further deterioration in income distribution evidently
resulted in very slow growth in the consumption of wage goods.

The evidence analysed here suggests that neither inflation nor the
occasional sharp increases in *per capita* food imports can be attributed
to the absorption of land by the export crops, with the exception of the
early 1920s when this process clearly did result in an increased import
bill. Even in this case, however, the transfer of land into export
production was rapidly reversed once the trend of relative prices
changed; no long-run effects were produced.

None of this, of course, implies that food production was 'adequate'
in a different sense. Consumption of calories *per capita* by 1938, the first
year for which we have data, was exceptionally low even for Latin
America at that time. Since the scanty evidence we have suggests
stagnation or slight fall in the lower levels of the income distribution
throughout most of the period we are here considering, and up to 1940,

then there is reason to think that such levels of malnutrition were typical of this period also, though possibly levels were somewhat better in the subsistence sector before population growth began to increase in the twenties and thirties. Expansion of exports did inevitably imply a failure to diversify, as the area cultivated figures have revealed; however, income distribution trends, themselves partly a result of the mode of export expansion, meant that the relatively slow growth of food production did not at this period have major macro-consequences. As we shall argue for a later period, it is possible that had the macro-consequences in fact been greater, the neglect of traditional agriculture might not have been so total.

7 Conclusion and Review

With the ending of the Chilean occupation in 1883 a new era in Peru's economic history began. Two sets of choices lay ahead as to the pattern this new era would follow. The first concerned the nature of the economy which was to replace the old guano-based system—whether the future lay with export-led growth or some alternative model; and if the former, whether exploitation of Peru's comparative advantage in the production of primary commodities for export was to generate dynamism also in other, non-export, sectors, or was to proceed with relatively slight spread effects for the rest of the economy. The second set of issues concerned the identity of the social and economic groups who would design, finance and control the new order, and in particular, the role of foreign capital and its relationship to domestic capitalists and to the State apparatus.

Given the period and the setting, it will come as no surprise to those familiar with Latin American history that the final outcome of Peru's post-war reconstruction and growth was outward-oriented growth with decreasing spread effects, dominated more and more as time passed by large foreign (mostly U.S.) capital operating in close alliance with the domestic upper classes. As we have seen, this control affected many areas of the economy, including sectors the early development of which had been undertaken by local capitalists in the 1890s. By the 1920s not only the mineral export sectors were foreign-controlled, but also a growing proportion of industry, banking and utilities. The developing Stock Exchange of the 1890s had suffered an absolute contraction,[1] suggesting a reduction in the local economy's ability to mobilise and efficiently allocate its surplus. In addition, regional imbalances had enormously increased; not only had many products suffered a collapse of their markets, but in two crucial sectors, mining and sugar, the degree of regional concentration had undergone a substantial increase. As many regional economies sank into depression with the decline of former export activities, the pre-eminence of Lima among the country's urban centres became increasingly evident.[2]

Whilst the historical inevitability of this outcome is hard to deny, it is an important conclusion of this study that Peru in 1890 had been adequately equipped to pursue alternative growth paths, had not international circumstances dictated otherwise. Our discussion of the 1890s demonstrated that, given a suitable conjuncture of circumstances,

Peru could produce a capable and effective class of entrepreneurs, could mobilise large resources for investment, and could sustain a process of balanced growth in which the profits of export sectors were channelled into the expansion of other areas of the economy.

Our discussion of the subsequent slide towards increased dependence confirms that the disintegration of this relatively autonomous model was not the result of any inherent inability of Peru to sustain its own capitalist growth process. Industrial growth slowed down not for lack of markets, finance or initiative, but because of unfavourable movements of relative prices, dictated by international trends. Export sectors became foreign controlled not because of constraints too great for local firms to overcome, but in one case because foreigners had a natural-resource monopoly, and in another because they were able to offer the Peruvians attractive terms.

The lack of viability lay on the international, not the local, front: in the contradiction between 'autonomous development' and the nature of the international system in which Peru was enmeshed. In the face of the options offered by the international system, only rather special circumstances could have preserved the vitality of Peru's development effort. Its preservation would have required, at the very least, an actively interventionist and protectionist policy, for which as we have seen there was no basis in the interests of any class. The economic élite had adopted the role of 'national bourgeoisie' in the 1890s in response to profit opportunities brought about by largely exogenous circumstances; but, with diferent circumstances, it was both simple and profitable to return to a narrower role. The existence of a relatively well-developed financial system aided the process of transfer of resources between sectors, thereby removing one possible source of resistance to the erosion of protection. When profitable export opportunities were seriously eroded in the twenties, so also was the financial and political position of the élite, an erosion which was partially responsible for their failure to fight for the creation of alternative profitable lines of productive activity.

The decline of industrialisation provided the most visible indicator of the decline of 'national capitalism' itself. With industrialists either dubious of the advantages of protectionism (because of their simultaneous interests as exporters and merchants) or else excluded from the inner councils of government, no political momentum was built up for pro-industry policies. Fiscal problems which might have driven the Government into raising tariffs were relieved during the first two decades of the century by the buoyancy of the export economy, and by the success of excise taxes which fell most heavily on lower-class consumers. As for the working-class movement, apart from the paternalism and patronage among its leadership which then and since have weakened it as a political force,[3] it could not begin to form a source of pressure for the encouragement of industry until industry was far more developed than it then was.

Perhaps the most difficult element of our discussion to this point has been the problem of isolating the role of foreign investment, particularly in view of the widespread tendency among 'dependency' writers to treat this as the primary or even sole cause of 'underdevelopment.' As we have several times emphasised, trends such as the changing modes of production, the processes of regional concentration, and much of the increase in income inequality, were dictated by wider parameters and affected only marginally by the issue of foreign versus national ownership. In certain cases where foreign ownership has explicitly been blamed for regional decline we have indicated that other factors were more important (this is clearest in the case of the sugar industry of La Libertad, where we have indicated both that the foreign-ness of the alleged 'foreigners' was in doubt, and that the fall in world sugar prices after 1920 was quite unrelated to the ownership of the industry in Peru). And finally, we have found that in periods of recession for the local economy, when profitable investment opportunities were limited, local capitalists could be just as liable to send their profits abroad as were foreign firms. For these reasons we stress that the exclusion of foreign investment could never *by itself* have constituted a sufficient condition for the maintenance or acceleration of the growth model of the 1890s, although it can be argued that such exclusion would have been a necessary condition.[4]

This said, we are left with two definite conclusions about the impact of foreign capital on the Peruvian economy. The first is that, using *ceteris paribus* assumptions (that is, asking what would have happened had all other external circumstances remained the same, but foreign investment been absent), we have argued that the net impact of foreign capital on Peruvian growth up to 1930 was negative—on balance, it is in our judgement probable that the economy would have reached a higher level of GNP[5] by 1930 without foreign capital than with it. This was because foreign capital entered Peru to develop activities which would otherwise have been developed by local capital. While it may be argued that foreign firms were in certain respects more efficient as producers, any gains on this score were outweighed by the heavy losses suffered by the economy as the result first, of the loss of a great part of export earnings as profits to foreign capitalists; and second, of distortions in the allocation of economic surplus resulting from the appropriation of an increasing fraction of the surplus by foreign firms, and the simultaneous exclusion of local capital from the economy's most thriving sectors.

Secondly, if we drop the *ceteris paribus* approach, foreign investment can be seen as an integral part of the whole process of reintegrating Peru into the world capitalist economy after the collapse of the Guano Age.

Had such reintegration been resisted (an unhistorical speculation, unless one posits the unlikely rise to power of a Peruvian Francia[6]) the Peruvian economy would have been totally different by 1930. Had reintegration been accompanied by a strong Peruvian drive to improve the terms of that process for the country as a whole, the role of foreign capital would have been greatly modified, and it might have been excluded from certain of the high-profit sectors. However, this would have required a constellation of class forces and a nationalistic commitment which Peru did not possess, nor could have been expected to possess, at that point in its history—partly, of course, because of previous history. In practice, foreign investment came as an inseparable part of the package, and was accepted because another component of the same package was an export-oriented State dominated by the pro-foreign classes of Peruvian society.

We have therefore been able to explain *why* the first of our two export-growth phases, from 1890 to 1930, ended without launching Peru on to an autonomous growth path. At the same time we have found no sign of the conditions which might have made possible a different outcome. This sense of the helplessness of Peru to change its own destiny, as much because of its lack of national will and its divided society as because of external constraints, brings us back to the central problem of dependence.

While we have blamed the failure of outward-directed growth up to 1930 as much upon policy biases as upon the impact of the international system, the Depression of 1930 represents a clear break in the trends which we have described for the years 1900–30. The international system fell into a state of crisis, while the Peruvian political scene changed dramatically with the fall of Leguía in August 1930 and the subsequent bid for power by the APRA Party, the most credible of the few possible vehicles for an alternative economic strategy. The next section of our study looks at the impact of these two changes, and the subsequent evolution of the economy.

Part III
The Opportunity for
Renewed Autonomy:
1930–48

Introduction

The World Depression of the 1930s marked a clear turning point in the economic history of most Latin American countries. Markets for export commodities fell steeply; the consequent balance-of-payments crises induced most countries to default on the large foreign debts accumulated during the 1920s; and the troubles of the metropolitan economies (especially the U.S.A.) resulted in a halt to foreign direct investment.[1] Obliged to engineer their own economic recoveries without outside assistance, many Latin American governments turned towards models of 'desarrollo hacia adentro,' with emphasis on government-aided import substitution and the expansion of government spending as a means of stimulating internal demand. The Second World War reduced the supply of manufactured goods imported from the industrialised countries, thereby providing additional impetus to industrialisation in Latin America. Throughout the continent, in addition, the period was one of political change, as parties associated with new and growing 'middle class' interests gained increasing access to power. Not until the late 1940s and the Korean War boom of 1950 did foreign investment activity and export-orientation fully revive.

The twenty years after 1930, in short, brought a general trend towards increased economic autonomy, followed by a tendency in the 1950s for patterns of 'dependence' to reassert themselves, although often in new forms. This picture, while somewhat stereotyped, undoubtedly indicates powerful forces working upon Peru as upon other Latin American countries. Our analysis of events will show, however, that the re-orientation of the Peruvian economy in the years following the Depression was slight by comparison with other Latin American countries, while at the end of the 1940s Peru was unique in Latin America for the enthusiasm with which export-led growth, economic liberalism, foreign investment, and the general reintegration of Peru with the U.S. economy, were welcomed and encouraged by policy measures. As Hunt[2] states, from 1948 on:

> In a continent that was witnessing ever-increasing state intervention in economic life in country after country, Peru . . . turned around to begin a march in the other direction that continued for the next 18 years.

This is not to say that important changes had not occurred in Peru from

1930 to 1948. The absence of new foreign investment during a period when opportunities were opening up in sectors such as gold, lead, zinc, fisheries, and even rubber, resulted in a considerable revival of local entrepreneurial activity in these areas. As export production again came largely under the control of local firms, the integration of export sectors with the rest of the economy was once more increased; while at the same time there took place a significant decentralisation of economic growth. The rise of lead, zinc and gold (see Chapter 8) brought new prosperity to widely-scattered areas of the Sierra; the economy of the Amazon Basin experienced its first signs of recovery after twenty years of depression; and one indicator of the centripetal forces acting in the economy—the rate of rural-urban migration into Lima—slowed down sharply by comparison with the periods preceding and following.[3]

Along with these changes in the economy went equally important changes in the nature of Peruvian politics, making possible the introduction of economic policies which would never have stood a chance of acceptance in the 1890s. In contrast to the close-knit oligarchic politics of the *civilista* republic. Peruvian politics after 1930 reflected the growing influence of new social groups commonly identified as 'middle class.' Mass politics, 'populist' parties,[4] and sharp ideological conflicts had made their appearance in Peru. The traditional ruling class maintained its power through the 1930s by the installation of military presidents and use of repression against the opposition; but the search for more viable long-run solutions led in the 1940s to tentative alliance with, and an attempt to co-opt the leadership of, the representatives of the new forces—particularly the APRA party. For most of the 1940s Peru was ruled by governments more or less committed to capturing and maintaining the support of the middle class and, for the first time in Peruvian history, policies of State economic intervention coupled with exchange and import controls made their appearance, aimed at extracting surplus from export sectors for the benefit of urban groups. The State also took steps to encourage the development of local enterprises in a variety of fields by the establishment of 'development banks' to provide cheap credit, and Peru's first 'Industrial Promotion Law' was passed by the Prado government in 1940.

However, by comparison with the development effort which had been mounted in the 1890s, or with events elsewhere in Latin America in the 1930s, Peruvian performance from 1930 to 1948 shows up poorly. Progress towards economic diversification was very limited, as we shall see in Chapter 10. Increased local participation in export production did not involve any displacement of foreign firms, which retained un-challenged control of the largest mineral deposits. The Depression struck Peru after the local economy had already become depressed (see Chapter 6) and the consequent shock was less severe than in most other Latin American countries. Most important of all, despite the broadening of entrepreneurial and political participation and the consequent opportunity to experiment with new policy directions, the record of unorthodox economic policies in Peru during the 1940s was a dismal one. Pressures for a change in economic strategy became effective with the election of Manuel Prado to the Presidency in 1939, and over the following years Prado and then Bustamante vastly increased government spending, introduced a fixed exchange-rate system with import controls and exchange rationing, and launched a grandiose scheme for a State-controlled iron and steel plant with associated industrial development in Chimbote. By 1948, however, the governing coalition was in disarray, the experiment with economic controls was generally recognised to have proved a failure, the economy faced an increasingly-acute balance-of-payments crisis, and rapid inflation had alienated much of the previous middle-class support for the new policies.[5] In August 1948 General Manuel Odría, backed by the traditional ruling class, seized power and swung the country firmly back towards the traditional policies of liberalism and outward-orientation.

At first sight, Peruvian experience during the 1930s and 1940s reproduced several of the trends which in the 1890s had led to the emergence of an autonomous growth model, and displayed in addition a willingness to adopt policy innovations which had been totally lacking at the turn of the century. Why then did the experiment with unorthodox policy end in failure, and why was the post-1948 return to *laissez-faire* liberalism so complete? The answers to these questions will emerge in the course of the next three chapters. In general we shall argue that Peru after 1930 was to a considerable extent the prisoner of its previous history. Having arrived at 1930 with an already-depressed economy, a moribund manufacturing sector, an unformed and inexperienced middle class, and a strong popular distrust of expansionary government finance as a result of Leguía's performance during the 1920s, Peru was relatively poorly equipped to respond to the new elements in the post-Depression situation. Only some of the economic preconditions for autonomy listed at the end of Chapter 3 were met during the 1930s and 1940s, and attempts to fill the gaps by means of new policy initiatives were poorly-conceived. Such nationalism as did emerge was too incoherent to provide the basis for a viable new economic philosophy; the alliance of local ruling groups with foreign capital was not demolished; and when a confrontation between local and foreign interests finally did emerge (over the International Petroleum Company's plans to explore the Sechura Desert for oil in 1946–7) the resulting disintegration of political consensus helped to bring down the Bustamante government.

The following chapters examine first the major export sectors, in order to understand the nature of their expansion and the implications for the rest of the economy. The analysis concentrates on the issues to which attention was drawn in Part I: the degree of integration into the economy, the availability of surplus, and the effect of developments within each sector on policy pressures and relative price movements. As the options for policy-making had increased with the broadening of the political base and the wider acceptability of interventionism, we give particular attention also to elements in the export sector histories which illustrate the 'style' and general competence of policy making, as well as the emergence of vested interests promoting particular policies.

We then move on in Chapter 10 to discuss policy-making in the light of the export sector histories, and to review how much was made of the opportunity for greater autonomy, in terms of the progress made in industry and domestic agriculture. In the light of this analysis we then attempt to explain the weakness and ultimate reversal of inward-oriented growth.

8 The Export Sectors, 1930–48: Part 1

8.1 AGGREGATE EXPORT PERFORMANCE

Table 8.1 shows the impact of the Depression and the subsequent recovery on the export earnings of Peru and five other Latin American countries. Peru, it will be seen, was one of the countries least affected by the Depression. First, although the initial fall was comparable with elsewhere (71 per cent, compared with an average of 72 per cent for the other countries shown), Peru recovered quickly after 1933, outpacing all those included here except Mexico and Chile (the latter had suffered an earlier collapse so extreme that even a relatively slight recovery sufficed to outpace Peru). Second, as shown in Table 8.2, while total export earnings fell 68 per cent from 1929 to 1932, returned value fell only 63 per cent, since much of the impact of the Depression fell upon the repatriated profits of foreign firms, rather than upon the local economy's foreign-exchange income. And third, in the mid-1930s one of the leading export products was cotton, exports of which exceeded their

TABLE 8.1 Latin America: comparative export performance of selected countries, 1928–48
(dollars, indices 1933 = 100)

	Peru	Argentina	Brazil	Chile	Ecuador	Mexico
1928	347	366	276	587	302	398
1933	100	100	100	100	100	100
1934	116	91	100	138	90	122
1936	137	114	111	164	98	154
1938	123	93	102	201	90	131
1940	106	113	108	203	82	117
1942	124	133	165	258	176	137
1944	138	180	236	283	299	179
1946	246	309	406	314	362	261
1948	258	411	506	478	439	384

Source: UN *Statistical Yearbook*, 1948, p. 331, and 1949, p. 365.

TABLE 8.2 Dollar value of major exports, 1927–39
(indices, 1929 = 100)

	Cotton	Sugar	Copper	Petroleum	Wool	Total	Estimated 'Returned value'
1930	71	67	60	71	60	71	75
1931	42	57	42	43	41	47	57
1932	35	41	12	47	25	32	37
1933	55	47	17	51	47	41	44
1934	91	45	25	80	48	60	59
1935	93	45	43	80	43	63	n.a.
1936	110	46	42	85	76	71	n.a.
1937	109	60	50	88	96	79	n.a.
1938	66	43	52	75	59	65	n.a.
1939	68	57	50	60	64	61	n.a.

Source: *Extracto Estadistico*, various years.

1929 level by 1936; the growth sectors thus included at least one with very high returned value and powerful income effects. The result was that, although Peru initially suffered the balance-of-payments troubles common to all Latin American economies, the effects were muted and short-lived. Default on the foreign debt in 1932, which doubled import capacity overnight, was sufficient (in combination with the rapid recovery of export earnings from 1933 on) to provide rapid relief from the crisis and to end downward pressure on the exchange rate—indeed, in April 1933 the exchange rate began to rise again, indicating that the critical period had already passed.[1]

These developments, which augured well for the future of export-led growth, were accompanied by a reversal of the trend which had dominated the export history of the preceding twenty years, namely, the tendency for foreign-controlled export sectors to dominate export growth while locally-controlled sectors fell behind. Table 8.3 traces the change; it can be seen that the foreign-controlled products, copper, silver and oil, which had accounted for 50 per cent of total export earnings in 1930, had fallen to 23 per cent by 1950, while the agricultural commodities sugar and cotton returned to a dominant role, rising from 29 per cent of exports in 1930 to 53 per cent by 1945. Wool and coffee, also locally-controlled sectors, maintained or slightly increased their shares, while a new locally-controlled sector, fishing, made its appearance among Peruvian exports. Finally, in Table 8.3 it can be seen that lead and zinc, two mine products which in 1930 had been virtually monopolised by the Cerro de Pasco Corporation, were hit hard by the Depression but picked up rapidly during the 1940s, accounting for 12

TABLE 8.3 Percentage shares of major exports by value, 1930 to 1950
(based on values at current prices)

	Percentage shares of total export earnings					
	Cotton and sugar	Wool and coffee	Fish prod- ucts	Copper and silver	Lead and zinc	Oil
1930	28.5	3.3	–	20.1	6.8	29.7
1935	34.4	3.0	–	17.7	2.2	37.8
1940	28.2	5.2	–	22.3	3.1	24.8
1945	52.9	3.3	0.9	9.6	7.4	12.5
1950	50.5	4.6	2.9	9.4	11.7	13.1

Sources: 1930 to 1945: Estadística del Comercio Especial for years shown. 1950: Banco Central de Reserva, Cuentas Nacionales, 1950–67, pp. 44–5.

per cent of export earnings by 1950. As is described later in this chapter, the increasing production of these two metals during the 1940s was due largely to the rise of a new generation of local mining companies, while gold-mining—a sector which does not figure in Table 8.3—was also the scene of a revival of local activity.

In summary, the proportion of Peru's exports produced by foreign firms fell from over 60 per cent at the end of the 1920s (if to the 50 per cent share of copper, silver and oil we add gold, vanadium, and the sugar from W. R. Grace's plantations) to 30 per cent or possibly less by the end of the 1940s. During those twenty years new opportunities opened up in various export sectors, and in the absence of foreign investment these opportunities were readily exploited by a new generation of local capitalists, a process reminiscent of the 1890s.

Returning to Table 8.1, however, it can be seen that following recovery from the Depression, the subsequent performance of Peruvian exports in the aggregate was rather sluggish, especially by comparison with the growth rates which had been characteristic of the period from 1890 to 1920. From 1933 to 1948 the average annual growth rate of exports in U.S. dollars was no more than three per cent, and by 1948 Peru was lagging badly behind the other countries shown in the table, despite the fact that several of those other countries had in the interim been concentrating on industrialisation rather than export promotion. In particular, it is evident that the Second World War failed to provide a recurrence of the commodity prices boom which had characterised the First World War. Given this slow overall growth of total export earnings, even the rising share of returned value did not suffice to generate the dynamic growth of local demand which we suggested in

Chapter 3 was one of the preconditions for a successful autonomous growth model.

In Chapter 10 we shall return to the implications of these overall trends in export performance for the rest of the local economy. First, however, a more detailed discussion is required of the histories of the main export sectors. We deal with the extractive sectors in this chapter, and with agricultural exports in the next.

8.2 METALS MINING: A LOCAL REVIVAL[2]

As the previous section mentioned, one of the important features of Peruvian economic growth during the post-Depression period was the appearance of a series of new investment opportunities, which local capital could exploit without competition from foreign firms. The most striking of these new opportunities lay in the development of metals mining. In this section, therefore, we look at the birth of a new generation of local mining companies, and ask what constraints they subsequently encountered to prevent their rising to equal the established foreign giants.

In Chapter 5 we described how between 1895 and 1905 the switch from production of precious metals to the 'new' metals copper and

TABLE 8.4 Shares of three large foreign firms in metals output[a], 1935–50 (percentages)

	Cerro share of		Northern Peru Mining	Vanadium Corporation	Total share of	
	Final output	Mine output			Final output	Mine output
1935	61	44	7	[b]	68	51
1942	63	25	4	3	69	31
1945	58	23	5[c]	2	65	29
1950	42	35	6	1	49	42

Source: National mining statistics for the years shown.
[a] The share of each of the companies in the total volume of each metal produced was first obtained, and this proportion was then multiplied by the total official valuation of Peruvian output of that metal. The values thus obtained for various metals were summed for each company, and the above percentages then calculated using as denominator the official total *valorizacion* of metals output. It should be noted that official values until 1958 were calculated using assay rather than recoverable content, and using international prices of the metals in their refined state.
[b] Closed down because of the Depression.
[c] Upper-bound estimate.

vanadium was accompanied by dramatic changes in the scale of mining operations, and the role of foreign capital. By 1929, the three leading foreign firms accounted for no less than 97 per cent of total metals exports.[3] The thirties brought a sharp reversal of this trend. By 1935 the share of the three foreign firms had fallen to 85 per cent,[4] while their share of total mining output had fallen much further, since the rapidly-increasing production of gold by local firms (see below) was only partly exported. By 1939 the foreign firms' share was below 70 per cent.[5] Table 8.4 provides some further indications[6] of the changing weight of the large foreign firms in mining production. These figures show their share in final output to have fallen from 68 per cent in 1935 to 49 per cent by 1950, while their share of the metal content in ores mined fell from 51 per cent in 1935 to only 29 per cent in 1945, recovering to 42 per cent by 1950. In a sense, the latter figures are more revealing than the former, for they indicate that the Oroya smelter (the commanding height of Peruvian mining at that time) moved from processing Cerro's own ores supplemented by some independently-extracted ore, to being ever more dependent upon ores mined by other companies. Cerro during these years was less and less a mining company, and increasingly a custom smelting enterprise serving the rapidly-expanding independent mining sector; by 1942, Cerro accounted for 63 per cent of final output, yet only 25 per cent of mine output.

The principal explanation for the reversal lies in the differential impact of the world crisis on the markets for different metals, shown in Table 8.5. It will be seen that whereas copper, the product which was most clearly monopolised by foreign firms in Peru (in terms both of actual production and control over large undeveloped deposits), was hit hard by the Depression, suffering a 69 per cent fall in price from 1929 to 1932, and showing only slow recovery until the end of the Second World War, other metals did better. In dollar terms the price of gold rose 69 per cent from 1932 to 1934, while at the same time silver prices recovered very rapidly in the mid-1930s before suffering a renewed fall. The two other base metals, lead and zinc, displayed greater price stability in the face of the Depression than did copper, and by the early 1940s had recovered to around their 1929 prices. Taking into account the depreciation of the Peruvian exchange rate during the 1930s (Part 2 of Table 8.5) it is evident that the prices received by local firms producing gold, silver, lead and zinc rose above the 1929 level by 1933, and for the rest of the thirties rose more rapidly than internal prices, as measured by the wholesale price index.[7] These metals could be produced from deposits which remained in Peruvian hands; and since the necessary technology was readily available, local firms were quick to take advantage of the good prices.

The Table also shows a feature of the 1940s to which we shall return later: namely, that dollar prices for metals remained frozen during the

Second World War due to U.S. Government price controls, while the Peruvian exchange rate was also frozen at S/6.50 to the dollar from 1939 to 1948, so that prices received in soles also stagnated. Local inflation in Peru, however, accelerated during the 1940s and by the end of the war the profit margins of local mining companies were under increasing pressure.

Copper was hit especially hard by the Depression for several reasons. The world's leading copper producers had several times formed cartels to hold prices above market levels, and the latest of these had been successful until late 1929 in holding the world price at record levels, generating a rapid increase in world supply,[8] much of which had come from new low-cost producing areas. These new entrants could afford to accept low prices for their copper, and the slump following the collapse of the cartel was correspondingly a severe one. In May 1932 the U.S.A. imposed a prohibitive duty on foreign copper, while shortly afterwards Britain announced preferential tariffs for Empire producers and France granted preference to Katanga, leaving Peruvian and Chilean copper to compete with African copper for what remained of the European

TABLE 8.5 Metals prices, 1929–1948
(indices, 1929 = 100)

Part 1. U.S. price in dollars

	Copper	Gold	Silver	Lead	Zinc
1929	100	100	100	100	100
1930	72	100	72	81	70
1931	45	100	54	61	56
1932	31	100	53	46	44
1933	39	121	66	56	62
1934	47	169	91	56	64
1935	48	169	121	59	66
1936	51	169	85	68	75
1937	72	169	85	88	69
1938	54	169	82	69	71
1939	59	169	74	74	78
1940	59	169	66	76	97
1941	60	169	66	85	115
1942	65	169	72	95	127
1943	65	169	84	95	127
1944	65	169	84	95	127
1945	65	169	98	95	127
1946	82	169	151	120	134
1947	116	169	136	220	161
1948	123	169	140	268	209

TABLE 8.5 (*continued*)

Part 2. *Equivalent prices in soles at current exchange rate*

	Gold	Silver	Lead	Zinc	Lima wholesale price index
1929	100	100	100	100	100
1930	113	81	91	79	96
1931	144	76	87	80	94
1932	188	99	86	82	91
1933	249	136	119	132	97
1934	278	157	97	111	101
1935	274	202	99	110	102
1936	264	137	109	121	103
1937	260	134	136	106	110
1938	295	146	96	98	110
1939	350	157	158	166	116
1940	401	162	198	252	133
1941	430	171	221	299	156
1942	425	188	247	330	197
1943	427	220	247	330	226
1944	427	220	247	330	234
1945	427	255	247	330	245
1946	430	393	312	348	263
1947	433	352	572	419	355
1948	433	365	697	544	445

Sources: Prices from *BCIM*, No. 117, pp. 117 and 251; and *Anuario de la Industria Minera*, 1948, pp. 77–8, 115, 132 and 144. Wholesale price index from *Anuario Estadístico*.

market.[9] Meantime the world price of silver, which in the past had contributed greatly to the profitability of copper mining in Peru, also slumped very heavily in 1930–1 following India's switch to the gold standard and subsequent heavy sales of silver bullion on the open market. Northern Peru Mining Company closed down its copper and silver operations in September 1931,[10] and by late 1932 Cerro had cut back its copper operations to 40 per cent of capacity.[11] World copper prices began to recover after 1935, but markets remained very competitive and U.S.-owned copper companies abroad had been hit hard by the discriminatory measures taken by their own Government in 1932. As a result, Cerro was slow to invest in further expansion of its copper production, which fell steadily again through the 1940s, and Northern Peru Mining never reopened the Shorey smelter,[12] although production of copper concentrates from Quiruvilca was resumed in 1940.

If the picture for copper was gloomy, that for gold was quite the opposite, as Table 8.5 has already indicated. The rapid depreciation of the Peruvian currency which began at the end of 1929 had again (as in the 1890s) brought a rise in the local gold price, while in the years 1933–4 there was a rapid increase in the international price as country after country was forced off the gold standard. In Peru the immediate beneficiaries of this rise of gold prices were the three foreign firms already engaged in gold production in 1929: Cerro (with gold included as a by-product in its copper bars), Northern Peru Mining Company,[13] and the Inca Mining Company.[14] Until 1935 these three remained at the top of the list of gold producers. New developments from 1930 on, however, came from a different direction. Local capital quickly became interested in gold mining, and in the climate of nationalism which followed the overthrow of the Leguía régime the Government decreed at the beginning of 1931 that all gold deposits not already held as concessions were reserved to the State (i.e. could not simply be staked out by the first-comer) and that access to these deposits would be granted preferentially to Peruvians, although foreign firms could submit applications for consideration.[15] Despite pressure from foreign capital for free access to Peruvian gold deposits[16] it was not until 1936 that the State reserves were thrown open again.[17] Meanwhile Peruvian interests staked claims to the bulk of the country's promising deposits and launched a wave of new companies to develop them.

The first of these ventures, while by no means the most successful, was symptomatic of the new atmosphere among Peruvian capitalists. At Ccochasayhuas, the Cotabambas Auraria company (the most successful of the local ventures launched at the turn of the century during the previous gold boom) had failed to find new reserves of ore and in early 1929, after several years of losses, the company went bankrupt.[18] The following year the mine was taken over by Fernando and Augusto Wiese, leading members of the Lima business élite, who invested large sums in mechanisation and electrification of the mine, and who in 1933 made mining history in Peru by transporting heavy equipment to the mine by air.[19] The Wiese brothers' example was quickly followed by other members of the national élite. Lists published in the late 1930s[20] gave details of thirty-eight new gold-mining companies formed in Peru from 1930 to 1938; of these, twenty-five were started in the three years 1933–5, and not less than twenty were formed with significant participation by the top echelon of local capitalists. Most active of these were five families: Wiese (in six companies), Fernandini (four), Boza (five), Alvarez Calderon (four), and Rizo Patron (two). Other élite names (Beltran, Aspillaga, Ayulo Pardo, Berckemeyer) were to be found among the lists of directors. Of the five leading families, three (Fernandini, Rizo Patron, and Boza) had previously been prominent in mining development.[21]

Among the successful promoters of gold-mining ventures during the 1930s only one group can be identified as foreign or quasi-foreign: a syndicate assembled by the US mining engineer Leon J. Rosenshine, who had come to Peru in the 1920s.[22] The syndicate included capitalists in both the U.S.A. and Lima, but with the U.S. element dominant, and between 1935 and 1946 it launched four successful gold companies. In the long run, the Rosenshine mines were to prove the most durable of the ventures launched at this time, but in the 1930s their role was relatively minor.[23]

By no means all, or even most, of the gold-mining companies launched during the 1930s were successful, but the record was strikingly better than that of the 1890s, largely because of technological advances which made the profitable development of gold mining more feasible than thirty years before. The two outstanding advances were the aeroplane, and development of the small-scale flotation concentrator (see the discussion below and in Note 27), which made possible the economic exploitation of relatively low-grade ores. To these two innovations should be added improvements in the technology of cyaniding gold ores, which had been in its infancy in the 1890s.

Of 1933 gold production of 3,010 kilos, the three leading foreign producers, Cerro, Northern Peru, and Inca Mining, accounted for 57 per cent and other minor foreign-controlled producers for one per cent. By 1939 production had risen to 8,471 kilos, of which only 22 per cent derived from the large foreign companies and a further seven per cent from the Rosenshine mines. The remaining 71 per cent was mined by Peruvian firms, mostly established since 1930.[24]

The peak year of gold production was 1941, when output reached 8.9 tons of fine gold; there was then a rapid fall to less than 3.5 tons in 1948, after which output stabilised through the 1950s at between 4 and 5 tons. Two factors constrained the expansion of gold production: first the limited size of high-grade gold deposits, and secondly the steady squeeze on profits during the 1940s as domestic inflation pushed up costs, while the gold price remained institutionally fixed (with the international price at $35, where it remained until 1972, and the Peruvian official exchange rate fixed at 6.50 until 1948).

The ending of the gold boom was overshadowed by the fact that again, as in the 1890s, a new area of opportunity for local capital had emerged. This time the new area was not copper, but lead and zinc. These metals are commonly found with silver in Peruvian ores and the silver smelters of the 1880s and 1890s had mostly produced lead-silver alloys. The decline of silver mining after 1897 had put an end to the early expansion of lead production. In the 1920s however, Cerro had begun diversifying its activities in Peru, beginning production of zinc concentrates at Casapalca in 1926, and opening a lead furnace at Oroya in 1927.[25] Both installations were closed down in 1931; but in 1933 a treaty signed in London by the world's main suppliers of silver committed them to official support for silver prices, and the subsequent rise in profitability led to the reopening of Cerro's Casapalca concentrator to treat silver-lead-zinc ores, and the re-starting of the lead furnaces at Oroya.[26]

By the 1930s, however, in contrast to the 1920s, Cerro was not the only firm interested in lead and zinc. The Peruvian Lizandro Proaño, who had played a leading role in the Morococha copper boom of 1894–1905, modernised and reopened his old smelter at Tamboraque to treat lead – silver ores in 1929–31, while, following the 1933 Silver Treaty, a number of silver-mining companies reopened old mines and installed new flotation plants capable of recovering lead and zinc as well as silver in the form of concentrates.

High lead and zinc prices, combined with the new horizons opened in Peru by the flotation concentrator,[27] soon attracted attention towards previously-neglected deposits with high grades of lead and zinc but little silver, and during the second half of the 1930s local capital began to move seriously into the establishment of new lead – zinc mining companies. Three of the new ventures of the 1930s are of special importance: Minas de Cercapuquio (1934), Compania Minera Atacocha (1936), and Sindicato Minero Rio Pallanga (1937). All were entirely Peruvian-owned,[28] and all three quickly built up efficient modern operations producing lead – zinc concentrates, coming into production during the first half of the 1940s. As these and other independent operators made their entry into lead – zinc production, the proportion of total production of ores and concentrates of those metals accounted for by independent local companies rose from 41 per cent in 1935 to 67 per cent in 1946, in the case of lead, and from zero to 64 per cent over the same period in the case of zinc.[29]

Production of lead reached 50,000 tons by 1940 and stabilised about this level for most of the rest of the decade, rising to 65,000 tons only in 1949, but zinc production expanded from around 20,000 tons at the beginning of the 1940s to over 60,000 tons by 1945 and 88,000 tons by 1950,[30] a fourfold expansion which made this the leading growth product in mining. Of the 40,000-ton increase in the first half of the 1940s only 2,000 tons were attributable to expansion by Cerro, the remainder coming from smaller independent mines.

This expansion was aided by governmental promotion. The rapid growth of Peruvian interest in mining during the 1930s had resulted in demands from owners of small mines for State support and intervention to encourage development, and the first move in this direction was made in 1938–9, when the mining section of the Ministerio de Fomento bought a 50-ton mill from Germany and installed it as a custom concentrator at Castrovirreyna.[31] The establishment of a national development bank for mining had also long been promoted in Peru, and in early 1941 the Prado Government promulgated the final legislation for the project, and set up the Banco Minero with capital of S/50 million and instructions to provide cheap credit for small national miners, operate custom concentrators to process the ores from small and medium mines, and establish assay offices and ore-buying agencies.[32] The Bank's activities thus extended well beyond simple finance; it took over the Castrovirreyna concentrator and during the 1940s opened others at Sacracancha and Huachocolpa, also in the central Sierra; it assisted local mining companies in obtaining scarce equipment from the U.S.A.,[33] and it participated actively in the negotiation of sales contracts with the U.S. Government during the Second World War.

The Peruvian expansion, then, was made possible by the opportunity to move into products not already dominated by foreign firms. That opportunity led to pressure for State support, which then reinforced the process. The increasing relative importance of local mining companies was also, however, due in some part to the reluctance of one foreign firm—Cerro—to resume its expansion, despite its access to lead and zinc deposits[34] and the apparent profitability of its operations by the late thirties.[35] By the forties, this abstention by foreign capital was coming to an end, beginning with renewed activity in the field of copper production.[36]

In the case of Cerro and Northern Peru Mining, the revival did not directly affect the new generation of local mining companies, since the established foreign firms already had under their control large mineral deposits suitable for development. The most important new venture of the 1940s, however, took the form of a joint venture of local and foreign interests. This was the Volcan Mining Company, established by Rosenshine to develop mines which he controlled at the Ticlio Pass on the Central Railway.[37] Although Rosenshine was Managing Director, the bulk of the capital was put up by Peruvian capitalists, led by the Beltran family (who retained control of the company into the 1970s).[38] Having been unable to import concentrating equipment during the war, the new company in 1944 obtained a lease of Cerro's idle concentrator at Mahr,[39] and in 1946 became the country's leading zinc producer and second lead producer.

Summing up, the revival of local entrepreneurship in the mining sector began with the Depression-induced rise of the gold price, and quickly moved on to lead and zinc. Because the deposits brought into production by the new local companies were those which had remained out of the hands of the large foreign companies, there was no basis for a clash of interests between local and foreign capital; on the contrary, the two groups existed amicably side by side, with local companies taking the lead during the 1930s not because they could displace foreign capital, but simply because foreign investment had temporarily come to a halt. The largest and richest mineral deposits in Peru, however, typically remained in the hands of large foreign firms, with the result that the new generation of local mining companies had access only to deposits of medium scale; their possibilities for future expansion were correspondingly limited.

Turning to the contribution of metals to total export earnings, the quantum data in Table 8.6 bring out clearly the importance of the rise of prices and production of lead and zinc during the 1930s in offsetting the prior decline of copper and silver. It can also be seen, however, that, with the exception of lead and zinc, metals production tended to decline during most of the 1940s, due to wartime shortages of materials and equipment as well as to the squeeze on profitability caused by rising local costs and the maintenance of a fixed exchange rate from 1940. Mining activity thus served to mobilise substantial sums of local capital for investment, and revived local capabilities and entrepreneurship in mining, but did not lead on to a dramatic gain in aggregate export earnings. Indeed, the growing economic crisis of 1946–8 both resulted in, and was aggravated by, a general recession of mining.

TABLE 8.6 Metal mining: the volume of exports, 1925–48
(indices, 1925–9 average = 100, 1953 prices)

	Copper	*Silver*	*Gold*	*Lead and Zinc*	*Total including other minor metals*
1932	48	16	110	7	45
1934	59	55	114	54	72
1936	69	95	130	242	108
1938	79	97	262	428	138
1940	80	87	297	308	134
1942	72	70	270	399	127
1944	67	54	129	605	122
1946	54	50	105	383	105
1948	35	26	82	468	82
Percentage share of total metals exports					
1925–9	62	36	8	7	100
1948	27	11	15	39	100

Source: Hunt (1973a), pp. 20–2.

One final point concerns the regional impact of the changed situation of the thirties and forties. As shown in Table 8.7, the first check to the ascendancy of the Central Sierra came in the 1920s, with the rapid

TABLE 8.7 Regional[a] distribution of mining output (metals) by value
(percentages)

	Centre	Mid-North	Mid-South	South-east	Far South	Other
1915	89.8	6.9	1.1	–	2.3	–
1920	90.2	6.2	1.5	–	1.8	–
1925	86.8	11.4	b	–	1.8	–
1929	81.5	17.1	b	–	1.4	–
1942	70.7	11.1	8.4	2.5	7.3	–
1945	73.0	14.9	4.4	0.6	7.0	–
1950	78.0	10.3	6.3	0.9	4.4	–

Sources: Annual mining statistics. 1925 and 1929 are shares of exports from *Estadistica del Comercio Especial*.
[a] *Definition of regions*: These are grouped as in the recent editions of the mining statistics, as follows:
Centre: Pasco, Junin, Lima, Huanuco
Mid-North: Cajamarca, La Libertad, Ancash, Amazonas
Mid-South: Ica, Huancavelica, Ayacucho, Apurimac
Southeast: Cuzco, Madre de Dios
Far South: Arequipa, Moquegua, Tacna, Puno.
[b] The small production from this region is included in Centre (exports through Callao).

expansion of mining output in La Libertad (in the north) by the Northern Peru Mining Company. The combined share of the Centre and Mid-North in total mining output remained about 96 per cent from 1920 to 1929, while the balance between the two shifted in favour of the latter. From 1929 to 1942, however, these two regions fell to 82 per cent of total output, while mining activity within both the Centre and the Mid-North became more decentralised, with the rise of new gold-mining companies in La Libertad and of new lead – zinc enterprises in the Centre. The gold-mining boom brought increased shares of total mining activity to the Mid-South and Far South, which rose from less than 2 per cent in 1929 to some 16 per cent in 1942.

8.3 PETROLEUM: END OF THE BOOM

The metals-mining sector, we have seen, played an important part in the post-Depression recovery of Peruvian exports, but failed to sustain its dynamism during the 1940s, although new opportunities for investment of local capital in the sector continued to be taken up, resulting in a dramatic increase in the share of local firms in output. The other mineral-export sector, petroleum, displayed a similar pattern of rapid recovery from the Depression, followed by stagnation and then decline during the 1940s; but the reasons for these trends were different, and the opportunities opened up for new entrants to the industry were very limited. Petroleum in Peru has always been the export sector most closely bound up with politics, and the period from 1930 to 1948 was no exception. As we shall see, the strong growth of production in the 1930s was primarily a response to political pressures, while the failure of exploration and investment activity during the 1940s was the direct result of a policy stalemate.

TABLE 8.8 Oil production and exports, 1925–49
(millions of barrels, annual averages)

	Production	Exports	Internal consumption[a]	Average Mid-Continent price of crude (cents per barrel)
1925–9	11.1	9.2	n.a.	166
1930–4	12.4	11.0	1.9	89
1935–9	16.3	14.0	3.0	110
1940–4	13.3	10.1	4.2	114
1945–9	13.6	6.4	6.5	195

Source: Estadística Petrolera del Perú, 1948–9, pp. 43, 117, 146–7. Exports were converted from metric tons to barrels using a conversion factor of 7.5. Prices are from *ibid.*, p. 191, average of annual price quotations.
[a] This includes imported oil products.

Table 8.8 traces the evolution of production and prices of petroleum; production, remarkably, soared to record heights in the second half of the 1930s, despite very depressed prices. The detailed figures on which Table 8.8 is based show the volume of exports to have recovered to above the 1929 level by 1933 and to have increased very rapidly thereafter. This expansion, conducted in the face of falling world prices,[40] provides eloquent testimony to the impact of two sets of political pressures on the International Petroleum Company in Peru. The first of these was the crisis in public finance which the Depression imposed on a country where taxation of foreign trade was still a major revenue source. The second was the rising tide of politically-effective nationalism, embodied in particular in the APRA party. The Benavides regime viewed increased oil exports as the key to its fiscal health, while the IPC was readily responsive to government urgings in this direction because of the company's fear of punitive taxation and possible expropriation should APRA come to power.

The motives of the Benavides Government in pressing for increased production are obvious enough. The Government had set its face firmly against deficit financing (see Chapter 10 below), and was endeavouring to balance the budget despite the strains of rearmament resulting from the brief war with Colombia over Leticia (1932). In the search for increased revenue, oil was one obvious target. By 1930 this sector accounted for over 80 per cent of all export taxes paid in the country, and for 4 per cent of total government income. Between 1930 and 1934, as oil exports were pushed up to record levels, the amount paid in export taxes by the industry nearly trebled, and the share of the oil export tax in total government income rose to 12 per cent, making this the most important single source of increased revenue during the first two years of the Benavides regime.[41] The rate of tax remained derisory (in 1934, when oil exports exceeded S/121 million, the sector's export tax totalled S/15 million, about 12 per cent); but for Benavides the immediate benefits of even a modest revenue increase clearly outweighed the heavy costs to Peru of such an expansion of production from an exhaustible resource in the face of falling prices.

For its part, the dominant firm in the industry, the IPC, had several equally clear reasons for maximising short-run output at Brea-Parinas. The 20-year exemption from additional taxes which had been granted in the 1922 'Award' was due to expire in 1942, and the company knew that it would then immediately be presented with an increased tax bill. Peruvian nationalists were becoming increasingly aware of the extraordinarily high profits which IPC was extracting from Peru, and the leader of APRA had placed on record his intention to revise the official attitude to such companies should his party attain power.[42] Barely defeated in the 1932 presidential elections, APRA was obviously a strong contender for the 1936 elections.

The result was that production was pushed to the technically feasible limit while new exploration was neglected. By the mid 1930s output at Brea-Parinas—83 per cent of total Peruvian output—was some 50 per cent higher than in the late 1920s. Without an enormous increase in exploration effort this level of output simply could not be sustained, and by 1938 production at Brea-Parinas was falling steeply, from a peak of 15 million barrels in 1936 to a 1940 low point of 10 million barrels. By intensive drilling IPC succeeded in holding output between 10 and 12 million barrels through the 1940s, but thereafter the trend towards declining productivity was irreversible, obliging IPC to secure its oil supplies by a joint venture with Lobitos (see below, Chapter 11).

With the country's main oilfield past its peak, Peru's future as an oil producer and exporter depended upon new exploration efforts to locate more oil deposits. Such exploration, however, could only proceed once an effective government policy had been evolved to guide the development of the industry. The most evident characteristic of the governments of the 1940s was their inability to achieve consensus on such a policy. It will be recalled that from 1910 to 1922 the granting of new exploration concessions in the most promising areas of the country had been blocked by an administrative and political logjam caused by the lack of adequate cadastral surveys, and the dispute with the IPC over its titles. The situation had been resolved eventually by the 1922 Petroleum Law which once again opened the most promising areas and fixed the terms under which concessions were to be granted. Any concession which was abandoned voluntarily would revert to the 'State reserves' and could not again be opened to private claim-staking without a specific decree. The original intention had been that in those areas where private enterprise failed to explore and develop, the State would have the second chance; and following the abandonment of the large number of Sechura desert concessions covered by the abortive Shell venture of 1924 (see Chapter 5) the State had indeed signed a contract with Phillips Petroleum for further exploration in 1927–8. With the withdrawal of Phillips, however, the entire area of the Sechura desert surrounding the existing productive oilfields of IPC, Lobitos and Piaggio lay idle in the hands of the State until 1934, when President Benavides set up a new State enterprise to explore and drill in the reserve areas. The Puno oilfield had also reverted to the State in 1924.

The effect of the above events during the twenty years preceding 1940 was that the only areas still open to claim-staking by private companies were the jungle and most of the Sierra, although even in the jungle large concessions taken out in the 1920s had since reverted to State reserves. In 1938 the first oil was struck in the jungle by the 'Ganso Azul' company,[43] and this stimulated renewed interest; in 1941 a new company formed by the coastal sugar planter Augusto Gildemeister secured a 34,000-hectare concession near Contamana,[44] under the very favourable terms of a special jungle-oil law passed by Benavides in 1937 for the benefit of Ganso Azul.[45] This, however, was the only oil concession granted by the Prado or Bustamante administrations, for Prado quickly took fright at the prospect of granting jungle concessions to large foreign firms under the very liberal terms of the prevailing legislation. Dependent upon a tacit political alliance with APRA, Prado felt unable to give his government's blessing to any 'sellout' of natural resources to foreign firms, and as a result all land which was not already a State oil reserve was withdrawn from private claim-staking until a new policy had been formulated. By 1943 international interest in the oil possibilities of the Amazon Basin was increasing rapidly, and the large international companies began to seek exploration concessions in Ecuador, Colombia, Peru and Bolivia. Some even began field surveys in Peru in expectation of obtaining official access.[46] But Prado firmly refused to open any area to denouncement, and the Bustamante régime (equally subject to nationalist pressure) took the same position.

The need for a new government strategy on oil exploration was obvious. Possible options included serious promotion of the State's own oil company, legislation reopening the country to private exploration on tougher terms than hitherto, or specific *ad hoc* contracts with private companies, bringing them in as partners of the State.

The route of direct State involvement in production had already been opened up by Benavides. In 1934 a 'Petroleum Department' had been set up[47] and instructed to begin exploring for new oilfields in the northeast. In 1936 the Department began sinking exploratory wells in areas around the Zorritos oilfield,[48] and in 1938 a small successful strike at Cope made the State the fourth oil producer in Peru. The State also conducted a drilling programme on the old Puno oilfield, with some shortlived success in 1939,[49] and at the beginning of 1939 it bought up the oilfield and refinery installations of the Piaggio company at Zorritos.[50] Rapid expansion followed, including the construction of a new $1.5 million refinery at Villar near Zorritos, opened in 1940.[51]

However, under both Prado and Bustamante, State development was pursued only in a desultory fashion. State exploration in the northwestern desert, initiated during the Benavides period, resulted in the discovery of commercial oil at Los Organos in 1943,[52] while a small-scale exploration programme in 1944 failed to find oil on a jungle reserve zone near the Ucayali.[53] These activities, however, were carry-overs from the momentum given to State oil exploration in the 1930s. Under both Prado and Bustamante the State venture, reorganised as E.P.F. in 1946, received low priority, while patronage appointments resulted in increasing incompetence and corruption among its employees. By 1947, whereas Lobitos Oilfields was pressing ahead with the development of its holdings adjacent to the State oil discovery at Los Organos, E.P.F. was moribund.[54] In his 1947 Annual Message Bustamante went so far as to state openly that his policy was to restrict E.P.F.'s activities lest foreign capital should mistakenly see in the company a threatening State monopoly in embryo.[55]

As for the second policy option, tougher ground rules, one half-hearted attempt was made. The first draft of Prado's 1942 oil tax law (see below) incorporated provisions empowering the Government to dictate to the holders of exploration concessions the rate at which they should conduct survey and drilling work and, in addition, permitting the compulsory purchase of as much as it wished of the output from new concessions at a fixed minimum price. Pressure from the oil companies secured the abandonment of these sections of the draft, however, and it was at this point that the Government froze all claim-staking pending new legislation.

The third policy option, that of *ad hoc* contracts for the development of specific areas by private capital in partnership with the State, produced the political *cause célèbre* of the 1940s: the Sechura Contract.[56] As noted earlier, by the end of the 1930s the productivity of the Brea – Parinas oilfield was falling and IPC was becoming aware of the need to secure new oil-bearing areas. The company was therefore in a receptive frame of mind when in early 1939 the Benavides government secretly proposed a joint venture to explore and develop five million hectares of State reserve areas in the Sechura desert. Negotiations on the contract began in March 1939,[57] but had not been concluded when Prado took over the presidency in the middle of the year. The project was then put in mothballs, and IPC from 1940 to 1946 devoted its attention and $22 million to an unsuccessful attempt to locate a new oilfield on the coast of Ecuador.[58] The departure of Prado in 1945 coincided with the abandonment of the Ecuadorean venture, and IPC proposed to the incoming Bustamante Government that the Sechura negotiations be revived. A draft Contract was agreed early in 1946 and presented to Congress for ratification; by July it had passed the Deputies and went on to the Senate. IPC, under the terms of this draft, agreed to pay an immediate $4.5 million advance on future taxes, spend S/8.5 million on public works in the area, maintain minimum rates of exploration and drilling, pay a $12\frac{1}{2}$ per cent royalty on all production, and be subject to prevailing tax legislation on the industry.[59] Bids were to be invited from other companies interested, and any competitor prepared to improve on the IPC's offer would receive the concession.[60]

In the Senate, the opponents of Bustamente seized on the Contract as a weapon with which to destroy the Government. The emotive connotations of the IPC name sufficed to convince many Peruvians that the Government was selling out the national interest yet again; among those labelling Bustamante a 'tool of U.S. imperialism' were not only the Left, but also the extremist Right-wing 'Alianza Nacional' led by Pedro Beltran, one of the chief architects of the 1948 coup which the Sechura debate helped to bring about.[61] Until Congress was broken up by an opposition boycott in late 1947, Sechura dominated the debates and discredited the Government. By the end of the year, the Contract was dead, and an attempt by Bustamante in 1948 to circumvent Congress by handing over to E.P.F. responsibility for signing the Contract was understandably rejected by IPC on grounds of political risk.[62]

The only policy area in which there was effective change during the 1940s was that of taxation. The twenty-year freeze on export taxes embodied in the Petroleum Law and IPC agreement of 1922 ended in early 1942, and in 1941 Prado sent to Congress a new draft Petroleum Law the key feature of which was a sharp increase in export tax rates. The law was specifically designed to remove a large part of the preferential tax treatment given to IPC in 1922 via exemption from production royalties. Under the new system all companies which paid royalties were permitted to offset these against their export tax liabilities, with the result that the new increase fell mainly on the IPC.[63]

(In production for the local market, however, IPC's exemption from the 10 per cent royalty remained a significant advantage.)

The immediate effect of the 1942 law was to raise export tax receipts from 12 per cent of the value of oil exports in 1941 to 26 per cent in 1942,[64] which, combined with some other minor new taxes, took the oil industry's total tax payments from 11 per cent to 16 per cent of total government revenues over the same period.[65]

To sum up, oil was a sector whose development was dominated by political considerations: first the IPC's fear of nationalism and the Government's need for revenue drove production up to a high level in the 1930s; then political hesitation and uncertainty blocked attempts to revive exploration activity in the 1940s, while increased taxation (and fixed prices in the internal market from 1939 on) probably contributed to the decline in production during the decade. Three new companies made their entry into the industry: one foreign (Ganso Azul), one local private venture (Gildemeister's El Oriente company) and one State company (E.P.F.); of these, two became successful producers, but only on a very small scale. The lacklustre performance of E.P.F. during the 1940s provided perhaps the clearest sign of the incapacity of the State to determine its priorities and then decree clearcut policies.

This political failure in the field of oil development is an interesting contrast to the various measures which were described earlier in this chapter in our discussion of mining development. Local metal-mining companies in the 1930s and 1940s were operating in an environment free of conflict over the issue of foreign control (since as was pointed out, the foreign and local sectors each enjoyed adequate opportunities during this period), and all that was required of the State was a degree of subsidy, in the form of cheap credit and various State-provided services. By contrast, oil was a sector the development of which depended directly upon strategic and highly-controversial political decisions. The Benavides régime of the 1930s had given a certain amount of momentum to an oil policy based upon an expanding State sector and the negotiation of *ad hoc* contracts with foreign capital, but the civilian régimes which followed were unable to develop any political consensus on oil policies (as on other vital economic issues), and their performance was characterised by legislative fumbling. It was not until the appearance in 1948 of another strong military President, Manuel Odría, that oil development policy again became positive and clearcut.[66]

9 The Export Sectors, 1930–48: Part 2 (Agriculture and Fishing)

9.1 SUGAR: FROM DEPRESSION TO LEADERSHIP

Sugar played no part in the recovery of export earnings during the 1930s. Free-market prices moved steadily downwards till 1937, and, more serious still, the Depression resulted in a series of bilateral trade agreements from which Peru was excluded. Preferential tariff treatment for British Empire suppliers drove Peruvian sugar out of the U.K. market in the second half of the 1930s,[1] while the long-established preferential tariff for Cuban sugar in the U.S. market was backed up in 1934 by the establishment of quotas for various suppliers of the U.S. market, Peru being given an initial quota of only 1,500 tons.[2]

Excluded thus from bilateral arrangements with the two strongest markets, Peruvian sugar producers faced a bleak outlook during much of the 1930s, since the main remaining outlet for Peruvian sugar, Chile, could absorb only a limited amount. Although Peru was too marginal a supplier to carry much weight in international sugar councils, the Peruvian delegates to the 1932 conference in London were among the most enthusiastic supporters of the 'Chadbourne Plan' to limit world supplies;[3] and throughout the 1930s one of the central planks of Peruvian trade policy was the negotiation of a bilateral treaty with Chile to secure preferential access there at least for Peruvian sugar.[4]

In 1934 a law was passed exempting sugar producers from several taxes;[5] but the most important source of relief for many growers was the possibility of transferring their land into the production of cotton, a crop which was doing relatively well during the 1930s (see below). It was in the 1930s that the displacement of sugar by cotton along most of the central and southern Coast reached its height. The area planted to sugar declined by more than 10 per cent during the 1930s (see Table 9.1). The disappearance of sugar cane from the valleys around Lima was assisted by special government credits announced in 1934 to facilitate the change over to cotton;[6] and penetration of the Lima market for white sugar by the new W. R. Grace and Company refinery at Paramonga finally drove out the last surviving sugar mill near Lima in 1938.

TABLE 9.1 Development of the sugar industry, 1930–49
(annual averages)

	(i) Production (000 tons)	(ii) Exports (000 tons)	(iii) Internal consumption (000 tons)	(iv) Area under cane (000 ha)	(v) Yields of cane per hectare — of land under cane (tons)	(vi) Yields of cane per hectare — harvested (tons)	(vii) Percentage of production coming from Lambayeque and La Libertad
1930–4	393	342	56	56.6	59.0	103.8	74.8
1935–9	383	297	75	50.6	62.5	105.8	79.3
1940–4	427	298	103	50.0	74.2	122.3	85.4
1945–9	428	300	147	50.2	73.4	122.8	83.9

Source: Sociedad Nacional Agraria, *Memoria* (annual). Figures are for coastal production only. The production series corresponds as closely as possible to the production of centrifugal sugar (excluding chancaca, concreto and cane alcohol).

This shift left the northern departments of Lambayeque and La Libertad firmly dominating sugar production, generating 85 per cent of output between them by 1940. It is possibly significant that it was 'the former department which took over the share of output previously represented by producers of the Centre. Lambayeque increased its share of total output from 21 per cent in 1930 to 29 per cent by 1945,[7] while La Libertad's share remained roughly constant. Producers in Lambayeque thus achieved an increase in output of more than 50 per cent in the decade of the thirties, despite the generally depressed condition of the market. The significance of this lies in the differences between the two regions. The sugar estates of La Libertad had been subject to a process of massive concentration from the 1870s through to the 1930s, in the course of which two enterprises (the U.S. company, W. R. Grace and Co., and the Gildemeister family) had achieved virtually complete control of the sector. The number of large estates milling their own cane had fallen from four (with four separate owners) in the early 1920s to three by the late 1920s, and these three were all under the control of the two leading firms by the end of the 1930s.[8] The few independent properties which remained became mere satellites of the big two. In contrast, Lambayeque represented a wider stratum of Peruvian capital,[9] and its relative success during the 1930s was possibly significant in helping to restore the political influence of the sugar sector entrepreneurs.

The Second World War dramatically improved the fortunes of the sector. The approach of war in Europe and the new International Sugar Agreement of 1937 had already brought some improvement of prices in the late 1930s, and cane yields rose by 25 per cent in 1939, due apparently to the spread of the new cane variety POJ2878[10] as well as to favourable weather conditions after several years of drought. In the early 1940s it became evident that sugar would be strongly favoured by wartime market conditions. The free market, characterised during the 1930s by oversupply, was now suffering from shortages, and by 1942 Peru was operating in a sellers' market, with the British and Chilean governments seeking to secure supplies by bilateral arrangements,[11] and the U.S.A. cutting its import duty on non-quota Peruvian sugar from 1.9 cents/lb to 0.9 cents.[12] Trade negotiations with Chile during the 1940s, in contrast to the 1930s, focused upon the exchange of cotton for wheat, with sugar barely mentioned.[13] Although Chile remained the leading single market, large sales were made also in other Latin American markets which had not previously been open to Peruvian sugar.

Despite the turnabout in market conditions, Table 9.1 shows that the volume of exports did not rise during the forties.[14] This was partly a result of wartime shortages of materials and post-war import controls, which hampered investment and modernisation,[15] and partly a measure of resistance to policy. Along with other export sectors, sugar was subjected to sharp increases in export taxation by the Prado Government, a situation which aroused bitter denunciations from planters who were enjoying a degree of prosperity not known for twenty years past, and were still paying off the debts incurred during the 1930s when the new tax law was passed.[16] In addition, the Government embarked on a policy of agricultural diversification, with priority assigned to production of foodcrops; for both cotton and sugar growers this policy implied a reduction in their supplies of guano fertiliser (rationed by the Government)[17] and government pressure for a reduction in the area of land under export crops.[18]

In addition, the Prado Government in 1941 decreed local-market quotas to be met by each sugar producer before any sugar could be exported—a measure designed to ensure adequate supplies to the urban market without allowing local prices to rise in line with international prices.[19] The producers, naturally enough, protested volubly; but the quota system probably in the long run constituted an incentive to increase output, since a producer could make large profits only on the exportable surplus left after the local-market quota had been filled.

Sugar planters were thus caught in a double bind, with incentives to increase production, yet restrained from doing so by government policies and wartime constraints on imported supplies of material and equipment. This frustration, combined with the increase in their economic base represented by wartime profits, resulted in their playing a leading role in the growing opposition to the Bustamante Government from 1945 to 1948 (see Chapter 10). Meantime, despite their new prosperity, sugar planters played no significant role as investors in other sectors. No doubt there was a significant surplus being generated by sugar exports, but the 'rules of the game' had to be changed before the sugar planters would show interest in mobilising that surplus.[20]

9.2 COTTON: THE KEY TO ECONOMIC ACTIVITY

In a frequently-quoted passage one observer, looking back on the 1930s, remarked of cotton:[21]

> 100,000 labourers work in the cotton fields, and if we take into account the associated industries (cottonseed and cottonseed oil) and the commercial interests involved, it can perhaps be said that almost half of the coastal population earn their living from cotton. All economic life is influenced by the harvest and the level of cotton prices. The value of land fluctuates in accordance with the premiums in the Liverpool market. The sol exchange rate weakens if export earnings from cotton fall. The buying power of large sectors of the urban population depends on cotton (a bad harvest, for example,

means fewer sales of hats . . . to cite but one example of a consumer good . . .); and even the inhabitants of the Sierra feel the effects, indirectly, of the classification of the cotton crop as 'strict good' or only 'good fair' . . . .

Even at the end of the 1940s, following a considerable reduction of cotton cultivation, it was estimated that 'approximately 15 per cent of the gainfully-employed population of the coast work in the cotton fields (and) . . . a much higher proportion of the area's income originates from cotton'.[22]

The high returned value[23] and relatively equal income distribution which gave cotton this key role as a determinant of the short-run buoyancy of the local economy were due, as Chapter 4 described, to the sector's labour-intensive and tenant-oriented mode of production. In this section we shall begin by considering the effects of changes in this mode of production which became increasingly evident during the 1930s.

The first such change was a relative decline in sharecropping and an increase both in direct working and in cash rentals. This trend represented not a desire to benefit from economies of scale, which would probably have led to income concentration similar to that in the sugar industry, but rather was a response to the growing political strength of tenants on the one hand, and the new credit system on the other. The increased degree of political mobilisation and awareness among tenants was in part a product of the growth of new mass parties which emerged with the collapse of the Leguía regime. In Piura, for example, the Partido Socialista was active in organising share croppers (*yanaconas*) into unions, and with support many tenants secured negotiated contracts.[24] Many landowners responded to this political mobilisation by abandoning sharecropping and moving towards either direct working of their land with wage labourers, or a system of cash tenancy (pressure from the tenants' unions was also orientated towards the latter goal).[25] The process was encouraged by the fact that credit appears to have been more difficult to obtain for large landowners who worked their land indirectly (with *yanaconas*) than for those working their properties directly.[26]

The exact timing and extent of such shifts is difficult to estimate; while in the North and Ica the process was observed in the thirties, in other areas it was delayed until the forties.[27] In any case, it remained true that cotton was still a small and medium cultivators' crop. A 1938 survey estimated that the two largest individual producers between them accounted for only five per cent of the total crop,[28] and at least one of these two (Okada) was using *yanaconas* to work part of his properties. More importantly, whether land was directly worked in large units or parcelled out among small peasant producers, the growing of cotton remained a labour-intensive activity—especially the harvesting, since the densely-covered high-quality Peruvian cottons were unsuited to mechanical harvesting, and have since remained so.[29] The cotton harvest therefore remained the most important single source of seasonal cash income for temporary migrants from the Sierra, and to a growing extent for the underemployed and unemployed of the Coast.

The increasing strength of tenants, and their consequent independence of the large landowners, contributed to a tendency for the process of cotton-ginning (formerly carried out on the *haciendas*) to become centralised in the hands of the merchant houses. 'Central gins' had handled less than one-quarter of cotton production in the 1920s; by 1940 their share had risen to 43 per cent. By 1970 it reached 90 per cent.[30] It would however be an error to regard this change as having been associated with an increase in the degree of monopoly power exercised by merchants. In the first place, growers were becoming less dependent upon merchants for rural credit during the 1930s, due to the expansion of the Banco Agricola (established in 1931). No less than 80 per cent of the total loans made by the Bank during the 1930s were to cotton growers.[31] In the second place, the power of the merchants was limited by the ease with which land could be transferred to other crops than cotton; this was increased by the centralisation of ginning, as landowners ceased to have capital tied up in gins of their own. The failure of the merchants to evolve a position of monopoly power was reflected in the large number and rapid turnover of the merchant houses—a process accentuated by the variety and changing relative importance of markets for Peruvian cotton, since the fortunes of particular cotton merchants in Peru has tended to be closely associated with the proportion of total cotton exports directed to markets with which a given firm had strong links,[32] because of nationality and/or favoured connections.

In general, thus, despite the trend away from 'pre-capitalist' relations of production in cotton growing, there was no great tendency for small-scale cultivation and labour-intensity of production to diminish; indeed, with the decline of the landowners' authority, there was if anything probably decentralisation and increased equality in the distribution of sectoral income.

World markets and Peruvian cotton

Given the widespread and rather equal distribution of the gains from cotton, it was of great significance for Peru that cotton was one of the very few commodities to benefit from a successful international price-support scheme during the Depression period. At the beginning of the thirties world cotton stocks were already heavy and prices falling. High world prices caused by the First World War, and subsequent world shortages of cotton in the early 1920s, had stimulated a worldwide

supply response which, combined with the recovery of the U.S. crop in
1925, brought a situation of chronic oversupply.[33] The Depression of
1930 resulted in a fall of world demand but no change in total
production, and the U.S.A., as the world's main cotton-exporting
nation, took steps to protect its farmers by financing the stockpiling of
cotton under the 'loan programme'.[34] By the end of 1932, U.S. stocks
had accumulated to over 70 per cent of annual production, and the
prospects for halting the decline by further stockpiling were bleak. In
May 1933, therefore, the Agricultural Adjustment Act (AAA) was
passed, authorising the U.S. Government to make farmers' eligibility
for the price-support programme conditional upon a reduction of their
area under cotton; and in April 1934 the Bankhead act reinforced the
acreage restrictions by imposing punitive taxes on excess production
above fixed quotas assigned to U.S. farmers.

The effect of the U.S. measures was that world cotton prices recovered
quickly after 1932, while the U.S. Government's refusal to sell export
cotton at prices below those of its support programme provided an
opportunity for other suppliers to capture an increasing share of the
world market by selling at slightly under the U.S. price and accepting
payment in currencies other than dollars. In 1932 the U.S.A. accounted
for 65 per cent of total world cotton exports and 60 per cent of
production. By 1939 the U.S. share had fallen to less than 30 per cent of
world exports, and less than 40 per cent of production.[35] As the leading
South American cotton exporter at the beginning of the decade, Peru
was the first to take advantage of the rapid improvement in market
prospects; from 1.5 per cent of world exports in 1932, Peru had
advanced to 2.8 per cent by 1935 and 3.0 per cent by 1939.[36] While this
left Peru very much a price-taker (even in the long-staple and extra-long-
staple cotton markets) the combination of rapidly-recovering world
demand and U.S. production restrictions made the decade a good one
for Peruvian growers. The most tangible sign of the improved position
was the development in 1934–5 of a strong market in cotton futures in
Peru, which enabled growers to avoid local shortage of credit by selling
all or part of their crop forward, often as much as nine months ahead,
thereby securing working capital.[37]

As contemporary commentators emphasised, not only were prevailing cotton prices after 1933 profitable (especially when the exchange rate
again began to depreciate), but in addition relative prices had moved in
favour of cotton. Taking the ratio of Tanguis prices to foodcrop prices
in 1929 as 100, the relative price of cotton had fallen to 74 by 1931, but
thereafter rose to 132 in 1934, at which stage there took place a massive
transfer of land into cotton. From 1935 on relative prices moved back
towards the 1929 level again; but only in the far North (where rice was
fostered as an alternative crop to cotton by deliberate government
policy) did cotton fail to consolidate its position as the dominant crop of

TABLE 9.2 Development of cotton-growing, 1925–49
(annual averages)

	Area under cotton (000 ha)	Production of raw cotton (000 tons)	Production of ginned fibre (000 tons)	Yield of raw cotton per ha (tons)
1925–9	123	141	53	1.15
1930–4	133	160	59	1.20
1935–9	171	227	84	1.33
1940–4	152	191	70	1.26
1945–9	133	182	67	1.37

Source: *Anuario Estadístico*, various years.

the decade.[38]

The scale of the swing into cotton is indicated by Table 9.2. Following the rapid expansion of cotton-growing during the First World War and early 1920s, the area under cotton remained virtually static between 1926 and 1933 at around 130,000 hectares. By 1938 however it had expanded to over 190,000 hectares—nearly half the total cultivated land of the Coast.[39] Yields per hectare, meantime, had by 1935 risen between 30 per cent and 40 per cent above the levels of the mid-1920s, with increased investments and use of guano fertiliser. Among various factors contributing to the rapid expansion, probably the most important was the rapid improvement in rural credit during the 1930s with the growth of the Banco Agricola.

The experience of the forties was very different. The case of world cotton markets brings out clearly the difference between the First and the Second World War for commodity-exporting countries such as Peru. In the First World War free markets were allowed to operate and wartime shortages of strategic commodities pushed prices up to a very high level, providing worldwide prosperity for commodity exporters and stimulating an immediate expansion of supply. In the Second World War the main participants entered the war with large stockpiles of many primary commodities; the Axis powers had developed extensive synthetics industries to substitute for natural raw materials; and the purchases of materials by Britain and the U.S.A. (the main two buyers for Latin American exports during the war) were handled by government agencies, paying fixed prices determined in bilateral agreements. As a result, prices, although firming as a result of the war, did not exhibit a surge comparable to that of the 1910s, and the export earnings of countries such as Peru rose only slightly during the 1940s. The only product for which wartime shortages in Latin America led to a major price rise was sugar, which we have seen was the leading Peruvian export in terms of value during the 1940s.

Whereas, thus, the First World War had precipitated a long-lasting international crisis of oversupply by stimulating production of cotton, the Second World War had the opposite effect. World production fell from 32 million bales in 1941 to only 22 million by 1947,[40] while world trade in cotton fell by more than half during the war years. By the end of the war, world production had fallen below consumption, and as postwar recovery was stimulated by reflationary policies throughout Europe and by Marshall Plan aid, commodity prices began to rise. Two factors, however, held back the expansion of non-U.S. cotton production: first, the fact that the U.S.A., as the nation financing the Marshall Plan, was in a position to capture for its own producers the European markets thus created, and second, the worldwide food shortages of the postwar period which, in Latin America as elsewhere, resulted in inflation led by food prices. With the relative prices of foodcrops improving, land continued to move out of cotton-growing, while growing world consumption was met by running down wartime stockpiles.[41] When in 1948–9 world cotton production finally began to move upwards again as the postwar food shortages eased, the memory of the 1920s and 1930s remained fresh enough to induce caution among growers, and fears of a new world recession led the U.S.A. in 1949 to reimpose acreage restrictions on the 1950 crop.[42]

How did Peru's experience fit into this world pattern? At first, the outbreak of war in Europe brought serious marketing problems for Peruvian cotton. Until 1940 Britain was the main buyer, taking between 40 per cent and 50 per cent of total Peruvian exports, while up to 1939 other European countries had accounted for a further 35–40 per cent. The war closed the German market immediately, and the remainder of Continental Europe in mid-1940, leaving only the British market.[43] The absence of buyers for either forward or spot cotton in 1939 and 1940 resulted in a local recession which the Government met in part by using the Banco Agricola to finance stockpiling of unsold cotton.[44] In March 1941 the situation abruptly changed when Japan, no doubt in anticipation of its entry into the war, began heavy purchases of cotton, and during 1941 accounted for 59 per cent of cotton exports. This market also was cut off by war at the end of the year.[45]

In early 1942, consequently, an alarmed Peruvian Government demanded assistance from the U.S. and British Governments in marketing Peruvian cotton, in return for Peruvian support against the Axis powers. In April a special agreement was signed with the U.S.A. under which the Commodity Credit Corporation (the U.S. Government buying agency) would guarantee to buy up, and if necessary store, all Peruvian cotton which could not be sold on the open market at above the agreed support price.[46] As part of the deal it was agreed that the support price would be raised one and a half per cent for every one per cent decrease in the area sown to cotton in Peru.

As matters turned out, the 1942 agreement proved less vital than had been anticipated. On one hand, the uncertainties and market difficulties of 1939–41, combined with fear of pests, was already leading to a swing of land out of cotton and into other crops whose prospects looked brighter, including flax[47] (in the valleys around Lima). On the other hand, new markets for Peruvian cotton opened up unexpectedly quickly in other Latin American countries, where the expanding textile industries found supplies from outside South America increasingly scarce.[48] By 1943, Latin American markets (headed by Chile) were absorbing 29 per cent of Peruvian cotton production, while exports to Britain had revived somewhat from the low levels of the early war years.[49] Virtually all Tanguis produced during the years 1942–5 was successfully sold without resort to the U.S. support-buying agreement, and it was the extra-long-staple Pima, grown in the far North, which had to be stockpiled heavily with U.S. money during the war; by 1945, when liquidation began, 98 per cent of the 17,000-ton stockpile consisted of Pima.[50]

The restriction of cotton planting in Peru by government decree followed hard on the heels of the April 1942 agreement. The Government announced that the area planted for the 1942–3 season must be 30 per cent less than that for 1941–2 (the reduction was subsequently modified to 20 per cent). A series of measures over the following years sought to enforce the planting to food crops of fixed minimum percentages of coastal properties. A decree of 1937 had already laid down that all agricultural properties in the Lima area must plant at least five per cent of their area to basic foodcrops; in 1942, as inflation took hold and food shortages developed in Lima, pressure began for generalised measures to force all coastal properties to grow more food.[51] The compulsory reduction of cotton acreage followed, and in 1943 the minimum foodcrop percentage for the entire Coast was raised to 40 per cent.[52]

At the same time cotton, in common with other export products, was subjected to sharply-increased export taxation by the Prado Government. The effect of all the above factors is evident in Table 9.2 (above). The area under cotton, from a peak of 180,000 hectares in 1940, had fallen to 125,000 hectares by 1943, a reduction of 31 per cent, while production suffered a similar decline. Yields in the early 1940s were 10–15 per cent down from the mid-1930s due to the effects of increased pests and disease, combined with the national shortage of guano fertiliser from 1941 on.[53] In short, the profitability of cotton-growing was eroded by low yields, increased taxation, the fixed exchange rate, and stagnant prices. These elements continued to operate through the period of the Bustamante régime, and it was not until 1949 that the area under cotton again began to expand rapidly.

9.3 FISH PRODUCTS: A NEW FIELD FOR LOCAL ENTERPRISE

The story of Peruvian fisheries and fish products belongs chiefly to the next period. As was seen in Table 8.2 above, fish products comprised a mere one per cent of exports in 1945 and as such have little part to play in our discussion of exports in terms of demand and the balance-of-payments before 1948. In terms of local enterprise, however, they were more significant, and must therefore receive brief attention, reserving the main story for Chapter 12.

The first, unsuccessful, proposals for industrialised development of fishing in Peru were made in the 1920s,[54] but it was in 1934 that the first successful cannery was established.[55] By the end of the 1930s three or four enterprises were in production, the main product being canned fish, with fishmeal and fish oil produced as by-products from the cannery residues.[56] Of these first ventures, one grew out of diversification by an Arequipa tannery into the production of sealskins, and another was an experimental venture by a group of leading Lima merchants and financiers. The aim was simply to supply local markets.

The Second World War, however, transformed the market situation for Peruvian fishery products. The war deprived the U.S. market of its main existing foreign suppliers of fish products (Japan and Scandinavia) and by 1942 U.S. firms were actively searching for new sources of supply—especially for canned fish and for fish-liver oil (the main source of Vitamins A and D for U.S. troops). The Wilbur Ellis Company, major U.S. dealers in these products, entered Peru as a buyer, and in the subsequent years until 1946 the small-scale fishing sector earned substantial profits from the production first of fish livers and then (in 1945–6) of smoked and salted fish for the European recovery programme.[57] In several cases these profits were used to finance a diversification into fish canning.

The first and most famous example of such diversification was that of a Lima physician who, having been successful as a fish-liver producer, started a canning enterprise in 1942 with financial assistance from the commercial banking sector.[58] Others followed and, despite wartime shortages of equipment and materials for canning,[59] by 1945 there were 23 canneries in operation along the Coast, of which six were plants of considerable size.[60] The distinctive feature of fish canning, and one which was to reappear in the development of fishmeal in the late 1950s, was that this was an activity with good market prospects and absolutely no barriers to entry, in which entrepreneurs of relatively modest means could hope to succeed.[61] In 1947 and 1948 there was a rush to establish canneries, and by 1950 (even after several of these hopeful ventures had failed) there were 49 plants in operation of which over 15 could be described as large.[62] Not more than two or three of these firms were controlled by the Peruvian élite[63] and only one (although that one was a leader in the industry) involved large foreign capital.[64] The remainder were ventures launched by middleclass entrepreneurs of Peruvian and immigrant origin.[65]

Thus the fishing industry, for all its relative insignificance in quantitative terms, was notable as the most rapidly-expanding area of local enterprise during the 1940s, and ranks with metals mining as a sector which at this time was spawning local firms which would play an important role in the Peruvian economy of later years. As in mining, foreign capital was relatively inactive, so that the field was left clear for local capitalists. However, in contrast to mining, which had attracted élite capital and participation during the 1930s and retained them in the 1940s, fishing embarked on rapid expansion during a period in which large local capital was also refraining from investment outside its established export sectors. This characteristic of the 1940s, which we shall analyse further in the next chapter, meant that in fishing, as in manufacturing industry, the new opportunities were taken up not by long-established capitalists possessed of the means to promote large-scale development, but by relatively small-scale new entrants to the capitalist class—often men from professional or small-scale commercial backgrounds. A certain amount of the finance for these new entrants came through the commercial banking system, and hence ultimately from export-sector profits; but the outstanding characteristic of the 1940s was that the undoubted opportunities which did emerge for diversification in the local economy did not suffice to tempt the upper level of the local bourgeoisie into promotional activity such as they had undertaken in their heyday of the 1890s. The consequent problems for local economic development provide the theme of the next chapter.

10 Economic Policy and the Non-export Economy, 1930—48

10.1 FORCES WORKING FOR AND AGAINST DIVERSIFICATION

In Chapter 3 we analysed the forces which in the 1890s had pushed the Peruvian economy towards increased autonomy and diversification, and suggested several prerequisites for the continuation of the process. Later chapters showed that those prerequisites were not present during the first thirty years of the century, and that the economy consequently drifted back to increased dependence and concentration on export production. As the last two chapters have shown, however, changed circumstances after 1930 revived a number of forces making for increased autonomy. The dominance of export production by foreign firms decreased; local entrepreneurs again became active in the development of several new export sectors; growth became more decentralised; and some of the trends which had made for worsening income distribution in the preceding period were reversed.[1]

To see how much was made of the renewed opportunity, we look first at the strength of the various forces which potentially can sustain and accelerate a shift to autonomy. As we identified them in Chapter 3, these are: a source of economic stimulus (from export earnings, investment, or fiscal policy); relative prices which do not result in a drain of capital and profits from non-export activities; organised interest groups which identify their fortunes with autonomous rather than dependent development; and government policy which, for whatever reasons, acts so as to steer the economy in that direction. We shall now consider which of these were present in the period 1930—48, and in the final two sections of the chapter we shall review the repercussions on industry and food agriculture.

The performance of exports has already been surveyed in the two preceding chapters. To summarise our findings, it is clear that Peru suffered less of a crisis in the World Depression than most other Latin American countries, and that export earnings recovered more rapidly from the Depression. The early revival of both cotton and petroleum exports (the former of special importance in supporting the balance-of-payments) was followed by a wave of local activity in new mining products and a forced pace of expansion of oil output by the IPC. These developments were sufficient to save Peru from the economic extremities suffered, for example, by Chile. They did not, however, suffice to trigger off a new growth boom. The late 1920s in Peru had not been a period of high prosperity, and a recovery of the export sectors' foreign-exchange earnings to the 1929 level did not, therefore, imply a return to a Golden Age. In addition, although the proportion of returned value from exports rose during the 1930s and 1940s, the recovery of exports in the early 1930s was not followed by continued dynamic growth; on the contrary, total export earnings increased at only a modest rate from 1935 to 1948. In part this was due to the continuing depression of certain formerly-important export sectors (particularly copper and sugar) during the 1930s, combined with a serious slump in earnings from cotton in 1938, and in part to the Allied price controls of the war years which discouraged export growth in the following decade.

With exports failing to resume their former dynamic role, what then of government policy? Here we must draw a sharp distinction between the two decades. In the thirties, Peru diverged significantly from the Latin American norm. In many Latin American countries the severity of the crisis in the early 1930s drove governments to adopt policies of the type soon to be identified with the name of Keynes: large budget deficits which sustained the level of demand and aided recovery and diversification, coupled with exchange controls and/or increased tariffs to direct the resulting stimulus towards import-substituting sectors. Such policies in Peru might have supplemented the limited but real gains in export performance, and pushed the economy towards a higher growth rate. In practice, however, the Peruvian Government moved in the opposite direction, with results dramatically apparent in Table 10.1, which shows Peru and Colombia to have been the only major Latin American economies in which government spending declined more rapidly than export earnings during the early Depression years, while even Colombia was ahead of Peru in restoring the role of the government sector in the late 1930s.[2]

To a large extent the political basis for this extremely inappropriate policy choice had been laid by the Leguía régime of the 1920s, with its unrestrained and extremely corrupt programme of foreign-financed public spending which appeared to have done the economy as much harm as good. The overthrow of Leguía in August 1930 was supported both by the conservative traditional élite, who hoped for a return to the days of the 'aristocratic republic,' and by the emerging populist movements of Sanchez Cerro and Haya de la Torre. While these improbable allies disagreed fundamentally over the issue of political power (the result being a short struggle from which the élite emerged

TABLE 10.1 The ratio of government spending to export earnings for six Latin American countries

	Peru	Argentina	Brazil	Chile	Colombia	Mexico
Ratio in 1928	0.82	0.37	0.59	0.50	0.87	0.48

Indices, 1928 = 100						
1932	67	178	193	460	79	173
1936	71	173	112	534	61	127
1940	70	251	178	672	121	181
1944	135	286	164	960	94	266
1948	127	235	122	1690	94	214

Sources: Export earnings from *U.N. Statistical Yearbook*, 1948 and 1949.
Government spending 1937–48 from *U.N. Statistical Yearbook*, 1948 and 1949.
Government spending 1928–36: Peru from *Extracto Estadístico*; Argentina and Chile from consular reports published by U.K. Department of Overseas Trade; Brazil from *Anuario Estadístico do Brasil*, 1939/40, p. 1409; Colombia from *Anuario General de Estadística* (Bogota); Mexico from *Anuario Estadístico de los Estados Unidos Mexicanos*.

triumphant[3]), they were unanimous in condemning the Leguía government, and particularly the fiscal profligacy which had been its trademark. Throughout the worst of the Depression the élite firmly supported fiscal retrenchment,[4] while the populist parties (basicallyAPRA) concentrated on nationalistic rhetoric and pressure for social and political reform. The populist parties, in addition, were themselves uneasy alliances of middle-class and mass interests, with the middle-class wing intensely nervous of radicalism, and readily persuaded to accept a strong and conservative régime when one emerged.

Adherence to such policies was further consolidated by the fact that they could be pursued without the drastic consequences which quickly forced their abandonment elsewhere in Latin America. The reasons were twofold: first, the relatively mild impact of the Depression on Peru, which meant that the export élite were at no point in urgent need of subsidy from the State, and second, the fact that the political and social forces likely to oppose such policies were still in an incipient stage of organisation after the long dictatorship of Leguía.[5] Social pressures were further weakened by the ease with which it was still possible for the urban population to return to or draw support from its rural base.

The assassination of Sanchez Cerro in 1933 opened the Presidency to General Oscar Benavides, a man who embodied élite interests and fiscal conservatism. The general lines of policy, though, had already been established before Benavides entered power. Government expenditure, having fallen 50 per cent between 1928 and 1931 with the cessation of foreign borrowing and the subsequent impact of the Depression on revenues, was cut by another 20 per cent in 1932,[6] while taxes were increased to finance help for the unemployed.[7] It was 1936 before a cautious expansion of public works was begun, and in 1937 government spending was still 25 per cent below the 1928 level in money terms (and considerably lower in real terms).

In summary, so far as economic stimulus was concerned, in the 1930s the export sectors generated only a limited amount, and the Government's fiscal policy partly counteracted what small stimulus there was. Further, relative price shifts did nothing to compensate by diversion of the stimulus towards internal growth, since one result of the maintenance of deflationary policies was that the balance of payments remained in approximate equilibrium through the decade, so that Peru by 1939 had experienced relatively little exchange-rate depreciation and no urgent need for import and exchange controls.

By the 1940s, however, as middle-class interests continued to develop, there was a growing undercurrent of dissatisfaction with this tight management of government spending, since the growth of white-collar urban employment was inevitably restricted by the Government's policies. When Benavides stepped down from power in 1939 his successor, Manuel Prado, was elected on a massive mandate which clearly included fiscal expansion. Prado's belief that the best way to combat the menace of APRA was to buy off the party's middle-class support[8] bore fruit in an abrupt about-face which, as Table 10.1 shows, made Peru during the Second World War one of the leading exponents in Latin America of an expanding government sector. From 1939 to 1948 government spending grew 4.6 times.[9]

This increase in government spending was partly financed by a new willingness to tax traditional export sectors (a result of Prado's urban-financial base). The tax burden on exports rose from 4 per cent of total earnings in 1939 to 14 per cent by 1945.[10] Export sectors were also taxed indirectly; for example, by the requirement that sugar and oil producers should supply the local market at fixed prices in a period of inflation, and by the maintenance of a fixed exchange rate.[11]

The government sector was thus operating after 1940 both to stimulate internal demand and to capture surplus from the export sectors (although the scope for the latter policy was limited by the effect of wartime commodity-price controls on the profitability of Peruvian export production). The availability of surplus for investment was further increased during the war years by the willingness of the labour force to accept a reduction of their share of national income during the wartime inflation,[12] which increased the share of profits in most sectors producing for the local market. Wartime shortages of many lines of imported goods might have been expected to provide a new opportunity for local industries to capture an increased share of the market. In fact, however, the outcome of these various new forces was not a favourable one. The period was characterised by rapid internal inflation;[13] no systematic attempt was made by the Government to manipulate relative prices in favour of non-export sectors; and the share of capital goods in the total import bill (a rough indication of whether internal investment was accelerating or slowing down) fell from 28 per cent in 1938 to 22 per cent in 1943.[14]

It must be admitted that, in certain areas, the Prado régime did initiate significant new promotional policies. An Industrial Promotion Law was passed in 1940, giving the Government a free hand to grant special incentives as and where it wished;[15] in practice the chief beneficiaries under this law were the Prado family's own enterprises and a few large foreign firms (notably the local Goodyear tyre-producing subsidiary, established in 1943[16]). As already described, a state Mining Bank was set up to provide credit assistance to local companies. In addition, in 1944 the Prado Government embarked on a grandiose scheme to develop the Marcona iron ores as the raw material for a large heavy-industrial complex planned for Chimbote.[17] This latter project, however, quickly fell victim to the Government's financial difficulties.

While undoubtedly important, these various policies did not add up to a coherent development strategy. In the absence of such a strategy, the economy's evolution was dominated by two underlying trends: uncertainty in the face of the mounting inflation and wartime problems, which meant that there was no attempt at a broad-based new initiative by local capital; and a revival of U.S. influence in Peru, actively encouraged by President Prado. This policy of close friendship with the U.S.A. was especially noteworthy, considering the relative decline of foreign capital in Peru during the 1930s, and the growth of Peruvian nationalism. It will be recalled that the rise of new locally-owned export enterprises in several sectors had occurred without any confrontation between local and foreign capital, with the result that the established alliance between the local élite and the foreign firms had not been fundamentally shaken. The Second World War, by cutting off many of Peru's former export markets, made the Government very conscious of the value of U.S. assistance—something which was particularly evident in the 1942 agreement for U.S. support buying of Peruvian cotton (see above).

On the other hand, the U.S.A. badly needed the raw materials produced by Peru, as Far East suppliers of products such as rubber, quinine and sugar were cut off, and as the need for mineral products such as copper, vanadium and molybdenum for war industries increased.[18] With the arrival in the Presidency of Prado, a firm friend of the Allies (in contrast to the earlier position adopted by Benavides[19]) the scene was set for a rapprochement. The 1942 support operation for cotton was part of a general trade agreement with the U.S.A.;[20] and it was followed by a lend-lease agreement[21] and a U.S. agricultural mission sent to oversee the development of jungle products such as rubber and quinine.[22] Another U.S. mission in 1941 had investigated the Peruvian fisheries as a possible source of supply of vitamins A and D. A major feature of the war period, thus, was an extension of U.S. influence in Peru, an influence which occurred at all levels: cultural missions, health advisers and military aid as well as economic agreements. This influence helped to cement strong pro-U.S. sympathies, even on the part of the formerly-nationalistic APRA party, which during this period underwent a total turnabout, dropping its attacks on U.S. imperialism, praising U.S. policy, and abandoning its attacks on capitalism in general.[23] The direct result of this dilution of nationalist sentiment during the war was that resistance to future renewed penetration of the local economy by U.S. capital was greatly weakened at the outset—a development which became very evident at the end of the 1940s.[24]

Another result of this growing influence was that the U.S.A. was able to win Peru's acceptance of wartime price controls on raw-materials exports, even in the case of minerals (where Peru's agreements with the U.S.A. reduced export earnings considerably below what could have been obtained on the open market[25]). The forgone profits meant that by the end of the war Peru had gained far less in foreign exchange reserves than had other major Latin American countries (see Table 10.2), while very little real progress had been made towards self-sufficiency.[26]

TABLE 10.2 Increase in foreign exchange reserves, 1940–45
(million dollars)

	Reserves at end of 1940	*Percentage change*
Argentina	430	+156
Brazil	68	+635
Colombia	25	+540
Chile	35	+214
Mexico	59	+480
Peru	20	+ 55

Sources: Ferrero (1946).

10.2 THE COLLAPSE OF CONTROLS, 1945–48

The Presidency of Jose Luis Bustamante y Rivero, elected in 1945 on the basis of an alliance with APRA, was in a sense the culminating political expression of the new social and economic forces which had emerged during the 1930s and 1940s. This was evident in several of the new régime's policies: continued expansion of the government payroll, the adoption of full exchange control in mid-1946,[27] legislated wage rises for organised labour, the determined maintenance of a fixed exchange rate despite a burgeoning black market in dollars, and a strong rhetorical commitment to economic growth. Unhappily for both Bustamante and the proponents of interventionist economic policy, the outcome was a shambles. Bustamante proved totally unable to produce any workable economic strategy which might have served to guide the administration of economic controls. Import licensing (introduced originally by Prado in 1945 as an emergency measure) was retained on a permanent basis as the means of defending the fixed exchange rate (which discriminated against exporting interests); but for the first two years the system appears to have operated entirely without criteria for its application. Only in mid-1947 did the Minister of Finance for the first time propose a detailed set of regulations,[28] at a time when the processing of applications was running six months behind demand. Even with this administrative delay, the number of licences granted consistently outran the available supply of foreign exchange.[29] These delays and shortages converted a policy which was presumably intended to help local industries, into a serious constraint on their expansion. Simultaneously, severe and increasing labour unrest (sparked off both by the increasing power of APRA and by the rising cost of living)[30] led to reduced production and an atmosphere of uncertainty and political tension. Even orthodox elements in the policy proved impossible to implement: Bustamante had several times declared his determination to cut public spending to a manageable level,[31] but when his first Finance Minister, Romulo Ferrero, embarked on a serious attempt to do so, he was at once censured and removed from his post by Congress;[32] no subsequent Minister of Finance seriously resisted fiscal expansion.

The combination of a frozen exchange rate, rapidly-rising internal wages and prices, import duties falling in real terms, and an import control system utterly without priorities or organisation, sufficed to deter the local élite from developing new industries, and to persuade them of the need to protect their more substantial interests elsewhere in the economy (eventually by open opposition to the Bustamante Government). Meantime, price controls had a strongly negative effect on agricultural production (see below), while the squeeze on the export sectors, severe as it was, served no useful purpose beyond that of subsidising urban middle-class consumption. The Banco Internacional summed up the economic climate of 1948 as follows:[33]

> The difficulties with which capitalists, agriculturists, merchants and industrialists have to contend in the development of their activities are

so numerous that the times are unfavourable for undertaking any work of importance.

In default of more positive aspects, the chief consequence of the experiment with interventionist policy was to strengthen the country's subsequent reversion to economic liberalism, and to breed such a resistance to controls in general that as late as the 1960s it was still being claimed that Peruvians would never again attempt such interventionism.

In explaining the total collapse of interventionist policies, it is helpful to begin by considering what the Bustamante government was *not*. In the first place, although we have described it as the peak expression of the new social and economic forces, this should by no means be taken to imply that it was the coherent reflection of a cohesive political base. It is true that the emergence of the National Democratic Front, whose candidate Bustamante was, reflected a desire for recognition of the rights of a broader stratum of the population than heretofore, but other elements were also essential to his election: first his position as Prado's chosen successor; and second the support provided by the conservative oligarchy, who misjudged in some degree the type of policy which was to follow.[34]

Secondly, it rapidly became apparent that the same lack of cohesiveness extended to the composition of the Government: Bustamante, himself an inexperienced politician, swiftly ran into conflict with his APRA-dominated Congress,[35] and by 1947 the situation was described as 'constitutional deadlock.' Congress was suspended in 1948 and the right-wing military coup of October of that year was greeted on many sides with a sense of relief.

In the light of this lack of base and of cohesiveness, the third negative quality of this Government is hardly surprising: the lack of coherent development strategy behind its policy of interventionism. Its peculiar weaknesses lay in two directions, both reflecting its antecedents. First, the impact of the growing U.S. influence depicted in the preceding section could be seen in the strong pro-U.S. and pro-foreign capital sentiments continually expressed both by Bustamante and by APRA. This orientation led among other things to a series of attempts at settlement of the outstanding foreign debt of the Leguía period (defaulted in 1932)[36] and to constant stress in the speeches of both Bustamante and Haya de la Torre on the need for foreign capital to develop the country.[37] Yet the policies of exchange rate, import and price control which were simultaneously implemented ran directly contrary to the philosophy and wishes of foreign capital. Foreign investors, mindful of Peru's pro-foreign investment attitude and rich resources, were described as 'sniffing around like bird dogs,' but without more favourable legislation and more security against controls they were not prepared to commit themselves.[38] The inherent contradictions in the situation were shown up nowhere better than in the crisis over oil policy which was described in Chapter 8, and which was a significant factor in the Government's fall.

Secondly, the interventionist policy could not be based upon existing experience, either of a developed public sector or of extensive controls. This was the heritage of the orthodoxy of the 1930s, in marked contrast to the experience of, say, Chile, where post-war interventionist policy was decidedly more successful, building on both experience and political base.

The lack of whole-hearted commitment to an interventionist policy implied by pro-foreign sympathies and a corresponding sensitivity to foreign pressure, added to the lack of experience with such policies, and the difficulties presented by the ongoing inflation when the Government took office, suffice to explain the total chaos which soon prevailed. In summary, the Bustamante period threw into sharp focus a problem which we shall encounter again in our discussion of the next phase of policy innovation in the early 1970s, namely, the absence in Peru, despite the 'rise of the middle classes' and the development of organised labour, of any single class or coalition of classes whose clearly-perceived interests could provide strategic guidelines for unorthodox policy. In the absence of such guidelines, policy instruments were deployed on an *ad hoc* and often mutually-inconsistent basis, and the reformist pretensions of the Government were swept away on a rising tide of economic crisis.

10.3 INDUSTRIAL PERFORMANCE, 1930–48

It will be evident from the above discussion of economic policy in general that industrialisation did not receive any determined support from government during this period, although certain specific policy measures, combined with outside circumstances such as the Second World War, clearly improved the relative position of manufacturing in the economy. Before going on to analyse how much industrial growth took place, we must first look briefly at certain further elements of policy which directly affected local industry.

The 1930s, despite the political pre-eminence of the export-oriented élite and the relatively slack state of internal demand, did produce some protectionist pressure in Peru. This was particularly evident in the case of imports of Japanese cotton textiles, which began to cause serious difficulties for the local textile industry in 1934.[39] Such competition was particularly strongly resented in view of the fact that the early years of the Depression had been a good period for many import-substituting industries, in contrast to the 1920s, and the textile mills had been operating at full capacity from 1930 to 1932.[40] Since this was an industry dominated by two large and powerful foreign merchant houses, its ability to secure government assistance was unusually great, and in 1935 import quotas were imposed on Japanese textiles.[41] Beneficiaries of this measure included not only the local mills but also U.S. and U.K. suppliers, whose share of the import market for quality textiles had been threatened.[42]

In 1936 a new tariff schedule was introduced, but the effect on the overall level of protection was minimal, the chief purpose of the new system being to consolidate into the scale of basic duties the large range of surcharges which had been accumulating since 1920.[43] The new schedule also confirmed the practice of charging duties on a weight-specific rather than an *ad valorem* basis, which (as we saw in Chapter 6) had already in the 1910s proved a dangerous system to use in periods of rising international prices. It proved so again with the outbreak of the Second World War, which led quickly to a rapid increase in import prices. As a result, despite an all-round 20 per cent tariff increase in 1941,[44] the total revenue from tariffs, as a proportion of the total value of imports, declined from 14 per cent in 1939 to eight per cent in 1945.[45] Not until mid-1947 did a further new tariff schedule come into force restoring the level of tariffs.

Industry was thus almost totally deprived of tariff protection during the 1940s, while the effect of the 1939 devaluation was quickly eroded and then reversed, the exchange rate becoming over-valued and imports consequently (when the necessary exchange was available) relatively cheaper. It might be thought that the general shortages induced by the war would have made the level of Peruvian tariffs irrelevant; but in fact what happened was that the more advanced Latin American economies—particularly Argentina and Brazil—seized upon the opportunity offered by the war to increase their exports of manufactured goods to neighbouring countries such as Peru.[46] Peru, already trailing behind these other economies in terms of industrialisation, provided a market into which they proceeded to expand, while local manufacturing displayed little dynamism; as already noted, the share of capital goods in total imports dropped from 28 per cent in 1938 to 22 per cent in 1943 (see above p. 186).

The lack of attempts to modify the unfavourable relative price situation was obviously partly related, by the 1940s, to such shortages of capital goods. But it was also, and more importantly, related to the continued lack of an industrial class identifying its interests with manufacturing *per se*. This lack was a product of the past weakness of manufacturing development, but also reflected the extent to which the economic élite retained other options throughout these two decades. We have seen the extent of élite involvement in the new local mining companies of the 1930s. Probably even more capital was devoted to real-estate purchases and to construction.[47] Several observers remarked on the rapid expansion of urban construction activity in Lima at the end of

TABLE 10.3 Cement production and consumption, 1929–48
(thousand metric tons)

	Total apparent consumption	Local production
1929	104	49
1930	54	25
1931	40	28
1932	29	21
1933	38	27
1934	60	46
1935	87	60
1936	112	75
1937	137	83
1938	142	101
1939	160	120
1940	143	125
1941	173	168
1942	190	189
1943	208	207
1944	250	249
1945	277	265
1946	289	261
1947	289	256
1948	289	282

Source: *Anuario de la Industria Minera*, 1948, pp. 246 and 249.

the 1930s,[48] a trend which was reflected in the rising sales of cement by the Lima cement plant established in the 1920s (Table 10.3). Table 10.4 provides a further indication of the scope found for investment in construction in the 1940s; the surge of new entrants into the construction industry from 1944 to 1947 shows up clearly.[49] Some capital was also financing the expansion of the public sector, as shown by the extent of sales of government bonds between 1940 and 1944.[50]

Given the above analysis, it is not difficult to predict the patterns revealed by the available statistics of manufacturing industry. Table 10.5 traces the performance of one of the leading import-substituting sectors, cotton textiles; it will be seen that, despite its initially depressed level, output rose only some six per cent annually from 1930 to 1936. Production initially rose rapidly in the early war years but then stagnated as competition from other Latin American manufacturers stiffened.

Table 10.6 indicates that consumer goods as a percentage of total imports fell considerably in the early 1930s, from around 30 per cent to 24 per cent, but that their share then stabilised as substitution ceased.

TABLE 10.4 New companies registered, 1938–47

	Industry		Agriculture		Mining		Construction	
	No.	*S/mil.*	*No.*	*S/ mil.*	*No.*	*S/ mil.*	*No.*	*S/ mil.*
1938	51	4.4	32	5.1	17	3.8	7	4.7
1940	55	2.5	24	2.3	10	1.3	21	1.7
1942	99	14.1	38	16.2	23	8.8	9	1.4
1944	141	46.0	49	11.9	7	0.7	58	39.1
1945	139	36.5	35	8.6	13	6.1	41	19.1
1946	117	30.9	36	30.8	8	2.8	62	59.2
1947	113	36.6	40	22.6	8	6.2	74	74.7

Source: Di Angeli (1949), p. 45 (based on data from the *Boletin de la Cámara de Comercio de Lima*).

TABLE 10.5 Volume of production and consumption of cotton textiles,
1928–45
(indices 1928 = 100)

	Domestic production	*Total consumption*[a]	*Domestic production as percentage of total*
1928	100	100	57
1930	93	97	55
1932	113	96	68
1934	121	127	55
1936	127	123	59
1938	120	114	60
1940	142	118	69
1942	216	139	90
1945	199	123	93

Sources and methodology: See Appendix 4.
[a] Production plus imports of cloth.

The early years of the Second World War saw a temporary further relative fall in consumer-goods imports as local industrial production benefited from shortages; but it is noticeable that the countervailing increase in other categories of imports was concentrated in intermediate goods, not capital goods—industry, in other words, was increasing the utilisation of installed capacity in response to short-run opportunities, but the investment ratio was if anything falling, largely, of course, because of shortages.

TABLE 10.6 Imports: percentage shares at current values, selected categories

	Consumer goods	Textile cloth	Other industrial inputs	Construction materials	Fuel	Capital goods	Total $ values (000)
1928	30	11	26	10	1	14	64,817
1935	24	9	29	7	2	18	43,120
1939	23	5	30	10	1	16	46,432
1942	21	5	39	7	3	14	51,130
1946	23	5	29	9	1	19	123,431

Source: Bertram (1976).

TABLE 10.7 The volume of industrial production, 1938–50

	Total	Export processing	Other consumer goods	Other intermediate goods
Percentage shares in 1938	100	19	65	16
		Indices 1942 = 100		
1938	74	63	79	75
1939	80	67	86	80
1940	87	72	92	87
1941	93	77	98	97
1942	100	100	100	100
1943	100	94	102	101
1944	110	97	114	112
1945	110	97	112	123
1946	112	95	121	122
1947	119	81	130	128
1948	124	81	132	141
1949	136	89	148	151
1950	135	93	144	162

Average annual percentage change, total:

1938–42	9
1942–46	3
1946–50	6

Source: Appendix 4. It is important to note that the methodology used is not accurate enough to allow any significance whatsoever to be given to year-to-year variations. Only the general trend should be considered.

Finally, Table 10.7 presents an index of industrial production for the years 1938—50; it will be seen that there was a spurt of rapid growth in import-substituting manufacturing between 1938 and 1942 under the protection of wartime shortages, exchange devaluation, and the 1941 tariff increase, but that the 10 per cent growth rate of those few years rapidly died out to near-stagnation in the years 1943—7. This pattern is confirmed by the fall in new industrial companies registered after 1944, and by their small size, as shown in Table 10.4 above. Only at the end of the decade were there some further signs of a recovery in the rate of industrial growth.

The pattern was thus clearcut. The early Depression years, with their accompanying balance-of-payments crisis, were good for local manufacturing firms, which had been operating with considerable excess capacity at the end of the 1920s. For several years output of light industries expanded rapidly, resulting in a significant degree of substitution in consumer-goods lines such as textiles, shoes, soap, pharmaceuticals, hats and paint.[51] Growth rates even during this period, however, were below those in other Latin American countries; with the leading sector in Peru, cotton textiles, growing at six per cent a year, it can safely be said that the average for manufacturing as a whole was considerably below this, whereas the overall average rate of industrial growth in Brazil was eight per cent (with the leading sectors far outstripping this) and in Argentina, seven per cent. Furthermore, Peru was beginning from a depressed condition at the end of the 1920s, while Argentina and Brazil were building on relatively advanced manufacturing sectors developed during the 1920s.[52]

During the second half of the 1930s, with local demand growing only slowly and the balance of payments (and hence import capacity) strong, industrial growth slowed again, despite the establishment in 1936 of the Banco Industrial to help new firms.[53] After 1935 the textile industry frequently suffered from excess capacity,[54] and the growth rate of its output was zero in *per capita* terms.[55]

With the Second World War came a new spurt in industrial growth with the emergence of several new industries, particularly tyres, toiletries, condensed milk and some basic chemicals. Three or four years of growth were followed, however, by renewed slowdown after 1942. This slowdown would appear to reflect a number of negative trends: decreasing competitiveness with imports, wartime shortages of machinery and spare parts, and the effects of export stagnation and falling real wages, which counteracted to a considerable extent the expansionary impact of government spending on middle-class incomes.

This general picture is confirmed by an examination of new ventures, which also demonstrates the continued weakness of élite interest in industry and the lack of an industrial class. In terms of ventures which can be described as large-scale, we can identify about a dozen during the period 1930–48.[56] Of these, seven or eight were promoted primarily by foreign capital and only four were backed to any extent by members of the Peruvian élite.[57] Other ventures were of generally lesser scale and promoted by sub-élite entrepreneurs, several of whom did very well for themselves as industrialists, but by the late 1940s these parvenu groups had not coalesced sufficiently to have much impact as an industrial class. Certainly there was no Peruvian equivalent of the new industrialist class emerging in Mexico. In summary, despite the generally slack pace of activity by foreign capital in Peru during the 1930s and 1940s, the half-dozen ventures which foreign firms did launch in manufacturing were nevertheless sufficient to dominate the list of large-scale promotions.

10.4 NON-EXPORT AGRICULTURE

As Chapter 6 has indicated, there was a fairly high elasticity of substitution between export and non-export crops on coastal irrigated land, although not in the Sierra (where apart from wool, no major export products originated). Coffee and cocoa were both products of the *montana* (high jungle). Difficulties for export crops resulting from the Depression might have been expected to lead to a more determined development of coastal production of food for local markets; while the expansion of local aggregate demand in the 1940s in a context of growing balance-of-payments difficulties might have encouraged development even in the Sierra by shifting relative prices in favour of food products. The main purpose of this section will be to explain why neither of these things happened.

To begin with the question of substitution of food for export crops on the Coast, Table 10.8 indicates that the worst Depression years from 1930 to 1932 brought an evident switch of land from cotton and sugar production into other crops (although the absolute figures shown in the Table should be treated with some care). This transfer, however, was quickly reversed by the recovery and subsequent expansion of cotton, described in Chapter 9. The trend was reversed again during the Second World War when cotton was encountering serious marketing difficulties and was subject to government-imposed acreage restrictions; and yet again, from the late 1940s on, as cotton entered a period of renewed expansion (see Chapter 12). Over the fifteen years 1929–44 the irrigated area along the Coast appears to have increased by up to 100,000 hectares, or 25 per cent, while the area under food crops was 67 per cent higher in 1944 than in 1929. Ignoring the fluctuations of the 1930s, this is equivalent to a 3.5 per cent annual increase in the area planted to food crops, while over the same period the area under export crops changed little. The available evidence on yields suggests that the total locally-produced food supply from coastal land cannot have increased much

TABLE 10.8 Area cultivated, 1929–52
(000 hectares)

	Area cultivated on the Coast				Non-Coast
	Total	Cotton & Sugar	Rice	Other	
1929	384	205	47	132	1080
1932	425	173	54	198	n.a.
1938	(450)[a]	244	42	(164)[b]	n.a.
1944	480	181	58	241	1006
1952	538	242	59	237	1138

Sources: Total Coastal area: Twomey (1972), p. 8. Individual crops and total cultivated area: *Extracto Estadístico* (various years), and Ministerio de Fomento (1932).
[a] Interpolated
[b] Obtained by subtraction from the interpolated total.

more than this.[58] Meantime, the total agricultural area in the Sierra did not expand at all, there was very little technical progress in the region, and population pressure inexorably increased.

The overall growth rate of food production was thus modest and for much of the 1930s supply was actually falling. This did not, however, result in any danger signals which might have induced the Government to introduce policies designed to achieve a breakthrough in food production. On the contrary, food imports *per capita* were very low compared to the level of the 1920s (Table 10.9); while food prices, after falling less rapidly than the aggregate wholesale price index during the early Depression years, showed no sign whatever of excess demand pressure during the remainder of the 1930s (see Table 10.10, column 1). This complete absence of pressure on food supplies is the clearest possible evidence of the impact on aggregate demand of the deflationary fiscal and monetary policies pursued throughout the decade. From 1930 to the early 1940s the internal terms of trade were moving steadily

TABLE 10.9 Index of food imports
per capita
(annual average, constant prices)

1925–9	100
1930–4	48
1935–9	60
1940–4	48
1945–8	78

Source (and notes): see Fig. 6.2.

TABLE 10.10 Ratios of price indices, 1929–49
(1934–36 = 100)

	Ratio of non-export food prices to wholesale prices	Ratio of beef prices to wholesale prices	Ratio of export crop prices to wholesale prices	Ratio of retail food prices to cost of living index	Ratio of retail food price index to wholesale food price index
1929	115		102	92	99
1930	121	137	95	95	102
1931	118	128	95	96	100
1932	114	123	89	101	106
1933	96	93	108	97	100
1934	100	101	105	101	99
1935	102	99	96	99	98
1936	104	99	103	101	104
1937	97	95	106	104	107
1938	101	106	107	101	104
1939	100	106	105	96	99
1940	91	101	92	97	100
1941	86	103	80	102	99
1942	75	88	73	102	95
1943	79	105	68	104	92
1944	87		66	103	96
1945	96	127	64	103	97
1946	103	121	68	102	95
1947	104	104	54	109	94
1948	96	88	58	112	100
1949	88	84	60	113	90

Source: Extracto Estadístico

against food products, while the situation for export crops improved due to high cotton prices and the falling exchange rate (Table 10.10, column 3).

Policies of government promotion for non-export agriculture, in consequence, were few and not very significant. The Leguía regime had introduced a protective tariff for rice in 1928, as a result of which cultivation of this crop in the far North expanded rapidly, but by the early 1930s rice was in excess supply.[59] (One result was that the recently-formed Banco Agrícola, after giving some priority to rice farmers in its first year of operation, withdrew its support and concentrated thereafter on credit for cotton-growers.)[60] Food agriculture was supplied with guano fertiliser at preferential prices, which may have somewhat offset the impact of declining terms of trade. Otherwise the only promotional measure of the 1930s was a programme of incentives for increased wheat cultivation,[61] which had no visible impact on either the area under wheat or the average yield.[62]

In the early years of the Second World War, the difficulties of the cotton sector resulted in a major swing back to food production, with a 50 per cent increase in the area under non-export crops along the Coast between 1938 and 1944 (Table 10.8). The most remarkable progress was registered by rice growing (the only subsidised sector). Taking 1935–9 = 100, the yield per hectare rose to 121 by 1940–4 and to 168 by 1945–9[63] –probably mainly the result of the entry of large producers formerly engaged in cotton growing.[64] What is significant about this new surge of food production is that it was in no sense a response to booming markets – as Table 10.10 shows, the internal terms of trade moved even more sharply against food crops in the early 1940s than in the early 1930s. Land was being squeezed out of export production, rather than attracted into food crop production. From the point of view of the Prado Government, this was a remarkably favourable development, since it meant that the expansionary fiscal policies of the early 1940s did not initially encounter any 'food bottleneck' which might have put pressure on the balance-of-payments (as Table 10.9 shows, food imports *per capita* actually fell in the early 1940s). The Government strongly encouraged the switching of land into food crops by decreeing a series of compulsory reductions in export crops (although it is to be doubted that such measures would have had much effect on their own).[65]

Ironically, although Table 10.10 clearly shows that food prices were lagging rather than leading in the inflation of the early 1940s (to some extent, of course, this merely reflected the impact of the price controls described below), it was upon food supplies to the urban market that most attention and policy intervention were directed. Price controls were imposed on food in March 1940,[66] and by the end of the same year food shortages in Lima began to develop.[67] As the situation worsened over subsequent years[68] accusations began to be heard again (as during the First World War inflation) that agriculturalists were unduly concentrating their land on production for export, and that firm controls were needed to enforce the planting of food crops. In March 1942 the Government decreed that the Banco Agricola would buy up several food products at fixed prices, and in May the Government took over rice marketing. These measures were followed by the compulsory reduction in cotton area discussed in Chapter 9. In mid-1943 a cooperative programme was set up with U.S. assistance to promote food production by supplying extension services, and further legislation was passed to raise the minimum food crop acreage on the Central Coast from 10 to 40 per cent.[69]

Shortages in the Lima market persisted despite the increasing scope of government controls over prices, marketing and land allocation.[70] As the above list of measures indicates, the first concern of both the Prado and the Bustamante Governments was to protect urban consumers from price increases, even at the cost of shortages. Tariffs on food imports were reduced or eliminated,[71] and in only one case—rice—did the Government use producer subsidies to mitigate the impact of price controls.[72] For producers of other foodstuffs, profitability fell steadily through the 1940s, and there was therefore no incentive to invest in improvements. Hardest hit by the price controls was beef production,[73] followed by cereals.[74] The controls become tougher still under the Bustamante government, while the growing strength of APRA-backed peasant movements in the Sierra from 1945 to 1947 constituted an additional disincentive for larger landowners.[75]

A 1947 observer commented that

> to produce, distribute and sell basic foodstuffs has become a nightmare, with a pervading and invading bureaucracy enthusiastically competing in driving the planter or distributer crazy until, in despair, he is forced to turn to some other form of activity.[76]

These were problems which affected not only the large land-owners: the incentive for peasant farmers to produce for the market was also greatly reduced in these years. Land reform, thus, although it might have improved the efficiency of utilisation of land in the Sierra, would not have solved the problem of marketed food supplies. It is noticeable that it was at this stage that APRA abandoned its last lingering commitment to agrarian reform, and pinned its hopes on large-scale capitalist development of agriculture.

The years after the Second World War witnessed growing shortages of basic foodstuffs as the price trends of the preceding years took their toll, and by 1947 food prices had at last begun to lead inflation (Table 10.10) while food imports rose threateningly. Beef, which had been 0.3 per cent of total imports by value in 1936, had risen to 3.5 per cent by 1948; wheat and flour were up from 9 per cent to 14 per cent over the same period.[77]

In summary, non-export agriculture failed to prosper except briefly in the early 1930s and possibly the early 1940s, in both cases as a by-product of the temporary decline of cotton. Meanwhile, the impact of government policy on the sector was strongly negative. It should perhaps be emphasised that the above discussion is not to be taken as support for the pure 'monetarist' view of inflation, since although price controls undoubtedly aggravated the food-supply problem of the late 1940s, a policy of price incentives could not by itself have provided any guarantee of rapid development given the existence of other problems for the sector—lack of credit, poor communications and infrastructure, shortages of inputs, and rising peasant unrest.

10.5 CONCLUSION: THE END OF THE EXPERIMENT

Given the disastrous consequences of the policy of intervention with regard to both industry and agriculture, the emergence of irresistible pressures to end it is hardly surprising. Centring around the sugar planters, who as we have shown had renewed their position of economic strength while at the same time suffering acutely from governmental policy, organised resistance built up, involving close cooperation between the élite and foreign capital.[78] A stronger contrast with the incoherence of the Bustamante period could hardly be found than the organised manipulation of policy by the élite after his overthrow.[79] Having supported, if not contrived, the right wing military coup in October 1948, the élite from then on left nothing to chance. A careful watch was kept over policy, and with skilful use of their foreign friends and manipulation of external pressures, the Government of General Odría was gently prodded in the desired direction. Step by step the exchange rate was totally freed in response to pressure, import restrictions were lifted the moment appreciation of the sol appeared likely, and contact maintained with the U.S. advisory mission called in to make recommendations on stabilisation, so as to make sure that the proposed policies tallied with élite interests. Major laws were encouraged guaranteeing and facilitating investment in mining and oil (on these see Chapter 11). By the early 1950s all signs of the 1940s experiment had disappeared, and Peru's system of trade and exchange was the freest in Latin America.

In summary, we have attempted to explain the totality of this commitment to a free economy in terms partly of the weakness of the alternative: the lack of prior progress in diversification, the missed opportunities of the 1930s, the contradictions and inefficiencies of the attempt to diverge from orthodoxy. To this we must now add the fundamental strength of the élite's economic position and the efficiency of their policy making, securely based as it was on a flourishing symbiotic relationship with foreign capital—which relationship is perhaps the key to understanding Peru's persistent adherence to this type of strategy through the ensuing twenty years, to which we now turn.

Part IV
Laissez-faire Export-led Growth: Disillusion and Reaction: 1948–77

Introduction

Peru's brief flirtation with nationalistic and interventionist policies having come to a definitive end in 1948, there now followed a remarkable twenty-year period of total integration into the international system, with complete commitment to the rules of the game. The economy from 1948 until the end of the 1960s was the example *par excellence* in Latin America of that dream of orthodox development economists: an export-led system in which cyclical balance-of-payments difficulties were handled by domestic demand restraint and exchange devaluation, in which the entry of foreign capital and the repatriation of profits were virtually unrestricted and in which government intervention and participation were kept to a minimum. In the 1950s Peru attracted U.S. investment at a rate above the Latin American average; followed to the letter the instructions of the IMF in the cyclical crisis of 1958–9; and hastened to remove the restrictions imposed on foreign trade and exchange markets during the mid-1940s. In the 1960s Peru offered tax and investment incentives of almost unbelievable scope to national and foreign firms engaged in the industrialisation process, while renewed balance-of-payments difficulties were met in 1967 with a major devaluation and effective policies of domestic demand deflation.

The volume of exports rose six per cent a year from 1948 to 1951, 10 per cent a year 1951 to 1959, and 21 per cent a year from 1959 to 1962, before falling back to around five per cent in the mid-1960s. Prices for Peru's main export products held up well during the 1950s and 1960s, with the brief exceptions of the international recessions of 1957–9 and 1966–7. GNP grew in real terms 4.7 per cent a year 1950 to 1959,[1] 8.8 per cent a year 1960 to 1962 as the export boom reached its peak, and thereafter at 3.9 per cent a year till 1968.[2] In *per capita* terms, these growth rates become 2.4 per cent p.a. for 1950 to 1959, 5.9 per cent for 1960 to 1962 and 1.3 per cent for 1963 to 1968.[3]

In short, Peru in 1968 would appear to have been an outstanding example of what could be achieved with orthodox, free-market policies. In that year the military seized power, announced their rejection of the *laissez-faire* growth model pursued up to that date, and embarked (with remarkably little opposition) upon a series of expropriations and controls which rapidly converted Peru into a State-dominated economy where foreign capital trod warily.

In terms of our initial framework, therefore, the period is of exceptional interest. Did the strength of export-led growth prove enough to spill over into a broader development of the economy? Or, as our analysis of earlier periods would lead us to predict, was there an increase in foreign domination and a weakening of forces making for autonomy? If so, was this related to the unusually violent reaction against the orthodox model seen in post-1968 economic strategy? What relation did the military's diagnosis bear to the underlying economic problems, and within what degrees of freedom has the new strategy been able to operate?

We shall find that this phase of export-led growth was considerably more complex than past phases. The interplay between underlying changes in the economy and society, policy-making and the changing interest of the multinationals, led to a significant structural shift in the economy, as analysed in Chapter 13, focusing upon the expansion of the industrial sector. This belated swing towards industrialisation, however, reflected not so much a major advance towards increased capacity for autonomous development, as the incorporation of Peru, along with the rest of Latin America, into the pattern which has been much discussed in recent years under the heading 'the new dependence'—industrialisation promoted by multinational firms, concentrating on consumer goods, heavily import-dependent, using imported technology and brand names, and achieved at the expense of major distortions in local markets. The economy's dependence upon export performance as the principal source of dynamism was not reduced, although in the 1960s (as in the 1870s and 1920s) increasing recourse to foreign borrowing made possible a rapid expansion of the government sector. Income distribution became more unequal through the period, while the aggregate savings and investment ratios (which according to some development theories should have been raised by such regressive income trends) dropped steadily from the mid-1950s on.

This last point, the decline in the investment rate, will emerge as crucial to an understanding of the underlying crisis of the late 1960s. In sector after sector we shall encounter evidence of an initially dynamic performance by local and foreign capital up until the late 1950s; thereafter, in sector after sector, new investment and promotional activity begins to fall, and we witness the 'decay of the national bourgeoisie' (a familiar theme of Peruvian social commentary during the 1960s).

Although the decay of investment also affected foreign firms, the impact was less striking, and during the 1960s, in consequence, the visible dominance of economic activity by foreign capital increased greatly. Our sector-by-sector discussion will indicate that the investment problem was caused not by any shortfall in the supply of *ex ante* savings, but by increasing constraints on profitable investment opportunities in the major productive sectors, as export growth for the first time began to encounter serious physical or structural bottlenecks, while non-export agriculture stagnated under the influence of adverse policy bias and growing rural unrest, and industrial growth was ever more closely linked with monopolistic competition among foreign firms. The resulting problems in the fields of production and investment, together with the impact of worsening income distribution, increasing dualism, fiscal crisis, and reviving nationalism, are reviewed in Chapter 14, which also discusses the analysis of these problems offered by contemporary Peruvian analysts, particularly the military. Chapter 15 then turns to the years following the coup of 1968, as the new military regime sought to come to grips with the economy's problems. First, however, we must turn in Chapters 11 and 12 to the continuing mainspring of the economy: the export sectors.

11 The Export Sectors, Part 1: the Extractive Industries

Table 11.1 demonstrates the sources of the rapid growth of exports which characterised the period 1948 to the mid-sixties. The expansion can be seen to have rested upon the recovery of copper and the development of new export products. The four most important such products (lead, zinc, fish products, and iron) had accounted for less than 7 per cent of total export earnings in 1930 (see Table 8.3). This rose to 15 per cent by 1950, 28 per cent by 1960, and 46 per cent by 1970. The corresponding relative decline of other export commodities first affected oil, which dropped from its position as the leading export in the 1930s to complete insignificance by the 1960s; and later the traditional agricultural products, cotton and sugar. The reasons for, and the implications of, these shifts in the relative importance of various commodities form the subject of this Chapter and the next. It is of interest to note at this

TABLE 11.1 Volume, value and composition of exports, 1945–74.

	Percentage share of total exports, current values							Export Indices (1929 = 100)	
	Cotton and sugar	Wool and coffee	Fish products	Copper and silver	Lead and zinc	Iron	Oil	Dollar earnings	Quantum index
1945	52.9	3.3	0.9	9.6	7.4	–	12.5	89	95
1950	50.5	4.6	2.9	9.4	11.7	–	13.1	165	103
1955	38.8	5.1	4.4	16.9	14.8	3.0	8.2	231	152
1960	27.8	5.9	11.5	27.5	8.9	7.6	4.1	370	283
1965	18.6	5.7	27.8	24.0	11.1	7.0	1.4	569	352
1970	11.2	4.6	32.2	31.5	7.8	6.3	0.7	894	395
1974	16.8	3.5	15.6	33.7	14.9	4.0	0.2	1297	306

Sources: Current values, 1945: *Estadística del Comercio Especial*. 1950 to 1970: Banco Central de Reserva, *Cuentas Nacionales*, 1950–67. 1974: *Boletín del Banco Central de Reserva*, Mar. 1975.
The data for the dollar earnings index are from *Anuario Estadístico del Perú*, 1934–1935 and BCR *Boletín*, June 1975. For the quantum index, see Table 12.9 below.

stage that the outcome of the changes in export composition from 1950 to 1972 was not the same as that which we have already discussed for the period 1890–1930. Whereas in the earlier period mineral exports became steadily more dominant relative to agricultural exports, with a corresponding trend toward dominance by foreign capital, during the period 1950 to 1970 this trend was much more muted, consisting mainly of the return of copper and silver to around one-third of total exports, from a low point of 10 per cent in the 1940s, and the development of iron exports, the bulk of which were produced by a new foreign firm. Offsetting these gains for foreign-dominated sectors (to which should be added a gradual increase in the proportions of lead, zinc, sugar and fish products produced by foreign firms) were two trends which were of fundamental importance to the export economy: the decline of oil, and the rise of fish products, the latter sector having been the most spectacular success story for local capital in Peru since the Second World War. As Table 11.2 indicates, the effect of these two developments was to maintain an approximate 50–50 balance between exports of mineral products and exports of 'agriculture-livestock-fishery' products, throughout the period from 1955 to 1972. As Chapter 12 describes, however, the fishmeal industry suffered a drastic collapse of production in the latter year, while other traditional agricultural staples were already in relative decline (see Table 11.2, Column 1). Meantime, the great bulk of the future growth of exports is expected to be in mineral production, suggesting that by the 1980s the balance will have swung

TABLE 11.2 Percentage breakdown of export earnings,[a] 1945–72

	Exports of 'traditional' commodities			Other ('non-traditional')[b]
	Crops	Livestock and fisheries	Minerals	
1945	60	5	33	2
1950	54	8	36	2
1955	45	8	44	3
1960	35	13	50	2
1965	24	30	45	1
1970	16	32	50	3
1972	18	29	47	6

Sources: 1945 to 1965 from *Estadistica del Comercio Especial*. 1970 and 1972 from the Ministry of Industry and Commerce, *Estadistica de Comercio Exterior, 1969–72*.
[a] Components may not total to one hundred due to rounding.
[b] The column for 'other' was obtained as a residual 1945–65. Metallic gold and money have been excluded.

decisively in favour of mineral sectors. The problem of ensuring that this swing does not lead to the same consequences as in the 1920s (see Chapters 5 and 6) has posed one of the central policy preoccupations of the post-1968 military regime.

11.1 THE MINING SECTOR, 1948–70

The fifties: the return to foreign domination
It will be recalled that we left the mining sector in the forties with the large foreign companies just recommencing expansion and consolidating their control of the largest deposits. The 1948 coup and the subsequent liberalisation of the exchange rate and of imports accelerated the investment plans of both local and foreign companies, and pressure was successfully brought to bear[1] to produce a new Mining Law. This was introduced in 1950, and liberalised the tax system applied to mining, as well as incorporating several special provisions of direct benefit to foreign capital.[2] The inflexible and increasingly heavy export taxes were replaced by taxes on net income, with generous allowances for depreciation and depletion. In addition to reducing the industry's Peruvian taxes, this change made it possible for U.S. companies to offset their Peruvian tax payments against their U.S. income tax liabilities, under double-taxation agreements.[3] Tax stability was guaranteed for 25 years. The best known of the provisions was Article 56, which authorised the Government to grant sweeping tax exemptions to companies which developed 'marginal' (high risk) ore deposits, in order to permit rapid amortisation of the initial investment.

Expansion was favoured not only by the new régime but also by good prices until 1957. Lead and zinc in particular were assisted by the U.S. Government's policy of strategic stockpiling of these metals, which kept prices artificially high. The ending of that policy in 1957 greatly intensified the effect on Peru of the world recession of 1957–9; the result was two years of poor metals prices which seem to have had a serious effect on local investment confidence, as we see below. In the meantime, however, expansion was rapid, particularly in the production of lead and zinc (see Table 11.3). The 1948 relaxation of exchange and import controls was followed immediately by a rush of new Peruvian mining companies to acquire and install mining and concentrating equipment, as local owners of small and medium-scale deposits followed the example of the pioneering local enterprises of the 1930s. Local companies held the lead in the development of non-ferrous metals production during the first half of the 1950s; in 1956, local companies accounted for 62 per cent of lead production and 47 per cent of zinc.[4] Of 24 significant new entrants into lead and zinc production between 1949 and 1953, only two were not locally controlled and financed.[5]

TABLE 11.3 Volume of production of six metals,[a] 1945–69
(annual average output; indices, 1929 = 100)

	Copper	Silver	Gold	Lead	Zinc	Vanadium
1945–9	46	62	112	249	490	169
1950–4	61	96	115	434	989	161
1955–9	92	138	149	592	1245	6
1960–4	332	186	121	650	1523	–
1965–9	362	197	83	733	2310	–

Source: annual mining statistics.
[a] Iron is excluded from this table since production began only in 1953.

The early 1950s stand out as a high point of local mining entrepreneurship in Peru,[6] largely because a backlog of investment opportunities had built up during the shortages and controls of the 1940s, when capital equipment was unobtainable and export prospects uncertain. The undeveloped deposits held by local interests were capable of rapid development once controls eased, and so it was that these projects took the lead after 1948. At the same time, however, the pendulum had already begun to swing towards renewed dominance of future mining development by foreign capital. The foreign firms held most of the country's very large deposits, which required a long gestation period before they could be brought fully into production, and it was into these giant projects of the future that foreign capital now began to move, beginning with the copper deposit of Toquepala.

The Toquepala project had been in the planning stage since 1948, when ASARCO established legal title to the property. In 1952 ASARCO set up a new company, Southern Peru Copper Corporation (SPCC) with three minority partners, including Cerro.[7] In 1954 a special contract was signed with the Government under Article 56 of the Mining Code, providing that SPCC would pay only a 30 per cent tax on net income until accumulated *net* profits (i.e. profits *after* subtraction of depletion and depreciation allowances) equalled the initial investment required to bring the mine into production. This simple drafting error[8] passed unnoticed at the time, since the tax rate specified was not significantly lower than that applying to all other mining companies in 1954. SPCC proceeded to arrange financing both from its shareholders and from the U.S. Export-Import Bank, and development work on the mine lasted for five years, production beginning early in 1960.

Meantime Cerro was rapidly developing its lead-zinc ores at Cerro de Pasco and Casapalca, and at the end of the 1950s began open-pit operations at the former mine. In the mid-1950s, however, even Cerro's expansion was eclipsed by the entry into production of the iron mines of Marcona.[9] The Marcona deposits had been known since the early twentieth century, and had several times been the subject of State-financed feasibility studies as the possible basis for a national iron and steel industry. The area was declared State reserve in 1929, and in 1945 was handed over to the Santa Corporation, a State enterprise set up by the Prado government to establish an iron and steel complex (see Chapter 10 above). Under subsequent presidents the Corporation had been accorded low priority and few funds, and by 1951 was practically bankrupt, and quite unable to finance the development of Marcona by itself.[10] In 1952 a 21-year contract was signed with the newly-formed Marcona Mining Company, the dominant participant being Utah Construction Company. The list of minority shareholders included the Prado family (whose links with the Santa Corporation had remained).[11]

The expansion of these and other projects, especially the growth of Cerro, brought a reversal of the previous trend towards local control of mining development. As shown in Table 11.4, the share of the five largest foreign firms in the final output of the sector reached a low point of 49 per cent of metals output by 1950, but by 1960 had risen to 73 per cent. The reasons for this reversal have in part already been indicated. We noted earlier that the new local mining enterprises of the 1930s and 1940s were able to establish themselves only because the foreign firms active in Peru during the first thirty years of the century had been selective in their purchases of mineral deposits, and had not taken control of most of the second-rank deposits of gold, lead and zinc. These deposits were consequently accessible to independent capitalists, and so long as the first-rank deposits were held out of production, or worked at

TABLE 11.4 Shares of five large foreign firms in metals output, 1945–70 (percentages)

	Cerro share of		Northern Peru Mining	Vanadium Corp- oration	Marcona	Southern Peru Copper	Total share of	
	Final output	Mine output					Final output	Mine output
1945	58	23	5[a]	2	–	–	65	29
1950	42	35	6	1	–	–	49	42
1955	38	37	6	n.a.	12	–	56	55
1960	25	17	2	–	11	34	73	65
1965	30	22	2	–	13	27	72	64
1970	24[b]	17	2	–	14	33[c]	73	66

Source: Calculated from data in *Anuario de la Industria Minera* for years shown. For methodology see notes to Table 8.4.
[a] Upper-bound.
[b] Including all smelted and refined gold and silver with the exception of 'lavaderos'.
[c] Excluding gold and silver which could not be disaggregated, and are all attributed to Cerro in this year.

a low level, the independents could capture the lead in terms of output. In the long run, however, access to deposits of first rank was essential if local mining enterprise were to escape from its confinement to a relatively small scale of operation. Only a nationalistic policy which broke the hold of foreign capital on the largest natural-resource assets could have opened the way for national enterprise to attempt a great leap forward.

That such a policy was unlikely to emerge is of course immediately obvious. Peruvian mining law had no tradition of expropriating unworked deposits, or even of penalising the owners of concessions for failure to develop, so that foreign firms were able to hold enormous areas 'in reserve.' The new Mining Law of 1950 made only the most feeble and ineffective gestures towards remedying this state of affairs. Neither the Odría administration nor its predecessors could have been expected to embark on the confrontation with foreign firms and governments which expropriations would have provoked; and in any case domestic political pressure for such a policy was entirely absent. Peruvian mining companies were perfectly happy to remain satellites of the foreign firms.

In some cases, of course, even freeing the access to mineral deposits would have made no difference—the development of Toquepala would never have been attempted by any private firm other than the international giants, though it need not have been developed on such generous terms. In other cases, foreign control obviously closed off alternative development options; this was particularly the case with the smaller copper deposits such as Cerro Verde, Magistral, Ferrobamba and Antamina, all of which have been since 1970 the subjects of State development projects.

The test case, and the most revealing case study, was the sole deposit of enormous scale and proven richness that had remained out of foreign hands: the Marcona iron ores. Development costs, at $8–10 million (see below), were modest for a mine of this size, and should have been well within the State's borrowing capacity. It seems probable that the decision to bring in private foreign capital was due more to the Odría régime's ideological distaste for State intervention in the economy than to any careful assessment of costs and benefits to Peru; but it must also be emphasised that Peruvian mining capitalists raised no objections to the 1952 Marcona contract and made no attempt to lobby for access to the deposits for themselves (although the success of this venture did encourage a group of Peruvians to invest in a subsequent iron-mining venture at Acari). Certainly the Marcona venture called for 'entrepreneurship'—the idea of bulk exports of iron ore over long distances was a relatively new feature in the world economy—and certainly also the close connections which the new Marcona Mining Company enjoyed with the U.S. steel industry helped it to secure

markets for its ore. There were, in other words, advantages enjoyed by
the foreign firm, which in the eyes of the Peruvian government of the day
sufficed to outweigh the relatively low returned value characteristic of
foreign-owned mining developments. But none of the obstacles to
Peruvian control of Marcona were insuperable, and it can be assumed
that had there been no foreign bidder for the deposits, some means
would have been found to develop them.[12] In this sense, the issues raised
by the Marcona contract are directly comparable to those raised by the
sale of the mines at Cerro de Pasco in 1901, discussed in Chapter 4.

Despite the resurgence of the foreign-controlled sector, however, the
spread effects from mining in the fifties were still considerable. This was
due in the first place to the prosperity of locally-controlled companies
with high returned value, which provided a market sufficiently promising to induce several Lima engineering works to move into the
production of simple capital goods for the sector—especially equipment
for flotation concentrators. As had previously occurred in the 1890s,
therefore, locally-controlled development provided a boost to the
domestic capital-goods industry. In the second place, the linkages
between Cerro (the oldest-established foreign mining firm) and local
suppliers increased very rapidly in the 1950s, the company having had
several decades to settle into the local scene and establish contacts
throughout the economy (in addition to which Cerro itself began to
diversify into the production of materials for the mining sector at this
time).[13] This new element in Cerro's operations emerges clearly in Table
11.5, which shows Cerro's returned value to have risen from around 58
per cent of gross earnings in the 1930s to 76 per cent by the 1960s, a rise
attributable almost entirely to the increase in local purchases of supplies
(while the rising share of taxation was offset by a falling share of wages).
By the late 1960s Cerro had participated in the establishment of several
backward-linkage projects supplying the mining sector[14] as well as in
forward-linkage ventures to utilise the output of the Oroya smelter.[15]

The sixties: the changing economic climate and its repercussions
The new entrants Marcona and SPCC were, however, very different,
being conspicuous for their high import propensities, high profits and
high repatriation rates. Their weight in the total was slight initially, but
by the 1960s, with both mines in full production, the scene was changing.
As important as the direct economic impact of these foreign firms was
their visibility, which contributed significantly to the changed atmosphere of mining development in the 1960s. Each was the subject of an
official commission of enquiry into allegations of excessive profit
repatriation.[16] In both cases the allegations were substantially upheld,
and subsequent studies by Lindqvist and Hunt indicate that figures
made public by both companies deliberately understated actual profit
rates—in the case of Marcona, by the underpricing of exports and use of

TABLE 11.5 Changes in Cerro's returned value, 1925–68
(percentage of gross dollar earnings[a])

| | Local expenditures by Cerro on | | | | Total returned value | Gross earnings (million dollars) annual average |
	Labour	Taxes	Custom ores and freight charges	Other supplies and services[b]		
1925–9	24	5	24	3	56	22.5
1930–7	33	7	17	2	58	10.6
1950–6	22	12	——27[c]——		61[c]	52.0[d]
1959–68	21	14	30	12	76	99.4
1971–2	26[e]	10[e]	29[f]	14[g]	79	141.5

Sources: 1925–37 from Table 5.6 and sources cited there. 1950–68 constructed from information supplied by the Lima office of Cerro Corporation. 1970–2 wage and tax data supplied by Cerro; custom ores and supplies from *El Comercio* (Lima), Jan. 1, 1973; gross earnings is the value of metals output as given in *Anuario de la Industria Minera*, 1970, pp. 5–6, 1971, pp. 5–6, and 1972, pp. 10–11.
[a] Percentage totals may not add exactly due to rounding.
[b] Including purchases of property.
[c] Total for returned value in this period is the total of dollars exchanged for soles plus payments made locally in dollars. 'Supplies and services' were obtained as a residual using this total.
[d] Sales only; 'other income' not available. For 1959–68, 'sales' were 98 per cent of gross earnings; hence any error will be minor.
[e] 1970–1.
[f] Ores only.
[g] Materials and capital goods.

accumulated gross investment (rather than investment net of depreciation and depletion) in calculating rates of return (as section 11.2 below notes, similar tactics were used by IPC in the late 1950s and early 1960s).

Both Marcona and SPCC were large capital-intensive operations. Evidence on their returned value is unfortunately somewhat incomplete, but some estimates are possible. To begin with SPCC, this company's operations over its first six years of production, 1960 to 1965, were subjected to detailed scrutiny by the 1966 congressional investigation, the source for the figures in Table 11.6.[17] Considering that it was now forty years after the golden age of petroleum exports in the 1920s when, as we have seen in Table 5.9, the foreign oil companies returned 19 per cent of their earnings to the local economy, it is striking to find that SPCC (the largest single development in mineral export production in Peru after the Second World War) recorded a returned value of only 21 per cent over its first six years of production, of which taxes accounted for no more than 7 per cent.[18] The regulation of large foreign capital in Peru had hardly toughened over the long run. Of foreign factor

TABLE 11.6 Returned value of Southern Peru Copper Corporation, 1960–5
(percentage of dollar value of sales)

	Local expenditures on			Total returned value	Expenditures abroad		Value of sales (million dollars)
	Labour	Taxes	Materials and services		Imports	Factor payments	
1960	6.9	5.4	5.5	17.8	22.1	60.1	72.3
1961	6.9	6.7	5.4	19.1	21.8	59.1	78.9
1962	9.0	4.5	5.7	19.2	22.9	57.8	65.1
1963	9.0	5.7	6.0	20.7	24.1	55.2	70.6
1964	10.1	6.5	5.8	22.4	23.1	54.5	72.9
1965	9.5	10.3	5.3	25.1	21.3	53.6	89.1
TOTAL	8.6	6.7	5.6	20.9	22.5	56.6	448.9

Source and Notes:

The figures were taken from Comisión Bicameral Multipartidaria, (1967), Anexo 23, and allocated where necessary using assumptions copied from Malpica (1968), p. 183, as follows:

Local payments to labour are the wage and salary bill in soles, plus 50 per cent of the salaries paid in dollars (i.e. the propensity of dollar receivers to spend locally assumed to be 0.5).

Taxes are assumed to have been entirely paid to the Peruvian as distinct from the U.S. government.

Factor payments abroad comprise net profits, depreciation, depletion, amortisation and interest, plus 50 per cent of the salaries paid in dollars.

Sales are as reported to the Peruvian government; it is not clear whether the figures are fob or cif, but circumstantial evidence (and comparison with valuation data in *Anuario de la Industria Minera*) tends to suggest the former. In any case, we assume that the 20–80 allocation of the residual item (see below) incorporates foreign freights if necessary.

Purchases of materials and services are taken as a residual, subtracting all identified items from sales. This residual is then assumed to be 20 per cent local purchases and 80 per cent imports (Malpica (1968), p. 183). We have accepted this estimate of Malpica's on the assumption that he had access to evidence from the investigation. It should be noted, however, that SPCC data for 1960 reproduced in *Peruvian Times*, Apr. 21, 1961, p. 3 stated that of $17,870,000 of purchases of materials and supplies, 60 per cent was spent locally. Applying this proportion to our data for 1960–65 would raise aggregate returned value to 32 per cent.

It should be noted that our results do not match exactly with those given by Malpica (1968), p. 183, owing to a double-counting error in his calculation of foreign factor payments; nor with the figures used by Lindqvist (1972), p. 226, since he does not use our assumption that 50 per payments totalling $254 million over the six years, the servicing of SPCC's loan from the Export-Import Bank absorbed roughly $40 million, and our estimate of foreign salary payments (50 per cent of dollar salaries paid) accounts for another $8 million. $206 million (46 per cent of the total value of sales) thus remained for the shareholders; of this, the company reported to the U.S. government that $135 million was net profit (the figure supplied to the Peruvian government was $69 million), the remainder being allocated to depreciation and depletion reserves.[19] Investment in the mine up to 1965 had totalled $250 million, of which $115 million came from an Export-Import Bank loan and the remaining $135 million represented funds committed by the shareholders.[20] The mine more than paid for itself in its first five years, and was widely regarded as one of the most profitable in the world. All loan commitments were paid off and dividend payments begun in 1966.[21]

The available information on Marcona has been assembled and discussed by Lindqvist and Hunt in attempts to determine the true rate of return on the company's investment.[22] Unfortunately, their figures do not enable us to derive usable estimates of returned value, and efforts to assemble detailed figures from the official mining statistics proved unavailing.[23] In Appendix 3, however, we have assembled data on the distribution of reported total income of the mining sector in Ica from 1963 to 1972 (of which Marcona accounted for 94 per cent during the years 1963–6) which form the basis for a provisional estimate of 50 per cent as Marcona's returned value.

The significance of these figures is obvious, in the light of our previous discussion of the effects of the rise of Cerro and Northern Peru Mining during the first decade of the century. Table 11.4 shows the share of Marcona and SPCC in metals production to have risen from zero in 1950 to 45 per cent by 1960; given their relatively low returned value, it is clear that the gains to the local economy from the rapid expansion of mineral exports were less than might appear at first sight. The aggregate estimates are shown in Table 11.7, where it will be seen that while gross output rose 227 per cent in dollar terms, the rise in returned value was only 174 per cent—still very rapid, but indicating the effect of increasing foreign control, as had previously occurred in the first thirty years of the century. However, it will be noted that the problem was not nearly so drastic as on the previous occasion, due to (*a*) the survival and continuing expansion of independent mining firms in the small and medium sectors (accounting for a consistent 30 per cent of output in the 1960s), and (*b*) the steadily-increasing returned value of Cerro, which helped to offset the extremely poor contribution of SPCC.

Another important implication should also be noted here. This was that, given the relatively low returned value of the recent foreign entrants, it was obvious that there was scope for increasing the local economy's participation in the benefits from these projects by govern-

TABLE 11.7 Aggregate returned value of mining, 1952–73

	Gross value of output (*$ million*)	Percentages of gross value of output				
		Wages & salaries	*Taxes & royalties*	*Other local factor payments*	*Local purchases*	*Total returned value*
1952	106					72
1960	228					53
1965	347					60
1966	373					63
1971	440	26	15	10	25	76
1973	791	21	19	19	22	81

Sources: For 1952–65, see Appendix 3; for 1966, *Peruvian Times*, Aug. 11, 1967, p. 9; for 1968–73, *La Mineria en el Peru*, 1975, p. 183.

ment action. In contrast to the 1920s, the Belaunde Government in the 1960s reflected the greater weight of sub-élite and nationalist groups, and in 1964 the Government moved to increase the income tax on mining companies.[24] Both Marcona and SPCC immediately came under close scrutiny from official commissions, and after some acrimonious public debate and a great deal of private negotiation, the Government succeeded in renegotiating the Toquepala contract in 1968, raising the company's tax from 30 per cent to 51 per cent of net profits.[25]

The impact of these and other government measures designed to push up the returned value from the mining sector is evident in Table 11.7, which shows the proportion of returned value to have risen from 53 per cent in 1960 (our estimate) to 63 per cent by 1966, 76 per cent by 1971, and a remarkable 81 per cent by 1973, under further pressure from the military régime. This of course was by itself equivalent to a 47 per cent increase in production, so far as the local economy was concerned. The rise in returned value, combined with very strong minerals prices in the late 1960s and early 1970s, helped to mask an underlying trend which had serious implications for long-run development of the sector, namely the dramatic slowing-down of new activity and investment in the decade following the recession of 1958.

This slowdown had two dimensions: firstly, a loss of dynamism among local firms in the small and medium-scale sectors, and secondly an investment strike by foreign firms in the *gran mineria*. We shall begin by considering the latter. The discussion of the development of Toquepala has already indicated that foreign companies, by persuading the Government to grant them special contracts as 'marginal operations' under the 1950 Mining Code, could obtain access to Peruvian mineral deposits under terms of extreme liberality, and hence profitability. The problem was that by the 1960s a growing section of articulate Peruvian opinion was taking note of the historical lessons of IPC and Cerro, as well as of the more recent performances of SPCC and Marcona. Just as in the 1940s the development of the oil industry had been blocked by the reluctance of the Prado and Bustamante governments to grant concessions to foreign firms and thereby risk nationalist criticism, so in the 1960s the willingness of Peruvian governments to invoke Article 56 for the benefit of foreign mining companies was increasingly limited. Since the companies, having observed the success of Toquepala, considered it worthwhile to hold out for equal treatment with SPCC, virtually all major new projects were held in abeyance while the companies waited for the Government to become more accommodating. This affected Anaconda's copper deposit at Cerro Verde, SPCC's copper deposits of Quelleveco and Cuajone, ASARCO's copper deposit at Michiquillay (purchased in the early 1960s from the discoverer), and a string of deposits owned by Cerro—Antamina, Tintaya, Ferrobamba, Magistral, Chalcobamba. During the 1960s the only major new mine to be brought into production was Cerro's Cobriza, exploitation of which was required to maintain the company's copper-smelting operations at Oroya at full capacity. Relations between the companies and the Government were not improved by the 1964 tax increase and the subsequent political scandal over Toquepala, and the stalemate persisted until the last months of the Belaunde régime, when it appeared that the Government was finally moving to meet the companies' demands;[26] the military coup, however, intervened and the new Government hardened the terms, the result being that the first contract (for Cuajone) was not agreed until late 1969,[27] while none of the other pending projects had been launched by the end of 1970 (when all undeveloped deposits were expropriated).

This lengthy investment strike did not initially affect the expansion of output, because of the long gestation periods characteristic of large-scale mining development. Of the expansion of mining output between 1952 and 1965, 40 per cent was accounted for by Toquepala, 22 per cent by the Marcona and Acari iron mines, and 27 per cent by expansion at Cerro. Because these projects followed one another very rapidly, the discontinuity of mining expansion was not immediately evident; but once the flow of new giant projects dried up, the long-run impact on growth of mining output was serious. By 1965–6 Peruvian mining production had reached a plateau (see Table 11.8), and with the large deposits whose development was technically feasible being kept in mothballs by the large foreign companies, expansion during the subsequent decade proceeded at a relatively slow pace.

The delay is not to be explained by depressed market conditions; world copper prices soared during the 1960s in response to the demand of the U.S. armaments industry, and Toquepala proved far more profitable even than expected. What was holding up the new generation

TABLE 11.8 Quantum index of mining output: six main metals, 1948–74 (1960 prices; all figures as percentages of 1960 total)

	Copper	Silver	Lead	Zinc	Iron[a]	Gold	Total
1948	4.8	3.5	4.3	3.5	–	1.7	17.9
1950	8.0	5.1	5.4	5.3	–	1.9	25.8
1955	11.6	8.8	10.5	10.0	5.0	2.6	48.4
1960	48.6	11.7	11.6	10.7	15.2	2.1	100.0
1965	48.3	13.9	13.6	15.3	22.3	1.6	115.0
1970	59.0	15.2	13.8	18.0	29.0	1.6	136.6
1974	63.2	16.1	17.2	24.8	25.1	1.6	147.9

Cumulative annual growth rates of total index:

1948–50	20.2
1950–5	13.4
1955–60	15.6
1960–5	2.8
1965–70	3.5
1970–4	2.0

Sources: *Anuario de la Industria Minera*, various years, and *La Minería en el Perú*, 1975, pp. 175 and 178.
[a] Exports.

of mining projects was simply the unwillingness of the multinational firms to commit more capital to Peru during the 1960s, apart from relatively small sums put into exploration and survey work. Given their global strategies the companies were happy to hold back until offered the right terms.[28] In addition to the country's copper deposits, similar factors delayed the development of the large phosphate deposits at Bayovar, controlled from 1963 by Texada Mines Ltd and from 1967 by Kaiser Aluminium.[29]

While new investment in large-scale mining fell during the 1960s, an even more dramatic loss of dynamism was displayed by local mining capitalists, who had led the sector's expansion from the 1930s to the mid-1950s. The turning point seems to have been the collapse of lead and zinc prices at the end of the 1950s, combined probably with the completion of development of the main unworked deposits in local hands. Whatever the precise reason, significant new initiatives by Peruvian mining companies after 1958 were few and far between, although the increased role of foreign capital throughout the economy was reflected in a series of new projects for the development of medium-sized mines. The last major venture to involve large amounts of Peruvian capital was Pan American Commodities, a syndicate formed in the mid-1950s to develop the Acari iron deposits; this company entered production in 1959 but went bankrupt (due to bad management and excessive gearing of investment) in 1966–7.[30] From 1957 to 1970 a survey of new developments in small and medium-scale mining reveals a striking contrast to the patterns of 1948–56 (discussed above). Of twenty new developments which we have identified from the annual mining statistics, no fewer than fourteen involved foreign capital in a dominant role and only three could be positively identified as new local ventures.[31] From 1961 to 1970 no significant new development by private Peruvian capital could be identified,[32] although the Banco Minero became increasingly active during the mid-1960s[33]—in a sense, the State was already beginning to compensate for the decline of local capitalism.

In summary, the performance of mining up to the early 1960s was dynamic, with rates of growth of output ranging between 13 per cent and 20 per cent a year; thereafter the pace slowed down to an annual rate of only 2 to 3 per cent (Table 11.8) as large foreign companies and local firms cut back on new investment, leaving foreign firms of medium scale as the only active element in the sector. This dramatic slowdown of growth was offset to a large extent during the mid- and late-1960s by the rise in the sector's returned value, from little more than 50 per cent in 1960 to over 80 per cent by the mid-1970s. The absence of large new projects entering production in the fifteen years after 1960, however, is very evident in Table 11.8; this trend was especially serious since, as we noted earlier, by the mid-1960s metals mining constituted virtually the only export sector capable of rapid large-scale expansion. In default of growth from this sector, export growth in general ran quickly into crisis, as Chapter 14 will discuss in more detail.

11.2 PETROLEUM, 1948–70

The pattern of weakening investment and stagnating growth which we have sketched above for the mining sector in the 1960s was repeated in the petroleum industry, but in this case the constraint was a straightforward lack of new resources to develop. The history of the oil industry from 1948 to 1970 was dominated by the failure to locate new commercial oilfields as the existing fields approached exhaustion; while, because of this constraint on production at a time of rising internal consumption, oil virtually disappeared from the list of Peruvian exports. As the sector's aggregate importance declined, the willingness of the Government to regulate the industry increased, with the result that by the 1960s the foreign firms which had dominated the industry during the previous half-century were pulling out.

It will be recalled that, by the time of the 1948 coup, the failure of the Government to work out a viable oil policy had brought new

TABLE 11.9 Oil production and exports, 1950–74
(millions of barrels, annual averages)

	Production	Exports	Internal consumption[a]
1950–4	16.1	7.2	9.9
1955–9	18.3	6.8	14.5
1960–4	20.9	4.8	21.9
1965–9	25.1	3.3	31.3
1970–4	25.3[b]	2.0[b]	n.a.

Sources: *Estadística Petrolera*, 1969, pp. 34, 104 and 126; *Petroleum Economist*, Jan. 1974, p. 10 and Jan. 1975, p. 10, Banco Central, *Boletin*, June 1975, p. 28.
[a] The total of exports and consumption exceeds total production due to imports.
[b] Converted from metric tons@7.5 barrels = 1 ton

exploration and development to a halt. Meantime, increasing local consumption of oil products had been stimulated by price controls imposed by the Prado and Bustamante régimes, and by the second half of the 1940s exports had fallen from nearly 90 per cent of total output in the 1930s to little more than half (see Tables 8.8 and 11.9). In 1948 the industry was in a state of great uncertainty. Nominally, the legislation of 1922 and 1937 remained in force, but in practice the granting of new concessions remained frozen, the state oil company E.P.F. had been severely weakened, and it remained unknown whether large oil deposits could be readily located in the Sechura desert or the jungle region.

Under the Odría regime steps were quickly taken to clarify the situation.[34] Draft legislation prepared under Bustamante[35] but never publicly debated was resurrected by Odría in 1949[36] and after two years of committee work was sent to Congress in late 1951. Despite criticism from the nationalist lobby, led by the newspaper *El Comercio*, the Government refused to allow the introduction of any amendments, and the new Petroleum Law, No. 11780, was promulgated in March 1952.[37]

Among the mass of technical provisions, the central features of the new Law were four.[38] First, it authorised the Government to grant new exploration and production concessions, and fixed the (generally very liberal) terms under which such concessions were to be held. Secondly, it abolished the existing State reserves, thereby reopening those areas to claim-staking, while retaining for the Government the power to declare any area a reserve if it saw fit. (The continental shelf was declared a reserve for the time being.)[39] Thirdly, the Law embodied an important advantage for native as distinct from foreign capital: namely, preferential rights of access to areas open to denouncement.[40] Fourthly, the Law, in common with other measures of this period, abolished the old system of export taxes and production royalties and substituted in their place a system of income taxes on oil companies, with generous exemptions for depreciation, depletion and reinvestment. (Under their existing concessions, Lobitos and Ganso Azul continued to be subject to royalties at the old level.)

In the conditions of 1952 the most important of these measures was the first, which once again gave local and foreign capital the right to explore for oil in the Sechura and the jungle; it is unlikely that the liberality of the terms affected the outcome one way or the other. As soon as the law appeared in June 1952, Peruvian and foreign companies began queueing up to obtain concessions in the Sechura, where great expectations had been aroused by the Los Organos oil strike of 1943 and the subsequent heat of the Sechura Contract debate. Of twenty-five applications received during the preferential period set aside for Peruvian companies, all but four concerned the Sechura.[41] On October 28, applications were opened to all comers, and areas subject to more than one application were auctioned off to the highest bidders in January 1953.[42] To the Government's evident astonishment, the auction raised no less than $2.5 million in five days, mostly from foreign companies eager to gain a place in the new rush.[43] At the end of the process, the Sechura was in the hands of seven foreign and five Peruvian companies.[44]

This sudden re-emergence of private Peruvian oil companies is the most striking aspect of the Sechura oil rush.[45] One company, 'El Oriente,' controlled by the Gildemeister family, had been active in jungle exploration since 1941 and had drilled unsuccessfully at two jungle sites in 1947–9.[46] A second, Petrolera San Miguel, revived the Cilloniz family's interest in the Sechura, where they had drilled in the 1920s (see Chapter 5). The three others were new ventures established specifically to take advantage of the privileges offered to national companies by the Petroleum Law. Petrolera Peruana was a syndicate of the leading élite figures of the day, headed by Augusto Gildemeister.[47] Petroleo Sullana represented the entry into oil of the Wiese brothers, leading Lima bankers and, as described earlier, gold-mine promoters of the 1930s. The last of the nationals, Sudamericana de Petroleo, was a minor venture by a group of middle-class entrepreneurs from Lima. As was the case in mining at this time, therefore, local capital was still active and capable, and in the event it was these Peruvian companies, given first choice of exploration areas, which made the few significant oil discoveries of the 1950s.

From 1953 to 1956 the Sechura was the scene of feverish prospecting, seismic surveys, and drilling.[48] Over thirty exploratory wells were drilled, thirteen of them by the private Peruvian firms.[49] The results were discouraging. In the Sechura itself only one small productive oilfield was located, on the Petrolera Peruana holding, making this the country's fifth oil producer.[50] Elsewhere, foreign firms drilling under contracts with EPF located two other insignificant oil deposits.[51] For the rest, the Sechura proved entirely barren, and by 1956 most of the concessions in the area were being abandoned. Twenty million dollars had been spent to no effect.[52]

In April 1953 the Government issued a decree opening most of the continental shelf (offshore areas) to claim-staking, again with special privileges for national firms.[53] The decree was almost certainly designed in close collaboration with the Gildemeister—Beltran group of capitalists, already operating two of the national oil firms; and it was this group, through its third venture (Petrolera del Pacifico SA) which secured the first large concession granted offshore in Peru. The company sank four wells offshore during 1954, of which two were successful, but full-scale development of the concession was left till 1959, while the group developed their onshore field: the technical difficulty of offshore development was considerable.

On the Coast, in summary, the oil rush of the 1950s failed to live up to expectations, while Peru's traditional oil surplus faded away under the impact of rising domestic demand. The need for new discoveries was as urgent as ever, and hopes now became pinned on the jungle. There, also, the 1952 Petroleum Law had been followed by a wave of applications for new concessions, although the competition was by no means as intense as in the Sechura. The leading participants were, on the whole, the same as in the Sechura,[54] and the pattern of events was also strikingly similar. Following an intensive period of surveying several of the concession-holders began drilling exploratory wells in 1955. In the following three years fifteen wells were drilled in various areas[55] and one new commercial oilfield was struck—at Maquia—by the Gildemeister company, 'El Oriente'.[56] The field was quickly developed to supply the government refinery at Iquitos and sell the products in the local market. Apart from this single find, the programmes of the major companies had proved disappointing by the end of the 1950s and many of the concessions were abandoned at this stage.[57]

The failure to locate large new oilfields (apart from the offshore reserves, which were not brought into full production for several years due to technical and marketing difficulties) had three major consequences for the industry. The first was the slow growth of output shown in Table 11.10, as Brea-Parinas reached exhaustion and was barely replaced by Lima Concessions[58] and the small finds in the jungle and offshore. By 1964 oil was a mere one per cent of exports, while imports of oil products rose steadily, to over four million barrels yearly by 1960. By 1968 the 'oil deficit' in foreign trade was $12.4 million.

The second consequence was the withdrawal of Peruvian enterprise from the oil sector. Faced with the difficulty and expense of developing offshore and Amazon basin oilfields,[59] company after company now

TABLE 11.10 Production of crude oil from main oilfields, 1930–71
(000 barrels, annual averages)

	Brea-Parinas (Negritos)	Lobitos-Lima Concessions	Zorritos & other E.P.F. onshore fields	Other coastal fields	Offshore	Jungle	Total[a]
1930–9	11,897	2,398	49	—	—	1	14,345
1940–9	10,968	2,395	90	—	—	66	13,518
1950–9	10,348	5,745	607	98	—	405	17,201
1960–9	7,230	9,972	1,797	193	2,612	1,156	22,961
1970–1	4,421	9,749	419	50	8,930	862	24,429

Source: Estadística Petrolera, 1951 p. 20A; 1969 p. 35; 1971 p. 30.
[a] Totals may not add exactly, due to rounding.

withdrew, beginning with the sale of one of the Gildemeister companies, Petrolera Peruana, to Belco Petroleum Corporation of New York. In the early 1960s Petrolera del Pacifico (another Gildemeister venture) and the Wiese brothers' Petroleo Sullana passed under the control of Peruvian Pacific Petroleum (Cities Service of the U.S.A.).[60] In the jungle, the 'El Oriente' company became increasingly a mere satellite of the German Group and of Mobil.[61] By the end of the 1960s the considerable array of Peruvian oil companies spawned in the 1940s and 1950s had vanished from the scene, leaving the State venture EPF as the only successful non-foreign oil operation. EPF meanwhile was making progress: the military government of 1962–3 launched a new period of growth for the agency, the central feature of which was the decision to build a new refinery at La Pampilla north of Lima to handle crude from EPF and other independents. After some delays the refinery was built by Japanese contractors in 1966–7 and proved commercially very successful.

The third consequence was that as oil paled into insignificance as an export product and as Peruvian capitalists' interest in the sector was reduced, so policy attitudes towards the sector veered towards toughness. This was evident above all in the growing campaign to expropriate IPC's Brea-Parinas oilfield, and force repayment to Peru of the value of the oil extracted since the 1922 Award.[62] The campaign, perhaps the best-known in Peru's history, ended in October 1968 when the military seized power and immediately took over all of IPC's assets in Peru, subsequently placing them in the hands of a new reorganised State company, Petroperu.[63]

Serious conflicts were also arising as to pricing policy. Prices of petroleum sold locally had remained frozen from 1931 until the late 1940s, when they had been only slightly adjusted upward by Odría in 1948–9 and 1953.[64] Obliged to supply the local market at the low fixed prices, IPC and Lobitos found that their exportable surplus was falling rapidly, and with it their profits.[65] Under heavy pressure from the companies to raise prices, the Prado Government set up a commission which reported, at the beginning of 1958, that the companies' costs had risen significantly since the last price increase;[66] but fearful of the political implications of a publicly-decreed increase, Prado tried to legislate it in concealed form as part of a tax increase in January 1958. The uproar when the manoeuvre was spotted obliged the Government to revoke the measure,[67] and the companies responded (as had IPC in a previous dispute in mid-1918) by cutting back on their drilling activities, alleging that the return on capital was insufficient to justify continued work.[68] In July 1959 the newly-appointed prime minister Pedro Beltran (whose family, as noted above, had been active participants in two of the new Peruvian producing companies) decreed substantial increases on the basis of a very pro-company report by an official commission.[69] This time the increase was successfully imposed and the foreign companies resumed drilling, but the congressional opposition immediately launched a head-on attack on the legality of IPC's 1922 Award—the opening shots in the battle which, as mentioned above, dominated the 1960s. The result was that while publicly the IPC fought to protect its position, both foreign firms prepared their exit. Lobitos Oilfields, the British parent of Compania Petrolera Lobitos, sold out to Burmah Oil in 1962,[70] while IPC used its breathing space during the years 1960–7 to repatriate most of its capital in the form of amortisation allowances; the company's book value as reported to the U.S. Department of Commerce fell from somewhere in the vicinity of $70 million in 1959 to less than $20 million by 1967.[71]

While these events contributed significantly to the growing antagonism to foreign penetration, new foreign firms were still moving in, but were taking care to maintain a low profile. Chief among these was Belco, which as mentioned above bought up Petrolera Peruana in 1959. The firm quickly established itself as the leading offshore producer, although for several years its development was held up by lack of marketing outlets (IPC-CPL had an effective monopoly on the local market, and export markets were difficult for a small independent to penetrate). During the decade 1960–9, Belco's 'Litoral' concession accounted for 60 per cent of offshore oil production, and the company firmly established its position by a 1967 contract with E.P.F. to operate the latter's offshore holdings, and a 1968 agreement with the other private offshore companies under which Belco took over the operation of their properties as well.[72] When in the 1970s offshore oil became the key to Peruvian supplies (with the virtual exhaustion of the old IPC-CPL fields), Belco was already placed to become the country's main producer, selling its output through Petroperu.

In the jungle region, the discovery of the Maquia oilfield in 1957 was followed in 1961 by new drilling programmes conducted by Cerro de Pasco Corporation and a consortium headed by Mobil. Cerro's venture failed, but Mobil struck a large gas field at Aguaytia in mid-1961, development of which was never undertaken because of the costs of constructing the necessary pipeline. After several years of further survey work, Mobil and Union oil launched a new programme of exploratory drilling in 1968 in the northern jungle, but failed to locate oil.[73] Overall, the pace of activity in the jungle during the 1960s was relatively leisurely, and it was not until after the massive oil discoveries in the jungle area of Ecuador that international interest in the Peruvian Amazon took on new urgency.[74]

The transformation of the oil industry from Peru's leading export sector to a mere supplier of the local market was a dramatic one, involving a sharp decrease in the industry's political influence as well as an end to the scandalous outflows of profits which had characterised the

TABLE 11.11 Data on International Petroleum Company, 1950–67
(U.S. $million)

	(1) IPC total sales	(2) Wages and taxes in Peru	(3) Total out- lays in Peru	(4) Col. 2 as % of Col. 1	(5) Col. 3 as % of Col. 1
1948	. .	. .		45.7	
1949	. .	. .		34.8	
1950	31.0	12.5		40.3	
1951	30.2	14.2		47.0	
1952	28.6	15.9		55.6	
1953	29.7	12.3		41.4	
1954	31.8	13.8		43.4	
1955	45.4	15.9		35.0	
1956	48.2	17.3		35.9	
1957	55.0	22.7		41.3	
1958	38.4	19.5		50.8	
1959	46.4	22.1		47.6	
1960	65.0	31.1		47.8	
1961	60.9	30.1	50.0	49.4	82.1
1962	42.7	32.5	54.6	76.1	127.9
1963	64.7	33.9	55.2	52.4	85.3
1964	75.5	37.4	63.7	49.5	84.4
1965	78.5	39.4	65.6	50.2	83.6
1966	84.6	40.9	73.4	48.3	86.8
1967	83.7	42.2		50.4	

Sources: Columns 1 and 2 assembled from *Estadistica Petrolera* annual volumes, converted to dollars at annual average exchange rates (weighted average for 1967). Total sales consist of exports plus local sales—i.e. oil products imported for sale are included in these figures. Taxes exclude gasoline tax. Wages include social-service payments by the company (estimated as S/30 million p.a. for 1950 and 1951).

Column 3 figures were prepared by IPC, published in *Peruvian Times*, Dec. 15, 1967, p. 2. Note that the IPC figures on wages and taxes do not coincide exactly with those used for Column 2; for 1966 (details of this year are given in the above source) IPC reported its tax bill in Peru as $26.1 million, while *Estadistica Petrolera* shows $21.3 million excluding gasoline tax (or $33.2 million including it). IPC shows its wage bill including social payments as $18.4 million, while *Estadistica Petrolera* shows $19.7 million. Orders of magnitude, however, seem acceptable.

period up to the Second World War. Table 11.11 presents some data on the operations of the IPC; local wages and taxes paid by the company had increased from less than 20 per cent of the gross value of output in the 1930s (Table 5.7) to around 40 per cent by the end of the 1940s, and 50 per cent by the late 1950s. Total operating costs (including imports) had increased from 30 per cent or less in the 1920s and 1930s to around 85 per cent by the early 1960s. These changes were caused partly by increased backward linkages and heavier taxation; but more importantly were due to the steady squeeze on profits as an increasing proportion of the company's output was compulsorily sold on the internal market at fixed prices. One result of this cheapness of fuel on the local market was a significant increase in the forward-linkage effects of the petroleum sector (both by encouraging industrialisation, and by subsidising consumers of kerosene and gasoline).

The very low returned value of the early days was thus reversed—but meantime petroleum had ceased to be a major export, with the result that the impact on the balance of payments of its decline was hardly significant, just as its earlier rise had contributed very little to the local economy. It would, however, be quite incorrect to attribute the decline of investment and stagnation of output to the political difficulties encountered by IPC at the end of the 1950s. The overriding feature of the oil industry's history from 1948 to 1970 was the fact that thirty years of exploration had failed to locate new oilfields. The supply constraint faced by the sector was neither a product of poor market prospects nor of the policy stances of government or companies. The rising tide of nationalism cannot be said to have deterred serious new investment, since the nationalist attack was single-mindedly concentrated on the IPC, while exploration meantime proceeded; the proven oilfields were exploited in so far as was possible. The hope that oil in large quantities might be discovered in the jungle sufficed to attract a large number of large foreign companies in the 1970s when a new exploration phase was launched; but the results of this exploration (as of 1977) were meagre, offering no hope of Peru again becoming a major oil exporter.

12 The Export Sectors, Part 2: Sugar, Cotton and Fishmeal

The discussion of mineral export sectors in the preceding chapter indicated that by the 1960s those sectors were encountering constraints on their further development: in mining, the reluctance of foreign firms to develop their large unworked deposits; in petroleum, the approaching exhaustion of the known reserves. Further, it emerged that the rise of foreign capital was accompanied by a stagnation or decay of local entrepreneurial effort and investment. It appeared also that, as the familiar problems of foreign-owned mineral sectors came to the fore again with the rise of Marcona and SPCC, the political reaction in the 1960s was more nationalistic than had been the case in the 1920s, with increasingly tough bargaining and heavier taxation of the foreign firms, and the build-up to expropriation of the IPC.

Certain of these tendencies appear also in the history of the non-mineral export sectors: sugar, cotton, and fishmeal. The 1960s witnessed, as we shall see, the emergence of physical or structural constraints on expansion, coupled with a perceptible decline in the dynamism of local entrepreneurship and investment. These trends, coupled with the more general anti-export bias in government policy from the late 1950s on, contributed powerfully to the general crisis of the economy in the late 1960s, discussed in Chapter 14 below. In dramatic contrast, the 1950s were a decade of exceptionally rapid growth in non-mineral export sectors, and it is with that growth that we begin.

12.1 AGRICULTURAL STAPLES: SUGAR AND COTTON

The increase of sugar and cotton production after the coup of 1948 was made possible primarily by renewed expansion of the area of irrigated land on the Coast. Under President Odría (who had much in common with Leguía)[1] the idea of large-scale government-financed irrigation works in the northern cotton-growing regions was revived, following a twenty-year gap since the abandonment of Leguía's giant Olmos project.[2] Within six months of seizing power in 1948, Odría had

TABLE 12.1 Allocation of irrigated land on the Coast
(000 hectares)

	(1) Total coastal agricultural	(2) Sugar	(3) Cotton	(4) Total sugar and cotton	(5) Other crops
1929	384	54	127	181	203
1932	425	58[a]	123	181	244
1944	481	49	129	178	303
1952	538	52	190	242	296
1962	640[b]	74	275	349	291
1967	667	83	180	263	404
1971	686[c]	84	136	220	466

Sources: Column 1 from Twomey (1972), Chapter 2, except 1961 which is from the agricultural census of that year. Column 2 from SNA *Memorias*. Column 3 from *Anuario Estadistico*, various issues. Column 5 is a residual.
[a] 1933.
[b] 1961.
[c] Extrapolated on the basis of 1961–7 trend.

launched these new irrigation works and strengthened the Banco Agricola to help finance expansion of crops such as cotton.[3] Largest of the Odría projects was Quiroz, in Piura, the first stage of which was completed in late 1953 at a cost of $11 million, providing irrigation for 31,000 hectares of cotton land.[4] Other public and private projects along the Coast increased the total irrigated area by 19 per cent between 1952 and 1962 (see Table 12.1). The entire increase was absorbed by the two leading export crops, cotton area increasing by 45 per cent, and sugar by 42 per cent (the implications for the domestic food supply are considered in Chapter 13 below). Over the same period, production of cotton increased by 59 per cent, and that of sugar 63 per cent;[5] it was thus the increase in area which accounted for most of the rise in both products, although increased yields were considerably more significant in sugar production than in cotton growing.

By contrast, from 1962 to 1967 the total increase in coastal irrigated area was no more than four per cent, and most of this increase together with 86,000 hectares of land formerly under cotton and sugar was allocated or reallocated to other crops, a trend which continued into the early 1970s. As Table 12.1 makes clear, the reallocation was in fact entirely of cotton land. From 1962 to 1967 total production of sugar fell four per cent and that of cotton fell 34 per cent; exports of sugar fell more heavily than output as internal consumption increased. A clear-cut pattern thus emerges of a rapid expansion of export crops up to the early 1960s, followed by both relative and absolute decline. The key to this emerging bottleneck of supply in the 1960s and 1970s, clearly, was the limited supply of irrigated land.

A recurring theme in the history of Peruvian exports during the 1960s is the reduced pace at which natural resources were brought into production, in comparison with the boom years of the 1950s; here the pattern appears as a reduction of investment in new irrigation projects. In part this reflected lack of financial resources; the Belaunde Government, in particular, gave greater priority to road construction and colonisation in the interior than to expansion of coastal agriculture. But more significant was the fact that the increments to total irrigated area which could be obtained by more efficient use of the country's westward-flowing rivers were becoming increasingly marginal. Future increases in coastal irrigation depended upon the diversion of rivers flowing down the eastern side of the Andes—and such projects, by their nature, were of very large scale and long gestation, requiring a major financial and organisational commitment by the State. (Note, however, that some of the present schemes, for example Chira-Piura, are still improving the utilisation of westward-flowing water.)

It is worth noting that while this represents the general view, it may be unduly pessimistic. In particular, the I.B.R.D. has produced estimates of the extent of salinity on the Coast and the probable cost of desalination, which suggest considerable potential for recovery of productive land.[6]

In the face of the reduced rate of expansion of irrigated area, the experience of the two main crops differed greatly, with cotton being displaced by other crops as relative prices moved against export production during the 1960s, whereas artificially high sugar prices in the protected U.S. market kept Peruvian production pressing against the resources constraint through the decade. We therefore discuss the history of each crop separately, before returning to consider their combined impact on the economy.

Sugar: investment, productivity increases and a protected market
The Second World War, followed by the Korean War boom, had brought a rise in sugar prices comparable to that of the First World War. After a delay imposed by the controls and shortages of the Bustamante period, the response was a wave of investment which rapidly raised yields and sent production soaring in the early years of the 1950s (see Table 12.2), despite the weakening of world prices which followed the Korean War. These improved yields reflected a variety of changes: improved irrigation, increased supplies of fertiliser, introduction of new cane varieties, wider use of herbicides and control of cane borer.

Increases in yields ceased about 1955, and until 1960 the continuing expansion of output rested upon the expansion of the area under cane, especially in Lambayeque. The increase involved not only expansion by the main sugar estates themselves, but also a rapid increase in the number and importance of independent *sembradores* who planted their

TABLE 12.2 Development of the sugar industry, 1945–74
(annual averages)

	(1) Production[a] (000 tons)	(2) Exports (000 tons)	(3) Internal consumption[b] (000 tons)	(4) Yields of cane per hectare of land under cane (tons)	(5) of land harvested (tons)	(6) Percentage extraction of sugar from cane milled	(7) Percentage of total area harvested
1945–9	428	300	147	73.4	122.8	11.6	60
1950–4	515	338	173	85.0	139.6	11.2	61
1955–9	683	459	226	102.0	162.1	10.9	63
1960–4	812	490	286	102.3	152.7	11.1	67
1965–9	740	399	349	92.2	151.4	9.8	61
1970–4	889	436	453[c]	n.a.	n.a.	10.5	n.a.

Sources: Columns 1 and 2: 1945–1964 from Sociedad Nacional Agraria, *Memoria* (annual) and *Estadistica Azucarera del Perú*, Table 7. 1965–74 from International Sugar Council, *Sugar Yearbook*.

Column 3: Sociedad Nacional Agraria, *Memoria*; *Estadistica Azucarera*, 1968, Table 7; and Kisic (1972) Table 30.

Columns 4–7: Areas and cane milled from SNA, *Memoria*; *Memorias* up to 1964; 1965–9 from *Anuario Estadistico*, 1968 and 1971.

[a] The series corresponds as closely as possible to centrifugal sugar (i.e. excluding *chancaca* and *concreto*, as well as cane alcohol). Up to 1949 the figures are for coastal production only, while 1950–74 they are for all centrifugal sugar output; this makes very little difference since only a tiny fraction of output of this type of sugar comes from the Sierra (mainly Huanuco).

[b] Excluding *chancaca*.

[c] Estimated, as production minus exports.

land to cane under contracts with the large estates, enabling the latter to increase the scale of their milling operations.[7]

These factors carried the expansion of the industry through the market collapse which followed the ending of the Korean War. The reappearance of world oversupply in 1952 prompted a new strengthening of bilateral arrangements, particularly British Commonwealth Preference, and tighter restrictions on non-Cuban suppliers of the U.S. market under the 1948 U.S. Sugar Act.[8] In 1953 a new International Sugar Agreement re-introduced export quotas for free-market exporters; and prices stabilised (although Peru refused to accept its reduced quota under this Agreement). The fall in prices helps to account for the fall in sugar's share of exports in the first five years of the decade, which was shown in Table 11.1 above. Also important, however, was the fact that domestic consumption was now rising to the point where it was significantly reducing the exportable surplus. The proportion of production exported had been 87 per cent in the early 1930s (Table 9.1 above); as can be seen in Table 12.2, it had fallen to 70 per cent by the 1940s, to 60 per cent by the early 1960s, and finally to less than half by the early 1970s. The rapid increase of domestic consumption of sugar has been due to the low initial level of consumption, to substitution of centrifugal sugar for the non-centrifugal varieties (*chancaca*) which are excluded from Table 12.2, and to the maintenance of internal prices at an artifically low level from the early 1940s. With internal demand rising at around 7 to 8 per cent annually, as it was doing by the late 1950s, a rapid and sustained expansion of production was required merely to hold sugar exports at around 400,000 tons annually, let alone to increase them.

During the 1950s Peruvian producers, having failed (as in the 1930s) to gain access to protected high-price markets, were reduced to selling in such areas of the free market as were available—mainly Chile, and to an increasing extent Japan. The period of rapid expansion of output (responding to the experience of the 1940s) thus coincided with years of poor prices. In 1960 both trends were reversed: rapid expansion of export supply began to tail off (owing both to a reduced growth of output and to the diversion of supplies to meet internal demand), while the external market situation abruptly brightened as a result of the Cuban Revolution of 1959. As U.S. opposition to Castro hardened, Cuba's sugar quota in the U.S. market was revoked, and replaced by new quotas allocated among pro-U.S. producers. Peru at that time was under a very conservative and extremely pro-U.S. government, and received a quota large enough to absorb virtually all of the available exportable supply. Throughout the 1960s Peruvian sugar was sold at the premium prices prevailing in the U.S.A., and by the late 1960s, as exportable supply was eroded by rising internal consumption and falling output (especially with the drought of 1968), Peru was encountering difficulty in filling even its U.S. quota, and had entirely ceased to sell on the free market.

The U.S. quota was vital in sustaining the profitability of sugar production during the 1960s. In 1968 an official study of the costs of production in Lambayeque[9] indicated that the fob cost of 96° sugar for export was about S/2.99 per kilo, or roughly 3.2 cents per lb. At that time the free-market world price had fallen to 1.98 cents per lb fob, significantly below Peruvian costs of production, while the price in the U.S. market to which Peru had privileged access was 6.54 cents per lb fob.[10]

This favourable position for local planters did not result in much increase in production, since yields were at a technological ceiling and irrigated land was scarce. Investment continued, however, in new techniques which reduced costs of production; in practice, this meant increased mechanisation and capital-intensity. One study of the process concludes that any innovation which proved itself cost-effective was rapidly adopted, and that this implied a strong trend towards labour-saving technology.[11] Changes in milling technology are difficult to trace,[12] but on the cultivation side the changes were clear-cut. The move towards mechanisation began in the late 1940s with the use of mobile cranes for loading the plantation railways,[13] and between 1954 and the end of the 1960s there occurred a general replacement of the relatively labour-intensive railways by large tractor-hauled trailers.[14] In 1955 a mechanical harvester designed in Hawaii was tested in Peru and, shortly after, the Grace-owned plantations switched to mechanical cutting, displacing the large work-force of *macheteros*. A new mechanical harvesting device, the pushrake, was widely adopted during the first half of the 1960s, reducing both the cost and the quality of cane supplied to the mills, and displacing labour.[15]

By the mid-1960s, however, the bulk of these innovations had been completed and the rate of investment was levelling off. In the absence of major new irrigation programmes, the capital-absorptive capacity of sugar production was falling, a trend paralleled, as we have seen, in several other export sectors. There also emerged at this time another highly significant trend: a tendency towards 'internationalisation' of the sector, as several of the Peruvian plantation-owners found it expedient to establish close links with 'foreign firms' as a means of transferring funds in and out of the country as the occasion demanded. A 1969 survey of the main estates[16] revealed not only the existence of considerable debts owed to U.S. banks, but also the fact that only two of the main plantations (Cayalti and Pomalca) were reported as 100 per cent locally-owned. Since the early 1900s the Gildemeister properties had had a considerable proportion of shareholders in Germany and Holland; but the 1969 survey showed certain other locally-controlled properties to have large blocks of shares registered in Panama, Nassau and Switzerland, causing inevitable speculation that Peruvians had been setting up foreign 'fronts' through which they could retain control while insuring themselves against exchange risk and possible expropriation.[17]

The cotton sector: expansion and contraction
When the Korean War and the associated rise in world commodity prices began in 1950, the world cotton supply situation was critical. Stocks were at a low point, and acreage restrictions combined with poor weather in 1950 had resulted in a 40 per cent fall in the U.S. crop. By early 1951 the fear of complete exhaustion of world stocks was causing panic buying by merchants and manufacturers.[18] High prices and the general impression of extreme scarcity encouraged agriculturists throughout the world to move land into cotton during 1950–1, and within a year world cotton markets were back to the situation of the early 1930s, with over-supply causing steady downward pressure on prices. The future of cotton was further clouded by the rapid expansion of the synthetic textiles industry, which had also benefited greatly from the Korean War.

In reaction to the post-Korea cotton problem the U.S. Government returned to its policies of the 1930s: acreage restrictions combined with stockpiling to maintain the support price.[19] During the first half of the 1950s, consequently, the U.S. Government kept world cotton markets in equilibrium by buying up surpluses; and once again non-U.S. growers, as beneficiaries of the political strength of the US South, were able to expand into the U.S.A.'s share of world cotton trade, while the U.S.A. unilaterally held prices up. From 1950 to 1956 total world trade in cotton remained stationary at 12–13 million bales, while the U.S. share of this trade fell from 45 per cent in 1950 to only 17 per cent in 1956.[20]

Although prices remained satisfactory through the first half of the 1950s, all cotton producers viewed with alarm the mounting size of the cotton stockpile held by the U.S. Government as a result of its price-support policies. Despite increasingly tight acreage restrictions, U.S. production fell only slightly while stocks mounted. In early 1956, faced with a slowdown in the expansion of the textile industries of the main industrial nations,[21] the U.S. Government abandoned its previous policy and began unloading its cotton stocks on to the world market, rapidly driving down the price of medium-staple cotton and attracting accusations of 'dumping.'[22]

Among the world's cotton producers those best placed to confront the crisis were Peru, Egypt and the Sudan—the producers of long-staple and extra-long-staple cottons, the market for which was differentiated from that for medium-staple cotton of the type produced by the U.S.A. The Suez crisis caused a diversion of a large part of Egyptian cotton exports from Western markets to the Soviet Union, leaving Peru with excellent prices in 1957; and in general long-staple prices held up better than those of other cottons into the early 1960s. In part this was due to the greater competitiveness of long-staple cotton with synthetics, and in part to the limitations on substitution of the increasingly cheap medium-staple cottons for LS and ELS varieties in the world's textile industries. At the beginning of the 1960s, two years of low U.S. crops, combined with recovery of the main industrialised countries from the 1958 recession, produced a revival of world cotton markets and renewed optimism among growers.

TABLE 12.3 Development of cotton-growing, 1945–74
(annual averages)

	Production of raw cotton (000 tons)	Production of ginned fibre (000 tons)	Yield of raw cotton per ha (tons)	Percentage of ginned fibre per ton of raw cotton
1945–9	182	67	1.37	37
1950–4	244	92	1.36	37
1955–9	304	111	1.32	38
1960–4	381	139	1.47	37
1965–9	299	110	1.57	36
1970–4	239	93[a]	1.72[a]	39[a]

Sources: Anuario Estadistico del Perú, 1940 p. 209; 1956–7 p. 396; 1966 p. 996; and 1971, p. 36. 1960 figures from *Memoria de la Camara Algodonera del Perú*, 1960. 1972–4 figures for output from Banco Central de Reserva, unpublished data.
[a] 1970.

Markets for Peruvian cotton were thus fairly consistently favourable during the 1950s, and the response was a rapid expansion of cotton growing (Table 12.3) which carried cotton back to the leading role among Peru's exports. From the 1947 low point of 120,000 hectares, cotton area had reached nearly 230,000 hectares by 1956, while output increased 75 per cent, the most rapid expansion taking place in the years 1950 to 1954. The early 1960s brought a further expansion to the all-time peak production of 400,000 tons of raw cotton in 1962–3.

As usual, however, the worldwide response to the recovery of 1960 was greater than the market could absorb, and between 1962 and the end of the 1960s the crisis of oversupply returned, aggravated by the steady inroads made by synthetic textiles into markets previously dominated by cotton. As in the 1950s, the U.S.A. unilaterally assumed the burden of supporting prices during most of the 1960s by stockpiling and restricting production, and this served to stabilise prices. This stabilisation, however, coincided with a worldwide tendency for food prices to move ahead of cotton prices, and in many cotton-growing countries land began to be switched to other crops. This trend was especially pronounced in Peru, where the exchange rate was held fixed from 1958 until 1967 while internal inflation proceeded. The ratio of cotton prices to wholesale agricultural prices in general fell by 40 per cent[23] between 1960 and 1966. By 1965, when a government study of production costs was carried out along the Coast, twelve of the twenty areas studied reported losses on cotton production, and all except two of the remainder were showing only small margins of profit.[24] Although the study's results were distorted by the fact that the year was one of abnormal climatic conditions[25] with exceptionally severe flood and pest damage to the crop in the North,[26] and although actual costs were inflated somewhat by the inclusion of imputed land rents and depreciation, the general picture of meagre profits appears reasonable. According to Zuñiga,[27] between 1956 and 1966 costs of production rose 90 per cent but the selling price in soles only 61 per cent.

The result was that between the early sixties and the early seventies the area under cotton was halved, and production fell by over one-third, as shown in Table 12.3. Exports, from 140,000 tons in 1962, had fallen to 50,000 tons by 1972 and were still falling in 1974.[28] In a sense, since this dramatic collapse had occurred as the result of reallocation of resources rather than as the result of any physical or structural constraints, the decline of cotton exports was not necessarily permanent; the central problem is that the land taken out of cotton was not transferred to some other export crop, but was instead devoted to the feeding of the urban population. Urban food demand continued to increase rapidly, while as of 1974 even the arrival of elements of the 'Green Revolution' did not appear to have made much difference to productivity in food production. To re-allocate this land back to cotton, therefore, would be to precipitate a severe crisis of urban food supply with a consequent steep increase in the import bill. Only a new phase of very rapid expansion of irrigated area along the Coast could make possible both the satisfying of domestic food needs and a revival of cotton exports to anything like their former importance.

Agricultural exports and the economy
Our discussion of cotton and sugar in Chapter 4 brought out a number of features which continued to characterise the two sectors into the 1960s. Cotton always figured as the more important employer, with labour-intensive production (particularly harvesting)[29] and a tenancy structure which resulted in a relatively widespread distribution of income. This income distribution, however, made the sector less prominent as a supplier of surplus for investment in other sectors.[30] Sugar, by contrast, was always a sector characterised by capital intensity, and this increased steadily after the Second World War. Income was thus more concentrated, and the sector remained important

as an accumulator of capital. Both sectors were closely integrated into the local economy, and their expansion during the 1950s provided complementary demand stimulus (from cotton employment) and investible funds (from sugar). Meantime, as growth proceeded, the differentiation between the two sectors in terms of production structure and power relations became increasingly clearcut. The growing strength of sharecroppers in cotton-growing areas continued to reduce the power of the large landowners and to erode the *hacienda* as an institution, whereas in sugar-growing areas the landowners consolidated their position as a dominant large-capitalist class. Consequently, in cotton-growing areas the issues of labour relations and income distribution involved a three-cornered struggle among landowners, tenants and labourers, while in sugar-producing regions the dominant relationship was that between employers and workers. Even the latter pattern, however, incorporated more complex developments.

During the late 1950s the spread of labour-saving innovations in the sugar industry coincided with a rapid increase in the supply of free wage-labour available to coastal agriculture as Sierra – Coast migration became less and less a temporary seasonal phenomenon.[31] The sugar estates, which had long supplemented their permanent labour force by attracting temporary migrants through the *enganche* system, began for the first time to encounter the problem of a labour surplus,[32] and *enganche* was generally abandoned by the end of the 1950s.[33] The first attempts by the plantations to lay off part of their permanent workforce, as their labour needs fell, coincided with the organisation of strong *aprista* unions on several plantations during the Prado administration of 1956–62,[34] and a consequent drive by the permanent workers to improve their working conditions and wages. The result, naturally enough, was severe labour trouble beginning in 1959 and continuing into the early 1960s.[35] As the unions established their right to exist, and secured for their members the effective application of labour legislation and social-security benefits, several estates accelerated their lay-offs of permanent field workers, hiring instead temporary contracted labour which did not qualify for the minimum wages and social benefits enjoyed by the unionised workforce.[36] This growing division between the permanent unionised workers and the unorganised *eventuales* was to carry over into the period following the agrarian reform of 1969, which converted the sugar estates into cooperatives owned by the members of the permanent labour force but excluding the non-unionised *eventuales*; the cooperative members, secure in their new position, have pressed ahead with labour-displacing investments at the expense of the temporary labourers.[37]

However, despite increasing capital intensity, sugar's high returned value made its expansion an important stimulus to growth. A study of returned value in the sugar industry as a whole was conducted in 1967,

TABLE 12.4 Distribution of gross value of sugar production, 1967

	Percentage of gross value of production
Local Expenditure:	
Wages and salaries	21.1
Interest payments	1.5
Rental payments	0.2
Purchases of goods and services	42.7
Taxes	9.0
Profits	8.8
Other	10.0
TOTAL RETURNED VALUE	93.3
Expenditure abroad:	
Wages and salaries	0.4
Interest payments	0.4
Remitted profits	1.7
Other	4.2
TOTAL SPENT ABROAD	6.7

Source: Unpublished Banco Central de Reserva data supplied by C. Scott. The low import content implicit in these figures is confirmed by the 1969 input – output table which gives direct and indirect imported inputs as 15 % of total inputs (Palma, *forthcoming*).

with results which appear in Table 12.4. The figure of 93 per cent, however, should not be treated as typical, since profits in 1967 were unusually low;[38] with 16 per cent of total profits being remitted abroad according to the Table, variations in profit rates were of considerable significance for returned value.[39] The sector's imports had also fallen with the ending of the main period of new investment during the preceding decade. It would, however, be reasonably safe to estimate that at least 80 per cent of export earnings from sugar could be classed as returned value during the years of export boom—a high enough figure to ensure the importance of the sector for general economic growth.

The sector also provided a stimulus via forward linkages, which were of growing importance, particularly on the estates controlled by W. R. Grace and Co. This firm had pioneered the making of paper from cane residue in the late 1930s,[40] and in the 1950s and 1960s had built up chemical complexes integrated with its sugar mills at Cartavio and Paramonga.[41, 42] A further forward linkage of importance was the use of molasses in the 1950s for the feeding of cattle; one of the pioneers in promoting this trade in an otherwise useless by-product was Luis Banchero, the later fishmeal magnate.[43]

By the 1960s a further issue arises in the relationship between agricultural exports and the economy: the lack of effective resistance to unfavourable trends in economic policy—particularly the fixed exchange rate, which discriminated against exporters with a high proportion of local costs. Traditionally, coastal landowners had been among the country's most powerful political interests, and their strength had generally increased during periods of export upswing. During the 1960s, however, the political weight of the sector appeared to wane, and an unmistakable drift towards agrarian reform set in, leading to decapitalisation of many agricultural properties.

In the case of cotton a number of possible explanations suggest themselves for this lack of political mobilisation. With one or two notable exceptions production was typically in the hands of small-scale and medium-scale tenants or smallholders, with slight political access, while landlords saw no need to intervene provided that their rents were paid. At least equally important was the flexibility of land use, which provided a simple escape route out of cotton and into foodcrops as, with given external prices, rising internal prices and a fixed exchange rate, relative prices swung against exports. The separation between the growing and ginning operations in cotton production, as processing facilities became increasingly concentrated in the hands of merchant houses, facilitated such a switch, and the merchants—the main direct victims—were powerless to prevent it.

In the case of sugar, characterised by larger-scale enterprises, the predominant factor was the existence of alternative profit opportunities outside the sector (although frequently linked to it, horizontally or vertically). In addition, the general anti-export bias implied by the fixed exchange rate was offset by the specific benefits obtained from a separate area of economic policy, namely, the direct negotiations with the U.S. Government over the size of Peru's quota in the U.S. market. The divergence between the premium prices available under the quota and the depressed world market price was of far greater significance than the exchange-rate issue, until the onset of the balance-of-payments crisis of 1967. In addition, issues other than exchange-rate policy preoccupied the sugar planters during the 1960s: pressure for increases in the local-market price of sugar, and manoeuvres to obtain exemption from agrarian reform.

Overshadowing the impact of exchange-rate policy on the agricultural export sectors, finally, was the overriding point that exchange stability was made possible until 1967 by an extremely rapid growth of aggregate export earnings. This was due in part to mineral exports, as long-run investment projects reached maturity, a process discussed in the preceding chapter. Still more important, however, was the fact that at the end of the 1950s a new export commodity had surged into the lead among Peruvian exports, and it was this commodity—fishmeal—which kept the export-led system afloat during the greater part of the 1960s.

12.2 THE FISHMEAL 'BOOM' AND ITS END

Of the new export products developed in Peru since the Depression the most important and spectacular was fishmeal.[44] As we saw in Chapter 9, fishery products were first exported in significant volume during the Second World War, but until the mid-1950s growth was relatively slow. By the mid-1960s, however, fish products had become the leading export sector, accounting for between 25 and 30 per cent of total export earnings. Peru had become the world's leading fishing nation in terms of volume,[45] with 18 per cent of the total world fish catch in 1964, and was producing around 40 per cent of the total world supply of fishmeal (used in the burgeoning animal-feed industry). The meteoric rise of the sector is shown by Tables 12.5 and 12.6, which bring out three major points: first, that the growth of the fishing sector until the middle of the 1950s was spear-headed by the production of edible fish products, especially

TABLE 12.5 Growth of Peruvian fish catch and production of fishmeal and canned fish
(000 metric tons, annual averages)

	Peruvian catch of		Peruvian production of	
	all fish varieties	anchovy	canned fish[a]	fishmeal[b]
1940–4	19	–	n.a.	[c]
1945–9	53	–	6[d]	[c]
1950–4	153	21	13	10
1955–9	1,027	638	21	117
1960–4	6,551	6,103	18	1,046
1965–9	9,215	8,964	9	1,622
1970–1	11,610	11,272	11	2,095
1972–3	3,534	3,108	12	663
1974[e]		3,644		841

Source: FAO, *Fisheries Yearbook*, annual issues 1947 to 1973. 1974 preliminary figures from *Latin American Economic Report*, Dec. 12, 1974, p. 197.
[a] Canned-fish figures up to 1961 are for all varieties of fish; from 1962 on, for tuna, bonito and mackerel.
[b] Fishmeal figures are for all varieties, including whalemeal (not of great importance, since anchovy meal dominates the picture).
[c] Less than one.
[d] 1947–9.
[e] Preliminary.

TABLE 12.6 Value of fish-product exports, 1940–74
(million dollars, annual averages at current prices)

	Canned fish	Fishmeal	Fish-oil	Other	Total
1940–4	0.2	–	–	0.1	0.2
1945–9	2.0	0.1	–	0.8	2.9
1950–4	5.3	0.8	0.2	1.5	7.8
1955–9	7.6	11.3	1.5	2.2	22.6
1960–4	6.3	87.5	10.9	2.0	106.7
1965–9	3.4	183.2	19.4	2.3	208.3
1970–3 ·	4.8	188.7	32.5	4.6	222.1

Source: FAO, *Fisheries Yearbook*, annual. Note that the FAO series use their own valuations, which may differ from those in the Peruvian official trade statistics.

canned fish; second, that the takeoff of fishmeal came in the second half of the 1950s, with growth continuing at a gradually-decreasing rate until 1970–1 when the peak was reached; and third, that after 1971 there was a dramatic decline in catches and production resulting from ecological problems. The three phases of the industry's history, corresponding to these trends, were: the establishment of the pioneering ventures up to 1955; the epic years of the fishing boom from 1956 into the 1960s; and the crises of excess capacity and overfishing which overtook the sector in the early 1970s, culminating in expropriation of all the private producers in 1973.

Expansion and its limits
As we saw in Section 9.3 above, in the forties the sector developed on the basis of small-scale enterprise concentrating chiefly on the processing of tuna. The industry experienced the first of its characteristic crises in 1948, when competition from Japanese supplies of canned fish in the U.S. market revived and the U.S. Government down-graded the classification of the Peruvian product from 'tuna' to 'bonito.'[46] Numerous bankruptcies followed, including some of the leading enterprises,[47] and the industry suffered difficulties for several years until in 1952–4 Peruvian producers successfully pioneered the marketing of canned bonito in Britain and expansion was resumed.[48] The renewed prosperity brought a new wave of middle-class entrants among whom was the future fishmeal giant, Luis Banchero Rossi.[49]

With fish canning the main activity, the by-product fishmeal had remained in the shadow until the late 1950s, being used mainly as a fertiliser. In the late 1930s the State-owned Compania Administradora de Guano, which was responsible for the supply of fertiliser to Peruvian agriculture, had become interested in fishmeal as a possible supplement to the increasingly inadequate supplies of guano,[50] and in 1941 the Prado government, having commissioned a report from a U.S. Fisheries Mission,[51] had purchased a large fishmeal plant to be operated by the Guano Company.[52] The experiment was, however, hamstrung by wartime shortages of parts[53] and following the departure of Prado the venture was allowed to die. In the early 1950s various private firms began to move tentatively towards specialisation in fishmeal and some of them, by beginning the fishing of anchovy for this purpose, incurred the wrath of the Guano Company which feared that the anchovy-eating, guano-producing bird population might be threatened by such fishing.[54] The ecological objections to anchovy fishing imposed a halt on its development until 1956.

The boom which began in the latter year was triggered by a combination of new market opportunities and technological innovation.[55] The key change in markets for fishmeal was the explosive growth in world production of feedstuffs for livestock (particularly pigs and poultry), which incorporated protein supplements such as soyabean meal and fishmeal. Fishmeal ceased to be regarded primarily as a fertiliser;[56] its price rose rapidly in response to the new demand, and fishmeal proved to possess an 'unidentified growth factor' which made it particularly valuable in the preparation of feeds. On the technological side, the Peruvian fishing fleet had by the mid-1950s been equipped with various technical items, including sonar equipment to locate fish shoals,[57] but was hampered by the use of nets made of cotton, which became heavy when wet and which rotted after only a few weeks' use. The technological break-through came with introduction of lightweight nylon nets in 1955,[58] which immediately replaced cotton and made possible the construction of a new generation of large fishing vessels (*bolicheras*).

The combination of nylon nets and growing external markets induced an immediate and dramatic response in Peru. In 1954 there had been seventeen factories in Peru producing fishmeal, of which nine were engaged in the processing of wastes from fish canning. By 1959 the number had risen to sixty-nine, and by 1963 to one hundred and fifty-four.[59] Fishmeal production expanded twenty times between 1954 and 1959, and more than trebled again by 1963. The expansion took place entirely in the processing of anchovy, which accounted for about half the fishmeal production in 1954, but 99 per cent by 1960.[60]

Two additional factors account for the extraordinary rapidity with which the fishmeal industry could be expanded in Peru. The first of these was the availability in the 1950s of very cheap second-hand capital equipment of good quality. This equipment came from the former sardine-fishing area of California, where a thriving fishmeal industry built up in the 1930s and 1940s had been wiped out in 1952 by the disappearance of the fish.[61] Entire factories were shipped down from

California, and the new Peruvian producers were enabled to start off with efficient modern machinery[62] at low cost.

The second contributory factor was the willingness of the Peruvian commercial banking sector to finance new fishmeal enterprises by means of short-term loans, renewed annually.[63] This ready availability of credit enabled a swarm of new enterprises with little initial capital to expand at an extremely rapid rate. The banks' reasons for financing the new sector were obvious enough. The years 1957 and 1958 were years of recession for most of Peru's export products, whereas fishmeal prices increased sharply in 1957, with world supply falling due to poor fishing in Scandinavia,[64] and demand growing rapidly. Peruvian fishmeal producers became so profitable at this stage that they were well able to support the short-term high-interest credit provided by the banks; with world prices for meal ranging between $120 and $140 per ton fob, the costs of production in Peru were not above $60 per ton, which left an ample margin to cover the servicing of short-term debt and provide a comfortable profit.[65]

The main result of the extremely high gearing ratios of most fishmeal enterprises was that their ability to survive even brief downturns in the market was very limited—rapid growth was a prerequisite if debts were to be repaid and a profit obtained—yet that same expansion continued to be financed on credit, perpetuating the financial vulnerability of the sector. By 1963, between 60 per cent and 80 per cent of the industry's total fixed assets and working capital was debt-financed.[66]

In 1963, after five years of meteoric expansion, the fishmeal industry suffered a severe crisis, due to local rather than external factors. A tax of S/25 per ton on fish caught for the industry was imposed on December 1962, to which the owners of fishing boats responded with a lockout in January 1963. This in turn led to a month-long strike by the fishing crews, and by the time the year's production got under way the best fishing months had passed and many of the companies were facing severe cashflow difficulties.[67] In May the commercial banks, alarmed at the prospect of a bad year for the industry, announced severe restrictions on the credit which would in future be made available to fishing companies[68] and by the middle of the year, as the credit squeeze coincided with unusually low fish catches,[69] large numbers of firms began to go bankrupt.

The year 1963 marked the end of the bonanza for new entrants to the industry. Although rapid expansion of output was resumed in 1964, the total number of fishmeal plants had stabilised at around 150, and from 1967 on began to decline, to around 100 by 1972.[70] Continued expansion of production was achieved by the introduction of a new generation of large *bolicheras* and by technical improvements in fishmeal processing.[71] As these technological improvements took effect, Peruvian fishmeal production began to press hard against the limits imposed by its natural-resource base: the fish population of the Humboldt Current.

This fish population was not infinite, and the maximum fish catch which could be sustained over the long run was limited by the reproductive capacity of the anchovy. Many of the world's former leading fisheries had been destroyed by over-exploitation,[72] and fears of a similar occurrence in Peru had been given weight by the Guano Company's demands for restrictions on anchovy fishing in order to safeguard the food supply for Peru's seabirds. From 1956 to 1962 the Prado administration, while allowing the development of anchovy fishing, had tried ineffectually to limit the industry's growth by a licensing system,[73] but the main result was a sharp rise in corruption and speculative dealings in licences, and the system was abandoned in 1962.[74] Proposals in 1960 for a closed season on fishing and the imposition of quotas were defeated by the fishing interests.[75]

By the mid-1960s there were signs of overfishing in the North and Centre of the country[76] and the growth of the industry after 1963 was concentrated in the relatively untapped fishing grounds of the south Coast.

In 1965 there occurred one of the occasional disturbances of the ocean currents which periodically disrupt marine ecology off the Peruvian coast, causing heavy seabird mortality and a fall in fishmeal production. The disruption consists of the intrusion of warm water from the north into the area normally occupied by the cold Humboldt Current; the phenomenon is known in Peru as '*El Niño*,' and occurred most notably in 1891 (when the resulting rains triggered the cotton boom in Piura), in 1925 (when floods wreaked havoc along the entire coast), in 1941 (when the phenomenon seriously misled the U.S. Fisheries Mission), and in 1953, 1957, 1965, and 1972.

The Government's biologists recommended that the annual fish catch should be limited to seven million tons (the 1965 level) by means of a closed season and imposition of quota limits on the total catch,[77] and in 1966 the Government, despite intense opposition from the industry, declared a three-month *veda* and indicated that annual catches would be restricted below eight million tons.[78] The industry, which by this time had installed capacity sufficient to process no less than 16 million tons of anchovy annually,[79] responded by heavy investment in new, larger fishing boats in a competitive struggle, with each firm striving to maximise its share of the national catch during the open season. Since the Government was unwilling to impose firm-by-firm quotas, this process of deliberate investment in excess fishing capacity proceeded until by 1970–1 the industry possessed capacity for a 30-million-ton annual catch (assuming a 300-day working year).[80] The obvious result was that maintenance of the 8-million-ton limit was impossible and the three-month *veda* increasingly ineffective as a production-limiting device. By 1968 the annual catch had soared above 10 million tons and the seabird population, from over 15 million in the early 1960s, was down to under 5 million. In 1970 an FAO mission warned that the long-run average catch could not be maintained for long above 9.5 million tons,[81] and an official limit of 10 million tons was decreed, but disregarded by the industry; the anchovy catch in that year rose above 12 million tons.[82] The following year increasingly stringent restrictions succeeded in bringing the catch back down to 10 million tons, but when in 1972 the ocean currents were again disrupted, the long-feared ecological collapse arrived, and fishmeal virtually disappeared from the list of leading Peruvian exports.

The central point to emerge from this story is that, of all the export industries of Peru in the 1960s, fishmeal was the one most clearly subject to an inflexible, long-run, natural-resource constraint. Experience appears to have demonstrated that the maximum extraction of raw material cannot exceed eight to nine million tons annually without threatening extinction of the fish, so that production can continue to expand only in so far as the yield of meal from that raw material can be raised.[83] By the late 1960s heavy investments in the sector were increasing excess capacity without making much difference to production, and the astonishing growth from 1956 to the mid-1960s could clearly not be repeated. Nor did profits remain at the bonanza levels of the years up to 1962. As the 1960s progressed, the abundance of Peruvian fishmeal on world markets steadily pushed down prices, whilst the Government and the work force both took steps to increase their shares in the industry's value added.[84] With the exception of 1965, when prices briefly went through the roof again, profits remained at more 'normal' levels after 1963.

Entrepreneurship and investment

Who were the leaders in the surge of growth in fishmeal? The most remarkable feature of the list of producers is the scarcity not only of the Peruvian capitalist élite, but also of large foreign capital. This is not to say that these groups were entirely absent; among the major enterprises of the 1950s can be identified at least two controlled by élite figures[85] and three controlled by foreign firms.[86] There is, however, no sign that these five firms enjoyed any competitive advantage due to their ownership; by 1963 two of the foreign firms had sold out and one of the élite firms had gone bankrupt.[87] The giant US and European dealers in animal feeds had not yet reached the point of direct foreign investment as a means of establishing control over their sources of supply of fishmeal. As for the established economic élite of the country, they appeared unwilling to play a direct entrepreneurial role in the new sector, preferring to participate indirectly in the profits of fishmeal by providing finance through the banking system, while leaving the new group of middle-class entrepreneurs to assume the risks.[88]

The fishmeal industry consequently passed through its period of most rapid growth without any significant attempt at penetration by the multinational feed producers; and given this open field, the leading local firms quickly reached maturity as large-scale producers. By the early 1960s there existed in Peru a powerful group of fishmeal capitalists, headed by native and immigrant entrepreneurs who, starting from middle-class origins, had established themselves in canning and were thereby well placed to lead the fishmeal boom. The outstanding figures in their group—Banchero, Elguera, Madueno, Del Rio—became operators of international importance in the fishmeal business when in 1960, led by Banchero, they formed a marketing cartel (the 'Consorcio Pesquero') controlling over 90 per cent of Peruvian production, which successfully handled a market slump and heavy speculative pressures against the fishmeal price during 1960–1 by holding supplies off the market.[89]

With the crisis of 1963, which as explained above was due to local factors and occurred in a favourable market context, the opportunity to buy up bankrupt enterprises was taken by a number of foreign firms and even some members of the Peruvian élite. Several observers have suggested that this was the beginning of a process of denationalisation which, by the end of the decade, had largely removed the sector from local control, with 'foreign' equity participation estimated to have increased from 12 per cent in 1960 to over 40 per cent by 1967.[90] This argument is of considerable importance, in view of the relative withdrawal of Peruvian entrepreneurial effort which we have already found in the cases of mining and oil, and to some extent in sugar. However, the figures quoted above are based on a misleading methodology, which treats as 'foreign' not only multinational firms entering the sector, but also locally-resident operators of immigrant origin.[91] More useful estimates come from a careful breakdown of 1968 fishmeal output by type of company carried out by Abramovich (see Table 12.7). Table 12.8 shows the results of applying the same definitions to the detailed data for the largest producers, published annually since 1966.

Two main conclusions emerge from these figures: first, that entrepreneurs of middle-class and immigrant origin (classed by Abramovich as *recien llegados*) remained the leading element in fishmeal production in the late 1960s, and together with members of the élite accounted for over 60 per cent of production in 1968, whereas wholly-foreign firms accounted for no more than 21 per cent (Table 12.7);[92] and second, that from 1966 to 1971 there was very little sign of any continuing process of denationalisation of the industry.[93] On the basis of our analysis of the leading firms (Table 12.8) the share of output

TABLE 12.7 Shares of 1968 fishmeal production by nature of ownership

Nature of ownership	Output (1000 tons)	Percentage of total output
Wholly-foreign firms	408.3	21.3
Joint ventures (foreign-Peruvian)	191.7	10.0
Traditional Peruvian élite	381.5	19.9
Non-élite local entrepreneurs	799.5	41.7
Cannery waste (not classified)	134.2	7.0
TOTAL	1,915.2	100.0

Source: Abramovich (1973), pp. 41–62.

TABLE 12.8 Share of the main firms in total fishmeal output, 1966–71 (percentages)

	Firms in the 'Top Producers' Lists			Producers not considered
	Wholly-foreign	Joint foreign-Peruvian	Peruvian	
1966	17.4	14.5	28.9	39.2
1968	23.1	9.9	40.9	26.1
1969	24.0	10.3	47.6	18.1
1970	20.4	5.1	49.1	25.4

Sources and Notes: Calculated from the lists of top producers published in *Anuario de Pesca* (1965–6), p. 148; *Peruvian Times*, Fisheries Number, Oct. 20, 1967, p. 7; Fisheries Supplement, Mar. 28, 1969, pp. 20–1; Fisheries Supplement, July 24, 1970, p. 57; and Fisheries Supplement, Mar. 3, 1972, p. 68.

The definitions used are copied from Abramovich (1973), and include certain problematic items, such as the classification of the Gildemeister company as 'wholly-foreign.'

Note that the 1968 figures do not agree exactly with those in Table 12.7, due to differences in the reported production of several firms between the two sources.

Firms in Column 4 were overwhelmingly Peruvian.

produced by wholly-foreign firms rose only slightly from 1966 to 1968, before falling again. Since it is clear from contemporary descriptions in the mid-1960s[94] that foreign penetration of the industry was proceeding at a rapid pace in 1964, following the bankruptcy of many of the first generation of producers, it seems fair to state that foreign participation in fishmeal production rose rapidly from a very low level (probably about 10 per cent) before 1963, to between 20 and 30 per cent by 1967,[95] but that foreign penetration then virtually ceased, and by the end of the 1960s foreign capital was withdrawing.

Detailed analysis of the foreign firms active in the fishmeal sector[96] reveals a high turnover of ownership (this was characteristic also of the Peruvian-controlled firms) and a failure by even the largest of the international feedstock companies to displace Peruvian firms from the leadership. The years 1963 and 1964 witnessed the entry to Peru of several large fishmeal-using multinationals (Ralston Purina, Heinz, Philipp, Cargill and U.S. Albumina Supply Co.) as well as other foreign firms attracted simply by the high profits (W. R. Grace, Harvey Smith, Mecom, DELTEC). Several of these and other new entrants started by buying bankrupt firms, but most also went on to build new plants of their own. Altogether we have been able to identify 13 large foreign entrants to Peruvian fishmeal between 1962 and 1965, but only four between 1965 and 1970, of which two were takeovers of enterprises from existing foreign firms. At least six large foreign firms withdrew from Peruvian fishmeal at the end of the 1960s.

In summary, the process of foreign penetration was concentrated in the years 1962–5, was limited in its extent, and went into reverse in the late 1960s. Effective control of the industry remained in local hands, and the dominant role of the Banchero enterprises was hardly challenged. Foreign firms, evidently, enjoyed no special advantages over local enterprise in fishmeal, an industry in which it was more important to insure against local risks by building plants in a number of widely-separated locations, than to seek to take advantages of economies of scale in a single location.[97]

Further, far from denationalisation reflecting a weakening of local investment, the local capital available for investment in the sector was far greater than the natural resource base would permit, even after the 1963 crisis, the result being the severe excess capacity already noted. This is particularly significant, since the urgency with which investment continued to be poured into this, the only really successful locally-controlled export sector of the period, confirms that it was not a 'savings constraint' which was holding back the development of other export sectors, but other constraints of a structural, physical, or external nature. An increasing proportion of the credit for the sector, it is true, came from the State through the loans made by the Banco Industrial (which bailed the industry out of its 1963 difficulties by arranging special financing terms);[98] but since State credit assistance was available for other sectors also, this does not modify the point made here. Further confirmation that fishmeal had become the only export sector able to absorb local capitalists' funds is provided by the behaviour of the most dynamic of the fishmeal entrepreneurs, Luis Banchero, when he decided to diversify his investments: among the list of interests acquired by

Banchero between 1962 and 1970 there were no export enterprises outside fishmeal.[99]

Fishmeal and the economy

In the late 1950s and through the 1960s, fishmeal was the key to the expansion of the export economy.[100] The sector's returned value was extremely high, and it generated backward linkages to the local capital-goods sector on a scale unprecedented in Peru's economic history.

Unfortunately, because of the fact that figures on the cost structure of the industry were generally produced for polemical purposes in the dispute between the industry and the Government over tax rates,[101] reliable statistics on the sector's returned value are rather scarce. Roemer, however, after a careful study of the sources available, produced estimates of the foreign-exchange leakages from fishmeal for the years 1964–6.[102] He found that leakages to pay for imported inputs, repatriated profits and interest paid abroad averaged $16.8 million annually for those years, while the average value of exports of fishmeal and fishoil was $177.4 million; hence the returned value for the industry, as we have defined it, was slightly over 90 per cent, which puts fishmeal near the top among Peru's export sectors on this count. If second-round imports of materials and equipment (i.e. the import-content of locally-purchased inputs) are subtracted, expenditure on local goods and factors remains 83 per cent.[103] Even taking account of third-round and subsequent leakages into imports, Roemer estimates that overall retention in Peru of the sector's earnings did not fall below 60 per cent. All of these figures, furthermore, should be marked up to allow for the net inflow of foreign capital into the sector during the mid-1960s.

One of the most important reasons for this very high transmission ratio (apart from the relatively small weight of foreign investment in the sector) was the extent of the sector's local purchases. After the initial wave of importation of second-hand processing machinery in the late 1950s, the great bulk of the industry's requirements were produced within Peru by a rapidly-expanding capital-goods sector. Some idea of the magnitude of these backward-linkage effects is provided by Roemer's Table of leakages into imports; he found that the total annual value of locally-produced inputs ($73 million 1964–6, excluding factor payments) was over six times as great as direct imports. The import content of such inputs was $23 million a year.[104] The implied import-content of local production of inputs for fishmeal, 32 per cent, is quite low, considering the degree to which imported technical equipment was used by, for example, the boatbuilding industry.[105]

The most spectacular case of backward linkage was boatbuilding, an activity as open to entry by small-scale operators as was fishing itself. Protected by a 60 per cent duty on imported fishing boats[106] and benefiting from the tax exemptions and other incentives provided in the

1959 Industrial Promotion Law, Peruvian shipyards grew with the fishmeal industry. Six new boats were produced for anchovy fishing in 1957; by 1960 the production figure was 305, and (after a recession in 1961) in 1963 a peak of 453 was reached.[107] Thereafter the pace slowed, and many of the smaller shipbuilders went out of business, while the large and more successful yards consolidated their dominant position. In shipbuilding, as in fishmeal processing, the leading local firm by the end of the 1960s was that of Luis Banchero.[108]

In certain areas the backward-linkage effects included the development in Peru of important new technology.[109] In general, the fishmeal boom generated new impetus for the light engineering industries in Peru, between their period of producing mining equipment in the 1950s and their concentration on consumer durables and motor-vehicle coachwork in the late 1960s. That impetus was accentuated and prolonged beyond what might have been expected (given the fishmeal industry's growth path) by the unnecessarily large amount of new investment in boats and processing plant during the 1960s.

So far as the labour force was concerned,[110] the fishmeal industry quickly generated a new sector of the 'labour aristocracy.' Wages for crews were high,[111] and most accounts agree that the marginal propensity to consume was high, which would suggest quite powerful multiplier effects from the industry's wage bill. A large part of the labour force was recruited among unskilled migrants from the Sierra, and fishmeal was one of the few factors operating to spread the impact of Sierra-Coast migration away from Lima; the growth of the northern city of Chimbote, in particular, took place at a breakneck pace.

Finally, we return to the point raised in the first part of this Chapter: the balance-of-payments situation. It was the dramatic growth of the value of fishmeal exports, more than any other single factor, which kept the balance of payments in equilibrium with only minor crises up to 1966, without depreciation of the sol, despite a huge growth both in imports and in debt servicing payments. Among other things, the fishmeal boom served throughout the mid-1960s to mask the underlying crisis which was gradually overtaking Peruvian export production.

12.3 REVIEW: THE EMERGING CRISIS IN EXPORT PRODUCTION

In the 1920s, although the Peruvian economy was in serious difficulties, the visible productive potential of the country had been only partially exploited, a point reflected in the frequency with which visitors and observers commented on the 'vast untapped wealth' of Peru. Copper and oil reserves were still large; huge deposits of lead, zinc and iron were known but undeveloped; the fisheries along the Coast had hardly been touched; cotton, sugar and wool producers were all hindered more by market problems than by physical constraints on output. During the 1930s and 1940s the groundwork was laid to bring into production this large range of untapped resources, and from the late 1940s to the mid-1960s the economy was swept forward on a wave of expanding export production. As Table 12.9 shows, export volume doubled from 1950 to 1959, and increased a further 65 per cent in the three years 1959–62 (an annual average rate of increase of no less than 18 per cent). After 1962 the pace of expansion slackened greatly; from 1962 to the peak year, 1968, the overall annual growth rate was no more than three per cent. The period of the Velasco Military régime was marked by a steady downward trend in export volume, falling 34 per cent between 1968 and 1975. In 1976 the volume index was still below its level in 1961.

TABLE 12.9 Quantum index of exports, 1929–74
(1929 = 100)

1953 weights		*1963 weights*	
1930	95	1960	276
1940	92	1961	320
1950	103	1962	338
1951	100	1963	328
1952	108	1964	363
1953	128	1965	352
1954	141	1966	349
1955	152	1967	362
1956	171	1968	407
1957	177	1969	368
1958	180	1970	395
1959	201	1971	362
1960	283	1972	386
1961	316	1973	300
1962	333	1974	306[a]
		1975	267[a]
		1976	309[a]

Source: The 1953-weighted index for 1930–62 is from Hunt (1973a) pp. 28–9. The 1963-weighted index is from *Anuario Estadistico*, 1969, p. 961 for 1960 to 1969, and unpublished Banco Central data thereafter. The indices were linked using their average ratio for 1960–2. The 1974–6 estimates are from IMF (1977).
[a] Estimates, from index 1972–5 = 100.

At the aggregate level, this stagnation of export growth after 1962 raises interesting questions. Were markets for Peru's main export commodities declining, or the terms of trade deteriorating? Were government policies biased unduly against exports? Or were there other

TABLE 12.10 Commodity terms of trade, 1960–73
(1963 = 100)

	Export price index	Import price index	Terms of trade
1960	94.8	103.5	91.6
1961	93.9	102.8	91.3
1962	96.6	101.4	95.3
1963	100.0	100.0	100.0
1964	112.1	98.0	114.4
1965	115.5	111.4	103.7
1966	133.3	115.3	115.6
1967	127.3	111.7	114.0
1968	129.9	108.4	119.8
1969	143.5	107.1	134.0
1970	162.0	108.6	149.2
1971	150.7	110.1	136.9
1972	149.4	119.8	124.7
1973	213.6	138.8	153.9

Source: Banco Central de Reserva, *Memoria*; indices are for prices in current dollars.

factors apart from market forces to account for the slowdown? The discussion of the leading sectors in these two chapters permits us to answer that the general tendency of markets during the 1960s and early 1970s was certainly not unfavourable, in contrast to the situation of the 1920s. World prices for most primary commodities were rising, and, as Table 12.10 indicates, the aggregate commodity terms of trade for Peru improved during the period.

The problems for the export-led model come into clearer focus if we take a slightly different approach and ask: what obvious areas of export production remained undeveloped in the mid-1960s—in other words, what form would further export expansion have taken? The most striking characteristic of the 1960s was that almost all of the 'untapped resources' noted by observers in the 1920s had been brought into production, while few new export possibilities had come to light. As we have seen, agricultural export staples had reached a high level of efficiency by world standards and were constrained by the inelastic supply of irrigated land. The more accessible high-grade deposits of iron, lead and zinc had been brought into production. Thirty years of exploration had failed to locate major new oilfields. Fish, the last great natural resource to be tapped, was reaching the ecological limits on extraction. The forest resources of the jungle region, which had excited such great expectations in the early twentieth century, had proved a disappointment from the point of view of profitable export production.

By the mid-1960s it was clear that in the absence of major new discoveries, Peru's future as a primary commodity exporter depended entirely upon the successful development of low-grade copper ores, of which large deposits existed in the hands of multinational corporations. From the opening of Toquepala in 1960 until the fall of Belaunde in late 1968 the pace of development of those deposits was determined by the corporate strategy of these firms, which also controlled copper deposits in many other countries of the world, and had no automatic reason for putting Peru at the head of the list for immediate development.[112] While the protracted war of manoeuvre between Belaunde and the companies proceeded, the momentum of export expansion faded away. When two more years of bargaining by the Velasco regime failed to speed up the pace of development, the Government resorted to expropriation in 1970, and eventually by 1973–4 several major projects were underway, the centrepiece being the Cuajone copper mine.[113] Given the long gestation periods characteristic of large-scale mining development, however, by the time the new generation of mines come into production in 1977, Peru will have lived for fifteen years without a single major new development in export production. How survival and even growth has been possible meanwhile, is analysed in Chapter 15, where we shall consider also the degree to which the new generation of mining projects can save the situation for export-led growth.

Two important conclusions emerge from the above discussion of export sectors during the years after 1948. The first is that local private capital, after playing a central role in export development during the 1950s, tended to withdraw from such activity during the 1960s. We have not been altogether successful in elucidating the reasons for this, although contributory factors were undoubtedly the decline in the profitability of new investment in several sectors as non-financial constraints were encountered, the impact on local confidence of the collapse of several manipulated international commodities markets in the late 1950s, and possibly the influence of the fixed exchange rate after 1958. To some extent this withdrawal of local initiative reflected a diversion of entrepreneurial effort towards industry and urbanisation, and to some extent it resulted from a general decline in the dynamism of the upper strata of the local bourgeoisie. Our analysis of fishmeal, the export sector which provided the exception to the rule of declining local initiative, served to confirm both the relative inactivity of the local élite (the sector was developed mainly by sub-élite operators) and the absence of any absolute savings constraint (since local funds were readily obtainable for investment through the financial system).

As this withdrawal by the local élite took effect, government policy towards export sectors exhibited a clear swing towards a more nationalistic stance. The promotional policies of the Odría regime had been based upon a tacit alliance between the local élite and foreign capital, both groups having a common interest in the development of export activities under special concessionary terms. As élite interest waned in the 1960s, the foreign firms which remained active in export development found that their leverage upon local politics had declined. Taxes were increased, terms for the development of mineral resources hardened, and policy on the exchange rate and the tariff system began to discriminate against exports. The reaction of the main foreign firms was to adopt a waiting game, in the hope that the policy pendulum would eventually swing back in their favour.

The short-run effect of these developments was slight, owing to the buoyancy of fishmeal and the entry into production of the Toquepala copper mine. In the longer run, the damage to the export-led growth model was severe, which brings us to our second major conclusion: the 1960s brought a fundamental change in the nature of feasible export growth. With the exception of fishing (the ecological constraint on whose growth was, and is, absolute) the growth of export sectors was slowing down primarily because of increasing constraints on small and medium-scale projects to expand production. The future lay with projects of very large scale, and the rapid increase in the minimum scale of practicable projects had evidently outrun the willingness or ability of the local élite to organise and invest in such development. The initiation of new projects consequently depended increasingly upon the willingness of the State and/or foreign capital to undertake the task. During the 1960s State investment was concentrated in non-export projects (particularly Belaunde's prized road schemes) and was subject to a severe revenue constraint, as the Government's foreign borrowing capacity was limited, and the political will to increase local taxation was entirely lacking. The virtual abstention of foreign capital during the decade therefore doomed Peru to a slow rate of export growth. Only following the coup of late 1968 did the new Government move towards full-scale state participation in export investment, using State capitalism to substitute for the failings of both local and foreign private capital during the 1960s.

In addition to this problem of the increased scale of projects, the future of the export economy had abruptly become almost totally dependent upon a single export sector: metal mining, and particularly copper. This probably could not have been foreseen at the beginning of the 1960s, given Peru's long tradition of highly-diversified exports; but it meant that during the decade, the failure to evolve a satisfactory policy for mineral development had a fatal impact upon growth prospects in the 1970s. As the importance of minerals for future growth increased, so did the importance of adequate governmental control over the mining sector. Combined with the technical problems of mining development, this meant that the nature of the export economy changed fundamentally in the 1960s.

13 Policy and the Non-export Economy, 1948–68

The coup of 1948 brought to power a Government which extended a positive and uncritical welcome to foreign capital, and staked the future of the economy on export-led growth in a *laissez-faire* framework. This general policy orientation established by the Odria regime remained until 1967 the guideline for economic strategy. A 1965 observer remarked that 'Peru today has the freest economy in South America, and perhaps the hungriest foreign investors.'[1] The maintenance of an orthodox liberal economic policy was made possible primarily by the spectacularly successful export growth analysed in Chapters 11 and 12, while in turn liberal policy undoubtedly contributed at least partly to the rate of export expansion.

Our earlier description of the effects of export growth in a *laissez-faire* policy environment before 1930 provides some predictions of the consequences which might be expected from a repetition of the process in the 1950s and 1960s. In particular, a progressively-increasing role for foreign capital could be anticipated—and the two preceding chapters have confirmed this trend for the main export sectors. A second prediction based upon the pre-1930 experience would be that as export-led growth proceeded, so the forces making for diversification and increased economic autonomy would tend to weaken. However, as we mentioned above in the Introduction to Part IV, this prediction is not at first sight borne out by the evidence. Table 13.1 shows how the relative weight of the different sectors moved over time. It will be seen that the share of manufacturing in GNP increased dramatically, from 14 per cent in 1950 to 20 per cent by 1968, and that those sectors reflecting more broadly the growth of the urban economy, such as banking, commerce, transport, power and services, all maintained or increased their share of the rapidly growing gross national product. Meanwhile the decline of agriculture was not compensated for by the rise of mining and fishing. The shift in the structure of employment was even more marked, as shown in Table 13.2, with the commerce and government sectors absorbing large numbers of the rising urban population. Further, when

TABLE 13.1 Real GNP: index and sectoral composition
(1963 prices)

	1950	1955	1960	1965	1968
GNP index 1950 = 100	100	134	165	226	245
Percentage shares:					
Agriculture	23	21	21	17	15
Fishing	0	1	2	2	2
Mining	4	5	7	6	6
Manufacturing	14	15	17	19	20
Construction	5	6	4	4	3
Electricity, etc.	1	1	1	1	1
Commerce[a]	15	14	13	14	14
Transport, etc.[a]	5	6	5	5	6
Banking, insurance[a]	3	3	3	4	3
Services[a]	12	14	13	16	15
House property	9	7	7	6	6
Government	9	8	8	8	9

Source: Banco Central, *Cuentas Nacionales del Perú*.
[a] These sectors are not disaggregated in the Central Bank's constant price estimates. They have been disaggregated here on the basis of the movement of their relative shares at current prices.

we look at policy, we find that the decade beginning in the late fifties was clearly distinct from, for example, the 1920s, in that a series of new policy initiatives were taken by successive governments with the express aim of promoting industrialisation and bringing about structural change in agriculture.

The task of this chapter is to evaluate the significance of these trends in structure and in policy. We look first at the emerging social trends which helped to induce the policy shift, and then turn to the two sectors most affected by the changing climate, industry and food agriculture. As in preceding sections, we are well aware of the extensive areas of the non-export economy which are thereby omitted from detailed study. In particular, we omit an evaluation of the apparent increase in employment in commerce and services, and its implications for under-employment and increasing dualism. However, we regard such omissions not only as inevitable given the already wide scope of the study, but also as reasonable, given the importance of the sectors chosen both as barometers for the degree of economic autonomy and as the immediate targets of the policy shift.

TABLE 13.2 Sectoral composition of the labour force, 1950, 1961, 1970[a]

	1950	1961 (BCR)	1961 (SERH)	1970
Agriculture	58.9	52.8	49.8	44.5
Mining	2.2	2.2	2.2	1.9
Manufacturing	13.0	13.5	13.2	14.5
Factory	–	–	4.5	5.4
Artisan	–	–	8.7	9.1
Construction	2.7	3.4	3.3	3.0
Commerce	6.6	8.6	8.9	10.9
Electricity	0.2	0.3		
Transport	2.7	3.1		
Banking	0.4	0.6	18.9	21.3
Government	4.0	5.5		
Other services	9.3	10.1		
Not specified	–	–	2.6	2.2
Aspirants[b]	–	–	1.1	1.1

Source: 1950 and 1961 (BCR) from *Cuentas Nacionales del Perú 1950–1965*; 1961 (SERH – Servicio de Empleo y Recursos Humanos del Min. de Trabajo) and 1970 from Tokman (1975), p. 147.
[a] The two different versions of 1961 have been given, to enable proper comparison to be made with earlier and later years. The Banco Central version appears to have allocated virtually all of the 'unspecified' and 'aspirant' categories to agriculture.
[b] This is not defined in the source, but presumably represents newcomers to the pool of unemployed, lacking an industrial classification.

13.1 SOCIAL TRENDS AND POLICY, 1948–68

Most important of the new social trends was the accelerating population growth and rise of middle-class groups, which in the 1940s had contributed to the rise of APRA and the election of Bustamante. Population growth had been 1.9 per cent annually in 1940; by 1950–1 it had risen to 2.2 per cent and by 1961 to 2.7 per cent;[2] meanwhile urbanisation proceeded apace, the population in cities of more than 2,500 rising from 18 per cent in 1940 to 39 per cent in 1961. Lima alone grew from half a million to some two million over that period.[3] Rural population pressure generated not only accelerating rural–urban migration, but also an increase in social tension in the countryside, which resulted in land invasions and sporadic guerrilla activity in the first half of the 1960s. As the urban population increased, the growing number of un- and under-employed became a serious problem for economic policy, while at the same time the increased urban population represented a larger potential market for local manufacturing industries. Urban growth naturally brought expansion of white-collar employment in the bureaucracy and the education system, and the consequent increase in the numbers of the middle classes inevitably produced a shift in the balance of politics.

The 1956 presidential elections, although fought within the policy framework laid down by Odría, bore witness to the renewed importance of the social forces which had produced the Prado and Bustamante Governments of the preceding decade. Opposed by a new middle-class party, Accion Popular, Prado won the election by reaching agreement with the old-established APRA, and his presidential term from 1956 to 1962 was marked by a *convivencia* which Bourricaud describes as follows:[4]

(the *convivencia* was) based on an agreement between APRA and certain conservative elements—the Pradists and a small group of Pedro Beltran's friends—who had gradually come to believe that the stability of power depended on reaching an understanding with a large popular party, reformist but not revolutionary . . . There was a prospect of large democratic reforms, particularly in the sphere of land tenure. In the main, however, it was intended that the basic rules of creole liberalism were to be observed . . .

Following an Aprista victory in the elections of 1962, the military intervened to prevent APRA taking power, the ensuing military Government[5] promising free elections within a year. With military approval, the 1963 election brought to power the Accion Popular party headed by Belaunde, with a platform which promised a fresh commitment to middle-class based populist policies, which although more progressive in tone than those of Prado, did not conflict with the 'creole liberalism' of economic and social policy.[6]

The changing complexion of politics, which brought with it limited and halting moves towards increased nationalism and a commitment to some economic diversification, was reinforced by basic trends in the economy. Despite the continued growth of export earnings up to the mid-1960s, we have seen how opportunities for profitable investment by the élite in export sectors were narrowing at the end of the 1950s, with the result that the élite became increasingly prepared to contemplate policy changes designed to create new profit opportunities in other economic sectors. A certain disenchantment with export dependence was also induced by the experience of price instability in foreign markets in 1953–4, and more sharply in 1957–8.

These various underlying trends brought a gradual shift in the focus of economic policy. The main new policy directions consisted of promotion of manufacturing industry, growing acceptance of the case for agrarian reform in the Sierra, and a steady increase in public spending and in the role of the State. The sections which follow look at the first two of these; the third will be discussed in Chapter 14.

13.2 THE PROCESS OF INDUSTRIALISATION, 1948–68

By 1950, for reasons already discussed, industrialisation had made less headway in Peru than in other South American economies of comparable size. The potential opportunities of the 1930s and 1940s had been largely neglected, and the 1948 coup which brought Odría to power represented a swing of policy towards export promotion, with low priority assigned to import-substituting industry. The new Government's orientation was evident in its promotional legislation for mining and oil, its considerable investment in new irrigation works in the North, and its failure to respond to pressures for the protection of local manufacturing. The sole major State-backed industrialisation venture of the 1940s—the Santa Corporation—was starved of funds.[7] The Banco Industrial's activities were restricted, and its share of total lending by the State development-bank sector fell steadily until 1955.[8] Once controls had been removed, imports grew rapidly, displacing local manufactures from a considerable segment of the internal market.[9]

This is not to say that industrial growth halted; on the contrary, as Table 13.1 has shown, the share of manufacturing in GNP rose slightly even in the period 1950 to 1955, and the annual rate of growth of industry was eight per cent. Much of this growth, however, was in export processing rather than in production for the local market. As Table 13.3 indicates, such processing activities moved from 18 per cent of industrial production in 1950 to 19 per cent in 1955. Furthermore, much of the rise in the importance of 'consumer durable and capital goods' during the first half of the 1950s represented activities directly linked to export growth—particularly to the expanding small-scale and medium-scale mining sector. Industrial growth in the early 1950s, therefore, was not import-substituting but export-supporting. The figures on import composition in Table 13.4 show that manufactured consumer goods remained around 15 per cent of total imports from 1945 to 1950 (although this conceals a fall in non-durables and a rise in durables), and that during the first half of the 1950s the share of both non-durables and durables tended to rise; only at the end of the 1950s did the trends again begin to indicate substantial substitution of consumer-goods imports. The share of industrial intermediate-goods imports fell from 1950 to 1955.

In 1953–4 an export recession put pressure on the exchange rate and seems to have convinced the Odría government of the advisability of a more positive attitude towards industrialisation. The Santa Corporation was revived by the appointment of a new president in 1954[10] and work was begun in 1955 on the drafting of a new industrial promotion law. In a generally more favourable climate, a number of significant new privately-organised industrial ventures made their appearance. One leading growth sector in the mid-1950s was cement, demand for which

TABLE 13.3 The composition of industrial production, 1950–68[a]
(percentages)

	1950	1955	1960	1965	1968
Export processing[b]	18.0	19.1	25.8	21.5	22.8
of which minerals	3.7	4.2	7.8	5.7	6.3
sugar	14.2	14.6	12.3	7.6	6.5
fishmeal	0.1	0.3	5.6	8.3	10.1
Other consumer goods[c]	50.7	49.4	42.4	40.8	39.3
Other intermediate goods[d]	19.0	19.6	19.0	21.8	25.1
of which paper	1.8	2.4	3.0	3.3	3.6
chem. products	4.1	4.1	5.5	8.0	9.5
petroleum products	4.4	3.7	2.9	2.4	2.3
Consumer durable and capital goods[e]	6.7	8.6	9.9	10.8	12.9

Source: Banco Industrial, *La Situación de la Industria Manufacturera Peruana en el año 1963, 1965, 1966, Censo Económico* (1963), *Anuario Estadístico*, and Banco Central (1961).
[a] For a comment on the sources see Appendix IV.
[b] Includes a small proportion processed for the local market.
[c] CIIU Nos. 20 (excluding 207, sugar & 20X, fishmeal), 21, 22, 23, 24, 26, 28, 39. Note: in the source used for 1950–65, 25 and 26 are given together. The procedure here was to assume the same rate of growth for each sector and take the absolute values from the 1963 census.
[d] CIIU Nos. 25, 27, 29, 30–33.
[e] CIIU Nos. 35–38'.This grouping is particularly weak, including also some intermediate goods. See the discussion in the text for the minute weight of 'genuine' capital goods in these sectors.

had been increasing rapidly with a renewed urbanisation boom in Lima during the early 1950s. From 1945 until 1952 cement production had risen 40 per cent; in the following four years, production increased a further 49 per cent.[11] In contrast to the cement industry's foreign-dominated origins in the 1920s, the new firms of the 1950s were mostly controlled and promoted by members of the local élite, and represented the first steps in a diversion of élite interest away from export activities and towards non-export sectors, including manufacturing.[12]

A turning-point for industrialisation can thus be identified in the last year or so of the Odría government, as a new generation of manufacturing ventures came on to the scene.[13] The new impetus can to a large extent be described as a spin-off from export expansion, as export interests moved towards greater horizontal and vertical diversification.

TABLE 13.4 Trends in import composition, 1945–73
(percentages of total imports by value)

	Consumer non-durable		Consumer durable	Industrial intermediate goods
	Food	Manufactures		
1945	8.1	9.8	4.7	37.0
1946	7.8	9.1	6.4	34.0
1950	9.6	6.0	8.6	36.6
1955	6.9	6.6	10.8	34.2
1960	6.2	6.0	9.4	34.8
1965	7.4	4.3	9.0	35.3
1970	6.4	5.1	2.6	45.8
1973	5.0	5.1	5.1	38.2

Source: Bertram (1976).

This was true not only of the local élite, but also of the old-established foreign firms Grace and Cerro. Grace's parent company in the U.S.A. had embarked after the Second World War upon a deliberate policy of diversification into chemicals, and the weight of chemicals production in Grace's worldwide operations grew from 3 per cent in 1950 to 55 per cent by 1958. In Peru, Grace's production of paper, paper products, chemicals, biscuits, machinery, textiles and paint was rapidly expanded during the 1950s, to the point where by 1958 the firm's local manager could speak of 'sugar as a by-product.'[14]

While Grace expanded horizontally, Cerro in the 1950s embarked seriously upon vertical diversification, with the establishment of Explosivos SA in 1956 and Refractarios SA (furnace bricks), both in partnership with local capitalists.[15] Other U.S. firms also began to move into local production for the Peruvian market during the second half of the 1950s, the leading new entrant being Goodrich's Lima Rubber Company, established in 1955. Figures on the book value of U.S. investments in manufacturing show a rapid increase beginning in 1954 and continuing until 1967,[16] while Table 13.9 below suggests that the number of new foreign firms entering manufacturing rose sharply from 1955 on.

As Table 13.3 shows, industrial expansion up to 1960 continued to be concentrated in export processing, and in the production of certain types of intermediate goods (particularly paper, chemicals, and cement) and capital goods (for the mining and fishing sectors). The drive came from a combination of the local élite and certain foreign firms, in some cases operating separately, but often in various forms of joint venture. The local élite were valued by foreign capital for the political and financial access which they could provide,[17] and it was common for foreign firms to invite élite figures to join the boards of their Peruvian subsidiaries. One example of the process is the Prado-Beltran-Ferreyros group of businessmen, who in addition to their own activities were involved with Wood Struthers of the U.S.A. in a project to set up a new industrial complex based on a sugar estate,[18] and with a foreign group including Cerro and Grace in the establishment of Fertisa, a petrochemical plant supplying fertiliser for commercial agriculture and chemicals for Cerro's explosives factory.[19]

Precisely what proportion of industrial production was directly a function of export growth by 1960 is difficult to say, but the order of magnitude is clear. Table 13.3 shows the share of export processing in total industrial production to have risen from 18 per cent in 1950 to 26 per cent by 1960, and according to the 1969 input–output table,[20] four per cent of industry's gross sales in 1969 consisted of inputs into primary activities; the 1960 proportion may well have been higher than this. Thus about one-third of manufacturing activity in 1960 was export-linked, and the links of ownership and control tying industrial ventures to the export sectors were of even greater significance. As large-scale export enterprises became also large-scale industrial ventures, the degree of concentration increased markedly both within industries and across industries, and the integrated 'industrial groups' which were to be characteristic of the 1960s made their appearance.[21]

Thus by the end of the 1950s the local élite and the established foreign firms—traditionally a bloc of interests concerned predominantly with export growth—had become involved in the promotion of non-export activities, although many of these remained linked closely to export sectors. In addition, there were the first signs of a move completely away from export-linked industries towards purely import-substituting ventures. Beginning with products such as paper, cement, tyres and textiles, the process was moving on by the end of the 1950s to plans for local production of consumer durables[22] and renewed interest in pharmaceuticals. The growing interest in industrialisation was stimulated by the widespread belief in Latin America that industrialisation was essential in order to expand employment and sustain economic growth (thus preventing social unrest), and by the experience of the export slump of 1958, which seemed once more to demonstrate the dangers of too great a dependence upon export sectors. Investment opportunities in the main export industries were also becoming less attractive (although fishmeal was to provide a temporary amelioration of this situation).

In addition, factors of the sort which we have used to account for previous surges of industrial investment operated during the 1950s. Exchange depreciation was one of the hallmarks of the Odría period, and the major devaluation of 1958 further strengthened the position of local industry *vis-à-vis* imports. Internal demand was growing rapidly as the export economy expanded; and while the diversion of this demand towards local supplies was less strong than in the 1890s, nevertheless it is clear that the profitability of manufacturing had improved sufficiently to attract renewed interest.

What was new in the situation of the late 1950s was that, in contrast to earlier periods when the élite had withheld their support from policies designed to favour industrialisation, now, for the reasons we have discussed above, they were prepared to support the promotion of industrial growth, by means of tariffs and tax exemptions. The key indicator of the changed climate was the Industrial Promotion Law drafted during Odría's last year in power, presented to Congress by Prado in 1956, and finally passed in 1959, following long debate and considerable amendment. By the time this bill became law it could claim 'favourable reaction from virtually all sectors of political opinion'[23] and it was clear that a sizeable fraction of the local élite, led by President Prado himself, was planning to shift its interests into manufacturing—preferably in alliance with foreign capital, the inflow of which was clearly foreseen in the new law.

The Industrial Promotion Law gave lavish incentives for investment in industry, principally by means of exemptions from import duties on equipment and intermediate goods, and provision for tax-free reinvestment of profits. Laws of this type were appearing throughout Latin America at that time, but usually with the intention of stimulating the growth of selected industries and/or regions. The Peruvian law was exceptional in its generosity and lack of selectivity. Most countries restricted incentives to new activities, or activities with high percentages of local inputs and/or local ownership. The Peruvian law however offered benefits to *all* sectors, to established firms as well as new ones; these benefits included complete exemption from import duties for all 'basic'[24] industries, *including* established firms, and the right to invest tax free 30–100 per cent of profits, depending on the region.[25] The incentives were explicitly made available to export processing activities, and their non-discriminatory nature made them more or less a straightforward subsidy to private enterprise. The most serious modification to the bill on its way through Congress was the elimination of a State agency, 'Corporacion Nacional de Fomento Industrial,' which was in the original proposal.[26] The Law was deliberately intended to encourage foreign investment,[27] and its unselective nature reflected the prevailing pro-private-enterprise, pro-foreign-capital ethos in Peru. The main argument advanced for the measure in the Congress debates was that it was 'unfair' for industry not to have a special law promoting it as other sectors did, and that, since promotional laws in other sectors had so successfully stimulated both foreign investment and rapid growth, the same recipe should now be tried for industry. Such an attitude precluded the discrimination among sectors which would have been essential for a rationally-planned industrialisation policy.

At the same time, tariff policy began to be modified to promote industry, more through the increases in effective protection resulting from exemptions granted under the new Law, than through a systematic reform of the tariff for this end. Peru had always been remarkable for a low level of tariffs;[28] beginning with the balance-of-payments crisis of 1958 tariffs were increased on several occasions, and in 1964 and 1967 entire new tariff systems were introduced. These tariff changes consisted largely of the raising of duties on consumer-goods imports—a trend particularly evident in a comparison of the tariffs of 1964 and 1967.[29] Higher duties on final goods, combined with exemptions under the Industrial Promotion Law, naturally brought massive increases in effective protection for import-substituting industries. Vehicles, for example, had 13 per cent effective protection in 1963 and 214 per cent in 1965; pharmaceutical products 18 per cent and 164 per cent for the same years.[30] Such increases far outweighed any negative effect of the stable exchange rate between 1958 and 1967.[31]

The policy context was thus prepared for a new burst of industrial growth in response to the significant increases in profitability implicit in these measures. Profitability was also sustained by the continued rise in the level of demand; as we have seen in the preceding chapters, export supply constraints had not yet affected the rate of growth of export value and, as the next chapter will show, government spending rose rapidly in the early sixties. But one further development was important in facilitating the response: the expansion of the financial system. Between 1961 and 1965 the stock of savings in financial institutions rose sharply, from 8 per cent to 12 per cent of GNP—far more rapidly than was typical elsewhere in Latin America—while the flow of annual personal savings held in such institutions rose from 2 per cent of personal disposable income in 1961 to over 4 per cent in 1965; this compares for example with an average of 2.5 per cent for Mexico from 1949 to 1963.[32]

This expansion reflects not only the development of new financial institutions, such as savings and loans and hire purchase associations, but a sharp increase in the dynamism of the banking sector, associated with a wave of foreign takeover. Banks effectively foreign-controlled represented 36 per cent of total bank assets in 1960, and 62 per cent in 1968.[33]

The increase in financial savings did not reflect a rise in the total savings effort; indeed, as we shall see in the following chapter, total private savings and investment were already falling by the mid-1960s as a percentage of GNP. Nor did it reflect an increase in real rates of return available on institutional savings; in fact rates became increasingly negative over the period.[34] Rather, it represented the infrastructural development which both reflected and facilitated the changing nature of the private sector in Peru in the 1960s. First, it facilitated the shift of funds by the élite out of export sectors, while allowing this to be compatible with the weakening of their entrepreneurial role which we have already observed in certain export sectors. Second, by the increase in provision of specialised financial institutions for housing it aided the expansion of their real-estate interests. Third, by the provision of finance for consumption purchases it greatly facilitated the switch to an import-substitution boom centred on consumer durables. And last, it facilitated the entry of foreign investment into manufacturing, by enabling foreign firms to borrow locally, usually at negative rates, so further enhancing their profitability.[35]

The result of these developments and of the policies we have already described was a massive wave of direct foreign investment in manufacturing, trebling between 1960 and 1966.[36] This brought the degree of foreign control in the manufacturing sector up to the high level demonstrated in Table 13.5:[37] over half of the total output of most products other than beer and printing were in foreign hands, and over three-quarters of production of intermediate goods and *metal mecanica*,[38] and this may well be an underestimate.[39] The extent to which this reflected an abrupt increase is reflected in the data on the year of entry of foreign firms shown in Table 13.6: of 242 foreign firms in the sector in 1969, no fewer than 68 per cent had entered since 1960. Only the small-scale unregistered industrial sector remained free of the web of foreign investment. Meanwhile domestic large-scale investors tended to play a subsidiary role. Unlike the more common Latin American pattern of the 1960s, this did not occur by means of takeover: as we see in Table 13.6, of the firms included only five per cent had entered by taking over an existing Peruvian firm.[40] The rise of foreign control in manufacturing (as in mining) thus reflected the fact that the new and growing enterprises were mostly foreign, using local finance and directors, while the bulk of locally-controlled firms displayed little dynamism.[41]

This increasingly weak role played by the obvious candidates for the part of the 'industrial bourgeoisie' lay behind the continued incoherence of government policy. We have seen that the Industrial Promotion Law approximated a generalised subsidy to manufacturing industry. While it incorporated certain inadequate incentives to regional decentralisation, the granting of exemptions and privileges was left to the discretion of the Government. In practice, the Government played a passive role, granting tariff exemptions to the sectors which mounted the most effective pressure campaigns. No consideration was given to the selection of industries on the basis of their real growth prospects, nor to the problem of avoiding diseconomies of scale in the limited Peruvian markets. (By 1966, for example, there were no fewer than thirteen

TABLE 13.5 Share of large and medium foreign and mixed companies in output[a], 1968.
(percentages)

	Non-durable consumer goods	Intermediate goods	Metal mecanica	Other
(i) In total output of registered industry[b]	33.5	57.6	44.1	17.4
(ii) In output of larger and medium firms	50.9	76.8	77.7	26.9
(iii) Excluding beer and printing from consumer goods	60.0	76.8	77.7	26.9

Source: calculated from Espinoza and Osorio (1972).
[a] Since we lack information on small companies, we give here in (i) and (ii) lower and upper bounds for the actual share of all foreign owned and mixed companies in total output. 'Mixed' includes firms with only 25 or 30 per cent foreign ownership. (In practice, a rather pragmatic criterion was used.) The meaning of the distinction between 'foreign' and 'national' is as follows: an individual or corporate shareholding is defined as national/foreign if the relevant individuals or firms sign a declaration that they wish such holdings to be regarded as Peruvian/foreign. 'Peruvian' holdings do not have the right to remit profits.
[b] This refers to firms with five or more employees.

TABLE 13.6 Major foreign manufacturing corporations (existing in 1969): year of entry into Peru

	Number entering	Number entering by takeover
Before 1940	14	5
1940–4	7	–
1945–9	14	1
1950–4	9	3
1955–9	23	4
1960–4	75	5
1965–9	89	3
No information	11	2
TOTAL	242	23

Source: Anaya (1975), p. 39, and information supplied by the author.

automobile assembly plants in a country with an effective market of, say, one million families.) A disproportionate number of exemptions were granted to the old-established and slow-growing textile and food industries, while high-import-content sectors like pharmaceuticals obtained preferential treatment. Nor was the State's own record in basic industry very impressive. E.P.F.'s new oil refinery at La Pampilla, development of the naval shipyard (SIMA) in Callao to build large freighters, the establishment of a large ammonium-fertiliser plant near Cuzco, the new cement plant at Yura near Arequipa, and a long series of plans for expansion of the Chimbote steel mill, were all ventures by the State into areas left vacant by private capital. But under the Prado and Belaunde régimes, only a few of these ventures (notably the La Pampilla refinery and the SIMA shipyard) were well-organised and efficiently-run; the Chimbote steel mill and the Cuzco fertiliser plant were conspicuous failures of the decade. The expanding role of the State and its significance is taken up again in the following chapter.

This weak and incoherent policy environment, combined with rapid expansion of foreign firms and facilitated by developments in the financial sector, had important consequences for the type of industrial growth which followed. The first consequence was an acceleration in the rate of growth of industry, to some nine per cent a year between 1960 and 1965, with the result that as shown in Table 13.1 above, the share of industry in GNP rose from 17 per cent in 1960 to 20 per cent by 1968. Table 13.3 above shows in which branches the most rapid increases occurred: however, we need to disaggregate further to understand its implications. The detailed examination of the 1968 industrial structure carried out by Saberbein[42] demonstrates clearly that true 'capital goods' are almost entirely lacking in *metal mecanica*, consumer durables comprising by far the larger part. He estimates machinery production as only one per cent of the gross manufacturing product. In fact the local production of capital goods was actively discouraged in the course of the 1960s as small mining declined[43] and as the high-linkage fishmeal sector reached the point of saturation. Further, although there was a significant expansion in chemicals, much of which was attributable to Grace's activities at Paramonga, the growth of packaging-type activities in pharmaceuticals was even more rapid.[44]

Further, as Table 13.7 shows, it was the rapidly-growing *metal mecanica* sector which was highly and increasingly dependent on imported inputs. The rising share of industries such as automobiles and consumer appliances was a major reason for the steady rise in the weight of intermediate goods in the total import bill shown in Table 13.4 above. This implied a significant increase in the inflexibility of economic management, given the importance of such goods in maintaining the level of activity. It also implied a further element in the weight of foreign control, since foreign firms were responsible for a high proportion of

TABLE 13.7 Structure of inputs in industry, 1954–72
(imported inputs as per cent of total inputs)

Type of industry	1954	1960	1967	1972
Mainly consumer goods[b]	31	27	29	31[a]
Mainly intermediate[c]	23	26	35	39[a]
Mainly consumer durable and capital[d]	77	70	77	58[a]

Source: *Estadistica Industrial*, various years.
[a] 1972 data exclude packaging. Packaging is probably included in the previous years, although this is not made clear in the source used. The 1972 ratios may therefore be biased downwards in comparison with earlier years.
[b] Sectors 20–24, 26, 28, 39 of the CIIU classification.
[c] Sectors 25, 27, 29–34.
[d] Sectors 35–38.

TABLE 13.8 Peru: indices of integration, 1969[a]

	Exports[b]	Domestic Agriculture	Manufacturing[c]		
			Consumption	Intermediate	Metal mecanica
Intersectoral sales ÷ total sales	0.9	0.12	0.22	0.69	0.33
Imported direct and indirect inputs ÷ total inputs[d]	0.22	0.15	0.36	0.35	0.67

Source: Calculated by G. Palma from INP (1973). For a more detailed study see Palma (forthcoming).
[a] Similar results using somewhat different definitions can be found in Fitzgerald (1976), Appendix I.
[b] Sectors 1, 6, 7, 9, 11, 27 of the input–output table.
[c] Consumption: Sectors 10, 12, 13, 15, 16, 18, 20, 32.
Intermediate: 17, 19, 21, 24, 25, 26.
Metal mecanica: 28–31.
[d] Inter- and intra-sectoral.

such imports. And it reflected the low[45] level of inter-industry linkages which we see in Table 13.8.

Implicit also in this evolution is another element familiar in analyses of post-1960 industrialisation in Latin America—increasing technological dependence. Such dependence has three interrelated dimensions: first, the vulnerability, reduced bargaining power, and decay in local capacities implicit in reliance on outside sources of technology; second, the distortions introduced in factor use by the availability of inappropriate technology (which in many cases locals then have to imitate); and third, the financial drain involved in servicing technology contracts. Unfortunately, no data exist which might enable us to measure the *increase* in technological dependence in Peruvian industry, although a series of studies carried out at the end of the 1960s established the extent of the phenomenon at that date.[46] As Table 13.9 demonstrates, the great majority of manufacturing firms were using imported knowhow by 1968.

TABLE 13.9 Percentages of firms obtaining foreign blueprints, etc.

Pharmaceuticals	81
Basic chemicals	80
Basic metals	80
Metal fabricating	71
Domestic electrical equipment	100
Textiles	90

Source: Espinoza *et al.* (1971), p. 49, quoting Consejo Nacional de Investigación (1970).

Such characteristics lead us to important conclusions concerning the significance of the undoubtedly rapid growth of industry during this period. Our discussion in Chapter 2 indicated that the potential significance of the expansion of the industrial sector as an agent of greater autonomy lies in its role in producing a more integrated economy and thereby increasing the extent to which the source of dynamism lies within the economy, and in its role as a source of capital goods and technological development. If its expansion also reflects an increase of the role of local interests as opposed to foreign, then it will also of course contribute to local control of the economic surplus.

We have seen here how the industrialisation process of the 1960s was neither integrated nor self-sustaining. Import content was high and increasing, and the sector's vulnerability to foreign-exchange constraints was consequently also increasing. Foreign control and associated external appropriation of the surplus was rising steadily. The amount of internal economic dynamism generated by mechanisms such as inter-industry linkages was minimal, and the growth sectors showed no sign of technological autonomy (with no more than one or two exceptions).[47] A large proportion of industrial activity remained tied to export sectors rather than the internal market – but as foreign control of the growing export sectors increased, and growth in the high-linkage fishmeal sector slowed, the export-generated demand for backward-linkage products such as capital goods was tending to weaken, and the economy's general dependence upon imported capital equipment was increasing. In the long run, we would hypothesise (on *ceteris paribus* assumptions, although in fact the political upheaval of 1968 disrupted economic trends), the industrialisation process of the 1960s would not have been self-sustaining, since the very high rates of investment on which it depended[48] were induced by policies which gave once-for-all very substantial increases in profitability, which could not have been continually repeated, and were to a large extent made possible by the scope for Peru to 'catch up' with other economies in terms of modernisation and re-equipment of industry;[49] once this backlog was exhausted, investment would naturally have slowed. This probability that industrial investment would have fallen off at the end of the decade, regardless of the events of 1968, should be borne in mind in appraising the problems faced by the military Government in attempting to revive industrial activity after 1968.

Having introduced so many criticisms of the industrialisation process during the 1960s, it is only fair to emphasise two of its more positive aspects. In the first place, the decade witnessed the most rapid diversification of the economy towards non-export activities achieved before or since; and while in the short and medium term the external dependence and distorted character of the new industrial sectors limited their growth potential, the years after 1959 undoubtedly brought a major expansion of the modern sector of the economy and the laying-down of a considerable amount of productive capital investment.

The second positive point is the employment record of industrial growth in Peru. A common theme in the writing of the dependency school has been the 'marginalisation' of labour as a result of the excessive capital-intensity and external technological dependence of the growing industrial sectors. In several Latin American economies, industrialisation (in the sense of an increase in the manufacturing sector's share of GNP) was not accompanied by any corresponding increase in the proportion of the labour force employed in the sector.

In the case of Peru, there is no doubt that the bias of the new industrial technology did lead to a significant increase in capital intensity,[50] with the direct result that industrial employment rose less rapidly than output; but since industrial output was itself growing extremely fast in the early 1960s, the expansion of employment was still rapid, resulting in a rise in the share of industrial employment in the total labour force. As Table 13.2 above shows, industry accounted for 13.2 per cent of the labour force in 1961, and 14.5 per cent by 1970. It further appears that this expansion did not represent a displacement of artisan and unregistered sector employment, since as the table shows such groups represented 66 per cent of industrial employment in 1961, and still 62 per cent in 1970. This unusual development by Latin American standards was partially responsible for the failure of urban un- and under-employment to increase over the period. Data for Lima *barriadas* in 1956 revealed that 5 per cent were unemployed and 25 per cent 'could be considered underemployed due to their unstable employment', giving a total of 30 per cent of the *barriada* labour force. In 1967 a new survey of the *barriadas* yielded remarkably similar results: a total of 31 per cent un- and under-employed (consisting of 3 per cent unemployed and 28 per cent underemployed).[51]

Conclusions

The rapid industrialisation of the 1960s significantly diversified the local economy, and marked a major turning-point in policy attitudes towards the promotion of non-export activities. It also brought increasing policy-induced distortions in the economy, vulnerability to foreign-exchange constraints because of the unintegrated and import-dependent character of the new industries and the resulting inflexibility in the import structure, and rapid decay of local capitalism as large foreign firms swarmed in to take advantage of the profit opportunities opened up by the policy shift. As had been evident since the turn of the century, the élite group of local capitalists, while prepared to take advantage of market opportunities, and on occasion to manipulate policy in their own interests, had no commitment to playing a role as a 'national bour-geoisie'; witness their unequivocal welcome to foreign capital during the 1960s, as at other periods. To a considerable extent, it was this lack of any clearly-perceived national priorities apart from those set by the strategic needs of the large multinational corporations, which accounts for the extraordinarily incoherent character of industrial promotion policy as it was applied by successive Peruvian governments. The impetus in the late 1950s towards the construction of a local industrial capitalism was rapidly overtaken by the wave of multinational invest-ment in import-substituting, branch-plant manufacturing which swept over Latin America as a whole in the 1960s, and in only the most limited sense was the real dependence of the Peruvian economy mitigated.

Industrialisation, in summary, came late, was externally-induced and controlled, relied heavily on artificial props to its profitability, was not subject to carefully-designed planning procedures or clearly-defined priorities, quickly encountered problems of scale, and failed to create a new class of dynamic local industrial capitalists. Judged against the expectations of many Peruvian advocates of industrialisation (including a growing group within the military) the process of the 1960s appeared a failure, dragging the economy towards increasing vulnerability, inefficiency and foreign dominance without yielding the anticipated compensating benefits. Despite the context of export growth and a rich natural-resource base, most of the new manufacturing sectors did not represent a clearcut step towards a more integrated, autonomous economy. As middle-class resentment over the role of foreign capital was fuelled by scandals and controversy in the mining and oil sectors, so feeling began to mount against the heavily-subsidised foreign firms in manufacturing, and by 1968 this nationalism had become a real force favouring a break with the previous growth model. As Chapter 14 will show, not all the nationalist criticisms were accurate (particularly the claim that national enterprises had been 'displaced' by foreign capital), but the problem at which they were directed was undoubtedly a real one.

13.3 DOMESTIC FOOD AGRICULTURE, 1948–68

Agriculture in Peru has always been the sector in which the dualism of the economy is most clearly manifested. During most of the period covered by this book, commercial modern-sector agriculture was concentrated on the Coast and oriented towards export crops (with the exception of rice-growing in the north, an activity which by the 1950s had become organised on a large-scale capitalist basis). Most food production for the internal market took place in the traditional sector of the Sierra, although as the urban population of the Coast grew, the opportunities for commercial farmers along the Coast to grow basic foodcrops at a profit became more attractive. As Chapter 10 described, in the 1940s a number of constraints hindered the expansion of export production, and the proportion of commercially-farmed land devoted to foodcrops rose accordingly, permitting an increase in levels of consumption. In the 1950s, however, export prospects were more attractive, and commercial agriculture was oriented primarily towards external markets, leaving expansion of the supply of food for the internal market dependent upon the traditional agricultural sector. In contrast to the rapidly-expanding, heavily-capitalised commercial agriculture of the Coast, historically the traditional sector has grown slowly, being deprived of resources, discriminated against in policy measures, and obliged to operate on the country's less-productive land resources.

Peru was by no means alone in Latin America in having a stagnant traditional agricultural sector; indeed, one striking feature of Peru in the 1950s and early 1960s was that the economic and social pressures generated by poor agricultural performance were much less severe than in several other neighbouring countries. The underlying problem, nevertheless, was a real one: in the long run, a growing urban population with rising living standards could be fed only if a breakthrough in agricultural production were achieved, or if export performance remained strong enough to permit the necessary food supplies to be imported. Our discussion in this section will show that the flexibility of the Peruvian economy, which enabled it to avoid a crippling food bottleneck until the 1970s, also enabled successive governments to ignore the real needs of agriculture, so that despite a new willingness to consider agrarian reform, policy nevertheless failed to promote agricultural development, and in some ways directly hindered it.

Statistics on food production and the movement of rural incomes outside modern-sector enterprises are scarce and unreliable before the 1960s. There is no doubt that, during the 1950s, parts of rural Peru experienced a growing integration into the national market and, as a result, some improvement in conditions not only in towns but in the countryside, particularly in the Mantaro Valley (close to Lima) and the Santa Valley in Ancash. But the evidence is limited; Webb's summary of the situation in the rural Sierra is as follows: 'The conclusion that incomes have grown must therefore be limited to those small farmers living in the narrower version of the coastal hinterland, that is, in Lima, Junin and Ancash, and it is more qualified in the case of Ancash.'[52] These areas contain only about 16 per cent of the small farmers in Peru.[53] Further, even within these areas some research suggests that while income levels have been maintained by wage employment outside agriculture, food production has been adversely affected by competition from the Coast.[54]

The difficulty in reaching any more general conclusion is the total unreliability of data on food crops prior to 1960. Series on most crops were published for the fifties by the Ministry of Agriculture, showing stagnation of output in *per capita* terms. However, when the 1961 Agricultural Census revealed large discrepancies in the Ministry's previous estimates at the departmental level of the area sown to different crops, a number of critical examinations were carried out, revealing wildly implausible year-to-year changes.[55] Statistical methods were significantly improved from 1963 on, but we are left with nothing solid for the previous decade. A revision carried out by the Departamento de Planeamiento of the Ministry of Agriculture, and adopted by the Iowa Mission and the Agrarian University[56] is used by Webb as the basis of his estimates of rural income trends in the 1950s; it shows a slow growth in output based on virtually constant yields and a small rise in cultivated area of somewhat over one per cent per annum for food crops excluding sugar. However, this latter estimate appears to be constructed on the assumption that the 1961 census under-recorded the area cultivated by about 10 per cent, but that the previous data for 1951 were broadly correct.[57] It rapidly becomes clear from inspection of the data, that any revision has to be too heavily guided by the statisticians' own expectations to provide independent evidence of trends in levels of

TABLE 13.10 Cultivated area in Peru, 1929–71
(000 hectares)

	Total cultivated arable area	Coastal cultivated area	Coastal area: food crops excl. sugar and rice[a]	Sierra + Selva, cult. area[a]
1929[b]	1464	384	240	1080
1943	1486	481	257	1005
1952	1676	538	242	1138
1961	1856	640	239	1216
1967	2042	667	325	1375
1971	2194	686[c]	366	1508

Source: Total cultivated area, and area devoted to sugar, cotton and rice: *Anuario Estadístico*. Coastal cultivated area: Twomey (1972), p. 8, except for 1961, which is taken from the Census of that year, as quoted in Zuñiga (1970), p. 4.
[a] Derived as residuals.
[b] The general view seems to be that 1929 was over estimated – which would make the apparent stagnation thereafter less extreme. See Twomey (1972), pp. 2–3.
[c] Extrapolated on the basis of the trend 1961–7.

consumption or area cultivated. As we show below, expectations formed in the mid-sixties as to trends were almost certainly too heavily influenced by the undoubted increase in food supplies occurring at that time as coastal land was switched out of cotton and into food. For what they are worth, figures on area cultivated over the long run are presented in Table 13.10, but it should be borne in mind that the country-wide totals embody errors of unknown magnitude. The estimates for the Coast can be used with greater confidence.

The slow growth of food supplies in the 1950s was accompanied by surprisingly low inflation, which after the spurt of price increases in the late 1940s ran at an annual rate of only seven or eight per cent between 1950 and 1960. Food prices admittedly led this inflation (Table 13.11), but the rate of increase was modest for a Latin American country at that time. Demand pressure was clearly not running far ahead of available supply.

One reason for this was the fact that rapid export expansion (including export crops) made possible the importing of foodstuffs to feed the urban population. Tariffs on food were steadily reduced during the 1950s and by the end of the decade had fallen to zero on most of the leading food products.[58] For part of the period imports of some products (for example, beef) were subsidised to restrain price increases, for the benefit of consumers. Despite these trends, however, the role of food imports should not be overemphasised. Table 13.12 traces the proportion of import expenditure devoted to food, and finds that

TABLE 13.11 Indices of retail prices in Lima and Callao
1950–74

	Cost of living	Food prices
1950	47	42
1960	100	100
1962	113	112
1964	132	135
1966	167	175
1968	218	227
1970	243	247
1972	278	284
1974	357	371

Annual rate of increase, per cent

1950–62	7.6	8.5
1962–8	11.6	12.5
1968–74	6.9	6.8

Source: 1950–70, *Anuario Estadistico;* 1972–4: Banco Central, *Boletin.*

TABLE 13.12 Food imports as per cent of total imports
(current values)

	1946	1951	1955	1960	1965
Wheat	8.2	7.6	6.8	7.0	5.3
Lard	1.1	1.4	1.2	1.3	0.3
Meat	1.0	1.8	1.0	0.4	2.6
Dairy products	1.6	1.6	2.0	1.6	2.0[a]
Rice	0.4	0.9	0.0	0.9	1.9
SUBTOTAL	12.3	13.3	11.0	11.2	12.1
TOTAL FOOD IMPORTS		13.6	15.7	14.4	16.0

Source: Estadistica del Comercio Exterior, various years.
[a] butter excluded.

although there was a moderate increase between 1946 and 1955, thereafter the weight of such imports fell. Thus there were no signs of acute pressure on supplies despite the diversion of much coastal land to export crops and the poor performance of the traditional sector.

We are left with one further possible explanation, which appears to be the key one: slow growth of food production was compatible with rapid GNP growth, low inflation and limited food imports because for a large segment of the population, income levels, and hence consumption of wage-goods, were growing slowly or not at all. [59] In 1956 and 1957, when severe droughts caused devastating crop losses and much rural hardship throughout the Sierra (especially in the poverty-stricken South), [60] food imports showed no tendency to increase, [61] while internal food prices remained moderate; the impact of the famine appears to have been absorbed entirely by a fall in mass living standards (certainly contemporary accounts confirm the reality of such a fall).

Table 13.13 presents the FAO production indices for Peru; these figures are based upon the unreliable official data for the 1950s, but are probably reasonably accurate from 1960 on. The stagnation of food production through the 1950s and into the early 1960s emerges clearly, as does an upturn beginning about the mid-1960s. It must be emphasised that this upturn did not represent any fundamental change in the growth rate of traditional agriculture, but simply the effects of the reallocation of land out of cotton and into food as relative prices swung during the 1960s (see Chapter 12 above). This once-for-all boost to food production had been completed by 1970; thereafter, in the absence of a breakthrough in the productivity of food agriculture, rising urban demand could be met only by increased imports – a problem to which we return in Chapter 15.

Apart from the issue of food supply, the lagging performance of agriculture began to affect also the supply of economic surplus for the rest of the economy. In addition to the long-standing role of export agriculture as a net supplier of funds for investment in other sectors, agriculture in general (including the traditional sector) had been subjected over the long term to a steady squeeze on its surplus as the terms of trade shifted in favour of urban sectors. The trend is illustrated for food crops in Fig. 13.1, and for export crops in Fig. 13.2. [62] Inspection of Fig. 13.1 suggests that, while the long-run trend is undoubtedly unfavourable to food agriculture, there are signs of short-run reversals of this trend in the mid-1940s and the mid-late 1960s—both periods in which food shortages in the urban market were sufficient to push up relative prices even in a context of general inflation.

Given these overall trends, what was the role of government policy towards agriculture, and particularly towards the traditional sector? As might be expected, in several critical areas policy continued to be biased against agricultural growth. The real needs of food agriculture, in terms of credit, technical advice, supply of inputs, and public investment in infrastructure, continued to be neglected. Small-scale agriculture, employing 80 per cent of the agricultural labour force, received on average only 24 per cent of the credit provided by the Banco de Fomento

TABLE 13.13 FAO production indices for Peru, 1952–74
(1961–5 = 100)

	Total agricultural output (crops)	Agricultural output per capita	Total foodcrops output	Foodcrops output per capita
	1952–6 weights			
1952	70	93	72	96
1953	74	96	77	100
1954	79	101	81	103
1955	79	98	82	102
1956	76	92	77	94
1957	77	91	79	94
1958	82	95	85	98
1959	85	95	86	97
1960	93	102	94	103
1961	96	102	96	102
1962	97	101	96	99
1963	100	100	98	98
1964	103	100	103	100
1965	104	98	107	101
1966	110	101	115	105
1967	110	97	118	104
1968	107	92	112	96
1969	109	90	117	98
	1961–5 weights			
1961	95	101	95	101
1962	97	100	96	99
1963	100	100	99	99
1964	104	101	105	102
1965	104	98	105	99
1966	109	99	112	102
1967	110	97	116	103
1968	104	89	108	93
1969	112	93	119	99
1970	121	97	129	104
1971	121	95	130	102
1972	120	91	131	99
1973	119	88	128	94
1974	118	84	125	89

Source: Production Yearbook, FAO (1970–4).

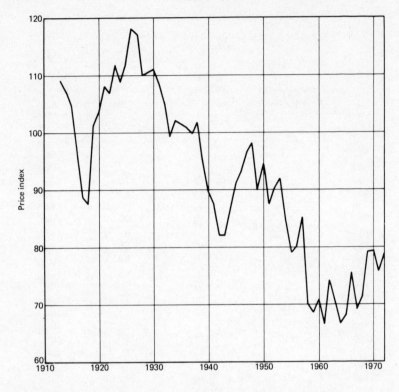

FIGURE 13.1 Terms of trade between food production and other sectors[a]
(Index, 1937 = 100)

Source: Anuario Estadístico.
[a] That is, the ratio between wholesale food prices and the general wholesale price index. After 1956, the latter was discontinued. We have used an unweighted average of the individual wholesale price indices published (clothing, construction and imported goods).

Agropecuario from 1948 to 1953, and 20 per cent in 1958–9, recovering again to 24 per cent in 1961–2.[63] Commercial bank credit went almost exclusively to large-scale agriculture,[64] and, in 1957, 93 per cent of all such credit was allocated to the Coast.[65] Of State credit in the same year, 81 per cent went to Coastal agriculture, and generally over two-thirds was provided to the cash crops cotton, sugar and rice.[66] As for technical assistance, Roel estimated that at the end of the 1950s there were only 40 extension agents and possibly 180 technical assistants in the entire country, against a need for at least 700. Imported fertiliser was available only on the Coast, and only 11 per cent of guano sales were in the Sierra.[67] Public investment was naturally concentrated on coastal

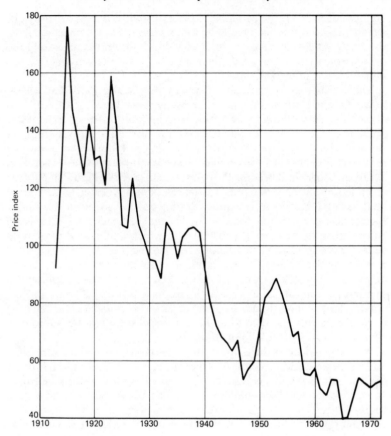

FIGURE 13.2 Ratio of export crop prices to general wholesale prices[a]
(index, 1934–6 = 100)

Source: Anuario Estadístico.
[a] The export crop index comprises sugar and cotton, weighted by their average share of
trade in 1934–6. For the wholesale price index after 1936, see note[a], Figure 13.1.

irrigation projects, in the departments producing cotton, sugar and
rice.[68]

Pricing policy during the 1950s had abandoned, in principle at least,
the controls and subsidies of the Bustamante regime. In practice,
however, the interests of urban consumers remained paramount in the
Government's mind, and prices were still subject to half-concealed
controls and subsidies. Officially these were limited to bread, but prices
of rice, meat and various other basic commodities were also subject to

manipulation.[69] Of the products subject to such controls, the only one which increased rapidly during the 1950s was rice, which benefited from the large irrigation projects in Piura. Most other branches of food production undoubtedly had their growth prospects seriously undermined by the price controls.[70]

The touchstone of agricultural policy during the 1950s and 1960s, however, was agrarian reform.[71] For many years, Peruvian radicals had argued that no solution to the problems of agricultural development was possible in the absence of an attack on the unequal distribution of the country's land resources, and on the exploitative labour relations which prevailed. By the mid-1950s, a rhetorical commitment to the principle of agrarian reform had become the common currency of Peruvian politics; all candidates in the 1956 presidential elections advocated some type of land reform. The victor, Manuel Prado, quickly set up a 'Comision Nacional de Reforma Agraria y Vivienda' (headed by a leading conservative landowner, Pedro Beltran), which deliberated for several years before producing two reports advocating, respectively, improvements in urban housing to accomodate migrants from rural areas, and colonisation of virgin lands east of the Andes as a long-run solution to overpopulation in the Sierra.[72] Redistributive reform, in the commission's view, should be avoided as far as possible, and only the most inefficiently-worked of large properties should be subject to expropriation, with full compensation.

It is easy to dismiss the Beltran commission as mere window-dressing, and such was undoubtedly its true intention (in particular, Prado's electoral alliance with APRA, long a vocal advocate of reform, required some cosmetic moves in that direction). The new consensus on the need to pay lip service to the idea of reform, however, was a development of considerable significance. On the one hand, it reflected the changing political reality of rural Peru, as landowners in the traditional sector became less powerful in national politics, and peasant groups became stronger and better-organised. By the early 1960s peasant invasions of large properties were spreading rapidly through the Sierra, as a result of which a *de facto* breakup of many such properties occurred, with landowners often unwilling to enter into open confrontation with their local peasantry.[73]

On the other hand, and of great importance for the future, the abandonment of opposition to agrarian reform *in principle* by the ruling group in national politics, led naturally to a general belief among landowners that genuine reform was only a matter of time (an expectation justified by subsequent events). With the partial exception of the sugar planters (who hoped to be able to preserve their large estates on efficiency grounds), the landowners of Peru entered the 1960s with the expectation that their properties would sooner or later be subject to expropriation, whether formally by government action, or informally as the result of peasant pressure. The most important result was that investment in agriculture fell and many landowners proceeded to decapitalise their properties, transferring their money into urban construction, finance or manufacturing. As one large landowner in Cajamarca observed in 1963,

The Agrarian Reform Law will soon be approved, and will certainly affect (the *hacienda*) Udima. Therefore we should plan to dedicate all our attention in the years in which the firm can still do so, to extracting the maximum possible surplus from the *coloniaje* and from the *hacienda*'s cattle. . . . We should eliminate the stables and the cheese factory, the alfalfa fields, land reclamation projects, etc., the purchase of feed concentrates and all the other activities which force the *hacienda* to spend money which is never transformed into profits.[74]

Added to this decline in investment was the spreading climate of social unrest in the rural areas, which further reduced the prospects for agricultural development in the short term. In 1962 the military junta which had overthrown Prado took steps to legalise a number of *de facto* land occupations, particularly in the La Convencion valley near Cuzco,[75] and in the following year agrarian reform was again a central issue in the presidential elections. The victorious candidate, Belaunde, had toured rural areas more widely than any previous politician, promising land to the peasants and distributing symbolic bags of soil.[76] In 1964, after heated debate, a detailed reform law passed Congress, but the exemptions and loopholes in this measure were so many, and the compensation provisions so generous, that very little real change was accomplished during the remainder of Belaunde's tenure of office.[77] The direct effects of the application of the law were less significant than the indirect effects: accelerated decapitalisation of agriculture; widespread evictions of tenants as landlords sought to protect themselves from the provisions of the law granting title to tenants; and the arousal of peasant expectations, which doubtless helped to accelerate the informal drift towards the breakup of large properties.[78]

In summary, from the mid-1950s until 1969 the development of Peruvian agriculture was largely paralysed by the general belief that agrarian reform had become inevitable in the long run. Landowners had no incentive to invest; peasants obtained control over land by informal *de facto* seizures which left them exposed to police reprisals, and deprived of governmental assistance. The long-run evolution of official policy towards radical reform was slow and fumbling, while the need for determined promotion of food production was concealed by the factors already discussed—slow growth of consumption, the strong balance of payments, and the gains in food production during the 1960s resulting from reallocation of land formerly under cotton. The famine of 1956 and 1957 had caused alarm among the local élite; but hopes of a solution were pinned on a combination of export growth and colonisation of the jungle region. By the mid-1960s colonisation had proved inadequate as an answer and export growth was slowing; at this stage hopes became centred instead on agrarian reform, which it was believed would lead to more efficient allocation of land resources, and hence substantial gains in production. Not until the effective application of agrarian reform in the early 1970s was it generally realised that the amount of productive land held idle by the *latifundios* of the Sierra was far less than had been universally believed,[79] and that agrarian reform could lead on to dynamic growth of agricultural output only if large resources were injected into the sector—a reversal of the historical tendency for agriculture to function as a net supplier of surplus to the rest of the economy.

13.4 CONCLUSION

The discussion of manufacturing and food agriculture in this chapter has shown that, during the twenty years of rapid export-led growth from 1948 to 1968, the nature of economic policy in Peru shifted gradually away from the *laissez-faire*, export-oriented, socially conservative stance adopted by the Odría regime after the 1948 coup. The policy shift was a response to emerging trends which the ruling groups felt obliged to accommodate: declining investment opportunities for local capital in export sectors, combined with the pressure of growing urban population, which the Government hoped to tackle by the promotion of industrialisation; and growing pressure from peasants and radicals on the traditional agrarian structure, which warned the élite of the wisdom of a strategic retreat from Sierra agriculture. In both cases (but particularly with respect to industrialisation) the shifting policy stance harmonised well with the changing role and interests of multinational firms active in the economy, as foreign investment became increasingly oriented towards import-substituting industry. In both cases, however, the policies which emerged were poorly-designed and wrongly applied from the standpoint of a possible advance towards more autonomous, self-sustaining economic growth. This was not surprising, given that the objective of these policies was not so much the promotion of autonomy and development, as the subsidising of the new activities of the élite and their foreign allies in industry, and the carrying-out of a rearguard action in traditional agriculture. The essential mechanism of the Peruvian economy remained the familiar one of export-led growth responding to external forces, and the new policies on non-export sectors brought about no major shift in the source of economic dynamism. Industry became more, not less, dependent upon successful export growth; while the failure to achieve a breakthrough in food agriculture implied equally a need for growing import capacity in order to make up the economy's food deficit. So it was that a breakdown in the central mechanism of export growth had critical implications for the entire economy in the late 1960s: a topic to which part of the next chapter is devoted.

14 The Emerging Crisis[1]

The years 1967 and 1968 brought the Peruvian economy to a turning-point. The process of economic growth was losing momentum; management of the economy was becoming increasingly difficult within the disintegrating political framework of 'creole liberalism;' and the general decay of Peruvian capitalism was reaching an advanced stage. By the late 1960s, however, these factors had by no means brought the economy to a point comparable to the crisis of the 1930s. Apart from the cyclical recession of 1967, there was no actual breakdown of the economic mechanism, no unavoidable need to default on the foreign debt, and no sign of heightened class conflict within Peruvian society. The problems of the economy were problems primarily for the top quartile or so of the population whose welfare was most directly linked to successful capitalist development, and it was to a great extent the inability of the civilian groups in this top quartile to agree on a revised economic strategy that opened the way for the Military seizure of power in October 1968. In this chapter we shall first draw together the various strands of the crisis and identify several problems whose solution was necessary if capitalist development were to continue in some form. We shall then look briefly at the analysis of the situation offered by Peruvian commentators at the time, with special emphasis on the policy stance adopted by the Military in the period following their seizure of power. By indicating the gaps and misconceptions in the ideology of the incoming Military Government, the chapter provides essential background to our interpretation of the successes and failures of policy since 1968, presented in Chapter 15.[1]

14.1 STRUCTURAL PROBLEMS

At the centre of the emerging crisis lay the failing dynamism of the export sectors. The first requirement of successful export-led growth is expanding production for export, at least over the long run (in the short run, improving terms of trade may partially compensate for stagnant production, as in fact occurred in Peru from 1963 to 1974). Growing export sectors generate effective demand in the economy, create incentives to maintain the rate of investment (and hence the rate of growth), and provide surplus funds to finance investment. By the mid-

1960s the main export sectors in Peru were failing to perform these roles, for reasons analysed at length in Chapters 11 and 12. Natural-resource constraints were being encountered more or less simultaneously on a number of fronts, although the only sector in which such a constraint was absolute was fishmeal. In other sectors the constraints could be overcome, and further expansion achieved—but only by indivisible projects of rapidly-increasing scale and sometimes riskiness. In a situation of this kind, unless there occurs a parallel increase in the capacity and willingness of some groups to undertake such large-scale investment projects, a point of crisis must eventually be reached. In Peru during the 1960s, local private investors did not appear able or willing to embark on the major projects required for continued export expansion. The numerous successful medium-scale export enterprises of the 1950s had failed to act as the seedbed for a new generation of larger local ventures.[2] Neither foreign investors nor the State were fully prepared to fill the gap (foreign firms because of their own strategic considerations, the State because of its financial and political weakness).

Crucial to an understanding of why local capital failed to mount a new developmental effort in export sectors is the fact that Peru, after nearly a century as one of the most diversified export economies of the continent, showed signs of becoming a virtual mono-export economy, dependent upon the mining sector. In discussing the turn-of-the-century history of mining (Chapter 5 above) we have already drawn attention to the fact that local firms, although perfectly capable of proceeding with the development of large-scale mining, had preferred to stand aside and leave the task to foreign capital. Again after the Second World War the same tendency had emerged, with foreign mining corporations retaining or taking over control of the best large mineral deposits. Precisely the sector in which the most straightforward and promising new large-scale export opportunities of the 1960s existed was thus the sector from which local capital had allowed itself to be excluded. In other sectors, the limitations on profitable investment were considerably more severe than in mining. No large new oilfields had been located; the fish catch was ecologically restricted; and further agricultural expansion required irrigation projects on a giant scale, each affecting several geographic regions and large numbers of landowners—projects, in other words, which could be undertaken only with State participation.

The slowdown in the rate of aggregate export growth from 1963 (see Table 12.9 above) fed through to the rest of the local economy in two main ways: first, by the impact on private capital formation; and second, by the steadily-worsening balance-of-payments problem which confronted the Belaunde Government. Data on private saving and investment in the economy as a whole are presented in Table 14.1. Private gross fixed capital formation, it will be seen, rose to a peak of around 20 per cent of GNP in the mid-1950s at the height of the export boom, but

TABLE 14.1 Savings and investment ratios, 1950–68
(percentages of GNP at current prices)

	1950–5	1956–7	1958–9	1960–4	1965–8
Private savings	15.4	21.5	19.5	16.1	14.6
less transfer to State	– 0.4	– 1.9	– 1.8	– 1.5	– 3.9
GIVES private gross capital formation	15.0	19.6	17.7	14.6	10.7
Public savings[a]	3.3	2.6	0.8	2.1	0.7
plus transfer from private sector	0.4	1.9	1.8	1.5	3.9
GIVES public gross capital formation	3.7	4.5	2.6	3.6	4.6
TOTAL gross capital formation	18.7	24.1	20.3	18.2	15.3

Source: Banco Central, *Cuentas Nacionales del Perú, 1950–65* and Fitzgerald (1976), p. 23.
[a] Includes public external borrowing, of which a small part is publicly guaranteed private debt.

the recession of 1958 brought a downturn. Thereafter the investment ratio for the private sector, and for the economy as a whole, fell steadily through the 1960s and into the early 1970s, despite an increase in investment by the State (much of it financed by transfers of savings from the private sector). The significance of these figures is very great; they reveal not only the depressing effect on capital formation of the falling absorptive capacity of export sectors, but also the inability or failure of potential investors to locate alternative investment opportunities in non-export sectors. Increased import-substituting industrialisation during the 1960s, despite the capital-intensive bias of the process, did not suffice to compensate for the tailing-off of new activity in export production and local agriculture.

The aggregate saving and investment ratios fell for both local and foreign capital—a trend which tends to confirm that the economy faced a capital-absorption rather than a savings constraint. The book value of U.S. direct investment in Peru showed a net increase of only 4 per cent from 1960 to 1964, compared with a 46 per cent rise from 1955 to 1960;[3] the slackening-off was due both to the lack of new investment in mining development, and to increased outflows on account of amortisation payments. Table 14.2 shows the trends in the composition of savings, on

TABLE 14.2 Structure of savings[a]
(percentages of GNP at current prices)

	1950–5	1956–7	1958–9	1960–4	1965–8
Private sector					
Personal	8.0	10.0	8.7	7.7	1.7
Corporate	9.4	9.1	8.3	11.2	13.9
External	1.5	5.4	4.3	0.1	1.8
TOTAL	18.9	24.5	21.3	19.0	17.4
Public sector[b]					
Domestic	2.6	1.2	1.7	1.5	−0.6
External	0.7	1.5	−0.1	0.6	1.4
TOTAL	3.3	2.7	0.8	2.1	0.8
TOTAL gross saving	22.2	27.2	22.1	21.1	18.2

Source : as for Table 14.1.
[a] Includes changes in stocks.
[b] Includes public external borrowing, of which a small part is government-guaranteed private debt.

the basis of the national income accounts,[4] indicating that private external savings accounted for much of the overall decline in the ratio. From 24 per cent of GNP in the mid-1950s, the private savings ratio had dropped to 17 per cent by the late 1960s; of the 7 per cent decline, about half was in external savings. This latter category is a net-flow item in the balance of payments, and was affected not only by the reduced inflow of foreign capital, but also by a growing net outflow of Peruvian funds. From 1961 on, Peruvian holdings of U.S. commercial bank deposits increased rapidly, and in 1963 the increase in such deposits corresponded to one quarter of the Peruvian current-account deficit.[5]

The decline in savings was not a result of inflation (although the rise in the cost-of-living index was somewhat more rapid in the 1960s than in the 1950s). On the contrary, as we have seen above, financial savings rose steeply in the early 1960s as new savings instruments became available.[6] With *per capita* income rising strongly at the same time, it is evident that aggregate savings were being depressed by poor investment performance, and not vice versa.[7]

Tables 14.1 and 14.2 also demonstrate clearly the failure of the State sector to make good the deficiencies of the private sector. Two possible sources of dynamism for the economy—exports and autonomous investment—were lagging; this left the Government to carry the burden of maintaining the level of activity. As Leguía had done in the 1920s, Belaúnde in the 1960s expanded the foreign debt in order to help finance public works and an increased government pay-roll, but the constraints on the government sector were considerable. All attempts during the 1960s to raise direct taxes were blocked by Congress, where the APRA was especially adamant in its opposition to tax measures, although lesser increases in indirect taxes were often approved as a substitute. As Table 14.3 clearly shows, the expansion of the Government's spending under Belaúnde was mainly financed from increased indirect taxation, with a consequent dramatic shift in the tax structure, and by a growing budget deficit, much of it financed from abroad.[8] Foreign borrowing capacity was limited, however, and became more so as Peruvian relations with the U.S. Government worsened over issues such as the IPC dispute and the purchase of French Mirage fighter planes in 1967.[9]

It is true that in a 'developmental' sense the State was beginning to come forward to supplement the deficiencies in the private sector in a number of areas—notably in mining. State development banks increased their share of total bank loans outstanding from 18 per cent in 1955 to 26 per cent by 1965.[10] Several State enterprises, such as the Corporation Peruana del Santa,[11] underwent significant expansion. But the base was tiny: in 1963 employment in State enterprises was well under one per cent of the labour force,[12] and a number of the enterprises in question were notoriously inefficient. In quantitative terms, the expansion was not enough to affect the picture in a 'Keynesian' sense. As Table 14.1 shows, public-sector gross capital formation under Belaúnde recovered to the same share of GNP as it had reached at the end of the Odría period; but with the Government accounting for less than one-third of total investment in the economy this did not suffice to offset the decline in the private sector.

Furthermore, to the extent that the Belaúnde Government used its foreign-financed deficit to expand local demand, it contributed to an emerging balance-of-payments problem, first because service payments on the foreign debt quickly began to absorb a considerable proportion of export earnings (18 per cent by 1967), and second because rising national income fed through to a very rapid increase in imports. With domestic food production stagnant (see Chapter 13), supplies of several basic foodstuffs, particularly beef, became increasingly dependent on imports, and when in 1967–8 total imports were finally cut back in the face of the balance-of-payments crisis, the weight of food in the total rose abruptly, as shown in Table 14.4. At the same time, the industrialisation of the 1960s was heavily dependent upon imported inputs and capital goods. The Table demonstrates the sharp rise in imports of intermediate products.

Table 14.5 illustrates the growing balance-of-payments problem,

TABLE 14.3 Government income and expenditure[a]
(percentage of GNP at current prices)

	1950–5	1956–7	1958–9	1960–3	1964–5	1966–8	1969–73
Direct taxation	5.2	4.4	4.6	4.9	3.8	4.3	5.9
Indirect tax etc.,	7.9	9.5	9.7	11.0	13.5	13.5	12.9
Current income	13.1	13.9	14.3	15.9	17.3	17.8	18.9
Current expenditure	10.5	12.7	12.6	13.6	17.7	20.8	17.9
Current surplus	2.6	1.2	1.7	2.0	−0.3	−3.0	+0.9

Source: as for Table 14.1
[a] Totals may not add exactly due to rounding.

TABLE 14.4 Percentage shares of certain import categories, 1955–70

	Foodstuffs	Semi-elaborated mineral products[a]	Semi-elaborated chemical products[b]	Total, three categories
1955	15.7	7.1	6.8	29.6
1960	14.7	8.3	7.1	30.1
1965	16.0	9.6	10.1	35.7
1968	20.1	10.3	13.3	43.7
1970	19.3	13.2	12.9	45.4

Source: Bertram (1976).
[a] Consists of CUODE categories 531, 532 and 533; mainly engineering and mechanical products.
[b] CUODE categories 552 and 553; the former dominates the figures.

TABLE 14.5 The balance of payments under three governments, 1950–68 (million dollars, annual averages)

	Odria	Prado		Belaunde		
	1950–5	1956–8	1959–62	1963–5	1966–7	1968
Exports	244	314	458	641	765	840
Imports	−234	−363	−382	−565	−811	−673
Visible trade balance	10	−49	76	76	−45	167
Net services and transfers	−20	−37	−35	−69	−72	−56
Profits and interest	−20	−36	−57	−75	−131	−138
CURRENT ACCOUNT BALANCE	−30	−122	−15	−68	−248	−28
Long-term capital: public	11	8	−1	83	178	74
private	15	79	22	21	11	−26
BASIC BALANCE	−3	−34	6	37	−59	21
Short-term capital	2	19	11	−20	39	0
Monetary movements and errors	1	15	−16	−16	20	−21

Source: Banco Central, *Cuentas Nacionales*, various issues. It should be noted that there are large discrepancies in the figures cited in different issues in respect of a number of capital account items. Parts do not always sum to the whole because of rounding errors.

comparing the situation under the three main Governments of the period 1950–68.[13] Several striking trends emerge. First, imports were rising increasingly rapidly, reaching a growth rate of 16 per cent a year in dollar value from 1960 to 1966. Despite improving terms of trade and a rapid increase in the volume of exports in the early 1960s, the visible trade balance showed little improvement. As the rate of growth of exports slackened from 1963, while that of imports was sustained, the commercial balance had swung into deficit by 1966. This deterioration of the commercial balance had ominous implications in view of other trends. As the years passed, the weight of profit and interest payments abroad grew from 8 per cent of export revenue in the Odría period to 15 per cent under Belaunde, while at the same time the inflow of private long-term capital fell dramatically from the high level of the mid-1950s (25 per cent of export earnings 1956–8) to only 1.4 per cent under Belaunde (and subsequently to minus 4 per cent under the Military, from 1969 to 1972).

As private capital inflow slowed, the management of cyclical export recessions became more difficult. The massive current-account deficit of 1956–8 had been financed by a wave of foreign private investment in Peru, coupled with a strong inflow of short-term private capital, so that the crisis was weathered with only minor government intervention. Other brief export recessions in 1953 and 1963 had also been handled relatively easily because of the support provided by private capital inflow.[14]

The worsening current-account deficit of the Belaunde years, on the contrary, was financed by a huge increase in government foreign borrowing. Once the growth of the deficit outpaced the Government's ability to borrow, and in the absence of a new surge of export expansion or foreign investment, it became imperative to limit the growth of imports in order to maintain balance-of-payments equilibrium. The difficulty was that controlling imports by the traditional methods of exchange devaluation and internal deflation had become very much more difficult.

In the crises of 1953 and 1956–8, with memories of the disastrous experience under a fixed exchange rate during the 1940s still fresh, there was a general willingness among the Peruvian upper and middle classes to acquiesce in exchange depreciation; and since in each case export recovery was sufficiently rapid to prevent the deflation from having serious adverse effects on production, a belief in the efficacy of orthodox policies was widely held.[15] By the 1960s, however, shifts both in the structure of the economy and in the Government's political base meant that there was much greater resistance to devaluation. As middle-class interests continued to gain strength and the memory of the 1940s receded, the problems resulting from an overvalued exchange rate were considered to be outweighed by the benefits.[16] These included low prices for the imported food consumed by the urban population, cheap inputs and equipment for the rapidly-expanding industrial sector, and assistance to the debtor Government in servicing its foreign obligations.

For reasons considered in Chapters 11 and 12, exporting interests were slow to mobilise serious opposition to the fixed rate. The result was that it remained unchanged from 1959 until 1967, while the internal price level rose by more than 80 per cent.

By late 1967, when devaluation finally became inevitable, the disequilibrium was acute and the political battle fierce—an investment strike by certain export sectors, withholding of goods by importers, currency speculation and capital flight.[17] In August 1967 the sol was devalued 42 per cent, import controls and new export taxes were imposed, and over the following year (at the cost of much of its popular support) the Government succeeded in putting through a series of deflationary measures.[18] The results brought out clearly the changes in Peru since Prado and Beltran had taken the same course ten years previously. The balance of payments did indeed swing to a large current-account surplus over the following four to five years (Table 15.3); but meanwhile economic growth came to a dead halt for three years,[19] and the Belaunde Government fell to a military coup in October 1968.[20] Export production showed no response whatever to the devaluation (Table 12.9).

14.2 THE ISSUES OF OWNERSHIP AND DISTRIBUTION

The growing malaise of the economy during the Belaunde era was evident to many Peruvians, and fear of a possible breakdown of the system became widespread among the politically-influential. As the decade proceeded a growing consensus emerged in support of the idea that Peru's economic difficulties could be traced to the influence of two small but powerful groups: foreign firms, which were alleged to be displacing Peruvian businessmen and draining the country of its resources; and the top stratum of the local élite (popularly described as the 'oligarchy') who were alleged to be obstructing attempts to reform the country's social structure and thus bring about a more egalitarian distribution of resources.[21] The 'structuralist' models of economic development which were popular in Latin America in the early 1960s gave special emphasis to the need for structural reforms to free resources for development purposes; in Peru, the main proposals were for agrarian reform to make more land available to the small agricultural sector, and tighter controls on foreign capital to prevent excessive pressure on the balance of payments from repatriated profits. In the original formulation of structuralism, these changes were to form part of an integrated and coherent economic strategy; but as the 1960s progressed without much to show in the way of reforms, the analytical focus was narrowed. The purpose which reforms were supposed to fulfil became obscured by the difficulty of achieving any reforms at all. By the late

1960s the emerging 'dependency' school, in Peru as elsewhere, was primarily concerned with identifying the groups whose power would have to be broken before serious reforms could be achieved. There was a tendency to suggest that a political assault on the 'oligarchy' and their foreign allies would be not merely a necessary condition for structural reform and economic growth, but also a sufficient condition. Among the younger, more radical officials of the military establishment the idea took root that any government strong enough to confront foreign capital and the oligarchy would be able, simply by decreeing 'structural reforms,' to guarantee a new surge of economic development for Peru. The appealing simplicity of this view provided a useful justification for the replacement of civilian by military government; but the true nature and complexity of the Peruvian economic problem tended to be overlooked. The mere transition from a 'soft' to a 'hard' state could not by itself provide an automatic shortcut to economic success, as the military were shortly to discover for themselves.

On the other hand, it is important to emphasise that structural reform was undoubtedly becoming an urgent necessity for Peru, whether as a means of salvaging the capitalist growth model or of beginning the transition to an alternative system. Before going on in Chapter 15 to analyse the shortcomings of the Military's post-1968 programme, therefore, we shall devote the remainder of this chapter to a discussion of the problems of ownership and distribution, and of the objectives which might reasonably be pursued by means of 'structural reform.'

So far as ownership was concerned, the great issue of the 1960s was the spread of foreign control in the economy. We have already discussed this process in export sectors and manufacturing industry. The proportion of exports produced by foreign firms rose from about 30 per cent in 1950 to 45 per cent in 1960, and 50 per cent by 1967.[22] In manufacturing, the book value of U.S. investment trebled between 1960 and 1964, and by the late 1960s something like 40 per cent of total fixed assets in the manufacturing sector were foreign-controlled.[23] As we have seen in Chapter 13, parallel with foreign investment in manufacturing went a dramatic denationalisation of banking, with the share of total banking assets under foreign control rising from 36 per cent in 1960 to 62 per cent by 1968.

To many observers at the time, figures such as these seemed to provide clear evidence of a massive takeover of local enterprises by foreign capital, with domestic entrepreneurs ('national bourgeois') being displaced by the inrush of foreign firms of superior strength. This was, however, a mistaken interpretation. In export sectors takeovers were the exception, and the increase in foreign control reflected simply the fact that the expansion of locally-controlled enterprises had slowed down, while the major new developments (especially in minerals) were carried out by foreign firms. As we have several times emphasised, in this period active displacement of local firms from resources desired by foreign firms was hardly ever necessary; the local élite generally agreed in welcoming foreign investment, and allying themselves with it where possible. In manufacturing, the survey by Anaya cited in Table 13.6 clearly shows that actual takeovers of local by foreign firms were few and far between; the essence of the process in this instance was not that local firms were pushed out, but rather that foreign firms were the ones which undertook new developments. Only in the banking sector can it be said that the process of takeover accounted for a significant part of the spread of foreign control, and there the entry of foreign capital, far from being opposed by local banking interests, was welcomed and even largely engineered by them.

The process described above was very different from the one described by many contemporary analysts. In a case where foreign capital comes into conflict with and drives out a dynamic national capitalist class, it may be reasonable to suppose that the exclusion of foreign capital would be a sufficient condition for a revival of local capitalism. Where foreign capital enters as the ally of local capital, and plays a complementary role in economic growth, no such conclusion can be drawn. An attempt to exclude foreign firms, far from clearing the field for local initiative, may serve rather to discourage local capitalists (by breaking up profitable joint-venture alliances) and to damage the general confidence of private investors. (Such in fact was to be the course of events in Peru after 1968.) In an economy where investment opportunities are viewed as increasingly difficult and risky by the local capitalist, partnership with a larger organisation may be essential if investment is to proceed. If partnership with foreign capital is prohibited, and local capitalism fails to produce a new generation of dynamic and well-funded private enterprises, then the burden naturally tends to fall upon the State sector as the logical replacement for foreign firms. An offensive against foreign capital in the Peruvian situation of 1968 necessarily implied a massive increase in the economic role of the State and a crisis of identity and confidence among local private investors. These problems were understood imperfectly or not at all by the architects and supporters of the 1968 coup.[24]

The second and closely related issue in the area of ownership was the wealth of the élite. It was widely believed that if the power of this group could once be broken, then it would be possible to achieve the structural reforms necessary to broaden the basis of growth and permit fairer access to its benefits, as well as reinforcing the dynamism of the economy by increasing the importance of the internal market.

The concentration of ownership of means of production in Peru was indeed very great, and inequalities of income distribution were correspondingly dramatic. Several recent studies have agreed in placing Peru among the world's most skewed income distributions in the

1960s;[25] Webb, for example, documents a greater degree of inequality than in Brazil or Mexico. In Peru the poorest 20 per cent receive only 3.5 per cent of personal income, well below the 5.6 per cent which is the average for 44 less-developed countries covered in a recent survey.[26] The modern sector generates 60 per cent of value-added in the economy, but employs only 23 per cent of the labour force.[27] Large sections of the population are thus dependent upon the trickle-down effects from the modern sector (especially from export industries).

But, just as we have argued that the prevailing view of the benefits from an assault on foreign ownership neglected the implications of long-run historical forces, so in the case of the concentration of local ownership and income the issue was over-simplified by a similar neglect. Present-day inequality in Peru is the natural outcome of two long-term trends, perceptible since at least the beginning of the century: on the one hand, the increasingly large-scale and capital-intensive nature of modern-sector production, which comprised a growing proportion of total production in the economy; and on the other hand, the growth of population, which swelled the numbers of those outside the modern sector and dependent upon the slower-growing 'traditional' sector. The process was clear in the early years of the century in export sectors such as mining (with the penetration of foreign capital and the introduction of foreign large-scale technology) and sugar. The trend was checked somewhat in the 1930s with the blossoming of small and medium mining and the growing importance of cotton growing; but by the end of the 1940s the long-run pattern had resumed. In the fifties and sixties both export production and the rapidly-growing manufacturing sector were characterised by increasing scale and capital intensity; and this trend (derived from pressures in the international system) was accentuated by the policies of successive governments. Capital intensity was encouraged by a variety of incentives; price policy discriminated against the traditional (labour-intensive) agricultural sector; and there was no attempt to restrict the privileged access to resources and opportunities enjoyed by the élite and their allies. Meanwhile the situation of labour scarcity which had afflicted most modern-sector activities in Peru at the turn of the century had come to an end by the 1920s as population growth accelerated; by the 1950s population pressure had become a serious problem, and by the 1960s un- and under-employment in Lima had risen to over 30 per cent of the labour force.

These trends are reflected in the available figures on the distribution of income through time, although such data cannot be extended back before 1950. Webb's data, which are summarised in Table 14.6, show an unambiguous worsening over time, with both rural and urban traditional sectors losing ground relative to the modern sectors. And, as we have remarked above in Chapter 13, Webb's figures for the poorest group, the 35 per cent of the labour force in non-coast rural areas, are

TABLE 14.6 Trends in *per capita* real income, 1950–66

Labour-force groups	Size of labour-force 1961		Annual per capita rate of income growth 1950–66
	(000)	%	%
Modern Sector[a]			
Wage-earners	255	8.4	4.9
Government employees	176	5.8	3.6
White-collar	172	5.7	3.3
TOTAL	603	19.9	4.1
Urban Traditional Sector			
Wage-earners	238	7.8	2.5
Self-employed	447	14.7	1.9
White-collar employees	102	3.4	1.8
Domestic servants	174	5.7	1.6
TOTAL	961	31.7	2.0
Rural Traditional Sector			
Coastal wage-earners	199	6.6	4.1
Sierra and Jungle, wage-earners	237	7.8	1.5
Small farmers	1,034	34.1	0.8
(a) Coast and hinterland	(240)	(7.9)	(2.0)
(b) Other regions:			
5–50 hectares	(120)	(4.0)	(2.7)
0–5 hectares	(674)	(22.2)	(0.0)
TOTAL	1,470	48.4	1.3
TOTAL OF ALL WORKERS	3,034	100.0	2.1

Source: Webb (1974b), p. 35.
[a] The 'modern' sector has been equated here with the reporting sector, *plus* government, *less* all agriculture except sugar.

based on optimistic estimates of the growth rate of food production for the 1950s.

This analysis carries strong implications for policies designed to distribute more widely the benefits from growth. Inequality being deeply rooted in the long-run evolution of the productive structure and its policy context, the massive shift of resources from modern to traditional sectors necessary to correct the imbalance implied not only ownership reforms, but also a major reform of the productive structure running completely counter to on-going trends; historically, resources have been sucked from the traditional sector into the modern sector, rather than the other way around. In a real sense, the objective of income redistribution would thus have to be achieved at the expense of growth in the modern sector. Although the loss to the modern sector might be more than compensated by the gains to the rest of the population, it must be remembered that the government operates in, and is primarily responsive to, the modern sector. There is a clear distinction to be drawn between 'structural reforms' which bring the State to the rescue of the modern sector (e.g. by organising and funding large investment projects) and those which aim to redistribute resources away from the modern sector to promote traditional-sector development. The rescue of the export-led model by the State, in other words, by no means implied any improvement in the relative position of the mass of the population. Nor would this be occasioned by measures which strengthened the position of modern sector workers *vis-à-vis* their employers. The potential beneficiaries of any 'structural reform' conducted within the modern sector constitute a limited and privileged group, falling entirely within the top quartile or so of the income distribution. It is important, therefore, that transfers to the modern-sector labour force should not be confused with transfers to the mass of the population.

Despite the erosion in the *relative* position of a large part of the population, it is important to note that the rapid growth of the Peruvian economy between 1950 and 1966 probably prevented any dramatic fall in absolute terms for those at the bottom of the ladder. Webb's figures in Table 14.6 show no group suffering an absolute decline in real income levels over time, although the lowest 22 per cent of the labour force experienced complete stagnation of their real income. While it is quite possible that the Table may hide falling incomes for some groups, the phenomenon of absolute decline does not appear to have been large-scale. Likewise we saw earlier that industrial growth in the modern sector had not been at the expense of any absolute decline in employment in traditional industry, although the relative importance of the latter had fallen. The significance of these points lies in the social and political implications of the worsening income distribution. Many observers of Peruvian society have viewed it as imminently threatened by mass revolt, reasoning that declining mass living standards would inevitably trigger-off revolutionary violence. In fact, the system has been noteworthy for its stability,[28] and even the peasant movements of the 1960s remained confined to limited objectives within local regions. In terms of national politics, this meant that the standpoint from which the majority of the population viewed 'structural reforms' was not that of a desperate and increasingly-impoverished mass seeking a saviour. Rather, it was the standpoint of groups who had been excluded from full participation in the gains from growth in the modern sector, but who hoped for more advantageous incorporation into the system in the future. A reforming government, thus, would find itself confronted not with a blindly-grateful peasantry and lumpenproletariat, but with a large number of calculating and often opportunistic groups anxious to maximise their own dividends from any reform. In order to operate successfully, therefore, a policy of sweeping reform (and specifically of agrarian reform) needed to begin from the realisation that the gains from any reform would of necessity be limited, and would have to be allocated among competing groups of potential beneficiaries.

Drawing together the conclusions of this section, and looking back to the analysis of industry and agriculture in the preceding chapter, it is evident that policies aiming to achieve economic development by means of reforms in the fields of ownership and income distribution needed to be formulated with great care. Apparently-straightforward slogans such as 'Peruvianisation' of ownership, or 'worker participation' in modern sector industry, or agrarian reform, concealed a complex social reality filled with traps for the reformer. For example, various commentators have suggested that income redistribution, by creating a mass market, could provide the basis for a great surge of industrialisation. In the Peruvian situation of 1968, while it was probably true that in the long run such redistribution would have permitted the development of a more rational and integrated industrial structure, the short-run situation was one where many lines of industrial expansion had been encouraged by excessive incentives—often promoting industrial activities which were orientated to a narrow luxury-consumption market and would not be much helped by income redistribution. Furthermore, the removal of 'obstacles to reform' (particularly the oligarchy and the large foreign firms) could open the path to the development of various sectors, but the problems of mobilising resources to finance development of traditional sectors, coping with the worsening internal terms of trade, and devising a new fiscal structure adequate to support the (inevitably increased) role of the State, would all remain to be tackled.

15 The Military Régime since 1968

15.1 THE VELASCO STRATEGY

On October 3, 1968, the Military seized power in Peru and sent President Belaunde into exile. Under the leadership of General Velasco, there followed a series of important reforms, aimed explicitly at bringing about a 'structural transformation' of the Peruvian economy and society, giving the country a more independent and nationalist stance in foreign affairs, and reducing 'dependence.' What was most striking about these reforms, and what quickly attracted attention throughout Latin America, was not so much the content of the legislation (embodying as it did ideas and proposals which had been widely canvassed and occasionally legislated during the 1960s), but the fact that the Military Government proceeded to apply the new measures with a determination previously unknown in Peru.[1] Expropriation without compensation of the International Petroleum Company assets in Peru,[2] the first major act of the new régime, was followed by reorganisation of the old state oil company EPF into the giant new Petroperu, which took over the north coastal oilfields and the Talara refinery, and subsequently pressed ahead with oil exploration in the jungle region, both on its own account and by means of production-sharing contracts with a series of large international oil firms.[3] The new Agrarian Reform Law, decreed in June 1969, was followed by immediate expropriation of the sugar estates of the north Coast—a direct blow at the country's most powerful agrarian interest group, who had previously been successful in obtaining explicit exemption for their properties in the half-hearted reform proposals and legislation of the Prado and Belaunde Governments. The reform was then steadily extended to other areas of the country, and by 1975 virtually all large private landholdings had been affected. The foreign mining companies, having again refused (after prolonged negotiations) to proceed with the rapid development of new large-scale copper mines, were deprived of their undeveloped concessions in late 1970, and the new state company Mineroperu was given a monopoly of mineral-export marketing, control of future projects in the area of metal refining, and the task of developing the mineral deposits recovered from foreign control.[4] In July 1970 the Industrial Reform Law decreed the establishment within modern-sector manufacturing enterprises of 'industrial communities' which, as representatives of the workers, would have a progressively-increasing share in the ownership, management and profits of the enterprise.[5] This law also required foreign capital in manufacturing companies to fade out to a minority ownership position, and foreshadowed the establishment of a new type of joint venture by the government and worker cooperatives, to be known as 'social property.'[6]

Subsequent legislation extended the idea of 'labour communities' to the fishing and mining sectors. In March 1971 the Fisheries Law established state control over the marketing of fisheries exports, required a fade-out of foreign capital from the sector, and laid the basis for worker participation. (Later, following the collapse of fishmeal production described earlier, the entire sector was taken over by the State in 1973.) In June 1971 the General Mining Law established labour communities in that sector also.[7]

Finally, in March 1972 the General Education Law appeared, with the declared objective of extending educational opportunities to all Peruvians.

At first sight, this is an impressive list, certainly sufficient to establish the radical-nationalist credentials of the new Government in the eyes of most observers. The impression was heightened by a series of *ad hoc* expropriations of large foreign firms active in the economy:[8] ITT in 1969, Chase Manhattan Bank in 1970, the Peruvian Corporation and the Conchan oil refinery in 1972, Cerro Corporation in 1974, Marcona Mining Company in 1975. At the same time, the Peruvian Government played a leading role in the formation of Andean Group policies to present a strong united front to foreign capital (the celebrated 'Decision 24'); while in the case of the automobile industry tough new regulations and the auctioning-off of concessions resulted in a dramatic reduction in the number of foreign car firms operating in Peru, and gave the Government a strong voice in planning the industry's future development.[9]

By the mid-1970s the State had assumed the role previously held by foreign capital in mining, oil, electricity and railways; had taken over much of the banking system, virtually all export marketing, and the entire fishing sector; and had pushed through reforms designed to benefit the employees of enterprises in the modern sector of the economy. The result was the major transformation of the ownership structure depicted in Table 15.1; according to Fitzgerald's calculations the weight of foreign capital in the economy was reduced to 40 per cent of its pre-reform level.

These measures, taken together, could be viewed as comprising in some sense an economic and social strategy, but it does not appear that the Government was ever really clear in its own mind either about its own priorities, or about the implications of its reforming policies.[10] In fact, policy evolved largely on an *ad hoc* basis as short-run pressures pushed the Junta first in one direction, then in another; the agrarian reform, in particular, was notable for successive changes of direction as the Government sought to accommodate the interests of antagonistic pressure groups.[11]

TABLE 15.1 The pattern of enterprise ownership in the modern sector
(value added as percentage of GNP[a])

	Pre-reform	*Post-reform*
State	11	26
Domestic private capital	30	22
Foreign capital	21	8
Co-operatives, etc.	–	6
TOTAL MODERN SECTOR	62	62

Source: Fitzgerald (1976), p. 36.
[a] Th figures have been standardised on the basis of the 1972 production structure.

One early attempt to define an economic strategy for the 'revolution' was the five-year Plan for the period 1971–75, published in 1971. The Plan made explicit the Military's belief that a reduction of the economy's external dependence was necessary if development performance were to be improved. The Plan proposed an end to

The subordination of the Peruvian economy to foreign centres of decision, where actions originate which fundamentally affect the economic life of the nation and prevent an autonomous development process geared to the achievement of national objectives.[12]

'Subordination' was to be ended by a radical revision of the terms under which foreign capital operated in Peru. Central to the Velasco Government's thinking was the idea that the weakness of export production and general lack of dynamism in the economy during the 1960s could be remedied by the assertion of national control over the economic surplus. By toughening the terms on which foreign capital was to operate in Peru, and judiciously expropriating foreign interests where necessary, more of the surplus generated by the foreign-controlled sectors would be made locally available. At the same time, by attacking the monopoly positions of the local 'oligarchy', the Government hoped to open up opportunities for a broad stratum of local entrepreneurs who were assumed to have been 'marginalised' by the excessive power and influence of the foreigners and their local élite allies. (The selection of foreign firms and the oligarchy as the targets of the new reforms had a political as well as an economic rationale: it was believed, with good reason, that the strongest opposition to reform of any kind stemmed from these two groups, and that the destruction of their power was therefore essential for any radical programme to succeed.)

For all its assertive nationalism, however, the 1971 Plan offered little in the way of a new economic structure for Peru. The focus of the Plan remained the old export-led growth model, with particular emphasis placed on the rational use of natural resources. The established export sectors were to lie at the heart of the policy, with the derived demand from export expansion,[13] reinforced by the demand stimulus anticipated from income redistribution in agriculture,[14] providing a wider market for renewed industrialisation; further stimulus to industrial development was to come also from 'the establishment of plants which permit the incorporation of greater value added in traditional exports.'[15] Accordingly, top priority was given to the major projects necessary to restore and sustain export expansion, and increase backward linkages. A subsidiary role was to be played also by expansion of domestic food production and the development of non-traditional exports to countries of the Andean Group.

None of these economic goals distinguished the Military Government from any of its predecessors since the 1940s. The novelty lay in the idea, already noted, that breaking the monopoly positions of the élite and the foreign firms would be a sufficient condition for the release of a great reserve of latent dynamism in the Peruvian economy. Such a mobilisation of resources by the allegedly marginalised private sector would provide the drive for the export-led expansion envisaged in the Plan; while in its turn the revival of the export economy was to 'contribute to the process of internal transformation.'[16] The implicit analogy was the breaking of a dam which had been obstructing the flow of resources; the problems of export sectors were envisaged as stemming almost entirely from the unwillingness of foreigners and the oligarchy to undertake investment, and merely breaking the dam should therefore lead directly to a revival of the investment ratio. Thereafter the Plan could come into its own as a means of channeling the subsequent surge of economic growth.

The flaws in the analogy of the dam, already pointed out in Chapter 14, were the biggest problem for such an economic strategy, as we shall describe below. Before passing on to the troubles of the 1970s, however, it is worth pausing here to consider the degree to which the Military Government actually enjoyed alternative options. It could well be argued[17] that the dependent status of the Peruvian economy imposed tight constraints on the government's freedom of manoeuvre. *We* would argue, on the contrary, that the first four years of the military régime were notable for the absence of the short-run pressures which had tied the hands of many previous governments.[18] Politically, the Military had been able to sweep away the Congress and leave the civilian parties in helpless disarray. Socially, the power of the élite had been immensely reduced and many of its leading members had left the country. Most important of all, the military régime enjoyed a large degree of freedom from economic crisis between 1968 and 1972, which provided ample room for manoeuvre. The initial expropriation of IPC provoked the customary U.S.-led freeze on credits from the main international agencies; but, as Table 15.4 below indicates, this was of little immediate concern, since the first five years of the new Government were marked by a large positive trade balance and the first sustained current-account surplus since the Second World War. The Belaunde Government in its last year of office had successfully pushed through the policies of devaluation, internal deflation, and tax increases which were the orthodox response to the economic problems of the mid-1960s, and the incoming Military therefore received the legacy of a stabilised and depressed economy with a strong balance of payments. While the recession continued, the Government could operate free from the problems of exchange crises, inflation, and fiscal bankruptcy. At the same time, international commodity markets were strengthening steadily, causing Peru's commodity terms of trade to improve rapidly; the consequent increase in export earnings served to disguise the continuing stagnation of export production.

The opportunity thus existed for the Military to carry through a fundamental reorientation of the social and economic structure of Peru, in pursuit of their declared goals of social justice and a more autonomous growth model. The most important single choice confronting the new Government was whether to mount a head-on attack on the dualistic structure of the economy, using intersectoral resource transfers to promote the development of the non-modern sectors; or whether, alternatively, to concentrate on reviving the flagging modern sectors—a strategy which implied a further concentration of resources in the development of capital-intensive growth poles. In Chapter 14 we suggested that a serious commitment to social justice in the short or medium term would have implied the former of these two alternatives; in practice, as the next section shows, the Military opted for the second.

15.2 THE IMPACT ON DISTRIBUTION

The 'structural reforms' decreed by the Government were mostly limited to redistribution within sectors rather than between sectors, and only one (the agrarian reform) had any direct impact on a traditional sector.

The principle vehicle of reform was the 'labour community,' a means of achieving worker participation in the profits of modern-sector enterprises. All such firms in industry, mining, fishing, and eventually commerce, were to allocate 10 per cent of profits each year in cash to the labour community (comprising all employees of the firm, including management) along with 15 per cent in shares in the enterprise, up to the point where 50 per cent of the share capital would be owned by the community. Apart from the fact that suitable manipulation of a firm's bookkeeping profits could delay indefinitely the moment of worker control, the scope of the possible redistribution implied by such measures was very limited. Figueroa has calculated that the Industry, Mining and Fishing Laws between them had the combined effect of transferring not more than two per cent of national income to a stratum of modern-sector workers comprising only eight per cent of the national labour force, and situated in the top quartile of the national income distribution.[19] Workers outside the registered sector were not affected by these reforms.

The Agrarian Reform went somewhat further, spanning the boundary between the modern and traditional sectors; but even this reform took a dualistic form. Modern-sector agricultural enterprises were transferred to their modern-sector workers organised in cooperatives, while the remainder of the rural population were to have access only to the poorer lands of the Sierra estates. Even in the latter case, *hacienda* lands were generally transferred to the permanent workforce, leaving independent peasantry and temporary labourers altogether outside the scope of the reform. The result, not surprisingly, was widespread discontent and uncertainty.[20] Despite the determined application of the expropriation provisions of the law, as of 1974 its effect was limited to the redistribution of about one-third of the country's total agricultural and pastoral land,[21] for the benefit of between one-quarter and one-third of the rural labour force.[22] The remainder of the rural population are excluded from the benefits of the reform. Furthermore, so long as agrarian reform was restricted to redistribution of income and resources within agriculture, rather than a net transfer of resources into agriculture from other sectors, its redistributive impact was inevitably limited by the low overall productivity of the agricultural sector. Using estimates made by Van der Wetering, Figueroa shows that even a transfer of 50 per cent of the total agricultural land would imply the transfer of no more than one per cent of national income to the rural poor—not enough to make a significant difference to the national income structure.[23]

Apart from direct reforms, the Military Government retained a number of established policies which had regressive effects on income distribution. The incentives to capital intensity embodied in the Industrial Promotion Law were continued, with the Government making explicit its belief that industrialisation must be capital-intensive (thus leaving employment problems to be solved by other means, despite statements to the contrary in the Plan). The drift to indirect taxation (see Table 14.2) was not reversed. Probably most revealing of the Government's priorities was the attitude towards allocation of resources to the post-reform agricultural sector—something which would have been crucial to any strategy of promoting traditional-sector growth. The Agrarian Reform Law of 1969 clearly anticipated a continuing net transfer of capital out of agriculture: the agrarian bonds paid to former landowners as part-compensation for their properties were intended to be used as collateral for industrial investments, while recipients of land under the reform were required to pay the purchase price over twenty years (the 'agrarian debt'). No major effort was made to improve the availability of agricultural extension services (which reached only about 4 per cent of Sierra small farmers in 1969[24]), while the provision of rural credit was assigned low priority,[25] and the credit available was channelled preferentially to the large-scale 'reformed enterprises' (cooperatives and 'SAIS') and away from small peasant producers.[26] At least one vital input—fertiliser—remained in short supply, and its allocation was hampered by bureaucratic rationing procedures.[27] To complete the picture, urban food prices were judged to be politically sensitive and were kept low, which in the absence of compensating subsidies to local producers[28] served to perpetuate the long-run unfavourable trend of the rural-urban terms of trade.

In summary, whatever their other virtues, the Military's policies left the traditional sectors to subsist as before on the 'trickle-down effects' from modern-sector growth. The existing relationships between modern and traditional sectors were to be left essentially unchanged, and the strategy was to stand or fall on the possibility of reviving modern-sector growth on a more 'autonomous' basis. The remainder of this chapter will be devoted to a discussion of the extent to which this goal has been achieved.

15.3 THE IMPACT ON GROWTH

The plan for the revival of the modern sector rested upon at least two crucial assumptions: first, that the traditional sectors could be left to their own devices without affecting the modern sector's growth; and second, that the primary constraint on investment performance in the modern sector was the monopolistic control of surplus, and that, with this revoked, domestic industrialists would respond. It was the failure of this latter assumption that provided the Government with its first major disappointment.

By 1970, having unveiled its structural reforms and asserted a nationalistic stance, the Government was anticipating a rapid revival of investment, and consequently of the rate of growth. The revival was to stem from two main sources: foreign firms in the mining sector, where the Government was applying heavy pressure to force the development of unworked mineral deposits; and local entrepreneurs freed from the influence of the 'oligarchy.' In the event, neither group acted in accordance with expectations.

Following the 1968 coup, and despite the hostile foreign reaction to the IPC expropriation, the Military continued the Belaunde Government's policy of negotiating with the large foreign mining companies over the development of their unworked concessions. Despite the Military's desire to take a tough line with foreign capital, it was accepted that the technical complexity and enormous costs of mining development made it imperative to bring in the multinational companies. The contradiction between the Government's nationalist rhetoric and its desire to retain the confidence of foreign investors produced considerable uncertainty, but in late 1969 a breakthrough came when Southern Peru Copper Corporation and the Government reached an agreement for the development of the Cuajone copper mine in the south.[29] The Cuajone contract contained a number of significant concessions to foreign capital, evidently in an attempt to establish the principle that foreign investment still had a role to play in Peru, under the new rules; the Government's willingness to make these concessions may also have been due to the pressing need to renegotiate the foreign debt.[30] Following the Cuajone agreement and successful debt re-negotiation, the Government attempted during 1970 to pressurise the other large mining companies into developing their unworked con-cessions, by announcing that deposits for which satisfactory develop-ment plans were not filed would revert to the State. Proposals satisfactory to the Government were not forthcoming, and at the end of 1970 all the major unworked deposits except Cuajone were taken over. Meanwhile, in April 1970 the Mining Law had established the new state company Mineroperu, initially conceived as a marketing agency; this company found itself at the beginning of 1971 placed in charge of the development of all the expropriated deposits. The point to emerge from these early moves of the Military Government in mining policy was that the original intention was not nationalisation, but partnership with foreign capital (a goal pursued with more success in oil exploration after 1971). Only after two years of negotiation and pressure had failed to result in the hoped-for new investment projects, did the Government decide to take over mining development itself. With the exception of the Cuajone contract, foreign firms had proved unwilling to commit capital to Peru under the terms offered by the Military.

Meantime, in 1970 the Government had been attempting to engineer a recovery from the economic recession by easing credit restrictions and providing some incentives for industrial investment. Here was the crucial test of the Military's belief that an attack on foreign and local large capital would open the way for a new stratum of dynamic local enterprises of medium scale.[31] To the Government's evident alarm, the response was negligible. An attempt to bring banking back under local control resulted only in the Government itself being forced to take over most of the banking system.[32] Investment in agriculture remained low, since in view of the fluidity of the agrarian reform situation, no private agriculturist could feel secure. With rare exceptions, local mining investment failed to revive.[33] Most damaging of all to government hopes, despite the apparent profitability of industry and increased tariff protection, local private investment in manufacturing remained very low. Industrial activity did pick up sharply in 1970, but this was expansion into unutilised capacity rather than the result of new investment. Apart from construction,[34] the dominant feature of private investment during the period 1969–72 was a continuation of the long-run decline in its share of GNP which had begun in the late 1950s (see Table 15.2).[35] Outstanding among the measures which were intended to reactivate local capitalism was the imposition of exchange control and obligatory repatriation of overseas funds, in May 1970.[36] Estimates of the inflow of private funds which resulted from this measure range as high as $400 million,[37] and the effect was to flood the local stock exchange, banks and real-estate market with funds. This dramatic increase in liquidity, however, produced virtually no effect on the level of productive investment.

Faced with this abstention by private capital, the Government had to move in to take over for itself the role of the economy's main investor. From the original aim of a mixed economy with a strong private sector, the Peruvian economy moved rapidly towards state capitalism. As shown in Table 15.1 above, Fitzgerald estimates that between 1968 and 1972 roughly 34 per cent of total modern-sector output was transferred from the private sector to the Government or to cooperatives, while at the same time roughly 42 per cent of modern-sector employment was similarly transferred. This took the state/cooperative share of modern-sector output from 18 per cent before the reforms to 52 per cent by 1972. The shift in control of investment decisions was correspondingly great; as Table 15.2 shows, the state sector came to account for more than half the total investment in the economy.

Financing this public investment, however, proved extremely difficult. The two obvious sources of funds within the economy were the large liquid savings of the private sector, and the profits of companies taken over by the State. The second of these proved a disappointment: most of the large foreign-owned enterprises nationalised between 1968 and 1975 were either perennial loss-makers like the Peruvian Corporation, or had been decapitalised by their foreign parent companies prior to expropriation (one major example of this, the IPC, was discussed in Chapter 11; another case in point was the Cerro Corporation's mining operations, nationalised in 1974). In most cases, following the nationalisation of major enterprises, the Government found itself faced with a heavy bill for urgently-needed investments, combined often with large compensation payments. In few cases were the enterprises profitable enough to finance these payments, let alone to subsidise other government projects.[38] Meantime the modern-sector labour force, its expectations aroused by government propaganda surrounding the creation of 'labour communities' and ending of 'foreign exploitation', began to press for a larger slice of the cake, thereby cutting still further into available profits (given that fear of accelerating inflation placed a restraint on price increases). Particularly in the mining sector, industrial unrest became a major problem in 1971 and 1972.

TABLE 15.2 Public and private investment as percentage of GDP, 1960–76

	1960–4	1965–8	1969–73	1974–6
Private saving[a]	16.1	14.6	9.9	8.1
less net transfer to State	− 1.5	− 3.9	− 2.2	− 1.6
gives PRIVATE GROSS FIXED INVESTMENT	14.6	10.7	7.7	6.5
Public savings[b]	2.1	0.7	2.7	7.2
internal			2.0	1.5
external[b]			0.7	5.7
plus net transfer from private sector	1.5	3.9	2.2	1.6
gives PUBLIC GROSS FIXED INVESTMENT	3.6	4.6	4.9	8.8

Source: Fitzgerald (1976), p. 23, and figures supplied by Fitzgerald from his forthcoming work.
[a] Net of stockbuilding. From 1969 only, public enterprise saving has been deducted and included in public savings.
[b] Includes public external borrowing, of which a small part is publicly-guaranteed private debt.

This left private-sector savings as the main source of domestic finance for the Government's plans. As Table 15.2 indicates, about one quarter of private saving was typically loaned to the State. But as government investment rose as a proportion of GDP, while private savings fell, the limitations of this source of finance became evident. 'Net transfers from the private sector' financed 85 per cent of state-sector investment under Belaunde, only 46 per cent in the period 1969—73, and less than 20 per cent in 1974–6. To make up the balance, other sources of funds were required. One obvious possibility was tax reform, which in principle at least had become a serious new possibility once the country's social and political power structure had been altered by the reforms. But to make effective changes in the yield of tax revenue inevitably meant either a sharp increase in profits tax—so discouraging the very groups on whom the reactivation policy depended—or a deep bite into the living standards of the middle classes, for example by ending the exemption from income tax of a large part of the earnings of government officials, or seriously taxing real estate. No such exercise was undertaken by the Military. Income tax had increased its share of total government revenues from 21 per cent to 28 per cent between 1965 and 1969, under the impact of the Belaunde reforms. By 1971, it had fallen back to 27 per cent.[39] The reason was not far to seek: the middle classes constituted the Military régime's main—and possibly only—reservoir of civilian political support. Mass mobilisation was always conspicuously avoided by the Military régime.

TABLE 15.3 External public debt, 1968–76
(U.S. $million)

	1968	1969	1970	1971	1972	1973	1974	1975[a]	1976[a]
Gross inflow	186	221	190	184	285	574	990	1046	1348
Servicing	129	134	167	213	219	347	343	474	511
Net inflow	99	132	69	28	121	309	740	762	1077
Outstanding debt	737	875	945	997	1121	1430	2170	3050	4127
Debt service as percentage of exports	15	16	16	24	23	33	22	34	32

Source: 1968–74: Fitzgerald (1976), p. 71.   1975–6: IMF (1977). The 1976 figures are preliminary estimates.
[a] 1975–76: includes a small figure for loans repayable in local currency. The figure comparable to $3,050 million in 1975 for total debt outstanding in 1974 is $2,288 million.

How then was the expansion of the state sector to be maintained at a sufficiently rapid rate to ensure sustained economic growth, in the absence of a recovery of private investment? The short-run answer is immediately evident from the figures presented in Tables 15.2 and 15.3. The continued rise in public investment in 1974–6 was financed entirely by public borrowing from abroad. Public foreign indebtedness increased from $945 million in 1970 to $2,170 million by the end of 1974, and $4127 million by the end of 1976 (see Table 15.3). The ratio of debt servicing to export earnings rose accordingly, as the Government made up for its inability or unwillingness to mobilise local surplus by turning

TABLE 15.4 Peruvian balance of payments, 1969–76
(U.S. $ million)

	1969	1970	1971	1972	1973	1974	1975	1976
Exports	880	1034	889	945	1112	1503	1290	1360
Imports	-659	-700	-730	-812	-1033	-1909	-2390	-2100
VISIBLE TRADE BALANCE	221	334	159	133	79	-406	-1100	-740
Financial Services								
Public	-37	-31	-48	-51	-66	-104	-231[b]	
Private[a]	-147	-117	-78	-70	-115	-114		-452
Non financial services and transfers	-37	-1	-67	-44	-90	-183	-206[b]	
CURRENT ACCOUNT BALANCE	0	185	-34	-32	-192	-807	-1537	-1192
Long term capital								
Public	124	101	15	116	314	693	793	480
Private[a]	20	-77	-43	-5	70	202	342	196
BASIC BALANCE	144	209	-62	79	192	88	-402	-516
Short term capital	-56	21	-80	24	-125	244	-173[c]	-351[c]
Monetary movements, errors and omissions	-88	-230	142	-103	-67	-332	575[c]	867[c]

TABLE 15.4 (*continued*)

	1969	1970	1971	1972	1973	1974	1975	1976
Export quantum index 1968 = 100	90	97	89	95	74	75	66	76
Commodity terms of trade 1968 = 100	112	125	110	98	144	156	115	n.a.

Source: Cuentas Nacionales del Peru 1960–1974 for balance of payments 1969–74; 1975–6 from Reynolds (1977) and from *Memoria del BCR* (1976). The quantum index is from Table 12.9. The terms of trade index is the Banco Central's export price index deflated by the import price index, from the Bank's *Memoria* and *Boletin*.

[a] Undistributed profits of foreign firms are here treated as outflows on current account and inflows on capital account, in accordance with present Peruvian practice. This table is therefore not directly comparable with Table 14.5. If undistributed profits are excluded, the current-account deficit is reduced to $7.2 million for 1971 and $18.8 million for 1972, with a correspondingly greater net outflow of long term capital.

[b] Services and transfers are aggregated in the Banco Central *Memoria*. They have been disaggregated here using the relative shares shown by Reynolds.

[c] Errors and omissions are included with short term capital in this year.

to international financiers.[40] The extent to which this reflected external borrowing to make up for a need for surplus rather than for foreign exchange is indicated in part by the rise in foreign exchange reserves in 1974.[41] Predictably enough, given the hostility of the World Bank and the U.S. government to the brand of radical nationalism displayed by Peru since 1968, ready access to the international capital market could be obtained only by moderating various elements of the Military's policies. In February 1974 Peru signed the 'Greene Agreement' with the U.S. Government;[42] the central feature of this agreement was payment by Peru of $150 million as full settlement of all outstanding disputes with U.S. business interests (including even the IPC),[42] in exchange for which the U.S.A. withdrew its opposition to the granting of loans to Peru. In addition to enabling the Peruvian Government to finance its operations, the agreement ended a four-year freeze on credits to Southern Peru Copper Corporation for the development of the Cuajone copper mine— the most critical of the export-expansion projects, completion of which had become dependent on the availability of U.S. finance through the Export-Import Bank.

By early 1975, however, the escape route of 1973–4 was closed, as the international banks reversed their easy lending policies and as the extent of Peru's economic crisis became gradually more evident. The ensuing three years provide compelling proof of the failure of the Military's attempt to construct a more autonomous growth model. As the debt service burden increased and the export crisis became more obvious, we find a recurrence of all the familiar problems which had bedevilled the Belaunde Government in the 1960s and which were described in Chapter 14. Balance-of-payments trouble resulted from the combination of stagnant export production, a cyclical decline in export prices, heavy dependence upon imports of foodstuffs and industrial intermediate goods, and an unmanageably-rapid increase in the burden of foreign debt. In turn, these problems flowed from the internal contradictions of the growth model pursued: failure to promote agricultural growth, inadequate integration and rationalisation of the structure of manufacturing industry, constraints upon rapid expansion of export supply, and the unwillingness of the Government to undertake tax reforms commensurate with its increased role in the economy. In addition the increase in defence spending provided a further burden, both internally and externally.

These problems are demonstrated in Table 15.4, as they affected the balance of payments. As the economy began to expand, the favourable trade balance which had provided early breathing-space for the Military régime began to shrink, while there was a corresponding rapid deterioration of the current-account balance, the deficit on which had by 1975 become equal to total export earnings. On the import side, there were two major problems. First, local manufacturing had remained very import-dependent despite the efforts at re-structuring undertaken by the Military, so that the increased capacity-utilisation of the early 1970s translated rapidly into increased imports of intermediate goods. The 'basic' industries reserved to the State include a number of intermediate goods, but the process of launching new projects was slow to get going. COFIDE[43] had overall responsibility for promoting new projects, but in its early years its budget went almost entirely on feasibility studies. Further, such State enterprises as were operating had not acted in such a manner as to reduce imports, continuing to purchase overseas 'on grounds of technical requirements.'[44]

In the second place, food production recorded a dismal performance, traced in Table 15.5; after 1971 (when the widespread transfer of coastal land out of cotton production and into food crops came to an end) foodcrop production remained almost stagnant, with a corresponding decline in *per capita* production. (With the exception of poultry production, the results in livestock production were similar.) So far as foreign capital was concerned, Table 15.4 shows that the increased foreign borrowing by the Government was offset to a considerable extent by the rise of debt servicing and the net outflow of private capital.

TABLE 15.5 Indices of agricultural production
(1968 = 100)

	All crops	Food crops	Food crops per capita
1968	100	100	100
1969	108	110	107
1970	117	120	113
1971	119	123	112
1972	118	123	110
1973	124	129	111
1974	121	126	107
1975	126	133	109

Source: Production and Trade Yearbook (FAO) (1975).

The other side of the coin was export performance. The Peruvian economy in fact had returned to a pattern familiar by now to any reader of this book: economic growth depended in the long run upon successful export expansion, with foreign borrowing able to serve only as a temporary stopgap. Having decided against an attempt at total reorientation of the economy at the end of the 1960s, the Military Government was inevitably obliged to assign ever-increasing priority to the task of carrying through a major expansion of export supply. Table 15.4 and Fig. 15.1 indicate clearly enough the difficulties encountered. Export earnings at current prices increased 71 per cent between 1969 and 1974, but this increase was made possible only by the improvement of world commodity prices; over the same period, the quantum index of export supply actually dropped by 17 per cent, while from 1969 to 1975 the fall was no less than 27 per cent. When the improvement in Peru's terms of trade was reversed in 1972, the continuing stagnation of export

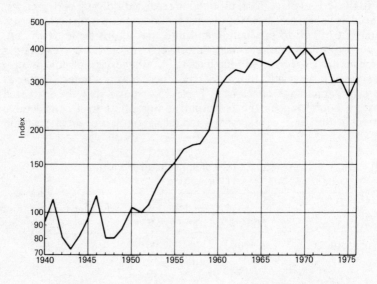

FIGURE 15.1 Quantum index of exports, 1940–74
(1929 = 100)

Source: as for Table 12.9.

production clearly spelt trouble. In 1975 export earnings fell while the rapid growth of import requirements continued.

Behind these figures lay the constraints outlined in Chapters 12 and 14, where it was shown that initially no increase in volume could be looked for in fishmeal or agriculture and livestock; even in the longer run the export prospects of these sectors were limited, despite the initiation by the Military Government of a new generation of large-scale coastal irrigation projects.

In effect, the urgent need for export expansion could be met only by a breakthrough in mineral exports, and the Military had staked everything on two groups of projects in this area: the attempt to locate new oilfields in the jungle such as those which made neighbouring Ecuador a leading oil producer in the early 1970s; and the development of a small number of giant copper mines, each of which required the concentration of enormous sums of capital, and highly advanced technology. Jungle oil exploration, in partnership with large foreign companies, began in 1971 and proceeded at an intensive pace until 1975. By late 1975, however, despite two successful oil strikes, the total reserves located amounted to only 550 million barrels—about three or four months' Venezuelan production—and the foreign companies began to withdraw.[45]

This left metals mining, and specifically copper, as the key to export expansion. As Chapter 11 indicated, however, mining development had by the 1960s become a matter of large scale projects and very long gestation periods. The development of the Cuajone copper mine by Southern Peru Copper Corporation under its 1969 contract was not completed until late 1976 (development work was slowed down somewhat by the refusal of U.S. Government agencies to assist with the financing until 1974). Government plans for the development of the ore deposits expropriated in 1970–1 were focused on the Cerro Verde copper mine, which has recently entered production, in May 1977; other state mining projects will not bear fruit until the end of the 1970s. The two key copper mines, Cuajone and Cerro Verde, should increase Peruvian copper production between two and three times, and will undoubtedly play a vital role in enabling the economy to survive its latest crisis (just as the opening of the Toquepala mine in 1960 provided relief from the crisis of 1958[46]).[47] But as of 1977, little or no relief had been experienced.

Drawing together these aspects, it will be seen that the combination of a higher debt service ratio, a more serious export situation, and possibly a more rigid import structure,[48] among other aspects, meant that once the panaceas of international prices and lending disappeared, the economy emerged as, if anything, more vulnerable than in earlier years. Not surprisingly, faced with this situation and under pressure from international creditors, the only option appeared to be the even more complete abandonment of innovative policies. In August 1975 the 'radical' President Velasco was replaced by the more cautious General Morales Bermudez, signifying a shift from the 'first' to the second 'phase' of the 'Revolution.' Despite assurances that the second phase represented continuance of the Revolution, in practice the significant features of the Velasco era were modified or abandoned, in a belated attempt to regain the support, politically and economically, of the private sector. In 1976 the Industrial Communities Law was revised, while 'social' property was gradually reduced to insignificance. However, this could do nothing to revive the private sector in the face of the economic depression which now followed stabilisation measures implemented in mid-1975, and with increased severity in mid-1976 and mid-1977—measures which, in the face of the Military's reluctance to cut its own spending, hit the private sector particularly hard.[49] The result was the by now familiar pattern of acute depression plus cost-push inflation; GDP *per capita* fell 0.2 per cent in 1976,[50] while by early 1977 the cost of living was rising at an annual rate of over 40 per cent.[51]

Thus it appears that the economic crisis of 1975–7 will probably yet again discredit, as in the 1940s, the ideas of autonomy, nationalism and reform, which had manifestly not provided the economy with adequate defences. While the parallel with 1948 is far from exact, it seems unlikely that a revival of export-led growth in the next decade will represent a major divergence from Peru's long-run historical path.

15.4 REVIEW AND CONCLUSION

The 'Peruvian Revolution' initiated by the Military in 1968 marked potentially the most important turning-point in the history of the Peruvian economy since 1890. A new Government held secure power, largely free from domestic opposition, and with room for manouevre provided by a temporarily strong balance-of-payments. Economic dependence and social injustice had been identified as the targets for a programme of structural reforms, and the Military stood ready to confront the country's most powerful interest groups in the pursuit of those goals. The climate in which foreign capital operated was rapidly changed, and the measure most widely regarded as crucial to the destruction of the old order—the agrarian reform—was pushed rapidly into effect. Clearly the new Military régime satisfied a number of the criteria set out in Chapter 2 in our discussion of the requirements for successful autonomous growth. Yet the results must be described as disappointing.

Income redistribution and other benefits of the reforms were limited mostly to the top quartile of the population—the participants in the modern sector. No new source of economic dynamism emerged to replace the traditional dependence upon export performance; and the expansion of the government sector, although successful in raising the level of economic activity during the first half of the 1970s, was accomplished only at the cost of a massive increase in the external debt. At the basic level of production and capital-formation, the growth performance of export sectors and food agriculture failed to improve, while the State's ability to finance the development of its newly-acquired interests throughout the economy proved inadequate. Policies dictated by political expediency (such as the payment of heavy import subsidies on food destined for the urban population), and the Government's failure to capture an increased share of national income by taxation, have resulted in misallocation of resources and unprecedented dependence on foreign borrowing—and with foreign finance have come the usual strings. In general, the move towards autonomy has been limited and the economy's external dependence has been moderated but not fundamentally altered.

Why has the 'Peruvian Revolution' produced such relatively unsatisfactory results?[52] Reviewing the material in the last two chapters, we would suggest a twofold explanation: the conceptual inadequacy of the Military's programme; and the harsh realities of Peru's position in the international system. The Military régime, we believe, correctly identified a number of the key problems for Peruvian development, but failed to tackle them from any consistent political or ideological stance—a trait which led one journal to report a major policy speech by President Velasco under the apt headline 'Neither Left, Right, nor Centre'.[53] By refusing to move to the left the Military lost their opportunity to mobilise mass support among the traditional-sector labour force, and to use major redistributive policies to promote a more inward-directed development strategy. At the same time, by attacking business interests and the Right, the Military lost the confidence and support of local capitalists and alienated foreign interests. As pressures from both sides mounted, a choice of direction was forced on the Government by its need for financial resources. A shift to the Left would have extended the state sector into the profitable consumer-goods sector which the Government had refrained from touching, and might have improved the internal mobilisation of resources by taxation, but would have brought severe problems in the external sector. A shift to the Right could bring in more foreign capital and open the way to a 'solution' in terms of orthodox economic management and the abandonment of social goals. As we have seen, this is in fact the road which has now been taken, although the resistance to orthodox policy has been so great (from the military and from private industry deprived of credit, as well as at the grass-roots level)[54] that recent developments have been characterised by policy incoherence as well as by increasing repression.[55]

Perhaps the most important lesson of the Peruvian experiment is that it is not sufficient for a government to have its heart in the right place (if we can so describe the Velasco Government with respect to autonomous development). Oversimplified models of social reality run the risk of merely shifting the focus of social conflict, on the one hand, while leaving essential economic weaknesses untouched, on the other. This is particularly true for an economy bound into the international system as closely as is that of Peru. For such an economy, periods of freedom from the pressures of the system come seldom and do not last long. The years from 1968 to 1972 were such a period, but it cannot be said that the policy innovations of those years were sufficient to launch a sustainable process of autonomous development. It may be some time before the opportunity recurs.

16 Conclusions

In the course of this book we have traced the evolution of the Peruvian economy from the War of the Pacific to the mid-1970s, in search of answers to two central questions: has Peru since 1890 been an example of a successfully developing country, and if not, why not?

Our answer to the first of these questions is easily summarised. Long-run growth has been slow (probably little more than one per cent a year in *per capita* terms), and associated with an overall worsening of income distribution. Growth was limited to the modern sector, and geographically concentrated on the coast. The dual structure of the economy hardened as the spread of capitalism discriminated among sectors and regions, and as disparities were accentuated by population growth. With economic growth paced by export performance, the country's economic history since independence has proceeded in a series of spurts of growth separated by periods of transition and uncertainty; these breakdowns of the export-led model have tended to occur roughly every fifty years, and to last about twenty years. No 'engine of growth' other than export earnings emerged to provide the basis for self-sustaining capitalist development; even industrialisation, despite its rapid advance in recent decades, has brought new elements of vulnerability and dependence without generating an autonomous economic dynamism.

The two main shortcomings of the Peruvian economy's performance since 1890 have been: first, the failure to achieve independent self-sustaining growth within the framework of a capitalist system; and second, the failure to distribute the gains from growth outside the modern sector to the impoverished mass of the population. We have several times suggested that these twin goals of autonomy and distributional equity are central to a process of genuine 'development', and in the remainder of this chapter we set out our main conclusions under these two headings.

The significance over the long run of achieving a greater degree of autonomy has been evidenced at a number of points in our study. We have defined the essential bases of autonomy as: local control over the surplus; local capacity to innovate and adapt technology; endogenous as distinct from external sources of economic dynamism; and policies which foster integrated growth. The consolidation of such a base might have permitted the economy to survive the periodic breakdown of the export mechanism without high cost in terms of growth, and might further have rendered the economy less vulnerable to domination on unfavourable terms by foreign investment. It would also have prepared the economy more successfully to tackle the increasingly large-scale and more complex investment projects required to sustain growth in the export sector.

Why then did the economy conspicuously fail to achieve a more autonomous or more broadly-based development? The answers lie partly in the nature of export-led growth itself. The most important conclusion to emerge from our study is that the economic trends set in motion by successful export growth have consistently eroded the potential for self-sustained development. The reasons, once identified, are fairly straightforward:

(i) The takeoff phase of each export boom rapidly generated cumulative forces drawing resources into the growing export sectors, and discouraging the parallel development of non-export industries. The normal working of the price mechanism accounts for much of this tendency. The increased relative profitability of export production served to attract resources from other sectors, while the strong balance-of-payments position created by export growth resulted in increased competition from imports in the local market, serving to depress the relative profitability of local industry. Export agriculture yielded a surplus sufficient to permit the neglect of non-export agriculture, with food shortages relieved by imports when necessary; food shortages in any case were muted by regressive trends in income distribution, which helped to limit the growth of domestic consumption. The availability of foreign exchange permitted capital exports and luxury consumption, both of which drained off economic surplus to unproductive uses. These forces can be observed at work both in the disintegration of the brief experiment with integrated development initiated during the 1890s, and in the period from 1948 to the 1960s. The latter period saw the gradual emergence of a countervailing tendency towards governmental support for import-substituting industrialisation, much of it in the form of heavily-protected branch plants of large multinational companies. The new protectionism, however, was not coherently planned, nor applied in such a way as to reduce the underlying dependence of the Peruvian economy; consequently the gains from industrialisation were slight and the costs high.

(ii) Over time, indigenous capabilities in the fields of entrepreneurship and technology, which in a closed economy might have been developed in the course of growth, suffered the opposite fate in an open system. The beginning of each phase of export growth led, predictably enough, to a reawakening of foreign interest in the opportunities thus opened up, and as the growth phase proceeded foreign capital, foreign technology and foreign advisers played an increasing role. While local capabilities were thus eclipsed by the obvious market superiority of things foreign, it cannot be said that this was accepted with any reluctance. On the contrary, the reasonable desire of local capitalists to have access to the most modern and 'efficient' techniques and equipment led naturally to the emergence of a close-knit alliance with foreign capital. During the growth phases, committed nationalists were the exception rather than the rule among Peruvian capitalists, and successful nationalists were scarcer still.[1]

(iii) In terms of policy formation, it is evident enough that the most powerful interest group to emerge from the process of export-led growth was precisely this coalition of local and foreign capitalists, eager to sustain the boom as long as possible without interference. In an élite-dominated political system, such as Peru remained until the 1960s, this point of view carried great weight in the formation of government policy. Periods of successful export growth rapidly consolidated the political power of those who reaped the benefits of comparative advantage, and thus ensured the supremacy of policies which served their interests, so that the familiar orthodox policy mix of *laissez-faire* liberalism and encouragement for foreign investment grew naturally out of export growth, rather than vice versa. Once adopted, of course, such policies thereafter produced acceleration of the growth of export-linked activities, encouraging the concentration of economic activity in part of the modern sector while the rest of the economy was left to drift.

(iv) Export-led growth quickly became closely associated with foreign direct investment, and government policy tended to encourage this trend. In several cases we have presented evidence which strongly suggests that the net contribution of foreign capital in various sectors was at times negative or negligible. Governments, however, were not prepared to embark on serious efforts to control or bargain with the foreign firms; and over time, as those firms became increasingly entrenched, Peru's ability to dispense with their presence was reduced. Given a conjuncture of unfavourable circumstances, reliance on external resources for the launching of one generation of key investment projects led, as already noted, to a decline in entrepreneurial orientation, which in turn ensured that external resources would be indispensable to the success of the subsequent generation of projects.

(v) The ending of each of the cycles of export growth quickly exposed the problems of the dependent, outward-oriented growth model. Solutions to those problems, however, were not readily thrown up by the system. This was due basically to three factors. In the first place, the reorientation of the economy which would have been required in order to switch to an autonomous growth model was very great, and unlikely to be accomplished overnight. The Peruvian economy in 1879, in 1930, and in 1968 was extremely dependent upon the dynamism provided by export sectors and foreign firms; the reconstruction of alternative growth poles and indigenous capabilities had to begin almost from nothing.

In the second place, the design and implementation of radically innovative economic policies requires a secure government with adequate skills at its command, and with a powerful social base among segments of the population who perceive autonomous growth as serving their own long-term interests. We have already stated however that the political effect of export-led growth was to consolidate the dominant position of the export-based élites, whose reluctance to abandon the traditional export-led model was strengthened by the degree to which, even in the difficult transition phases, their major interests remained concentrated in export sectors or closely-allied activities. Unwilling to initiate a policy switch away from the orthodox model, the élite were nevertheless prepared at some periods during the transition phases to acquiesce in certain innovations; but the design and implementation of such policies was left to other groups lower down the social and economic scale: in the 1940s, the emerging middle classes and organised labour; in the 1960s, the Military. But it was intrinsic to the situation that such groups were ill-prepared or underdeveloped. In all three major periods of transition covered in this book (the 1890s, the 1940s and the early 1970s) the class base for innovative policies was ill-defined and policy itself consequently lacked any clear strategic orientation—a pattern which recurs in the debate between free-traders and protectionists in the 1890s, in the factionalism and vacillation of the Bustamante regime in the 1940s, and in the well-intentioned but contradictory policies of the Military after 1968. The lack of clear guidelines meant that priorities were uncertain, that much policy was made by *ad hoc* response to pressing circumstances rather than in pursuit of consistent principles, and that the hegemony of traditional interests could readily be reasserted once the expansion of the export economy was resumed.

The opening for innovative policies was, almost by definition, provided by the onset of periods of economic and social crisis: the collapse of guano and the War of the Pacific; the Great Depression and the Second World War; the failure of export growth and capital formation in the 1960s. The impact of these economic crises provides the third, and in a sense the basic, reason for the failure of the Peruvian system to throw up an alternative development model. We have already argued that the phases of rapid export growth tended to accentuate the degree to which the dynamism of the economy depended on exports; while export success also naturally led to an improvement in Peru's international credit rating and hence to heavy foreign borrowing to finance the public sector, coupled with an influx of private foreign capital. The periods of transition resulting from the collapse of each export boom were consequently also periods of great difficulty for the management of the economy, not only because its mainspring (export growth) was no longer operative, but also because of the balance-of-payments repercussions of the preceding growth pattern. Innovative régimes embarking on the attempt to reorient the economy during the 1940s and 1970s were required simultaneously to cope with short-run economic pressures, which quickly eliminated any temporary freedom of manoeuvre enjoyed by the government. Freedom of manoeuvre was ample, of course, at the height of each growth phase—but, at those times, comparative advantage and élite hegemony ensured the survival of orthodox policies.

Thus, while on the one hand each period of rapid growth by its very success sapped the capacity of the economy and society to rise above the subsequent crisis, on the other hand the innovators brought to power by the crises have been ill-organised and uncertain, with their options restricted by short-run economic pressures and their class base incoherent. The consequent 'failure' of interventionist policy has then helped to consolidate the forces making for a return to liberalism when export growth revived. Small wonder that in Peru the record of orthodox policy appears strong and that of unorthodox policy weak; small wonder also that in Peru, as in much of Latin America, the theorists of dependence have tended to discount the possibility of breaking out of the pattern. Peru has been the prisoner not only of external economic trends, but also of its own history, with the collapse of radical policies at time of crisis reinforcing the conservatism of policy during the subsequent boom.

The above reflections on Peruvian experience prompt two further conclusions concerning the reasons for the extraordinary resilience and durability of the Peruvian model. The first is the system's ability to coopt its potential critics; the second the elements of circularity within that process.

The issue of cooption lies at the heart of the failures of economic policy discussed above. Over the long run, the phases of export growth have been marked by the incorporation into the modern sector (and hence into the benefits of export growth) of those new social groups which might otherwise have provided the base for a coherent radical policy. We have already discussed the harmonious relations which prevailed between local and foreign capital; similar patterns, it must now be added, emerged at lower levels of the social pyramid. The process of incorporating organised white-collar and blue-collar workers into, respectively, the bureaucracy and the labour aristocracy, and their leaders into the political spoils system, is perfectly illustrated by the historical evolution of APRA from its original role as revolutionary opposition around 1930, to its close partnerships with Manuel Prado in the late 1950s, and with Manuel Odría in the 1960s. This cooption process meant that criticisms of the orthodox model were voiced weakly or not at all, because of the fragmentation of the classes which might otherwise have launched a political movement or movements committed to non-traditional policies. At the same time, the failure to promote more diversification of the economy slowed down the development of precisely those classes which would have been most likely to press for diversification. This is one among many examples of the self-reinforcing nature of economic and social processes in Peruvian history. For example, the capacities necessary to manipulate the international system were constantly undermined by the operation of the international system itself. And again, the lack of a social base led to the continual apparent failure of interventionist policy, which in turn strengthened support for orthodox liberalism.

Finally, having dealt at length with autonomy, we return to the second deficiency in Peruvian growth, and perhaps its most glaring defect: the virtual failure to improve the situation of the poorest groups of the population. To some extent, this failure flowed directly from the same characteristics of export-led growth which blocked progress towards a more autonomous capitalism and slowed the long-run average rate of growth below what might have been achieved. Export-led growth naturally focused on the modern sectors, produced a workable macro-economic equilibrium which eliminated much of the possible incentive to develop traditional sectors (particularly food agriculture), and created powerful vested interests opposed to even minimal programmes of social reform and structural change. In addition, the modern sector's use of imported techniques helped to consolidate dualistic patterns of employment and productivity. It is important, however, not to over-estimate the extent to which the historical trend towards dualism could have been modified simply by greater autonomy within the existing capitalist mode of production[2] Greater autonomy would have implied stronger and more beneficial trickle-down effects for traditional sectors, and hence somewhat more satisfactory integration of those sectors into the process of modern-sector growth. But expansion would still have been focused upon modern-sector growth poles, within the framework of options and pressures determined by the international market. The question of how far it was inevitable that capitalist development should lead to the emergence of dualism is impossible to answer satisfactorily, but we would suggest that so far as the position of Peru's poor was concerned, the difference between autonomous and dependent capitalism would have been of degree rather than of kind.

It therefore appears that the suggestion of some 'dependency' writers, that a more autonomous development process would both promote and rest upon greater equality, applies to an option beyond the reach of the case we have been discussing. It may be true that a determined drive to achieve greater autonomy would have brought about greater equality, but such a programme would have had to be undertaken in defiance of (not in cooperation with) the forces of the local and international market system. Such defiance requires a political base—but as we have indicated, one of the great strengths of the dependent export-led model has been its ability to divert challenges by means of cooption. The picture in some dependency writing of 'marginalised' social groups waiting in the wings to provide political and economic backing for a new order could hardly be further from the truth.

A further pessimistic note is in order also. One hundred years of dependent dualistic development have left a cumulative centripetal tendency firmly built into the Peruvian system. The present poverty of the mass of participants in the traditional sectors cannot be adequately explained in terms simply of present or recent 'exploitation,' and the removal of identifiable 'exploiters' therefore does not provide a solution to the problem of poverty. Any attempt to achieve an economic takeoff for the traditional sectors must rest upon a radical redistribution of resources from the modern to the traditional sectors, a redistribution which would fly in the face of history, and would be possible only in a situation where the social and political, as well as the economic, legacies of the past century had been put aside. The failure of the present military Government to confront the problem of dualism is thus understandable enough.

Where, then, does Peru stand in the middle of the 1970s? The 'Revolution' of 1968 was able to accomplish very striking reforms in the structure of ownership in the modern sector, and to take some steps towards the construction of a more autonomous, state-capitalist development model. But such reforms could neither solve the pressing short-run crisis of the export-led economy nor offer much hope of overcoming dualism in the longer term. [3] As the windfall export price boom of the early 1970s faded, familiar tendencies began ominously to reappear. The focus on a breakthrough in export production became accentuated; the usual arguments in favour of private enterprise and liberal orthodoxy gained ground both inside and outside the government; there was talk of 'squeezing the peasants;' and signs began to emerge of a rapprochement between the Military and the more conservative of the old civilian political parties, notably the APRA. Despite the Military's repeated claims that Peru has definitively broken with its past, the issue remains in doubt.

Appendix 1
Estimating the Value of the Main Exports, 1880–1910

Official trade statistics were published for only a few of the years 1880–99, and their accuracy has been subject to some doubt, particularly as regards their valuation techniques. Detailed official statistics appeared for 1887, 1891, 1892, and for all years from 1897 on. In addition, retrospective official series exist showing the value of total exports for all years through the 1890s.[1] As it turns out, our results indicate that these official series are reliable for the trend of exports, although they were evidently biased upwards by overvaluation.

We decided to construct annual estimates of the value of major export products by assembling figures on the volume of exports, and multiplying these by current world prices to obtain estimated cif values. Table A.1.1 reproduces the volume series used, Table A.1.2 contains the world prices, and Table A.1.3 shows the results of the exercise. It will be seen that we have confined ourselves to only eight export products; these however accounted for the great bulk of export earnings during the period, and their total value is the best proxy available to us for total exports. The most serious omission is guano, data on which we have included in Table A.1.1. Unfortunately we have not had available to us a price series for guano, and it has therefore been excluded from Table A.1.2. We have, however, included an extra column in Table A.1.3 showing the value of guano exports at the 1900 price given by Hunt.

It will be noted that our quantity data up to 1900 have been drawn with very little modification from the pioneering study by Hunt. For 1900 to 1910 we have drawn upon the official volume data as well as upon Hunt, but we have rejected the suspect official series for copper exports in favour of annual copper production as reported in the mining statistics; this has the result of overstating the figure for copper exports somewhat for the years 1902–4 (when considerable quantities of ore were being stockpiled at Cerro de Pasco) and understating it somewhat for 1906–7 (when those stockpiles were run down).

TABLE A.1.1 Volume of major exports, 1880–1910
(metric tons)

	Sugar	Cotton	Wool	Alpaca	Coffee	Silver	Copper	Rubber	Guano
1880	57,610	2,339	522	641	212	63		84	
1881	44,469	2,031	713	805	34	52		95	
1882	44,943	2,157	586	1,441	391	52		151	
1883	34,514	2,117	822	638	410	61		155	83,767
1884	34,307	1,612	2,184	3,072	548	64		541	23,932
1885	46,260	2,175	1,212	1,708	491	67		1,041	19,075
1886	43,760	3,605	1,022	1,754	308	78		1,228	69,858
1887	36,240	2,514	1,159	1,938	319	79		828	12,158
1888	40,579	3,736	855	1,797	470	77		2,045	41,971
1889	52,667	3,439	1,320	2,048	282	83		1,177	39,100
1890	39,077	4,172	1,086	1,413	383	83	180	1,164	—
1891	38,445	4,766	1,429	1,813	293	79	336	1,582	12,451
1892	47,975	9,837	1,223	1,841	465	88	348	1,635	30,300
1893	44,367	8,008	1,651	2,042	347	96	552	1,153	67,599
1894	34,455	4,465	1,374	2,053	452	99	528	1,294	39,161
1895	58,723	5,038	1,228	1,653	544	98	540	1,105	17,371
1896	71,735	4,718	1,469	1,649	713	118	888	1,338	16,460
1897	105,463	5,586	1,393	2,064	1,240	101	1,198	2,614	20,301
1898	105,713	6,712	924	1,763	1,245	162	3,649	2,334	31,272
1899	103,707	5,876	1,104	1,921	1,215	200	6,195	1,952	43,516
1900	112,223	7,246	969	1,922	1,454	209	9,865	1,728	11,280
1901	114,637	8,011	1,434	2,422	1,556	197	11,414	1,724	
1902	117,362	6,684	1,258	2,460	1,657	184	9,096	1,701	
1903	127,673	7,651	1,489	2,711	1,352	185	9,497	2,108	
1904	131,958	7,532	1,279	2,328	1,047	186	9,504	2,221	

TABLE A.1.1 (*continued*)

	Sugar	Cotton	Wool	Alpaca	Coffee	Silver	Copper	Rubber	Guano
1905	134,234	9,561	1,599	2,912	1,028	59	12,213	2,540	
1906	136,729	10,445	1,730	2,837	605	115	13,474	2,576	
1907	110,615	12,339	1,429	2,384	839	114	20,681	3,029	
1908	124,892	16,019	1,146	1,913	735	139	19,854	2,516	
1909	125,352	21,305	1,408	2,391	334	127	20,068	2,802	
1910	122,856	14,106	1,716	3,013	443	252	27,375	2,651	

Sources: Up to 1900 the series are based upon Hunt (1973a), Part 2. Sugar, cotton, wool, alpaca and coffee from Table 14 of this source (sugar 1897–1900 corrected to include *chancaca*). Silver from Table 21; converting to kilos using 4.4 marks = 1 kilo. Rubber also from Table 21. The series for copper in *ibid.*, Table 14, was rejected as obviously far too high for the 1880s and early 1890s (Hunt shows substantial exports of 'refined copper' for years when no copper smelters were operating, or had been operating for decades). Copper, therefore, is the figure for U.K. imports from Peru (*BCIM*, No 14, p. 36) marked up 20 per cent to allow for exports to other markets.

For 1900 to 1910 official figures (as summarised in *Extracto Estadístico, 1934–5*, p. 135 are used for sugar, cotton, and wool (the last disaggregated between alpaca and sheepwool using data in Hazen, 1974, Table 1). Silver is from Hunt (1973a), Table 3; copper is the production series from *BCIM* 82, p. 74; coffee from Hunt (1973a), Table 1, using the constant-price index applied to 1900 volume. Rubber 1903–1910 is the official series; 1901 and 1902 filled in by estimation.

TABLE A.1.2 Prices used to value exports

(£)

	Sugar (ton)	Cotton (ton)	Wool (ton)	Alpaca (ton)	Coffee (ton)	Silver (kilo)	Copper (ton)	Rubber (ton)
1880	20.13	44.53	125.58	154.46		7.63	61.61	
1881	20.87	41.32	127.42	156.72	56.58	7.63	60.73	249.88
1882	19.64	42.54	112.75	138.68	45.27	7.63	64.84	284.28
1883	18.66	36.90	110.92	136.43	37.12	7.48	61.77	324.57
1884	13.01	38.50	110.92	136.43	42.10	7.48	52.91	253.05
1885	13.26	36.13	91.67	112.75	37.12	7.18	42.77	170.21
1886	11.54	32.92	83.42	102.61	34.40	6.60	39.37	183.79
1887	11.54	35.29	92.58	113.87	48.44	6.60	45.20	217.28
1888	12.77	35.68	89.83	110.49	63.37	6.31	80.11	198.72
1889	15.71	38.11	89.83	110.49	58.85	6.31	48.85	172.02
1890	12.77	38.50	94.42	116.14	72.43	7.04	53.29	199.18
1891	13.26	30.09	85.25	104.86	86.01	6.60	50.55	239.92
1892	13.26	26.89	79.75	98.09	90.53	5.87	44.84	223.17
1893	14.00	29.71	79.75	98.09	63.37	5.28	42.99	194.20
1894	11.05	24.45	77.92	95.84	74.24	4.25	39.65	202.35
1895	9.82	24.45	74.25	91.33	66.54	4.40	42.21	209.14
1896	10.56	27.72	77.00	94.71	66.09	4.55	46.07	204.15
1897	9.08	25.28	73.33	90.20	50.25	4.11	48.25	222.26
1898	9.33	21.24	74.25	91.33	33.95	3.96	50.90	249.88
1899	10.31	22.84	78.83	96.96	29.42	3.96	72.37	281.11
1900	11.05	35.29	87.08	107.11	30.33	4.11	72.31	287.45
1901	9.08	30.48	68.75	84.56	33.50	3.96	65.79	233.13
1902	7.12	31.31	68.75	84.56	29.42	3.52	51.63	223.62
1903	8.35	38.69	76.08	93.58	29.42	3.67	57.12	250.33
1904	10.07	42.35	79.75	98.09	31.69	3.96	57.97	309.18
1905	10.80	32.66	85.25	104.86	39.84	4.11	68.36	335.88
1906	8.35	38.18	93.50	115.00	38.93	4.55	85.86	353.09
1907	9.08	42.03	94.42	116.14	35.76	4.40	85.53	346.75
1908	9.58	36.70	85.25	104.86	34.40	3.67	58.95	266.17
1909	10.07	40.62	87.08	107.11	33.95	3.52	57.81	315.97
1910	10.80	51.33	93.50	115.00	35.76	3.67	56.14	452.67

Sources: Sugar from Deerr (1949–50), p. 531, London raw price. Cotton from Mitchell (1962), p. 491; Peruvian cotton price assumed 70 per cent of the American Middling price in Liverpool. Wool from Mitchell (1962), p. 496, British average import price. Alpaca is the wool price multiplied by 1.23. Coffee from *Statistical Abstract of the United States*, 1908, p. 460 and 1921, p. 622, U.S. average import price. Silver from *Quin's Metals Handbook*, 1938, pp. 328–9, London price. Copper as for silver. Rubber as for coffee.

FIGURE A.1.1 Comparison of two export series

Source: Table A.1.4.

TABLE A.1.3 Value of eight export products, 1880–1910
(£000)

	Sugar	Cotton	Wool	Alpaca	Coffee	Silver	Copper	Rubber	Total	(Guano)[a]
1880	1,160	104	66	99	12	481		21	1,943	
1881	928	84	91	126	2	397		24	1,652	
1882	883	92	66	200	18	397		41	1,697	
1883	644	78	91	87	15	456		50	1,421	340
1884	446	62	242	419	23	479		137	1,808	97
1885	613	79	111	193	18	481		177	1,672	77
1886	505	119	85	180	11	515		226	1,641	284
1887	418	89	107	221	15	521		180	1,551	49
1888	518	133	77	199	30	486		406	1,849	170
1889	827	131	119	226	17	524		202	2,046	159
1890	499	161	103	164	28	584	10	232	1,781	–
1891	510	143	123	190	25	521	17	380	1,909	51
1892	636	265	98	181	42	517	16	365	2,120	123
1893	621	238	132	200	22	507	24	224	1,968	274
1894	381	109	107	197	34	421	21	262	1,532	159
1895	577	123	91	151	36	431	23	231	1,663	71
1896	758	131	113	156	82	537	41	273	2,091	67
1897	958	141	102	186	36	415	58	581	2,477	82
1898	986	143	69	161	42	642	186	583	2,812	127
1899	1,069	134	87	186	37	792	448	549	3,302	177
1900	1,240	256	84	206	37	859	713	497	3,892	46
1901	1,041	244	99	205	49	780	751	402	3,571	
1902	836	209	86	208	46	648	470	380	2,883	
1903	1,066	296	113	254	49	679	542	528	3,527	

TABLE A.1.3 *(continued)*

	Sugar	Cotton	Wool	Alpaca	Coffee	Silver	Copper	Rubber	Total	(Guano)[a]
1904	1,329	319	102	228	43	737	551	687	3,996	
1905	1,450	312	136	305	42	242	835	853	4,175	
1906	1,142	399	162	326	40	523	1,157	910	4,659	
1907	1,004	519	135	277	22	502	1,769	1,050	5,278	
1908	1,196	588	98	201	29	510	1,170	670	4,462	
1909	1,262	865	123	256	25	447	1,160	885	5,023	
1910	1,327	724	160	346	12	925	1,537	1,200	6,231	

Source: Tables A.1.1 and A.1.2.
[a] Guano valued at the 1900 price of £4.06 per ton (Hunt (1973a), p. 63).

TABLE A.1.4 Comparison of our eight-product total
with official series for exports
(£000)

	Our series	Official series
1880	1,943	
1881	1,652	
1882	1,697	
1883	1,421	
1884	1,808	
1885	1,672	
1886	1,641	
1887	1,551	1,275
1888	1,849	
1889	2,046	
1890	1,781	1,820
1891	1,909	1,753
1892	2,120	2,513
1893	1,968	1,928
1894	1,532	1,100
1895	1,663	1,406
1896	2,091	2,095
1897	2,477	2,779
1898	2,812	3,027
1899	3,302	3,073
1900	3,892	4,497
1901	3,571	4,319
1902	2,883	3,704
1903	3,527	3,858
1904	3,996	4,067
1905	4,175	5,757
1906	4,659	5,696
1907	5,278	5,745
1908	4,462	5,479
1909	5,023	6,493
1910	6,231	7,074

Sources: Column 1 from Table A.1.3. Column 2 from *Extracto Estadístico*, 1934–5, p. 76.

In Table A.1.4 we compare our series with the official series for total exports, and the data are reproduced in Fig.A.1.1. It should be noted that the official series excluded guano (as does our series) for all years except 1902–10.[2] It should also be noted, that the official export statistics for the 1890s incorporate a serious underestimate of the true value of rubber exports, implying rather considerable overvaluation of other export products, even if we treat the official figures as cif rather than fob estimates of value (they purport to be fob except for minerals).

To reduce our figures to an fob basis (which we have not done here) a subtraction of roughly 20 per cent from cif value would be appropriate. It is only fair to warn the reader that our data are far from definitive. The prices used have been those in the British market where possible (coffee however is valued at the U.S. import price), but actual prices received by Peru in various markets around the world would have differed; this is particularly the case, for example, with sugar sold to Chile. Furthermore, the price series available to us are averages based upon quality grades which are not necessarily appropriate for Peruvian exports. We have made some very crude adjustments in an attempt to take account of this, on the basis of Hunt's comparisons of British and Peruvian prices in 1900.[3] Hunt guessed that the true value of Peruvian cotton exports was 0.69 the British import price; we have used a figure of 0.7 times the average price of American Middling (Upland) cotton, the main British import variety. Wool we have valued at the British average import price, although this appears very much higher than the reported Peruvian price for 1900 (£87 per ton as compared to £55 per ton). Alpaca prices we have estimated by assuming a 23 per cent premium on the British average wool price (on the basis of the 1900 alpaca prices reported by Hunt). Rubber is valued at U.S. import prices (which were available on a year-by-year basis) although this gives a prices series considerably below the 'fine hard para' price in the U.K.[4] The net effect of these various discrepancies is probably to overvalue wool somewhat, and possibly to undervalue rubber by as much as 30 per cent; although, since Peruvian rubber was generally exported in relatively little-processed forms, its actual export value was probably well below the U.K. price for good para rubber, and the undervaluation is likely to be far less than 30 per cent, and probably not very significant.

Appendix 2
Some Long-run Data Series: Foreign Investment, Foreign Debt, Output of Basic Commodities[1]

TABLE A.2.1 Estimated book value of foreign direct investment, 1880–1973 (millions of U.S. dollars)

	(1) U.S. and British capital	
	Total amount	*Average annual percentage change over preceding decade*
1880	17	—
1900	30	2.9
1910	84	10.9
1919	161	7.5
1929	209	2.6
1935	128	−1.3
	(2) U.S. capital only	
	Total	*Annual change*
1929	143	
1943	71	−3.9
1950	145	10.7
1960	446	11.9
1970	688	4.4
1973	793	4.8

Sources: 1880 from Rippy (1959). 1900–35 British data from *South American Journal*, Sep. 21, 1935, p. 273, adjusted downwards to allow for over-valuation of Peruvian Corporation shares (see Bertram (1974), p. 29). 1900–19 U.S. capital from Lewis (1938). 1929–35 U.S. capital estimated as the average of figures given by Lewis (1938) and those of the U.S. Department of Commerce. 1943–73 U.S. capital from U.S. Department of Commerce *Survey of Current Business* and U.S. Treasury Department (1947).

Tᴀʙʟᴇ A.2.2 Trends in the public external debt, 1850–1973

	Percentage change in external indebtedness	Outstanding debt at end of period (millions)	
1850–9	−22.1	(£)	5.3[a]
1860–9	88.7		10.0
1870–9	226.9		32.7[b]
1880–9	c		c
1890–9	−		−
1900–9	d	($)	10.4
1910–9	17.8		12.3
1920–9	776.4		107.8
1930–9	c		c
1940–9	c		125.3[e]
1950–9	58.8		187.7
1960–9	356.3		856.4
1970–3	74.1		1,490.6

Sources: Nineteenth-century debt estimates based upon Rippy (1959) pp. 20–32.
1909 estimate comprises the three large foreign loans of 1906 and 1909 (2).
1919 and 1929 figures from *Extracto Estadistico*, 1934–5, p. 301.
1949 from *Anuario Estadistico*, 1950 p. 653.
1959 from *Anuario Estadistico*, 1966, p. 1554.
1969 from *Anuario Estadistico*, 1971, p. 454.
1973 from Banco Central *Memoria*, 1973, p. 115.
[a] 1862
[b] 1877
[c] In default
[d] Starting from zero, hence cannot be meaningfully calculated
[e] Value of previously-defaulted bonds plus accrued interest.

TABLE A.2.3 Production of sugar, cotton and petroleum, 1880–1930

	Sugar production (000 tons)	Cotton production (tons)	Cotton purchased by local textile mills (tons)	Output of crude petroleum (000 barrels)
1880	73			
1881	59			
1882	60			
1883	50			
1884	49			6
1885	61			8
1886	59			8
1887	51			16
1888	56			16
1889	68			18
1890	54			31
1891	53			114
1892	63			167
1893	59			114
1894	75			95
1895	79			95
1896	92			95
1897	125			99
1898	126			151
1899	124			204
1900	140			289
1901	135	9,611	1,600	295
1902		8,524	1,840	243
1903	153	9,651	2,000	281
1904	157	9,882	2,350	293
1905	162	10,765/12,061	1,204/2,500	376
1906	169	12,637	2,192	536
1907	141	14,484	2,145	758
1908	157	18,719	2,700	953
1909	158	23,805	2,500	1,424
1910	172			1,270
1911	179			1,478
1912	188			1,768
1913	179			2,070
1914	223			1,854
1915	258			2,603
1916	271	27,426	3,200	2,617
1917	248	27,125	3,400	2,627
1918	283	30,687	3,695	2,536
1919	282	33,558	3,351	2,639
1920	314	38,396	3,053	2,825
1921	269	40,352	2,850	3,699

	Sugar production (000 tons)	Cotton production (tons)	Cotton purchased by local textile mills (tons)	Output of crude petroleum (000 barrels)
1922	319	43,120	2,781	5,304
1923	320	45,996	3,149	5,690
1924	317	46,582	3,371	7,915
1925	276	45,467	3,050	9,235
1926	376	53,374	3,470	10,804
1927	375	53,254	4,087	10,148
1928	362	48,682	3,900	12,048
1929	428	65,591	3,700	13,450
1930	400	58,695	3,600	12,533

Sources and Notes: 1) Sugar production: 1880–93: Exports from Appendix 1 plus 15,000 tons.
1894: Garland (1895), p. 29.
1895–99: Exports from Appendix 1 plus 20,000 tons.
1900: The Times (London), Aug. 20, 1901.
1901: Garland (1902a) p. 6.
1902–7: Málaga (1908), p. 70.
1908–10: Martin (1911) p. 157.
1911: FAO (1961), Table 1.
1912–30: Extracto Estadístico, 1934–5, p. 158.
Series includes Chancaca.
2) Cotton production:
1901–9: Exports from Appendix 1 plus local mill purchases from Column 3.
1916–30: Extracto Estadístico, 1934–5, p. 168.
3) Local mill purchases of cotton:
1901–2: Marie (1904), pp. 36 and 58; the assignment of the latter figure to 1902 is circumstantial.
1903–7: Málaga (1908), p. 75.
1905: higher alternative figure from Garland (1908), p. 212.
1908: Romero (1949), Vol. 2, p. 196.
1909: Martin (1911), p. 176.
1916–17 and 1928–30: Extracto Estadístico 1934–5, p. 371.
1918–27: Tizón y Bueno (1930), p. 17.
4) Crude oil output: Boletín del Cuerpo de Ingenieros de Minas, No. 122.

Appendix 3
Estimates of Returned Value for Marcona and for the Mining Sector

As discussed in Note 11.23, no direct estimate of returned value (RV) for Marcona was possible. However, since Marcona accounted for 94 per cent of reported total income in the mining sector in Ica from 1963 to 1966, we present here data on the distribution of that income, as the basis for a provisional-estimate of Marcona's RV. The figures are given in Table A.3.1. It will be seen that according to the reported data, wages, taxes and royalties absorbed 38 per cent over the decade while openly-repatriated profit absorbed 9 per cent. Depreciation, of which an unknown proportion would have left the country as repatriated earnings or payment for imported capital goods, took 16 per cent. The remaining 36 per cent went to pay for materials, services, etc. To obtain a working figure, we assume that 50 per cent of depreciation and purchases went abroad and the remainder was returned, in which case the total RV would be 64 per cent of reported income. If income was 25 per cent under-reported, then actual RV would have been around 50 per cent. In the mine's first decade of operation, 1953 to 1962, the company's official figures supplied to Lindqvist indicate openly-repatriated profits to have totalled $25.8 million (14 per cent of $183 million reported income) in addition to which at least another $10 million can be assumed to have been taken out as amortisation and service on the Utah Construction Company's loan to its subsidiary.[1] Hunt's figures from the company accounts filed in the U.S.A indicate net post-tax profits for this first decade to have totalled $65 million ($38 million of it reported by Marcona Mining Company itself, the rest by its marketing and shipping branches)[2]; these profits include the gains from undervaluing exports and also the difference between fob and cif prices. On the basis of the above figures we feel safe in estimating that repatriated profit during the first decade absorbed between 20 per cent and 30 per cent of the reported value of exports. Reasonable assumptions about the level of imports required to launch and expand the venture suggest that RV in this earlier period would certainly have been no higher than in the second decade of

TABLE A.3.1 Distribution of gross income of the mining sector, in Ica, 1963–72

	Gross value of output, $ million	Percentages of gross value of output				
		Wages & salaries	Taxes & royalties	Production inputs	Depreciation	Profit and interest
1963	33.5	22	17	38	14	9
1964	40.6	23	17	39	15	7
1965	46.9	21	21	27	22	9
1966	55.5	18	17	35	14	10
1967	65.8	17	19	31	15	12
1968	72.8	19	20	32	12	17
1969	76.9	20	20	32	15	12
1970	78.9	21	12	44	15	8
1971	69.3	25	16	41	22	0.4
1972	75.4	27	17	39	16	1
TOTAL	615.6	21	17	36	16	9

Source: Sectoral data in *Anuario de la Industria Minera* for years shown. Note that, for 1963–6, gross value of output totalled $176.5 million, while Marcona's reported income for the same period (Lindqvist (1972), p. 242) totalled $165.5 million.

operations, which points to 50 per cent as a provisional working estimate.

Combining this estimate with the other data on RV given in the Chapter 11 enables us to derive an estimate of RV for the sector. We take the information in Tables 11.4, 11.5 and 11.6 on market shares and RV, and estimate a figure of 80 per cent RV for firms other than Cerro in 1952. For 1960 and 1965 we take an estimate of 21 per cent RV for SPCC and a generous 60 per cent for Marcona. For other mining companies we again assume 80 per cent; since the weight of foreign firms in medium size mining had meanwhile increased greatly, this overstates the growth of RV. We can now derive the estimates shown in Table 11.7 in the text.

Appendix 4
Data on Industrial
Output in Peru

The first comprehensive attempt to estimate the volume of industrial output in Peru was made by a CEPAL team in 1957,[1] for the period 1945–56. Later indices, such as those published by the Banco Central in 1966[2] and the Banco Industrial – Instituto Nacional de Promocion Industrial in 1960,[3] all begin in 1950, and show an increase from 1950 to 1955 which is identical with that shown in the original CEPAL work (45–46 per cent). Since no indication is given of the methodology used in either of those sources, it seems reasonable to suppose that the CEPAL work has remained the basis of the 1950–5 estimate. Both series were continued thereafter, the former till the mid-1960s, the latter up to the present. Meanwhile, estimates of the current value of output began with 1950, stemming from two sources: the Banco Central (henceforth BCR) has made estimates from its own questionnaire, which forms the basis of the national income accounts, and the Ministry of Industry and Tourism (M.I.T.) has conducted a separate survey, published regularly in *Estadistica Industrial*. M.I.T. also now makes estimates of the volume of output, which have appeared in *Anuario Estadistico*.

This appendix concerns itself with two main problems: first, how we may extend these estimates back to an earlier period, and second, how we may evaluate and handle existing contemporary data.

The two main sources that permit reconstruction for earlier years are: first, the kind of input data used by CEPAL, combined occasionally with direct output estimates of particular products; and second, censuses of numbers of establishments, which were reasonably frequent in Peru. The following two sections describe briefly what we have done on the basis of these two types of material; the final section turns to certain problems in using contemporary data.[4]

ESTIMATING OUTPUT FROM INPUT DATA

This methodology involves many problems; in particular, it has to assume a constant input–output ratio over time, it has to use patchy information as a basis for correctly weighting the share of imports and exports, to deduct or add them, as the case may be, and it may involve the aggregation of a group of inputs with shifting composition over time. Further, the actual determination of what is an input and disaggregation of inputs used by more than one sector may frequently present problems. It is also difficult to determine the frame of reference for the data: are we estimating modern factory production or total industrial production including artisan and small-scale enterprises? The problem is that using input data sometimes gives us a proxy for *total* production, while such output data as there are tend to refer only to organised factory production. The CEPAL estimates tend to be a mix of the two.

In the text, we have used in Table 10.7 our own estimate of industrial production 1938–55, based on extending the CEPAL methodology back to 1938. In the course of this exercise we also attempted to evaluate the seriousness of the problems faced by the CEPAL methodology, and to make corrections where we found them to be necessary.

The details of the estimation, the sources used, and the full results, are given in a working paper (Thorp 1976b). Table A.4.1 compares the aggregate indices for overlapping years. It will be seen that our adjustments have somewhat reduced CEPAL's estimate of the rate of growth. The detailed paper reveals that the chief adjustments were in wood products, artificial fibres, pharmaceutical products and glass; in some of these cases the CEPAL estimate was simply wrong, in others it was unclear how it could have been derived, and we used our own method. Overall, we conclude that our estimates may be taken as reasonable for general trends, but definitely not for year-to-year

TABLE A.4.1 Indices of industrial output, 1945–54: A comparison of our estimates with CEPAL's

	CEPAL's	Ours
1945	55.1	67.0
1946	55.4	68.5
1947	60.3	72.6
1948	64.3	75.6
1949	70.4	83.1
1950	72.5	82.2
1954	100.0	100.0
Percentage change:		
1945–50	31.6	22.7
1950–4	37.9	21.7

Sources: See text.

fluctuations. The data refer as far as possible only to organised factory production.

In the case of cotton textiles, it was possible to take the production series back much further, partly because there are reasonably frequent estimates of total yards of cloth produced, partly because there was no artisan sector, and partly because we have a continuous series for cotton consumed by the mills from 1916, and partial estimates for earlier years. Tables 3.4, 6.5 and 10.5 represent a combination of direct output estimates and figures based on inputs of cotton, plus imports of cotton yarn. In the case of textiles, the ratio between ginned cotton and cloth output is an unusually constant one, affected principally by humidity and by waste rather than by technique. To obtain the necessary conversion ratios, we looked at data for Egypt in the 1930s and for Peru post-1940, as well as double-checking by means of the occasional output estimates. Imports of yarn used for weaving were not always clearly distinguishable in the import data, but the series proved not to be sensitive to exactly which types were included.

INDUSTRIAL CENSUS DATA

There were five censuses of manufacturing industry carried out in Peru in the early twentieth century. These comprise Garland (1902a), Garland (1905), Jimenez (1922, referring to 1918), Dunn (1925), and Hohagen (1936 referring to 1933). These 'censuses' represent surveys carried out by individuals, sometimes at government request, but essentially relying on personal observation and, furthermore, on personal judgement as to which sectors should be included and what size of establishment should constitute a 'factory.' Unfortunately it is beyond doubt that there is considerable variation in both elements. For example, the 1918 census uses in general a far wider definition than did Garland as to size of plant, but excludes the capital goods sector entirely, for reasons which are not explained. Awareness of developments outside of Lima also varies with the author: Dunn in his 1923 revision of the 1918 census is the only author to have spent time researching regional developments and this is reflected in the much more thorough coverage of his figures.

In Table A.4.2 we present the unrevised figures; in the case of 1902, 1905 and 1923 these have been compiled from data scattered throughout the respective books. Then in Table A.4.3 we present our revised version. This Table forms the basis for Table 6.6 in the text. 'Interpolated' figures are approximate figures based on trends in other components of the Table. Other adjustments are explained in the footnotes to the Tables. It will be noted that in deciding on interpolated values we have given little weight to Dunn's 1923 estimates: the extensive

TABLE A.4.2 Number of factories reported active in the manufacturing sector, 1902–33

Activity	(1) 1902	(2) 1905	(3) 1918	(4) 1923	(5) 1933
Cotton textiles	7	7	10	10	10
Woollen textiles	4	4	5	5	6
Knitting mills	2	2	1	2[a]	6
Hat manufacture	2	1	4	3	4
Shirt making, etc.	9[b]	9[b]	n.a.	14[c]	11
Tanneries	16	17	35	46	40
Shoe factories	2	1	7	37	11
Candles & wax	15+	10	19	67	10
Soap		19	58		65
Paper	1	0	3	3	1
Cardboard boxes	0	1			1
Cigarettes	9	9	1	1	0
Matches	2	1	1	1	0
Brooms & brushes	2	2	n.a.	10	2
Furniture	2	3	n.a.	30[d]	19[d]
Glass & crystal	0	0	0	2	1
Pottery & ceramic	1	1	n.a.	3	n.a.
Bricks	2	2	n.a.	20	1
Plaster factories	n.a.	n.a.	n.a.	1	n.a.
Marble & stone	n.a.	n.a.	n.a.	7	6[e]
Sawmills	4	5	n.a.	15	4
Coachworks	1	1	n.a.	n.a.	3
Foundries	8[f]	8[f]	n.a.	20	6
Soft drinks	3	5	71	41[g]	90
Wine & liquors	5	4	33	33	
Breweries	6	5	10	9	4
Rice mills	25	n.a.	59	41	60
Flour mills	8	14	8	22	4
Spaghetti	20	22	26	21	29
Biscuits	1	2	29	28	40
Chocolate & caramel	n.a.	7			
Freezing works	0	0	0	0	1
Canning plants (meat)	0	0	0	2	n.a.
Lard	9	n.a.	n.a.	n.a.	6
Pharmaceuticals	0	0	0	1	3[h]
Cement	0	0	0	1	1
Rubber goods	0	0	0	0	1
Metal fabricating	0	0	0	0	4
Polishes & waxes	0	0	0	0	1
Paint factories	0	0	0	0	1

TABLE A.4.2 (continued)

Activity	(1) 1902	(2) 1905	(3) 1918	(4) 1923	(5) 1933
TOTALS TO THIS POINT	166	162	380	496	452
Cottonseed oil mills[i]	7	8	25	24	24
Sugar mills	60	n.a.	33	35	25
Cocaine	21	22	n.a.	6	n.a.
TOTALS	254	192	438	561	501

Sources: 1902–Garland, (1902a) (compiled from data scattered throughout the book). 1905–Garland, (1905), (compiled from data scattered throughout the book). 1918–Jimenez, (1922). 1923–a count of enterprises mentioned in Dunn (1925). 1933–Hohagen (1936).
Notes:[a] Including the knit-goods section of the Santa Catalina mill.
[b] Lima-Callao only.
[c] All clothing factories.
[d] Including brass beds and billiard tables.
[e] Including two mosaic factories.
[f] Including boiler makers.
[g] Including some wine bottling plants.
[h] Including one perfumery.
[i] Including cottonseed oil refineries.

TABLE A.4.3 Number of factories, 1902–1933: revised estimates

Activity	1902	1905	1918	1923	1933
Cotton textiles	7	7	10	10	11[a]
Woollen textiles	5[b]	5[b]	5	5	7[c]
Knitting mills	2	2	1	2	6
Hat manufacture	2	1	4	3	4
Shirt making, etc.	9	9	10*	14	11
Tanneries	16	17	35	46	40
Shoe factories	2	1	7	37[d]	11
Candles & wax	5[e]	10	19	67	10
Soap	10[e]	19	58		65
Paper	1	0	3	3	1
Cardboard boxes	0	1			1
Cigarettes	9	9	1	1	1[f]
Matches	2	1	2[g]	2[g]	0
Brooms & brushes	2	2	2*	10	2
Furniture	2	3	11*	30	19
Glass & crystal	0	0	1*	2	1
Pottery & ceramic	1	1	2*	3	3*
Bricks	1	2	2	20[d]	1
Plaster factories	0	0	1*	1[h]	1*

TABLE A.4.3 (*continued*)

Activity	1902	1905	1918	1923	1933
Marble & stone	1*	1*	4*	7	6
Sawmills (Lima-Callao only)	4	5	4*	15[i]	4
Coachworks	1	1	2*	2*	3
Foundries	8	8	8*	20[d]	6
Soft drinks	3	5	71	41	90
Wines & liquors	5	4	33	33	
Breweries	6	5	10	9	4
Rice mills	25	31*	59	41	60
Flour mills	8	14	8	22[d]	7*
Spaghetti	20	22	26	21	29
Biscuits	1	2	29	28	40
Chocolate & caramel	7*	7			
Freezing works	0	0	0	0	1
Canning plants (meat)	0	0	0	2	1*
Lard	9	9*	6*	6*	6
Pharmaceuticals	0	0	0	1[h]	3
Cement	0	0	1*	1	1
Rubber goods	0	0	0	0	1
Metal fabricating	0	0	0	0	4
Polishes & wax	0	0	0	0	1
Paint factories	0	0	0	0	1
TOTALS TO THIS POINT	174	204	435	505	463
Cottonseed oil mills	7	8	25	24	24
Sugar mills	60	55*	33	35	25
Oil refineries	2	2	2	2	2
Cocaine	21	22	10*	6	0
TOTALS	264	291	505	572	514

Sources: as Table A.4.2.
Notes: (N.B. The data in this table are from Table A.4.2, with the revisions indicated here. The information footnoted in Table A.4.2 is not repeated here.
* Interpolated estimate (see text).
[a] Including the Sullana cotton mill, missed by the Census.
[b] Including the Urcos woollen mill, missed by the Census.
[c] Including the Huascar woollen mill, missed by the Census.
[d] Dunn's coverage is obviously much wider than that of the others. But revision downwards could only be on a very arbitrary basis.
[e] The total for candles, wax and soap given by Garland has been split on the basis of their relative shares in 1905, to permit the inclusion of soap in 'export by-products'.
[f] Missed by the Census.
[g] Including the Paramount plant in Arequipa, missed by the Census.
[h] Clearly a very incomplete estimate.
[i] Including the rest of the country as well.

regional coverage of his work makes it invaluable for other purposes but not very comparable with our other sources here. For this reason we have omitted his figures entirely in Table 6.6.

PROBLEMS WITH POST-1950 DATA

As described above, the main sources are M.I.T., BCR and INPI-BIP (up to 1968). As M.I.T. is the only source which covers the entire period since 1950, and which gives full disaggregation both by sector and by components of value-added, it would appear the sensible choice, which has been our general policy. However, while the methodology and general handling of the data have become much more systematic since 1965, before that date there are many problems with the figures. Even after that date, certain problems have remained which complicate interpretation. The chief problem areas comprise the treatment of export-processing, the variable coverage of the data, and the definition of gross output and value-added. Since these problems affect Tables 13.3, 13.10 and 13.11, they are discussed briefly here. For a fuller discussion, see Thorp (1976a).

Export-processing. A problem arises because of the difficulty of separating refining and extracting activities in sectors such as mining, petroleum, sugar and fishing. In the M.I.T. data no deduction is made for that part of output which represents extraction.[5] This inflates the share of export-processing sectors.

Variable coverage. The M.I.T. data refer only to those enterprises appearing in their industrial register. There are two main problems here. First, the M.I.T. procedure varies, since their published data sometimes refer to firms with five or more employees, sometimes only to those with ten or more, while estimates are occasionally included for non-reporting firms. Second, the number of firms included in the register increases sharply and erratically with time, with a discontinuity in 1964–5 as the benefits available under the Industrial Promotion Law were increased and made conditional on a firm being registered.

Implications. One consequence of these two problems is that estimation of the composition of industrial output over time was found to be not possible from the current price M.I.T. data. For this reason, Table 13.3 in the text was estimated by taking the volume indices produced by INPI-BIP and applying them to the 1963 value added figures from the manufacturing census. For 1965 and 1968 the volume indices given regularly in *Anuario Estadístico* were used.

A further consequence is that the increasing coverage over time makes data such as average size of establishment or share of wages in value added even more difficult to interpret meaningfully than it normally is.

This problem is discussed in the text with reference to Table 13.10 and 13.11.

Definition of value-added. The problem here becomes evident when the absolute figures for value-added for a given year are compared from M.I.T. and the Banco Central. Despite the wider coverage of the Bank's data, its estimate is significantly less than that of M.I.T., even after allowing for M.I.T.'s inflation of export-processing. This problem is discussed more fully in a working paper: briefly, the answer most probably lies in M.I.T.'s inflation of both gross output and input figures in comparison with the Bank[6]—for example, by the inclusion on both sides of 'products sold without transformation' and of work subcontracted out, which the Bank's methodology counts as a service to the sector.

This again raises difficulties in correctly estimating the share of manufacturing in total output, and in interpreting such data as the share of wages in value-added. Since there is no reason to suspect a change in practice over time, however, the trends shown in the text Tables can presumably be meaningfully discussed—subject to the problem of coverage, as we have already explained.

Notes and References

CHAPTER 1

1. Griffin (1969), pp. 46–8 and 63–5.
2. This has required much tedious reconstruction of data, the details of which have been confined, as far as possible, to appendices and working papers.
3. If we deflate dollar values by an import price index, in foreign currency, we obtain an extremely rough guide to purchasing power. This gives 0.8 per cent a year. The method of calculation of the import price index is explained in Table 6.9. However, we must stress the difficulty of any such long-run calculations, with changing commodity baskets and relative prices, as well as deficient data series: what is particularly disturbing is that the quantum index of exports calculated by Hunt shows a higher 'real' growth rate, although the two approaches should yield a similar result. More research is clearly needed here.
4. See Table A.2.3 in Appendix 2. For surveys of the history of the foreign debt see McQueen (1926a), Yrigoyen (1928), and Suarez and Tovar (1967).
5. See Table A.2.1, Appendix 2, for estimates of foreign investment. Using total export earnings as a denominator (in the absence of capital-stock or GNP estimates prior to the 1940s), the book value of US investment in Peru rose from 77 per cent in 1908 to around 150 per cent by the early 1930s, fell back to 77 per cent in 1950, rose to 107 per cent in 1960, and had fallen again to 63 per cent by 1970. It should be noted that in the 1960s, high gearing ratios and the decline of the oil industry biased the figures downward.
6. For a fuller introduction see Owens (1963), and Weil *et al.* (1972), Ch. 3.
7. The 1940 census found 25 per cent of the then population of 6.2 million to be residents of the coast (Dirección General de Estadística (1944) Vol. 1, p. cxlix). By 1961 the coast had 39 per cent of a total population of 9.9 million, and the first results from the 1972 census suggest a coastal population of around 45 per cent of the Peruvian total of 13.5 million. (*Anuario Estadístico*, 1969, p. 271; Oficina Nacional de Estadística y Censos, 1974, Vol. 1, Table 2).
8. Until the recent agrarian reform—although the latter has affected the form of tenure rather than the size of holding (Chapter 15).
9. The urban population of Lima-Callao accounted for roughly five per cent of total population at the turn of the century. This rose to 10 per cent by 1940, 18 per cent by 1961, and nearly 25 per cent (over half the population of the coast) by 1972. (Bromley and Barbagelata (1945), pp. 117–18, and other sources as for note 7 above). The proportion of the total population resident in urban areas of over 20,000 was 15 per cent in 1940, 30 per cent in 1961, and 43 per cent in 1972 (Fox (1972), p. 9).
10. Millones (1973), p. 34.
11. Thus in the 1890s and early 1900s *El Economista* flourished, while in the

Sierra *El Minero Ilustrado* was a flourishing local paper until U.S. investors arrived. In the 1930s and 1940s again we have *El Economista Peruano*.

CHAPTER 2

1. On the diverse experiences of European countries, see Gershenkron (1962).
2. Prebisch (1950).
3. Kuznets (1965), pp. 177, 186.
4. Myrdal (1958).
5. The most influential members have been Enrique Cardoso, Teotonio Dos Santos, Celso Furtado and Osvaldo Sunkel, and outside of Latin America, Samir Amin. For a full bibliography, see Chilcote (1974). For a good summary of the main ideas, see O'Brien (1975).
6. Sunkel and Paz (1970), describe what was happening as a realisation that structuralism was still using the framework and concepts of the orthodox school whose assumptions it was attacking (p. 36).
7. Pinto and Kñakel (1972) provide a useful summary of these changes.
8. The phrase 'surplus' is used deliberately in the dependency school's writing, rather than, say, 'net profits', to denote resources *potentially* available for investment. As the term 'potential surplus' is used by, for example, Baran, it includes two principle elements. First it refers to the possibility of re-allocating existing funds between consumption and investment, and different types of investment. This might occur with different ownership systems, including a varying role for the State, within the capitalist mode of production. Secondly it refers to the increase in the surplus which could occur with a different (i.e. socialist) mode of production, where certain types of expenditure could, it is argued, be altogether eliminated (e.g. advertising and other so-called 'unproductive' occupations). In the context of dependency writing, and generally in the context of our own analysis, it is the first of these areas which is relevant.
9. Many writers do make such an equation—Furtado (1971) and Frank (1967), for example. We find this unhelpful, if not actively confusing.
10. Cardoso (1973).
11. Frank (1967).
12. This position is taken by Lall (1975). Weisskopf (1976) takes a similar but more qualified view: 'It is more appropriate to view dependence as aggravating conditions of under-development that are inevitable under capitalism, than to view dependence as a major cause of under-development' (p. 21).
13. It will be noted that here and elsewhere we avoid the word 'national', as it suggests a single definable interest—a concept inapplicable to a fragmented society. Action in the 'local' interest implies action furthering the pursuit of greater autonomy in the sense above defined. On the 'foreign/domestic' distinction, see the discussion on p. 17.
14. The other main example was the 1971–73 Allende government in Chile, the objectives of which were explicitly socialist.
15. Cross-country comparisons over long periods are what are required. But first a detailed understanding of the economic history of particular countries has to be achieved.
16. Lewis, Ranis and Fei being the chief representatives.

17. For references to models of export-led growth which underlie this summary, see Roemer (1970), Chap. 2, and Caves (1965).
18. On the meaning of this term, see Note 2.8.
19. Returned value is estimated either by summing all the local expenditures of an export sector (including profits accumulated locally), or by subtracting from exports the amount of imported inputs and repatriated/expatriated profit. For a discussion of the concept see Reynolds (1965) and Pearson (1970).

PART II INTRODUCTION

1. On the Guano Age see Bonilla (1967–8), (1970), (1973); Hunt (1973b); Levin (1960); Maiguaschca (1967); Mathew (1968); Yepes (1972).
2. Greenhill and Miller (1973).
3. On this period see Pike (1967), Chapt. 6; Ugarte (1926), pp. 182; 197; and Basadre (1963–4), Vol. VI, Chaps 107–14.
4. On the negotiations, and the significance of the Contract see Miller (1976).
5. An article in the *Mexican Financier* of July 4, 1891 listed 21 companies formed within the past few years with British capital to operate in Peru. Of these, 13 were in mining and oil, 5 in railways (Peruvian Corporation subsidiaries) and 2 in manufacturing. (See Foreign Bondholders Protective Council Inc. (1950), press cuttings file, Guildhall Library, London).
6. The course of the dispute between the British Government and the Peruvian Government is documented in the file of press clippings accumulated by the Council of Foreign Bondholders in London, and now held in the Guildhall (Volumes 16 and 17 of the Peru collection), as well as in the *Annual Reports* of the Peruvian Corporation during the period. For a bitter attack on the Corporation's record from a Peruvian observer see Alejandro Garland, 'The Peruvian Corporation from a Peruvian Point of View' in *South American Journal*, June 28, 1902.
7. For example Cisneros and García (1900) pp. iv–v; *The Times* (London), Aug. 20, 1901; *Buenos Aires Standard*, Sept. 13, 1901 (from Foreign Bondholders File, Guildhall Library, London).
8. See Garland (1908), pp. 247–8 on the manufacturing sector; McQueen (1926a), p. 16 on the 'beneficial' results of Peru having been 'forced to rely upon its un-assisted efforts.'

CHAPTER 3

1. Basadre (1963–4), Vol. VII, pp. 3105–6.
2. For the detailed figures and methodology, see Appendix 1.
3. See Appendix 1, Table A.1.2.
4. *Extracto Estadístico del Peru*, 1934–5, p. 37.
5. The great bulk of Peru's imports came from gold-standard countries; the fall of silver prices not only caused a devaluation of the sol against the currencies of

those countries, but also reduced the buying power of Peru's leading export product, silver.

6. See the detailed discussion in Chapters 4 and 5.

7. Garland (1895), pp. 23–4.

8. *El Economista*, July 2, 1898, p. 665. This level of employment in mining was not reached again until the late 1950s. Silver mining in particular was a relatively small-scale activity, and widely-dispersed regionally.

9. Leading examples were the Santa Barbara plant at Yauli (1899–1900) and the Tamboraque smelter below Casapalca (1904–6); see *El Economista*, June 9, 1900, p. 634; and Pacheco (1923), p. 49. On the problems of the Lima foundries in the face of strong US penetration of their markets after 1900 see Bollinger (1971), pp. 30–1.

10. At Cerro de Pasco, reinvestment of silver miners' profits was discouraged by drainage problems. At Morococha and Casapalca, areas served from 1889 on by the large custom smelter of Backus and Johnston at Casapalca, few mine-owners felt it worth investing in plants of their own. In addition, throughout the Central Sierra, silver exports were held up by a major washout of the Central Railway in 1889 which was not repaired until 1891; large accumulated stocks were thus exported on the eve of the market collapse, the income received from these exports being probably diverted away from mining investment (Peruvian Corporation *Annual Report* (1890–1), p. 9).

11. *South American Journal*, Sep. 23, 1899.

12. In 1898 a government commission was appointed to enquire into the reasons for the increased cost of living. See Basadre, (1963–4), Vols. 7 and 9, pp. 3434 and 4698.

13. This is evident from the history of labour protest in the period: strikes for higher wages, provoked by the rising cost of living, constantly failed because other workers could be brought in. On this see Blanchard, (1975). The lag in wages is also discussed in the Peruvian Corporation's *Annual Report* for 1891–3.

14. Purser (1971), p. 97.

15. Between 1899 and 1908 three sugar planters became Presidents of Peru— Lopez de Romana, Pardo, and Leguía.

16. A survey of the *Arancel de Aforos*, published every few years during the nineteenth century, indicates this as the date of the first increase; modest increases proceded steadily through the 1880s.

17. *Estadística General del Comercio Exterior del Perú*, 1891, p. xxxvi.

18. *Estadística General del Comercio Exterior*, 1892, p. ix; British Consular Report Annual Series No. 1318.

19. *Diario de los Debates*, Senado, 1894 Legislatura Ordinaria, pp. 1015 ff.

20. *Diario de los Debates*, Senado, 1895 Legislatura Ordinaria, p. 1033.

21. Garland (1896) pp. 19–20; 'Importación y Manufactura de Fósforos,' in *La Industria* (Lima), Aug. 1901, p. 669.

22. Gubbins (1899), pp. 11–12. The *Arancel de Aforos* for 1856 and 1872–3 shows cotton textiles with duties of 20 per cent. In 1874–5 this rose to 26 per cent, and by 1890 the rate had reached 40 per cent.

23. J.M. Rodríguez in *Estadística General del Comercio Exterior*, 1892 (published 1895), p. xvii; see also *Panama Star and Herald*, May 25, 1889 (Council of Foreign Bondholders, press cuttings file, Guildhall Library, London) for a discussion of an early Government drive against an organised smuggling ring;

and Garland (1900), p. 13, on the continuing problem in the late 1890s.
24. Rodriguez (1895), p. xvii.
25. Rodriguez (1895), p. xvii.
26. Garland (1900), p. 13.
27. *The Times* (London), Apr. 4, 1895. Analysis of the figures in *Estadística del Comercio Exterior*, 1900, shows 28 per cent of imports by value to have been duty-free, comprising almost entirely machinery, raw materials and some intermediate goods. Ten per cent more, comprising similar items, were subject to duties of 10–20 per cent. Forty-seven per cent of imports, made up of consumer goods of various kinds, were subject to 40 or 45 per cent duties, while luxury goods were subject to still higher rates. For a discussion of the high effective protection provided to a number of specific industries, see Gubbins (1899), pp. 4–14.
28. For contemporary comment on the rapidity of industrial expansion, see *Sinopsis Geográfico y Estadístico del Perú, 1895–1898*, pp. 178–96.
29. The main published contributions were Garland (1896) (1900) (1901), Gubbins (1899) (1900) and Barreda y Osma (1900). The Chamber of Deputies in 1900 gave its support to the principle of protection for infant industries (*Diario de los Debates*, Camara de Diputados, Legislatura Ordinaria de 1900, pp. 929–32).
30. The factory was originally named 'La Nacional.'
31. Mainly the Lima weekly journal *El Economista*.
32. Yepes (1972), pp. 175–80.
33. See p. 35.
34. In any case, world silver prices had stabilised by the end of the decade, so that the exchange rate would have remained steady even without the change to the gold standard.
35. For a fuller treatment of the early period of industrialisation in Peru see Thorp and Bertram (1976). Some material will also be found in Rippy (1946).
36. A history of Callao published in *West Coast Leader*, Aug. 18, 1936, supplement p. 23, lists a string of engineering and related enterprises started by British interests: the repair shops of the Pacific Steam Navigation Company in 1843; the English Dock Company in the 1860s, the Lima and Callao Gas Company in 1865, the Eagle Iron Works (D. Coursey and Co.) in 1866 (see also Basadre 1963–4, Vol. V, p. 2044, and *West Coast Leader*, March 12, 1921, p. 2), and the Fundicion de Chucuito, later the William White works, in the same year (see also Basadre 1963–4, Vol. VII, p. 3193). In Lima, the Fundicion de Acho was started by Richard Ashworth in 1872 (Bollinger (1971), p. 31) while John (Juan) White had a Foundry by 1884 (Bollinger (1971), p. 79).
37. Notably Backus and Johnston's Brewery (1881), the Santa Catalina woollen mill (1889) and the Malatesta cotton textile mill in Ica (1892). (See Fuentes (1950), p. 102; Dunn (1925), p. 377.)
38. One familiar example is the D'Onofrio ice-cream and confectionery factory, established in the late 1890s.
39. On the difficulties of the artisan sector during the guano era see Hunt (1973b).
40. See the lists in Bollinger (1971), pp. 79–81.
41. Gubbins (1899), pp. 18–19.

42. 'Importacion y Manufactura de Fosforos' in *La Industria* (Lima), Aug. 1901, pp. 668–70, and Sept. 1901, pp. 688–92.

43. One-third was taken by the Pardos 'La Victoria' factory and one-third by the British Cotton Manufacturing Company.

44. In 1891, of total cotton textile imports of 3,565 metric tons, *tocuyo* accounted for 827 tons (23 per cent); by 1902, with the total at 3,424 tons, *tocuyo* had fallen to 226 tons (7 per cent), and by 1905 the proportion was down to 3 per cent. Other cheap grades showed similar reductions. (Figures taken from *Estadística del Comercio Especial* for years shown.)

45. Garland (1902a) *passim*. Garland's detailed results are included in Table 6.6 below.

46. These figures are only very partial evidence, however, because (i) they do not take account of possible turnover of firms in the sector (some would no doubt have been going out of business during the 1890s) and (ii) we have made no attempt to weight firms according to their size, nor to identify the period in which they achieved factory scale of operation (which need not coincide with date of origin). The census data are significant only when taken in conjunction with the evidence of import composition cited above.

47. This was the Empresa Transmisora de Fuerza Electrica, set up by Mariano Ignacio Prado to supply power for the Santa Catalina woollen-textile mill in which he had been a partner since 1890 (*Peru Today*, June, 1911). The company was later renamed Empresa Electrica Santa Rosa.

48. Sociedad de Alumbrado y Fuerza Motriz de Piedra Liza (1900) and Compania Electrica de Callao (1901). For a full history of the early development of electricity and tramways see 'Lima in the Dawn of Electricity' in *West Coast Leader*, May 24, 1927, Special Electrical Supplement.

49. Compania del Ferrocarril Urbano de Lima (1898), Ferrocarril Urbano de Lima y Callao (1903), Tranvia Electrica de Lima y Chorrillos (1902) and Compania Nacional del Tranvia Electrica (c. 1905). Prior to the arrival of electricity, urban transport had been provided by the horse-drawn trams of the Empresa del Tranvia de Lima (1876) and the steam-drawn trains of the Lima Railway Company (1865).

50. Basadre (1963–4), Vol. 7, p. 3432. For the official history of the firm see Empresas Eléctricas Asociadas (1966).

51. The only British utilities company as of 1900 was the moribund Lima Railway Company, which in 1906 leased its lines to the new Empresas Eléctricas Asociadas.

52. For Payan's biography, see Camprubi (1967).

53. The Banco Italiano (1889), tactfully renamed the Banco de Credito during the Second World War.

54. Camprubi (1967), pp. 25–7.

55. The reorganisation involved a merger of the Banco del Callao with the London Bank of Mexico and South America. The bank thus became jointly owned by Peruvian and foreign capital; in 1914 ownership was 30 per cent Peruvian, 44 per cent French, and 16 per cent British (Bollinger, 1971, p. 234). The local board, and the manager Payan, had far greater influence on policy than these ownership figures indicate, however.

56. Banco Internacional (1897), started by a group of agricultural, mining, commercial and financial operators; and Banco Popular (1899), started by a

similar group headed by Mariano Ignacio Prado y Ugarteche. Historical material on the banks and insurance companies listed here and in note 57 below can be found in *Perú en su Centenario* (1921), Basadre (1963–4, Vol. VII), Karno (1970) and Halsey (1918). Many of the boards of directors are listed in Yepes (1972), pp. 175–80.

57. Compañía de Seguros Internacional (1895, Payan); Compañía de Seguros Italia (1896, Banco Italiano); Compañía de Seguros Rimac (1896); Compañía de Seguros Urbana (1902); Compañía de Seguros La Nacional (1904); Compañía de Seguros Popular (1904); Compañía de Seguros del Perú (1903); for sources see the previous note.

58. Bolsa Comercial de Lima, started by Payan in 1896 (Camprubi (1967), p. 69).

59. Most important of these were the Sociedad Recaudadora de Impuestos started by Payan in 1896 (McQueen (1926a), p. 22), the Compañía Salinera started by Payan in 1901 (Basadre (1963–4), Vol. 7, p. 3391), and the Caja de Depositos y Consignaciones (now Banco de la Nación) started by the banks on the initiative of Payan and Leguia in 1905 (Karno, 1970, p. 53; Camprubi, 1967 p. 69).

60. *Extracto Estadístico del Peru*, 1934–5, p. 66. This source contains assembled statistics of the banking system from 1897 on.

61. Pierola's Annual Message of 1899, cited in *South American Journal*, Sep. 23, 1899. For the names and capital of companies floated during the late 1890s see Basadre (1963–4) Vol. 7, p. 3188.

62. Bolsa Comercial de Lima, *Memoria* for 1900.

63. The account which follows is drawn from Karno (1970), pp. 52–6.

64. See the dividend rates listed in *Extracto Estadístico* 1934–5, p. 67. As Karno notes (1970, p. 52) profitability was greatly assisted by the fact that banks were subject to a tax rate of only 5 per cent of net profits. In 1903 the Banco Perú y Londres and Banco Italiano paid 15 per cent dividends on their share capital (note that the *Extracto* series uses capital plus reserves as denominator, and hence understates actual dividend rates), while the lowest dividend, 12 per cent, was paid by the more recently-established Banco Popular.

65. See Pierola's Annual Message, in *South American Journal*, Sep. 23, 1899.

CHAPTER 4

1. Especially interesting is the contrast with Cuba and Brazil, countries with seasonal patterns of sugar harvesting, where the growing of cane remained in the hands of relatively small-scale independent growers, while large central mills handled the processing. In Peru, the turn of the century saw some interest in the establishment of such a system of *colonos* and *centrales*, but this was quickly swamped by the advantages of large-scale cultivation. See Albert (1976), p. 41.

2. Note, however, that in the early period a large proportion of the labour force were temporary migrants, hired for three months or so through the system of *enganche*; a permanent stable labour force evolved only gradually, with *enganche* being finally discontinued only at the end of the 1950s.

3. For more detailed discussion of this process see Albert (1976).

4. This case is documented by Klaren (1969), Chapter 2, from which the following summary is taken.

5. Grace and Gildemeister were both diversified merchant houses with considerable capital of their own; the Larco family, to finance their expansion, formed an alliance with the British house Graham Rowe and Company (Klaren (1969), p. 24).

6. Parker (1919), pp. 435–7; Paz Soldan (1917), p. 132.

7. Karno (1970), p. 79. Swayne apparently immigrated about 1860, and was a leading figure in the sugar industry in the 1860s and 1870s. See Basadre (1963–4), Vol. 8, pp. 3672 and 3554; and Martin (1911), p. 155.

8. Notably Lurifico near Chimbote, taken over by the French firm Dreyfus (*West Coast Leader*, Feb. 1, 1919, p. 1) and Andahuasi near Huacho (Fraser Luckie and Co.) (Dunn (1925), p. 107).

9. See however Horton (1973), and Albert (1976).

10. In Cañete, following Swayne's death in 1898, his heirs formed the British Sugar Company in partnership with the enterprise's sugar-buyers and creditors, the Liverpool house of Lockett (Basadre (1963–4), Vol. 8, p. 3554); both Santa Barbara and the San Jacinto estate in Nepena were modernised by the new company. The Barreda y Laos family of Supe floated the Compania Agricola San Nicolas in 1896, with capital of £80,000 and participation from the leading Peruvian bank of the time, the Banco del Perú y Londres (Basadre *op. cit.* p. 3,187; *Perú en su Centenario*, 1921, pp. 49–51). In Pativilca the Canaval family passed their Paramonga estate to the new Sociedad Agricola de Paramonga in 1898 (*ibid.*, pp. 66–9), while in the Chicama valley the modernisation and expansion of the Cartavio mill was undertaken not by the owners (W.R. Grace and Co.) but by the new 'Ingenio Central de Cartavio' company headed by the Lambayeque planter Antero Aspillaga (*El Economista*, Lima, June 24, 1899, pp. 642–5).

11. For some examples of the latter, see Bertram (1974), p. 73.

12. Bertram (1974), p. 73.

13. Bertram (1974), p. 79; Klaren (1969), p. 37.

14. See, for example, Mariategui (1971), pp. 20 and 54; Ruth (1964), pp. 85–6. (Note that Mariategui was careful to emphasise that many plantations remained in local hands, but he regarded this control as largely nominal.)

15. See, for example, remarks in Garland (1895) p. 14.

16. Appendix 1, Table A.1.2.

17. Garland (1905) p. 53 estimated that the cost of production in the leading mills had been reduced from 15 shillings per quintal in 1880 to 5s. 6d. per quintal by 1905.

18. Stewart (1951); Levin (1960).

19. Unión de Productores de Azucar (1945) p. 11; Albert (1976).

20. By 1875 the industry had invested heavily on the basis of bank credit, with debts totalling around £3 million, and the commercial banks of the period had a dangerous proportion of their capital tied up in loans to sugar planters. In the crisis of the late 1870s, the widespread defaults and bankruptcies among planters contributed significantly to the collapse of the banking system. In the 1880s, consequently, not only were there few credit institutions in existence, but there was an understandable reluctance to lend to the sugar industry. See Garland (1895), p. 13; Levin (1960).

21. Garland (1895), p. 14.
22. See for example Garland (1895), pp. 35 and 45–9; and Moreno (1900), pp. 14–17. Both writers called for agrarian reform to break up large holdings, in the belief that sugar planting could be most efficiently developed by a new class of medium-scale *colonos* on the Cuban model.
23. Garland (1895), pp. 42–3. Surprisingly, in his historical survey Ruth (1964), p. 84, claimed to be unable to discern the reasons for the sugar boom; he could find no relation between sugar output and British prices, world prices, or the spread of railways. Ruth ignored, however, the political and exchange situation in Peru and tariff changes in Chile.
24. Garland (1902a), p. 7; and Garland (1905), pp. 52–9.
25. Garland (1895), p. 22; full capacity defined as a 12-hour day.
26. Garland (1895), p. 23. Total capital for the whole country, including Sierra and Montana, was given as S/35, 170,000 (p. 33). Garland valued machinery at replacement cost rather than original cost, while land was valued at market value. The obvious result of the first practice was to understate the subsequent investment in the industry, since a large part of the existing mill machinery was obsolete and was later scrapped.
27. 'El Nuevo Año de 1897' in *El Economista*, January 2, 1897, p. 242.
28. Garland (1902a), p. 7.
29. Klaren (1969), p. 32.
30. Martin (1911), p. 148.
31. Garland (1895), p. 22.
32. Garland (1902a), p. 6.
33. Garland (1895), p. 22.
34. From Garland (1902a), pp. 6–7.
35. Prinsen-Geerligs (1912), p. 270.
36. Sedgwick (1906), pp. 78–82.
37. The Brussels convention of 1902, in response to the crisis, banned the dumping of beet sugar on to world markets. From 1903 until the First World War this international agreement held prices up to near the 1900 level.
38. Ministerio de Fomento (1902).
39. Garland (1905), p. 60 gives the area as 16,160 *fanegadas*.
40. See Garland (1905), pp. 54–8.
41. Martin (1911), p. 149.
42. Prado (1908), pp. 59–60.
43. Klaren (1969), p. 33; Prinsen-Geerligs (1912), p. 271.
44. Martin (1911), pp. 157–60; Paz Soldán (1917), p. 132; Albert (1976).
45. The concentration of cane growing in the ecologically most favourable areas of the Coast contributed to the increases in average yields which occurred at this time.
46. Bertram (1974), pp. 77.
47. Respectively, the estates were Infantas, Puente Piedra, Santa Barbara and Tambo Real; the sellers W.R. Grace and Co., Milne and Co., W. and J. Lockett, and Barber, Vargas and Co. The buying syndicates were headed by the Banco Italiano group; Manuel Mujica (former Cerro de Pasco mine-owner); Pedro Beltran and Oscar Ramos Cabieses; and Rollin Thorne. See Bertram (1974), pp. 72–3 and 77.
48. For figures on the world sugar crisis of the 1920s see FAO (1961) Tables 1

and 15; for analysis see Nogaro (1936), Gutiérrez (1935), and Timoshenko and Swerling (1957).

49. Bertram (1974), p. 79.

50. 'The Economic Future of Peruvian Sugar' in *West Coast Leader*, Sep. 22, 1925, p. 21.

51. *Peru Today*, Nov. 1909, p. 26; Bollinger (1971), pp. 30–3.

52. This trend is probably largely the result of the fact that the figures are not corrected for the effects of the regional shift in production; the relatively high-wage departments of the central Coast were those from which sugar production was vanishing. The conclusion remains the same: expansion of sugar did not imply equivalent expansion of the local market.

53. The fact that after 1880 wage labour was mobilised from the Sierra by the somewhat peculiar system of 'enganche' should not be allowed to conceal the fact that the change represented an increase in the real wage, sufficient to attract labour which had formerly resisted recruitment for coastal work. The enganche system had the obvious advantage, from the point of view of the migrant worker, that payment was made in advance and a contract signed, thus removing the element of uncertainty which otherwise existed for anyone moving to the Coast in search of work. For the employers, the system had the advantage of obtaining labour at a wage probably below that which would have been necessary in an unstructured labour market.

54. *Extracto Estadístico*, 1934–5, p. 283.

55. The recorded foreign-currency deposits of the Peruvian banks rose from £627,000 in 1917 to £1.5 million in 1918 (Bertram (1974) p. 39). Deposits in foreign banks were undoubtedly far in excess of this figure.

56. Bertram (1974), p. 79.

57. Klaren (1969) traces the origins of Apra to the economic effects of the sugar industry on the regional economy, but his emphasis is on the distortions caused by monopoly capital, rather than on the economic difficulties of the sugar industry as a whole. We believe that in fact the latter was more important.

58. Lopez de Romaña, Pardo and Leguía.

59. For an incisive critique of the sugar planters as 'intermediaries' of international capital, see Mariátegui (1971), p. 54–5, and the discussion in Albert (1976) pp. 44–7.

60. Cotton is grown mostly in the far north, where ecological conditions are suitable for 'extra-long-staple' varieties, and along the Coast from southern Ancash to Ica, where 'long-staple' and 'medium-staple' varieties predominate. (Length of staple is an important quality variable, according to which world cotton markets are differentiated.) The departments of Lambayeque, La Libertad, and northern Ancash are more suited to sugar and rice, although until the 1920s Lambayeque was a significant cotton producer.

61. See Moreno (1900), p. 94, on Piura; Leubel (1861) on Lambayeque about 1860; Matos Mar (1967) on Chancay; and Hammel (1962), pp. 21–4, on Ica.

62. Ruth (1964), p. 51; Cisneros (1906), p. 156.

63. For a detailed description of the operation of this system in Ica see Hammel (1962), pp. 24 ff. For a general discussion of the institution of *yanaconaje* see Romero (1949), Vol. 2, pp. 195–7. On Cañete, see López Aliaga (1908), pp. 13–16.

64. For example, Moreno states that thirty landowners dominated Piura

(Moreno (1900), p. 20). For an example of an attempt by landowner interests to equate small-scale cultivation practices with egalitarian property distribution see SNA (1935).

65. On the politics of irrigation water in Ica see Hammel (1962), pp. 27–30. On Piura, see Bell (1976).

66. In Ica, Hammel claims that whereas in 1905 large owners held 2.6 times as much cultivated land as smallholders, by 1918 the ratio had risen to 5.8 times as much (Hammel, 1962, pp. 23–4; no source given). In Piura the main beneficiaries of the new irrigation schemes of the 1890s and 1900s were, naturally enough, the large landowners who had promoted the projects (Bell, 1976).

67. A demonstration of the difficulties a foreign firm did encounter when, on a rare occasion, one ventured into the unfamiliar environment of the Peruvian rural labour market, is given in an account of the Peruvian Corporation's problems in running the Chira irrigation scheme in the 1900s. The labour force eventually left wholesale, their number falling from 850 to 40 (Dubosc, 1905).

68. Gerbi (1941) p. 138.

69. *El Economista* (Lima), January 9, 1897, p. 293, reported a project to launch a Banco Agricola in Lima with capital of $2 million; prominent among the promoters was a 'Sr Seminario', no doubt from the Piura cotton family.

70. Gerbi (1941), pp. 341–6.

71. Hammel (1962), p. 35; Moreno (1900), p. 46; Ruth (1964), p. 52.

72. Ruth (1964), p. 52; Martin (1911), p. 172; Robinson Wright (1908), p. 332.

73. Dunn (1925), pp. 352, 362, 375, and 460.

74. See Chapter 6.

75. *Perú en su Centenario* (1921), pp. 31–7.

76. Dunn (1925), p. 375.

77. Dunn (1925), p. 365.

78. Cf the list in *West Coast Leader*, Special Cotton Number 1925, pp. ix–xv.

79. At least eight major houses by the 1920s, comprising four different nationalities (British, North American, Chinese, Japanese).

80. Cumberland (1922) shows these items of repatriated profit as £300,000 for January–June 1922. Sugar and cotton exports for the full year totalled £8.9 million.

81. *West Coast Leader*, Jan. 8, 1924, p. 1, and July 1, 1924, p. 23.

82. Romero (1949), Vol. 2, pp. 200–1 attributes this new trend to greater efficiency of large scale production. Hammel (1962), p. 25 states that credit became more difficult to obtain for landowners whose land was worked by *yanaconas*.

83. Clavero (1896), p. 48.

84. Ruth (1964), p. 49 dates strong demand in the British market for this type of cotton as having begun in 1884.

85. See Appendix 1, Table A.1.2. Exchange depreciation, of course, mitigated the effects.

86. The cake was used for cattle-feed in Britain; by 1900 its price had reached £5 per ton, cif, with freight costs of £2.5.0 per ton. Although seed and cake were never more than marginal contributors to the total value of cotton-industry exports (5 per cent in 1908), this was almost pure profit.

87. *West Coast Leader*, Mar. 5, 1921, p. 14.

88. Nogaro (1936), p. 104.

89. See the discussion in Chapter 6.

90. The average yield of unginned cotton per hectare was 1.4 tons in 1916; fell to 1.0 tons in the mid-1920s; recovered to 1.4 tons again by the mid-1930s; and was still 1.5 tons in the first half of the 1960s (*Extracto Estadistico* 1934–5, 1966).

91. Moreno (1900), pp. 32–3; Dubosc (1905), p. 5.

92. Such rains, associated with the '*El Niño*' disruption of ocean currents along the north Coast, were believed at the time to display a pattern of seven-year cycles. See Moreno (1900), pp. 45 and 92; Robinson Wright (1908); Marie (1904), p. 7.

93. Moreno (1900), p. 33, notes particularly the projects of the communities of Catacaos and Sechura, and of the landowners Checa and Romero.

94. Cisneros (1906), p. 143; Basadre (1963–4), Vol. 7, p. 3476, and Vol. 9, p. 4139.

95. Among other things, the legal issue of private access to water rights made large integrated schemes impossible to organise privately, since the planning had to encompass entire river basins.

96. Published in the *Boletin del Cuerpo de Ingenieros de Minas y Aguas*.

97. Hammel (1962), p. 22; López Aliaga (1908), p. 4.

98. Varieties such as Mitafifi and Sea Island had been grown for many years in the central Coast. The greater part of the expansion of cotton exports from 1900 to 1909, however, involved the higher-priced but disease-prone Aspero and Semi-aspero native cottons, the latter being the mainstay of cotton-growing in Ica (Martin (1911), p. 177). On the wilt problem, see Uranga (1924), (1925).

99. Basadre (1963–4), Vol. 8, pp. 3861–3; Barlow (1952), p. 120; *Peru, Cradle of South America*, Sep. 1924, p. 92.

100. Nelson Rounsevell in *West Coast Leader*, Jan. 8, 1924, p. 1.

101. Hinds (1926), p. 4.

102. In the case of *yanacona* sharecroppers, the landowner was responsible for supplying seed, and could hence influence the selection of varieties.

103. Barlow (1952), p. 113.

104. By 1927 it was reported that cotton prices were failing to meet production costs, although there are grounds for some scepticism as to the accuracy with which growers would have reported their costs to the Government (Despatch No. 742G, Miles Poindexter to US Secretary of State, May 12, 1927, D.F. 823.51/401).

105. By the early twentieth century these seasonal migrations of labour from the Sierra for the cotton harvest were becoming organised on a massive scale in several areas; see, for example, Roberts (1974a), p. 7, on migration from the Mantaro Valley to Cañete and Ica.

106. For example, McQueen (1926b); Despatch No 43G, Matthew E. Hanna to U.S. Secretary of State, Aug. 7, 1928, D.F. 823.51/415.

107. Employment and wage data are from Hunt (1974c), Tables 4-8 and 4-17. The employment increase is significant in terms of the economy as a whole, from 38 per cent to 47 per cent of the registered agricultural labour force.

108. Twenty-eight per cent in real terms between 1916 and 1920, if the data in *Extracto Estadístico* are to be believed. Our scepticism is based on the room for error with compositional shifts, the possibility of variation in the length of seasonal employment, and the fact that sugar wages did not rise, while workers on sugar estates were more militant and in as strong a position in terms of

market at this period. See Blanchard (1975), Chap. 9, for an account of rural workers' militancy during the period of export boom.

109. *Estadistica del Comercio Especial* 1930, p. 404; 'From Cottonseed to Lard: a Peruvian Industry' in *West Coast Leader*, Sep. 9, 1927, Supplement, p. 1.

110. This point is double-edged, however: many Peruvian textiles did not require such a high-quality cotton, and some experts have argued that Peru should have exported the Tanguis and imported a lower quality for the making of rough cloth.

111. Two examples were Santiago Poppe, active in urbanisation companies and the pioneering Compania Peruana de Marmoles (*West Coast Leader*, Oct. 30, 1923, Supplement, p. 2, and Oct. 19, 1926, Supplement, p. 2) and Luis Albizuri, also involved in the Compania de Marmoles, and also banking (*West Coast Leader*, June 21, 1927, p. 27) and the construction of the Hotel Bolivar in Lima (*West Coast Leader*, May 13, 1924, p. 1).

112. *Extracto Estadistico*, various years.

113. The sector's history is also interesting for the current debate on modes of production, as the description in the text makes clear. This has been discussed elsewhere by one of the authors (Bertram, 1974b, 1976; see also Bradby, 1975).

114. Figures taken from annual volumes of *Estadistica del Comercio Especial*, converted to dollars at current exchange rates. Note that the total-exports figure *excludes* Bolivian exports brought down by the Southern Railway and passed through the port at Mollendo.

115. Sotillo Humire (1962), p. 110, estimated that in the early 1960s some 75 per cent of alpaca production remained in Indian hands. Stordy (1921), p. 126 stated that 'practically all' alpaca production at that time came from small producers. These two references, especially Sotillo, provide good surveys of the general structure and characteristics of the sector. See also Barreda y Ramos (1929).

116. There has always existed in the Peruvian Sierra a substantial internal market for wool, which is used as the raw material for a large range of artisan textiles as well as by the few large woollen textile mills. Estimates of the proportion of total wool production consumed locally vary very widely; observers in the 1920s advanced estimates ranging from one-third (*West Coast Leader*, Aug. 10, 1926, p. 19) to three-quarters (F.E. Ross, 'Peruvian Wools', in *West Coast Leader*, June 4, 1921, p. 20). Data published during the 1940s in the annual *Memoria* of the Junta Nacional del la Industria Lana indicated a minimum of 50 per cent local consumption, and since the Junta's estimates for artisan consumption of alpaca are patently too low, the actual figure must have been above this.

117. Indian producers showed considerable price responsiveness to the boom conditions of the First World War by this means. See Stordy (1921), p. 126; F.E. Ross, op. cit. above.

118. For detailed discussion of the problems of modernisation in the South during the 1920s see Bertram (1976a). For a more general analysis of this problem in Peru, based particularly on the experience of the Central Sierra, see Martinez-Alier (1973).

119. Cf Chevalier (1966), Piel (1967), Craig (1967), Hazen (1974).

120. Hazen (1974), p. 18.

121. Quiroga (1915), cited by Hazen (1974), p. 133, reported that the number of

haciendas in Puno increased from 703 in 1879 to 3,219 by 1915. Similar data is given in Maltby (1972). By 1940 the number had dropped again substantially, to 1,691 *haciendas* (Hazen, 1974, p. 133).

122. Hazen (1974), Chapters 2 to 5; Maltby (1972); Piel (1967); Diez Bedregal (1955).
123. *Peru Today*, Oct. 1909; *West Coast Leader*, June 4, 1921, p. 1. The property, located in the Central Sierra near the Central Railway, was also on occasion spelled as Atocsaico.
124. Liga de Hacendados de Puno-Arequipa (1922); Piel (1967), pp. 388–94; Bertram (1967a); Stordy (1921).
125. Barreda (1970) summarises the history of the model ranch. Bertram (1967a) discusses its performance during the 1920s.
126. "Huacauta Sheep Ranch", in *West Coast Leader*, March 16, 1926; Bertram (1976a).
127. Bertram (1976a).
128. *West Coast Leader*, Nov. 27, 1919, p. 4; Manners (1922).
129. Thomson (1914); Basadre (1963–4), Vol. 8, pp. 3654–8.
130. Garland (1908), p. 223; Cisneros (1906), p. 175.
131. Garland (1908), p. 224–5.
132. Knorr (1945), Chapter 2; MacFadyean (1944), Chapter 1.
133. See Appendix 1, Table A.1.2.
134. *West Coast Leader*, May 9, 1933, pp. 19–20.
135. Appendix 1, Table A.1.1.
136. Dunn (1925), p. 510; *South American Yearbook*, 1913, p. 587. This bank was taken over in 1917 by the Anglo-South-American Bank, which was active in Lima (*Stock Exchange Yearbook* (1920), p. 520). In 1931 the Iquitos branch was liquidated, leaving the Amazon region without a bank (*Memoria de la Superintendencia de Bancos*, 1931, p. 16).
137. Torres Videla (n.d.).
138. North (1973).
139. On Fitzcarrald's career see *El Comercio* (Lima), July 8, 1972 p. 5; Dunn (1925), p. 491; Basadre (1963–4), Vol. 8, pp. 3209–10.
140. On Arana see Basadre (1963–4), Vol. 8, pp. 3603, 3654–8; Karno (1970), pp. 131–3.
141. *El Economista* Jan. 2, 1897, p. 243.
142. Garland (1908), p. 224.
143. During 1900 a total of 500,000 hectares of rubber concessions were approved (*South American Journal*, Oct. 19, 1901).
144. Garland (1908) p. 225; *West Coast Leader*, Nov. 13, 1920.
145. *West Coast Leader*, May 9, 1933, pp. 19–20.
146. *West Coast Leader*, Feb. 15, 1922, p. 1.
147. *West Coast Leader*, May 9, 1933, p. 19.
148. Victor Solaini, in *West Coast Leader*, Feb. 19 1924, p. 23.
149. In addition to wool and rubber, discussed above, we should mention the decline of coffee production in the Chanchamayo Valley and of cocaine production in La Libertad, as well as the decline of silver mining throughout the Sierra, discussed in Chapter 5 below.
150. See especially Haya de la Torre (1970).

CHAPTER 5

1. Regional shares of mining output by value are not available for years before 1914. However, product-by-product volume data from the official statistics show the two central departments of Junin and Lima to have increased their share of total silver production from 50 per cent in 1905 to 72 per cent in 1915, while their share of copper production rose from 93 per cent to 95 per cent over the same period. Much of the regional concentration, however, had already taken place before 1905, as the old silver-mining sector went into decline throughout the Sierra.

2. On the history of mining up to the 1890s see Purser (1971), Chapters 2 and 3.

3. One example was the installation in 1816 of Trevithick steam engines to pump out the mines at Cerro de Pasco; see Peruvian Mining Company (1825), and Purser (1971), p. 83.

4. *El Economista*, Jan. 9, 1897, pp. 258–9.

5. Purser (1971), p. 91.

6. Basadre (1963–4), Vol. 8, p. 3803; Paz Soldan (1917), pp. 71–2.

7. Proaño, Valentine, Stuart, Azalia, Miculicich and others. See Masias (1905); Bollinger (1971), pp. 207–11.

8. Purser (1971), p. 96; Malaga Santolalla (1904a), pp. 63–6; Malaga Santolalla (1904b), pp. 52, 60, 62; Masias (1905), pp. 24–5.

9. Purser (1971), pp. 96–7. An earlier form of leaching process for silver ores had been tried, without success, in the mid-nineteenth century (see Romero n.d., Vol. 2, p. 123). The Patera process was first introduced at Hualgayoc in 1890 (Malaga Santolalla (1904a), p. 66).

10. Article by F.C. Fuchs and L.G. Marquina in *El Economista*, Mar. 26, 1898, pp. 438–9; Apr. 2, 1898, p. 454; Apr. 9, 1898, p. 472; and Apr. 16, 1898, p. 488; and Malaga Santolalla (1904a), pp. 66–7.

11. *El Economista*, July 24, 1897, pp. 714–16.

12. Bollinger (1971), pp. 174–6.

13. *El Economista*, Jan. 2, 1898, pp. 246–7.

14. Established in 1890, at the height of the silver boom, this company went bankrupt in the early twentieth century, when the workings reached the water table at a time when the company lacked finance for drainage works. See Purser (1971), pp. 96 and 106–7, and Enock (1906).

15. See A.R.P., 'Los Minerales de la Zona Seca en el Cerro de Pasco' in *El Economista*, Jan. 9, 1897, pp. 258–9.

16. See Appendix 1, Table A.1.2.

17. *El Economista*, Apr. 24, 1897, p. 493, and Aug. 21, 1897, pp. 773–4. The mint had been paying 10 per cent above the market price; its closure provoked an immediate commercial crisis in Cerro de Pasco.

18. Appendix 1, Tables A.1.1 and A.1.3.

19. Table 5.1. The decay of most of the smaller mining centres during the first decade of the twentieth century is evident from the descriptions in Velarde (1908).

20. The detailed history of this and other gold mining ventures of the period has been covered in a working paper, Bertram (1975).

21. On the failure of the El Gigante venture see De Lucio (1905), pp. 28–30. On

the similar failure of an ill-designed cyanide plant installed at the Santo Domingo mine in 1914, see Woods (1935), Chapter 13; and Dunn (1925) pp. 456–90.
22. For the mine's history see Woods (1935).
23. Purser (1971), pp. 57 and 106.
24. The Poto deposits came at this time into the hands of the Peña family, who controlled them until the 1970s.
25. Bertram (1975), pp. 35–6.
26. Andaray (Candamo-Leguia-Aspillaga), and Cotabambas Auraria, formed in 1902 by Isaac Alzamora and Nicolas de Pierola to develop Ccochasayhuas (*El Economista*, July 17, 1897, p. 695; Karno (1970), p. 63).
27. Purser (1971), p. 90; *Boletin del Cuerpo de Ingenieros de Minas*, No. 29, pp. 10–13.
28. An attempt at copper smelting by the Pfluckers at Morococha in the mid-nineteenth century had failed for these reasons, and in 1877 the Pfluckers had given up control of the Morococha copper deposits rather than pay the small annual surface tax (Masias (1905), p. 17).
29. Masias (1905), pp. 21–3.
30. Appendix 1, Table A.1.2.
31. *El Economista*, July 31, 1897, p. 795.
32. McArver (1970).
33. *El Economista*, Apr. 7, 1898, p. 467.
34. *El Economista*, July 31, 1897, p. 796.
35. *El Economista*, Apr. 30, 1898, p. 518. The two smelters operating were Huamanrauca (formerly a silver/lead smelter) and Pucayacu.
36. Bollinger (1971), p. 173.
37. Velarde and Denegri (1904), pp. 21 and 34.
38. Matte is copper ore enriched by smelting to a copper content of 40 per cent or more (in the 1890s, although present-day technology produces mattes of closer to 90 per cent). This product could be obtained from relatively simple water-jacket furnaces such as the Lima capital-goods industries were supplying at the end of the 1890s. Blister copper is obtained by passing ore or matte through a high-temperature Bessemer-type converter, which raises the copper content to 95–99 per cent. The final stage of processing is refining, usually by an electrolytic process.
39. Bollinger (1971), p. 184.
40. Bollinger (1971), Chapter 4.
41. Dávalos y Lissón (1901) mentions a '*gran bomba*' which at one time had been used at the Mesapata mine; this may, however, be a reference to the Trevithick experiment.
42. The cost problems of Cerro de Pasco about 1900 were the subject of an extensive literature: Basadre (1899) and Davalos y Lisson (1901) were the main contributions.
43. Bollinger (1971), p. 173.
44. McArver (1970), Bollinger (1971), pp. 172ff.
45. Of all the ventures floated in the Lima capital market at the turn of the century, the Empresa Socavonera was the most interesting. Its board brought together leading mine-owners, bankers, merchants, planters and promoters in an enterprise whose history reads as a remarkable success story. Begun as a

project to solve the Cerro de Pasco drainage problem, the company became, after the mines were bought by U.S. capital, a skilful and effective blackmailer of the foreign firm, pushing the tunnel to completion against strong opposition, and forcing the U.S. firm to buy them out in 1908. (McArver (1970); Bertram (1974), pp. 83–4 and 184.)

46. Cerro de Pasco was only one of the areas where high-grade copper ores were available for development.

47. The events summarised in this paragraph are described in detail in Bollinger (1971), Chaps 4 and 5, and Bertram (1974), Chapter 3.

48. The only survivors appear to have been two small lead smelters in an isolated region of Ancash.

49. These were the Huaraucaca smelter of Eulogio Fernandini, and the San Jose smelter of the Compagnie des Mines de Huarón (the latter, French-owned, had been opened only in 1916). A tiny smelter at Huacracocha, owned by Juan Galliver, functioned sporadically until the mid-1920s.

50. *Boletin Oficial de Minas y Petroleo*, (1928), No. 26, p. 8.

51. The 'La Docena' mine at Cerro de Pasco, owned by Manuel Mujica and Ignacia de Sal y Rosas, reputedly earned S/10 million profit in roughly a decade of operation to 1918. Fernandini's Colquijirca mine was reported in the mid-1920s to be generating profits of S/3–4 million annually (Bertram (1974), p. 186).

52. In the event the railway was completed in 1904, the smelter in 1906, and the tunnel in 1908.

53. *El Minero Ilustrado* (Cerro de Pasco) Feb. 27, 1901, p. 365.

54. Dávalos y Lissón (1901), p. 585.

55. Dávalos y Lissón (1901), p. 584.

56. This was not the first time Haggin had taken an interest in Peru: in 1897 he and other New York capitalists had seriously considered investing $30 million in gold exploration in Puno (*El Economista*, Sep. 18, 1897, p. 758).

57. *El Minero Ilustrado*, Oct. 23, 1901.

58. Bollinger (1971), p. 394.

59. Roughly $6 million was spent by Cerro on mine purchases at Cerro de Pasco and Morococha between 1901 and 1912 (Mayer (1913)). Research in the company's archives at Oroya and Cerro de Pasco indicates that this sum, equivalent to £1.2 million, was divided between the two areas roughly in the proportions of £700,000 in Cerro de Pasco and £400,000 in Morococha. See Tables 5.4 and 5.5.

60. About 60 per cent of it (*BCIM* annual statistics). Production at Morococha rose 56 per cent in the two years 1904 and 1905.

61. Langdon (1968), pp. 50–1. The family's 'Santa Inez' silver mines at Castrovirreyna were also in a poor state by 1905 (*The Times* (London), July 30, 1906) and were later sold to a Lima merchant.

62. Proaño had held large, but not majority, interests in the Compania Industrial Minera de Yauli (in partnership with Valentine, Stuart, Tealdo and Pehoaz) and Compania Minera Copaycocha (with Valentine and Stuart). Following Cerro's acquisition of majority shareholdings in these companies from Proaño's partners, he was forced out of all his management positions and eventually induced to sell. (Bertram (1974), pp. 12 ff).

63. For discussion of this remarkable legal case, which dragged on from 1912

until 1923, see Bertram (1974), pp. 85–7, and Bollinger (1971) p. 211n. For Proaño's version see Proaño (1918), (1923).

64. At Morococha, for example, the Alpamina and Sacracancha silver mines of the Gildemeister—De Osma family, and the Gertrudis and Alejandria mines of the Sociedad Minera Puquiococha (Jose Miculicich, Severino Marcionelli, and Jose Hanza) remained independent, but as silver producers these mines were in decline until the 1930s (when the lead and zinc content of their ores brought a revival). See Masías (1903), p. 37 and (1905), p. 23.

65. Fernandini owned the Colquijirca silver-copper mines some miles south of Cerro de Pasco itself; he had no drainage problem, and owned his own modern smelter at Huaraucaca. In Cerro de Pasco he took advantage of the 1901 recession to buy up a number of copper mines on his own account; these mines were later leased to Cerro. One other independent producer later became important at Cerro de Pasco: the La Docena mine of Manuel Mujica and Ignacia de Sal y Rosas, which was staked out after the entry of Cerro, and the ores from which were sold to Cerro from 1910 until the mine was exhausted in 1917. (*BCIM* No. 95, p. 177).

66. The discussion which follows is based upon Bertram (1974), pp. 81–97, and Bollinger (1971), pp. 206–29.

67. *West Coast Leader*, Mar. 25, 1920, p. 16.

68. In secondary mining areas, also, there was considerable foreign penetration, mainly by British capital. British firms tried their hand at gold mining at Chuquitambo (1901 to c.1926), Aporoma (1910–14), Inambari (1912–13) and Pataz (1914), while the Anglo-French Ticapampa Silver Mining Company entered Ancash in 1903, and the Lampa Mining Company began operation in Puno in 1906. The French-owned Compagnie des Minas de Huaron, as noted earlier, began operations in 1915–16.

69. It is worth emphasising that despite contemporary accusations that those who sold mines to foreigners were often 'speculators' who had bought up mines merely to re-sell them, our story above indicates that the leading mine-vendors were well-established and capable mine operators. The great majority of the Cerro de Pasco surnames listed in Table 5.4 are to be found also in the mining *padrones* of the 1870s (see Fuentes (1879), and *La Minería y la Agricultura al Punto de Vista del Progreso* (1876)).

70. E.g. Hymer (1960), Kindleberger (1969), Chapter 1.

71. Bollinger (1971), pp. 167–9.

72. Skelton (1937) describes the history of these cartels. The price collapse of 1901 was the direct result of the failure of a cartel organised by John D. Rockefeller.

73. Bertram (1974), p. 380 indicates a lower-bound estimate for imports of about $1.6 million p.a. 1922–37.

74. Reynolds (1965), p. 378, column 81.

75. That is, Cerro's actual returned value of $207 million, plus the profits and U.S. taxes repatriated by the company, totalling (at least) $110 million.

76. See Geddes (1972) and Klein (1965). Tin-mining in Bolivia, in contrast to copper in Chile and Peru, was not subject to denationalisation in its infancy because U.S. international mining companies had no experience with, nor much interest in, tin. British foreign investment was by the early twentieth century little interested in countries such as Bolivia.

77. Using our earlier figure of $317 million returned value out of gross earnings of $375 million for a 'counterfactual' local sector identical to Cerro.

78. Eighty-five per cent returned value from $244 million is $207 million.

79. This assumes that none of the money received by sellers of mines was subsequently invested in the construction of the Socavon; in fact, it seems likely that former mine-owners would have been among purchasers of the Empresa's bonds.

80. $9 million received from Cerro minus $0.5 million capital losses.

81. See, for example, Prado (1906), pp. 75 ff on the debate over the effects of foreign borrowing.

82. Cf Adler (1965) and Stevens (1971) on the determinants of capital-absorptive capacity in underdeveloped economies.

83. Cf Griffin (1970).

84. Baran (1960), Chapter 2. See Chapter 2 above.

85. Low (1976).

86. Steel, Languasco, Villaran, Perez, Stuart, Pfluckers, Valentine.

87. Pehoaz, Tealdo, and Sociedad Minera Puquiococha.

88. Palomino, Ortiz, Lagravere, Martinench, Montero.

89. One family studied by Low, the Rizo Patrons, received only £4,660 from Cerro but over £17,000 from the independent Cerro de Pasco operator Eulogio Fernandini; their subsequent investment record, while impressive, was thus financed more by a transfer of local capital than by an infusion of foreign money.

90. Our conclusion obviously rests upon several unstated assumptions, firstly about the net contribution to Peru from the $10 million capital formation (which we believe translated into a much smaller gain in realised aggregate investment); and secondly about the appropriate discount rate to be used in comparing a net gain of (say) $5–10 million 1900–1916, with losses of $100 million 1916–1937. The assumptions required to make the gains outweigh the losses are so extremely unrealistic that we feel justified in sparing the reader a detailed discussion; see however Bertram (1974), pp. 174–80.

91. For example, the Compania Salinera, established by Payan in 1901, with nominal capital of £100,000, which attracted £1,200,000 in subscriptions when the shares were offered publicly (Basadre (1963–4), Vol. 7, p. 3305).

92. See Chapter 6 below.

93. Bertram (1974), Chap. 5 and Appendix F.

94. This was because our cost-benefit model measured net contributions to national income, rather than gains for the balance of payments. In calculating national-income effects we encounter difficulties with concepts such as the shadow wage rate, opportunity cost of capital, non-marginality of the enterprises considered, and shadow-pricing in general, so severe as to suggest that formal complexity in a case such as this adds very little to commonsense arguments.

95. Cerro, as the foreign mining company most closely linked into the local economy, compared favourably in returned-value terms with Northern Peru Mining Company, which to judge from scattered data in the mining statistics during the 1920s was returning 50 per cent or less of its earnings to Peru in the 1920s, even taking into account lump-sum payments to local mine-owners for properties purchased during the period. Excluding such capital inflows from returned value reduces Northern Peru Mining to a level of returned value similar to that of the copper companies in Chile (see Note 74 above). In the south, the returns to Peru from Anaconda's possession of the Cerro Verde copper deposit were limited to a brief period of exploration investment at the end of the First

World War, and the surface tax of S/30 per claim paid by the U.S. company to retain its control over the deposit. Practically any local venture which brought the deposit into production would have scored better.

96. The basic sources for the early history of oil in Peru are Moreno (1891), Marsters (1907), Garland (1902b), Kay (1924) and Jochamowitz (1939).

97. *El Economista*, June 18, 1898, p. 626. The company made a deal with the merchant house Duncan Fox and Company in London which permitted the repayment of debts totalling £40,000, of which £36,000 had been owed to Michael P. Grace.

98. Large amounts of technical data on the refineries are given in the annual statistics from 1924 to 1929, published in the *Boletin Oficial de Minas y Petroleo* (BOMP).

99. Purser (1971), p. 92.

100. On Meiggs' death in 1874 his enterprise (in which some $150,000 had been invested) was taken over by J.B. Mullor and Co. of Lima, who built port works at Talara.

101. Jochamowitz (1939), p. 24.

102. Tweddle had previously been involved in an attempt to obtain a Rockefeller-style pipeline monopoly on the Russian Baku oil fields in 1875 (Moreno (1891), p. 42).

103. Two attempts were made by a Peruvian, Francisco Miranda, to develop a small field at Quebrada Heath near Zorritos. Both were joint ventures dependent on foreign financing: Heath Petroleum Company (British) in 1891, and Compagnie Française du Pétrole de l'Amérique du Sud in 1897–8. The latter company spent 3.5 million francs on refinery construction before running out of working capital; in any case, the very limited quantities of oil struck did not justify the installation of a refinery. Other attempts to enter oil production during the 1890s were the Mancora Peru Petroleum Syndicate (Peruvian-British, 1891); the Peruvian Petroleum Syndicate (1894), E.L. Doheny (U.S., in 1895) and Federico Blume (Peruvian, in 1900). See Kay (1924).

104. *BCIM*, No. 81, p. 26. This company was Chilean-financed, and operated in close alliance with London and Pacific.

105. The 1904 mining statistics reported Taiman as a small-scale producer at La Breita; *BCIM*, No. 24 (1905), p. 38.

106. Kay (1924); Jochamowitz (1939) p. 79; *BCIM*, No. 83, p. 50. In addition to these ventures on the north Coast, a series of companies worked the Pirin field in Puno; see *Estadística Petrolera del Perú*, 1948–9, p. 94.

107. *BCIM*, No. 81 (1914) p. 18; Kay (1924), p. 27; Jochamowitz (1939), p. 79.

108. The 1911 break up of the Standard Oil Trust by the U.S. Supreme Court left Jersey Standard with control of a Canadian subsidiary Imperial Oil, with a refinery at Vancouver on the Pacific Coast. This refinery had formerly been supplied from Standard's California oilfields, which now passed into the hands of a separate company, Standard Oil of California. In order to restore a vertically-integrated source of supply for the Vancouver refinery, Jersey Standard quickly decided on obtaining control of the producing coastal oilfields of Peru, and began working towards this in 1912. (Lewis (1972), p. 14).

109. It should be noted that IPC retained the name of London and Pacific Petroleum Company for its Peruvian operations from the takeover in 1913 until 1924. During that period the actual ownership of the Hacienda La Brea-Parinas

remained vested in the heirs of William Keswick, former head of London and Pacific, who leased their interests to London and Pacific. In 1924 IPC finally consolidated its control by buying out the Keswicks' surface rights. The London and Pacific Petroleum Company actually went into liquidation in 1917 (*Oil and Petroleum Yearbook*, 1929, p. xlii).

110. It is worth noting that Peru was the leading oil producer in South America until 1924, when Venezuela became a large-scale producer. See American Petroleum Institute (1937), pp. 56–7. After the end of the First World War, several of the large international oil companies sent representatives to Lima in 1920 to investigate the possibility of large-scale new concessions (Bertram (1974), p. 213).

111. Jochamowitz (1939), p. 30.

112. The Shell venture was described in *West Coast Leader*, Feb. 3, 1925, p. 1 and June 23, 1925, p. 36. The agreement with Esso was indicated in Despatch No. 399, Miles Poindexter (Lima) to U.S. Secretary of State, D.F. 823.6363/78.

113. *West Coast Leader*, Aug. 2, 1928 p. 1; Jan. 10, 1928, p. 28; July 21, 1928, p. 1 and Nov. 27, 1928, p. 3. See also Normand (1962), p. 282.

114. Jochamowitz (1939), pp. 30–33.

115. *West Coast Leader*, Feb. 19, 1924, p. 2; *BOMP*, No. 15, p. 17.

116. Bertram (1974), p. 368, compares average labour productivity in the Piaggio company and in IPC, finding that the two were virtually identical until 1920, although thereafter Piaggio fell behind, for reasons unconnected with the efficiency considerations discussed here.

117. Manners (1922) p. 13.

118. Penrose (1968).

119. For detailed treatment of IPC's economic contribution from 1916 on see Bertram (1974), Chap. 4 and Appendices B, C and D.

120. Bertram (1974), Chap. 6, especially pp. 243–54.

121. Gurney (1930).

122. The valuation of oil exports in the Peruvian official statistics is the main problem; although definite statements to this effect are very hard to find, it seems probable that, for a number of the earlier years covered, oil exports were valued at cif rather than fob prices by the authorities. However, given the nature of world oil markets and the wide divergence among regional prices even within the U.S.A., it is difficult to say how significant the notional distinction between fob and cif really was in the case of oil; all IPC exports had the character of intra-company transfers. On the side of returned value, it should be noted that our figures include a 10 per cent write-up for possible unrecorded expenditures, which almost certainly gives the expenditures series an upward bias as well.

123. There is a conceptual problem in discussing returned value in the context of a firm which sells locally as well as abroad. One definition of returned value would allocate costs proportionally between exports and local sales, and take the local costs of export production as returned value. Another possibility is to treat income from local sales as a subtraction from returned value, in which case returned-value would here be zero. A third version, and the one which we use for 'returned value' in our discussion here, treats local import-substituting sales as equivalent to exports, and all local-economy costs as returned value.

124. See particularly Pinelo (1973), pp. 35–40, and Bertram (1974), Chap. 6. The IPC made frequent loans and occasional grants to the government, the

largest being the $1 million paid for the 1922 Laudo. The Sanchez Cerro regime was rescued in its hour of greatest financial crisis in 1931 by an IPC loan. On a more personal level, Alberto Salomon (the Minister responsible for the key negotiations with IPC during the Leguía regime) was regarded by the British as a company agent (see the documents on the 1921 Laudo negotiations in FO371/5609, especially FO371/5609/A5687; and Despatch No. 73, C.H. Bentinck to Foreign Secretary, Apr. 24 1930, F0 371/14252/A4124), and in the 1930s was accused and convicted of illegal personal enrichment (i.e. accepting IPC bribes) by the Tribunal of National Sanction. The sentence was later set aside by a higher court on a technicality (*West Coast Leader*, Mar. 8th, 1938, p. 5).

125. For example, during the IPC's oil blockade of 1918; and again in 1930–31 when the oil companies mounted a joint offensive with other foreign firms to have suspected Apristas purged from the Sanchez Cerro cabinet, the main casualty being the Minister of Government, Jimenez. (On the latter affair see the British diplomatic correspondence in FO371/14254.)

126. IPC returned value plus repatriated profits, from Table 5.8.

127. Local sales of $62 million plus exports of $10 million = total sales $72 million. Import costs at 14 per cent of total sales = $10 million.

128. Bertram (1974), Chapter 4 and Appendix D.

129. When IPC was eventually, in 1968, expropriated without compensation, the results were a massive withdrawal of foreign capital, and a five-year campaign by the U.S. Government to block lending to Peru by the international aid agencies. See Chapter 15 below.

130. The complex legal history of the La Brea-Pariñas (Negritos) oilfield has been the subject of a number of studies, particularly Laurie Solis (1967), Furnish (1970), Lewis (1972), and Pinelo (1973). The account here is a summary of Bertram (1974), pp. 204–7, and the general discussion which follows is based on *ibid.*, Chapter 6. Strong legal arguments for regarding the 1824 title as null *ipso jure* are given by Furnish (1970) pp. 376–9.

131. The revelation was made by Ricardo Deustua, an oil engineer, in a lecture to the Sociedad Geografica de Lima. See Deustua (1912), p. 26 and (1914), pp. 209ff.

132. The U.S. Ambassador, on instructions from Washington, delivered a mild verbal protest but notified the State Department of his opinion that the IPC had been evading its legal tax obligations. Washington took no further action in the matter. (See Cable of Apr. 12, 1915 from William H. Libby of Standard Oil (NJ) to the State Department, and the Department's instructions to Lima in U.S. State Department Decimal Files D.F. 823. 6363/5; and Cable of Apr. 17 from McMillin to Secretary of State, D.F. 823.6363/6.)

133. The British Foreign Office remained unaware until March 1919 that IPC was controlled not by British but by U.S. capital. By the time their error was discovered, the British Government had already become firmly committed to the IPC's cause. (See Memo P.E.561 of Mar. 13, 1919 from Petroleum Executive to Foreign Office, F.O.371/3893.)

134. Lewis (1972), p. 16.

135. Bertram (1974), pp. 227–9.

136. One of the Peruvian Government's main creditors, the British-owned Peruvian Corporation, brought strong pressure to bear on the U.S. Government to stop the loan contract being approved unless the proceeds were preferentially

earmarked for repayment of Peruvian Corporation claims. W.R. Grace and Co. assisted the Corporation in pressuring the National City Bank, which was to have granted the loan. (Bertram (1974), p. 229n.)

137. 'Petroleum Famine' in *West Coast Leader*, Jan. 12, 1918, p. 1. Pinelo (1973), p. 37, reports that material in the U.S. State Department archives shows the 'requisition' never to have occurred, so far as the Canadian Government was concerned; the decision to withdraw the tanker was a unilateral one by the oil company.

138. Bertram (1974), pp. 232–3.

139. Bertram (1974), pp. 233–4. Many later commentators have been mystified by the apparently inexplicable decision of Congress to pass the arbitration bill without debate and virtually without dissent; see, for example Basadre (1963–4), Vol. 8, pp. 3893–5, where Barreda y Laos (the leader of Congress at the time, and a cousin of President Pardo) seeks to present the Congressional about-face as the result of imperialist pressure. In fact, as material in the British diplomatic archives makes clear, the arbitration bill was drafted by the IPC solicitors and put through Congress under a secret agreement between Pardo and the deputies. IPC and Pardo were both anxious to take the heat out of the local issue, while the members of Congress were anxious to distinguish themselves by rhetorical flourishes of nationalist outrage. The deal reached in October 1918 satisfied all three. In addition, the bill included a clause, much attacked by later Peruvian commentators, providing that any agreement reached between the Government and the company (represented by the British Government) would be binding on the international 'arbitral tribunal,' thus enabling the parties to the dispute to pre-empt the process of arbitration—clearly a recipe for secret negotiations.

140. Pinelo (1973), p. 22; Bertram (1974), p. 234. The evidence of Shell financing for Leguía is in the U.S. State Department archives: Cable of Mar. 15, 1920, W.H. Smith (Lima) to Secretary of State, D.F. 823.6363/22, and Confidential Enclosure in Despatch No. 264 of Aug. 5, 1920, Carlton Jackson (Lima) to Secretary of State, D.F. 823.6363/32.

141. Bertram (1974), p. 239. For the text of the 1922 Agreement see League of Nations, *Treaty Series*, Vol. 10, 1922, pp. 464–9.

142. See especially Kindleberger (1969).

CHAPTER 6

1. To the orthodox theorist of international trade, of course, this tendency would come as no surprise, given the presumed comparative advantage of Peru in the production of export staples. Our point here, however, is that the dynamic process of transforming export growth into wider development of the local economy could operate successfully only where such trends were checked in some way.

2. To obtain the *net* stimulus to demand attributable to government spending, it is of course necessary to take account of how that expenditure was financed.

3. Beginning with the 1901 purchases of mines by the Cerro de Pasco Mining Company and continuing with the financing of expansion of foreign-owned mineral export sectors. Other elements in the inflow of capital were the £600,000 foreign loan obtained by the Government in 1905, and the resumption of railway

expansion by the Peruvian Corporation in 1907.

4. As Chapter 5 above describes, Cerro brought in £1.1 million for the purchase of mining properties between 1901 and 1906.

5. For the changing composition of export earnings see Table 3.2 above.

6. Calculated from *Extracto Estadistico*. A detailed table is given in Thorp and Bertram (1976), p. 66.

7. For a summary of public works spending during the 1920s, as reported by Garland Duponte (n.d.), Capunay (1951), Labarthe (1933), and Jochamowitz *et al.* (1930), see Bertram (1974), pp. 48–50.

8. Bertram (1974), pp. 52–3.

9. On the balance-of-payments crisis of 1925–6 see McQueen (1926b).

10. The lack of a national population census between 1876 and 1940 makes it difficult to date the point at which population growth rates took off. The careful assembly of data from special censuses by Hunt (1974c, see pp. 2–3 especially) make it possible to conclude that rates increased from the 1900s on, rising from 1 per cent or so in the first decade to well over 2 per cent by the 1920s. The abrupt cessation of contemporary comment on the labour-shortage problem after the first decade supports this.

11. Nearly half the increase in modern sector agricultural employment.

12. See Chapter 4 on the regional concentration of sugar by the 1920s and its implications.

13. Juan Leguía's best-known coup was the collection of $520,000 in commissions in 1927 from Seligmans, the New York investment bankers, as payment for his assistance in passing them two large foreign-loan contracts in that year (see Seligmans cable of March 21st, 1927 to their Lima representative in U.S. State Department Decimal Files, 823.51Se4/5, microfilm file M746 Roll 21, Frame 130). A more direct case of his participation in public-works money was an Lp 88,000 profit from fraudulent land 'expropriation' deals connected with the Olmos irrigation project in 1929; see Labarthe (1933), p. 66.

14. Imports of motor-cars rose from Lp 210,000 in 1919 to Lp 588,000 in 1929. Possibly of more importance than such familiar types of import-intensive luxury consumption was the tendency to transfer funds abroad during the 1920s. The evidence for such capital flight is mainly qualitative (the phenomenon attracted a good deal of contemporary comment), but is confirmed by the strong downward pressure on the exchange rate which persisted even when the balance of payments should have been in equilibrium. (See Bertram (1974), pp. 283–91).

15. The public sector wage and salary bill was only about 15 per cent of the wage bill in agriculture, and this does not take account of the numerous small independent operators in agriculture, especially in cotton.

16. The recession was caused by the acute depression in the United States; for a discussion see Prado (1908).

17. The most convincing evidence is that after 1907 the flow of published commentary on Peru's industrial progress, which had been such a feature of the early 1900s, dried up completely. Surveys of the economy written during the 1910s and 1920s generally gave very low priority to manufacturing, and emphasised its backwardness and lack of dynamism.

18. The only ventures of long-run significance established during the years 1906–10 were the Gunther Tidow breweries in Cuzco (1908) and Arequipa (1909)—now Compania Cervecera del Sur.

19. Bollinger (1971), p. 33. The increasing foreign control of mineral export sectors undoubtedly contributed to this process of decline, because of the tendency of foreign firms to purchase capital goods in their home countries rather than locally.

20. At least one of the cotton mills was established by a merchant firm for the explicit purpose of relieving a supply shortage (Chaplin (1967), p. 237).

21. Two foundries and an unsuccessful attempt to establish a cement factory were the only new ventures outside the category of light industry. See *West Coast Leader*, Jan. 15, 1921, Supplement p. 1, and Apr. 16, 1921, Supplement p. 2, for the two foundries; and Rospigliosi (1967), p. 3 and *West Coast Leader* Nov. 11, 1924, p. 36 on the cement company.

22. These are surveys done by individuals, sometimes at Government request, but essentially relying on personal observation. The different sources are listed in the notes to Table 6.6.

23. See Bertram (1974), pp. 260–70, and Thorp and Bertram (1976). As the construction firm responsible for most of the Leguía Government's public-works programmes, the Foundation Company, had an obvious interest in vertical integration into the cement industry; while the freezing works was a case of horizontal integration growing directly out of the firm's construction interests. (Among other things, the building of the freezing works helped to strengthen the case for more roads into cattle and sheep-rearing districts of the interior—roads in whose construction the Foundation Company would be involved.) On the company's operations in Peru see *West Coast Leader*, July 28, 1925, p. 1.

24. See below for further discussion of this case. Foreign firms were also responsible for the establishment of a large sawmill near Iquitos in 1923 (*West Coast Leader*, Mar. 15, 1927, p. 10), and for Peru's first large chemicals plant, which quickly failed in the conditions of the 1920s (*West Coast Leader*, Oct. 27, 1925, p. 5; Trant (1927), p. 37). Peruvian residents started one new cotton mill in 1924, which was quickly taken over by Duncan Fox and Co., and one large new flourmill which caused an immediate and drastic crisis of oversupply in the industry (*West Coast Leader*, July 16, 1929, p. 6).

25. There were new tariffs in 1901 and 1910, but these were designed as administrative improvements. The 1900 revision was carried out primarily to improve the valuation of imports. Contemporary remarks about the 'protectionism' of this tariff referred not so much to any very dramatic increase in protectionism as to the maintenance of the existing rates of duty ruling in the late 1890s. On this tariff, see the introductory section in *Arancel de Aforos* 1901, and in *Estadística del Comercio Especial del Perú* 1901. The 1902 trade statistics provide a condensed summary of the rates under the new tariff, pp. xix-xxii. The 1910 tariff revision involved the switch from *ad valorem* duties, being an exercise in the conversion of the existing rates of duty. On this revision see *Memoria del Ministerio de Hacienda* (1912); *Estadística del Comercio Especial*, 2 semestre 1910, p. ix; and *Boletín de Aduanas*, No. 115, Sep. 21, 1912, especially p. 535.

26. The system is described in Rutter (1916).

27. See the forceful criticisms of the 1910 tariff by Oscar Arrus (head of the statistical department) in *Estadística del Comercio Exterior*, 1915 pp. iii–iv.

28. Compare the 1916 *Memoria del Ministerio de Hacienda*. The problem was

concealed by the fact that the import statistics were constructed using fixed official prices.

29. *Diario de los Debates*, 1915, Camara and Senado, *passim*.

30. The contrast here with Colombia is interesting. Colombia, like Peru, had an export performance which far outstripped that of the more successful industrialisers of this period. But since the funds generated in Colombia far exceeded what the sector could absorb, and the sector was locally owned, protectionist pressure was generated which, together with other important factors such as an unusually equal income distribution in coffee, generated more industrial growth than was experienced in Peru. See Thorp and Bertram (1976), pp. 63.

31. See Chapter 3.

32. Taxes on alcohol, sugar, tobacco and matches were the principal sources of the increase.

33. Rutter (1916). The ending of the exemption of mining and petroleum and the size of sugar profits forced acceptance even on the still-powerful sugar producers.

34. See Basadre's survey of the history of the labour movement (Basadre (1963–4), Vol. X, p. 4748). The cost of living was explicitly an issue in the General Strike of 1919. See Gallo (1970) for a parallel argument—undoubtedly of more significance in the case of Argentina, where the degree of organisation and numbers involved were far greater.

35. Salomon (1919); Fishlow (1972).

36. Goetz (1973).

37. In cotton textiles, for example, the Japanese share of Peruvian imports rose from zero in 1913 to eight per cent by 1918–19.

38. The process of tooling-up factories for capital-goods production was a long-term one, and the duration of the war could not be forecast, while local entrepreneurs could be certain that with the ending of hostilities the established preference for U.S. or European machinery would quickly reassert itself. Furthermore, it should be noted that since several of the key export sectors had laid down large amounts of capital investment in the years prior to the war, shortages of capital goods were not sufficiently critical to induce a search for local sources of supply.

39. Bertram (1974), Chap. 7.

40. As a debtor, this was in the Government's interest.

41. Bertram (1974), pp. 39–46.

42. On the 1923 tariff see *Estadística del Comercio Especial*, 1923, p. ii. A table in *ibid.*, p. xvi, permits a rough comparison of the change in the incidence of duties on the main types of goods which resulted from the imposition of the new scale of duties in mid-1923. The most significant increases were on clothing, woollen textiles, leather goods, furniture and beverages; the last showed the most dramatic increase, from 27 per cent to 62 per cent. Duties collected on capital goods show a decrease in incidence. It is of interest to note that the duties on cotton textiles, which had been around 40 per cent at the beginning of the century, were down to only 13 per cent overall incidence before application of the 1923 tariff, and 16 per cent after application (*ibid.*). An 'emergency tariff,' which was later formalised as the new tariff schedule of 1928, came into effect at the beginning of 1927 (the relevant law was promulgated in November 1926). An

analysis by the U.S. Commercial Attaché, in *West Coast Leader*, Jan. 11, 1927, p. 7, indicates important increases in the duties on textiles, clothing, leather goods, furniture and beverages—virtually the same sectors benefited by the 1923 increases. There were also, however, a number of increases obviously designed as revenue measures rather than for protection, i.e. on automobiles, musical instruments, cameras and various other luxury items. A detailed analysis of the revised duty schedule which became the new formal tariff of 1928 is in *West Coast Leader*, Apr. 10, 1928, p. 5.

43. The number of looms controlled by foreign firms in cotton textiles was 55 per cent of the total by 1918, and had risen to 76 per cent by 1931.

44. *West Coast Leader*, Apr. 10, 1928, p. 5 discussed the effects of this campaign.

45. Bollinger (1971), pp. 234–53.

46. Bertram (1974), p. 271; Bolsa Comercial de Lima, *Memoria*.

47. Twomey (1972), p. 60.

48. In 1924, 11,243 tons of beef were moved on the Central Railway, while Lima's consumption in the same year was 13,100 tons (Twomey (1972), p. 45). Unfortunately the Central Railway statistics do not indicate direction or distance; we only know that the average distance was 200 km.

49. Basádre (1963–4), Vol. VII, p. 3381.

50. A variety introduced in 1916 maintained its resistance only while still cultivated on a small scale.

51. In the 1960s wheat on irrigated land on the Coast was yielding 6,497 soles a hectare, compared with 17,161 soles for sugar and 16,882 for cotton (Twomey (1972), p. 63). Wheat admittedly used less water, but this far from compensated for the lower yield.

52. The problem of preference was very great. Klinge (1946) claimed that the effect of improved transport had been to increase Sierra consumption of coastal flour, not vice versa.

53. In 1929, 88 per cent of the cattle population was in the Sierra or Selva, principally the former (calculated from Ministerio de Fomento (1932)). Unfortunately this census gives no data on size of holdings, but, in 1961, 73 per cent of cattle were held on units less than 10 hectares in size.

54. These possibilities are explained by Klinge (1946), p. 726.

55. *West Coast Leader*, May 7, 1921, p. 1 and Aug. 21, 1923, p. 1.

56. Prado (1908), pp. 59–60; Blanchard (1975), Chap. 3, p. 2; U.K. Parliamentary Papers, 1908, Vol. CXV, p. 33. Poor weather in 1905 was supplemented by earthquakes in the Sierra which interrupted food supplies and caused increased rural-urban migration. The year 1907 was one of severe drought.

57. Twomey (1972), p. 33, makes a comparison of tariff levels over time.

CHAPTER 7

1. Bertram (1974), pp. 270–2.
2. Mariátegui (1971), Essay No. 6.
3. See Stein (1973).
4. The reaction of the Peruvian private sector to the policies of the post-1968 Government further demonstrates this point. See Chapter 14, Section 14.2.

5. The distinction between GNP and GDP is of significance in this conclusion, given the great importance of payments abroad to foreign factors of production.
6. Francia seized power in Paraguay in 1814 and for nearly forty years kept his country virtually isolated from the outside world. Paraguay being isolated and poor in natural resources, this was a relatively simple task; to close Peru off from international events would have been the achievement of a superman indeed.

PART III INTRODUCTION

1. U.S. Department of Commerce estimates indicate that the total book value of U.S. investments in Latin America and the Caribbean, having risen from $2 billion in 1919 to $3.6 billion in 1929, had fallen to $2.5 billion by 1940 and recovered to the 1929 level again only in 1947. By 1949 the total had reached $4.8 billion as the post-war surge of U.S. investment began (*Survey of Current Business*, Jan. 1951, p. 22).
2. Hunt (1974a), p. 2.
3. Bromley and Barbagelata (1945), pp. 117–18 show that the population of Lima-Callao doubled between 1920 and 1931 (from 249,000 to 500,000), but increased only 18 per cent from 1931 to 1940 (reaching 590,000 in the latter year). Using a slightly broader definition of the urban boundaries, *Anuario Estadistico*, 1969, p. 267 shows a 183 per cent increase in the population of Lima-Callao from 1940 to 1961. Annual average rates of growth based on these figures are 6.5 per cent 1920–31; 1.9 per cent 1931–40; and 3.0 per cent 1940–61.
4. The main parties were those of Sanchez Cerro, an Army officer with wide popular support who overthrew the Leguía régime in August 1930; and the Alianza Popular Revolucionaria Americana (APRA) led by V. R. Haya de la Torre, a former student leader exiled by Leguía who returned to Peru in 1931 to stand for the Presidency.
5. On the economic crisis of 1947–8 see Dragisic (1971) and Hayn (1957).

CHAPTER 8

1. *Extracto Estadistico*, 1934–5, p. 43.
2. For general surveys of mining in the thirties see Gerbi (1941), pp. 219–81, and for the forties see Fuentes (1950), Chapter 9; Sainte Marie (1945), pp. 175–240; and Pan American Union (1950), pp. 93–108.
3. Calculated from *Estadistica del Comercio Especial*, 1929, pp. 390–5. The output attributed to foreign large capital consists of copper bars, lead and bismuth bars of the types produced by Oroya, silver and gold concentrates and precipitates exported through Salaverry, zinc concentrates exported through Callao, and all vanadium exports. This results in some overestimation, particularly in relation to Northern Peru Mining's exports through Salaverry, but this is unlikely to have a significant effect upon the figures. (Note that, of Cerro's export revenue, about 10 per cent was passed on to suppliers. Bertram (1974), pp. 168–9).
4. *Estadistica del Comercio Especial*, 1935, pp. 229–32. On methodology see

Note 3; the overestimation problem is more serious in this year than in 1929 owing to the entry of new firms into lines of output formerly monopolised by the foreign firms, such as zinc concentrates and silver/gold precipitates.

5. *Estadística del Comercio Especial*, 1939, pp. 223–7. See Notes 3 and 4 above. The items listed in Note 3 sum to 73 per cent, but by now include substantial amounts of concentrates and precipitates actually produced by independents and exported through Salaverry and Callao.

6. The figures in Table 8.4 are constructed using the assay content of various metals in mining products, weighted by the current price of each metal in its refined state. This use of refined-metals prices to value metals actually contained in ores, concentrates, and unrefined smelter products, means that our figures understate Cerro's share in the actual value of final output, since the Oroya smelter turned out products of higher unit value than those of the independent mining sector. This accounts for the discrepancy between Table 8.4 and the figures on export value cited above.

7. Copper is not included in Part 2 of the Table since it was the dollar price which determined the decisions of the foreign firms, whose profits accrued in dollars rather than soles.

8. For the history of the cartels and the events of the thirties, see Skelton (1937); also *West Coast Leader*, Jan. 6, 1931, p. 3.

9. *West Coast Leader*, Apr. 26, 1932, p. 19; May 24, 1932, p. 1; June 7, 1932, p. 1; Nov. 29, 1932, Supplement p. 4.

10. *West Coast Leader*, Sep. 1, 1931, p. 1 and Sep. 22, 1931, p. 1.

11. *West Coast Leader*, Nov. 29, 1932, Supplement p. 4.

12. The smelter had been bought second-hand in Chile (*BOMP* No. 26, p. 8) and had suffered from severe technical difficulties, particularly the poor quality of the local coal on which it had to operate.

13. *West Coast Leader*, Nov. 25, 1924, p. 1; and Oct. 26, 1926, p. 4. Also *BOMP*, No. 8, p. 60, and No. 26, p. 8. Northern Peru took over several old gold mines at Pataz in 1924 and brought them into production in 1926 as part of the company's integrated activities in La Libertad.

14. Woods (1935); *West Coast Leader*, Dec. 30, 1930, p. 1. The mine had been taken over and rehabilitated by a new owner in 1927–28.

15. *West Coast Leader*, Jan. 20, 1931, p. 10. For the *Reglamento* of this law, No. 6909, see *West Coast Leader*, June 7, 1932, p. 5. A further law, No. 7601 of October 18, 1932, granted tax exemptions to encourage gold-mine development (Arias Schreiber, 1967, p. 5, Alvarado Garrido, 1939, p. 25). The texts of the *Reglamentos* of these laws appeared also in the 1935 mining statistics (*BCIM*, No. 117, pp. 97–126).

16. E.g. an attempt in 1932 by William Braden to persuade the Sanchez Cerro regime to grant him liberal terms for large-scale gold development (*West Coast Leader*, Aug. 9, 1932, p. 30).

17. A bill to this effect passed Congress in September 1935 (*West Coast Leader*, Oct. 8, 1935, p. 7).

18. Dunn (1925), p. 174 and *BOMP*, No. 8, p. 191 describe the successful operations of this company in the early 1920s. *West Coast Leader*, June 26, 1934 pp. 15–16 and Basadre (1963–64), Vol. 10, p. 4719 describe the problems and bankruptcy.

19. On the formation of the new Compania Explotadora de Cotabambas see

West Coast Leader, July 25, 1933, p. 13. On the 'airfreight spectacular' see *West Coast Leader*, June 20, 1933, p. 19 and June 26, 1934, pp. 15–18. The company was launched with a capital of S/30 million.

20. *BCIM*, 117, pp. 127–55; *West Coast Leader* Annual Industrial Number, Feb. 1938, p. lxxxvi; Hohagen (1937), pp. 78–80.

21. Fernandini and Rizo Patron were names familiar from the heyday of national enterprise around Cerro de Pasco at the turn of the century. The Bozas had been the leaders in development at the Millhuachaqui silver mines during the First World War but had sold out to ASARCO in 1924. (Note that in mentioning two Rizo Patron companies we are including here their Compania Minera Chanchamina which, although not listed in the sources given in Note 20 above, was the leading gold-mining company of 1938–9). Of the other two leading families in gold, the Alvarez Calderon family had become interested in mining as a result of Alfredo Alvarez Calderon's position as nominal President of Northern Peru Mining (he was a lawyer for the company).

22. So far as we are aware no study has yet been written of Rosenshine's fascinating career in Peruvian mining from 1920 to 1970. See, however, the article in *Peruvian Times* Mining and Petroleum Number, June 1953, p. 130.

23. Rosenshine succeeded in entering gold mining by buying or leasing deposits already staked out under the 1931 legislation by local companies.

24. Based on tables in 'La Industria Minera en Perú 1932–33' (BCIM No. 111), p. 19, and *Anuario de la Industria Minera en el Perú* (1939), p. 56. Note that the 1933 figure apparently does not take account of the contribution of custom ores to Cerro's production; this, however, was relatively low in 1933. If the 1939 figure is reconstructed on the basis of control of final output, the share of Cerro rises from 12 per cent to 30 per cent, due mostly to the inclusion in Oroya output of the production of the largest independent Peruvian mine, that of Carlos Rizo Patron at Chanchamina.

25. Bertram (1974) p. 164.

26. *West Coast Leader*, Jan. 30, 1937, p. 17; Nov. 6, 1934, p. 17; and Dec. 3, 1935, Supplement, p. 5.

27. The flotation concentrator was surprisingly slow in making its impact in Peru. The basic technology of the process had been proven by the First World War and a pioneering flotation plant had been installed by the Boza family at their La Guardia silver mine in 1918. During the 1920s, however, almost the only flotation plants built and operated in Peru were those of the large foreign firms— Cerro, Northern Peru Mining, and Vanadium Corporation. With the revival of national enterprise in gold, lead and zinc mining during the 1930s, the number of flotation concentrators in operation rose very rapidly. In 1935 there were nine base-metals concentrators operating (*BCIM* No. 117, p. 276, adding the Vanadium Corporation plant). By 1942 the number had risen to 17 (*Anuario de la Industria Minera*, 1942, pp. 70–3), while by 1954 there were 47 concentrators for lead and zinc alone (*Anuario de la Industria Minera*, 1954, pp. 160–3). The great advantage of the concentrator was that it could be installed at the mine site, and had very small fuel needs, since water power could be harnessed to run it. This was in sharp contrast to the smelters which had been the 1890s' equivalent of the concentrator; smelter after smelter in Peru had failed because of problems of fuel supply and location. Two other points about the concentrator deserve notice here: first, that its ability to recover zinc opened up an entirely new line of

mine production in Peru (since zinc was not recoverable by basic smelting technology); and second, that it made local mining companies less dependent upon the large central processing plants such as Oroya, since concentrates could be exported directly and sold on international markets.

28. For the history of these companies, see *Vademecum del Inversionista*, various years, and *Anuario de la Industria Minera*, 1947, p. 133; 1948 p. 139; and 1949, p. 185.

29. Based on company-by-company production data in the mining statistics.

30. *Anuario de la Industria Minera*.

31. *Peruvian Times*, Feb. 21, 1941, p. 8; and May 22, 1942, p. iii.

32. See Sainte-Marie (1945), pp. 191–8; *Peruvian Times*, Oct. 9, 1942, p. 17; *Peruvian Times*, Feb. 25, 1966, p. 15.

33. Carlos del Solar, in *Engineering and Mining Journal*, Apr., 1942.

34. Cerro's properties at Casapalca and Cerro de Pasco included the country's largest known lead and zinc deposits.

35. As indicated by the Corporation's *Annual Report and Balance Sheet* (see Table 5.7).

36. Northern Peru, as already noted, reopened its Quiruvilca mine in 1940. In 1943 Cerro began development of the Yauricocha mines (*Peruvian Times*, July 9, 1943, p. 49) and opened the new Paragsha concentrator at Cerro de Pasco (*El Serrano*, No. 59, Aug. 1954, pp. 3–4). Following the end of the war, despite severe shortages of imported materials, Cerro pushed ahead with new large-scale projects; the Yauricocha railway and a large electrolytic copper refinery at Oroya were both completed in 1948 (*Peruvian Times*, May 16, 1947, p. ii, and Sep. 10, 1948, pp. 5–6). In that year, also, Cerro finally embarked upon very rapid expansion of lead and zinc production from its own mines, and succeeded in trebling production of both metals by 1953.

37. *Peruvian Times* Mining and Petroleum Number, June 1953, p. 130.

38. *Anuario de la Industria Minera*, 1946, p. 146; Purser (1971), p. 132.

39. *Anuario de la Industria Minera*, 1945, p. 185.

40. Prices were under downward pressure at this time not only due to depressed demand but also as a result of the entry of cheap oil from East Texas and the Soviet Union on to the world market.

41. *Extracto Estadístico*, various years.

42. Haya de la Torre (1970).

43. The actual discovery was accidental: a U.S. geologist on a flight from Lima to Iquitos in 1929 spotted an eroded dome structure on the Pachitea River, and in early 1931, having obtained the backing of a Californian syndicate, he staked out a claim on the area. Survey work was completed by 1936. The first well struck oil, and the company went into commercial production in 1939. Although the limited size of the local market constrained expansion, by 1944 the company had seven producing wells and a 600-bpd refinery. For the early history of Ganso Azul see *West Coast Leader*, July 21, 1936, p. 15; Oct. 26, 1937, p. 13; and Industrial Number 1938–9, pp. 106–7; also *Peruvian Yearbook*, 1941 and 1944, p. 10; and *Estadística Petrolera*, 1948–9, pp. 62–4.

44. This was the Compania de Petroleo El Oriente, for the early history of which see *Peruvian Times*, June 22, 1945, front cover; and *Vademecum del Inversionista*, 1958–9, pp. 499–501. The company failed to find oil until the mid-1950s, despite several survey and drilling programmes.

45. On Decree-Law 8527 of Apr. 1937 see Jochamowitz (1939), pp. 85–6, and *West Coast Leader*, Apr. 27, 1937, p. 10.

46. *Peruvian Times*, Jan. 14, 1944, p. 2; June 22, 1945, front cover; Oct. 4, 1946, front cover; June 20, 1947., p. viii; and Feb. 13, 1948, front cover.

47. Jochamowitz (1939), pp. 84–5.

48. Jochamowitz (1939), p. 109; *West Coast Leader*, Sep. 22, 1939, p. 14.

49. *Estadística Petrolera*, 1948–9, p. 94; Despatch of Aug. 17, 1939, Homer Brett to State Department, D.F. 823.6363/204.

50. The Piaggio company had already made repeated but unsuccessful efforts to sell the field to IPC. Projected sale to Chilean interests in 1936 and Japanese interests in 1937 were both blocked by the Government on national security grounds (the oilfield being close to the frontier with Ecuador). After a year's negotiation the Government finally bought out the Piaggio firm for S/3 million, most of which was used to repay the company's heavy indebtedness to the Banco Italiano. Apart from solving the company's problems, the purchase provided the State venture with port and refinery installations, as well as a group of experienced technicians and workers. The details of the purchase are to be found in the U.S. diplomatic correspondence, particularly Despatch 861, Feb. 2, 1939, Laurence A. Steinhardt to State Department, D.F. 823.6363/196; Despatch 926, March 20, 1939, Steinhardt to State Department, D.F. 923.6363/200; and Despatch of Mar. 15, 1939, Homer Brett to State Department, D.F.823.6363/199. See also *Peruvian Times*, Jan. 28, 1941, p. 25.

51. *Peruvian Times*, Jan. 28, 1941, p. 25; Ramírez Novoa (1964), pp. 134–5. In 1946, on the basis of 1939 legislation, the State enterprise became 'Establecimientos Petroleros Fiscales' (E.P.F.).

52. An unenthusiastic Prado noted the discovery in his Annual Message for 1944; see *Peruvian Times*, Aug. 25, 1944, p. 5.

53. *Peruvian Times*, Sep. 15, 1944, p. 7.

54. This is especially evident in the drilling footages recorded by the company (see *Estadística Petrolera*, 1955, p. 39, and 1969, p. 66). From a peak of 26,000 feet drilled in 1940, E.P.F. had fallen to only 7,000 feet by 1944. Drilling activity was not revived from this low level until the 1950 regeneration of the company by Odría.

55. *Peruvian Times*, Aug. 1, 1947, p. 1.

56. On the political battle over the Sechura, see Pinelo (1973), pp. 44–8; Pike (1967), pp. 285–6; Carey (1964).

57. 'Confidential' enclosure in Despatch 926, March 20, 1939, Steinhardt to State Department, D.F.823.6363/200.

58. *Peruvian Times*, Feb. 14, 1947, p. 1, and July 11, 1947, p. 7.

59. *Boletín Oficial de Minas y Petroleo*, Año 6, No. 80, Oct., pp. 61–88, especially pp. 70–1 and 84–5.

60. See Bustamante's Annual Message for 1946, in *Peruvian Times*, Aug. 1–9, 1946, p. 13. It should be noted that compared with the terms on which the Sechura was eventually explored during the 1950s these terms were very favourable to Peru.

61. *Peruvian Times*, Oct. 24, 1947, p. 1; Oct. 31, 1947, p. 1 and 15–17.

62. The new policy involved reorganisation of E.P.F. as 'Empresa Petrolera Fiscal' by a decree of April 2, 1948, which empowered the new firm to make contracts on its own account with private capital; and a further decree of April

29, 1948, handing over control of the Sechura reserves to E.P.F. (For texts of these measures see *Anuario de la Industria Minera*, 1947, pp. 167–79.) On the failure of the policy see the article by W. M. Jablonski in *New York Journal of Commerce*, Apr. 16, 1948, reprinted in *Peruvian Times*, Apr. 30, 1948, p. 1.

63. For IPC's heated protests at the proposed new tax rate, supported by similar complaints from Lobitos, see *Peruvian Times*, Nov. 4, 1941, pp. 17–19; and Dec. 19, 1941, pp. 7 and 10. IPC's views were also forcefully communicated to the U.S. Embassy; see 'International Petroleum Company's Views of the Severity of the New Peruvian Petroleum Tax Law', Despatch 3197 of March 26, 1942, Henry F. Norweb to State Department, marked 'Strictly Confidential', D.F.823.6363/237. For discussion of the terms of the law see the speech by Mariano Velasco (Director of Mines and Petroleum) published in *La Prensa* (Lima), July 15, 1946, and reproduced in *Anuario de la Industria Minera*, 1945, p. 208. The tax law was promulgated as Law 9485.

64. Export tax payments from *Anuario de la Industria Minera*, 1942, p. 155, and 1944, p. 195. These are somewhat higher figures than those given retrospectively in *Estadística Petrolera*, 1948–9, p. 117.

65. Oil industry taxes are from *Anuario de la Industria Minera*, 1942, p. 155 and 1944, p. 195. Total revenues are from *Anuario Estadístico*.

66. The post-1968 oil policies of the military (on which see below, Chapter 15) were in this sense an extension of the same pattern: civilian governments incapable of producing workable oil policy, alternating with military régimes which pressed ahead with exploration by granting access to large international oil companies, while simultaneously building up the State sector.

CHAPTER 9

1. Imperial Preference for sugar was announced in Britain in 1934, at a time when (due to import and exchange controls in Chile) the British market was taking some 60 per cent of Peruvian exports. (*West Coast Leader*, Apr. 24, 1934, p. 11). In April 1934 the British Government agreed to discuss with Peru a possible bilateral trade treaty to give Peru a quota for sugar sales to Britain (SNA *Memoria*, 1934–5, p. 11); but when in late 1936 a trade treaty between the two finally emerged, it covered only cotton, wool and cinchona bark among Peru's exports; sugar gained no preferences (*West Coast Leader*, Oct. 6, 1936, p. 14). Australian and Indian production proceeded to displace Peruvian sugar from the British market (*West Coast Leader*, Apr. 4, 1937, p. 8).

2. SNA *Memoria*, 1934–5, p. 10. In 1935 this quota was raised to 7,000 tons (*West Coast Leader*, Jan. 8, 1935, p. 21), and in 1937 to 53,500 tons (*West Coast Leader*, Aug. 10, 1937, p. 21). 1938 sales to the U.S. were limited to 52,000 tons (*West Coast Leader*, Sept. 6, 1938, p. 9).

3. *West Coast Leader*, Mar. 22, 1932, p. 1; SNA *Memoria* 1931–2, p. 10.

4. *West Coast Leader* Jan. 31, 1933, p. 24; Mar. 20, 1934, p. 17; Sep. 4, 1934, p. 6; Feb. 5, 1935, p. 7; Nov. 12, 1935, p. 7; SNA *Memoria*, 1934–5, p. 11. The treaty, based upon the exchange of sugar for wheat, was signed in March 1934 and ratified (after strong opposition in the Peruvian Congress) in late 1935.

5. This followed an intense campaign by the sugar interest for tax relief. For successive memoranda on the issue submitted to the Government see *West Coast*

Leader, Aug. 1, 1933, p. 23; Oct. 9, 1934, p. 23; Nov. 6, 1934, Supplement p. 9; and SNA *Memoria* 1934–5, pp. 69–73.

6. For the text of Law 7920, SNA *Memoria*, 1934–5, pp. 73–5; for the debate and the Minister's statement, *West Coast Leader*, Nov. 13, 1934, pp. 1 and 6. For subsequent SNA complaints that the law did not go far enough, SNA *Memoria*, 1935–6, Anexo 4.

7. Calculated from SNA *Memorias*.

8. These estates were Roma (Larco family), Laredo (Chopitea family), Casagrande (Gildemeisters) and Cartavio (Grace). The Gildemeisters took over Roma in 1927, and Laredo about 1937.

9. The area was dominated by four élite families: the Aspillagas, Pardos, de la Piedras and Izagas.

10. *Unión de Productores de Azucar* (1945), p. 20. The increased concentration of cane-growing into the ecologically most-favoured regions is also said to have contributed to the rise in average yields; probably the droughts of the mid-1930s prevented this effect from showing up in the yield series earlier. On cane varieties see also *Peruvian Times*, Apr. 7, 1944, p. 13–16.

11. *Peruvian Times*, Apr. 3, 1942, p. 13.

12. *Peruvian Times*, May 5, 1942 p. 3; and June 26, 1942, p. 15.

13. *Peruvian Times*, June 25, 1943, p. 14; and Jan. 9, 1948, p. 8.

14. Production did better, but the increase was absorbed by local consumption, as the Table shows.

15. However, 1946 (the year before the exchange crisis really began to bite) did witness widespread installation of new milling machinery (*Pan American Union* (1950), p. 76).

16. Export taxes were levied on the difference between the officially-determined cost of production and the prevailing fob price—i.e. these were designed as simple profits taxes. The increases took two forms. One, explicit, form was the imposition in early 1942 of an additional tax of 10 per cent of any price excess over $1.30 per quintal fob (*Peruvian Times*, Jan. 2, 1942, p. 4; and Apr. 7, 1944, p. 15). The other, covert, increase consisted in the refusal of the Prado government to allow any increase in the notional 'production cost' of $0.90 per quintal, despite the fact that during the early 1940s inflation in Peru was rapidly pushing costs above this level, with the exchange rate fixed from 1940 on. The rate of tax on the industry's profits thus rose quite steeply, until in 1946 the notional-cost figure was finally raised to $1.70; but at the same time the rate of tax was sharply raised (*Pan American Union* (1950), pp. 81–3). Sugar export taxes collected as a percentage of the value of sugar exports, evolved as follows:

1939	0	1945	8
1940	2	1946	26
1941	1	1947	32
1942	7	1948	20
1943	10	1949	10
1944	9	1950	20

Source: *Anuario Estadistico*

For the planters' complaints against tax policies see *Memoria de la SNA*

(1944–5), pp. 72–6; (1945–6), pp. 68–74; and *Peruvian Times*, Feb. 1, 1946, pp. 12–13.

17. The supply of guano was in any case falling in the 1940s due to heavy mortality of guano-producing seabirds in 1941 when the '*El Nino*' ocean current disrupted ecological conditions in their feeding areas. For complaints that the sugar industry was not receiving its due share of the restricted supplies in the late 1940s, see *Memoria de la SNA* (1947–8), pp. 112–13. In 1943–4 the entire supply was allocated to foodcrops, with cotton and sugar plantations receiving none at all (*Peruvian Times*, Aug. 18, 1944. pp. 7–10).

18. As will be shown below, this affected cotton more than sugar, in so far as it was effective at all.

19. As late as June 1941, the planters were still regarding the local market as their most profitable outlet, and calling for government measures to stimulate consumption (*Memoria de la SNA* (1940–1), p. 11). By 1945, however, the fixed local price had become a major grievance; the *Memoria de la SNA* (1945–6), p. 30 claimed that besides being only one-quarter of the international sugar price, the local price was in fact below the current cost of production. One natural result of the system of quotas combined with low internal prices was the development of a flourishing contraband trade in sugar, with merchants buying on the local market at cheap prices and smuggling the sugar out to neighbouring countries (*Memoria de la SNA* (1946–7), pp. 89–92); by 1947 the local price was claimed to be only 10 per cent of the export price, which offered smugglers a good profit.

20. Augusto Gildemeister, however, invested at this point in the purchase of *La Prensa*, as a deliberate manoeuvre to extend his influence on policy and opinion. On this purchase and the thinking of both Beltran and Gildemeister on contemporary developments see the *Klein Correspondence* file. On this file, see Note 79 of Chapter 10, below.

21. Gerbi (1941), p. 130 (our translation).

22. Pan American Union (1950), p. 84. For similar remarks on the mid-1960s, when 130,000 worked in cotton and 600,000 were dependent upon it, see Zuniga (1970), p. 96.

23. Over the five years from 1930 to 1934, oil exports were worth $102 million and cotton exports were worth $61 million. Yet the returned value from cotton was at least $52 million (85 per cent) while that from oil was no more than $23 million (22 per cent).

24. Collin-Delavaud (1968), pp. 207–8; Harding (1975), p. 227.

25. Harding (1975), p. 227, quoting Castro Pozo: 'The northern landowners mean to avoid all the problems arising from the demands being made upon them by suppressing *yanaconaje* on their estates and cultivating the land themselves.'

26. Hammel (1962), p. 25, claims this to have been true of Ica.

27. In the Centre, *yanaconaje* remained the dominant institution in the thirties, with Japanese sharecroppers playing a major role. An article in the *West Coast Leader* (Aug. 17, 1937, p. 7) states that in the Rimac valley, where by 1935 over 80 per cent of the land was under cotton, no less than 90 per cent of the *yanaconas* were of Japanese descent, while the independent smallholders tended to be Peruvian. Matos Mar (1967), pp. 347–52, describes the importance of Japanese groups in Chancay in the 1930s, and notes (p. 347) that the wealthy Japanese and Chinese, who by 1934 had rented half of the valley's *haciendas*

from their Peruvian owners, relied during the 1930s upon the system of *yanaconaje*, with their countrymen obtaining many of the contracts. With the dispossession of the Japanese in Peru in 1942, *haciendas* in the Centre moved towards direct cultivation.

28. *Fortune*, Jan. 1938, p. 122. The two were Nikumatzu Okada, with 11,000 acres in Chancay, and the Cilloniz family, with 9,600 acres in Chincha.

29. Zuniga (1970), p. 102.

30. Calculated from the annual *Memorias* of the Camara Algodonera.

31. Gerbi (1941), pp. 344–5. On the origins of the Bank see Trant (1927) p. 53 and Gurney (1931), p. 13.

32. Lists of cotton dealers published annually in the Camara Algodonera *Memoria* from 1940 to 1971 make it possible to trace these shifts. British houses such as Locketts, Eccles and Milne were at the peak of their importance before the Second World War; U.S. houses such as Anderson Clayton increased their role in the 1930s but on the whole failed to establish a dominant position (the U.S.A. was never a very large buyer); Japanese merchants displayed a burst of activity in 1940–1; Peruvian, German and Argentinian firms were most important in the 1950s and 1960s.

33. For analysis of the long-run situation see Nogaro (1936).

34. U.S. farm price-support policy began with the Agricultural Marketing Act of March 1929. For a survey of the policy see El-Sarki (1964), pp. 21ff.

35. Calculated from *Cotton: World Statistics*, Apr. 1963.

36. From 1935 on, Peru was rapidly overtaken and outpaced as a cotton exporter by Brazil, whose exports increased from 5,000 bales in 1933 (compared to Peru's 215,000) to 1.6 million bales by 1939 (against Peru's 351,000). For comments on the benefits for Peru from the AAA and the Bankhead Act, see *Memoria de la SNA*, 1934–5, pp. 11–12; and *West Coast Leader*, Jan. 7, 1936, p. 5.

37. The 1933 cotton crop was the first for some years to sell well, with immediate benefits for the exchange rate and the business climate (*U.S. Commerce Reports*, July 1, 1933, p. 5 and Dec. 2, 1933, p. 356). The first reports of futures trading appeared in the business press in early 1935 (*West Coast Leader*, Mar. 12, 1935, p. i). An article by Manuel Montero Bernales discussing the appearance 'in recent years' of futures trading is in *West Coast Leader*, Mar. 1, 1938, pp. 5–7.

38. Relative price calculations from the price indices in *Extracto Estadístico*.

39. Ferrero (1938), p. 7, estimated the total of coastal cultivated land as 430,000 ha; of this, cotton occupied 44 per cent, sugar 12 per cent and rice 9 per cent.

40. *Cotton: World Statistics*, Apr. 1963, pp. 14–16.

41. *Cotton: Monthly Review of the World Situation* Apr. 1948, p. 158.

42. *Ibid.*, Sep. 1949, p. 1 and Oct. 25, 1949, p. 1.

43. *Memoria de la Camara Algodonera del Perú* (1940), p. 8. Freight rates to Britain, however, were rising steeply.

44. *Memoria de la Camara Algodonera del Perú* (1940), pp. 12–13.

45. *Memoria de la Camara Algodonera del Perú* (1941), pp. 6 and 9.

46. *Memoria de la Camara Algodonera del Perú* (1942), pp. 3–5.

47. On the high hopes initially aroused by the new flax industry see *Peruvian Times*, Oct. 31, 1941, p. 21; and *Memoria de la Camara Algodonera del Perú* (1940) and (1941). For the subsequent disillusionment, *Peruvian Times*, Feb. 5, 1943, p. 11; Nov. 17, 1944, p. 17, and Feb. 14, 1947, p. 9; also *Memoria de la*

Camara Algodonera del Perú (1943), p. 10.

48. *Memoria de la Camara Algodonera* (1942), p. 8; *Peruvian Yearbook*, June 1944, p. 51 .
49. *Memoria de la Camara Algodonera* (1943), p. 7 and Anexo 26.
50. *Peruvian Times*, Apr. 20, 1945, p. 1.
51. *El Economista Peruano*, Mar. 1, 1942, p. 588.
52. *El Economista Peruano*, May 1943, p. 178. The legislation was extended explicitly to sugar plantations in March 1943 (sugar ceasing to be accepted as a 'basic foodcrop'). For a survey of this and subsequent similar legislation in Peru see Sociedad Nacional Agraria (1964).
53. *Peruvian Yearbook* (1944), p. 51.
54. *West Coast Leader*, Aug. 19, 1924, p. 1, reported a scheme by a U.S.-Peruvian syndicate to establish a cannery in Ilo. *West Coast Leader*, Feb. 3, 1925, p. 1 and July 6, 1926, p. 3, reported the granting, and subsequent rescinding, of a government monopoly concession for fishing development to a private group.
55. Iparraguirre Cortez (1965), pp. 13–15; Edmonds (1972), p. 6.
56. For descriptions of these early ventures see *West Coast Leader*, May 4, 1937, p. 15; May 25, 1937, p. 10; Mar. 1, 1938, p. 13; and National Products Number, 1939, p. 30; also Edmonds (1972), p. 6.
57. *Peruvian Times*, Oct. 31, 1941, p. 1; Dec. 28, 1945, p. 7, and Fisheries Number, 1950, p. 6; Jan. 10, 1958, pp. 12–13.
58. Thorndike (1973), pp. 86–7; Abramovich (1973), pp. 116–17. The company was Industrial Pesquera SA in Callao, the founder Miguel Capurro, and the bank the Prado's Banco Popular.
59. *Peruvian Times*, Aug. 21, 1942, p. 5.
60. Uriarte (1960) p. 10; *Peruvian Times*, Dec. 28, 1945, p. 7.
61. The average investment in the largest canneries established at this time was less than $100,000, while small plants could be built for a tiny fraction of this amount (*Peruvian Times*, Nov. 1, 1946, p. 1).
62. *Peruvian Times*, Fisheries Number, 1950, pp. 5–6; and Jan. 10, 1958, p. 13.
63. Juan Gildemeister's Compania Maritima Pesquera at Chancay was the main example.
64. This was Empresa Pesquera Ilo, begun in 1945 by the Wilbur-Ellis Company with Peruvian partners. The management, and subsequently control, of the enterprise was put in the hands of one of the Peruvians, Manuel Elguera. The pioneer Miguel Capurro was also involved (*Peruvian Times*, Apr. 6, 1945, cover; and Southern Peru Number, 1951, p. 45).
65 Abramovich (1973), p. 16 notes the arrival in the 1940s of a group of exiled Spanish fishermen who later pioneered the fishing of anchovy in Peru.

CHAPTER 10

1. For example, the export sectors in which capital-intensity had been increasing most rapidly, namely sugar production and copper mining, fell back relative to activities which had more equal distribution of income, such as cotton-growing, fishing, and small or medium-scale mining.
2. It should be noted that several of the countries which display high rates of

growth of their government sectors relative to exports during the 1930s in Table 10.1 were also achieving more rapid export growth than Peru (Table 8.1).

3. As Stein (1973) demonstrates, Sanchez Cerro while President relied almost entirely on advisers drawn from the élite.

4. They were more divided over the issues of exchange-rate depreciation (which obviously suited the export producers rather well) and default on the foreign debt (which as all could see, did little damage in the context of the 1930s and certainly eased the external problem).

5. See Stein (1973).

6. *Extracto Estadistico*, 1934–5, p. 279. In addition to direct cuts, the payment of public-sector wages and salaries was subject to increasing delays until the necessary revenues were forthcoming (*U.S. Commerce Reports*, Aug. 26, 1933, p. 137).

7. Basadre (1963–4), Vol. XI, p. 89.

8. See, for example, Prado's Annual Message for 1940, in *El Economista Peruano*, July 31, 1940, p. 307, in which '*todas las inteligencias y todos los brazos*' of Peru were offered government posts provided they supported Prado.

9. *Anuario Estadistico* (1950), pp. 628 and 638. For an example of early alarm at the inflationary consequences, see *El Economista Peruano*, Feb. 29, 1940, p. 227 and Dec. 31, 1940, p. 379.

10. Data from *Extracto Estadistico*. The increase came both from the explicit increases in export taxes legislated in 1941, and from the manipulation of the official shadow-costs estimate. The tax was imposed on the margin between this shadow cost and the actual price received; holding down the cost figure in this way, while inflation proceeded in the real world, had the immediate result of increasing the real tax burden.

11. The average exchange rate for 1934–6 was S/4.18 to the dollar. After considerable depreciation in 1939, and at a time of acute crisis (with the Central Bank's holdings of convertible foreign exchange representing less than five days' imports) stabilisation was undertaken at a rate of S/6.50 (*West Coast Leader*, Dec. 3, 1944, p. 19). The rate is generally considered to have been set too low, adding fuel to the inflation of the subsequent two years; see Ferrero (1946).

12. Alexander (1957), p. 230, describes the Communist-led trade union movement's policy of cooperation with the Government during the war. Warren (1976) calculates the fall in real wages in the industrial sector to have been roughly 15 per cent between 1940 and 1944. He finds also a rise of between 30 per cent and 45 per cent in the share of gross surplus in gross output in six industries between 1940 and 1945. Other sources also document the decline of real wages during those years.

13. From 1940 to 1945 the cost of living index increased by 70 per cent (*Anuario Estadistico*).

14. Bertram (1976), Table 4. 'Capital goods' here includes industrial machinery and heavy transport equipment. Excluding transport, the drop was from 19 per cent at the 1938 peak to less than 15 per cent in 1943.

15. *Ministerio de Industria y Turismo* (hereafter *M.I.T.*) (1974), Part II, p. 22. Despite its title, the law was not specifically designed to promote industry, and was in fact used to benefit enterprises in commerce and agriculture as well as manufacturing.

16. *Peruvian Times*, Jan. 15, 1943, p. 1. The factory was established to use

rubber produced in the Amazon under a U.S. promotional scheme.

17. On the Santa Corporation project see *Peruvian Yearbook*, 1943–4, pp.12–13.

18. Carey (1964), p. 107.

19. Pike (1967), p. 277.

20. *Peruvian Times*, Apr. 24, 1942, cover; and Aug. 7, 1942, pp. i-ix (Prado's Annual Message for the year).

21. Carey (1964), p. 107. Peru received considerably more lend-lease aid than did other Andean countries.

22. *Peruvian Times*, Feb. 1, 1946, Supplement, p. ii, covers the history of the U.S.-backed revival of the Amazon rubber industry during the war. Production was raised from 65 tons in 1941 to 2,300 tons by 1945, but following the end of the war the industry again sank into depression.

23. Pike (1967), p. 277.

24. Hunt (1974a), p. 4 remarks that 'The deposed President Bustamante, sitting down in exile to write a defense of his administration, produced a political testament that never once mentioned foreign companies. . . . With the United States standing at its zenith, only *termacefalos* would think of attacking North American investments in postwar Peru.'

25. Ferrero (1957), p. 26.

26. A critique of Peru's economic performance during the Second World War, written by Francisco Tudela y Varela and making essentially the points discussed above, appeared in *El Economista Peruano*, Mar. 1944, pp. 297–8.

27. *El Economista Peruano*, June–July 1946, pp. 555–6; *Peruvian Times*, July 12, 1946, p. 1.

28. *Peruvian Times*, Apr. 18, 1947, pp. 15–16.

29. Hayn (1957) gives a full description of the experience with import controls and the degree of disorganisation which prevailed. See also *Peruvian Times*, June 13, 1947, p. 14.

30. See, for example, *Peruvian Times*, Feb. 7, 1947, p. 18.

31. See, for example, his first presidential manifesto, in *El Economista Peruano* July 31, 1945, p. 450.

32. *El Economista Peruano*, Aug.–Sep. 1945, pp. 466–7, *Peruvian Times*, Aug. 17, 1945, p. 1 and Oct. 5, 1945, p. 1.

33. Quoted in *Peruvian Times*, Feb. 20, 1948, p. 16.

34. Gildemeister and Beltran, for example, were happy with the result, confident in and amused by the deradicalisation of APRA. Gildemeister described how Aprista agents had gathered his workers at Trujillo 'and told them everything would remain as it was, no partition of the land or other properties or money, but creation of new wealth for the whole country thro' them all. It is really funny.' (Gildemeister to Beltran, July 5, 1945, Klein correspondence file.) On this file, see Thorp (1974).

35. Initially by naming a Cabinet not dominated by Apristas; but the issues became increasingly broad. See Pike (1967), p. 283–90.

36. Negotiations for this purpose were begun in 1945, in an attempt to clear the way for a $25 million Export-Import Bank loan which had been negotiated in 1941, but blocked since then pending some agreement on the defaulted debt (*Peruvian Times*, Nov. 30, 1945, Supplement p. 1). The opening of negotiations was greeted by the immediate granting of a new $30 million Export-Import

credit (*Peruvian Times*, Dec. 14, 1945, p. 1). The proposed settlement terms, however, were rejected by the powerful U.S. Foreign Bondholders' Protective Council in 1947 (*Peruvian Times*, Mar. 14, 1947, p. 7), and it was several more years before a mutually-satisfactory agreement was finally reached in the early 1950s.

37. See the post-election interviews with these two politicians published in *Peruvian Times*, July 6, 1945, p. 1.

38. *Wall Street Journal*, quoted in *West Coast Leader*, June 27, 1947.

39. *West Coast Leader*, Oct. 30, 1934, p. 7.

40. *West Coast Leader*, Nov. 20, 1934, Supplement, pp. ii–iii.

41. *West Coast Leader*, May 14, 1935, p. 7.

42. *U.S. Commerce Reports*, June 29, 1935, p. 425 commented with satisfaction that the quota had meant an increase in orders for U.S. manufacturers.

43. *West Coast Leader*, Jan. 21, 1936, p. 5. A report in *U.S. Commerce Reports*, Mar. 7, 1936, p. 128 was confident that U.S. exports to Peru would not be affected by the new schedule.

44. *West Coast Leader*, Nov. 28, 1941, p. 21 and Dec. 19, 1941, p. 1.

45. Calculated from data in *Extracto Estadistico*.

46. Only one per cent of Peruvian imports of cotton textiles in 1939 came from Latin American suppliers; by 1943 the figure had risen to 60 per cent. Shortages which might have induced further rapid expansion of the local industry were thus largely mitigated. Textile exports from Peru were non-existent.

47. Wilson (1934), p. 6, described the beginning of expansion in private construction as being concentrated on medium-sized houses and villas, many of them for renting and representing 'in large part' the deliberate investment of funds which people did not like to leave liquid either in Peru or abroad.

48. For example *West Coast Leader*, Feb. 23, 1937, p. 11 compared the state of the building trade with 'the boom days of the Leguía regime.'

49. The absolute figures in Table 10.4 should be given no weight, considering the problems of classification and valuation of capital. The relative swing towards construction and agriculture, and the obviously relatively small scale of manufacturing promotions (indicating their sub-élite character) are the important points.

50. *El Economista Peruano*, Aug. 1, 1941, pp. 483–4; *Peruvian Times*, Dec. 17, 1943, p. iii and Nov. 24, 1944, p. 5.

51. Descriptions of this brief burst of activity are to be found in the 'Annual Industrial Numbers' published by the *West Coast Leader* in 1936 and February 1938. In one case, pharmaceuticals, the very rapid increase in the number of small laboratories operating resulted in an increase in imports of semi-elaborated chemical products from 1.8 per cent of total imports in 1928 to 3.0 per cent in 1935 (Bertram, 1976). A list of some of the pharmaceuticals ventures launched during the 1930s and 1940s is in Fuentes (1950) p. 148. It may be noted that by the end of 1936, total employment in manufacturing was estimated by the SNI as 26,000 (*West Coast Leader*, Special Industrial Number, Feb. 1938, p. lxxxiv) compared with 14,000 in the 1933 census (Hohagan (1936), p. xvii). Part of this increase, however, was no doubt attributable to the use of different definitions of industrial employment.

52. For Brazil, see Fishlow (1972); for Argentina, Diaz Alejandro (1970), p. 95.

53. A speech by Ricardo Madueno, managing director of the new bank, reported in *West Coast Leader*, Dec. 14, 1937, pp. 26–7, was filled with good intentions but devoid of definite proposals or strategies for industrial promotion. A survey of the Bank's outstanding loans at the end of 1938 (*West Coast Leader*, Annual Industrial Number, 1938–9, p. xxi) showed 8 per cent of the S/5.8 million loaned to cotton gins, and 42 per cent more to textiles and tanning. Textiles alone accounted for 34 per cent.

54. *U.S. Commerce Reports*, Mar. 3, 1936, p. 188; Dec. 4, 1937, p. 958; Feb. 5, 1938, p. 122. Substitution of rayon for cotton, which gathered force during the 1930s, accounted for only a small part of this stagnation.

55. The same pattern appeared in imports of machinery for the textile industry; the U.K. *Annual Statement of Trade*, Vol. 3 for years 1932 to 1938, shows that the peak year for spinning machinery imports to Peru was 1933, after which they fell steadily.

56. Namely the Los Andes woollen mill in Huancayo (1931), W. R. Grace's paper mill at Paramonga (1939), Fleischmann's yeast factory in Lima (1941), General Milk Company's 'Leche Gloria' plant in Arequipa (1942), Goodyear's tyre factory (1943), W. R. Grace's chemicals plant at Paramonga (early 1940s), Lanificio woollen mill (1944–6), a planned cement factory for Arequipa (1941–5), Rayon Peruana (1946). Other ventures of slightly lesser rank were Papelera Peruana (1936–7), Grace's extension to the Inca textile mill (1939), Productora Peruana chemical plant (1943), Coca Cola bottling plants in Lima and Arequipa (1946) and a joint venture of Grace and Arthur Field y La Estrella to rebuild the latter's burnt-out factory (1947).

57. Namely Los Andes (the Pardo family), Lanificio (Wiese brothers), the proposed Arequipa cement factory (families including Ugarteche, Bustamante, Belaunde, Romana, Gibson, Said, Diaz), and Rayon Peruana (Dibos, Berckemeyer, Gildemeister, Ferreyros, Larranaga). The difficulties encountered by the Arequipa cement venture are symptomatic of the reasons for élite abstention from industrial investment; established in 1941, the company was still in 1945 endeavouring to obtain the necessary imported equipment. (*Peruvian Times*, Feb. 4, 1941, cover; May 7, 1943, p. 7; and Mar. 16, 1945, p. 7.)

58. No time-series data disaggregated by area are available. But such evidence as there is on yields suggests very little change in either Coast or Sierra. Thus, yields in maize and wheat stayed constant between 1929 and 1943, and in rice, potatoes and barley rose between four and seven per cent over the same period. Annual series for wheat and rice show that the two years were not abnormal. (Data for 1929, Ministerio de Fomento y Obras Públicas (1932); for 1943, Pan American Union (1950) and *Anuario Estadistico*.)

59. *West Coast Leader*, July 5, 1932, p. 13.

60. *West Coast Leader*, Jan. 24, 1933, p. 23.

61. A 1930 law authorised the Government to buy up to 100 per cent of the harvest of new wheat varieties which they wished to encourage in certain areas (Furnish and Muñoz Cabrera (1966), p. 33), and wheat benefited from a preferential freight rate on the Central Railway, while wheat-carrying lorries were exempt from tolls (*West Coast Leader*, May 30, 1933, p. 21). In 1934 local flourmills were ordered to purchase a fixed quota of local wheat, and in 1936 further measures were enacted to enforce this (*West Coast Leader*, Oct. 2, 1934, p. 7, and Jan. 7, 1936, p. 6). In 1937 an experimental station started under

Leguía was revived to try to develop a rust-resistant wheat suitable for the Coast (*West Coast Leader*, Mar. 30, 1937, p. 21).
62. As mentioned in note 58, the wheat yield did not change during this period. The average area under wheat was 118,000 ha in 1926–30, and 123,000 ha in 1936–40 (*Anuario Estadistico*, 1951, p. 248).
63. Calculated from *Anuario Estadistico*, various years.
64. In the early thirties rice was generally described as a peasant crop (see, for example, *West Coast Leader*, May 31, 1932, p. 7). By the 1960s, on the contrary, less than 10 per cent of producers were responsible for 75 per cent of output (Shepherd, Prochezka and Furnish (1967), p. 36).
65. See, for example, Klinge (1946), p. 405, on the problems encountered by these laws. A survey of this and subsequent legislation is in *Sociedad Nacional Agraria* (1964).
66. A description of the design and application of food price controls during the war years is 'Comunicado de la Contraloria General de Precios' in *El Economista Peruano*, Apr. 1944, pp. 319–20.
67. *El Economista Peruano*, Nov. 30, 1940, p. 365.
68. The failure of the 1941 rice crop had a particularly severe impact (*Peruvian Times*, Apr. 1, 1943, p. 2).
69. These measures are all documented in the regular reports in *El Economista Peruano*. See particularly Mar. 1, 1942, p. 588, Apr. 1, 1942, p. 1, June 1, 1942, pp. 34–5, June 1943, p. 187, May 1943, p. 178.
70. *El Economista Peruano*, Feb. 1944, p. 286; Apr. 1944, p. 311; Dec. 31, 1946, p. 597; May –June, 1947, p. 637; and Nov. –Dec., 1947, pp. 671–3.
71. Twomey (1972), p. 33. It should be noted also that food was the only category of imports excluded from the 1941 tariff adjustment (*El Economista Peruano*, Sep. 1, 1941, p. 502).
72. In this one case, however, the effort was substantial. By 1946 the rice subsidy was accounting for 5 per cent of government spending (estimated from data in Shepherd and Furnish (1967), p. 32, and Merrill and Prochezka (1967), pp. 36–7; Government expenditure from Hunt (1971)).
73. A considerable amount of coastal land which in the 1930s had been used for cattle-bearing was switched to crops from the late 1930s on.
74. Furnish and Muñoz Cabrera (1966), p. 25.
75. Harding (1975); Alberti (1970).
76. *Peruvian Times*, Jan. 24, 1947, p. 1.
77. *Estadistica del Comercio Especial*, 1936 and 1948.
78. A dramatic early manifestation of this opposition was the attempt by the Peruvian Ambassador in Washington, Pedro Beltran, to force a devaluation on the Peruvian Government via the recommendations of a U.S. economic mission sent to Peru in late 1945. When the manipulation came to light Beltran was immediately dismissed, following which he returned to Lima to edit *La Prensa* and orchestrate opposition to the regime. (On the devaluation affair see *Peruvian Times*, Dec. 28, 1945, Supplement p. 1).
79. The role of pressure from the élite, in close cooperation with foreign capital, is clearly illustrated in the Klein correspondence, a correspondence file from the Gildemeister sugar estate now held in the Centro de Documentación Agraria, Lima. The file is labelled 'Klein' since many of the letters concern the 1949 mission mentioned in the text, known as the Klein–Saks mission. The

letters comprise the correspondence of Augusto Gildemeister with Pedro Beltran and with Douglas Heddon Allen, a New York business consultant with interests in the Amazon. Thus, for example, foreign pressure is mobilised over the exchange rate. Beltran is asked to mobilise Cerro in New York: 'Perhaps we might get them as allies so as not to be the only ones who are complaining about putting the brakes on deliveries of dollars' (A.G. to P.B. Aug. 10, 1948). Care is taken that such pressures should appear to be independent. The U.S. Chamber of Commerce is persuaded to cable approval of the freeing of the exchange (Nov. 11, 1949). The Klein Mission is carefully supervised, directly and indirectly (D.H.A. to A.G. Nov. 21, 1948, A.G. to P.B. Nov. 3, 1950) and used to apply pressure for the lifting of import controls. These are only a few of many examples (the correspondence is reviewed in Thorp (1974) (mimeo)).

PART IV INTRODUCTION

1. The only series for the 1940s is at current prices, and in any case not very reliable. For what it is worth, the growth rate given by the series for 1948 to 1950 is 4 per cent or 17 per cent, deflating in one case by the wholesale price index and in the other (much less appropriately) by the cost of living (*La Renta Nacional del Peru 1942–4*, p. 24).
2. During the first five years of the military government, 1969–73, growth was maintained at 6 per cent by means discussed in Chapter 15 below.
3. Taking the rate of population growth as 2.3 per cent p.a. for 1950–9, 2.9 per cent p.a. for 1960–2, and 2.5 per cent p.a. since 1962, on the basis of series in *Anuario Estadístico* 1969, p. 215, for years to 1961, and the 1972 census result for 1962–72.

CHAPTER 11

1. Goodsell (1974), pp. 153–4 indicates that the Law was 'greatly influenced, if not dictated, by the wishes of Cerro' and other mining interests. That ASARCO was also directly involved in pressing for favourable new legislation to cover the Toquepala project is evident from speeches and meetings of a group of top ASARCO executives who visited Peru in early 1949; see, for example, *Peruvian Times*, Jan. 21, 1949, cover.
2. The text of the Law with an English translation appeared in *Peruvian Times* Mining and Petroleum Number, June 1953. For discussion of its terms and implications see Samamé Boggio (1971) and Purser (1971), Chap. 11.
3. Hunt (1974b), pp. 11–12.
4. Calculated from *Anuario de la Industria Minera*, 1956. Cerro accounted for 22 per cent of lead production and 38 per cent of zinc; and minor foreign firms produced the remainder.
5. See the company-by-company production data in annual issues of *Anuario de la Industria Minera*. The two non-local entrants were Compania Minera Buenaventura (a joint venture by Cerro and a local engineer) and the new Northern Peru Mining Company mine at Chilete. The most successful of the

new local firms was Compañia Minera Milpo, which entered production in 1951.

6. *El Economista Peruano*, Jan. – Mar. 1954, p. 202.

7. For the history of SPCC see Purser (1971), Chap. 5; Ballantyne (1974); Goodsell (1974), pp. 154–5.

8. This at any rate is Hunt's interpretation – Hunt (1974b), p. 12.

9. For the history of Marcona see Purser (1971), Chap. 5, and Ballantyne (1974).

10. *El Economista Peruano*, Aug. – Oct. 1952, p. 108; *Peruvian Times*, Sep. 26, 1958, Supplement.

11. Purser (1971), p. 156.

12. The necessary geological and engineering studies had been completed by the Santa Corporation, the road from the mines to the port of San Juan constructed, and a start made on the port works, by early 1950 (*El Economista Peruano*, Jan. – Mar. 1950, pp. 819–20). When the mines were leased to the Marcona Mining Company in 1952, less than a year's further development work was required before production started (in May 1953). Lindqvist (1972), p. 246, estimates that the Santa Corporation spent roughly $2 million on early development work, and that by the end of 1953 (at a point when exports had already yielded gross profits of $4.0 million) the Marcona Mining Company had invested an additional $7–8 million. Thereafter, the mine's profits were sufficient to finance all subsequent investment. To complete the development of the project, in other words, the Peruvian Government would have had to raise no more than $8 million, of which $4 million could have been paid off in the first year. Instead, the leasing of the mines was followed by a drastic cutback in the Santa Corporation's activities in other areas as well, with all current projects except the Santa hydroelectric plant either hived-off or closed down (*El Economista Peruano*, Aug. – Oct. 1952, p. 108). It may be noted that the Quiroz irrigation scheme of the early 1950s (see below) cost the Government $11 million, more than the cost of developing Marcona.

13. Beginning with an explosives factory 'EXSA', which opened in 1959 (*Peruvian Times*, Aug. 14, 1959, p. 3).

14. Explosivos SA (established 1956, production began 1959); Compania Peruana de Electrodos Oerlikon SA (1960, welding rods); Metalurgica Peruana SA (1961, grinding balls); and Refractarios Peruanos SA (1950s, furnace bricks).

15. E.g. Industrias de Cobre SA (1952, copper wire and cables); Compania Industrial del Centro (1966, copper rods and sulphuric acid); Metales Industriales del Peru SA (1964, extrusions); and Fundicion de Metales Bera del Peru SA (late 1960s, lead alloys).

16. The results of these two enquiries are summarised in Malpica (1968), pp. 174–202. The Santa Corporation's report on Marcona was never published; but the Congressional committee report on Toquepala, with a separate volume of documentary evidence, appeared in 1967 (Comisión Bicameral Multipartidaria, etc. (1967)). Lindqvist (1972), pp. 224–53, surveys the figures from both reports and adds additional data of his own. Hunt (1974b) also contributes calculations on the profitability of the two companies.

17. Consolidated results obtained from the same source appear also in Malpica (1968), p. 183, Lindqvist (1972), p. 226, and Ballantyne (1974).

18. The figures in Table 11.6 are not particularly sensitive to changes in our

assumptions. Even lowering the assumed import-content of materials purchases to 60 per cent would raise returned value only slightly above 30 per cent. If the sales figure were to turn out to be a cif rather than a fob figure, a 20 per cent downward adjustment in this figure would increase returned value only to 26 per cent.

19. Comisión Bicameral, etc. (1967), Anexo 23, 'Recuperacion de Inversiones 1960–65.'

20. *Peruvian Times*, Apr. 16, 1965, 'Toquepala Supplement', p. v. The original investment as of 1960 was $205 million, a figure which the investigating commission considered to have been artificially inflated for accounting purposes (see Lindqvist (1972), p. 229).

21. *Peruvian Times*, Dec. 15, 1967, p. 1. It must of course be recognised that the enormous scale of the investment in Toquepala meant that as a percentage return on capital its earnings were lower than had been the case with the oil companies in the 1920s.

22. Lindqvist (1972), pp. 240–53; Hunt (1974b), pp. 35–8. Hunt estimates the internal rate of return for Marcona 1952–71 as 28 per cent.

23. The main difficulties are two: first, that no breakdown of costs between local purchases and imports is available, and second, that Marcona used undervalued transfer prices as a means of extracting roughly half of its actual profits during its first decade of operation, with the result that the value of sales as reported to the Peruvian authorities and shown in the official trade statistics is about 25 per cent too low (Lindqvist (1972), pp. 249–51). Lindqvist's figures are confirmed by the more detailed discussion in Hunt (1974b).

24. Hunt (1974b) p. 16.

25. *Peruvian Times*, June 21, 1968, p. 1.

26. Law 16892 of Feb. 24, 1968, laid down the basis for the negotiation of future contracts under Article 56 (*Peruvian Times* Mar. 1, 1968, pp. 1–2; and Mar. 8, 1968, p. 2). Negotiations were then renewed, and in mid-1968 SPCC and Anaconda announced their willingness to proceed with Cuajone and Cerro Verde, respectively (*Peruvian Times*, June 28, 1968, p. 1; and July 5, 1968 p. 3). The contracts had not been finalised before the government fell.

27. Figures published annually in the US *Survey of Current Business* show that from 1955 to 1959 the net capital inflow generated by US mining companies in Peru totalled $130 million, while repatriated profits were $45 million. For 1960–4 the corresponding figures were $25 million and $85 million; the foreign companies had thus become net extractors of surplus on the balance of payments. For 1965–9 capital inflows rose to $115 million while repatriated earnings soared to $415 million; and for 1970–2 capital inflows were minus $27 million while repatriated earnings were $105 million.

28. On multinational strategies in minerals see Girvan (1970). The attitude of Anaconda was summed up in a 1967 article: 'Between 1918 and the early 1960s this particular deposit at Cerro Verde did not appear profitable in comparison with other deposits available to Anaconda. But in accordance with mining company practices all over the world, the company maintained its claims, in case higher prices should justify Cerro Verde's exploitation' (*Peruvian Times*, Aug. 18, 1967, p. 3.)

29. *Peruvian Times*, June 18, 1965, p. 1; and May 19, 1967, p. 1.

30. *Peruvian Times*, Oct. 11, 1968, p. 2.

31. The events considered worthy of note here were the entry as producers of lead, zinc, gold and/or copper of the Santander (1959), Condor* (1959), Minera Cerro* (1960), Natomas (1962), Raura (1963), Condestable (1964), *Cobre SA* (1965), Cobriza (1966), Chavin (1967), Santa Rita (1968), Santa Luisa (1968), Gran Bretana (1969), Canaria* (1969), *Cata* (1971), *Atalaya* (1972) and Madrigal (1972) mines. Of these sixteen, Peruvian firms are marked with an asterisk and unidentified firms are italicised. The other four events consisted of takeovers and subsequent development of existing mines: Chapi (1960), Huanca (1965), Lampa Mining Company (1966) and Katanga (1968). The 1966 takeover of the Huanzala mine by the Japanese firm Mitsui appears in the first set under 'Santa Luisa.' The leading firms were Mitsui, the St. Joseph Lead Company, Hochschilds and the Homestake Mining Company.

32. One partial exception being the Ballon family's new zinc mine at Vitoc, opened in 1970. As high officials in the military regime's mining administration, the family were in an unusually secure position.

33. Purser (1971), pp. 254–5.

34. In addition to the Petroleum Law discussed below, these included a reorganisation of E.P.F. followed by rapid expansion of its activities (*Anuario de la Industria Minera*, 1948, pp. 166–70; *Peruvian Times*, Sep. 23, 1949, p. 1; *Estadística Petrolera*, 1948–9, pp. 16, 56 and 82A, and 1950, pp. 14A and 27). The Government also imposed a local-market quota on the Lobitos company, leading directly to a merger of Lobitos with IPC, beginning as a partnership in 1950 and culminating with IPC's purchase of a 50 per cent share in CPL in 1957 (Pinelo, 1973, p. 52; *Peruvian Times*, July 18, 1958, p. 22).

35. A New York oil consultant employed by the Government prepared an extremely liberal draft (*Anuario de la Industria Minera*, 1945, p. 211) which Bustamante had accepted in principle (*Peruvian Times*, Aug. 1 1947, p. 20).

36. *Peruvian Times*, Jan. 7–14, 1949, p. 11; *El Economista Peruano*, Oct. – Dec. 1949, pp. 799–802.

37. *El Economista Peruano*, Oct. – Dec. 1951, p. 49; and Jan. – Mar. 1952, p. 63. The first of these references contains a summary of nationalist criticisms voiced in the Chamber of Deputies.

38. Full texts of the Law in English and Spanish are reproduced in *Peruvian Times*, Mining and Petroleum Number, June 1953, pp. 89–101.

39. E.P.F. retained control of the areas granted to it in Bustamante's decrees of 1948. It may be noted that, like the 1922 law, that of 1952 provided that abandoned concessions reverted to state reserve.

40. Article 6 of the law defined 'national' companies as those with a minimum of 60 per cent local capital. Their privilege was the right to put in applications for exploration areas during a preliminary 'Peruvians-only' period before foreign bids were considered. National companies were also to have preferential access to state reserve areas.

41. *Estadística Petrolera*, 1952, p. 118.

42. *Peruvian Times*, Jan. 23–30, 1953.

43. *Peruvian Times*, Mining and Petroleum Number, June 1953, Supplement, p. iv.

44. See the list of concessions granted up to the end of 1953 in *Estadística Petrolera*, 1953, pp. 117–18. A map of these companies' holdings appeared in the *Peruvian Times*, Mining and Petroleum Number, June 1953, p. 3. Largest of

the foreign-held concessions was that of Richmond Oil, followed by Seaoil Ltd., IPC, and Gulf Oil.

45. For details of the capitalisation and membership of the various companies see *Peruvian Times*, Mining and Petroleum Number, June 1953, Supplement, p. iii.

46. The company's jungle exploration and drilling from 1945 to 1952 are described in *Peruvian Times*, June 22, 1945, cover; and Nov. 7, 1947, Supplement, p. ii; *Estadística Petrolera*, 1948–9, p. 17; 1950, p. 28; and 1952, p. 43.

47. The board of directors of this enterprise indicates eloquently the strength of its local backing: as well as Gildemeister we find Alfredo Ferreyros, Felipe Thorndike, Gustavo Aspillaga, Enrique Ayulo, Ernesto Baertl, Felipe Beltran, Gustavo Berckemeyer, Elias Fernandini, Carlos Moreyra Paz Soldan, Juan Pardo, Carlos Rizo Patron, and Waldemar Schroeder. For a summary history of the firm see Malpica (1968), pp. 256–61.

48. On the initial stages see *Peruvian Times*, Mining and Petroleum Number, June 1953, p. 118. The subsequent history of the Sechura exploration can be followed in the *Estadística Petrolera*, volumes for 1953, 1954, 1955, 1956 and 1957.

49. Data assembled from *Estadística Petrolera*, 1953, pp. 113–14; 1954, pp. 32 and 52–3; 1955, pp. 19 and 35–6A; and 1956, p. 40A.

50. Production reached 188,000 barrels in 1956, roughly 1 per cent of the national total (*Estadística Petrolera*, 1956).

51. The two firms involved were Peruvian Pacific Petroleum (a Cities Service subsidiary) and Petrolera Amotape, a small company owned by an individual U.S. operator. See *Estadística Petrolera*, 1953, pp. 147–58; and 1954, p. 42.

52. *Peruvian Times*, Apr. 17, 1959, p. 2.

53. For the text of the decree see *Estadística Petrolera*, 1953, pp. 136–7. For a discussion of the terms see J. E. Rassmuss, 'Regulations for Oil Concessions on the Continental or Submarine Shelf' in *Peruvian Times*, Mining and Petroleum Number, June 1953, p. 120.

54. For lists of concession-holders in the jungle see, for example, *Estadística Petrolera*, 1953, p. 118; 1955, p. 125; and 1959, p. xviii–3. Maps showing the location of jungle concessions appeared in *Peruvian Times*, Mining and Petroleum Number, June 1953, p. 2 and *Estadística Petrolera*, 1953, facing p. 116.

55. *Estadística Petrolera*, various issues.

56. *Vademecum del Inversionista*, 1962–3, pp. 536–8; Malpica (1968) p. 265. Following the death of Augusto Gildemeister, 'El Oriente' had become associated in 1954 with a group of German companies including Erdoel.

57. Texaco, the most active of the international companies in the jungle during the 1950s, gave up in mid-1959 after spending $4 million on exploration in the Sechura and Jungle (*Peruvian Times*, June 12, 1959, p. 1).

58. A neighbouring joint venture between Lobitos and IPC.

59. Philip (1975), p. 104.

60. Peruvian Pacific acquired operating rights on the 'Humboldt' field (Petrolera del Pacifico) in 1960 (*Peruvian Times*, Mar. 18, 1960, p. 3). See also Philip (1975), pp. 103–4. Peruvian Pacific developed the fields in a joint venture with Cabeen Exploration in 1965 (*Peruvian Times*, June 25, 1965, p. 3).

61. *Peruvian Times*, Feb. 1, 1963, cover and pp. 3–4; June 21, 1963, pp. 2–3.
62. The first sign of trouble came in 1957, when the IPC unsuccessfully applied to have its operations placed under the terms of the 1952 law. The company was seeking to jettison the legal embarrassment of the 1922 Agreement, which had long since served its purpose of providing super-profits and was now merely an administrative nuisance (Pinelo (1973), p. 53).
63. The IPC dispute of the 1960s is not further analysed here. The reader is referred to the studies by Pinelo (1973), Chapters 5–7; Olson (1972); Lewis (1972); Peterson and Unger (1964); Ramírez Novoa (1964); Zimmerman (1968); Dirección General de Información (1968); Goodsell (1974); and Philip (1975).
64. Pinelo (1973) p. 43.
65. It should be borne in mind that Rippy (1959), pp. 131–2, estimates that during the years of peak production 1935–8 IPC's annual profits averaged over 100 per cent on capital.
66. Gonzales del Valle (1958).
67. Pinelo (1973), pp. 65–71.
68. *Peruvian Times*, June 6, 1959, p. 2.
69. Comisión Especial Nombrada para el Estudio de la Crisis de la Industria del Petróleo (1959); *Peruvian Times*, July 31, 1959, p. 2; Pinelo (1973), pp. 72–3. The subsequent debate on the accuracy of the commission's report revolved largely around the question of how much capital IPC had invested in Peru, with estimates ranging from $70 million up to $250 million; since the Government had committed itself to the maintenance of a 6.6 per cent rate of return on capital, this was a crucial issue. IPC persistently overstated its net worth during the debate by giving figures for its accumulated gross investment in Peru without subtracting accumulated depreciation and depletion allowances. See Pinelo (1973) p. 74; *Peruvian Times*, May 15, 1959, pp. 14–15; Nov. 13, 1959, p. 15; and Mar. 11, 1960 pp. 14–15. For a direct criticism of IPC's failure to show its

(U.S. $million)

	Book value of U.S. investment	Net capital flows into Peru	Net earnings for the year
1959	79	− 9	5
1960	79	− 5	10
1961	71	−12	7
1962	66	− 7	7
1963	56	−14	10
1964	60	4	10
1965	60	11	19
1966	29	− 2	10
1967	35	16	11
1968	39	4	10

As a matter of interest, it may be noted that the compensation eventually paid to IPC in 1974 for its expropriated assets in Peru, totalled $22 million (*Petroleum Economist*, Feb. 1975, p. 75).

investment net of depreciation see J. E. Rassmuss, 'Peruvian Oil Prospects' in *World Petroleum*, Dec. 1962.
70. *Peruvian Times*, Nov. 30, 1962, p. 1.
71. The following figures are drawn from the annual surveys of U.S. investments abroad, published in the U.S. Department of Commerce *Survey of Current Business* every year. They cover the operations of U.S. oil companies active in Peru (almost entirely IPC in 1959; IPC and Belco plus some minor interests by 1967). See table at foot of p. 400.
72. *Peruvian Times*, Sep. 15, 1965, p. 2; and Feb. 23, 1968, cover.
73. *Peruvian Times*, Aug. 4, 1961, p. 2; Jan. 18, 1963, p. 19; June 21, 1963, pp. 2–3; Dec. 1, 1967, p. 1; Nov. 17, 1967 p. 2.
74. *Peruvian Times*, Feb. 16, 1968, p. 1.

CHAPTER 12

1. Odría was evidently aware of this; Leguía's image was rehabilitated in the early 1950s. See Capunay (1951) and *El Economista Peruano*, Jan.–Mar. 1949, pp. 754–5.
2. On Olmos, see Labarthe (1933). The project was ended both by lack of funds, and by political conflicts—by threatening to reduce the amount of water controlled by the Lambayeque sugar plantations, Olmos brought them into sharp conflict with the Leguía government in the years 1928–30, culminating in an assassination attempt in April, 1930.
3. *El Economista Peruano*, Jan. – Mar. 1949, p. 751. The Bank was renamed 'Banco de Fomento Agropecuario,' its present title, at that time.
4. *El Economista Peruano*, Nov. – Dec. 1953, p. 196; *Peruvian Times*, Sep. 7, 1962, pp. 2–5.
5. Figures from *Anuario Estadístico*, various issues.
6. International Bank for Reconstruction, etc. (1975).
7. Collin-Delavaud (1967), pp. 261–2, estimates that in 1964 the mills of Tuman, Pomalca and Pucala in Lambayeque were grinding cane from 5,750 hectares of independently-owned land as well as from 20,000 hectares of their own. In the case of Tuman, detailed figures supplied by Christopher Scott show that the estate began obtaining cane from independent 'outgrowers' in 1952, in the wake of the Korean War, and that by 1962 no less than 37 per cent of the cane ground by the mill came from independents. The proportion declined again during the 1960s, to 28 per cent by 1967. In the early 1970s it was estimated that 20 per cent of the total cane area in the country was outside the 'agro-industrial complexes' (Kisic (1972), p. 20).
8. Scott (1972), pp. 32–3; Pan American Union (1950), pp. 70–1.
9. Data supplied by Oficina Sectoral de Planificación Agricola (Lima) in 1969. Similar figures are cited by Kisic (1972), p. 26.
10. The prices are on a Caribbean fob basis; Peruvian fob prices would probably have been slightly lower (from *Lamborn's Sugar Data*). For similar calculations see Kisic (1972), p. 26.
11. Rodriguez Pastor (1972). See also Horton (1973), p. 77.
12. No study of this subject could be located. It should be noted, however, that

although there was no increase in the physical extraction ratio of sugar cane over the fifty-year period from the First World War to the 1960s, there were important innovations introduced over time to lower costs and increase the efficient scale of operation in the mills—automatic contrifuges, the change from steam power to electricity, and so on. The only important innovation directly orientated to increasing the physical extraction ratio, the· 'diffuser,' was introduced in Casagrande only in the late 1960s. It may be noted that a study in the mid-1960s found sugar milling to be the most capital-intensive industry in the sample (Clague (1967)).

13. Collin-Delavaud (1967), p. 261; Scott (1972), p. 36.

14. Collin-Delavaud (1967), p. 261. The railways required a large labour force to move and lay the portable tracks. Also Horton (1973) p. 11.

15. Information from Christopher Scott. The largest plantation, Casagrande, switched over from manual cane-cutting and the plantation railway to pushrake harvesting and use of trailers, in 1965. As a result of this and other innovations the plantation reduced its labour force from over 7,000 in 1960 to less than 4,000 by 1969, creating a large local pool of unemployed labour (Rodriguez Pastor (1972), p. 84).

16. Results of the survey for nine leading estates are in Kisic (1972), Table 12.

17. The case of the Pardo family's overseas 'fronts' was discussed in *Oiga*, Sep. 26, 1969.

18. *Monthly Review of the World Cotton Situation*, Jan.–Feb. 1951, p. 1.

19. *Ibid*, May–June 1952, p. 4.

20. *Cotton: World Statistics*, various issues.

21. *Cotton: Monthly Review of the World Situation*, Apr.–May 1956, p. 1.

22. Ibid., Apr.–May 1956, p. 4; Ferrero (1956b).

23. *Anuario Estadistico*, 1966 and 1969.

24. CONESTCAR (1965), especially p. 3.

25. As Section 12.2 notes, 1965 was a year of the '*El Nino*' current which occasionally disrupts oceanographic and climatic conditions along the north.

26. *Peruvian Times*, Oct. 15, 1965, p. 16.

27. Zuñiga (1970), p. 102.

28. Banco Central, *Boletin*, May 1975, p. 31.

29. Zuñiga (1970), p. 102. This is not to say that no mechanisation had taken place; the study by CONESTCAR in 1965 found that the wage bill made up only 33 per cent of total costs, whereas in the thirties labour costs had been nearer 50 per cent (estimated from *Extracto Estadistico*). Matos Mar (1967), p. 354, remarks on the degree of mechanisation and modernisation in Chancay since the landowners began moving towards working their properties directly in the early forties.

30. Although not by any means negligible; see for example Matos Mar (1967), p. 356.

31. Soler (1963).

32. Miller (1967) p. 143; Horton (1973) p. 45.

33. Casagrande closed its last *enganche* offices in the Sierra in 1959 (information from Colin Harding). Horton (1973), p. 50, attributes the ending of *enganche* in Pomalca to union pressures.

34. Payne (1965), p. 35; Miller (1967), pp. 202–3; Horton (1973) pp. 48–9.

35. A major strike accompanied by serious violence (5 dead, 50 injured) at

Casagrande in 1959 was triggered off by disputes over the manning of cranes (*Peruvian Times*, Sep. 11, p. 1.) The following May there was a violent strike at Paramonga protesting against the installation of time-clocks in the mill (*Peruvian Times*, May 13, 1960, p. 1) with 3 dead and 16 injured. Early 1962 saw seven strikers shot by police at Pomalca (*Peruvian Times*, Jan. 26, 1962, p. 4) while later in the same year San Jacinto was closed by a long strike for improved wages and conditions (*Peruvian Times*, Sep. 7, 1962, p. 15). It need hardly be said that the great bulk of the casualties in all these strikes were inflicted by police guns.

36. Rodriguez Pastor (1972), p. 28, gives figures on the substitution of temporary for permanent field labour in a Lambayeque plantation.

37. Scott (1972).

38. The year was one of economic crisis at the end of nearly a decade of fixed exchange rate, and aggravated by a drought in the sugar-producing regions.

39. It should be noted also that as an increasing proportion of production was sold on the low-price open market, overall profitability would have been depressed.

40. The Paramonga paper mill opened in September 1939 and was thereafter one of the leading local producers (*Peruvian Times*, Jan. 8, 1943, p. 18; July 8, 1966, p. 2; Jan. 8, 1967, pp. 6–7).

41. Grace established a small caustic-soda plant at Paramonga in 1946, but large-scale expansion of chemical manufacture was undertaken only in the early 1960s. From caustic soda, chlorine and other basic chemicals, Grace went on to the production of plastics from sugar by-products in the mid-1960s (*Peruvian Times*, Feb. 3, 1961, p. 2; Nov. 17, 1961, cover; Apr. 24, 1964, p. 2 ; June 26, 1964, p. 10; Aug. 13, 1965, p. 8; and Mar. 11, 1966, p. 1). The company also began producing multiwall paper bags for the fishmeal industry in the mid-1960s. For a general survey of Grace's chemical and paper industries associated with the sugar industry see *Peruvian Times*, Sep. 20, 1968, pp. 11–14.

42. A 1957 Peruvian-foreign joint venture to establish an integrated *bagasse*-using wallboard industry in Nepeña. however, failed to make progress after the expropriation in 1960 of its Cuban associate, which had been developing the technology (*Peruvian Times*, Jan. 31, 1958, p. 1, and Sep. 23, 1960, p. 3).

43. Thorndike (1973), pp. 73–4.

44. Because of its remarkable growth performance, the fishing sector has been the subject of a number of thorough studies, and only the general trends require coverage here. The main studies are Roemer (1970), Edmonds (1972) and Abramovich (1973).

45. Edmonds (1972), pp. 11–13.

46. Abramovich (1973), p. 17; Roemer (1970), p. 82; Thorndike (1973), p. 88.

47. Among these was Miguel Capurro (Thorndike (1973), p. 87).

48. *Pacific Fisherman*, Nov. 1957; *Peruvian Times* Jan. 10, 1958, p. 13. Figures given in *Estadística del Comercio Exterior* indicate sales of canned fish to Britain rising from zero in 1950 to over 6,000 tons p.a. by 1956.

49. For Banchero's biography see Thorndike (1973); also *Peruvian Times*, Fisheries Supplement, Mar. 28, 1969, pp. 30–1.

50. *West Coast Leader*, Mar. 1, 1938, p. 15.

51. *Peruvian Times*, Jan. 7, 1941, cover; Fiedler (1943).

52. *Peruvian Times*, Apr. 25, 1941, cover; Oct. 31, 1941, p. 1; and Aug. 7, 1942, p. 1.

53. *Peruvian Times*, Dec. 28, 1945, p. 7; and Nov. 1, 1946, p. 1; Abramovich (1973) p. 18.

54. *Peruvian Times*, July 4, 1947, cover; and Feb. 21, 1964, pp. 11–12; Abramovich (1973), p. 17; Thorndike (1973), p. 95.

55. See Roemer (1970), Chap 5, and Edmonds (1972), Chap 5 and 6.

56. *Peruvian Times*, Dec. 2, 1960, p. 4.

57. Edmonds (1972), pp. 59–60; *Peruvian Times*, Fisheries Number, 1950.

58. *Peruvian Times*, Sep. 18, 1959, p. 3; Edmonds (1972), pp. 60–2; Roemer (1970), p. 83.

59. Vasquez Aguirre (1964–5), p. 35.

60. Vasquez Aguirre (1964–5), p. 34.

61. The cause appears to have been overfishing. See 'Peru's Fishery Plant' in *Pacific Fisherman*, Nov. 1957, and *Peruvian Times*, Jan. 24, 1958, p. 15.

62. Fishmeal technology changed little from the early twentieth century until the innovations of the 1960s (Dávila (1972), p. 64); the Californian plants, although as much as a decade old by 1957, were thus not obsolete.

63. Edmonds (1972), pp. 25–9. Prevailing banking legislation prohibited the commercial banks from making long-term loans.

64. *Peruvian Times*, Aug. 21, 1959, p. 11.

65. Edmonds (1972), pp. 38–40. Roemer (1970), pp. 152–3, emphasises also the banks' long experience in financing export sectors.

66. Sixty per cent was the lowest estimate cited by Edmonds (1972), p. 25. Eighty per cent was the contemporary estimate of the Banco Continental (*Peruvian Times*, Nov. 8, 1963, p. 11). The variability of these estimates is due to disagreement over the magnitude of total investment in the industry, and hence of the denominator used to calculate the percentages (Edmonds (1972), p. 25). It should be noted that in addition to commercial bank credit, the sector financed its expansion also on suppliers' credits, at 25–30 per cent per annum (Edmonds (1972), p. 27). On the capital structure of the sector see also Roemer (1970), pp. 147–55; his estimate is a 3:1 gearing ratio.

67. On the development of the 1963 crisis, *Peruvian Times*, Jan. 4, 1963, p. 2; Jan. 25, 1963, p. 3; Feb. 1, 1963, p. 1; Feb. 8, 1963, p. 1; Feb. 22, 1963, p. 2; Mar. 1, 1963, p. 1; and Mar. 8, 1963, p. 2. The peak year for fishmeal investment was 1963 (Roemer (1970), p. 128); in that year the sector absorbed over 15 per cent of gross investment. Indebtedness was correspondingly high.

68. *International Commerce* (Washington, DC), Aug. 26, 1963; *Peruvian Times*, Sep. 6, 1963, p. 4; Banco Continental, third-quarter survey in *Peruvian Times*, Nov. 8, 1963, p. 11; Edmonds (1972), p. 28.

69. Debate raged over whether the disappearance of the fish was due to natural causes or overfishing (*Peruvian Times*, Aug. 9, 1963, p. 1).

70. Edmonds (1972), pp. 23–4; *Anuario de Pesca*, 1964–5, p. 24; *Peruvian Times*, Fisheries Supplement, 1972, pp. 63–4.

71. Edmonds (1972), pp. 64–6.

72. For a list see *Report of the Fourth Session of the Panel of Experts on Stock Assessment in Peruvian Anchoveta (Boletín del Instituto del Mar*, Vol. 2, No. 10, 1974), p. 711.

73. *Peruvian Times*, Aug. 21, 1959, p. 11, and Feb. 5, 1960, p. 5.

74. *Peruvian Times*, Sep. 14, 1962, p. 11; Sep. 28, 1962, p. 8; and Mar. 22, 1963, pp. 13–14.

75. *Peruvian Times*, July 1, 1960, p. 4.

76. The most definite sign was an ominous downward trend in the seabird population beginning in 1963; see *Boletin del Instituto del Mar* (Callao), Vol. 2, No. 6, 1970, p. 367; and Vol. 2, No. 10, 1974, p. 650. Also Roemer (1970), pp. 136–7 on the decline of guano production.

77. *International Commerce* Feb. 28, 1966; *Peruvian Times*, Mar. 11, 1966, p. 10; Edmonds (1972) p. 13.

78. *Peruvian Times*, May 13, 1966, p. 2; May 20, 1966, p. 1; June 3, 1966, p. 2.

79. *Peruvian Times*, June 17, 1966, p. 25; July 29, 1966, pp. 1–2.

80. Abramovich (1973), p. 80; Dávila (1972), p. 62. Edmonds (1972), p. 19, states that potential capacity of the fishing fleet had reached 14 million tons (above the 1970 peak actual catch) by 1963.

81. *Boletin del Instituto del Mar*, Vol. 2, No. 2, 1970, p. 359.

82. *Peruvian Times*, Fisheries Number, 1972, p. 21.

83. Technical improvements in fishmeal processing during the 1960s did indeed achieve improvement in the yield; according to Edmonds (1972), p. 22, the quantity of raw fish required for the production of a ton of meal dropped from 5.41 tons in 1961 to 5.33 tons in 1968. By 1972, although the average yield for the industry had not fallen further, the most efficient plants were obtaining ratios of 4.5 : 1, and plan targets for the industry were to achieve an average of 5.1 : 1 (*Peruvian Times*, Fisheries Supplement, Mar. 3, 1972, p. 21). Edmonds (1972), p. 66, indicates a technical limit of around 4.3:1.

84. Edmonds (1972), pp. 38–41, surveys the available (very unreliable) statistics on the increases in the industry's costs during the 1960s, and (pp. 76–80) sets out the most important tax changes.

85. Namely the Gildemeisters' Compania Maritima Pesquera and Rafael Graña's Grupo Pacifico.

86. Compania Pesquera Coishco (taken over in the mid-1950s by Star Kist of California); Wilbur-Ellis; and Westgate-California. For the list of producers in 1963, see *Peruvian Times*, Fisheries Number, Oct. 28, 1963, pp. xxiv–xxvi and xxxvi. Two locally-controlled firms also brought in foreign partners to finance expansion in the 1950s.

87. Wilbur-Ellis and Westgate-California sold out; Graña failed.

88. The reasons for this reluctance are not altogether clear, but probably included some aversion to entering an industry where competition was extremely strong and the construction and exploitation of monopolistic positions quite impossible. For some remarks on the issue see Bourricaud (1969), pp. 31–2.

89. On the 1960–1 crisis and the success of the Consorcio: *Peruvian Times*, Mar. 10, 1961, p. 10; Apr. 28, 1961, p. 3; May 5, 1961 p. 2; July 21, 1961, p. 14; Mar. 30, 1962, p. 10; and June 22, 1962, p. 14. Also Thorndike (1973), pp. 180–204; Roemer (1970), pp. 84–5; Edmonds (1972), pp. 34–6.

90. See especially Sociedad Nacional de Pesquería, *La Crisis de la Pesquería*, cited by Edmonds (1972), p. 98; and Brundenius (1973), pp. 3–4.

91. The detailed data on which Brundenius' calculations were based can be found in Espinoza and Osorio (1971).

92. Similar estimates presented in *Peruvian Times*, Fisheries Supplement, Oct.

20, 1967, p. 4, showed wholly-foreign firms with 18 per cent of total 1966 production, joint ventures with 14 per cent; these figures are compatible with those in Table 12.8.

93. See Alejandro Bermejo, 'Time to Clean Up', in *Peruvian Times*, Fisheries Supplement, Mar. 28, 1969, p. 9: 'The feeling among a number of Peruvian producers that the industry is being taken over by foreign interests is just not borne out by the facts.' Also Roemer (1970), pp. 153–4.

94. *Business Week*, Feb. 20, 1965; *Peruvian Times*, Mar. 5, 1965.

95. Roemer (1970), p. 154.

96. Based on a file of data accumulated from various sources.

97. Cf remarks in Roemer (1970), pp. 99–107 and 157, on the absence of scale economies at outputs of over 20,000 tons/year.

98. Edmonds (1972), pp. 89–96.

99. Dávila (1972), pp. 116–27.

100. For a full analysis of the economic effects of the fishmeal sector, see Roemer (1970), Chaps 7 to 10.

101. Edmonds (1972), pp. 39 and 76.

102. Roemer (1970), pp. 160–3. It will be noted that this period included one year of extremely high profits (1965).

103. Roemer (1970), p. 127.

104. From the input-output Table for the industry in Roemer (1970), pp. 112–13.

105. Cf. remarks in Edmonds (1972), p. 88 on 1963 data for the boat-building industry, showing import content of only 25 per cent. However, Roemer (1970), p. 116, estimates a 50 per cent import content for boatbuilding.

106. Roemer (1970), p. 124.

107. Roemer (1970), p. 11.

108. The Banchero shipbuilding enterprise, PICSA, was begun in 1962 (*Peruvian Times*, Fisheries Supplement, Mar. 28, 1969, p. 31).

109. Notably the helical-impeller fish pump (Edmonds (1972), pp. 21 and 67; Roemer (1970), p. 119) and the process of pelletising fishmeal and treating it with a deoxidant, to permit bulk shipping (*Peruvian Times*, Jan. 6, 1968, cover, and Fisheries Supplement, Mar. 28, 1969, pp. 28–30).

110. Roemer (1970), pp. 139–47.

111. For 1968, Edmonds estimates a total labour force in fishing and processing of 38,000, in addition to a further 20,000 employed in service activities linked to fishmeal (Edmonds (1972), p. 29). In that year the boat crews, totalling 23,000–28,000, received wages totalling U.S. $25 million, or an average of roughly $900 (S/39,000) each. Captains of boats averaged $4,800 each. These sums were earned in 170 working days (between five and six months); during the *veda*, other sources of income would no doubt have been tapped as well (Edmonds (1972), p. 17).

112. For a good discussion of the international strategies of mining companies see Girvan (1970).

113. See Chapter 15.

CHAPTER 13

1. *Miami Herald*, quoted in *Peruvian Times*, Mar. 5, 1965, p. 16.
2. Arriaga (1966), p. 222.
3. Chaplin (1967), p. 33 and Appendix B.
4. Bourricaud (1970), p. 287. APRA's participation in the Prado regime illustrated the swing from Left to Right which this remarkable party performed during the 1940s and 1950s without losing its mass base. This ability to retain strong working-class support while espousing a very conservative ideology made APRA in the long run one of the most negative influences in the development of Peruvian political life, and does much to account for the weakness of Peruvian working-class politics.
5. Even in their short span of office, the military too revealed themselves in tune with the underlying shift in politics, and foreshadowed something of what they would attempt after 1968. The two most significant moves were the founding of the Instituto Nacional de Planificación and the introduction of an Agrarian Reform Bill.
6. On the politics of the 1960s see Astiz (1969).
7. See Chapter 11 on the decline of the Corporation in the early 1950s. The early years of the Odría regime brought a shortlived attempt to revive the Corporation, with preliminary development work at the Marcona iron mines and a 1951 contract with a French group for financing and construction of the Chimbote steel mill (*El Economista Peruano*, July 28, 1951, p. 4). From 1952 to 1954, however, the Corporation was in virtual suspended animation.
8. Using as denominator the total outstanding loans of the three *fomento* banks for mining, agriculture and industry, the percentage share of the Banco Industrial evolved as follows:

1950	25.7	1955	9.5	1960	24.5
1951	27.2	1956	16.2	1961	26.2
1952	21.6	1957	24.9	1965	38.9
1953	16.6	1958	22.5	1970	31.0
1954	17.4	1959	25.8		

(Figures from *Anuario Estadístico*, 1956–7, p. 237; 1969, p. 1021; 1971, p. 361). The contrast between the Odría and Prado regimes is immediately evident. After 1963, the State banks' share of total credit grew quite rapidly.
9. Figures assembled by the Banco Industrial, and cited in Jelicic (1955) p. 31, showed local industries to have supplied 67 per cent of internal demand for manufactures in 1942 and 77 per cent in 1945. By 1950 they had fallen back to 65 per cent, and by 1952 to 59 per cent. Similar (though not directly comparable) data in Saberbein (1973), p. 137, indicate a return to a share of 65–70 per cent for the period 1958–65.
10. *El Economista Peruano*, Jan.–Feb. 1955, p. 256 described the new contract with the French suppliers of equipment for the mill. *Peruvian Times*, Apr. 25, 1958, p. 1, and Sep. 26, 1958, Supplement, described the construction and entry into production of the mill. The new president appointed by Odría in 1954 was Max Peña Prado, a relative of future President Manuel Prado.
11. *Anuario de la Industria Minera*. For the new plants, see *Peruvian Times*, Feb. 14, 1958, pp. 13–14.
12. The Lima cement plant was controlled in the mid-1950s by a group headed

by Fernando Berckemeyer, and was subsequently taken over by the Prado interests. Cemento Chilca was a Nicolini venture; Cemento Andino at Tarma was owned by the Rizo Patron family; and Cemento Chiclayo by the Aspillagas.
13. For a discussion of the changed climate in manufacturing after 1954, see *Board of Trade Journal*, Jan. 17, 1958, article reprinted in *Peruvian Times*, Feb. 14, 1958, pp. 13–14.
14. Title of a lecture reported in *Peruvian Times*, Apr. 18, 1958. Sugar production for export had formerly been Grace's main activity in Peru. It should be noted that this process of diversification by foreign firms established in export sectors was not altogether new. In the 1940s Grace had set up chlorine and caustic soda plants, expanded paper production and launched a paint factory, while Cerro had begun production of copper sulphate (1941) and white arsenic (1942) (*Peruvian Times* May 21, 1943, p. 13). The quantitative significance of these developments, however, was limited.
15. On Cerro's ramifying interests see Brundenius (1972).
16. U.S. Department of Commerce data assembled in Anaya (1975), pp. 23–4.
17. Malpica (1968) traces the major role of élite figures in the banking sector; see the figures in Table 13.12 below.
18. *Peruvian Times*, Jan. 31, 1958, p. 1. This venture, known as 'Primadera Nepeña SA,' eventually failed; see Note 12.42 above.
19. *Peruvian Times*, Dec. 26, 1958, p. 1.
20. I.N.P. (1973).
21. These industrial groups are identified and analysed in Espinoza and Osorio (1972) and Torres (1975).
22. The lead in this sector was taken by the élite-controlled Industrias Reunidas (INRESA) in 1959; see *Peruvian Times*, June 19, 1959, p. 3.
23. *Peruvian Times*, Oct. 16, 1959, p. 9. The debates on the bill, which can be followed in the congressional *Diario de los Debates* for the sessions of 1957 and 1959, were notable for the complete absence of any organised opposition to the principle of industrial promotion; the bulk of amendments were concerned with the distribution of the spoils from a promotion system.
24. A term whose coverage was continually increased in subsequent decrees. Further, the law was almost immediately extended to consumer durables and even to the consumption goods sector.
25. Farnworth (1967) gives a Table comparing the provisions of such laws in seven different countries, from which the striking generosity of the Peruvian Law may be seen. The lesser benefits to non-basic industries typically took the form of a reduced number of years (e.g. 10 as against 15) during which a benefit would apply—not a serious handicap given the typical time horizon of an industrialist.
26. Ministerio de Industria y Turismo (1974).
27. Its chief proponent in Congress was a lawyer well known for his involvement in the legal affairs of foreign firms, patents, etc.
28. Macario (1964) compares levels of nominal protection at the end of the 1950s for Peru, other Latin American countries, and the E.E.C. Peru has by far the lowest level of the Latin American countries (average 34 per cent, p. 75), the two closest being twice as high, while for example Chile's average rate is 138 per cent, Colombia's 112 per cent.
29. Ministerio de Industria y Turismo (1974).

30. Marquez and Carcelen (1968), p. 54 and p. 47.

31. Of course, as local manufacturing became more dependent upon imported materials and equipment during the 1960s, a stable exchange rate, when combined with increased final tariffs, increasingly favoured industrial profits, since the cost of inputs was held relatively steady while internal prices rose.

32. The basis for these calculations is explained in Thorp (1972).

33. A bank was classified as foreign if it was generally accepted that there was foreign control, rather than relying on a specific degree of foreign ownership of assets. The sources were newspaper and business periodicals.

34. The real rates of return on savings and term deposits in 1968 were −4.5 per cent and −2.5 per cent respectively (Deltec Panamericana, 1968). As inflation accelerated during the sixties, so rates had become increasingly negative.

35. Chudnovsky (1974) demonstrates for the Colombian case the increased profitability of foreign firms able to borrow locally. This issue seems to have been somewhat less significant in Peru, where bank credit was less absurdly cheap than in Colombia, and where industrial profits were in any case high enough to permit investment to be financed by reinvested profits.

36. Anaya (1975), p. 23.

37. Taking comparable samples of large industrial firms for Peru and Chile, we find that in 1969 foreign-controlled firms account for 80 per cent of the total in Peru, and only 40 per cent in Chile (Peru: Espinoza (1972); Chile: Pacheco, in Munoz (1972)).

38. This useful phrase is difficult to translate exactly, its nearest equivalent being 'light engineering.' It comprises sectors 35–38 of the CIIU classification: metal manufactures, machinery including instruments and electrical appliances, and transport equipment.

39. Footnote a to Table 13.5 explains how 'foreign' is defined in the source used. The actual degree of effective foreign *control* may well be higher.

40. Of the takeovers which did occur, the majority were in fishmeal processing rather than in manufacturing for the local market; among the existing élite-controlled industrial enterprises, only those controlled by the Prado family (whose power was waning rapidly after 1962) were takeover-prone. Their soap company, Pacocha, was sold to Lever Brothers in the early 1960s. Their cement plant, Cemento Lima, was taken over by foreign interests after a series of shady manoeuvres in the mid-1960s. (The company's application for a price rise was rejected by a congressional commission, despite pressure on the members by the Prado family's Banco Popular. The commission report recommended technical advice to improve the firm's very low level of efficiency, and Holderbank was brought in as a major shareholder as part of a technical-assistance package.)

41. The atmosphere of the sixties is vividly illustrated in the remark made by Augusto Weise, distinguished member of Peru's business élite, as he decided in 1964 to move into fishmeal in partnership with Mecom, a Texan oilman: 'This whole fishmeal business has always smelled highly to me. But if Mr. Mecom is interested, why then, it smells like a rose' (*Peruvian Times*, 5th Mar., 1965, back inside cover). For an illuminating analysis of the role of the élite, see Fitzgerald (1976b). The failure of an independent industrial bourgeoisie to emerge is further discussed in Ferner (1975).

42. Saberbein (1973), pp. 211–19.

43. Bravo Bresani (1968), pp. 148–9.

44. In 1960 special incentives were introduced for the sector; by early 1961 ten new foreign firms had entered the sector and 46 more had applied to do so (*Peruvian Times*, Aug. 5, 1960, p. 5; Apr. 28, 1961, p. 9).
45. For example, Palma (forthcoming) shows that the ratio of direct and indirect imported inputs to total inputs in the manufacturing sector is 0.19 in Chile, 0.42 in Peru.
46. Ocampo (1973); Consejo Nacional de Investigacion (1970); Espinoza *et al.* (1971); and Anaya (1975), Chap. 4.
47. Such as the locally-owned firm Moraveco, which relied on ingenious imitation of foreign products in preference to patent licences, and managed to raise local content in products such as refrigerators and stoves to 80 per cent. (Interview with the head of Moraveco, Samuel Drassinower. The firm's success was based upon the technical expertise of a La Molina engineer, Sr Ramos.) But the fundamental problem remains: that they were still imitating foreign technology.
48. The high rate of investment in manufacturing is quite consistent with the declining aggregate investment ratio which we discuss in the next chapter.
49. Calculations made from *Estadística Industrial* confirm the lack of any clear correlation between rates of investment and rates of growth of output. Qualitative evidence on the modernisation of slow-growth traditional sectors such as flourmilling and cotton textiles during the sixties is ample.
50. We have no direct evidence for this. The clear downward trend in the share of wages and salaries in value added is indicative, but could be simply the product of the increase in profitability which clearly also occurred. (Data from *Estadística Industrial*; the trend is clearly observable *despite* the increasing coverage of the sample, which would *ceteris paribus* have led to a rise in the ratio, as more small firms were included in the sample.)
51. The data and quotation come from the very careful study by Lewis (1973); he takes great trouble to assess problems of comparability before reaching the conclusions noted here.
52. Webb (1974a), p. 27.
53. Webb (1974a), p. 21.
54. See the analysis of the Mantaro Valley carried out by Samaniego (1974).
55. See Hunt (1964) and Watson (1964).
56. See pp. 132–3 of the report by the Convenio de Cooperación Técnica (1969).
57. Adjustments were made to particular crops to give more 'plausible' growth rates 1951–61, but in such a way as to cancel each other out. See the comparative Table, p. 133 of Convenio de Cooperación (1969).
58. Twomey (1972), p. 33.
59. Official data on traditional-sector incomes are very unreliable, but show a rise of no more than 5 per cent over ten years in per capita food consumption for the economy as a whole. Webb rejects these data as incompatible with the official trends in income distribution, but himself concludes that the incomes of 22 per cent of the population did not rise at all during the 1950s. The data are discussed further in Thorp (1969) and Webb (1974b).
60. See *Fortnightly Review*, May 5, 1956; Apr. 19, 1956; Nov. 10, 1957; and Nov. 24, 1957.
61. By comparison with the 15.7 per cent of total imports in 1955 (Table 13.15),

food accounted for 12.5 per cent in 1956 and 13.3 per cent in 1957.
62. Unfortunately, in constructing Fig. 13.1 we have not had data on farmgate prices; the trend could possibly be misleading if the cost of transport between the farm and the wholesaler had fallen steadily at a rate sufficient to compensate the farmer for the downward trend in relative wholesale prices. We do not believe this to have occurred, but further research on this issue would be welcome.
63. CIDA (1966), p. 342.
64. CIDA (1966), p. 338.
65. Roel (1961), pp. 245–6.
66. Alvarez Salomón (1974), p. 54.
67. CIDA (1966), p. 331.
68. Alvarez Salomón (1974), p. 66.
69. Shepherd and Furnish (1967), pp. 50 ff., give a full account of the means used to control or influence prices. For data on producer prices see Merrill and Prochazka (1967), p. 36.
70. For the case of beef, see Vandendries (1967). While supplies of meat were responsive to short-run price fluctuations (for example, prime minister Beltran's decreed price increase in 1960 resulted in a sharply-increased rate of slaughtering), unfavourable long-run price trends clearly contributed to the stagnation of the sector.
71. For surveys of policy developments see Horton (1974), pp. 34–45, and Petras and LaPorte (1971).
72. Summaries of the reports are in *Peruvian Times*, Mar. 7, 1958, pp. 16–22; July 15, 1960, p. 6; and Oct. 7, 1960, p. 1.
73. On the events of this period seé Neira (1964); Tullis (1970); Handelman (1975).
74. Quoted in Horton (1974), p. 44.
75. On the events in La Convención see Craig (1967) and Hobsbawn (1970).
76. Horton (1974), p. 36.
77. Reportedly, between 1964 and 1969 fewer than 15,000 families benefited, many of them receiving only the *minifundios* which they had previously worked as *feudatarios* (Harding (1975), p. 234). In 1961, according to CIDA (1966), p. 455, there were 897,000 families in need of land.
78. Horton (1974), p. 46.
79. Harding (1975), p. 233, cites cases of cooperatives (SAIS – Sociedades Agrarias de Interes Social) under the recent reform who have found that the poor quality of the land held by the former *haciendas*, and the need for rotation, make it necessary to leave large areas fallow.

CHAPTER 14

1. Both this chapter and the one which follows owe much to the invaluable work of Fitzgerald – in particular his analysis of the crisis in the old model of accumulation, and the attempt after 1968 to replace it with a new one. See Fitzgerald (1976) and his forthcoming study, which develops the point more fully.
2. Again the main exception, fishmeal, is instructive: the very uniqueness of

Banchero's success emphasises the more general failure of Peruvian capitalists to achieve the transition to a new stage of large-scale entrepreneurship.

3. Anaya (1975), p. 23. Between 1965 and 1969 there was, however, a sharp increase in the reported book value of U.S. mining companies in Peru, apparently due largely to development of the existing operations of Cerro and Marcona.

4. It must be stressed that the data in Table 14.2 are mostly estimated as a residual in the national accounts, and are correspondingly unreliable. The magnitude and consistency of the trends revealed, however, appear to justify the conclusions we draw from the Table.

5. *Cuentas Nacionales del Perú, 1950–65*, p. 49. The growing tendency to place funds abroad was paralleled by the 'internationalisation' of the leading sugar companies described earlier (Chapter 12). In 1970 an enforced repatriation of deposits held abroad by Peruvians netted $400 million, which must have represented only a fraction of the funds actually sent abroad during the 1960s (*Peruvian Times*, May 22, 1970, p. 1; Ayala and Ugarteche (1975)).

6. See Thorp (1972).

7. A further point emerging from Table 14.2 but not discussed in the text is the shift from 'personal' to 'corporate' savings in the private sector during the 1960s; this was due to the growing practice of retaining company profits in liquid form and investing them through the banking system (with which most large companies had close ties). This made it possible for shareholders to avoid paying corporate taxes, which were collected only when profits were distributed or capitalised within the firm. The extent of this practice was indicated by the outcry from business interests when in 1963 an attempt was made by the government to introduce a measure under which company profits neither distributed nor capitalised after six months would be taxed as if they had been distributed. The measure was revoked. (*Peruvian Times*, Jan. 25, 1963, pp. 13–15; and Mar. 29, 1963, p. 1).

8. The public external debt rose from $93 million in 1960 to $621 million in 1967 (*Anuario Estadístico*, 1969, p. 1098).

9. Goodwin (1969).

10. Banco Central, *Boletín*, June 1975, pp. 17, 20–1.

11. Centro de Documentación Económica y Social (1965), pp. 7–34.

12. *Ibid.*, p. 211.

13. The military junta of 1962–3 has been ignored, with 1962 considered a 'Prado year' and 1963 a 'Belaunde year'. The Prado period has been divided between the trade recession of 1956–8 and the boom years 1959–62. For an analysis of this recession and boom see Thorp (1967).

14. The 1963 recession was concentrated in one sector—fishmeal—while other export industries remained relatively buoyant, and capital inflow produced an actual increase in foreign-exchange reserves.

15. See Thorp (1967) for a further discussion, where it is demonstrated that the export recovery was a function of long-run forces, not of the orthodox programme.

16. This is not to say that Odría and Prado had been unconcerned about the impact of devaluation on middle-class consumers. As Dragisic (1971) shows, the swing was a gradual one. On Prado's resistance to devaluation, see *Peruvian Times*, July 18, 1958, p. 3, and May 2, 1958, pp. 11–12.

17. Fishmeal producers delayed shipments abroad. The mining companies withheld investments. All who could, withheld dollars from the market. As Astiz describes it, the warning in 1967 was that 'if the President does not accept the request of the fishing industry (for devaluation and/or tax relief), the pressure of the exporting and financial groups may reach really dangerous levels' (Astiz (1969), p. 120).

18. The mix of policies adopted in 1967 and 1968 brought out the great difficulty for the Belaunde government of obtaining a political consensus. While the Government's middle-class base was alienated by the devaluation, conservative interests which might have rallied to support a full-scale swing to the Right were offended by other elements in the package. Restrictive monetary and fiscal policy was combined with import licensing, import controls and a proposed tax on exporters (*Peruvian Times*, Sep. 8, 1967, p. 1; Oct. 13, 1967, p. 1; Mar. 8, 1968, p. 1) as well as measures to restrict local borrowing by foreign firms and curb the unplanned expansion of the automobile industry (*Peruvian Times*, May 26, 1967, p. 2; June 30, 1967, p. 1). Political discord was thus increased to the point where for nine months the Government was unable to secure approval of the budget.

19. Real GNP in 1970 was less than 7 per cent above the 1966 level, and *per capita* GNP was up only 3 per cent (*Cuentas Nacionales*, 1969–1972, p. 11).

20. Other factors of course, contributed to the fall of Belaunde, particularly the IPC affair, and the political tensions induced by the approach of the 1969 elections. See Astiz (1969).

21. Influential academic contributions to the debate included the analysis of the 'oligarchy' in Bourricaud *et al* (1969), and the 'Gran Empresa Pequeña Nación' focus of Bravo Bresani (1968).

22. The 1950 figure is from Chapter 10 above. For 1960, we treat cotton, coffee and wool as locally-controlled, assume foreign firms accounted for one-third of sugar exports, all oil exports, and 10 per cent of fish products; and use Table 11.4 to estimate the foreign-controlled proportion of metal mining at 73 per cent for large firms and a further 10 per cent for small and medium-scale ventures. For 1967 the same proportions are assumed except for fish products, where the foreign share in 1967 is estimated as 25 per cent (see the previous discussion in Section 12.2). Shares of total exports by value are calculated from data in *Cuentas Nacionales 1969*, p. 42.

23. Estimated on the basis of a 1969 survey by the Ministerio de Industria y Comercio (1973, pp. 61 and 63), which found 56 per cent of the net fixed assets of large-scale manufacturing (sample of 174 firms accounting for 49 per cent of industrial value added, 28 per cent of manufacturing employment, and 4 per cent of the total number of manufacturing firms) to be foreign-controlled. We have assumed that the proportion of foreign control in the rest of the manufacturing sector was in the vicinity of 25 per cent, giving an overall average of 40 per cent. It should be noted that the U.S. Department of Commerce data on book value of U.S. direct investment in Peru show U.S. capital in manufacturing as only $92 million—around 10 per cent of the 1969 total capital stock of Peruvian industry in 1969 as reported in *Estadistica Industrial*; this figure seriously understates actual U.S. control, since it does not take into account (*a*) gearing-up of U.S. capital by means of loans from local banks, nor (*b*) joint ventures bringing in local equity capital but controlled by U.S. firms.

24. These arguments might be thought to qualify our earlier case against a 'developmental' role for foreign capital in the early years of the century, which rested in part upon the adequacy of the local supply of entrepreneurship. In fact it provides a further example of the point argued there (for instance p. 222), that the mere exclusion of foreign capital *by itself* is unlikely to be sufficient for development—especially once such traditions of collaboration and identification are well-established. The *long-run* cost of the foreign presence may be particularly great, precisely because it makes impossible the kind of short-run reversal that at this date policy makers still thought would be effective.

25. Chenery *et al.* (1974), Chap. 1; Adelman and Morris (1975), pp. 152 and 161.

26. Webb (1972a), p. 4.

27. Fitzgerald (1976), Appendix II.

28. Chaplin (1968).

CHAPTER 15

1. For a survey of the reforms and their immediate effects see Lowenthal (1975). For a summary of the effects on the structure of ownership and control in the economy see Fitzgerald (1976), Chap. 3.

2. Technically, compensation was provided by payment of funds into a blocked account, with the promise that these funds would be released when IPC paid Peru a much larger sum to compensate for past excess profits. Eventually, in early 1974, compensation of $22 million was paid.

3. Philip (1975).

4. On metal-mining policies see Ballantyne (1974). Full texts of mining legislation are published annually in *Perú Minero*.

5. For details of the profit-sharing arrangements see Figueroa (1973), p. 9.

6. *Peruvian Times*, Aug. 7, 1970, pp. 2–4. The full Social Property Law appeared in May 1974 (see *Latin American Economic Report*, May 31, 1974, p. 84).

7. *Peruvian Times*, June 18, 1971, p. 5.

8. Hunt (1974b) surveys these expropriations, with the exception of Marcona.

9. *Peruvian Times*, Aug. 21, 1970, pp. 2–3, and Jan. 22, 1971, pp. 5–6.

10. In mid-1974 President Velasco made public the 'Plan Inca,' which he claimed to have had written before the coup of 1968. The official version of the antecedents of the Plan are given in Zimmermann Zavala (1975), along with the full text (*ibid.*, pp. 322–53). The Plan lists 31 areas for action, each dealt with in isolation from the others on an *ad hoc* basis. No set of priorities is provided to guide policymakers in the event of a clash between two or more of the stated objectives of the Plan; nor are any general principles spelled out beyond the declaration that the Peruvian Revolution should be 'nationalist, independent and humanist' and free from the influence of imported dogmas. The slogan 'neither capitalist nor communist' recurs in many of Velasco's speeches, and echoes the policy-stance of Haya de la Torre and his APRA party around 1930.

11. Philip (1975), Chap. 4, has discussed in detail the early divisions and disagreements in the Military, and the victory of the more radical officers over the conservative faction in early 1969. Harding (1974, 1975) analyses the

evolution of the agrarian reform policy under pressure of events.

12. Quoted by Fitzgerald (1976a), p. 68.
13. Instituto Nacional de Planificación (1971), Vol. I, p. 40.
14. Instituto Nacional de Planificación (1971) Vol. I, p. 27.
15. Instituto Nacional de Planificación (1971) Vol. I, p. 18.
16. Instituto Nacional de Planificación (1971) Vol. I, p. 28.
17. See, for example, Fitzgerald (1976a), p. 104.
18. We are speaking here of the type of short-run pressures that effectively block innovative long-run policymaking—not to be confused with the much lighter pressures which caused an already-vacillating military government to chop and change its policies in practice (see above, p. 303).
19. Figueroa (1973) p. 15. See also Webb (1974), Chap. 6.
20. Harding (1974).
21. This uses the careful estimate in standardised hectares made by Caballero (1976), p. 3. The reform goal is 48 per cent.
22. Estimates of the proportion of the rural population excluded from the benefits of the reform range from two-thirds (Harding (1975), p. 220) to three-quarters (Fitzgerald (1976), p. 31). The *goal* is to benefit nearly 40 per cent (Caballero (1976), p. 4).
23. Figueroa (1973), pp. 14–15. His figures are constructed on the extreme assumption of land redistribution carried to the point of overall equality.
24. Webb (1974a), p. 42.
25. Total loans and investments of the Banco de Fomento Agropecuario increased 149 per cent 1968–74, compared with a 231 per cent increase in Banco Industrial loans (Banco Central *Boletin*, June 1975, p. 21). Ayala and Ugarteche (1975), p. 55, note that the Banco de Fomento Agropecuario suffered a drain of nearly half its total deposits between 1969 and 1972, as former large landowners transferred their funds elsewhere (particularly into mortage bonds). Agriculture, they show (Table 18A), had received 80 per cent of total government development loans in 1955, 38 per cent in 1968, and still only 39 per cent in 1972. Meantime, commercial banks which had been lending 10 per cent or more of their portfolio to agriculture until 1968, had reduced this to only 4 per cent by 1973 (*ibid.*, Table 8A).
26. Horton (1974), p. 99.
27. Horton (1974), p. 100.
28. There were some food subsidies, but these were mainly on imports.
29. *Peruvian Times*, Jan. 29, 1971, pp. 27–35 carried the text of the contract.
30. Hunt (1974a), pp. 26–7.
31. For a statement of the Government's belief that rapid privately-financed growth should follow from the structural reforms, see the speech by Finance Minister Morales Bermudez in *Peruvian Times*, Mar. 6, 1970, p. 1.
32. See Thorp (1972). In 1969 tough restrictions were announced on foreign-owned banks unless they transferred 75 per cent of their share capital to local ownership. The effects were slight, and the Government began to pressurise the locally-owned banks into mergers to improve their competitive strength, by raising the minimum capital requirements. The main result was an attempt by the Prado family's Banco Popular to arrange a merger with one of the foreign-controlled banks; and in June 1970 the Popular was nationalised. Other banks

followed. (See, for example, *Peruvian Times*, May 15, 1970, p. 1; June 19, 1970, p. 1; and Aug. 28, 1970, p. 1.)

33. The exceptions were the Ballon family's San Vicente zinc mine, developed in mid-1970 at a time when David Ballon was an important mining official in the Government (*Peruvian Times*, May 15, 1970, p. 2 and May 29, 1970, p. 1); and the 1971 purchase by fishmeal producer Luis Banchero of Minsur (a subsidiary of Grace and Lampa Mining Company) (*Peruvian Times*, Mar. 26, 1971, p. 2).

34. See the sectoral investment estimates in Fitzgerald (1976) p. 23.

35. Finance Minister Morales Bermudez, speaking in mid-1971, complained about 'the failure of private investors to respond to the stimuli which should have been provided by a balanced budget, tight monetary control and curbed inflation. Instead of rising by 37 per cent, as expected, private sector investments actually fell by 3 per cent (in 1970)' (*Peruvian Times*, June 11, 1971, pp. 4–5). The target for 1970 gross investment had been 23.5 per cent of GNP: in the event, the actual figure was only 13.1 per cent.

36. *Peruvian Times*, May 22, 1970, p. 1.

37. Ayala and Ugarteche (1975), p. 41.

38. The problems remained evident in 1975, when the Marcona Mining Company was taken over following a period of intensive decapitalisation achieved by the exploitation of penalty clauses in the company's export contracts. For six months following the nationalisation, Peru was unable to sell iron ore on the world market as a result of opposition from Marcona; in the absence of revenues from sales, the entire cost of maintaining the mine became a charge on the Government.

39. Webb (1972b), p. 2. For an evaluation of tax changes under Velasco see *ibid.*, pp. 27–31.

40. The ease of this course of action was greatly increased by the boom in international bank lending to countries such as Peru in 1973–4. On this see Kuczynski (1976).

41. 'In part' because availability of funds in the form of foreign exchange, not soles, probably influenced purchasing decisions.

42. *Latin American Economic Report*, Mar. 1, 1974, p. 33.

42. The Rockefeller interests associated with IPC had already in 1971 received some covert compensation via the Government's purchase of the Chase Manhattan Bank interests in Peru (see Hunt 1974b). Of the $150 million covered by the Greene Agreement, some $22 million was allocated to IPC by the U.S. Government, with the tacit consent of the Peruvians (*Petroleum Economist*, Feb. 1975).

43. Corporación Financiera de Desarrollo. See Ayala and Ugarteche (1975) for an analysis of COFIDE's performance in its first three years.

44. Fitzgerald (1976a), p. 25.

45. *Petroleum Economist*, Nov. 1975, p. 436; *Latin America Economic Report*, Mar. 12, 1976, p. 42.

46. Thorp (1967).

47. It is important not to over-estimate the extent to which the new mining projects will rescue the rate of growth of exports. In 1969, when the development of Cuajone began, copper accounted for around 30 per cent of export earnings, so that even a trebling of the output of this commodity would result in only a 60 per cent increase in total export earnings, if prices remained at 1969 levels. This

would represent a major contribution to an export economy whose other sectors were also growing; but such was not the case with Peru in the 1970s. While the mining projects moved slowly towards production, fishmeal exports (25 per cent of total earnings in 1969) suffered a permanent fall of roughly half (enough to nullify about one-fifth of the contribution of the new mines), while cotton, oil and wool continued their historic declines, and only non-ferrous metals such as lead, zinc and silver recorded any increases (Banco Central, *Boletin*). A trebling of copper production would thus imply (still at 1969 prices) only a 50 per cent or smaller gain for total export earnings, with a gestation period of up to a decade before full production is reached. The long-run trend of export earnings up to the end of the 1970s thus appears unlikely to rise above five per cent, although this growth will be concentrated in the last few years of the decade and may generate cumulative further growth.

48. In the sense that defence commitments were larger—at least 20 per cent of imports in 1975—and even fewer non-essentials were imported than pre-1968.

49. In the first year of stabilisation, 1975–6, public spending continued to rise in real terms and the entire burden of deflation was felt in credit restrictions on the private sector. In 1974 public sector and private sector imports rose by 126 per cent and 72 per cent respectively in dollar terms. In 1975 the figures were 69 per cent and 8 per cent (figures supplied by C. Boloña from his forthcoming study).

50. IMF (1977) (estimated).

51. *Latin America Economic Report*, May 27, 1977.

52. Not all observers are pessimistic. Fitzgerald, for example, has argued that 'the Peruvian strategy, for all its shortcomings, is the only realistic one' (Fitzgerald (1976), p. 104).

53. *Peruvian Times*, July 31, 1970, p. 1.

54. See the account in *Latin America Political Report*, 15 July 1977.

55. See the report in *Latin America Political Report*, 5 Aug. 1977, of the President's speech on 28 July, 'promising to combine financial orthodoxy with price controls and a 'flexible' attitude towards wage bargaining'; also of repressive measures taken.

CHAPTER 16

1. It should be emphasised again here that we are in no way suggesting that the 'oligarchy' were in any sense inadequately entrepreneurial, or too unresponsive to opportunity, or too 'precapitalist' in outlook, to promote the economy's development. Our argument has been that, given the dominant trends in international commodity and capital markets, the Peruvian élite responded intelligently as their interests dictated—and often with great entrepreneurship.

2. We emphasise again, as in Chapter 2, that we have deliberately confined our discussion within the framework of capitalist development, which we take to have been the only historical path open to Peru during the first half of the twentieth century. To measure the actual achievements of the economy against what might have been possible under a hypothetical socialist development plan would be an exercise in pure wishful thinking; we press quite hard enough against the borders of the historically-feasible in our discussion of why autonomous capitalist development was not pursued with more enthusiasm.

3. This conclusion is reached also by Fitzgerald (1976).

APPENDIX 1

1. *Extracto Estadistico del Perú*, 1934–5, p. 76.
2. Ibid., footnote.
3. Hunt (1973a), pp. 60–2.
4. For 1900, the U.S. price of £287.45 per metric ton was only 65 per cent of the London price of fine hard para, £440. It should be noted, however, that the reported Peruvian export price in late 1899 (Hunt (1973a), p. 61) was only £250.

APPENDIX 2

1. We give here those series which are least easily drawn from the standard sources. Mining is well covered in the official statistics.

APPENDIX 3

1. Lindqvist (1972), pp. 251–2.
2. Hunt (1974b), Table 4.

APPENDIX 4

1. U.N. Economic Commission for Latin America (1959).
2. In *Cuentas Nacionales del Perú*, 1950–65.
3. *La Situacion de la Industria Peruana en el año*—, published annually for the years 1962–8 by the Instituto Nacional de Promocion Industrial and the Banco Industrial del Peru (henceforth INPI-BIP).
4. The detailed working papers which the sections summarise are all available in microfiche from the Latin American Centre, Oxford University.
5. This is made clear by comparison of the M.I.T. figures and those of the Banco Central. The Bank practice is to calculate that portion of activity which represents refining on the basis of labour-force shares. This gives for, for example, petroleum, value-added in 1971 of 311 million soles, compared with 3,209 million in the M.I.T. data.
6. This should not be taken to imply that the Bank's figures are *in general* more reliable. Besides being highly aggregated, they are drawn from a smaller sample, for example, and we have not been able to examine the likely biases in the data very closely.

Bibliography

Items marked with an asterisk are cited in the text. Books without named authors are given under the initial of the first word of the title (excluding definite and indefinite articles). Periodicals and statistical series are listed separately, under their titles.

BOOKS AND ARTICLES IN JOURNALS CONSULTED

*Abramovich, J. (1973)
La Industria Pesquera en el Perú: Genesis, Apogeo y Crisis (Lima: Imprenta La Popular).

*Adelman, I. and Morris, C. T. (1975)
Economic Growth and Social Equity in Developing Countries (Stanford: University Press).

*Adler, J. H. (1965)
Absorptive Capacity: the Concept and its Determination (Washington D.C.: Brookings Institution).

Alayza Paz Soldan, F. (1933)
La Industria: Estudio Económico, Técnico y Social (Lima: Imprenta Torres Aguirre).

*Albert, W. (1976)
An Essay on the Peruvian Sugar Industry 1880–1922, and the Letters of Ronald Gordon, Administrator of the British Sugar Company in the Cañete Valley, 1914–1919, (Norwich: School of Social Studies, University of East Anglia).

*Alberti, G. (1970)
'Los Movimientos Campesinos' in Keith, R. G. et al., El Campesino en el Perú (Lima: Moncloa Editores).

*Alexander, R. J. (1957)
Communism in Latin America (New Jersey: Rutgers University Press).

*Alvarado Garrido, A. (1939)
La Industria Minera en el Perú: Breve Reseña sobre su Estado Actual (Lima: Imprenta Torres Aguirre).

*Alvarez Calderón, A. (1934)
'El Problema de la Plata y el Con-

*Alvarez Salomón, E. (1974) venio de Londres: Memorandum' (Lima: MS). 'La Agricultura Alimenticia Peruana 1960–1970' (Lima: Bachiller thesis, Universidad Católica).

Alzamora Silva, L. (1931a) *El Billete de Banco en el Perú* (Lima: Imprenta Gil).

Alzamora Silva, L. (1931b) *La Situación Económica y Fiscal del Perú* (Lima).

*American Petroleum Institute (1937) *Petroleum Facts and Figures* (New York, 5th ed.).

Anales del Congreso Nacional de la Minería (1921) (Lima: Imprenta Torres Aguirre) (7 vols).

Anales del Primer Congreso de Economía Nacional: Octubre 1957 (1958) (Lima: Universidad Nacional Mayor de San Marcos).

Anales del Primer Congreso de Irrigación y Colonización del Norte (1929) (Lima: Imprenta Torres Aguirre (4 vols).

*Anaya Franco, E. (1975) *Imperialismo, Industrialización y Transferencia de Tecnología en el Perú* (Lima: Editorial Horizonte).

Apuntes Monográficas de Morococha: Apuntes para una Monografía de la Provincia de Yauli (1930) (Morococha: Imprenta S. Camargo Moreno).

Arana, V. M. (1921) 'El Estado de Nuestra Industrialización,' *Mundial* (Lima), July 28.

Arca Parró, A. (1945) *El Medio Geográfico y la Población del Perú* (Lima: Imprenta Torres Aguirre).

*Arias Schreiber P. M. (1967) 'El Rol Promocional de la Legislación Minera' in Rodríguez Hoyle, D. (ed.) *Perú Minero, 1967* (Lima: n.p.).

*Arriaga, E. E. (1966) 'New Abridged Life Tables for Peru: 1940, 1950–51 and 1961,' in *Demography*, Vol. III, No. 1, pp. 218–37.

Arrús, O. (1925) *El Costo de la Vida y Causas de su Carestía* (Lima: Imprenta Americana).

Arrús, O. (1943) 'El Indice de Precios en el Peru,' *Estadística* (Washington: Inter-American Statistical Institute).

Aspíllaga Anderson, I. (1926)   *La Industria Azucarera Peruana* (Lima: F. E. Rosay).

*Astiz, C. (1969)   *Pressure Groups and Power Elites in Peruvian Politics* (Cornell: University Press).

*Ayala, M. and Ugarteche, O. (1975)   *International Comparative Analysis of Financial Markets in Colombia and Peru, 1965–1972* (London: MS, Graduate School of Business Studies).

Bain, H. F. and Read, T. T. (1934)   *Ores and Industry in South America* (New York: Harper).

*Ballantyne, J. (1974)   'The Political Economy of the Peruvian *Gran Mineria*' (Cornell University: Ph.D. thesis, Business School).

*Banco Central de Reserva (BCR) (1961)   *Actividades Productivas en el Perú* (Lima).

Banco de Perú y Londres (1927)   *Breve Reseña Histórica de la Fundación y Desarrollo del Banco del Perú y Londres al Cumplirse el Cincuentenario de su Establecimiento* (Lima: Imprenta Gil).

*Baran, P. (1960)   *The Political Economy of Growth* (New York: Prometheus Books).

Bardella, G. (1964)   *Setenta Anos de Vida Económica del Perú* (Lima: Banco de Crédito).

*Barlow, F. D., Jr. (1952)   *Cotton in South America: Production, Marketing, Consumption, and Developments in the Textile Industry* (Memphis: National Cotton Council).

*Barreda C., J. A. (1970)   'Cincuenta Anos de Labor en la Granja Modelo de Chuquibambilla,' *Boletin Informativo* No. 1 (Puno: Direccion de Proyección Social, Universidad Técnica del Altiplano).

*Barreda y Osma, F. (1900)   *Los Derechos de Aduana y las Industrias Nacionales* (Lima: Imprenta E. Moreno).

*Barreda y Ramos, C. (1929)   *La Industria de Lanas en el Perú y el Departamento de Puno* (Lima: Imprenta Torres Aguirre).

*Basadre, J. (1899)   'Aspecto Industrial del Cerro de Pasco', *Boletin de la Sociedad Na-*

cional de Mineria Ano 2, No. 21, Sep. 30, 1899.

Basadre G., J. (1948)   *Perú, Chile y Bolivia Independientes* (Barcelona and Buenos Aires: Salvat Editores).

*Basadre G., J. (1963–4)   *Historia de la República del Perú*, 11 vols, 5th ed. (Lima: Ed. 'Historia').

Basadre G., J. and Ferrero, R. (1963)   *Historia de la Cámara de Comercio de Lima* (Lima: Santiago Valverde).

*Bell, W. S. (1976)   'The Transition to Agrarian Capitalism in Northern Peru: Piura 1840 to 1920' (*MS*, Paper prepared for British Sociological Association Development Study Group).

*Bertram, I. G. (1974)   'Development Problems in an Export Economy: a Study of Domestic Capitalists, Foreign Firms and Government in Peru, 1919–1930' (Oxford: D.Phil., thesis).

Bertram, I. G. (1974a)   'Entry of the Cerro de Pasco Mining Company to Peru' (Oxford MS).

Bertram, I. G. (1974b)   'New Thinking on the Peruvian Peasantry', *Pacific Viewpoint* (Wellington) Sep.

*Bertram, I. G. (1975)   'Metal Mining in Peru since the Depression' (Oxford University: MS).

*Bertram, I. G. (1976)   *End-Use Classification of Peruvian Imports, 1891–1972* (Microfiche, Latin American Centre, Oxford).

*Bertram, I. G. (1976a)   'Modernisation and Change in the Wool Industry of Southern Peru 1919–1930: a case of Development Failure' (unpublished).

*Blanchard, P. (1975)   'The Peruvian Working Class Movement 1883–1919' (London: D.Phil. thesis).

*Bollinger, W. A. (1971)   'The Rise of U.S. Influence in the Peruvian Economy, 1869–1921' (U.C.L.A.: M.A. thesis).

*Boloña, C. (1976)   *Las Importaciones del Sector Público en el Perú 1971–74* Universidad del Pacífico, Trabajo de Investigación No. 5

*Bolsa Comercial de Lima   *Memoria* (Lima: annual).

*Bonilla, H. (1967–8)   'La Coyuntura Comercial del Siglo

*Bonilla, H. (1970)

*Bonilla, H. (1973)

Bourricaud, F. (1965)

*Bourricaud, F. (1969)

*Bourricaud, F. (1970)

Boza Barducci, T. (1961)

*Bradby, B. (1975)

Bravo, J. J. (1925)

*Bravo Bresani, J. (1968)

*Bromley, J. and Barbagelata, J. (1945)

*Brudenius, C. (1972)

*Brundenius, C. (1973)

Bureau of the American Republics (1895)

XIX en el Perú,' *Revista del Museo Nacional* Vol. 35 (Lima).

'L'Histoire Economique et Sociale du Pérou au 19e Siècle, 1821–1879' (University of Paris: doctoral dissertation).

Guano y Burguesía (Lima: Instituto de Estudios Peruanos).

'Structure and Function of the Peruvian Oligarchy', *Studies in Comparative International Development*, Vol. 2, No. 2 (St. Louis: Washington University).

'Notas sobre la Oligarquía Peruana' in Bourricaud, F., *et al., La Oligarquía en el Perú* (Lima: Instituto de Estudios Peruanos/Moncloa Editores).

Power and Society in Contemporary Peru (London: Faber).

Situación Actual y Perspectives del Algodón Tanguis: Posibilidades e Inconveniencias del Cultivo de Otras Variedades en el Perú (Cañete: MS).

'The Destruction of Natural Economy,' *Economy and Society* (May).

'Informe sobre los Humos de La Oroya,' *Boletín del Cuerpo de Ingenieros de Minas*, No. 108.

'Gran Empresa, Pequeña Nacion,' in Matos Mar, J., *et al., Perú Problema*, No. 1 (Lima: Francisco Moncloa).

Evolución de la Ciudad de Lima (Lima: Imprenta Lumen).

'The Anatomy of Imperialism: the Case of the Multinational Mining Corporations in Peru,' *Journal of Peace Research* Vol. 9, 1972, pp. 189–207 (Oslo).

'The Rise and Fall of the Peruvian Fishmeal Industry,' *Instant Research on Peace and Violence*, Vol. 3, No. 3, pp. 149–58 (Finland: Tampere).

Handbook of Peru (Washington DC: Senate Executive Documents I Sess.

*Caballero, J. M. (1976) 52 Cong. Vol. 7, No. 149, Part 9). 'Agrarian Reform and the Transformation of the Peruvian Countryside,' (Cambridge University: M.S.).

*Camprubi Alcázar, C. (1967) *Jose Payán y de Reyna (1844–1919): su Trayectoria Peruana* (Lima: P.L. Villanueva).

*Capunay, M. (1951) *Leguía: Vida y Obra del Constructor del Gran Perú* (Lima: Imprenta Bustamante).

Capunay Mimbela, C. (1965) *El Endeudamiento Público del Perú* (Lima: Universidad Nacional Mayor de San Marcos).

*Cardoso, F. H. (1973) 'Associated-Dependent Development: Theoretical and Practical Implications,' in Stepan, A. (ed.) *Authoritarian Brazil: Origins, Policies and Future* (New Haven and London: Yale U.P.).

*Carey, J. C. (1964) *Peru and the United States* (University of Notre Dame Press).

Cavero, E. (1971) 'Smelter: lo que Resta de la Antigua Fundición,' *El Serrano*, Vol. 30, No. 262, Sep.

*Caves, R. E. (1965) 'Vent for Surplus Models of Trade and Growth', in Baldwin, R.S. *et al., Trade, Growth and the Balance of Payments* (Amsterdam: North Holland Press).

*Centro de Documentación Económica y Social (1965) *Las Empresas Estatales en el Perú* (Lima: Santiago Valverde).

Centurión Herrera, E. (1939) *El Perú en el Mundo* (Brussels: Etablissements Généraux d'Imprimerie).

Cerro de Pasco Corporation (1952) 'Cincuenta Años de la Cerro de Pasco Corporation,' *Cultura Peruana* (Lima), Vol. 11, No. 54, May-June.

*Chaplin, D. (1967) *The Peruvian Industrial Labor Force* (Princeton: University Press).

*Chaplin, D. (1968) 'Peru's Postponed Revolution,' *World Politics*, Vol. 20, No. 3, Apr., pp. 393–420.

Chávez-Delgado Carrasco, G., (1973) 'La Industrialización Peruana: el Caso del Sector Textil' (Lima: Bachiller thesis, Universidad Católica).

*Chenery, H. B. *et al.*, (1974) *Redistribution with Growth* (London:

*Chevalier, F. (1966)

*Chilcote, R. H. (1974)

*Chudnovsky, D. (1974)

*CIDA (Comité Interamericano de Desarrollo Agrícola) (1966)

*Cisneros, C. B. (1906)

Cisneros, C. B. (1908)

Cisneros, C. B. (1911)

Cisneros, C. B. (1912)

Cisneros, C. B. and García, R. E. (1898)

*Cisneros, C. B. and García, R. E. (1900)

*Clague, C. (1967)

*Clavero, J. G. (1896)

Colley, B. T. (1945)

*Collin-Delavaud, C. (1967)

*Collin-Delavaud, C. (1968)

Oxford University Press).
'Témoignages Littéraires et Disparité de Croissance: L'Expansion de la Grande Propriété dans le Haut Pérou au XXᵉ Siècle,' *Annales*, No. 4, July–Aug. (Paris).
'Dependency: a Critical Synthesis of the Literature,' *Latin American Perspectives*, Vol. 1, No. 1.
Empresas Multinacionales y Ganancias Monopolicas en una Economia Latinoamericana (Mexico: Siglo Veintiuno).
Tenencia de la Tierra y Desarrollo *Socio-Económico del Sector Agricola: Perú* (Washington DC: Pan American Union).
Reseña Económica del Perú (Lima: Imprenta La Industria).
Frutos de Paz (Lima: 'La Opinion Nacional').
Monografía del Departamento de Lima (Lima: Carlos Fabori).
Sinopsis Estadística del Perú 1908– 1912 (Lima: Imprenta Unión).
Guía del Viajero: Callao, Lima y sus Alrededores (Lima: Imprenta del Estado).
El Perú en Europa (Lima: Guzman Editores).
'An International Comparison of Industrial Efficiency: Peru and the United States,' *Review of Economics and Statistics*, Vol. 49, No. 4, Nov., pp. 487–93.
El Tesoro del Perú (Lima: Imprenta Torres Aguirre).
'The Haciendas of the Cerro de Pasco Copper Corporation,' *Mining and Metallurgy*, Nov.
'Consecuencias de la Modernización de la Agricultura en las Haciendas de la Costa Norte del Perú' in Favre, H. *et al., La Hacienda en el Perú* (Lima: Instituto de Estudios Peruanos).
Les Regions Cotières du Pérou Sep-

*Comisión Bicameral Multipartidaria Encargada de Revisar el Convenio entre el Gobierno y la Southern Peru Copper Corporation (1967)

*Comisión Especial Nombrada para el Estudio de la Crisis de la Industria del Petróleo (1959)

Compania Manufacturera de Tejidos 'La Nacional', (1899)

*CONESTCAR (Convenio de Cooperación Técnica, Estadística y Cartográfica) (1965)

CONESTCAR (1968)

*CONESTCAR (1969)

*Consejo Nacional de Investigación (1970)

Consejo Provincial de Lima, Officina Municipal de Estadística (1916)

Cotler, J. (1967–8)

*Craig, W. W. (1967)

*Cumberland, W. W. (1922)

tentrional (Lima: Institut Francais d'Etudes Andines).

Dictamen and *Anexos* (2 vols) (Lima)

Causas y Factores Determinantes de la Crisis Actual de la Industria del Petróleo, su Magnitud y Posibles Derivaciones y Medidas Propuestas para Solucionarla (Lima: MS).

Estatutos, (Lima: Imprenta Gil).

Aspectos Económicos en el Cultivo del Algodón en el Perú (Lima: Ministerio de Agricultura).

Costos de Producción de Azúcar: Departamento de Lambayeque (Lima: Ministerio de Agricultura).

Peru. Proyecciones a largo plazo de la Oferta y Demanda de Productos Agropecuarios Seleccionadas, 1970–1975–1980 (Lima: Universidad Agraria, Ministerio de Agricultura).

Estudio sobre Transferencia de Tecnologia: Informe Preliminar (Lima).

Anuario Estadística de la Ciudad de Lima 1915 (Lima: Tip. Lartiga).

'The Mechanics of Internal Domination and Social Change in Peru,' *Studies in Comparative International Development* Vol. 3, No. 12 (St Louis: Washington University).

From Hacienda to Community: an Analysis of Solidarity and Social Change in Peru (Cornell: University Latin American Dissertation Series, No. 6).

'Economic Position of Peru in the Middle of the Year 1922' (typescript

	enclosure in Despatch No. 877, F.A. Sterling to Secretary of State, Sep. 12, 1922, in US National Archives Records Group 59, Decimal File 823.51/269).
*Dávalos y Lissón, p. (1901)	'Revista Anual sobre la Industria de Plata y Cobre del Cerro de Pasco, con la Estadística de sus Productos, Gastos y Utilidades,' *Boletín de la Sociedad Nacional de Minería* (Lima), Vol. 4, No. 39, Mar. 31.
Dávalos y Lissón, P. (1919)	*La Primera Centuria: Causas Geográficas, Políticas, y Económicas que han Detenido el Progreso Moral y Material del Perú en el Primer Siglo de su Vida Independiente* (4 vols) (Lima: Imprenta Gil).
Davies, Thomas M., Jr. (1974)	*Indian Integration in Peru: a Half-Century of Experience 1900–1948* (University of Nebraska Press).
*Dávila, M. A. (1972)	*Oligarquía y Pesca* (Lima: Universidad Católica, Taller Urbano-Industrial).
De Clairmont, A. (1907)	*Guide to Modern Peru: its Great Advantages and Vast Opportunities* (Toledo, Ohio: Barkdull Print).
De la Torre, J. O. (1925)	*El Presidente Leguía: su Espíritu y Labor Constructiva* (Lima).
De Lavalle, H. (1919)	'La Gran Guerra y el Organismo Económico Nacional,' (Lima: Bachiller thesis, Universidad Nacional de San Marcos).
*De Lucio, F. (1905)	'Recursos Minerales e Importancia de la Provincia de Pataz,' *Boletín del Cuerpo de Ingenieros de Minas* (Lima) No. 21.
*Deerr, N. (1949–50)	*The History of Sugar* (2 vols) (London: Chapman and Hall).
*Deltec Panamericana (1968)	*El Mercado de Capital en el Perú* (Mexico: Centro de Estudios Monetarios Latinamericanos).
Denegri, M. A. (1905)	*Estudios de Minería Práctica* (Lima: Imprenta La Industria).
Dennis, L. (1930)	'What Overthrew Leguía: the Responsibility of American Bankers for

	Peruvian Evils,' *The New Republic*, Sep. 17.
*Deustua, R. A. (1912)	'The Present Condition of the Petroleum Industry in Peru,' *Peru Today* (Lima), Apr. Vol. IV, No. 1, pp. 25–31.
*Deustua, R. A. (1914)	Memorandum addressed to Peruvian Government on the subject of the La-Brea-Parinas oilfield, reproduced in: Ministerio de Hacienda (1928), *Arreglo y Pago de las Reclamaciones Extranjeras* (Lima: Imprenta Americana).
Deustua, R. A. (1921)	*El Petróleo en el Perú* (Lima: Imprenta Americana).
*Di Angeli, G. (1949)	*Ensayo sobre la Industrializacion del Perú* (Lima: Editorial Lumen).
Diaz, J. A. (1945)	*La Situación Económica y Financiera del País* (Piura: Imprenta Minerva).
Diaz Ahumada, J. (n.d.)	*Historia de las Luchas Sindicales en el Valle de Chicama* (Trujillo: Editorial Bolivariano).
*Diaz Alejandro, C. (1970)	*Essays on the Economic History of the Argentine Republic* (New Haven: Yale University Press).
Dickens, P. D. (1930)	*American Direct Investments in Foreign Countries* (Washington DC: U.S. Department of Commerce Trade Information Bulletin No. 731.)
Dickerson, M. O. (1975)	'Peru Institutes Social Property as Part of its "Revolutionary Transformation",' *Inter-American Economic Affairs*, Winter (Washington).
*Diez Bedregal, F. (1955)	'Los Levantamientos de Indios en Huancané' (Cuzco: Thesis, Universidad Nacional San Antonio Abad).
Diez Canseco, E. (1953)	'Cuarenta Años de la Minería,' *La Crónica* (Lima), Apr. 7.
*Dirección General de Estadística (1944)	*Censo Nacional de Población y Ocupación de 1940* (12 vols) (Lima).
*Dirección General de Información (1968)	*Petroleum in Peru—For the World to Judge: the History of a Unique Case* (Lima).
Dirección Nacional de	*Estadística de Precios y Numeros In-*

Estadística (1930) — *dicadores* (Lima: Imprenta Americana).

Dirección Nacional de Estadística y Censos (1966–7) — *Primer Censo Nacional Económico* (Lima).

*Dragisic, J. (1971) — 'Peruvian Stabilisation Policies, 1939–68' (University of Wisconsin: Ph.D. thesis).

*Dubosc, L. (1905) — 'Apuntes sobre el Valle de Chira,' *Boletín del Ministerio de Fomento* (Lima) Ano 3, No. 11.

*Dunn, W. E. (1925) — *Peru: a Commercial and Industrial Handbook* (Washington DC: U.S. Deartment of Commerce Trade Promotion Series, No. 25.)

*Edmonds, D. C. (1972) — 'Reasons Underlying Development of the Peruvian Fishing Industry in the Post World War II Period' (American University: Ph.D. thesis).

Elejalde Zea, A. (1966) — *La Industria Pesquera* (Lima: Empresa Gráfica Sanmarti).

Elliott, W. Y. *et al.* (1937) — *International Control in the Non-Ferrous Metals* (New York: Macmillan).

*El-Sarki, M. Y. (1964) — *La Monoculture du Coton en Egypte et le Développement Économique* (Geneva: Libraire Droc).

Empresa Agrícola Chicama Ltda (1946) — *Estatutos* (Lima).

*Empresas Eléctricas Asociadas (1966) — *60 Años de Empresas Eléctricas Asociadas* (Lima: Imprenta Santa Rosa).

*Enock, C. R. (1906) — 'Peru in Transition,' *The Times* (London), July 30.

Enock, C. R. (1908) — *Peru* (London: T. Fisher Unwin).

*Espinoza Uriarte, H. and Osorio, J. (1971) — 'Dependencia y Poder Económico: Caso Minería y Pesquería' in Espinoza Uriarte, H. *et al.*, *Dependencia Económica y Tecnólogica: Caso Peruano* (Lima: Universidad Nacional Federico Villareal).

*Espinoza Uriarte, H. and Osorio, J. (1972) — *El Poder Económico en la Indústria* (Lima: Universidad Nacional Federico Villareal).

Fábrica Nacional de Tejidos de Algodón La Victoria 1899–1924 — (Lima: San martí y Cía).

*Farnworth, C. (1967)　　'The Application and Impact of Tax Incentives for Industrial Promotion in Peru 1960–66' (Lima: MS, Banco Central)

*Fernández, A. (1923)　　'Los Humos de la Fundición de La Oroya', *Boletín Oficial de Minas y Petroleo* (Lima), No. 3.

*Ferner A. (1975)　　'The Evolution of the Peruvian Industrial Bourgeoisie' (Lima: MS, ESAN).

*Ferrero, R. A. (1938)　　*Tierra y Poblacion en el Perú: la Escasez de Tierras Cultivadas y sus Consecuencias* (Lima: Banco Agrícola).

Ferrero, R. A. (1943)　　*Perspectivas Económicas de la Post-Guerra* (Lima: Editorial Lumen).

*Ferrero, R. A. (1946)　　*La Política Fiscal y la Economía Nacional* (Lima: Editorial Lumen).

Ferrero, R. A. (1952a)　　*Estudio Comparado de los Impuestos a la Renta en el Perú y los Demas Paises de América* (Lima: Imprenta Gil).

Ferrero, R. A. (1953)　　*La Historia Monetaria del Perú en el Presente Siglo* (Lima: n.p.).

Ferrero, R. A. (1956a)　　*Comentarios Acerca de los Impuestos en el Perú* (Lima: Tipografia Peruana).

*Ferrero, R. A. (1956b)　　*La Situación Algodonera Mundial y las Exportaciones del Perú* (Lima: Banco Continental).

*Ferrero, R. A. (1957)　　*La Renta Nacional* (Lima: Tipografia Peruana).

*Fiedler, R. (1943)　　*La Pesca y las Industrias Pesqueras en el Perú, con Recomendaciones para el Futuro Desarrollo* (Lima: Imprenta Gil).

Figueroa, A. (1972)　　*Asignación de Recursos, Empleo y Distribución de Ingresos en la Economía Peruana* (Lima: Universidad Católica, CISEPA Documento de Trabajo No. 5).

*Figueroa, A. (1973)　　*El Impacto de las Reformas Actuales sobre la Distribución de Ingresos en el Perú* (Lima: Universidad Católica,

CISEPA Documento de Trabajo No. 8).

Figueroa, A. (1975) 'Income Distribution, Demand Structure and Employment: the Case of Peru,' *Journal of Development Studies*, Jan., Volume XI, No. 2, pp. 20–31.

*Fishlow, A. (1972) 'Origins and Consequences of Import Substituting Industrialisation in Brazil,' in Di Marco, L.E. *et al.* (ed) *International Economics and Development: Essays in Honor of Raul Prebisch* (New York and London: Academic Press).

*Fitzgerald, E. V. K. (1976) *The State and Economic Development: Peru since 1968* (Cambridge: University Press).

*Fitzgerald, E. V. K. (1976a) *Some Aspects of Industrialisation in Peru 1965–1975* (Cambridge: University Latin American Centre, working paper No. 22.)

*F⁚.zgerald, E. V. K. (1976b) 'Peru: the Political Economy of an Intermediate Regime,' in *Journal of Latin American Studies*, Vol. 8, part 1, pp. 1–21.

*Fitzgerald E. V. K. (1976c) 'The Search for National Development: The Political Economy of Peru 1956–76' (Cambridge: MS).

*Food and Agriculture Organisation (FAO) (1961) *The World Sugar Economy in Figures, 1880–1959* (New York: United Nations).

Ford, A. G. (1956) 'Argentina and the Baring Crisis of 1890,' *Oxford Economic Papers*, Vol. 8, No. 2, pp. 127–50.

Ford, T. R. (1955) *Man and Land in Peru* (Gainesville: University of Florida Press).

*Foreign Bondholders Protective Council Inc. (1950) *Report for Years 1946 through 1949* (New York). (Also subsequent years.)

*Fox, R. W. (1972) *Urban Population Growth in Peru* (Washington DC: Inter-American Development Bank Urban Population Series, No. 3).

*Frank, A. G. (1967) *Capitalism and Underdevelopment in Latin America* (New York: Monthly

Fuchs, F. G. (1918)

Review Press).
'Yacimiento Mineral del Cerro de Pasco,' *Boletin de la Sociedad Geográfica de Lima*, Vol. 34, Trimestre II, June 30.

*Fuentes, M. (1879)

Estadística de las Minas de la República del Perú en 1878 (Lima: Imprenta del Estado).

*Fuentes Irurozqui, M. (1950)

Sintesis de la Economía Peruana (Lima: Sanmartí).

*Furnish, D. B. and Muñoz Cabrera, R. (1966)

Legal Research Series on Agricultural Marketing Structures in Peru: III, Wheat (Lima: Iowa Universities Mission)

*Furnish, D. B. (1970)

'Peruvian Domestic Law Aspects of the La Brea y Parinas Controversy,' *Kentucky Law Journal*, Vol. 59.

*Furtado, C. (1971)

'Dependencia Externa y Teoria Económica,' *El Trimestre Económico*, Vol. 38(2), No. 150, April–June 1971.

Galarza, E. (1931)

'Debts, Dictatorship and Revolution in Bolivia and Peru,' *Foreign Policy Reports*, May 13.

*Gallo, E. (1970)

'Agrarian Expansion and Industrial Development in Argentina 1880–1930;' in *Latin American Affairs*, ed. R. Carr, St. Antony's Papers No. 22 (Oxford: University Press).

*Garland, A. (1895)

Estudio Económico: la Industria Azucarera en el Perú (1550–1895) (Lima: Imprenta del Estado).

*Garland, A. (1896)

Las Industrias en el Perú (Lima).

*Garland, A. (1900)

El Fisco y las Industrias Nacionales (Lima).

*Garland, A. (1901)

Articulos Económicos (Lima: Imprenta La Industria).

*Garland, A. (1902a)

Reseña Industrial del Perú (Lima: Imprenta del Estado).

*Garland, A. (1902b)

'La Industria del Petróleo en el Perú en 1901,' *Boletín del Cuerpo de Ingenieros de Minas* (Lima), No. 2.

*Garland, A. (1905)

Reseña Industrial del Perú en 1905 (Lima: Imprenta La Industria).

*Garland, A. (1908)

Peru in 1906 (Lima: Imprenta La Industria).

*Garland Duponte, A. (n.d.)	*Lo Que el Oncenio Hizó por el Peru bajo el Mando del Presidente Leguía* (Lima: Imprenta Gil).
*Geddes, C. F. (1972)	*Patiño, the Tin King* (London: Robert Hale).
*Gerbi, A. (1941)	*El Perú en Marcha: Ensayos de Geografía Económica* (Lima: Banco de Credito).
Gerbolini, J. F. (1969)	*La Industria Manufacturera* (Lima: Editorial Gráfico Labor).
*Gershenkron, A. (1962)	*Economic Backwardness in Historical Perspective* (Cambridge, Mass: Harvard U.P.).
Gilbert, D. (1971)	'Power and Progress: One Hundred Years of Oligarchy in Peru' (Cornell University: MS).
*Girvan, N. (1970)	'Multinational Corporations and Dependent Underdevelopment in Mineral Export Economies,' *Social and Economic Studies*, Vol. 19, No. 4, Dec.
Glade, W. P. (1969)	*The Latin American Economies: a Study of their Institutional Evolution* (New York: Van Nostrand).
Gleason, D. (1974)	'Profit and Peril in Peru: the Gottfried Affair, 1898–1900,' *Inter-American Economic Affairs*, Winter.
*Goetz, A. (1973)	'Industrialisation in Argentina' (Oxford: MS).
Gotnez-Cornejo Ponsignon, M. O. (1974)	'Historia del Movimiento Obrero Textil' (Lima: Bachiller thesis, Universidad Católica).
*Gonzales del Valle, L. (1958)	*Estudio sobre Costos de Producción, Refinación Distribución y Venta y Transporte, de las Diversas Companias Productores de Petróleo en el Perú* (Lima: MS).
*Goodsell, C. T. (1974)	*American Corporations and Peruvian Politics* (University Press: Harvard).
Goodsell, C. T. (1975)	'The Multinational Corporation as Political Actor in a Changing Environment: Peru,' *Inter-American Economic Affairs*, Winter.
*Goodwin, R. N. (1969)	'Letter from Peru,' *The New Yorker*, May 17, pp. 41–109.

*Greenhill R. G. and Miller, R. M. (1973) — 'The Peruvian Government and the Nitrate Trade, 1873–1879,' *Journal of Latin American Studies*, Vol. 5, part I, May 1973, pp. 107–31.

*Griffin, K. B. (1969) — *Underdevelopment in Spanish America* (London: Allen and Unwin).

*Griffin, K. B. (1970) — 'Foreign Capital, Domestic Savings, and Economic Development,' *Bulletin of the Oxford University Institute of Economics and Statistics*, May, Vol. 32 (1970), pp. 99-112.

Grunwald, J. and Musgrove, P. (1970) — *Natural Resources in Latin American Development* (Baltimore: Johns Hopkins Press).

*Gubbins, J. R. (1899) — *Lo Que Se Vé y Lo Que No Se Vé* (Lima: n.p.).

*Gubbins, J. R. (1900) — *'Más Luz'. Estudio Económico-Social* (Lima: Imprenta del Estado).

The Gum Industry in Peru: Official Publication for Capitalists, Tradesmen and Settlers (1903) — (Lima: Imprenta del Estado).

*Gurney, W. M. (1930) — 'Summary of Events Relating to the Passing by Congress of the Petroleum Monopoly and National Refinery Bill' (Enclosure in Despatch No. 38, C.H. Bentinck to Foreign Secretary, Mar. 8, 1930, in British diplomatic archives, FO371/14252/A2500).

*Gurney, W. M. (1931) — *Report on the Economic Conditions in Peru* (London: HMSO).

*Gutiérrez, V. (1935) — *The World Sugar Problem 1926–35* (London: Norman Rodgers).

*Halsey, F. M. (1918) — *Investments in Latin America and the British West Indies* (Washington DC: U.S. Department of Commerce Special Agents Series, No. 169).

*Hammel, E. A. (1962) — *Wealth, Authority and Prestige in the Ica Valley, Peru* (Albuquerque: University of New Mexico Publications in Anthropology, No. 10).

Hammel, E. A. (1969) — *Power in Ica: the Structural History of a Peruvian Community* (Boston: Little, Brown).

* Handelman, H. (1975)	*Struggle in the Andes: Peasant Political Mobilisation in Peru* (University of Texas Press, Latin American Monographs Series No. 35).
Handley, W. W. (1915)	'Peru,' *Supplements to U.S. Commerce Reports*, No. 46A, July 27.
* Harding, C. (1974)	*Agrarian Reform and Agrarian Struggles in Peru* (Cambridge: University Centre of Latin American Studies, Working Paper No. 15).
* Harding, C. (1975)	'Land Reform and Social Conflict in Peru,' in Lowenthal, A. (ed.) *The Peruvian Experiment: Continuity and Change under Military Rule* (Princeton: University Press).
Hardy, O. (1917)	*Peru's Financial Problem* (Washington DC: Government Printing Office).
* Haya de la Torre, V. R. (1970)	*El Antiimperialismo y el APRA* (2nd ed.) (Lima: Imprenta Amauta).
* Hayn, R. (1957)	'Peruvian Exchange Controls, 1945–1948,' *Inter-American Economic Affairs*, Vol. 10, Spring, pp. 47–70.
* Hazen, D. C. (1974)	'The Awakening of Puno: Government Policy and the Indian Problem in Southern Peru 1900–1955' (Yale University: Ph.D. thesis).
Hernández Zubiarte, A. (1934)	*El Estanco de la Sal: Legislación, Historia y Economía del Impuesto en el Perú* (Lima: La Prensa).
Herrera, C. (1909)	'Estado Actual de la Minería en Huarochirí,' *Boletín del Cuerpo de Ingenieros de Minas*, No. 72 (Lima).
Hill, A. J. (1923a)	*Report on the Finance, Industry and Trade of Peru, September 1922* (London: HMSO).
Hill, A. J. (1923b)	*Report on the Finance, Industry and Trade of Peru, August 1923* (London: HMSO).
* Hinds, W. E. (1926)	*Informe sobre la Producción de Algodón en el Valle de Cañete* (Cañete: Imprenta Chenyek).
* Hobsbawm, E. J. (1970)	'La Convención, Peru: a Case of Neo-Feudalism,' *Journal of Latin American Studies*, Vol. 1.

Hobsbawm, E. J. (1974)   'Peasant Land Occupations', *Past and Present*, Feb.

* Hohagen, J. (1936)   'Las Industrias en el Perú', *Boletín del Cuerpo de Ingenieros de Minas* No. 114 (Lima).

* Hohagen, J. (1937)   'El Oro en el Perú', *Boletín del Cuerpo de Ingenieros de Minas* No. 118 (Lima).

* Horton, D. E. (1973)   *Haciendas and Cooperatives: a Preliminary Study of Latifundist Agriculture and Agrarian Reform in Northern Peru* (University of Wisconsin: Land Tenure Centre Research Paper No. 53).

* Horton, D. E. (1974)   *Land Reform and Reform Enterprises in Peru*, Report submitted to the Land Tenure Centre and the International Bank for Reconstruction and Development (Wisconsin: Land Tenure Centre).

* Hunt, S. J. (1964)   'Peruvian Agricultural Production 1944–1962' (Lima: MS).

* Hunt, S. J. (1971)   'Distribution, Growth and Government Economic Behaviour in Peru,' in Ranis, G. (ed.) *Government and Economic Development* (New Haven: Yale University Press).

Hunt, S. J. (1972)   *Some Tasks in Peruvian Economic History, 1880–1930* (Princeton University: Woodrow Wilson School Research Program in Economic Development, Discussion Paper No. 25.)

* Hunt, S. J. (1973a)   *Price and Quantum Estimates of Peruvian Exports, 1830–1962* (Princeton University: Woodrow Wilson School Research Program in Economic Development, Discussion Paper No. 33).

* Hunt, S. J. (1973b)   *Growth and Guano in Nineteenth-Century Peru* (Princeton University: Woodrow Wilson School Research Program in Economic Development, Discussion Paper No. 34).

* Hunt, S. J. (1974a)   *Direct Foreign Investment in Peru: New Rules for an Old Game* (Princeton University: Woodrow Wilson

	School Research Program in Economic Development, Discussion Paper No. 44).
*Hunt, S. J. (1974b)	*Direct Foreign Investment in Peru under the Ancien Régime* (Cambridge University: Mimeo paper presented to Symposium on Foreign Investment in Latin America, June 1974).
*Hunt, S.J. (1974c)	'Real Wages and Economic Growth (in Peru),' (Princeton: MS).
*Hymer, S. (1960)	'The International Operations of National Firms: a Study of Direct Investment' (Massachusetts Institute of Technology: Ph.D. thesis).
*IMF (1977)	*Peru – Recent Economic Developments* (Washington DC: International Monetary Fund)
Instituto Nacional de Planificación (INP) (1971)	*Plan Nacional de Desarrollo para 1971–1975* (Lima).
*Instituto Nacional de Planificación (INP) (1973)	*Relaciones Inter-industrales de la Economia Peruana – Tabla Insumo-Producto 1969* (Lima).
*International Bank for Reconstruction and Development (1975)	'*Agricultural Sector Survey: Peru*' (Washington).
International Petroleum Company (1947/49)	'The International Petroleum Company and the Economic Development in Peru,' in *Peruvian Times*, Dec. 12, 1947, and June 3, 1949.
*International Sugar Council (1963)	*The World Sugar Economy: Structure and Policies* (London).
*Iparraguirre Cortez, J. (1965)	*Política Económica de la Pesquería del Perú* (Lima: Ministerio de Agricultura).
*Jelicic, J. (1955)	*La Economía Peruana en 1954–1955* (Lima: Tipografía Peruana).
*Jimenez, C. P. (1922)	'Estadística Industrial del Perú en 1918,' *Boletín del Cuerpo de Ingenieros de Minas* (Lima), No. 105.
Jimenez, C. P. (1924)	'Reseña Historica de la Minería,' in Ministerio de Fomento, *Sintesis de la Minería Peruana en el Centenario de Ayacucho* (Lima: Imprenta Torres Aguirre).
Jochamowitz, A. (1909)	'La Industria Minera en Morococha

438　　　　　　　　*Peru 1890–1977*

*Jochamowitz, A. *et al.* (1930)

*Jochamowitz, A. (1939)

Kapsoli, W. and Reátagui, W. (1972)

*Karno, H. (1970)

*Kay, L. L. (1924)

Keith, R. G. *et al.* (1970)

Kemmerer, H. W. *et al.* (1931)

*Kindleberger, C. P. (1969)

*Kisic, D. (1972)

*Klaren, P. (1969)

*Klein, H. S. (1965)

Klinge, G. (1924)

Klinge, G. (1937)

*Klinge, G. (1946)

*Knorr, K. E. (1945)

en 1909,' *Boletin del Cuerpo de Ingenieros de Minas* (Lima), No. 65. *Album Obsequiado al Sr A.B. Leguia, Presidente de la República, por el Personal Directivo del Ministerio de Fomento, Mostrando las Diversas Obras Llevadas a Cabo de 1919 a 1930* (Lima: Imprenta Torres Aguirre). 'El Problema Petrolífera en el Perú,' *Boletín del Cuerpo de Ingenieros de Minas* (Lima), No. 125. *El Campesinado Peruano 1919–1930* (Lima: Universidad Nacional Mayor de San Marcos). 'Augusto B. Leguia: the Oligarchy and the Modernisation of Peru, 1870–1930' (U.C.L.A.: Ph.D. thesis). 'The Oil Coast of Peru,' in *West Coast Leader*, 10 weeks beginning February 19, 1924. *La Hacienda, la Comunidad y el Campesino en el Peru* (Lima: Moncloa Editores). *Report on the Public Credit of Peru* (Lima: Banco Central de Reserva). *American Business Abroad* (New Haven: Yale University Press). 'Aspectos Socioeconómicos de la Industria Azucarera Peruana' (Lima: bachiller thesis, Universidad Católica). *La Formación de las Haciendas Azucareas y los Orígenes del APRA* (Lima: Moncloa). 'The Creation of the Patiño Tin Empire,' *Inter-American Economic Affairs*, Vol. 19, No. 2, Autumn. *La Industria Azucarera en el Perú* (Lima: Imprenta Torres Aguirre). *Evolución Histórico de los Precios de Algodón y sus Tendencias Actuales* (Lima: Banco Agrícola). *Política Agrícola-Alimenticia* (Lima: Imprenta Torres Aguirre). *World Rubber and its Regulation*

	(Stanford University Press).
Kubler, G. (1952)	*The Indian Caste of Peru, 1795–1940* (Washington DC: Government Printing Office, Institute of Social Anthropology Publication No. 14).
*Kuczynski, M. (1976)	'Latin America and the Dollar', seminar paper, Oxford Latin American Centre, 26 November 1976.
*Kuznets, S. (1965)	*Economic Growth and Structure* (London: Heinemann).
Labarthe, P. A. (1930)	'El Mas Grande Escándalo de Ingeniería en Suramérica', *El Comercio* (Lima), Sep. 5.
*Labarthe, P. A. (1933)	*La Política de Obras Públicas del Gobierno de Leguía* (Lima: Imprenta Americana).
Laite, A. J. (1972)	*Industrialisation and Land Tenure in the Peruvian Andes, Part 2* (MS, paper presented to Symposium on Land and Peasant in Latin America and the Caribbean, Cambridge University, Dec. 1972).
*Lall, S. (1975)	'Is "Dependence" a Useful Concept in Analysing Underdevelopment?', in *World Development*, Vol. 3, Nos. 11 and 12, pp. 799–810.
*Langdon, G. (1968)	*Don Roberto's Daughter* (London: Chatto and Windus).
Larkin, E. P. (1866)	*Report of the General Superintendent to the Board of Directors of the Peruvian Petroleum Company of New York* (New York: L.H. Biglow).
*Laurie Solis, L. (1967)	*La Diplomacía del Petróleo y el Caso de La Brea y Parinas* (2nd ed.) (Lima: Universidad Nacional de Ingeniería).
*Leubel, A. C. (1861)	*El Perú en 1860, o sea Anuario Nacional* (Lima: Imprenta de El Comercio).
*Levin, J. (1960)	*The Export Economies: their Pattern of Development in Historical Perspective* (Harvard: University Press).
*Lewis, C. (1938)	*America's Stake in International Investments* (Washington DC: Brookings Institution).
Lewis, C. (1945)	*Debtor and Creditor Countries: 1938,*

*Lewis, R. A. (1973) — *1944* (Washington DC: Brookings Institution).
Employment, Income and the Growth of the Barriadas in Lima, Peru (Cornell: University Latin American Dissertation Series, No. 46).

*Lewis, S. (1972) — *The International Petroleum Company Versus Peru: a Case Study in Nationalism, Management, and International Relations* (California State College: MS, Department of Political Science).

*Liga de Hacendados de Puno-Arequipa (1922) — *La Verdad sobre la Cuestión Indígena: Memorandum que Presenta la Liga de Hacendados de Puno-Arequipa al Supremo Gobierno, Mayo 2, 1922* (Arequipa: Tip. S. Quiroz).

*Lindqvist, S. (1972) — *The Shadow: Latin America Faces the Seventies* (London: Penguin Books).

Long, N. and Roberts, B. (1974) — 'Regional Structure and Entrepreneurial Activity in a Peruvian Highland Valley: Final Report Presented to Social Science Research Council' (University of Manchester: MS).

Long, R., Sobradillo, A., Ugarteche, O., and Barnes, J. (1975) — 'Cerro de Pasco Copper Corporation—a Financial Analysis (1941–1952)' (London Business School: MS)

*López Aliaga, F. (1908) — 'El Algodón en el Valle de Cañete,' *Boletin del Ministerio de Fomento* (Lima) Ano 6, No. 12, Dec. 31.

López Aliaga, F. (1924) — 'La Fundición de La Oroya: una Grave Amenaza para la Ganadería Nacional,' *La Vida Agrícola*, Vol. 1, No. 1, Jan.

*Low, A. (1976) — 'The Effect of Foreign Capital on Peruvian Entrepreneurship' (Oxford: B.Phil. thesis).

*Lowenthal, A. F. (ed.) (1975) — *The Peruvian Experiment: Continuity and Change under Military Rule* (Princeton: University Press)

*Macario, S. (1964) — 'Protectionism and Industrialisation in Latin America,' *Economic Bulletin for Latin America* Vol. IX, No. 1, Mar. 1964, pp. 61–102 (U.N. Economic Commission for Latin America).

*McArver, C. H. (1970) 'The Role of American Economic Interests in the Development of Cerro de Pasco, 1877–1907' (University of North Carolina: M.A. thesis).

*MacFadyean, A. (ed.) (1944) *The History of Rubber Regulation, 1934–1943* (London: Allen and Unwin).

Macedo Mendoza, J. (1960) *Nacionalicemos el Petróleo!* (Lima: Ediciones Hora del Hombre).

McLaughlin, D. H. (1945) 'Origin and Development of the Cerro de Pasco Copper Corporation,' *Mining and Metallurgy*, Nov.

*McQueen, C. A. (1926a) *Peruvian Public Finance* (Washington DC: U.S. Department of Commerce Trade Promotion Series No. 30).

*McQueen, C. A. (1926b) 'Causes of the Exchange Slump in Peru,' *West Coast Leader* (Lima, Nov. 30).

*Maiguashca, J. (1967) 'A Reinterpretation of the Guano Age, 1840–1880' (Oxford University: D.Phil. thesis).

*Málaga, F. E. (1908) 'Producción de Nuestras Principales Industrias Agropecuarias en 1907,' *Boletín del Ministerio de Fomento* (Lima), Ano 6, No. 10, Oct. 31.

*Malaga Santolalla, F. (1904a) 'El Asiento Mineral de Hualgayoc,' *Boletín del Cuerpo de Ingenieros de Minas* (Lima) No. 6.

*Malaga Santolalla, F. (1904b) 'La Provincia de Cajatambo y sus Asientos Minerales,' *Boletín del Cuerpo de Ingenieros de Minas* (Lima) No. 10.

*Malpica, C. (1963), (1968) *Los Dueños del Perú* (1st, 3rd ed.) (Lima: Ediciones Ensayos Sociales).

*Maltby, L. L. (1972) 'Indian Revolts in the Altiplano: the Contest for Land, 1895–1925' (Harvard University: Honours thesis)

*Manners, F. W. (1922) *Report on the Finance, Industry and Trade of Peru to October 31, 1921, Together with a Report on the Com-*

Marett, R. 1969

*Mariátegui, J. C. (1971)

*Marie, V. (1904)

*Marquez, P. and Carcelen, J. (1968)

*Marsters, V. F. (1907)

*Martin, P. F. (1911)

*Martinez-Alier, J. (1973)

*Masías, M. G. (1903)

*Masías, M. G. (1905)

*Mathew, W. M. (1968)

*Matos Mar, J. (1967)

*Mayer, D. (1913)

*Merrill, W. C. and Prochezka, G. (1967)

Mikesell, R. F. (1973)

mercial Aspects of Southern Peru (London: HMSO).
Peru (London: Benn).
Seven Interpretive Essays on Peruvian Reality (trans. M. Urquidi) (University of Texas Press).
'La Producción del Algodón en el Perú,' *Boletín del Ministerio de Fomento* (Lima), Año 2, No. 4, Apr.
'Estudio sobre Protección Efectiva,' (Lima: MS, Banco Central de Reserva).
'Informe Preliminar sobre la Zona Petrolifera del Norte del Perú,' *Boletín del Cuerpo de Ingenieros de Minas* (Lima), No. 50.
Peru of the Twentieth Century (London: Edward Arnold).
Los Huachilleros del Perú (Paris: Ruedo Ibérico).
'Informe sobre los Trabajos Efectuados en el Asiento Mineral de Yauli,' *Boletín del Cuerpo de Ingenieros de Minas* (Lima), No. 5.
'Estado Actual de la Industria Minera de Morococha,' *Boletín del Cuerpo de Ingenieros de Minas* (Lima), No. 25.
'The Imperialism of Free Trade: Peru 1820–1870,' *Economic History Review*, Vol. 21, No. 3, Dec.
'Las Haciendas del Valle de Chancay,' in Favre, H. *et al.*, *La Hacienda en el Perú* (Lima: Instituto de Estudios Peruanos).
The Conduct of the Cerro de Pasco Mining Company (Lima: Asociación Pro-Indígena).
Estableciendo Precios de Arroz en el Perú: Informe Resumido (Lima: Iowa Mission special report).
'Southern Peru Copper Corporation's Profits from Toquepala: an Economic and Normative Analysis' (University of Oregon: MS).

Bibliography

443

Miller, R. (1974)   *The Peruvian Government and British Firms, 1885–1930* (MS, paper presented to Symposium on Foreign Investment and External Finance in Latin America, Cambridge University, 1974.)

*Miller, R. (1976)   'The Making of the Grace Contract: British Bondholders and the Peruvian Government, 1885–1890,' in *Journal of Latin American Studies*, Vol. 8, Part 1, May, pp. 73–100.

*Miller, S. (1967)   'Hacienda to Plantation in Northern Peru: the Process of Proletarianisation of a Tenant Farmer Society,' in Steward, J.H. (ed.) *Contemporary Change in Traditional Societies* (Urbana, Ill.: University of Illinois Press).

*Millones, O. (1973)   'La Oferta de los Productos Agrícolas Alimenticios a la Zona Urbana' (Lima: Universidad Catolica, CISEPA working paper No. 11).

*La Minería y la Agricultura al Punto de Vista del Progreso (1876)   (Lima: Imprenta de El Comercio).

*Mines and Mining in Peru (1903)   (Lima: Imprenta del Estado)

*Ministerio de Fomento y Obras Públicas (1902)   *La Crisis del Azúcar: Informe de la Comisión Oficial* (Lima).

Ministerio de Fomento y Obras (1903)   *Peru: a Sketch for Capitalists, Tradesmen and Settlers: a Report on the Industries that can be Developed and on Those that Might be Introduced* (Lima).

*Ministerio de Fomento y Obras Públicas (1921)   *Resúmenes del Censo de las Provincias de Lima y Callao* (Lima: Imprenta Torres Aguirre).

Ministerio de Fomento y Obras Públicas (1924)   *Sintesis de la Minería en el Centenario de Ayacucho* (2 vols) (Lima: Imprenta Torres Aguirre).

*Ministerio de Fomento y Obras Públicas (Dirección de Agricultura y Ganadería) (1932)   *Estadística General Agro-Pecuaria del Perú del Año 1929* (Lima: Imprenta Gil).

* Ministerio de Hacienda (1912) — *Ley de Tarifas de Derechos de Aduanas* (Lima).

* Ministerio de Hacienda (1922) — *Documentos Relativos al Proyecto de Tarifa de Derechos de Importación Formulado por la Comisión Nombrada por Disposición Suprema de 13 de Abril de 1921* (Lima: Casa Nacional de Moneda).

* Ministerio de Industria y Comercio (M.I.C.) (1973) — 'Sectores Industria y Comercio, Enero – Diciembre, 1972' (Lima: MS).

* Ministerio de Industria y Turismo (M.I.T.) (1974) — 'Efectos de la Política Industrial sobre la Inversión en el Sector' (Lima: MS).

Ministerio de Relaciones Exteriores (1937) — *The Progress of Peru* (Lima).

* Mitchell, B.R. (1962) — *Abstract of British Historical Statistics* (Cambridge: University Press).

Monografía Geográfica e Histórica del Departamento de La Libertad (1935) — (Trujillo: Imprenta La Central).

* Moreno, F. (1891) — *Petroleum in Peru from an Industrial Point of View* (Lima: F. Masias).

* Moreno, F. (1900) — *Las Irrigaciones de la Costa* (Lima: Imprenta del Estado).

* Muñoz O., *et al.* (1972) — *Proceso a la Industrialisación Chilena* (Santiago: Ediciones Nueva Universidad).

Muñoz de la Cruz, N. (1963) — 'Economía Algodonera del Departamento de Ica' (Lima: Bachiller thesis, Universidad Nacional Mayor de San Marcos).

* Myrdal, G. (1958) — *Economic Theory and the Underdeveloped Regions* (London: Duckworth).

* Neira, H. (1964) — *Cuzco, Tierra y Muerte* (Lima: Ediciones Populares).

* Nogaro, B. (1936) — *Les Prix Agricoles Mondiaux et la Crise* (Paris: Libraire Générale du Droit et de Jurisprudence).

* Normand, E. (1962) — 'El Petróleo en el Perú,' in Paz Soldán, J.P. (ed.) *Vision del Peru en el Siglo XX* (Lima: Ediciones Librería Studium).

* North, L. L. (1973) — 'The Origins and Development of the

Noticias sobre la Historia de Barranco y su Servicio de Agua Potable (1907)

*O'Brien, P. J. (1975)

Peruvian Aprista Party' (University of California at Berkeley Ph.D. thesis).
(Lima: Imprenta El Lucero).

'A Critique of Latin American Theories of Dependency', in Oxaal, I. *et al.* (eds), *Beyond the Sociology of Development* (London: Routledge and Kegan Paul).

*Ocampo, R. E. (1973) — *Imperialismo y Pacto Andino* (Lima: UNFV).

*Oficina Nacional de Estadística y Censos (ONEC) (1974) — *Censos Nacionales VII de Población, II de Vivienda, 4 de Junio de 1972: Resultados Definitivos* (Lima).

*Olson, R. S. (1972) — *The Politics of Threat and Sanction: the United States and Peru in the IPC Expropriation Dispute of 1968–1969* (University of Oregon: MS).

Otero, J. G. (1906) — 'Información Agro-Pecuario de la Costa del Perú,' *Boletín del Ministerio de Fomento* Ano 4, Nos. 6, 7 and 8 (June, July, Sep.) (Lima).

*Owens, R. J. (1963) — *Peru* (London: Royal Institute of International Affairs).

*Pacheco, B. A. (1923) — *Cabezas Dirigentes del Alto Comercio del Perú* (Lima: Sanmartí).

*Palma, G. (forthcoming) — 'Growth and Structure of the Chilean Manufacturing Industry from Independence to 1970' (Oxford University: Thesis in progress).

*Pan American Union, Division of Economic Research (1950) — *The Peruvian Economy: a Study of its Characteristics, Stage of Development, and Main Problems* (Washington, DC).

*Parker, W. B. (1919) — *Peruvians of Today* (Lima: Hispanic Society of America).

*Parra del Riego, M. (1945) — *Sintesis Monográfica del Perú* (Lima: Imprenta Torres Aguirre).

Partido Democrático-Reformista (1935) — *Lima 1919–1930* (Lima).

Paulet, P. E. (1943) — 'Información sobre las Condiciones Económicas y Sociales del Perú y sus Problemas Fundamentales,' in *Pro-*

                              ceedings of the Eighth American
                              Scientific Congress, Vol. 11 (Washing-
                              ton, DC: Government Printing
                              Office).

*Payne, J. L. (1965)   *Labor and Politics in Peru: the Sys-
                              tem of Political Bargaining* (New
                              Haven: Yale University Press).

*Paz Soldán, J. P. (1917)   *Diccionario Biográfico de Peruanos
                              Contemporáneos* (Lima: Imprenta
                              Gil).

Paz Soldán, J. P. (ed.) (1963) *Visión del Perú en el Siglo XX*
                              (2 vols) (Lima: Ediciones Librería
                              Studium).

*Pearson, S. R. (1970)   *Petroleum and the Nigerian Economy*
                              (Stanford: University Press).

*Penrose, E. (1968)   *The Large International Firm in
                              Developing   Countries: the
                              International Petroleum Industry*
                              (London: Allen and Unwin).

Pepper, C. M. (1906)   *Panama to Patagonia: the Isthmian
                              Canal and the West Coast Countries
                              of South America* (Chicago: A. C.
                              McClurg).

Perales, B. A. (1972)   'Desarrollo y Burguesía: la Indus-
                              trialización Tipo "Ensamblaje"'
                              (Lima: Bachiller thesis, Universidad
                              Católica).

*Perú en su Centenario: Infor- (Lima: Sanmartí).
maciones Mercantiles e Indus-
triales* (1921)

*Peruvian Mining Company   *Address from the Directors of the
(1825)   Peruvian Mining Company to the
                              Shareholders* (London: W. Phillips).

*Peterson, H. C., and Unger, T. *Petróleo: Hora Cero* (Lima: n.p.).
(1964)

*Petras, J., and LaPorte, R. *Peru: Transformación Revolucionaria
(1971)   o Modernización?* (Buenos Aires:
                              Ediciones Periferia).

Phelps, C. W. (1927)   *The Foreign Expansion of American
                              Banks* (New York: Ronald Press).

*Philip, G. D. E. (1975)   'Policymaking in the Peruvian Oil
                              Industry: with special reference to the
                              period since 1968' (Oxford: D.Phil.
                              thesis).

Philip, G. D. E. (1976)   'The Soldier as Radical: the Peruvian

	Military Government 1968–1975,' in *Journal of Latin American Studies*, Vol. 8, No. 1, pp. 29–51.
Pickering J. C. (1908a)	'Transportation, Costs and Labor in Central Peru,' *Engineering and Mining Journal*, Mar. 21.
Pickering J. C. (1908b)	'Recent Developments at Cerro de Pasco, Peru,' *Engineering and Mining Journal*, Apr. 11.
Pickering, J. C. (1908c)	'The Mining Districts of Central Peru,' *Engineering and Mining Journal*, May 16.
*Piel, J. (1967)	'A Propos d'un Soulevement Rural Péruvien au Début du Vingtième Siècle: Tocroyoc (1921),' *Révue d'Histoire Moderne et Contemporaine*, Oct.–Dec.
*Pike, F. B. (1967)	*The Modern History of Peru* (London: Weidenfeld and Nicholson).
*Pinelo, A. J. (1973)	*The Multinational Corporation as a Force in Latin American Politics: a Case Study of the International Petroleum Company in Peru* (New York: Praeger).
*Pinto, A., and Kñakel, J. (1972)	'The Center-Periphery System Twenty Years Later,' in Di Marco, L. E., *et al.* (ed), *International Economics and Development* (New York: Academic Press).
Prado, J. (1937)	*Bosquejo de la Evolución Bancaria en el Perú* (Lima: Editorial Huáscar).
*Prado y Ugarteche, M. I. (1906)	*Emprestito de £3,000,000 para la Construcción de Ferrocarriles: Discursos Pronunciados en la H. Cámara de Diputados por el Dr. Mariano I. Prado y Ugarteche, Diputado por Lima* (Lima: Imprenta La Industria).
*Prado y Ugarteche, M. I. (1908)	*Balance Económico del Año 1907 en el Perú* (Lima: Imprenta La Industria).
*Prebisch, R. (1950)	*The Economic Development of Latin America and its Principal Problems* (New York: United Nations Economic Commission for Latin America).
*Prinsen-Geerligs, H. C. (1912)	*The World's Cane Sugar Industry,*

448   *Peru 1890–1977*

Past and Present (Manchester: Norman Rodgers).

*Proaño, L. A. (1918)   *Sociedad Minera Alapampa Ltda: la Titulada Memoria del Ex-Directorio de la Minoría de la Sociedad* (Lima: Tip. de El Lucero).

*Proaño, L. A. (1923)   *Lizandro A. Proaño y la Sociedad Minera Alapampa: Pruebas y Fundamentos del Recurso Presentado ante la Corte Suprema Pidiendo Nulidad de la Sentencia Revocatoria de la de Primera Instancia que Declaro Fundada la Demanda y la Inexistencia del Contrato de 17 Enero de 1913, así como los Daños y Perjuicios* (Lima: Casa Editora La Opinion Nacional).

Proaño, L. A. (1934)   *La Industria Minera Nacional de 1903 a 1931: Estadística de su Producción y su Correspondiente Valorización* (Lima: Sanmartí).

*Purser, W. C. F. (1971)   *Metal Mining in Peru, Past and Present* (London: Praeger).

Quijano Obregón, A. (1968)   'Tendencies in Peruvian Development and in the Class Structure,' in Petras, J. and Zeitlin, M. (eds.); *Latin America: Reform or Revolution?* (New York: Fawcett).

Quijano Obregón, A. (1971)   *Nacionalismo, Neoimperialismo y Militarismo en el Peru* (Buenos Aires: Ediciones Periferia).

Quijano Obregón, A. (1973)   'El Perú en la Crisis de los Años Treinta' (Lima: MS, Universidad Católica).

*Quiroga, M. A. (1915)   *La Evolución Jurídica de la Propiedad Rural en Puno* (Arequipa: Tip. Quiroz Perea).

Ramírez Gastón, J. M. (1926)   *Perú y Chile: Estudios Politicos y Económicos* (Lima: Imprenta Americana).

*Ramírez Novoa, E. (1964)   *Recuperación de La Brea y Parinas* (Lima: Ediciones 28 de Julio).

Randall, H. M. (1929)   'Status of Manufacturing Industries in Peru,' *West Coast Leader* (Lima), Jan. 29.

Rey de Castro, C. (1913)   *Antagonismos Económicos: Protección y Libertad – Tratado de Com-*

*Reynolds, C. W. (1965) — *ercio entre el Perú y el Brasil* (Barcelona: Imprenta Vda de Luis Tasso). 'Economic Problems of an Export Economy: the Case of Chile and Copper,' in Mamalakis, M. and Reynolds, C. W., *Essays on the Chilean Economy* (New Haven: Yale University Press).

*Reynolds, C. W. (1977) 'Social Reform and Foreign Debt: the Peruvian Dilemma,' mimeo, memo to Wells Fargo Bank.

Richards, H. I. (1936) *Cotton and the AAA* (Washington DC: Brookings Institution).

*Rippy, J. F. (1946) 'The Dawn of Manufacturing in Peru,' *Pacific Historical Review*, Vol. 15, June.

*Rippy J. F. (1959) *British Investment in Latin America, 1822–1949: a Case Study in the Operations of Private Enterprise in Retarded Regions* (Minneapolis: University of Minnesota Press).

Rivera y Piérola, N. (1924) *El Algodón en el Perú* (Lima: Imprenta Torres Aguirre).

*Roberts, B. R. (1974a) *Urban Migration and Change in Provincial Organisation in the Central Sierra of Peru* (University of Manchester Department of Sociology: MS).

Roberts, B. R. (1974b) *The Social History of a Provincial Town: Huancayo 1890–1972* (University of Manchester Department of Sociology: MS).

*Robinson Wright, M. (1908) *The Old and the New Peru: a Story of the Ancient Inheritance and the Modern Growth and Enterprise of a Great Nation* (Philadelphia: George Barrie).

*Rodríguez, J. M. (1895) Introduction to *Estadistica del Comercio Exterior del Perú Durante el Año de 1892* (Lima: Imprenta Gil).

Rodríguez Hoyle, D. (ed.) (1967) *Perú Minero 1967* (Lima: n.p.).

Rodríguez Hoyle, D. (ed.) (1969) *La Minería Metálica en la Economía Peruana* (Lima: Litografía La Confianza).

Rodríguez Hoyle, D. (1972) — *La Minería Metálica Peruana 1971* (Lima: Litografía La Confianza).

Rodríguez Pastor, H. (1969) — 'Caquí: Estudio de una Hacienda Costeña' (Lima: MS, Instituto de Estudios Peruanos).

*Rodríguez Pastor, H. (1972) — 'Inovaciones Tecnológicas y su Impacto Social en las Plantaciones Cañeras' (Lima: MS).

*Roel, P. V. (1961) — *La Economía Agraria Peruana: Hacia la Reforma de Nuestro Agro* (2 vols) (Lima: Talleres Graf Color).

Roel, P. V. (1971) — *Esquema de la Evolución Económica* (Lima: Biblioteca Amauta).

*Roemer, M. (1970) — *Fishing for Growth: Export-Led Development in Peru, 1950–1967* (Harvard: University Press).

*Romero, E. (1949) — *Historia Económica del Perú* (2 vols) (Buenos Airés: Editorial Universo).

Romero, F. (1958) — *La Industria Peruana y sus Obreros* (Lima: Imprenta del Politécnico Nacional José Pardo).

Rondón, C. A. (1974) — 'Política Arancelaria y Sustitución de Importaciones en el Perú' (Lima: Bachiller thesis, Universidad Católica).

Rose Ugarte, L. (1945) — *La Situación Alimenticia en el Perú 1943–1944* (Lima: Ministerio de Agricultura).

Rosenfeld, A. R. (1926) — *La Industria Azucarera en el Perú* (Lima: Talleres de La Crónica).

*Rospigliosi, C. (1967) — 'Cemento', in Rodríguez Hoyle, D. (ed.) *Peru Minero 1967* (Lima: n.p.); 2nd ed. (Lima: University Press).

Rowe, L. S. (1920) — *Early Effects of the War upon the Finance, Commerce and Industry of Peru* (New York: Oxford University Press).

*Ruth, R. L. (1964) — 'The Cotton and Sugar Industries of Mexico and Peru: a Comparative Study' (University of Wisconsin: Ph.D. thesis).

*Rutter, F. R. (1916) — *Tariff Systems of South American Countries* (Washington DC: U.S. Department of Commerce Tariff Series, No. 34).

*Saberbein Chevalier, G. A. (1973) 'Industrie et Sous-Développement au Pérou' (Université des Sciences Sociales de Grenoble: Doctorat thesis).

*Sainte-Marie, S. (1945) *Perú en Cifras 1944–45* (Lima: Editorial Internacional).

Saint-Pol Maydieu, C. P. (1973) 'Minería, Empleo y Tecnología' (Lima: Bachiller thesis, Universidad Católica).

*Salomón, A. (1919) *Peru – Potentialities of Economic Development* (Lima: n.p.).

*Samamé Boggio, M. (1971) *La Mineria Peruana* (Lima: Ed. La Confianza)

*Samaniego, C. G. (1974) 'Local Social and Economic Differentiation, and Peasant Movements in the Central Sierra of Peru' (University of Manchester: Ph.D. thesis).

Sample, C. C. (1936) 'Peru's Gold-Mining Industry Grows,' *Engineering and Mining Journal,* Dec.

*Schlote, W. (1952) *British Overseas Trade from 1700 to the 1930's* (Oxford: Blackwell).

Schurz, W. L. *et al.* (1925) *Rubber Production in the Amazon Valley* (Washington DC: U.S. Department of Commerce Trade Promotion Series, No. 23).

*Scott, C. (1972) 'The Political Economy of Sugar in Peru' (University of East Anglia: MS).

*Sedgwick, T. F. (1906) 'La Industria Azucarera en el Perú,' *Boletín del Ministerio de Fomento* (Lima) Ano 4, No. 3, Mar.

*Shepherd, G. and Furnish, D. B. (1967) *The Economic and Legal Aspects of Price Controls in Peruvian Agriculture* (Lima: Iowa Mission Special Report).

*Shepherd, G. Prochezka, G. T. and Furnish, D. B. (1967) *Rice Marketing Problems and Alternative Solutions,* (Lima: Iowa Mission Special Report).

Sinopsis Geográfico y Estadístico del Perú. 1895–1898 (1899) (Lima: Imprenta El Tiempo).

*Skelton, A. (1937) 'Copper,' in Elliott, W. Y. *et al., International Control in the Non-Ferrous Metals* (New York: Macmillan).

Smetherman, B. B. and Smetherman, R. M. (1973)

'Peruvian Fisheries: Conservation and Development,' *Economic Development and Cultural Change*, Jan.

Sociedad Agrícola Casa Grande Ltda (1899)

Estatutos (Lima).

Sociedad Agrícola Nepeña Ltda (1921)

Estatutos (Lima).

*Sociedad Nacional Agraria (SNA) (1935)

Como se Produce el Algodón en el Perú (Lima: Empresa Periodística SA).

*Sociedad Nacional Agraria (SNA) (1964)

Resoluciones y Decretos Supremos Relacionados con el Sembrío Obligatorio de Articulos Alimenticios (Lima).

Sociedad Nacional de Industrias (1924)

Guia Fabril del Perú (Lima: Imprenta Incazteca).

Sociedad Nacional de Industrias (1928)

Directorio de la Sociedad Nacional de Industrias (Lima: SNI Cartilla No. 6).

Sociedad Nacional de Industrias (1936)

Guia Fabril del Perú 1936 (Lima: SNI).

Société de Publicité Sud-Américaine Monte Domecq et Cie (1922)

El Perú en el Primer Centenario de su Independencia (Berlin: Gebr. Feyl).

Soenens, G. (1975)

'Economic Policy in Peru, 1950–1968' (Cambridge University: MS).

*Soler, E. (1963)

'Fuentes de Migración al Complejo Agrícola-Industrial de Paramonga,' in Dobyns, H. F. and Vasquez, M. C., *Migración e Integración en el Perú* (Lima: Editorial Estudios Andinos).

Sonnenblick, M. (1972)

Notas sobre las Relaciones Laborales en la Hacienda Cayalti, 1859–1972 (Lima: Universidad Católica, Taller de Investigación Rural Documento de Trabajo No. 2).

*Sotillo Humire, H. (1962)

'Los Auquénidos en la Economía del Sur' (Arequipa: Bachiller thesis, Universidad Nacional San Agustín).

*Stein, S. (1973)

'Populism and Mass Politics in Peru: the Political Behaviour of the Lima Working Classes in the 1931 Presidential Election' (Stanford University: Ph.D. thesis).

Stephens, R. H. (1971)

Wealth and Power in Peru (Me-

	tuchen, N.J.: Scarecrow Press).
*Stevens, W. J. (1971)	*Capital Absorptive Capacity in Developing Countries* (Leyden: A. W. Sijthoff).
Stewart, W. (1946)	*Henry Meiggs, Yankee Pizarro* (Duke University Press).
*Stewart, W. (1951)	*Chinese Bondage in Peru: a History of the Chinese Coolie in Peru 1849–1874* (Durham, N.C.: Duke University Press).
*Stordy, R. J. (1921)	'The Breeding of Sheep, Llama and Alpaca in Peru,' *Journal of the Royal Society of Arts*, Jan. 14.
*Suárez, G. and Tovar, M. (1967)	*Deúda Pública Externa* (Lima: Banco Central de Reserva).
Sulmont, D. and Haak, R. (1971)	'El Movimiento Obrero Minero Peruano' (Lima: MS, Universidad Católica, Taller Urbano-Industrial).
*Sunkel, O. and Paz, P. (1970)	*El Subdesarrollo Latinoamericano y la Teoria del Desarrollo* (Mexico: Siglo XXI).
Tanguis, F. (1925)	'Como Formé una Variedad de Algodón,' *West Coast Leader*, Annual Cotton Number.
*Thomson, N. (1914)	*The Putumayo Red Book* (London: N. Thomson).
*Thorndike, G. (1973)	*El Caso Banchero* (Barcelona: Barral Editores).
*Thorp, R. (1967)	'Inflation and Orthodox Economic Policy in Peru,' *Bulletin of the Oxford University Institute of Economics and Statistics*, Vol. 29, Aug.
*Thorp, R. (1969)	'A Note on Food Supplies, the Distribution of Income, and National Income Accounting in Peru,' *Bulletin of the Oxford University Institute of Economics and Statistics*, Vol. 31, Nov.
*Thorp, R. (1972)	*La Funcion Desempeñada por las Institutiones Financieras en el Proceso de Ahorro Peruano 1960–1969* (Lima: Comision Nacional de Valores).
*Thorp, R. (1974)	'The Klein Correspondence' (Oxford: MS).

*Thorp, R. and Bertram, I. G. (1976) 'Industrialisation in an Open Economy: the case of Peru 1890–1940,' in *Social and Economic Change in Modern Peru*, ed. R. Miller, C. T. Smith and J. Fisher (University of Liverpool: Centre for Latin American Studies, Monograph Series No. 6).

*Thorp, R. (1976a) 'Interpreting Recent Peruvian Industrial Output Figures' (Oxford Latin American Centre, microfiche).

*Thorp, R. (1976b) 'The Estimation of Peruvian Industrial Output 1938–1954' (Oxford: Latin American Centre, microfiche).

*Thorp, R. (1976c) 'Valuation Problems in Peruvian Trade Data 1895–1930' (Oxford Latin American Centre, Microfiche).

*Timoshenko, V. P. and Swerling, B. C. (1957) *The World's Sugar: progress and Policy* (Stanford: University Press).

*Tizón y Bueno, R. (1930) 'La Industria Textil Algodonera,' *El Comercio* (Lima), Sep. 11.

*Tokman, V. (1975) *Distribución del Ingreso, Tecnología y Empleo: Análisis del Sector Industrial en el Ecuador, Perú y Venezuela* (Santiago: Cuadernos de Instituto Latino americano de Planificación Económica y Social) No. 23.

*Torres Videla, S. (n.d.) *La Revolución de Iquitos (Loreto-Perú)* (Para: Tip. Espana).

Torres, Z., J.A. (1974) *Analisís de la Estructura Económica de la Economía Peruana* (Lima: Universidad Católica, CISEPA Documento de Trabajo No. 17).

*Torres, Z., J.A. (1975) *Estructura Económica de la Industria en el Perú* (Lima: Editorial Horizonte).

Torres Z., J.A. (1976) *Protecciones Efectivas y Sustitución de Importaciones en Perú* (Lima, Univ. Católica CISEPA documento de Trabajo No. 33)

*Trant, J. P. (1927) *Report on the Commercial, Economic and Financial Conditions in Peru, October 1926* (London: HMSO).

*Tullis, F. L. (1970) *Lord and Peasant in Peru: a Paradigm of Political and Social Change* (Harvard: University Press).

*Twomey, M. (1972) — *Ensayo sobre la Agricultura Peruana* (Lima: Universidad Católica, CISEPA Documento de Trabajo No. 7).

*Ugarte, C. A. (1926) — *Bosquejo de la Historia Económica del Perú* (Lima, Imprenta Cabieses).

Ugarteche, P. (1969) — *Sanchez Cerro* (3 vols) (Lima: Editorial Universitaria).

*Unión de Productores de Azucar (1945) — *El Azúcar Peruano* (Lima: Sanmartí).

United Nations Department of Economic Affairs (1951) — *Productividad de la Mano de Obra en la Industria Textil de Cinco Países Latinoamericanos* (New York: UN).

United Nations Economic Commission for Latin America (1959) — *Analisis y Proyecciones del Desarrollo Económico: VI: El Desarrollo Industrial del Perú* (Mexico: UN).

United States Federal Trade Commission (1916) — *Report on Trade and Tariffs in Brazil, Uruguay, Argentina, Chile, Bolivia and Peru, June, 30, 1916* (Washington DC: Government Printing Office).

*United States Treasury Department (1947) — *Census of American-Owned Assets in Foreign Countries* (Washington DC: Government Printing Office).

*Uranga, F. (1924) — 'Como se Formó y Seleccionó el Algodón Tanguis,' *La Vida Agrícola* (Lima), Vol. 1, No. 1, Jan.

*Uranga, F. (1925) — 'El "Cotton Wilt," las Variedades Resistentes, la Seleccion y el Tanguis,' *West Coast Leader*, Annual Cotton Number.

*Uriarte, C. (1960) — 'La Evolución de la Industria Persquera en el Peru,' *Pesca* (Lima), No. 1, Oct.

Valdevieso Montano, L. M. (1972) — 'La Gran Minería y el Crecimiento Económico en el Perú' (Lima: Bachiller thesis, Universidad Católica)

Van der Wetering, H. (1969) — 'Agricultural Planning: the Peruvian Experience,' in Thorbecke, E. (ed.) *The Role of Agriculture in Economic Development* (New York: National Bureau of Economic Research).

*Vandendries, R. (1967) — *An Analysis of the Evolution of Peru's Beef Imports from 1950 to 1966*, (Lima: Iowa University Mission).

Van Zeeland, P. (1922) — 'La Banque de Réserve du Pérou', *Révue Économique Internationale* (Brussels), Year 14, Vol. 4, No. 3.

*Vasquez Aguirre, I. (1964–5) — 'Nuestra Pesquería y su Futuro,' *Anuario de Pesca* (Lima).

*Velarde, C. E. (1908) — *La Minería en el Perú* (Lima: Tip. de La Opinión Nacional).

*Velarde, C. E. and Denegri, M. (1904) — 'Informe de la Comisión del Cerro de Pasco,' *Boletín del Cuerpo de Ingenieros de Minas* (Lima), No. 16.

Vélez Picasso, J. (n.d.) — *Ricardo Bentín (1853–1953)* (Lima: Imprenta Torres Aguirre.)

Vernal, A. (Peru) Consultores (n.d.) — *Directorio de Gerentes: Quien es Quien en el Perú* (Lima).

Villarán Rincón, L. (1959) — 'La Companía Petrolera Lobitos y la Industria del Petróleo en el Perú,' in Instituto de Ingenieros de Petróleo del Perú, *Anales de la Primera Convención Técnica de Petróleo* (Lima).

Vuskovic, P. (1958) — *El Informe Preliminar de la CEPAL sobre el Desarrollo Industrial del Perú* (Lima: Imprenta Gil).

Walle, P. (1908) — *Le Pérou Économique* (Paris: Colin)

*Warren, W. (1976) — *Inflation and Wages in Underdeveloped Countries* (London: Frank Cass).

*Watson, E. (1964) — 'Situación de las Estadísticas Agropecuarias en el Perú' (Lima: MS, Universidad Agraria – Ministerio de Agricultura).

*Webb, R. C. (1972a) — *The Distribution of Income in Peru* (Princeton University: Woodrow Wilson School Research Program in Economic Development Discussion Paper, No. 26).

*Webb, R. C. (1972b) — *Tax Policy and the Incidence of Taxation in Peru* (Princeton University: Woodrow Wilson School Research Program in Economic Development, Discussion Paper No. 27).

*Webb, R. C. (1974) — 'Government Policy and the Distribution of Income in Peru 1963–1973' (Harvard: Ph.D. thesis) (To be published).

*Webb, R. C. (1974a) *Government Policy and the Distribution of Income in Peru, 1963–1973* (Princeton University: Woodrow Wilson School Research Program in Economic Development, Discussion Paper No. 39).

*Webb, R. C. (1974b) *Trends in Real Income in Peru, 1950–1966* (Princeton University: Woodrow Wilson School Research Program in Economic Development, Discussion Paper No. 41).

*Weil, T. E. *et al.* (1972) *Area Handbook for Peru 1972* (Washington DC: The American University).

*Weiskopf, T. E. (1976) 'Dependence as an Explanation of Underdevelopment; A Critique' (University of Michigan: MS).

Wilde, C. N. (1923) *The Republic of Peru: its Development and Commercial Opportunities* (Ottawa: Department of Trade and Commerce).

Wils, F. M. (1972) *Agricultural and Industrial Development in Peru: some Observations on their Interrelationships* (The Hague: Institute of Social Studies Occasional Paper No. 19).

Wils, F. M. (1975) *Industrialists, Industrialisation and the Nation State in Peru* (The Hague: n.p.).

*Wilson, D. (1934) *Economic Conditions in Peru* (London: U.K. Department of Overseas Trade, HMSO).

Winkler, M. (1929) *Investments of U.S. Capital in Latin America* (Boston: World Peace Foundation).

*Woods, J. (1935) *High Spots in the Andes: Peruvian Letters of a Mining Engineer's Wife* (New York: Putnam).

Wyatt, F. J. (1959) 'Origin and Development of the Fishing Industry of Peru,' *Peruvian Times*, Aug. 7.

Wynne, W. E. (1951) *State Insolvency and Foreign Bondholders*, Vol. 2 (New Haven: Yale University Press).

*Yepes del Castillo, E. (1972) *Perú 1820–1920: un Siglo de De-*

*Yrigoyen, M. (1928)   *sarrollo Capitalista* (Lima: Ediciones Campodónico).
'Bosquejo sobre Empréstitos Contemporáneos del Perú,' *Revista Universitaria* (Lima), Year 22, Vol. 2.

Ysita, E. (1948)   'The Economic Role of Peruvian Cotton, 1916–1948,' *Commercial Pan America* (Washington DC) No. 182, Sep.

*Zimmerman Zavala, A. (1968)   *La Historia Secreta del Petróleo* (Lima: Editorial Gráfico Labor).

*Zimmerman Zavala, A. (1975)   *El Plan Inca. Objectivo: Revolución Peruana* (Barcelona: Ediciones Grijalba).

Zink, D. W. (1973)   *The Political Risks for Multinational Enterprise in Developing Countries: with a Case Study of Peru* (New York: Praeger).

*Zuñiga Trelles, W. (1970)   *Peru: Agricultura, Reforma Agraria y Desarrollo Económico* (Lima: Editorial Imprenta Amauta).

PERIODICALS, JOURNALS AND STATISTICAL SERIES CONSULTED

Annual Statement of the Trade of the United Kingdom (London: Board of Trade, 1853–   ).

Anuario de la Industria Minera en el Perú (Lima: Ministerio de Fomento, 1939–   ).

Anuario de Pesca (Lima).

Anuario Estadístico do Brasil, IBGE –Conselho Nacional de Estadística (Rio de Janeiro).

Anuario Estadístico de los Estados Unidos Mexicanos (Mexico).

Anuario Estadístico del Perú (Lima: Direccion Nacional de Estadística, 1944–   ).

Anuario General de Estadistica (Bogotá).

Arancel de Aforos (Lima: Ministerio de Hacienda y Comercio).

Boletin de Aduanas (Lima).

Boletin del Banco Central de la Reserva (Lima).

Boletin de la Cámara de Comercio de Lima (Lima).

Boletin del Cuerpo de Ingenieros de Minas y Aguas (Lima, 1903–   ).

Boletin del Instituto del Mar (Callao).

Boletin del Ministerio de Fomento (Lima, 1903–   ).

Boletin Oficial de Minas y Petroleo (BOMP) (Lima: Ministerio de Fomento, 1922–   ).

Boletin de la Sociedad Nacional de Mineria (Lima, 1890s).

Bulletin of the Institute of International Finance (New York).

Cerro de Pasco Copper Corporation Annual Report and Balance Sheet (New York, 1916–   ).

Commerce Reports (Washington DC: U.S. Department of Commerce, 1915–40, thereafter *Foreign Commerce Weekly*).

Cotton: Monthly Review of the World Situation (Washington DC: International Cotton Advisory Committee, 1949–   ).

Cotton: World Statistics (Washington DC: International Cotton Advisory Committee, 1949–58).

Cuentas Nacionales del Perú (Lima: Banco Central de Reserva; volumes cover 1950–65, 1950–67, 1960–9, 1960–73 and 1960–74).

Diario de los Debates, Camara de Diputados (Lima: annual report of proceedings in Peruvian Chamber of Deputies).

Diario des los Debates, Senado (Lima: annual report of proceedings in Peruvian Senate).

El Comercio (Lima).

El Economista (Lima, weekly, 1896–?).

El Economista Peruano (Lima, irregular, 1909–59).

El Financista (Lima, 1912–?).

El Minero Ilustrado (Cerro de Pasco).

El Serrano (Lima, Cerro de Pasco Copper Corporation).

Engineering and Mining Journal (New York).

Estadística Azucarera del Perú (Lima: Sociedad Nacional Agraria, 1960s).

Estadística del Comercio Especial del Perú (Lima: Ministerio de Hacienda y Comercio, most years from 1891. Title varies, e.g. *Estadística del Comercio Exterior*)

Estadística Industrial del Perú (Lima: Ministerio de Fomento, 1942–   ).

Estadística Petrolera del Perú (Lima: Ministerio de Fomento, 1948–   ).

Estadística de la Producción de Algodón en el Perú (Lima: Ministerio de Fomento, 1916–?).

Estadística de la Producción de Azúcar y Azúcar de Caña en al Perú (Lima: Ministerio de Fomento, 1912–22).

Extracto Estadístico del Perú (Lima: Dirección Nacional de Estadística, 1918–43; subsequently *Anuario Estadístico del Perú*).

Foreign Commerce and Navigation of the USA (Washington: Department of Commerce).

Fortnightly Review (London: Bank of London and South America).

Fortune (New York).

La Industria (Lima: Sociedad Nacional de Industrias, 1931–   ).

Industria Peruana (Lima: Sociedad Nacional de Industrias, 1900–?).
International Commerce (Washington).
Lamborn's Sugar Data (New York), annual.
Latin America (London, 1967–   ).
Latin American Economic Report (London, 1973–   ).
Memoria del Banco Central de la Reserva (Lima).
Memoria de la Bolsa Comercial de Lima (Lima).
Memoria de la Camara Algodonera del Perú (Lima, 1940–71).
Memoria de la Junta Nacional de la Industria Lanar (Lima, 1940s).
Memoria de la Sociedad Nacional Agraria (Lima, 1922–72).
Memoria de la Superintendencia de Bancos (Lima, 1931–   ).
Memoria del Ministerio de Hacienda (Lima).
La Minería en el Perú: Anuario Minero Comercial (Lima, 1964–
).
Oiga (Lima).
Oil and Petroleum Yearbook (London).
Pacific Fisherman (Seattle, Washington).
Peru, Cradle of South America (London: Peruvian Embassy, 1920–2).
Peru Minero (Lima).
Peru Today (Lima, monthly 1909–14).
Peruvian Corporation Annual Report (London).
Peruvian Times (Lima, weekly 1940–74).
Peruvian Yearbook (Lima, 1940s).
Petroleum Economist (London).
Quin's Metal Handbook and Statistics (London: Metal Information
      Bureau).
La Renta Nacional del Peru (Lima: Banco Central de Reserva, covers
      years 1942–60).
La Situación de la Industria Manufacturera Peruana en el año – (Lima:
      Banco Industrial-Instituto de Promoción Industrial, 1962–8).
Statistical Abstract for the United Kingdom (London: Board of Trade).
Statistical Abstract of the United States (Washington: U.S. Department
      of Commerce).
Statistical Yearbook (Geneva: United Nations, 1931–45, 1949–
).
Stock Exchange Official Intelligence (London).
Stock Exchange Yearbook (London).
South American Journal (Buenos Aires).
South American Yearbook and Directory (London, 1913–   ).
Sugar Yearbook (London: International Sugar Council).
Survey of Current Business (Washington: U.S. Department of
      Commerce).
Treaty Series (New York: League of Nations, 1920–47).
U.K. Parliamentary Papers (London; contain annual consular reports
      from Peru 1890–1920s).

Vademecum del Inversionista (Lima).

West Coast Leader (Lima, weekly 1913–40).

World Petroleum (Los Angeles, New York).

Yearbook of Fisheries Statistics (Washington: Food and Agricultural Organisation of United Nations).

Yearbook of Food and Agricultural Statistics (Washington, Rome: Food and Agricultural Organisation); continued as *International Yearbook of Agricultural Statistics*; then *Production and Trade Yearbook*.

Index